THE ELEMENT ENCYCLOPEDIA OF SECRET SOCIETIES

John Michael Greer

THE ELEMENT ENCYCLOPEDIA OF SECRET SOCIETIES

the ultimate
a-z of ancient mysteries,
lost civilizations and
forgotten wisdom

HARPER element

HarperElement
An Imprint of HarperCollins*Publishers*
77–85 Fulham Palace Road,
Hammersmith, London W6 8JB

www.harpercollins.co.uk

HarperElement is a trademark of HarperCollins*Publishers* Ltd

The material in this book is taken from *The Element Encyclopedia of Secret Societies and Hidden History*, first published by HarperElement in 2006

This production 2013

A catalogue record of this book is available from the British Library

ISBN-13 978-0-00-793145-3

Printed and bound in England by
Clays Ltd St Ives, plc

Contents

Introduction vii

The Element Encyclopedia of Secret Societies

A – Accepted Mason to Aurum Solis 3
B – Babeuf, François "Gracchus" to Burlesque Degrees 75
C – Cabala to Culdees 107
D – Damcar to Dualism 141
E – E Clampus Vitus to Extraterrestrials 161
F – Fabian Society to Fundamentalism 181
G – Gematria to Guilds, Medieval 209
H – Hall, Manly Palmer to Hollow Earth 223
I – Illuminates of Thanateros to Isiac Mysteries 243
J – Jacobites to John Birch Society 251
K – Kabbalistic Order of the Rose+Cross to Ku Klux Klan 265
L – Labor Unions to Loyal Order of Moose 287
M – Mackenzie, Kenneth to Mysteries, Ancient 309
N – Nan Madol to Nine Unknown Men 337
O – Occultism to Osiris, Mysteries of 353
P – P2 to Pythagorean Brotherhood 379
R – Raggi to Russian Revolution 403
S – Sabbat to Synarchy 447
T – Temple of Set to Trilateral Commission 493
U – UFOs to Urban Design 511
V – Vehm to Vril Society 523
W – Weishaupt, Adam to Worshipful Master 527
Y – Yale Secret Societies to Young Italy 545
Z – Zero Point Energy to Zos Kia Cultus 551

Bibliography 555

Dedication

On a spring afternoon some years ago, as I waited in the anteroom of an aging lodge building for my initiation into one of the higher degrees of a certain secret society, an elderly man in the full ceremonial uniform of that degree came in and looked at me for a long moment. "You know, John," he said finally, "you must be the first man ever initiated into this degree who wears his hair in a ponytail."

"Yes," I said, "and we'd better hope I'm not the last, either."

He nodded after a moment and went past me into the lodge room, and the ceremony began a few minutes later. The old man's name was Alvin Gronvold; during the few years I knew him before his death, he was a friend and mentor as well as a lodge brother. To him, and to all the men and women of his generation who kept the secret societies of the western world alive when they were ignored, ridiculed, or condemned by almost everyone else, this book is dedicated.

Introduction

Behind the ordinary history of the world, the facts and dates that most of us learn in school and forget immediately thereafter, lies a second, hidden history of secret societies, lost civilizations, sinister conspiracies and mysterious events. This shadow side of history has become a pervasive theme in the popular culture of recent years. In an age of politicians who manipulate facts for their own benefit, scientists who invent data to advance their careers, and scholars who let their prejudices all too obviously shape their judgment, only the foolish – or those with agendas of their own – accept the claims of authority blindly.

Like the Holy Grail of legend, though, the truth behind commonly accepted realities is easier to seek than to find. Since the 1960s, when alternative visions first broke through into the cultural mainstream of the western world, the hidden history of the world has become the storm center of a flurry of uncertainties. What were the real origins of Christianity, the Freemasons, or the French Revolution? Do secret societies actually control the world, and if so, what do they plan to do with it? Does the hidden hand behind history belong to a cartel of bankers, a Gnostic secret society, the Catholic Church, the benevolent masters of the Great White Lodge, alien reptiles from another dimension, or Satan himself? Look at any five books or documentaries on the subject, and you can count on at least six mutually contradictory answers.

Fortunately, there are pathways through the fog. No secret society is completely secret, and even the murkiest events of hidden history leave traces behind. Theories about the shadow side of history have a history of their own. Current ideas about the Bavarian Illuminati or the lost continent of Atlantis, to name only two examples, mean one thing in the hothouse environment of the modern alternative-realities scene, and quite another in context, as ideas that have developed over time and absorbed themes and imagery from many sources. Errors of fact and disinformation can often be traced to their origins, and useful information unearthed from unexpected sources. All this can be done, but so far, too little of it has been done.

The Element Encyclopedia of Secret Societies is an alphabetic guide to this shadow side of history, and it attempts to sort out fact from the fictions, falsifications, and fantasies that have too often surrounded the subject. True believers and diehard skeptics alike may find themselves in unfamiliar territory, for I have not limited myself to the usual sources quoted and challenged in the alternative reality field; the material in this book has been gathered through many years of personal research, using scholarly works as well as more unorthodox sources of information. A bibliography at the end, and the suggestions for further reading following many of the articles, will allow readers who are interested in checking facts to do so.

Another resource I have used, one that will inevitably raise the hackles of some readers, stems from my personal involvement in secret societies and the occult underground of the modern world. I am a 32° Freemason, a Master of the Temple in one branch of the Golden Dawn tradition and an Adeptus Minor in another, the Grand Archdruid of one modern Druid order and a member of three others, and an initiate of more than a dozen other secret societies and esoteric traditions. The world of hidden history has been a central part of my life for more than 30 years. I make no apologies for this fact, and indeed some of the material covered in this book would have been much more difficult to obtain without the access, connections, and friendships that my participation in secret societies has brought me.

Many people have helped me gather information for this volume or provided other assistance invaluable in its creation. Some of them cannot be named here; they know who they are. Among those who can be named are Erik Arneson, Dolores Ashcroft-Nowicki, Philip Carr-Gomm, Peter Cawley, Patrick Claflin, Gordon Cooper, Lon Milo DuQuette, John Gilbert, Carl Hood Jr., Corby Ingold, Earl King Jr., Jay Kinney, Jeff Richardson, Carroll "Poke" Runyon, Todd Spencer, Mark Stavish, Donna Taylor, Terry Taylor, and my wife Sara. My thanks go with all.

Note: Readers will notice the occasional use of a triangle of dots instead of an ordinary period. This is because I have followed the Masonic punctuation practice when abbreviating Masonic terms.

THE ELEMENT ENCYCLOPEDIA OF SECRET SOCIETIES

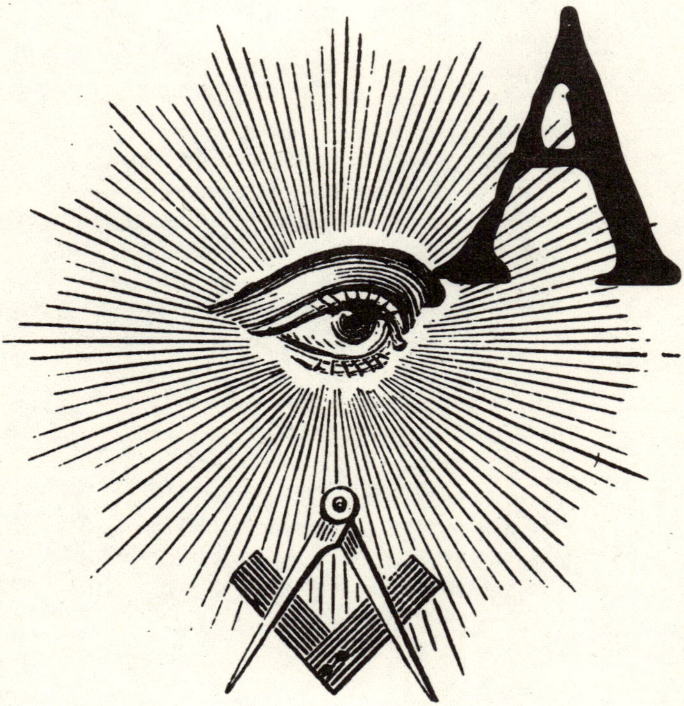
A

Accepted Mason

A member of a lodge of Masons who is not an operative Mason – that is, a working stonemason – but has joined the lodge to take part in its social and initiatory activities. The first accepted Masons documented in lodge records were Anthony Alexander, Lord William Alexander, and Sir Alexander Strachan of Thornton, who became members of the Edinburgh lodge in 1634. Sir Robert Moray, a Hermeticist and founding member of the Royal Society, became a member of the same lodge in 1640; the alchemist and astrologer Elias Ashmole was another early accepted Mason, joining a lodge in England in 1646. They and the thousands who followed them over the next century played a crucial role in the transformation of Freemasonry from a late medieval trade union to the prototypical secret society of modern times. See **Ashmole, Elias**; **Freemasonry**; **Moray, Robert**.

Further reading: Stevenson 1988.

Adonis, mysteries of

A system of initiatory rites originally practiced in the Phoenician city of Byblos, in Lebanon, to celebrate the life, death, and resurrection of the old Babylonian vegetation god Tammuz, lover of Ishtar and subject of a quarrel between her and her underworld sister Ereshkigal. Local custom used the Semitic title Adonai, "lord," for the god; after Alexander the Great's conquests brought Lebanon into the ambit of Greek culture, the god's name changed to Adonis, while Aphrodite and Persephone took the places of the older goddesses. In this Hellenized form the mystery cult of Adonis spread through much of the Middle East.

According to Greek and Roman mythographers, Adonis was the son of an incestuous affair between Cinyras, king of Cyprus, and his daughter Myrrha. He was so beautiful that the love goddess Aphrodite fell in love with him, but while hunting on Mount Lebanon he was gored to death by a wild boar. When he descended to Hades, Persephone, the queen of the underworld, fell in love with him as well and refused to yield to Aphrodite's pleas that he be allowed to return to life. Finally the quarrel went before Zeus, king of the gods, who ruled that Adonis should live six months of the year in the underworld with Persephone and six months above ground with the goddess of love.

Brief references to the mystery rites suggest that initiates carried out a symbolic search for the lost Adonis, mourned his death, and then celebrated joyously when he returned to life. All this follows the standard pattern of Middle Eastern vegetation myth, with the deity of the crops buried with the seed and reborn with the green shoot, only to be cut down again by a sickle the shape of a boar's tusk. The same pattern occurs in the Egyptian legend of

Osiris, the myths behind the Eleusinian Mysteries of ancient Greece, and arguably in the Gospel accounts of the life and death of Jesus of Nazareth as well. See **Christian origins**; **Eleusinian mysteries**.

Many scholars during the eighteenth and nineteenth centuries recognized the common patterns behind these myths and many others, and argued that worship of the life force expressed through the fertility of vegetation, crops, and human beings was the source of all religion. These ideas found a ready audience in secret societies of various kinds, and similarities between contemporary secret society rituals and surviving information about the mysteries of Adonis encouraged secret society members to draw connections with this and other classical mystery cults. Older works on the origins of Freemasonry commonly list the mysteries of Adonis as one of its possible sources. See **fertility religion**; **Freemasonry, origins of**.

Adoptive Masonry

A system of quasi-Masonic rites for women, Adoptive Masonry appeared in France in the middle of the eighteenth century; the first known Lodge of Adoption was founded in Paris in 1760 by the Comte de Bernouville. Another appeared at Nijmegen, the Netherlands, in 1774, and by 1777 the adoptive Rite had risen to such social heights that the lodge *La Candeur* in Paris had the Duchess of Bourbon as its Worshipful Mistress, assisted by the Duchess of Chartres and the Princess de Lamballe. Its basic pattern came partly from Freemasonry and partly from earlier non-Masonic secret societies in France that admitted men and women alike. See **Freemasonry**; **Order of the Happy**; **Order of Woodcutters**.

The degrees of Adoptive Masonry take their names from corresponding Masonic degrees, but use an entirely different symbolism and ritual. The first degree, Apprentice, involves the presentation of a white apron and gloves to the new initiate. The second, Companion, draws on the symbolism of the Garden of Eden, and the third, Mistress, on that of the Tower of Babel and the ladder of Jacob. The fourth degree, Perfect Mistress, refers to the liberation of the Jews from bondage in Egypt as an emblem of the liberation of the human soul from bondage to passion, and concludes with a formal banquet. The entire system focuses on moral lessons drawn from Christian scripture, a detail that has not prevented

Christian critics from insisting that Adoptive Masonry is yet another front for Masonic devil worship. See **Antimasonry**.

Despite its ascent to stratospheric social heights, Adoptive Masonry faced an early challenge from the Order of Mopses, a non-Masonic order for men and women founded in Vienna in 1738 after the first papal condemnation of Freemasonry. The chaos of the French Revolution and the Napoleonic Wars finished off the Mopses but left Adoptive Masonry tattered but alive, and it remains active in France at the present. Attempts to launch it in other countries had limited success, although the example of French Adoptive Masonry played a major role in launching the Order of the Eastern Star and similar rites for women in America. See **Order of Mopses**; **Order of the Eastern Star**.

African-American secret societies

The forced transportation of millions of Africans into slavery in the New World set in motion an important but much-neglected tradition of secret societies. The West African nations from which most slaves came had secret societies of their own, and these provided models that black people in the New World drew on for their own societies. See **African secret societies**.

The first documented African-American beneficial society was the African Union Society, founded by a group of former slaves in Providence, RI in 1780. The Union provided sickness and funeral benefits to members, raised money for charities in the black community, and networked with similar organizations locally and throughout the country. Like most of the earliest black societies in the New World, it attempted to raise money and hire ships for a return to Africa. Despite the obstacles, projects of this sort managed to repatriate tens of thousands of African-Americans to West Africa, and founded the nation of Liberia.

By the time of the Revolution, though, most American blacks had been born in the New World; their goals centered not on a return to Africa but on bettering themselves and securing legal rights in their new home. The rise of a large population of free African-Americans in the large cities of the east coast inspired new secret societies and beneficial organizations with less direct connections to African tradition. Among the most important of these were Masonic lodges, working the same rites as their white equivalents. From 1784, when African Lodge #459 of Boston received a dispensation from the Grand Lodge of England, Prince Hall lodges – named after the founder of African-American Freemasonry – became a major institution in African-American communities and provided a vital social network for the emergence of the earliest black middle class. By the beginning of the

American Civil War Prince Hall lodges existed in every state in the North, and had a foothold in the few Southern states with a significant free black population. See **Prince Hall Masonry**.

Freemasonry was not the only secret society of the time to find itself with a substantial African-American branch. A social club for free blacks in New York City, the Philomathean Institute, applied to the Independent Order of Odd Fellows (IOOF) in 1843, intending to transform their club into an Odd Fellows lodge. The IOOF rejected their application, and the Institute then contacted the Grand United Order of Odd Fellows in England and received a charter. With its innovative system of sickness and funeral benefits, Odd Fellowship found an immediate welcome among African-Americans, and expanded into the West Indies and black communities in eastern Canada as well. See **Odd Fellowship**.

While Prince Hall Masons and Grand United Order Odd Fellows were the most popular fraternal societies among African-Americans before the Civil War, many other societies emerged in the black community during that period. Secret societies faced competition from public voluntary organizations rooted in Protestant churches, however the same cultural forces that drove the expansion of secret societies in the white community helped African-American secret societies hold their own and expand, especially in Maryland, Virginia, New York, and Pennsylvania, where more than half the free black people in America lived between 1830 and the Civil War.

The years after the American Civil War saw vast economic and cultural changes across the defeated South, as former slaves tried to exercise their new political and economic rights and conservative whites used every available means to stop them. The Ku Klux Klan used secret society methods to unleash a reign of terror against politically active African-Americans. While the Klan's power was broken by federal troops in the early 1870s, "Jim Crow" segregation laws passed thereafter imposed a rigid separation between black and white societies south of the Mason–Dixon line. Ironically, this led to the rise of an educated black middle class in the South as black communities were forced to evolve their own businesses, banks, churches, colleges – and secret societies. See **Ku Klux Klan**.

Masonry and Odd Fellowship were joined by more than a thousand other fraternal societies among Americans of African ancestry. Most of these grew out of the black community itself and drew on African-American cultural themes for their rituals and symbolism, but some borrowed the rituals and names of existing white fraternal orders as an act of protest. The Improved Benevolent and Protective Order of Elks of the World (IBPOEW), for example, came into being in 1898 in Cincinnati, Ohio when two African-

American men, B.F. Howard and Arthur J. Riggs, were refused membership in the local Elks lodge because of their race. Riggs obtained a copy of the Elks ritual, discovered that the Elks had never copyrighted it, and proceeded to copyright it himself in the name of a new Elks order. Despite lawsuits from the original Elks order, the IBPOEW spread rapidly through African-American communities and remains active to this day. See **Benevolent Protective Order of Elks (BPOE)**.

During these same years fraternal benefit societies became one of the most popular institutions in American culture, offering a combination of initiation rituals, social functions, and insurance benefits. Americans of African descent took an active role in the growth of the new benefit societies. They had more reason than most to reject the costly and financially unsteady insurance industry of the time, since most insurance companies refused to insure black-owned property. Since nearly all fraternal benefit societies founded by whites refused to admit people of color, blacks founded equivalent societies of their own. See **fraternal benefit societies**.

Between 1880 and 1910, the "golden age" of African-American secret societies, lodges vied with churches as the center of black social life, and became a major economic force in the black community. One example is the Grand United Order of True Reformers, founded by the Rev. W.W. Browne in 1881 at Richmond, Virginia. In the two decades following its founding, the order grew from 100 members to 70,000, expended more than $2 million in benefits and relief funds, and established a chain of grocery stores and its own savings bank, newspaper, hotel, and retirement home.

The problems that beset most American fraternal benefit societies in the years just before the First World War did not spare the African-American societies; like their white equivalents, few used actuarial data to set a balance between dues and benefits, and aging memberships and declining enrollments became a source of severe problems. The True Reformers were not exempt, and went bankrupt in 1908. The support of the black community kept many others going, until the Great Depression of the 1930s and the mass migration of blacks to northern industrial cities during the Second World War shattered the social basis for their survival and left few functioning. Sociologist Edward Nelson Palmer commented that "[a] trip through the South will show hundreds of tumble-down buildings which once served as meeting places for Negro lodges" (Palmer 1944, p. 211) – a bleak memorial to a proud heritage of mutual aid.

Like its white equivalent, black Freemasonry found a new lease of life in the 1950s, as servicemen returning from the Second World War sought active roles in their communities, but few other African-American secret societies benefited much from this. In the second half of the twentieth century, civil rights organizations such as the National Association for the Advancement of Colored People (NAACP), radical groups such as the Black Panther Party, and new religious movements such as the Nation of Islam (also known as the Black Muslims) absorbed much of the energy that had driven secret societies a century earlier.

Further reading: Harris 1979, Palmer 1944.

African secret societies

Like other traditional societies around the world, the cultures of sub-Saharan Africa possess a rich and varied body of secret society traditions, many of which still exist today. The sheer diversity of the hundreds of distinct African cultures makes generalizations about African secret societies risky at best, and continuing prejudices and misunderstandings on the part of people in the industrial world cloud the picture further. It is just as inaccurate to think of all African secret societies in terms of masked "witch doctors" and fire-lit dances, as it is to think of all Africans as tribal peoples living in grass huts.

In reality, just as traditional African societies include everything from tribal hunter-gatherer bands to highly refined, literate, urban cultures, African secret societies include initiatory traditions that focus on the education and ritual transformation of children to adults; craft societies governing trades such as blacksmithing and hunting; religious and magical societies that teach secret methods of relating to supernatural powers; secret societies of tribal elders or leading citizens that play important roles in the government of many African communities; and many other forms of secret society as well. While most African secret societies are specific to particular cultures or nations, a few, such as the Poro and Sande societies of West Africa, have spread across cultural and national boundaries. See **Poro Society**; **Sande Society**.

During the four centuries of European colonialism in Africa, African secret societies faced severe challenges from the cultural disruptions caused by the slave trade and colonial incursions, from the efforts of Christian and Muslim missionaries, and from colonial governments that often identified secret societies as a potential threat to their rule. During this time, African slaves deported to the New World brought several secret societies with them, and they and their descendants created new secret societies of their own, influencing the development of fraternal secret societies in America and elsewhere. Nor did this process of exchange go in only one direction; several secret societies of European origin, including Freemasonry and the Loyal Orange Order, established themselves in the nineteenth century among European-educated

Africans and remain active, especially in the large cities of West Africa. See **African-American secret societies**; **Freemasonry**; **Loyal Orange Order**.

Today many traditional African secret societies survive in a more or less complete form, and the twilight of western colonialism enabled some to reclaim the roles they once had in their own cultures. Thus the Mau Mau society, derived from older oath-bound societies in Kenya, played an important role in freeing that country from colonial rule, while the Poro Society in Sierra Leone was able to impose and enforce a "Poro curfew" during the Sierra Leone civil war of the 1990s that protected local communities from the attacks both of rebels and government soldiers. African-descended communities in the New World have also preserved a number of African secret society traditions, and these have become more popular with the decline of Christian control over governments and the spread of religious freedom. See **Mau Mau**.

Further reading: Mackenzie 1967.

AGES OF THE WORLD

Since ancient times many cultures have divided the history of the world into a series of distinct ages, separated by cataclysms. The oldest documented teaching about ages of the world in the West appears in the writings of the Greek poet Hesiod, who wrote sometime in the eighth century BCE. According to Hesiod, history began with the Golden Age, when people lived without sorrow or toil; they became earth spirits, and their age ended. Next came the Silver Age, inhabited by people who refused to worship the gods and so were destroyed. The Bronze Age followed, and its people were savage warriors who ended the age by exterminating one another. The fourth age was the Age of Heroes, the setting for all the Greek heroic myths, and ended when the heroes either died in battle or went to the Elysian Fields in the far west of the world. Finally came the Iron Age of Hesiod's own time, an age of poverty, toil, and bitter suffering. Later Greek and Roman writers suggested that the Iron Age would end with a return to the Golden Age, but Hesiod holds out no such hope; in his vision the Iron Age is fated to worsen until the gods finally abandon the world and the human race perishes.

A similar scheme appears in India, where a sequence of four *yugas* or world-ages sets the beat for a cosmic clock. First in the sequence comes the Satya Yuga or golden age of righteousness of 1,728,000 years, then the Treta Yuga or silver age of

1,296,000 years, then the Dvapara Yuga or bronze age of 864,000 years, and finally the sinister Kali Yuga, the iron age of darkness and ignorance, lasting a mere 432,000 years. The Kali Yuga ends in catastrophe, after which the entire cycle begins again.

Another scheme of the same type can be traced in Native American traditions. A set of myths found from Oregon to Peru divides time into world-ages called suns, of which the present is the fifth. Each sun lasts about 5125 years and ends with a disaster. The current Fifth Sun, according to the Mayan calendar, began on August 11, 3114 BCE, and will end in catastrophe on December 21, 2012. See **Mayan calendar**.

What lies behind these numbers, according to many scholars, is the precession of the equinoxes, a slow wobble in the earth's orbit that moves the equinoctial and solstitial points backwards through the zodiac at the rate of one degree every 72 years: 2160 years, one Great Month, takes the markers through an entire sign of the zodiac, and 25,920 years, one Great Year, completes the full precessional cycle. For convenience, the position of the sun at the spring equinox is used to track the entire process; when the cast of the 1960s musical *Hair* sang about the dawning of the Age of Aquarius, they were referring to the shift of this position out of Pisces, where it has been for a little more than 2000 years, into the sign of Aquarius.

The same numbers govern most other systems of world-ages. The Fifth Sun of the Mayan calendar, for example, is almost exactly one-fifth of the Great Year, and the Kali Yuga consists of 200 Great Months. Even shorter cycles such as the system created by the German Renaissance wizard Johannes Trithemius of Sponheim (1462–1516) unfolds from the precessional cycle; the seven angels of Trithemius's system each rule over a period of 307 years and 7 months, so that the full cycle completes in one Great Month.

Not all secret society teachings about world-ages, however, follow the movements of the precessional cycle. For more than two thousand years, Chinese revolutionary secret societies have postulated a simplified system of world-ages as part of their ideology. The length and number of previous ages vary from one secret society to another, though a three-age system is the most common. Of central importance, though, is the transition from the present dark age – identified with the then-current Chinese imperial dynasty – to the bright new age that will dawn as soon as the dynasty is overthrown and the secret society's leader becomes the next emperor. See **White Lotus societies**.

A remarkably similar system can be found in nineteenth- and twentieth-century European secret societies, which borrowed it from the medieval Italian mystic Joachim of Floris. Joachim's system originally postulated an Age of God the Father, ruled by the principle of law and lasting from the fall of Adam and Eve to the crucifixion of Jesus; an Age of God the Son, ruled by the principle of love and lasting from the crucifixion to Joachim's own time; and an Age of God the Holy Spirit, ruled by the principle of liberty and lasting from Joachim's time to the end of the world. Later Joachimite theologians flipped the first two to produce a more satisfying drama, in which an original blissful Age of Love gave way via the fall of Adam and Eve to the bitterness of the Age of Law, which was about to yield to the redemption of a utopian Age of Liberty.

Stripped of its theological framework, this latter scheme became the most common system of world-ages in the modern West. Karl Marx and Friedrich Engels redefined it in economic language to become the basic historical scheme of communism, with primitive communism as the Age of Love, capitalism as the Age of Law, and the workers' paradise of communism as the future Age of Liberty. Aleister Crowley used Egyptian mythology rather than political economy to define history in terms of the Aeons of Isis, Osiris, and Horus, with himself the prophet of the latter. A string of feminist writers, in turn, subjected gender relationships to the same scheme and saw the Age of Love reflected in their hypothetical ancient matriarchal utopias, the Age of Law in Indo-European patriarchy, and the future Age of Liberty in a "Partnership Society" of gender equality in which, to adapt George Orwell's phrase, women would be noticeably more equal than men. See **Communism**; **Crowley, Aleister**; **Matriarchy**.

These two grand schemes – the precessional cycle and the myth of fall and redemption – define most of the systems of world-ages circulated in secret societies during the last four hundred years or so, but the sheer creativity of the secret society underground has guaranteed a hearing for other, unique systems. One of the best examples is the work of Sampson Mackey (1765–1843) of Norwich, a shoemaker and self-taught cosmologist, who argued that Earth's poles gradually turned over in a vast cycle no less than 2,332,800 years in length. When the poles were perpendicular to its orbit, Earth basked in perpetual springtime; when the poles were parallel to the orbital plane, it entered an "Age of Horror" in which its inhabitants alternately froze and fried in nights and days that were each six months long. This vision of prehistory found a home in the teachings of the Hermetic Brotherhood of Luxor, an influential magical secret society of the late nineteenth century. See **Hermetic Brotherhood of Luxor (H.B. of L.)**.

The popularity of teachings about world-ages shows no signs of ebbing at present, and recent discoveries about natural catastrophes in the distant and not-so-distant past have provided a good deal of fodder for present and future theories about ages of the world. Whatever else can be said about the present world-age, it is one in which world-ages are a perennially hot topic!

Further reading: de Santillana and von Dechend 1977, Godwin 1993, Hesiod 1973.

Agharta

An underground city supposedly hidden away somewhere in the vastnesses of central Asia, Agharta – also spelled Aghartta, Agharti, Agartha, and Arghati – has become a fixture of modern occultism, the secret teachings of numerous secret societies, and the further shores of contemporary conspiracy theory. Unlike its twin and rival Shambhala, which has deep roots in Tibetan Buddhist traditional lore, the hidden city of Agharta was concocted out of Norse mythology and thin air by two nineteenth-century French authors. Its invention and spread is one of the most remarkable tales in hidden history. See **Shambhala**.

The story begins with Louis Jacolliot (1837–90), a French official in Chandernagore, India, who eked out a sparse salary by writing for the popular press. Jacolliot made several contributions to the field of rejected knowledge; the Nine Unknown Men, one of many groups claimed as the secret masters of the world, was another of his inventions. One of Jacolliot's favorite themes was euhemerism, the idea that ancient mythology recounted events from even more ancient prehistory. In 1871 he published a bestseller, *Le Fils de Dieu* (*The Son of God*), supposedly recounting the 15,000-year-old history of India, as revealed to him by friendly Brahmans. See **Euhemerism**; **rejected knowledge**.

Suspiciously, the "history" in Jacolliot's book has almost nothing in common with the traditional history of India as recounted in Hindu scriptures and epics, and almost everything in common with the Norse mythology then wildly popular in Europe as a result of the folklore collections of the Brothers Grimm and the operas of Richard Wagner. The city of Asgartha, capital of the ancient Indian empire at the center of Jacolliot's history, is a case in point. This is simply Asgarth – an alternative spelling of Asgard, the home of the Norse gods – with an *a* tacked on the end to make it look like a Sanskrit word.

The success of Jacolliot's book put Asgartha on the map in French popular culture, but it is not quite clear how the city came into the hands of the next major figure in the Agharta saga, the eccentric French occultist J.-A. Saint-Yves d'Alveydre (1842–1909). Saint-Yves claimed that he was taught about Aghartta (his preferred spelling) by Haji Sharif, whom Saint-Yves called "a high official in the Hindu church" but who had a Muslim name and seems to have been a parrot-shop proprietor in Le Havre. According to the researches of Joscelyn

Godwin, one of the few capable historians to explore the Agharta myth, Haji Sharif taught Sanskrit to Saint-Yves, and also passed on some material derived from Jacolliot's book. From there, Saint-Yves went on to create the entire modern mythology of Agharta.

In 1886 Saint-Yves privately published a book about Aghartta titled *Mission de l'Inde en Europe* (*The Mission of India in Europe*). He then became convinced he had revealed too much, recalled the entire edition, and had all but two copies burned. Not until 1910, a year after his death, was the book reissued. It proved to be an account of astral journeys in which Saint-Yves went in search of Aghartta and found a living city deep underground, inhabited by millions of people under a Sovereign Pontiff whose absolute rule was backed up with technological marvels as well as mystical powers. Much of the book expounds Saint-Yves' political philosophy of synarchy, and the whole account shows obvious borrowings from Jacolliot's *Le Fils de Dieu*, Edward Bulwer-Lytton's occult novel *The Coming Race*, and the "Mahatma letters" circulated by the Theosophical Society. See **synarchy**; **Theosophical Society**.

Well before *Mission de l'Indé*'s reissue, rumors about Agharta circulated in occult circles in Paris, and the Martinist order headed by Papus (Dr. Gérard Encausse), one of Saint-Yves' closest students. The republication of the book instantly made the hidden city a hot topic throughout the European occult underworld. This was probably the channel by which it reached its next major publicist, Polish adventurer Ferdinand Ossendowski. After traveling through central Asia in the throes of the Russian Revolution and the civil war that followed it, Ossendowski published the sensational bestseller *Beasts, Men, and Gods* (1922). Large portions of the first three chapters were plagiarized from Saint-Yves' book, though Ossendowski changed the spelling of most of the proper names: Saint-Yves' Aghartta, for example, became Agharti in Ossendowski's tale. See **Martinism**.

Ossendowski's book was published in several languages and brought Agharta into a blaze of publicity that has never really faded. The Traditionalist philosopher René Guénon took time from his abstruse studies of Vedanta to write *Le Roi du Monde* (*The King of the World*, 1927), turning the story of Agharta into vehicle for subtle analyses of symbolism and myth. On the other end of the cultural spectrum, the pulp science fiction magazine *Amazing Stories*, under its legendary editor Raymond Palmer, made room for stories about Agharta in the 1940s. See **Palmer, Raymond**.

In the second half of the twentieth century, Agharta became a fixture in New Age and alternative reality circles in America and elsewhere, and found itself associated and at times confused with Shambhala, the other mysterious city in central Asia.

During these same years, however, most serious occult secret societies dropped the entire superstructure of occult alternative history that had accumulated during the "Theosophical century" (1875–1975), and few if any magical secret societies include teachings about Agharta at present.

Further reading: Godwin 1993, Guénon 1983, Kafton-Minkel 1989.

Akhenaten

Pharaoh of Egypt, *c.*1400–*c.*1350 BCE. The second son of Amenhotep III of Egypt's 18th Dynasty, the future Pharaoh Akhenaten was originally named Amenhotep. There may have been ill feeling between father and son, as the young Amenhotep is never named or portrayed alongside his siblings on his father's monuments, but he became crown prince after the death of his older brother Thothmes and took the throne a few years later as Amenhotep IV.

Shortly after his enthronement, he proclaimed that the gods of Egypt's polytheism were lifeless and powerless, and the only real god was Aten, the physical sun. In the first four years of his reign he imposed a religious revolution on Egypt, abolishing the priests and temples of all gods but his own and changing his name from Amenhotep, meaning "Amen is satisfied," to Akhenaten, "spirit of Aten."

In the fifth year of his reign, Akhenaten abandoned the capital city at Thebes and built a new capital for himself nearly a hundred miles down the Nile, at Tell el-Amarna, across the river from the ancient city of Hermopolis. Akhetaten, "Horizon of Aten," contained a huge temple to Aten and a grandiose palace for Akhenaten himself, built and decorated in a style that flouted the traditional geometries of Egyptian art. Surrounded by his courtiers and favorites, the pharaoh pursued his religious vision and isolated himself from the world outside Akhetaten's walls.

The last decade of his reign was a period of continual crisis, as the burden of rising taxes and forced labor for Akhenaten's building programs crushed the Egyptian economy, and the rising power of the Hittite Empire in what is now Turkey challenged a military already stretched to the limit by Egypt's own internal troubles. Meanwhile epidemic disease swept through Egypt, adding another strain to a crumbling society. Many Egyptians believed that the gods were abandoning Egypt because Egypt had abandoned the gods.

In the midst of these crises, Akhenaten died. Three short-lived successors – a shadowy figure named Smenkhare, the boy-king Tutankhamen, and Akhenaten's elderly Prime Minister Ay – struggled with the situation without resolving it. Finally, on Ay's death, the throne passed to Horemheb, commander of the army. Often tarred as the villain of Akhenaten's story, Horemheb was a canny realist who understood that Akhenaten's disastrous experiment had to be reversed if Egypt was to survive. During Horemheb's 25-year reign, Egypt returned to peace and prosperity, but the price was the total destruction of Akhenaten's legacy. Akhetaten was razed to the ground, the temples of Aten were torn down stone by stone to provide raw materials for new temples to the old gods of Egypt, and every trace of Akhenaten's reign, his image, his name, and his god was obliterated.

The destruction was systematic enough that historians afterwards had only scattered references to "the accursed one of Akhetaten" and a confused legend of a time of troubles to suggest that something unusual had happened near the end of the 18th Dynasty. Not until the 1840s did the wall of silence raised by Horemheb break down, as European archeologists carried out the first surveys at Tell el-Amarna and found puzzling images of people worshipping the sun's disk, carved in a style utterly unlike traditional Egyptian art. Curiosity about these so-called "disk worshippers" led to systematic digs at Tell el-Amarna and the gradual uncovering of the facts about Akhenaten.

The discovery of the tomb of Akhenaten's son, the boy pharaoh Tutankhamen, in 1922 finished the process and catapulted the "heretic pharaoh" into public awareness throughout the western world. Akhenaten's monotheism guaranteed that most portrayals of his life and reign during the early twentieth century were strongly favorable, and this made him an easy target for retrospective recruitment. H. Spencer Lewis of AMORC and Savitri Devi, the first major theoretician of the neo-Nazi movement, were among the many who found a place for Akhenaten as a forerunner of their own ideas. See **Ancient Mystical Order Rosae Crucis (AMORC)**; **National Socialism**; **retrospective recruitment**.

Further reading: Aldred 1988, Redford 1984.

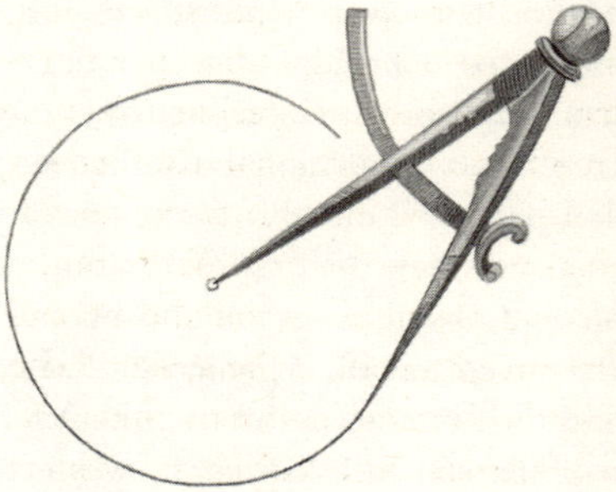

Albigensians

A common term for the Cathars, derived from the town of Albi, where the Cathar faith first established itself in France. See **Cathars**.

Alchemy

One of the core elements of the western esoteric traditions, the science of alchemy has had an important part in the teachings of secret societies from ancient times up to the present. Today's popular culture and the publicists of modern western science portray alchemy as a failed predecessor of chemistry that wasted centuries in an attempt to turn lead into gold by hopelessly inadequate means, but alchemy was much more than this.

A comprehensive philosophy of matter, alchemy included physics, chemistry, biology, meteorology, medicine, herbalism, embryology, the environmental sciences, psychology, economics, and mystical religion. Alchemists in China more than a thousand years ago successfully extracted steroidal sex hormones from human urine and used them to treat cases of hormonal insufficiency, and produced metallic aluminum. In the same way, the first distillation of alcohol, the discovery of phosphorus, the invention of organic fertilizers, and the first successful treatment for syphilis can be credited to western alchemists.

Nor is it certain that the central goal of western alchemy, the transformation of base metals to silver or gold, is entirely a will-o'-the-wisp. Such transmutations were witnessed more than once by qualified and skeptical observers, who used the best available technology to check their results. Nature doubtless has nooks and crannies that modern western science has not yet discovered, and alchemists in the past might have stumbled across one or more of those. The alchemists themselves claimed that a mysterious substance called the "secret fire" was necessary for transmutation; might this have been electricity, produced by simple lead-acid batteries, and transmutation akin to the "cold fusion" that set the scientific world on its ear a few years ago? No one knows.

Alchemy first surfaced in China, India, and Hellenistic Egypt around the second century BCE. The question of its origins remains wide open; scholars have argued inconclusively for many years whether it began in one of these areas and spread to the others, whether it emerged independently in all three, or if it originated in some other area that has not yet been traced.

Common to all alchemical traditions is the use of symbolism and evasive language to communicate alchemical secrets to those who already know the craft, while hiding them from all others. According to all accounts, the only way to understand the core secrets of alchemy is to receive them from an experienced alchemist, or to grasp them through a sudden flash of insight after careful reading of alchemical texts. Alchemists themselves claimed that openly publishing the secrets of their art might literally bring about the destruction of the world. Since those secrets are still hidden today, the reality behind these dire warnings remains anyone's guess.

While these common themes connect all the different branches of alchemy, the art went through many changes in its history. The Chinese alchemical tradition spread throughout the Far East but had only indirect contact with traditions further west until recent times. It focused on creating the elixir of life. The original *wai dan* or "Outer Elixir" school, which attempted to create this substance in the laboratory, was largely replaced in medieval times by a newer *nei dan* or "Inner Elixir" school, which used meditation, breathing, and subtle energy exercises (*qigong*) to create the elixir within the body using the body's own internal substances. Important elements of Taoist meditation, Chinese medicine, and "internal" martial arts such as tai chi developed out of this alchemical tradition. Chinese secret societies such as the White Lotus societies adopted many of these practices in past centuries and some offshoots of the White Lotus tradition still teach them today. See **White Lotus societies**.

In India, alchemy paid more attention to the creation of gold, but underwent the same transformation as in China. The art of laboratory alchemy, known as *rasayana* in India, was cultivated using simple equipment but complex vegetable compounds, while on the internal side alchemy fused with yoga and Tantric spirituality to create subtle sciences of physiological and psychological transformation.

In the West, the alchemy of Hellenistic Egypt failed to catch on in Greece or Rome, but found eager pupils among the Arabs. Arabic alchemists such as Jabir ibn Hayyan (*c.*720–810 CE) focused their efforts on metallic alchemy and invented most of the later toolkit of the western alchemist, perfecting the athanor (the alchemist's furnace) and making important advances in laboratory technique. Beginning in the twelfth century, Arabic alchemical writings made their way to medieval Europe and launched a widespread alchemical movement there.

During the Renaissance, the golden age of European alchemy, tens of thousands of alchemists bent over retorts and crucibles in an attempt to wrest the secrets of gold-making from mute matter. Most of these were "puffers," untaught novices motivated by greed, but some of the greatest alchemical writings of all time came out of the ferment of the Renaissance – works such as Salomon Trismosin's *Splendor Solis,* Basil Valentine's *Triumphal Chariot of Antimony,* and the lavishly illustrated writings of Michael Maier. These same years saw alchemical studies expand to include almost every branch of human knowledge from theology to agriculture.

It was the alchemy of the late Renaissance that flowed into secret societies in the early modern period, as the spread of the scientific revolution forced all occult sciences underground and esoteric secret societies tried to salvage everything they could of the occult traditions before they were lost forever. The complexity of Renaissance alchemical studies means, though, that a secret society that claims to teach and practice alchemy may be doing almost anything. When the eighteenth-century German *Orden des Gold- und Rosenckreuz* (Order of the Golden and Rosy Cross), an influential Rosicrucian order of the time, boasted of its alchemical teachings, it meant that its initiates spent long hours in laboratories over crucibles and retorts, attempting to create the philosopher's stone that enabled common metals to be turned into gold. When the Octagon Society, an American esoteric order founded in the 1920s, refers to its alchemical teachings, it means that its initiates practice a system of psychological healing meant to turn the "lead" of painful memories and unproductive mental states into the "gold" of mental healing and joy. Both of these can be very worthwhile pursuits, but they have little in common beyond the label "alchemy" and a handful of symbolic themes drawn from alchemical teachings. See **Octagon Society**; **Order of the Golden and Rosy Cross**.

After many years when alchemy was practiced only in secret, alchemical studies saw a revival in the late twentieth century. To some extent this was the work of psychologist Carl Jung (1875–1961), whose studies of alchemical literature convinced him that the old alchemists had been studying depth psychology concealed as folk chemistry. While this is true only of a small portion of alchemical writings, it made alchemy respectable again and encouraged scholars and occultists alike to take another look at the complex symbolism of alchemy.

At the same time, though, several occult secret societies in the early twentieth century began the process of reviving a tradition of laboratory alchemy. During the first decades of the century, a secretive occult order in Paris, the Brotherhood of Heliopolis, helped reintroduce practical alchemy into French occult circles. Inspired by this, the American Rosicrucian order AMORC taught classes in laboratory alchemy at their San Jose headquarters in California during the 1940s and circulated information on alchemical practice through its widespread network of initiates in America and elsewhere. During the late twentieth century, a lively alchemical revival took off from these beginnings; many classic works of alchemical literature are again in print, and alchemical studies are once more spreading through secret societies and the occult community as a whole. See **Ancient Mystical Order Rosae Crucis (AMORC)**.

Further reading: Albertus 1960, Anonymous 1994, Fulcanelli 1971, Grossinger 1983, Trismosin 1991.

Aldworth, Elizabeth

According to contemporary accounts, Elizabeth Aldworth (née St Leger), the daughter of Viscount Doneraile, was the first woman to be initiated into Freemasonry. In 1710, at the age of 17, she walked into a room in her father's mansion near Cork where a lodge meeting was in progress. The members of the lodge put her in the anteroom, debated the issue, and decided that the only way to prevent her from revealing their secrets was to initiate her and swear her to secrecy. She was duly initiated, and remained a supporter of Masonry until her death in 1773 at the age of 80. Masons referred to her after her marriage as "our sister Aldworth."

Similar accounts describe the admission of a handful of other women to Masonic lodges in the eighteenth century. The first lodges of Adoptive Masonry, a branch of the Craft specifically for women, were founded in France in 1760, and several irregular jurisdictions of Masonry have admitted women to the standard Craft degrees since the middle of the nineteenth century. See **Adoptive Masonry**; **Co-Masonry**.

All-American Association

Founded in 1923 in Memphis, Tennessee, the All-American Association was one of many organizations that rose in opposition to the revived Ku Klux Klan. Its official objects were to promote patriotism and combat intolerance and bigotry. Members pledged themselves to gather information on the Klan's illegal activities and expose the individuals involved. It went out of existence sometime after the Klan's implosion in the late 1920s. See **Knights of Liberty**; **Ku Klux Klan**; **Order of Anti-Poke-Noses**.

Allegory

One of the core elements in secret society ritual, symbolism, and literature is allegory, the creation or use of a story with a hidden meaning concealed beneath the obvious one. Allegory was one of the most popular literary devices in the Middle Ages and Renaissance; few works of literature from those times failed to have at least one allegorical meaning, and Jewish, Christian, and Muslim scholars all treated their respective scriptures as allegorical books in which many levels of hidden meaning could be found beneath the literal interpretation. While allegory was driven out of philosophy and science around the time of the scientific revolution, it remained a common feature in popular literature until the beginning of the twentieth century.

Secret societies picked up the habit of allegory early on. Freemasonry drew from its roots in operative masonry the habit of thinking of its tools as the emblems of moral ideas; for example, the level, used by operative masons to check the set of stones, became a symbol of equality – the idea that all "are on the same level." Similar connections link other working tools and objects in a Masonic lodge to moral concepts, and this led the designers of Masonic degrees to weave allegorical stories early on. In many Masonic degrees, events from history or legend have been turned into moral allegories. See **Freemasonry**.

Complexities enter the picture because the same story can have more than one allegorical meaning, and such meanings can change without any alteration to the ritual itself. Nor is it easy to tell what any particular allegory is intended to mean. The Masonic legend of Hiram Abiff, the master builder of King Solomon's Temple, is a case in point. Most modern Masons interpret it as an allegory of faithfulness in the face of death, but Jacobite Freemasons in France used it as an allegory for the execution of King Charles I of England in 1649, which they hoped to avenge; revolutionaries of many nations in the nineteenth century saw it as an allegory of their countrymen's sufferings under the rule of foreign overlords; Theosophist mystics in Co-Masonry in the early twentieth century understood it as an account of the fall of the spirit into matter; while certain modern writers on the origins of Freemasonry insist that it refers to events in the distant past, ranging from the assassination of an obscure Egyptian pharaoh to the destruction of the planet Mars by asteroids. See **Hiram Abiff**.

The unpopularity of allegory in modern philosophy and literature has much to do with the spread of speculative theories about secret societies. In nineteenth-century Britain and America, when allegory was still popular, people handled it with some degree of sophistication and rarely fell into the trap of thinking that because an allegory seems to make sense, it must have been intended by the author. Too many people nowadays lack this awareness. Much of the wilder modern literature on secret societies assumes that if a story can be interpreted allegorically, the hidden meaning must not only be intentional, but true. This has added to the entertainment value of today's alternative reality literature, but does little to make it accurate or even reasonable. See **rejected knowledge**.

Alpina

See **Grand Loge Alpina**.

Alta Vendita

In some nineteenth- and twentieth-century conspiracy theories, the name of a secret society conspiring to overthrow monarchy and private property across Europe. The name is actually the title used by national grand lodges of the Carbonari, an early nineteenth-century political secret society with liberal aims. See **Carbonari**.

Altar

One of the most common pieces of lodge furniture in secret societies of all kinds is an altar, usually placed at the center of the lodge room, draped with an altar cloth, and provided with one or more symbolic objects. The existence of altars in lodge rooms is one of the facts most often pointed out by Christian critics of secret societies to claim that the latter practice a non-Christian religion. In some cases this claim is justified, in most it is not; in all cases, though, the symbolism and function of a lodge altar set it apart from altars in Christian churches and Pagan temples alike. See **Antimasonry**; **lodge**.

A lodge altar forms the symbolic focus of the lodge. The most important events in initiation rituals and other lodge ceremonies take place at it; core symbols of the lodge rest on it; new initiates go on symbolic journeys around it. In nearly all lodges, the line connecting the seat of the presiding officer with the altar is not to be crossed except when the ritual specifically directs it.

The shape of the altar, the color of the altar cloth, and the items put on the altar have provided the creators of secret societies with a wide field for their symbolic art. Rectangular altars are most common, but secret societies that use threefold symbolism, such as Royal Arch Masonry and the Knights of Pythias, commonly have triangular altars. Altar cloths range from solid colors, such as the plain black cover of the altar in a temple of the Hermetic Order of the Golden Dawn, to complicated patterns and designs with extensive symbolic meanings. See **Hermetic Order of the Golden Dawn**; **Knights of Pythias**; **Royal Arch**.

The symbolic objects on the altar provide the lodge designer with enormous freedom, though it's not always used. Most American fraternal secret societies, for example, simply place an open Bible on the altar. On the other hand, not all secret societies have an altar in the lodge at all. In lodges of the Independent Order of Odd Fellows, for example, the center of the lodge room is empty, and the open Bible rests on a podium at the chaplain's station. The empty space at the center of the lodge forms a symbolic focus in Odd Fellows ritual, however, and important objects and actions are located there at various points in the degree work. See **Odd Fellowship**.

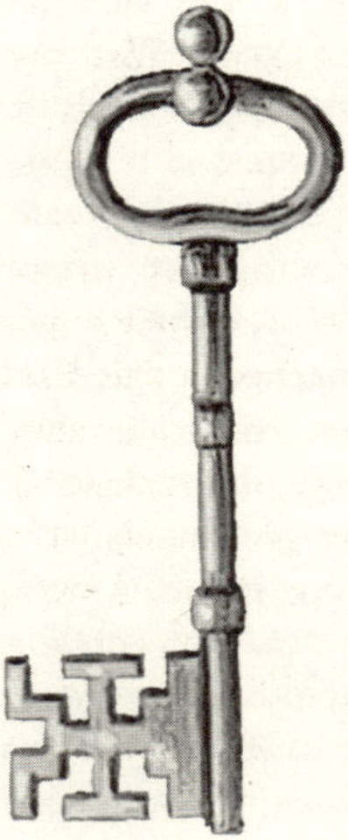

Alternative 3

On June 20, 1977, a British television network, Anglia TV, ran a mock-documentary titled *Alternative 3*, perhaps the most successful science-fiction spoof since the radio broadcast of H.G. Wells' *The War of the Worlds.* According to the show and the 1979 book that followed it, the earth's governments had discovered that air pollution would shortly doom the earth and its inhabitants. Three plans had been devised to save the human race. Alternative 1 used nuclear explosions to blast pollutants into space; Alternative 2 mandated the creation of underground habitats into which survivors could retreat from the dying surface of the planet.

Both these alternatives had proven unworkable, however, leaving only Alternative 3 – the emergency colonization of Mars. Working in total secrecy, a joint American–Russian space program had reached Mars in 1962. In order to provide a labor force for the huge project, many thousands of ordinary people had been kidnapped, turned into mindless slaves by brain surgery and drugs, and shipped to Mars via two concealed lunar bases. These "Batch-Consignment Components" were directed by small crews of "Designated Movers" under the command of an international leadership. Anyone who attempted to leak the truth about Alternative 3 was targeted for assassination via laser "hot job."

Although the show displayed a prominent notice that it had originally been scheduled for April 1, and listed a cast of professional actors in its credits, *Alternative 3* quickly became a hot topic among conspiracy theorists. A flurry of magazine articles and at least one book, Jim Keith's *Casebook on Alternative 3* (1994), argued that even though the film itself was fiction, all its allegations were true. Some writers suggested that the TV show was "gray disinformation" meant either to help build a social consensus in favor of an Alternative 3-type evacuation, or to make people dismiss the idea as fiction so Alternative 3 could continue unhindered. Like so many elements of modern conspiracy theory, the Alternative 3 story seems destined to keep playing out in the collective imagination for a long time to come. See **Disinformation**; **unidentified flying objects (UFOs)**.

Further reading: Keith 1994b, Watkins 1979.

America, discovery of

Since Christopher Columbus sighted a small island in the West Indies and mistook it for part of Asia, the possibility that America was visited by Old World voyagers before his time has been hotly debated. The first discovery of America, of course, happened tens of thousands of years before his time, when the ancestors of today's Native American peoples reached the New World. In recent years, though, the probability that others made the trip before 1492 has become a certainty. One set of transatlantic crossings has been firmly proven by archeology; three others are supported by significant evidence, and at least three contacts across the Pacific Ocean have solid backing as well.

The best documented voyages across the Atlantic before 1492 were those of the Vikings. In 1000 CE Leif Ericsson, the son of the man who led the Norse settlement of Greenland, sailed along the coasts of what is now eastern Canada and spent the winter on the continent before sailing home to Greenland. A few years later, inspired by his example, several shiploads of Greenlanders sailed to L'Anse aux Meadows in Newfoundland and built a settlement. Troubles with local Native Americans forced the settlement to be abandoned a few years later; it was uncovered by Canadian archeologists in the 1970s, proving a Norse presence in America.

The other probable Atlantic voyages also took the northern route. That route may have been opened by Irish voyagers, sailing westwards in hide-covered boats that have been navigated from Ireland to America in modern times; the early medieval *Voyage of St Brendan* includes good descriptions of icebergs and other North Atlantic sights on a saint's voyage to the "Land of Promise" in the west. Canadian writer Farley Mowat's book *The Farfarers* presents a good case for a migration from ancient Scotland via Iceland and Greenland to Newfoundland, partly drawn by rich resources ahead of them and partly driven by the Viking presence behind. If he's right, maritime Canada saw immigrants from far off long before the seventeenth century.

Later on, as European shipbuilding improved, fishing craft ventured further into the North Atlantic. Several historians have pointed to evidence that British, French, and Portuguese fishing fleets used harbors along the northeast coast of North America as stopping places where water casks could be refilled and food restocked by barter with the native peoples. Some of the enigmatic stone ruins along the coast may have been built by fishermen who over-wintered in the New World, or set up facilities to process catches before sailing home to Europe.

The voyage of Henry Sinclair, Earl of Orkney, to the shores of America in 1398 followed these fishing routes. According to the record of his Venetian navigator Niccolo Zeno, the main source for the voyage, Sinclair sailed west from Orkney with 12 ships, wintered over in Nova Scotia, and sailed south as far as Massachusetts before returning to Europe. Here the evidence of Zeno's written account combines with something far more concrete – the image of a figure in fifteenth-century armor, hammered painstakingly into a rock face near Waterford, Massachusetts, where it can still be seen today. According to Zeno's account this was the burial effigy of Sir James Gunn, one of Sinclair's companions. See **Sinclair family**.

The Pacific Ocean may seem like a much greater barrier than the Atlantic, but solid evidence exists for crossings to America from the west. Several plant crops from southeastern Asia, such as cotton and sweet potato, were grown in Mexico and South America before 1492; crops don't cross oceans by themselves, so clearly somebody brought them. The most likely candidates are the Polynesians, who crossed vast stretches of open ocean centuries before European mariners first dared to sail out of sight of land. Linguistic and technological evidence suggests that several Polynesian voyages reached America well before Columbus did.

Japanese and Chinese sailors seem to have accomplished the same feat. The Kuroshio Current, one of the great Pacific currents, sweeps past Japan and the eastern shores of Asia, arcs across the northern Pacific, and flows down the western coasts of North and South America. Most people who grew up near the beaches of Washington and Oregon state, as the present author did, remember beachcombing for blown glass fishing-net floats from Japanese fishing vessels; lost in the Aleutians or the waters off Japan, the floats followed the Kuroshio around to the beaches of the Pacific Northwest. The same current brought scores of Japanese fishing vessels to America in historic times, and doubtless did so earlier as well. The language of the Zuñi people of New Mexico shares hundreds of words with medieval Japanese, and Zuñi religion and culture combine Japanese and Native American elements; in her book *The Zuñi Enigma*, Nancy Yaw Davis has argued that the Zuñi emerged out of the fusion of a native tribe with voyagers from Japan who landed on the California coast in the Middle Ages and moved inland.

Chinese contact with the New World may date back many centuries further. Old Chinese myths speak of a wonderful land across the Pacific, the paradise of the goddess Hsi Wang Mu, and voyagers seeking the peaches of immortality sailed east from China's shores in search of that far country for more than two thousand years. Physical traces ranging from Chinese coins to stone anchors from Chinese oceangoing junks have been found along the coasts of North and South America. While some recent claims for Chinese overseas voyages appear overstated, a Chinese presence on the western shores of the New World is hard to dismiss.

All these are tolerably well supported by evidence. The literature on voyages to the New World before 1492, however, includes literally thousands of other claims. Some of these may well be true. The fact that some people from the Old World reached America before Columbus, though, does not mean that all the claims are true. This should be obvious, but today's alternative history literature demonstrates that it is not obvious enough. Claims that the Knights Templars had an overseas empire in the New World, for example, are based on a series of unlikely assumptions about seventeenth-century pirates and Masonic symbolism, a legend about a non-existent Templar Atlantic fleet, and very little more, except the fact that books on Templars are a hot commodity in the alternative scene nowadays. Equally, claims that ancient Egyptians (who stopped building pyramids around 2000 BCE) must have crossed the Atlantic to teach the Mayans (who started building their own, very different pyramids around the beginning of the Common Era) rest on wild assumptions, not evidence. See **Egypt**; **Knights Templar**; **skull and crossbones**.

Further reading: Davis 2000, Pohl 1974.

American Order of Clansmen

A competitor to the Knights of the Ku Klux Klan, the American Order of Clansmen was founded in San Francisco in 1915 as a "patriotic, social and benevolent secret society." The year is significant, since 1915 saw the appearance of the movie *Birth of a Nation*, a masterpiece of racist propaganda that portrayed the original Ku Klux Klan of the post-Civil War South as heroic defenders of white culture against bestial black hordes. *Birth of a Nation* inspired Col. William Simmons to launch the Knights of the Ku Klux Klan, the most successful Klan revival, in Georgia, and probably played the same role on the other side of the country in bringing the American Order of Clansmen into being. See **Ku Klux Klan**.

Under pressure from the revived Klan, the American Order reorganized itself as a fraternal beneficiary order in 1919, discarded the white robes and hoods of the original Klan, and focused on patriotic causes. Never very large or successful, it seems to have gone out of existence sometime in the 1920s.

American Party

See **Know-Nothing Party**.

American Protective Association [APA]

Founded at Clinton, Iowa in 1887, the APA was an anti-Catholic secret society motivated by fears that the Roman Catholic Church sought to dominate American politics and erase barriers between church and state. It pursued immigration restrictions, removal of tax exemption from Catholic churches, and "public inspection of all private institutions where persons of either sex are secluded, with or against their will" (a reference to media stories about Catholic monasteries and nunneries). By 1896 it had a membership between one and two million, and could count 20 known members in the US Congress. See **Roman Catholic Church**.

Unlike the revived Ku Klux Klan, which took up the anti-Catholic banner after the First World War, the APA did not combine its anti-Catholicism with racism; in northern states, black men were admitted to full membership, while south of the Mason–Dixon line the APA organized separate white and black Councils (local lodges). The APA remained a significant force in American politics until the First World War but was eclipsed thereafter. See **Ku Klux Klan**.

American Protective League [APL]

A secret society organized and operated by the US government, the American Protective League was founded in 1917 after the American declaration of war on Germany. Under the auspices of the Federal Bureau of Investigation (FBI), responsible for counterintelligence work on US soil, the APL recruited volunteers as unpaid secret agents for the duration of the war. Each member had a number, and reported suspicious activities to his or her captain, who forwarded them to the local FBI office.

The APL had 250,000 members by the end of the war. In February 1919, the FBI dissolved it and issued colorful certificates to each of its members. As far as can be determined, the APL's activities did not result in the arrest of a single spy or the prevention of a single act of sabotage. When the Second World War broke out, the experiment was not repeated.

American Revolution

The successful insurgency of American colonists against British rule between 1775 and 1782 has been cited far more rarely by historical conspiracy theorists as an example of secret society interference in politics than the French Revolution that broke out less than a decade later. This is ironic, because – while the role of secret societies in the French Revolution is ambiguous at best – the American Revolution was unquestionably planned and carried out by well-documented secret societies.

The origins of the American Revolution can be traced to British colonial policy under the Tory governments favored by King George III. British attempts to restrict colonists' westward expansion combined with unpopular tax policies to produce widespread resentment against British rule. The British responded with military repression, and the colonists countered with boycotts and the first outbreaks of violence.

In the midst of this rising spiral of confrontation, at least two significant secret societies took shape. The first of these organizations was the Committees of Correspondence. Largely drawn from the landowners and educated classes, the Committees coordinated political action across the 13 colonies and kept each colony abreast of radical activities and British government responses throughout America. Many members of the Committees ended up becoming delegates to the Continental Congresses of the war years and the Constitutional Convention that followed. See **Committees of Correspondence**.

The second of these organizations was the Sons of Liberty, a radical organization centered in Boston, the hotbed of colonial radicalism. The Sons of Liberty drew most of its membership from the urban middle classes and pursued a radical line, favoring independence while most colonists still hoped for an improved relationship with Britain. Terrorist actions against British property were a Sons of Liberty hallmark, with the famous Boston Tea Party – the dumping of three shiploads of imported tea into Boston Harbor to protest a tax on tea – their most famous act. During the last months before the outbreak of war, the Sons of Liberty organized armed bands that became the nucleus of the colonial army. See **Sons of Liberty**.

Both these societies had connections to Freemasonry, but the role of the Craft in the American Revolution was an ambivalent one. Most of the upper-level leadership of American Masonry on the eve of the Revolution sided with Britain, but many ordinary Masons supported independence. George Washington was a Mason, as were 32 other generals in the Continental Army and 8 members of Washington's personal staff. Benjamin Franklin, ambassador to France and architect of the Franco-American alliance that won independence, was not only a Freemason but a member of the prestigious Loge des Neuf Soeurs in Paris, as well as a member of the Friars of St Francis of Wycombe, better known as the Hell-Fire Club. See **Franklin, Benjamin**; **Freemasonry**; **Hell-Fire Club**.

The war years saw the Sons of Liberty and Committees of Correspondence absorbed completely into the Continental Army and the emerging government; once their purpose was fulfilled, these secret societies faded away. Freemasonry became popular during and after the Revolution, but its popularity did not prevent it from becoming the target of a New England witch-hunt in the late 1790s and a systematic attempt at extinction by the Antimasonic Party of the 1830s. See **Antimasonic Party**; **Antimasonry**.

Anarchism

A major political force in the nineteenth and early twentieth centuries, anarchism was communism's most important rival in the struggle to define and control the Left, and gave rise to important political secret societies. Its principal founder was French philosopher Pierre-Joseph Proudhon (1809–65), who argued that all legal systems are methods by which the rich oppress the poor, and a just society could only be founded on the basis of voluntary associations. Proudhon's famous *What is Property?* (1840) argued that "property is theft" and that systems that give ownership of land and other necessities to a few are simply methods of institutionalized robbery.

After Proudhon, anarchism developed in two main directions, and the most important figure in each was a Russian. Prince Pyotr Kropotkin (1842–1921), the doyen of pacifist anarchism, argued for an ideal state in which government and private property would alike be abolished, removing the causes of crime and violence. His older contemporary Mikhail Bakunin (1814–76) argued instead for the violent overthrow of every government. Bakunin was the head of the International Brothers, a revolutionary secret society, and his writings helped inspire a wave of political violence in the late nineteenth century carried out by anarchist and Nihilist secret societies. See **International Brothers**; **Nihilists**.

All through the late nineteenth century, anarchist and communist groups struggled for control of labor unions and left-wing political parties in Europe and America, and only the victory of the Bolsheviks in the Russian Revolution of 1917 and the Russian civil war that followed it made communism the standard doctrine of the far left in the middle years of the twentieth century. Despite a small resurgence of interest during the 1960s, anarchism never regained the ground it lost and remains mostly the concern of historians of ideas today. See **Communism**.

Further reading: Joll 1980, Wells 1987.

Ancient and Accepted Scottish Rite [AASR]

The most influential of the concordant bodies of Freemasonry in the United States and one of the most important Masonic rites worldwide, the Ancient and Accepted Scottish Rite was founded in Charleston, South Carolina in 1802 by a group of Freemasons who had received a charter to work the Rite of Perfection, a system of high degrees from France that claimed descent from the medieval Knights Templar but actually had their roots in the Jacobite Masonry of the mid-eighteenth century. They obtained several additional degrees from various sources, expanding their Rite from the 25 degrees worked by the Rite of Perfection to 33. Recruitment was slow, and for decades the Scottish Rite ranked as one of the minor rites in American Freemasonry. It has two jurisdictions in America, Northern and Southern; the Northern, despite the name, includes only those northern states east of the Mississippi River, so that Scottish Rite Masons in Alaska belong to the Southern Jurisdiction. See **Freemasonry**; **Jacobites**; **Rite of Perfection**; **Scottish degrees**.

The transformation that turned the Scottish Rite into one of the world's most successful Masonic rites was the work of one man, Albert Pike (1809–91). Pike joined the Scottish Rite in 1853 and rose quickly through its ranks, becoming Sovereign Grand Commander of the Southern Jurisdiction in 1859. He completely rewrote the Rite's initiation rituals, replacing dull and turgid language with genuine poetry and inserting a great deal of occult philosophy into the ceremonies. In addition, his *Morals and Dogma* (1871) – a commentary on the Scottish Rite degrees – is one of the classics of nineteenth-century occultism. It has been said, with some justice, that Pike "found the Scottish Rite in a log cabin and left it in a Temple." See **Pike, Albert**.

Pike envisioned the Scottish Rite as the university of Freemasonry, a body in which those Masons interested in the philosophical and spiritual dimensions of the Craft could work their way through degrees that summed up the moral and intellectual heritage of the western world. During his time, Scottish Rite lodges met in buildings owned by other Masonic bodies, and Pike wrote movingly of the simplicity and dignity of the rituals. Under Pike and his successors, the Rite spread to many other countries, and Supreme Councils were chartered in Europe, South America and Australasia.

Pike's immediate successors in the American jurisdictions lacked his vision, but for the most part they followed the precedents he had set. Starting in the decades after Pike's death, however, the Rite gradually took on a more active political stance and entered into a long-running feud against the Roman Catholic Church. Masonic bitterness about the Vatican's hostility toward Masonry goes back centuries, but in early twentieth century American opposition to Catholicism also served to cloak racist attitudes toward Irish, Italian, and Hispanic immigrants. Successive Sovereign Grand Commanders in the Southern Jurisdiction used the Rite's resources to disseminate anti-Catholic propaganda and lobby against parochial schools. See **Roman Catholic Church**.

The Scottish Rite's opposition toward Catholicism became a severe liability in the 1920s when it brought the Rite into a tacit alliance with the revived Ku Klux Klan. The Klan shared the Rite's anti-Catholic sentiments, and white Masons' hostility toward black Prince Hall Masonry rendered the Rite's leadership as well as its ordinary members vulnerable to the Klan's blandishments. During the mid-1920s several members of the Southern Jurisdiction's Supreme Council were also Klansmen, and one of them simultaneously headed the Scottish Rite and the Klan in his home state. As the Klan's dubious activities came to light in the media in the second half of the decade, embarrassed Scottish Rite leaders and members alike concealed their Klan involvements, but the Rite's reputation suffered. See **Ku Klux Klan**; **Prince Hall Masonry**.

The difficulties caused by the Rite's short-lived rapprochement with the Klan proved to be transitory. By the end of the twentieth century, though, the Rite in America faced problems that offered no easy solutions. The roots of the predicament reached back to the beginning of the century, and grew out of the soaring popularity of the Scottish Rite in those years. Faced with hundreds of enthusiastic new members, most American Scottish Rite units began to confer the degrees as theatrical performances in which new members simply sat through a series of ritual plays, standing at intervals to join in when it was time to take the obligations of each degree. At the same time, the once-mandatory time between degrees went by the wayside, and new rules allowed most of the degrees to be skipped, so that only five degrees – 4°, 14°, 18°, 30°, and 32° – were required. By the middle of the twentieth century new members of the Rite in America went from 3°, Master Mason, to 32°, Master of the Royal Secret, in a single weekend, or even a single day, by sitting in an auditorium and watching five rituals performed on stage.

These changes went as far as they did because the Scottish Rite in America during this time had become economically dependent on another Masonic concordant body, the Ancient Arabic Order of Nobles of the Mystic Shrine. The Shriners had golf courses and other members-only recreational facilities that offered a powerful draw to the middle-class and middle-aged men who made up the majority of American Masons. Membership in the Shrine was available only to Masons who held either the 32° of the Scottish Rite or the Knight Templar degree of the York Rite, but most Shriners had little interest in Freemasonry – in the late 1950s, 92 percent of Shriners never set foot inside a Masonic lodge meeting and 95 percent never attended meetings of Scottish Rite or York Rite bodies after their initiation. The Scottish Rite capitalized on this by simplifying the process so that Master Masons could qualify for Shrine membership after a single weekend of Scottish Rite degrees. This brought the Rite a steady income from hundreds of thousands of members who had no interest in the Rite itself but paid their dues every year to maintain their standing in the Shrine. See **Ancient Arabic Order of Nobles of the Mystic Shrine (AAONMS)**.

All this changed abruptly in 2000 when the Shrine, faced with declining membership on its own account, changed its rules to allow Master Masons to join without going through the Scottish or York Rites first. Enrollment in the Scottish Rite, already dwindling at that time, plummeted thereafter. While the Rite's survival in the United States is probably not at risk, it seems likely to shrink to a small percentage of its peak size during the next few decades.

Outside the United States, the Rite's history has followed different paths. In Latin America, the Scottish Rite is far and away the most popular branch of Masonry, and most Masonic lodges are affiliated with it. In the years following the Soviet Union's collapse the Rite succeeded in expanding into eastern European countries formerly closed to Masonry, including Russia itself, and seems to be taking a similar role there. In Britain, by contrast, the Rite has restricted its membership to Christians, limited access to its degrees, and dropped the word "Scottish" from its name, referring to itself as the Ancient and Accepted Rite; it remains a relatively small Masonic body there.

Further reading: Brockman 1996, Hutchens 1995, Pike 1871.

Ancient Arabic Order of Nobles of the Mystic Shrine [AAONMS]

The premier burlesque order in Freemasonry, the Ancient Arabic Order of Nobles of the Mystic Shrine – the Shriners, for short – was founded in New York City in 1871 by Dr. Walter Fleming (1838–1913) and a circle of Masonic friends who met for lunch at the Knickerbocker Cottage, a popular restaurant. In its early years, the new organization claimed to be exactly what it was – a social drinking club for high-ranking Freemasons invented in the early 1870s – and for that reason attracted little attention. See **burlesque degrees**; **Freemasonry**.

In 1877, however, Fleming realized that this was a mistake and invented a romantic origin story for the Shriners, tracing it back to an Arab secret society of the Middle Ages that allegedly still had branches all over the Muslim world. Official letters from these branches were published in the Shrine's official proceedings for several years; despite historical and linguistic howlers most high school students of the time would have easily caught, they gave the Shriners the exotic origin and history that potential candidates wanted. See **origin stories**.

The result was an immediate and dramatic expansion in Shriner numbers, and the founding of dozens of new Temples (local lodges) across North America. The Shrine restricted its membership to Freemasons who had received either the 32° of the Scottish Rite or the Knight Templar degree of the York Rite, but even this attempt at exclusivity failed to slow down the Shrine's expansion. The Scottish Rite simply streamlined its initiation process to enable Master Masons to qualify for Shrine membership after a single weekend of Scottish Rite degree ceremonies, and profited handsomely from initiation fees and annual dues paid by men whose access to the Shrine depended on Scottish Rite membership. See **Ancient and Accepted Scottish Rite**; **York Rite**.

For the first half of its existence, if not more, the Shrine existed primarily as an excuse for partying and drinking on a heroic scale. By the early 1880s the annual convention of the Imperial Council, the international governing body of the Shrine, had already earned a reputation as the wildest party in American fraternalism. "Water from the well of Zumzum" and "camel's milk," the standard Shriner euphemisms for alcohol, flowed with such abandon at Shrine events that other Masonic bodies criticized the Shrine for its effect on the reputation of Freemasonry.

The Shrine's role as the premier Masonic drinking club, though, gave way to charitable fundraising as the twentieth century went on. Charitable projects became a focus of Shrine activity from 1888, when Shriners raised money nationwide to help Jacksonville, Florida deal with a devastating yellow fever epidemic. In 1930, the Imperial Council launched a program to build and fund free children's hospitals. More than 20 Shrine hospitals and burn clinics in cities around North America now provide free treatment to children in the largest charity program operated by any fraternal organization in the world.

These programs cost immense amounts of money, and Shrine Temples across the continent invested equally large sums in golf courses, clubhouses, and recreational facilities to attract and keep members. During the first two-thirds of the twentieth century this strategy paid off handsomely, but the social changes of the 1960s posed challenges that an organization composed mostly of middle-aged, socially conservative, white businessmen was poorly equipped to face. Membership peaked in the 1970s and began an inexorable decline. In 2000, in an attempt to boost membership, the Imperial Council removed the longstanding requirement for Shriners to hold high Scottish Rite or York Rite degrees. This had a drastic impact on the Scottish Rite, which suffered sharp membership losses thereafter, but had little impact on the decline in Shrine membership. While Shrine hospitals, burn centers, and other charities have large trust funds supporting them, the survival of the Shrine itself is more and more in question.

In the realm of American conspiracy theory, however, the Shrine has come to play an increasingly important part in recent years. Like the other branches of Freemasonry, it has attracted plenty of attention from antimasonic crusaders, and more recently it has been listed as one of the organizations suspected of stage-managing the New World Order. Several recent books have claimed that Shrine Headquarters in Chicago contains a working replica of the original Ark of the Covenant, which top-level Shriners use to communicate with aliens from other worlds – an interesting claim, since the Shrine moved its headquarters to Tampa, Florida in 1978. See **Ark of the Covenant**; **extraterrestrials**; **New World Order**.

Further reading: van Deventer 1964.

Ancient and Archaeological Order of Druids [AAOD]

A short-lived but influential British Druid order, the AAOD was founded in 1874 by Robert Wentworth Little (1840–78), an avid Freemason who also founded the Societas Rosicruciana in Anglia (SRIA). Like many Masons of his time, Little believed that Freemasonry had inherited the assembled wisdom of many ancient Pagan mysteries, and he was also influenced by theorists in the Druid Revival who presented ancient Celtic Druidry as a system of initiation parallel to Freemasonry. Another influence was the Ancient Order of Druids, founded outside Masonry in 1781. See **Ancient Order of Druids (AOD)**; **Druid Revival**; **Societas Rosicruciana in Anglia (SRIA)**.

While many members of the original AAOD came from within Masonry, Masonic affiliation was not originally required to join. In 1886, however, the governing Grand Grove of the order voted to change its name to the Ancient Masonic Order of Druids (AMOD) and expel all members who were not Master Masons in good standing. Nearly two-thirds of the order's members quit at that point, and formed a new organization under the original name, which continued in existence until sometime around 1900. The AMOD still exists as a Masonic side degree in Britain.

Ancient Druid Order [ADO]

See **Druid Circle of the Universal Bond**.

Ancient Illuminated Seers of Bavaria

See **Bavarian Illuminati**.

Ancient Mystical Order Rosae Crucis [AMORC]

The most successful of American Rosicrucian orders, the Ancient Mystical Order Rosae Crucis was founded in 1925 in Tampa, Florida by Harvey Spencer Lewis (1883–1939), an advertising executive with a longtime interest in the occult. He claimed Rosicrucian initiations from Europe and a lineage dating back to Akhenaten, the "heretic pharaoh" of Egypt, but the actual origins of AMORC are a good deal less exotic. The process of AMORC's evolution began in 1904, when Lewis founded an organization called the New York Institute for Psychical Research. Despite the scientific name, this was an occult study group with a particular interest in Rosicrucian traditions. See **Akhenaten**; **Rosicrucians**.

In 1915, Lewis contacted Theodor Reuss, founder and head of the Ordo Templi Orientis (OTO), and received a charter for an OTO lodge. This action brought him into the middle of the feud then under way between Reuss and Aleister Crowley, over the latter's attempt to turn the OTO into a vehicle for his new religion of Thelema. Crowley, who spent most of the First World War in America, attempted to recruit Lewis in 1918 but was rebuffed. Lewis's efforts on behalf of Reuss's branch of the OTO had little effect, however. In 1918 the New York City police raided his offices and arrested Lewis, charging him with selling fraudulent initiations. The charges were dropped, but Lewis relocated to San Francisco immediately thereafter. In 1925 he moved to Tampa, Florida and formally established an occult secret society of his own, the Ancient Mystical Order Rosae Crucis (AMORC). He soon discovered that the market for occult correspondence courses was concentrated on the west coast, and relocated to San Jose, California in 1927. AMORC's international headquarters remained there until 1990, and its North American operations are still based there. See **Crowley, Aleister**; **Ordo Templi Orientis (OTO)**; **Reuss, Theodor**.

Like most American occult orders of the time, AMORC used the correspondence-course model for recruitment and training. Advertisements in popular magazines offered a series of study-by-mail courses to prospective members, and those who completed the introductory courses were authorized to join a local group if one existed in their area, or help found one if one did not. Another standard procedure was the use of different titles and privileges for local lodges depending on their number of members, as an incentive to local recruitment; in AMORC's case it took 15 members to form a Pronaos, 30 to form a Chapter that could work the first of the Temple degrees, and 50 to form a Lodge that could confer the degree rituals.

Lewis's prior experience in the advertising industry gave him an advantage over his competitors. By the early 1930s AMORC was the largest occult order in America, and was expanding into foreign markets as well. The order did particularly well in France. Through this French connection AMORC unwittingly played a minor role in launching one of the most colorful hoaxes of recent years; see **Priory of Sion**.

Though AMORC's overseas expansion drew on the same methods that had made it successful in the American market, connections with existing European secret societies also played a part. Lewis built on his links with OTO lodges in Germany, headed by Heinrich Tränker (1880–1956) after Theodor Reuss's death in 1921, and also pushed the organization of an international Rosicrucian federation, the Fédération Universelle des Ordres et Sociétés Initiatiques (FUDOSI). These links with French occult sources brought Lewis into contact with the Martinist movement, and he quickly established a Martinist organization, the Traditional Martinist Order (TMO), open only to AMORC members. See **Martinism**.

AMORC's rapid expansion brought it unfriendly attention from its main American competitor, R. Swinburne Clymer's Fraternitas Rosae Crucis (FRC). From 1928 on, Clymer made common cause with disaffected ex-members of AMORC and circulated allegations that Lewis's order was simply a moneymaking scheme with no right to call itself Rosicrucian. Lewis responded in kind. The American occult press was enlivened for years by vitriolic blasts and counterblasts from the two orders, with Max Heindel's Rosicrucian Fellowship an occasional target from both sides. See **Fraternitas Rosae Crucis (FRC)**; **Rosicrucian Fellowship**.

During the 1930s AMORC expanded its San Jose headquarters to include a planetarium, a museum, and a college for Rosicrucian studies, where courses on practical laboratory alchemy were taught during the following decade. Lewis also found time to involve himself in lost continent literature, publishing a book on Lemuria under a pseudonym. Longtime residents of the Mount Shasta area have described AMORC expeditions in the 1930s searching for entrances to the Lemurian cities in the mountain. See **Alchemy**; **Lemuria**.

On Lewis's death in 1939, his son, Ralph M. Lewis, became Grand Imperator of AMORC. Under the younger Lewis's leadership, AMORC continued expanding into the international market, translating its correspondence-course material into scores of languages and marketing the order in any country that allowed it. By the time Ralph Lewis died in 1987, AMORC had members in over 100 countries and a secure place in the American occult scene.

Lewis was succeeded as Grand Imperator by Gary L. Stewart. In 1990, however, Stewart was deposed by AMORC's board amid charges of embezzlement. He was replaced by Christian Bernard, the head of AMORC's French branch, who remains Imperator as at the time of writing. The legal wrangling around Stewart's removal from office brought AMORC a certain amount of bad publicity and some loss in membership, and the attrition suffered by most of the older occult secret societies since the 1970s has also taken its toll. AMORC nonetheless remains a significant presence worldwide.

Further reading: Lewis 1948, McIntosh 1997.

Ancient Noble Order of Gormogons

A short-lived rival to Freemasonry, the Ancient Noble Order of Gormogons surfaced in the fall of 1724, announcing itself to the world in a London newspaper. The announcement claimed that the Gormogons were founded "many thousand years before Adam" by Chin-Quaw Ky-Po, the first emperor of China, and had just been brought to England by a Chinese mandarin. The article solicited new members but warned them that Freemasons would only be admitted if they renounced Masonry and were expelled from their lodges. A later article announced that the same mandarin was on his way to Rome, where he expected to initiate the Pope and the entire College of Cardinals into the Gormogons. See **Freemasonry**.

Behind these claims lay a complex political drama. The founder of the Gormogons was Philip, Duke of Wharton, a leader of the Jacobites, the supporters of the exiled House of Stuart. Wharton had a complex career in the secret societies of early eighteenth-century England. He founded the Hell-Fire Club in London in 1719 and closed it down in 1720. Apparently reformed, he was elected Grand Master of the Grand Lodge of England in 1722, but stormed out of Masonry the following year upon the publication of the first Book of Constitutions, which committed the Craft to "obedience to the civil government" and closed lodges to religious and political agitation. The Gormogons was his attempt at a rival organization, linked with the Stuart cause. See **Hell-Fire Club**; **Jacobites**.

The Gormogons carried on a lively propaganda campaign against Freemasonry, backed by money from Jacobites in the gentry and nobility. The order was never more than a private project of Wharton's, however, and on his death in 1731 the Gormogons seem to have quietly disbanded. The idea of a Stuart Masonry, however, was taken up in France a few years later with Andrew Ramsay's famous oration of 1736 and the creation of the first versions of Templar Masonry. See **Knights Templar**; **Ramsay, Andrew Michael**.

Ancient Order of Druids [AOD]

The oldest firmly documented Druid organization in the world, the Ancient Order of Druids was founded in 1781, probably by a London carpenter, Henry Hurle, and a group of friends. Looking for a name and appropriate imagery for his new group, Hurle hit on the ancient Druids, who had become a fashionable property in the romantic fiction of the time. An initiation ritual was soon devised, extolling the exploits of the ancient Druid leader Togodubeline – a name concocted from the first half of Togodumnus, an ancient Briton mentioned by Julius Caesar, and the second half of Cymbeline, the title character in one of Shakespeare's plays.

The AOD in its early days used the King's Arms tavern in central London as their meeting place, but the order soon found itself chartering new groves (local lodges) and established a Grand Grove to administer the order. Growth led to controversies; many of the new order's members, like its founder, came from the working classes, and by 1800 many groves were agitating for the establishment of a system of sickness and funeral benefits modeled on those of the Odd Fellows, the premier working-class secret society in Britain at that time. The leaders of the AOD, mostly drawn from the gentry, rejected this plan and tried to limit recruitment from the working classes. Finally, in 1833, most of the order's members broke away from the AOD to found a new society, the United Ancient Order of Druids (UAOD). The UAOD quickly eclipsed its parent in size and influence and went on to become the largest Druid order in the world for more than a century. See **Odd Fellowship**; **United Ancient Order of Druids (UAOD)**.

The AOD survived the defection of its working-class members, and continued to work along its original lines. Through much of the nineteenth century it drew most of its membership from the London theatrical world. The dubious social standing of the theatre at that time inspired the Freemason and Rosicrucian Robert Wentworth Little (1840–78) to found a competing Druid organization, the Ancient and Archaeological Order of Druids (AAOD), in 1874. Despite this competition, the AOD has remained quietly active up to the present. See **Ancient and Archaeological Order of Druids (AAOD)**.

Ancient Order of Druids in America [AODA]

Originally chartered as the American branch of the Ancient Masonic Order of Druids (AMOD), the Ancient Order of Druids in America was founded by American physician and Freemason Dr. James Manchester in Boston, Massachusetts on the summer solstice of 1912. Its membership at first came from within Masonry, but in the course of the twentieth century it drifted gradually away from a Masonic connection. In 1942 it changed its rules to allow the initiation of anyone vouched for by a Master Mason, and began admitting women; the first female Grand Archdruid, Dr. Juliet Ashley, took office in 1954. In 1976 it removed its last formal connection with Masonry and redefined itself as an esoteric religious order teaching Druid spirituality. In 2004 it incorporated as a Druid church.

Today, like most Druid organizations rooted in the eighteenth- and nineteenth-century Druid Revival, AODA keeps its initiation rituals private, but has few other traces of its secret society ancestry. Its teachings and most of its rituals are public. Its training program focuses on meditation, seasonal rituals, nature awareness, and lifestyle changes to help the environment, and it has a substantial online presence. See **Druid Revival**.

Ancient Order of United Workmen [AOUW]

The first and one of the most popular of the insurance lodges of nineteenth-century America, the Ancient Order of United Workmen got into the insurance business almost by accident. Its founder, John Upchurch, hoped to create an organization to help mediate the growing disagreements between business and labor in late nineteenth-century America. As an incentive for workers to join his order, he set up an insurance plan into which each member put $1 on joining and another $1 any time a member died. Out of that fund, an insurance payment of at least $500 went to the surviving family of each deceased member. The order never had much impact on labor disputes, but the insurance benefit proved extremely popular and made the AOUW an immediate success. See **fraternal benefit societies**.

Upchurch was a Freemason, and the symbols and rituals of his order were heavily influenced by Masonry. Even the Masonic square and compasses found a place in AOUW symbolism. See **Freemasonry**.

By 1895, when the order was at its peak, it had nearly 320,000 members and lodges all over the United States and Canada. By that time its insurance benefit had been copied by many other orders, and its original aim of managing disputes between business and labor had helped inspire the labor union movement. The twentieth century saw the AOUW share in the decline of most fraternal orders, however, and by the beginning of the twenty-first century it counted only a few hundred members in a handful of lodges in Washington State. See **labor unions**.

Annunaki

Originally the Babylonian word for "god," this word acquired a new meaning in many corners of the alternative-realities scene in Europe and America with the publication of Zecharia Sitchin's book, *The 12th Planet*, in 1976. Sitchin argued, based on his reinterpretation of Mesopotamian mythology, that the gods of ancient Sumer and Babylon were actually extraterrestrials from Nibiru, a previously unknown planet orbiting the sun in an elliptical orbit like that of a comet. The Annunaki, who were also the biblical Nephilim, established a base on Earth in the Middle East during the Ice Ages, and manufactured humanity from the local apes as a labor force to mine minerals for shipment back to Nibiru.

Like most ancient-astronaut theories, Sitchin's depends on the euhemerist assumptions that any divine miracle must be the product of something analogous to twentieth-century technology, and that all mythology is garbled history, lacking any more symbolic or spiritual meaning. While Sitchin believes that his theories explain Mesopotamian mythology, a case could equally be made that he has simply retold myths in the medium of science fiction. See **Euhemerism**.

Despite these difficulties, Sitchin's theories have attracted a substantial following in today's alternative-realities scene, and several other authors have borrowed liberally from his work to bolster their own theories. Among the most successful of these is David Icke, whose efforts to create a universal conspiracy theory embracing all alternative viewpoints did not neglect the Annunaki. Icke identified Sitchin's extraterrestrial gods with the reptilians that, in his belief, are the secret masters of the world. See **Reptilians**.

Further reading: Icke 1999, Icke 2001, Sitchin 1976, Sitchin 1980, Sitchin 2002.

Antarctica

The forbidding icebound continent at the bottom of the world was a target for speculation long before its existence was even certain. Many maps from the Middle Ages and Renaissance show a continent of the right shape at the southern end of the world. In the age of European exploration, many attempts were made to find this *Terra Australis Incognita* ("Unknown Southern Land"), and Australia got its name when Dutch navigators thought they had happened upon its northernmost reaches. Only in the nineteenth century did sailing vessels finally brave the bitter seas and ice floes to map out the coastline of the seventh continent, yet those coastlines appear on maps from the sixteenth century and before – one of several pretty puzzles posed by the impossible knowledge in old maps. See **lost civilizations**.

Its inaccessibility made Antarctica a favorite setting for adventure fiction in the late nineteenth and early twentieth centuries. The coldest weather on earth and a three-mile-thick ice cap posed little trouble for writers used to spicing their stories with geographical improbabilities. The handful of barren ice-free areas along the Antarctic coast turned, in these tales, into forests hidden behind walls of ice, teeming with woolly mammoths and similar livestock; alternatively, the ice gives way to barren uplands in which lost cities wait to be discovered. In the best of these tales, H.P. Lovecraft's *At the Mountains of Madness*, explorers find an obsidian city millions of years old on an ice-free plateau. Its former inhabitants, an alien race from the stars, prove to be a good deal less extinct than they look.

The appeal of Lovecraft's story, and its many equivalents, guaranteed that its themes would find their way into twentieth-century alternative-reality theories. A document called the Hefferlin Manuscript entered circulation by the 1940s, describing the hidden Rainbow City in Antarctica, one of a network of underground cities built by Martians some two and a half million years ago. The Martians' enemies, monstrous reptiles from Venus, also have a hidden city in Antarctica where thousands of them sleep in suspended animation, waiting for human members of sinister serpent-worshipping cults to awaken them. The name of the reptiles' city, Kadath, is only one of many direct borrowings from Lovecraft. See **Rainbow City**.

Other speculations have dealt with Antarctica's forbidding climate by suggesting that the continent was free from ice at various points in the past – a claim that has some support from science, though the current consensus rejects it. One of the old maps to show Antarctica, the Oronteus Finaeus map of 1532, portrays the Ross Sea as it would look with open water in place of the present ice sheet. Several early twentieth-century occult orders taught that Antarctica's original name had been Isuria, and that it was ice-free and inhabited by an advanced society until it was destroyed by an immense catastrophe. Recent alternative-history literature argues similarly that Antarctica was the original Atlantis, and that it was not drowned beneath the oceans, as nearly all other accounts suggest, but flattened by a comet and then buried beneath ice as a result of the climate changes that followed. See **Atlantis**; **earth changes**.

These themes have seen their most colorful use in the neo-Nazi mythology of the "Last Battalion," a secret Nazi military force hidden away in some secret location in the Third Reich's last days to re-fight the Second World War. This story surfaced in the popular media in the summer of 1945, alongside claims that Hitler himself escaped Berlin and fled to an overseas refuge via U-boat. The rapid spread of variants of this story suggests that disinformation may have been involved, though Hitler's admirers in Europe and elsewhere proved themselves ready to clutch at straws in an effort to believe their hero was still alive. See **Disinformation**; **National Socialism**.

By the 1970s accounts in neo-Nazi circles claimed that the Antarctic base was equipped with flying saucers – allegedly, secret weapons designed and tested by the Third Reich during the war years – and had links to secret underground installations in remote corners of South America and South Africa. The German scientific expedition to Antarctica in 1938 and 1939 was redefined as a reconnaissance mission to locate sites for emergency bases in case Germany lost the approaching war, while the joint American–Soviet expedition headed by Admiral Byrd in 1946 and 1947 entered the mythology as a failed attempt by the Allies to conquer the hidden Nazi redoubt. Much of this material was circulated, and may have been invented, by the pro-Nazi writers Ernst Zundel and Wilhelm Landig to encourage loyalty to the failed Nazi cause. In recent years it has been adopted by several neo-Nazi secret societies, and blended with the "occult Hitlerism" of Miguel Serrano and Savitri Devi in the new racial mythology of the Black Sun. See **Black Sun**; **neo-Nazi secret societies**; **unidentified flying objects (UFOs)**.

Further reading: Godwin 1993, Goodrick-Clarke 2002, McKale 1981.

Anthroposophical Society

Founded by Austrian mystic Rudolf Steiner (1861–1925), the Anthroposophical Society was established in Dornach, Switzerland, in 1912 as a vehicle for Steiner's system of occult theory and practice. Called Anthroposophy ("wisdom of humanity," from Greek *anthropos*, "human," and *sophia*, "wisdom"), this system derives partly from Steiner's background as a Theosophist, partly from his intensive study of the writings of the German polymath

Johann Wolfgang Goethe (1749–1832), and partly from Steiner's wide acquaintance with the occult traditions of his own time. Standard Theosophical concepts such as karma, reincarnation, lost continents, root races, and spiritual evolution play a very large role in Anthroposophy, but share space with a strong if idiosyncratic Christian spirituality, in which the crucifixion of Jesus of Nazareth forms the central turning point in human evolution, an equivalent for the earth and humanity of the mystery initiations of ancient Greece. See **mysteries, ancient**; **Theosophical Society**.

Steiner evolved many of these ideas during his years as a Theosophist, during which he rose to the position of General Secretary of the Theosophical Society in Germany. In 1912, he broke with the Theosophical Society over the latter's promotion of Jiddu Krishnamurti as the next World Teacher, and founded the Anthroposophical Society as an alternative. More than 90 percent of German Theosophists followed him into the new society. Steiner obtained a charter for a lodge of the Rite of Memphis and Misraim – an occult branch of Freemasonry – from German Masonic promoter Theodor Reuss, but the Anthroposophical Society ended up taking Theosophy as its model and abandoned the secret society tradition in favor of a public teaching organization with an active publishing arm. See **Order of the Star in the East**; **Reuss, Theodor**; **Rite of Memphis and Misraim**.

Unlike many of the offshoots of Theosophy, Steiner's evolved a distinctive set of meditative exercises designed to foster spiritual clarity and non-physical perceptions. It also helped to inspire a remarkable range of practical applications. Steiner's work on biodynamic agriculture helped launch the modern organic farming movement, his Waldorf schools remain a popular alternative to conventional schooling, and eurhythmy, a performing art combining dance and gesture with the spoken word, has a small but devoted following in Europe and America.

All these movements have helped channel people into the Anthroposophical Society, which remains active today. Headquartered still in Dornach, in a building designed by Steiner, the Society focuses its efforts wholly on preserving and publicizing Steiner's legacy. This has had the predictable effect of stopping any further growth of the tradition in its tracks. As a result, while many of the practical manifestations of Steiner's work have seen immense development over the years, Anthroposophy remains where it was at the time of Steiner's death, and the Society has had trouble attracting followers in recent years.

Further reading: Herrnleben 2000, Steiner 1994.

ANTICHRIST

According to Christian mythology, a human servant of Satan who plays a major role in the events just before the Second Coming of Christ and the end of the world. He is described in the Book of Revelations as the Beast whose number is 616 or 666 (the earliest surviving versions of the text differ on this point), and who persecutes Christians for 42 months. He receives an apparently fatal wound but then recovers. His rule finally ends when Christ returns, defeats him in the battle of Armageddon, and casts him and his minions into a lake of fire.

Many modern Bible scholars interpret the Beast as a veiled description of the Roman emperor Nero (37–68 CE), who launched the first great persecution of Christians. Believers in more fundamentalist versions of Christianity, however, treat the Book of Revelation as an accurate account of events that will happen in the future. For most of two millennia, Christian propaganda has focused on the claim that these predictions are about to be fulfilled, and identifying the Antichrist has therefore been a popular sport since the Middle Ages. Religious differences provided the material for Antichrist-baiting for most of this time; it became an item of faith for many medieval Christians that the Antichrist would be Jewish, while during the Reformation, both Martin Luther and the Pope were labeled Antichrist by their opponents.

In recent centuries, however, religious candidates for Antichrist have been outnumbered by political ones. During the English Civil War, for example, Roundhead authors named Charles I as the Antichrist, while Royalists nominated Oliver Cromwell for the same position. In the same vein, American rebels of the Revolutionary War era noted that the phrase "royal supremacy in Britain," translated into New Testament Greek, added up to 666. Popular candidates in the nineteenth and twentieth centuries included Napoleon Bonaparte, Napoleon III of France, Kaiser Wilhelm II of Germany, Lenin and Josef Stalin, Benito Mussolini, Adolf Hitler, Franklin D. Roosevelt, and President Anwar el-Sadat of Egypt. Before his defeat in the second Gulf War, many American fundamentalists considered Saddam Hussein a major contender for the title.

In another category are volunteers for the position, a rare breed before 1900 but fairly common since then. The best known of these was English occultist Aleister Crowley. Raised in a fundamentalist Christian family where the Antichrist and the Second Coming were everyday topics of conversation, Crowley convinced himself that he was the Beast 666 whose new religion of Thelema ("will") would replace Christianity. See **Crowley, Aleister**.

Belief in the imminent appearance of the Antichrist has played a major role in spreading conspiracy theories in the western world. The idea that all the real and imaginary enemies of Christianity are in league with one another, under the direction of Antichrist or his agents, has been used to justify persecution of religious minorities for centuries, from the massacres of Rhineland Jews in the eleventh century to the attempts by today's fundamentalists to deprive Pagans of their religious liberties. Inevitably, Christian versions of the popular "New World Order" conspiracy theory feature Antichrist as a major player. See **Antisemitism**; **fundamentalism**; **New World Order**.

Further reading: Boyer 1992, Fuller 1995, Goldberg 2001, O'Leary 1994.

ANTIENT—MODERN SCHISM

The most significant split in English Freemasonry since the founding of the first Grand Lodge in 1717, the schism between the Antients (or Ancients) and Moderns started in 1751, when a group of Irish Freemasons living in London founded the "Grand Lodge of England according to the Old Institutions." The Antient Masons, as they called themselves, insisted that the lodges affiliated with the other Grand Lodge had abandoned the ancient landmarks of Masonry, and that they possessed the only true Masonry. A minority of English lodges left the Modern grand lodge, as the Antients called their rivals, to affiliate with the Antient grand lodge, and for more than six decades England had two feuding grand lodges of Masonry. See **Freemasonry**; **grand lodge**.

The reasons for the split were complex, and ranged from minor organizational and ritual differences to some of the most heated political issues of the day. The organizational differences reached back to the foundation of the first Grand Lodge of England in 1717. Founded by four London lodges, the Grand Lodge won the allegiance of numerous other lodges in the years that followed, but other lodges remained independent. Many members of the latter resented Grand Lodge's claim to govern all English Freemasonry, and this resentment helped fuel the birth of the Antient Grand Lodge.

The ritual differences had their origin in 1730, when Samuel Prichard's *Masonry Dissected* was printed. Prichard's antimasonic book revealed words and symbols of certain Masonic degrees, and the Grand Lodge of England responded by changing the order of the passwords in their ritual, to prevent readers of Prichard's book from passing for Masons. This break with tradition was rejected by the Antients, as well as by the older European Masonic jurisdictions. The Antients also had secret material that was not part of the Modern ritual at all, including an early form of the Royal Arch Degree. See **Antimasonry**; **Royal Arch**.

Behind these formal differences lay others, cultural and political. Through most of the eighteenth century English society was split between the Whigs, supporters of the victorious House of Hanover, and the Tories, who had backed the defeated House of Stuart. The Modern Grand Lodge was closely affiliated with the Whigs, the Antients with the Tories. The Antient Grand Lodge may in fact have been founded, as were many European Masonic bodies from the same time, by Jacobites (Stuart supporters) trying to recover their position after the disastrous defeat of the 1745 Jacobite rising. See **Jacobites**.

Only when the nineteenth century arrived and new political issues cut across the old divide did the breach between Antient and Modern Masons come to an end. The final resolution came in 1813, when the Antient Grand Lodge elected as Grand Master the Duke of Kent, one of the brothers of King George IV. The Grand Master of the Moderns at that time was the Duke of Sussex, another of George IV's brothers, and the two worked out a compromise that created the United Grand Lodge of England, the present governing body of regular English Masonry.

The feud between Antients and Moderns had a reflection on the other side of the Atlantic. American Masonry was founded by members of both sides of the quarrel, and for many years Antient and Modern grand lodges quarreled over jurisdictions in America. The creation of the United Grand Lodge of England encouraged a resolution of these disputes, and the last state in the Union with two rival grand lodges, South Carolina, saw the two sides unite in 1817. Nearly the last remaining trace of the old quarrel is a variation among American Masonic titles; some jurisdictions refer to themselves as Free and Accepted Masons (F∴&A∴M∴), others as Ancient Free and Accepted Masons (A∴F∴&A∴M∴).

ANTIKYTHERA DEVICE

In 1900 a sponge diver in the waters off the little Greek island of Antikythera, between Kythera and Crete at the western entrance to the Aegean Sea, discovered the sunken remains of an ancient Roman ship. Along with pottery amphorae of olive oil and wine, divers found marble statues and a strange object of corroded bronze and wood. The device remained unidentified until the 1950s, when American historian Derek de Solla Price recognized it as an astronomical machine. After years of work, de Solla Price was able to show that the hand-cranked device used dials, pointers, and gears to predict movements of the sun, moon, and planets.

The Antikythera device was quickly adopted by writers in the rejected knowledge field as evidence for the presence on earth of ancient astronauts from other planets, though the idea of aliens relying on a hand-cranked bronze computer for their astronomical calculations seems unlikely. Ironically, the Roman author and statesman Cicero mentions a similar device in his writings, but scholars before de Solla Price's time had dismissed the claim as fanciful. See **rejected knowledge**.

Antimasonic Party

The first significant third political party in American history, the Antimasonic Party emerged out of the furor over the abduction and murder of William Morgan, a New York Mason who broke with the Craft in 1825 and wrote a book, *Illustrations of Masonry*, revealing Masonic rituals. Morgan disappeared in Canandaigua, New York on 12 September 1826, three months before the publication of his book, and was never seen again. See **Morgan abduction**.

The light sentences meted out to those convicted of Morgan's abduction shifted attention from Morgan and his fate to claims that Masons had infiltrated state and local governments and could commit crimes with impunity. Public meetings in upstate New York, close to the scene of Morgan's disappearance, gave rise to an organized movement. In its first days the movement was largely religious in tone, backed by the same conservative churches that have been the core of American antimasonry since colonial times. See **Antimasonry**.

By 1828, though, the movement had a more political cast, and set out to drive Masons from public office and pass laws proscribing Masonry. During the brief lifetime of the Antimasonic Party, from 1828 to 1838, it put one candidate in the US Senate, 24 in the House of Representatives, and one each in the governors' mansions of New York, Vermont, and Pennsylvania. In Connecticut, Massachusetts, and Pennsylvania Antimasons launched investigations of Masonry in state legislatures, and in Massachusetts, Rhode Island, and Vermont, the party passed state laws outlawing Masonic oaths.

As a national party, though, the Antimasonic Party failed dismally. It became a real force in only five states (Connecticut, New York, Pennsylvania, Vermont, and Rhode Island) and established significant party organizations in two others (Ohio and Massachusetts). It never penetrated into the southern states at all. In its sole presidential campaign, in 1832, it ran William Wirt of Maryland as its candidate and carried only the state of Vermont. After this fiasco most of its political leaders moved into the new Whig party, helping it to victory over the Democrats in 1840, while its diehard members went on to support the Know-Nothing Party's crusade against the Catholic Church in the following decade. See **Know-Nothing Party**; **Roman Catholic Church**.

Its effects on Masonry in the United States were significant but shortlived. Faced with public pressure, sometimes backed by mob violence, Masonic lodges in the states most affected by the Antimasonic Party went into hiding, and membership in Masonic lodges declined steeply during the late 1830s and early 1840s. After the Antimasonic Party dissolved and its adherents turned their attention to new bogeymen, however, Masonry recovered swiftly, and re-established itself as America's premier secret society.

Further reading: Vaughn 1983.

ANTIMASONRY

Just as Freemasonry has been the most widely copied model in the world of secret societies, reactions against it have served as a model for most agitations against secret societies. Opposition to the Craft dates back at least to the end of the seventeenth century, when the handful of existing Masonic lodges were barely noticeable in the welter of clubs and societies that filled the British social scene of the time. A London flysheet of 1698, among the first known antimasonic publications, warned "all Godly people" that "[the Masons] are the Anti-Christ which was to come leading them from fear of God. For how should they meet in secret places and with secret Signs taking care that none observe them to do the work of God; are not these the ways of Evil-dom?" (quoted in Roberts 1972, p. 59). See **Antichrist**; **Freemasonry**.

The traditional secrecy of the Craft attracted particular attention from religious authorities concerned that it might serve as a cloak for heresy. Pope Clement XII began the long tradition of Catholic antimasonry in 1738 by issuing his bull *In Eminenti*, excommunicating all Freemasons in the Catholic Church and restricting the power to forgive them to the Pope alone. The bull cited Masonic secrecy and rumors of Masonic misconduct, as well as the Craft's role in bringing men of different religions together. Similar logic drove the Presbyterian Church in Scotland in 1757 to forbid its members to become Masons. See **Roman Catholic Church**.

Clement's bull also referred to "other just and reasonable motives known to us" but left unnamed. Evidence suggests, though conclusive proof is lacking, that these unstated motives revolved around the exiled House of Stuart, whose claim to the British throne had Clement's support. During the years just before *In Eminenti* appeared, a power struggle in French Masonry replaced Jacobite (pro-Stuart) leaders with a younger generation that sought closer ties with the Grand Lodge in London, a bastion of support for the ruling House of Hanover. A similar shift took place in Florence, where Jacobite influences in Florentine Masonic lodges yielded to a new pro-Hanoverian leadership with close ties to the English ambassador. See **Jacobites**.

If an undercurrent of eighteenth-century politics moves through Clement's bull, it marks what would become a central theme of antimasonry thereafter: the political dimension. Attacks on Masonry in the 1740s pick up this theme. *Les Francs-Maçons Écrasés* (*The Freemasons Collapsed*), a piece of sensational journalism from 1747, claimed that Masonry was founded by Oliver Cromwell as part of a vast conspiracy aimed at universal equality and liberty, to be achieved by exterminating monarchs and aristocrats, and that a secret inner core of Masonic leaders still pursued these goals unbeknownst to the majority of Masons, who were kept in the dark and manipulated by the inner circle. All this echoes the great waves of antimasonic agitation of the next century, but it took a dramatic event to bring these ideas into the limelight.

This event was the exposure of the Bavarian Illuminati in 1784–6. The Illuminati had been launched in 1776 by Adam Weishaupt, a professor at the University of Ingolstadt, and a handful of his friends, using secret society methods to promote a liberal cultural and political agenda in conservative, Catholic Bavaria. As the Illuminati expanded, it infiltrated Masonic lodges in Germany, Italy, and elsewhere, and recruited influential Freemasons; advancement beyond the grade of Illuminatus Minor, in fact, required the aspiring member to join a Masonic lodge and receive the three degrees of Craft Masonry. In 1784 the Bavarian government got wind of the Illuminati and launched a campaign of repression against it. A large cache of Illuminati documents came to light in 1786 and was immediately published, provoking a furor and making conservatives across Europe worry that Freemasonry might harbor initiates with sinister agendas. See **Bavarian Illuminati**.

The outbreak of the French Revolution turned these suspicions into an article of faith. In 1797, in the wake of the Revolution, two writers, the French Catholic Augustin de Barruel and the Scottish Presbyterian John Robison, produced books arguing that the Illuminati had been behind it all and planned to carry out similar uprisings in every other European state; Robison claimed an Illuminati presence in America for good measure. Neither author offered any verifiable evidence for these claims, but to the conservatives of the time they offered a convenient explanation for the traumatic events in France and a useful club to belabor political opponents.

The results appeared first in New England, where a full-blown Illuminati panic, backed by conservative Christian churches, targeted Masonic lodges from 1797 to 1799. The Rev. Jedediah Morse, a leading figure in anti-Illuminati circles in New England, prefigured Senator Joseph McCarthy by claiming "I now have in my possession … an official, authenticated list of the names, ages, places of nativity, [and] professions of the officers and members of a society of *Illuminati*" (cited in Goldberg 2001, p. 6). While it had little impact on Masonry at the time, the Illuminati panic helped lay the foundations for later American antimasonic activities.

In Britain, fears of Illuminati activity helped push the notorious Unlawful Societies Act of 1799 through Parliament, though ironically Freemasonry was exempted from the provisions of the Act. Until 1832, when agitation over the case of the Tolpuddle Martyrs finally forced the repeal of the act, harmless fraternal benefit societies such as the Odd Fellows and Druids risked drastic legal penalties, while revolutionaries flocked to London and plotted uprisings across most of Europe from the safety of the British Library reading room. The close alliance between Masonry and the political establishment in England helped stymie the hopes of antimasons in the British Isles until the late twentieth century.

In the United States, however, the fractured politics of the early Republic and the presence of powerful, conservative churches hostile to Masonic principles of toleration and free thought made open warfare on Masonry a political possibility. This first became apparent after the Morgan abduction of 1826, a celebrated case in which a Mason who had written a book revealing Masonic secrets was abducted and allegedly murdered by other Masons. The Morgan affair launched a crusade against Masonry, first by conservative Christians and then by the first significant third political party in American history, the Antimasonic Party. In the decade of the party's existence, it managed to pass laws banning Masonic oaths in several states, and public pressure and occasional mob violence by party members and supporters forced many lodges to disband or operate in secret. See **Antimasonic Party**; **Morgan abduction**.

The Antimasonic Party collapsed in the early 1830s as new crises, above all the rising debate between North and South over the issue of slavery, took antimasonry's place in the public eye. By the time of the American Civil War, Masonry had recovered all the ground lost during the 1820s and 1830s, and the end of the war in 1865 marked the beginning of the golden age of American fraternal orders. By 1920, when fraternalism peaked in America, 50 percent of all adult Americans – counting both sexes and all ethnic groups – belonged to at least one fraternal order. During those years Freemasonry was always either the largest or the second largest secret society in America, with the Independent Order of Odd Fellows its only serious rival for the top position. Antimasonic agitation continued during this period as a pet cause of Christian fundamentalists, but found few listeners outside those circles. See **Odd Fellowship**.

In continental Europe and Latin America, by contrast, antimasonry remained a live issue all through the nineteenth and twentieth centuries. The hostility of the Catholic Church toward Masonry helped drive antimasonic movements, but another important factor was the role of Masonry as an institution of the educated middle classes. In England and the United States, these classes already had a share in government and Freemasonry quickly lost any political agenda it might have had. Wherever aristocrats or the military monopolized political power, however, Masonic lodges tended to serve as the seedbeds for middle-class political organizations and revolutionary movements. Thus political conservatives denounced Freemasonry as a liberal conspiracy, while Catholic priests condemned it as an anti-Christian religion. Where these two came together, the results were sometimes comical; Léo Taxil's remarkable Palladian hoax of the 1880s, which sent devout Catholics hunting for an imaginary secret society of Satanist sex fiends, is a case in point. Still, as the events of the following century proved all too clearly, such claims contained an enormous potential for human tragedy. See **Palladian Order**.

These forms of antimasonry entered public discourse worldwide once the Russian revolution of 1917 cleared the way for a new outburst of conspiracy theories. Conservatives who had dismissed Marxism as a hopeless folly backed only by idealists panicked when Russian Marxists overthrew the most autocratic regime in Europe. The trauma of revolution and the real threat posed by Russia's new rulers to the stability of a Europe shattered by the First World War fed into old fantasies of subversion by secret societies. Freemasonry inevitably came in for its share of the resulting paranoia, even though the Communist government in Russia suppressed Masonry savagely once it seized power. See **Communism**.

Nesta Webster (1876–1960), the doyenne of twentieth-century British conspiratologists, played a central role in this process by reworking the old claims of de Barruel and Robison to fit a new era. Her *Secret Societies and Subversive Movements* (1922), the most influential conspiracy-theory book of the century, argued that every secret society, past and present, pursued a common plan of subversion and revolution against the political and religious establishments of the world. Webster saw Freemasonry as one wing of the vast Jewish-Satanist-Communist conspiracy, but singled it out as a significant force in the French Revolution and the deliberate destruction of the British Empire. In Germany a similar set of ideas became the foundation of Nazi ideology and provided justifications for the Nazi suppression of Freemasonry. See **National Socialism**.

After the Second World War, these views became central to the worldview of extreme conservatives everywhere. In a startling twist, the same ideas found a new home on the far left in the 1970s, as the collapse of Marxist orthodoxy after the failure of the New Left of the 1960s left a vacuum that was readily filled by conspiracy theories. By the last years of the twentieth century, the far left and far right both believed that an invisible government of bankers and industrialists, descended from the Bavarian Illuminati, functioned as the world's unseen puppet masters, the driving force behind the dreaded New World Order, and Freemasons were cited by both camps as one arm of the universal conspiracy. Ironically, even the extreme right-wing John Birch Society has been tarred as an agent of the New World Order because some of its members have been Freemasons. See **John Birch Society**; **New World Order**.

At the same time, and once again at both ends of the political spectrum, these views blended with a dizzying range of alternative-reality claims to create conspiracy theories resembling exotic science fiction. The leading figure in this movement is the British writer David Icke, a former football commentator and Green Party candidate turned conspiracy hunter, whose many books argue that the world is secretly controlled by a race of shape-shifting alien lizards from the constellation Draco who disguise themselves as human beings. The House of Windsor, the Bush family in America, and essentially every other family in the world with political or economic influence, according to Icke, belong to this reptilian race. Freemasonry once again plays a significant role in these ideas, as a major reptilian stronghold. As weird as these claims may seem, they have attracted a sizeable following in recent years. See **Reptilians**.

Another source of exotic claims about Freemasonry is the Satanic ritual abuse industry, which claims that thousands or millions of children are being raped and ritually murdered by elusive cultists. While these accusations are usually aimed at Satanists, a subset within the industry accuses Freemasons of engaging in these crimes. Partly overlapping with the Satanic ritual abuse furor is Christian fundamentalism, which has long taken offense at Freemasonry's advocacy of tolerance and freedom of conscience. A vast amount of fundamentalist literature condemns Freemasonry as a non- or even anti-Christian religion. Acting on these arguments, the Southern Baptist Convention – one of the largest conservative Protestant bodies in North America – adopted policies in 1993 and 1998 defining Freemasonry as incompatible with membership in Baptist churches. Several other conservative Christian churches in America and elsewhere have taken similar stands. See **fundamentalism**; **Satanism**.

Less focused but more pervasive is a widespread feeling among the general public in most of the world's nations that Freemasons are powerful, sinister, and suspect. Recent demands by British politicians that Masonic lodges should be forced to submit their membership lists to the police, and that Masons should be excluded from any public position where they might treat other Masons with undue favoritism, stem from this sense. Ironically, these suspicions have become widespread just as Masonry itself has become weaker, losing members and influence in an age that offers little support to fraternal orders of any kind.

Further reading: Ankerberg and Weldon 1990, Roberts 1972, Vaughn 1983.

Antisemitism

One of the oldest and most pervasive conspiracy theories in the western world is the claim that people of the Jewish faith are engaged in a sinister plot against the rest of the world. While antisemitism as it exists today is mostly a product of the repeated clashes between Judaism and its prodigal offspring, Christianity, prejudice against Jews has ancient roots. In Hellenistic Egypt, centuries before the birth of Jesus of Nazareth, native Egyptians believed that Jews served the evil desert-god Set; their logic seems to have been that since Jews refused to worship the Egyptian gods, they must be on the side of the traditional enemy of the gods.

These attitudes were adopted into Christianity early on, and, in fact, Egypt's role as an early center of Christianity may have helped start the long and inglorious tradition of Christian antisemitism. By the early Middle Ages, certainly, many Christians had convinced themselves that Jews worshipped Satan and were personally responsible for the crucifixion of Jesus. These attitudes helped fuel bouts of persecution and mass murder of Jews through the course of the Middle Ages, especially in Germany, where entire Jewish communities in cities along the Rhine were massacred at the end of the eleventh century by Christians on their way to the First Crusade.

The Black Death of 1345–50 brought a new wave of persecutions as Jews, among other outcast groups in medieval society, were accused of causing the pandemic by poisoning wells. By the fifteenth century, though, Christians had turned their attention to a new set of scapegoats, as the age of witchcraft persecutions began. Jews continued to suffer from persecution during the later Middle Ages and the Renaissance, but in western Europe, at least, popular opinion turned gradually against the more extreme forms of antisemitism as the narrow religiosity of the Middle Ages broke down. See **witchcraft persecutions**.

At the beginning of the nineteenth century, though, this process went into reverse in many parts of Europe, as industrialization disrupted traditional economies and shattered the old social order. Ethnic, national, and religious prejudices of all kinds blossomed as immigration and the rise of huge urban centers redefined the cultural landscape of most European countries. Jews made a convenient target for the frustrations of those left behind by the new industrial economy, since a handful of Jewish families, such as the Rothschilds, prospered with industrialization and many of the skilled professions included large numbers of Jews. By the beginning of the twentieth century, antisemitic secret societies and political parties had emerged in Germany and elsewhere, proclaiming loudly that Jews were responsible for all the ills of the modern world. See **Germanenorden**; **Ordo Novi Templi (ONT)**.

These beliefs coalesced around one of the most influential documents of the twentieth century, the *Protocols of the Elders of Zion*, a forgery manufactured out of several older documents by the Russian aristocrat and Theosophist Yuliana Glinka in Paris before 1895 and first printed in Russia in 1903. The *Protocols* claimed to be a set of secret plans adopted by a supreme council of Jewish rabbis intent on taking over the world. Distributed worldwide in the aftermath of the Russian revolution of 1917, they featured in the propaganda of every antisemitic movement in the world in the first half of the twentieth century and were enthusiastically circulated by influential conspiracy theorists such as Nesta Webster. In Germany, where the Nazi movement embraced them with open arms, they became justifications for the most brutal massacres of Jews in modern history. See **National Socialism**; **Protocols of the Elders of Zion**.

The defeat of the Third Reich and the worldwide exposure given to Nazi atrocities against the Jews made the more virulent forms of antisemitism socially unacceptable in most western countries. Recent years, though, have seen the old prejudices find their way back into popular culture via the spread of neo-Nazi movements and, more worryingly, via conspiracy theories that disguise their antisemitic elements beneath various labels. *The Protocols of the Elders of Zion* have been reworked and reprinted as blueprints for world domination by the Illuminati or reptiles from other planets, but connections to Judaism – via the Rothschild family, for example – are never absent. See **neo-Nazi secret societies**; **Reptilians**.

During the heyday of antisemitic conspiracy theory in the early twentieth century, most of the important revolutionaries and secret society leaders of the past were redefined as Jews to justify their membership in the alleged "Jewish world conspiracy." Adam Weishaupt, founder of the Bavarian Illuminati, and Russian revolutionary Vladimir Lenin were among those who underwent postmortem conversions to Judaism at the hands of antisemites, in a curious parallel to the secret society practice of retrospective recruitment. Though neither Weishaupt nor Lenin had any trace of Jewish ancestry, these claims are still recycled in popular books today. See **Bavarian Illuminati**; **retrospective recruitment**.

Further reading: Cohn 1967.

Apron

The essential regalia of a Freemason, the apron in its basic form consists of a rectangle of white lambskin with a triangular flap along the top, and ties on the upper corners allowing it to be tied around the waist. Masons who have served a term as Worshipful Master of a lodge have the right to wear an apron with blue trim and an emblem on the flap; those who hold current or past offices in a Grand Lodge wear much more ornate aprons with gold braid and embroidered emblems. See **Freemasonry**.

The concordant bodies of Freemasonry also use aprons, with their respective colors and symbolism replacing the plain white or white-and-blue of the symbolic lodge. In those bodies with many degrees of initiation, such as the Ancient and Accepted Scottish Rite with its 33 degrees, the regalia for most of the degrees include a distinctively decorated apron – a custom that puts significant demands on the ingenuity of the Rite's creators. See **Ancient and Accepted Scottish Rite**.

During the eighteenth and early nineteenth centuries, Freemasonry's immense popularity led many other secret societies to adopt aprons as well, though most abandoned the practice later in the nineteenth century in an effort to distinguish their members from Masons. Among other fraternal secret societies, Odd Fellows lodges often wore aprons, along with the ornate collars Odd Fellowship uses as marks of membership and rank, and the Patrons of Husbandry also used aprons early on for male members. Both orders discarded aprons long before the nineteenth century was over. See **Odd Fellowship**; **Patrons of Husbandry (Grange)**.

Arcane School

Founded by American occultist Alice Bailey (1880–1949) and her husband Foster Bailey in 1923, the Arcane School teaches the system of occult philosophy received by Alice Bailey in trance from an entity calling himself the Tibetan master Djwal Khul. The Arcane School aims at initiating and training a "New Group of World Servers" to assist in the work of the Masters of the Great White Lodge. Many of its teachings derive from Theosophy, which Bailey studied extensively before setting up her own school, and its course of study focuses on meditation, study, and service to the Great Plan as a way of life. See **Bailey, Alice**; **Great White Lodge**; **Masters**; **Theosophical Society**.

The Arcane School seems to have avoided the complex organizational superstructures and bitter politics that beset most of the occult correspondence schools of its time, and remains quietly active at the present. It consists of a series of small study groups and individual students scattered across most of the world, studying Alice Bailey's extensive writings and practicing her forms of meditation. Ironically, despite its small size and inoffensive activities, the Arcane School has been claimed by some fundamentalist Christian conspiracy theorists as the secret controlling body behind all the other conspiracies in the world. See **New World Order**.

Archons

In ancient and modern Gnostic literature, the ignorant and demonic ruling powers of the world of matter, created by the dark lord Ialdabaoth to help him maintain his dominion over human souls and keep them from escaping back to their home in the world of light. Many of the surviving Gnostic scriptures provide lists of the archons, who range in number from 7 to 365; clear but complex symbolic links connect the archons to the seven planets known to ancient astronomy, while their opponents, the aeons of the world of light, correspond to the fixed stars. See **Gnosticism**.

Argenteum Astrum [A.·.A.·.]

One of two secret societies closely associated with the legacy of British occultist and would-be Antichrist Aleister Crowley (1875–1947), the Argenteum Astrum (Latin for "silver star") was created by Crowley in 1908 following the instructions of the Book of the Law, the revelation Crowley believed he had received in 1904 from the ruling powers of the world in the new Aeon of Horus. The Book of the Law instructed him to salvage what he could from the rituals of the previous Aeon of Osiris; in Crowley's view, these included those of the Hermetic Order of the Golden Dawn, the secret society in which Crowley received most of his magical training. See **Crowley, Aleister**; **Hermetic Order of the Golden Dawn**.

The major innovation Crowley brought to the A.·.A.·. was a shift from formal lodge initiation to personal spiritual practice and experience as the means of advancement through the grades. To some extent this was forced on him by limits of the resources at hand, since during Crowley's lifetime the A.·.A.·. never amounted to more than Crowley himself and a handful of students. However, the transformation of the Golden Dawn grades from initiatory ranks to stages in the process of spiritual growth was an important contribution to the tradition, and had a strong influence on later Hermetic secret societies. See **Hermeticism**.

After Crowley's death a handful of his students, notably the German occultist Karl Germer, revived the A.·.A.·. and started teaching and initiating students on their own. The order has no formal organization at present, and consists of individual initiate-teachers and their students working with many different variants of Crowley's teachings.

The order is occasionally misnamed the Atlantean Adepts as a result of a British reporter's incorrect guess. During Crowley's lifetime the meaning of the initials "A∴A∴" was a secret imparted by him to initiates under an oath of secrecy; one of the many newspaper exposés of the Great Beast guessed at the meaning, and missed.

Ark of the Covenant

The most sacred property of the ancient Israelites, the Ark of the Covenant was a large wooden chest covered with hammered gold, carried on two poles, and topped by a pair of golden angels. According to the Book of Exodus, it was made by the Israelites during their wanderings in the Sinai peninsula after their escape from Egypt, following a set of exact specifications given by Yahweh, the god of the Jews, to Moses; the specifications may be found in Exodus 25:10–22. The Ark was kept in the tabernacle before the building of Solomon's Temple, and in the Holy of Holies of the temple thereafter. See **Temple of Solomon**.

Its fate during and after the Babylonian captivity of the Jews is uncertain. It may have been included in the "vessels of the temple" that were looted from the temple by the Babylonian king Nebuchadnezzar in 586 BCE and restored to the Jews by the Persian king Cyrus in 526 BCE, but it is not specifically mentioned in the biblical accounts. An Ark of the Covenant was present in the rebuilt temple, though this may not have been the original. That ark disappeared when Jerusalem was sacked by the Romans in 70 CE and all the Temple treasures were pillaged by the victorious Roman general Vespasian. Various theories have been proposed for their fate, but the most likely is that they were melted down and turned into coins during the repeated financial crises of the late Roman Empire.

The Ark has been an important part of the symbolism of Orthodox Judaism and Ethiopian Christianity for many centuries, but its role outside those traditions was minor until the eighteenth century, when inventors of new Masonic degrees began ransacking the Bible for raw material for initiation rituals. The importance of the Temple of Solomon in Masonic symbolism guaranteed the Ark frequent appearances in these rites. As degree performances became more theatrical in the nineteenth century, Arks of the Covenant became part of the equipment of many lodges inside and outside Masonry, and most commercial lodge-supplies catalogues carried several different models. See **Freemasonry**; **high degrees**.

Despite this, it took the George Lucas film *Raiders of the Lost Ark*, which featured cinema star Harrison Ford battling Nazis for possession of the Ark of the Covenant, to make the Ark a hot property in the world of rejected knowledge. One of many resulting theories is the claim that the Shriners, a branch of Freemasonry best known for wild parties and lavishly funded children's charities, have an exact copy of the original Ark hidden away in their Chicago headquarters, where high-ranking Masons use it to communicate with aliens from other planets. Those familiar with Shriners may suspect them of communing with pink elephants more often than gray-skinned extraterrestrials, and their national headquarters has been in Tampa, Florida for many years. Still, such factual issues rarely penetrate into the hermetically sealed world of modern conspiracy theories. See **Ancient Arabic Order of Nobles of the Mystic Shrine**; **extraterrestrials**; **rejected knowledge**.

Armanen

According to the theories of Guido von List (1848–1919), the father of Ariosophy and the spiritual forerunner of Nazism, the ancient Germanic tribes were divided into three castes, with the Armanen, or hereditary priest-kings, as the highest caste. He got the term "Armanen" from a misreading of the Roman author Tacitus, who lists the Irminones as one of three German tribes in the wilderness north and east of the Roman imperial border. List's vision of a priestly caste among the Germanic tribes, however, drew extensively from popular eighteenth- and nineteenth-century accounts of the ancient Celtic Druids. Since the classical sources on Druidry insisted that the ancient Germans had no Druids, an equivalent caste had to be invented; the Armanen filled that role. See **Druids**; **Druid Revival**.

The popularity of List's writings on the runes and ancient Germanic magic encouraged various people in the central European occult scene to claim Armanen connections and launch Armanen secret societies. List himself was out in front of this trend, recruiting members from his fan club, the Guido von List Society, for a magical secret society named the Höhere Armanen-Orden (Higher Armanen Order, HAO). Under the leadership of Heinrich Himmler, the SS drew much of their symbolism from Armanist sources, and right-wing occult circles since the Second World War have continued to make use of List's legacy. See **Höhere Armanen-Orden (HAO)**; **National Socialism**; **neo-Nazi secret societies**; **SS (Schutzstaffel)**.

ART OF MEMORY

One of the forgotten sciences of the pre-industrial world, the art of memory was a system of mental training that enabled practitioners to memorize quickly and accurately recall very large amounts of information. The basic methods of the art were devised by the Greek poet Simonides of Ceos sometime in the sixth century BCE and became part of the standard training for orators in ancient Greece and Rome. Lost to the western world during the collapse of the Roman Empire, it was recovered from a handful of surviving texts in the twelfth century CE and became an important part of medieval and Renaissance education, while Hermetic occultists such as Giordano Bruno reworked it into a powerful system of magical meditation. See **Bruno, Giordano**; **Hermeticism**.

The core method of the art was the use of visual imagery as a code for information to be remembered. Practitioners would memorize the inside of one or more buildings until they could walk through each room in imagination and see every detail clearly in the mind's eye. The rooms would then be stocked with images representing the words or facts to be remembered. Textbooks of the art included many rules for creating memory images designed so that the practitioner could encode large amounts of information in a single image, and stressed that the images should be funny, shocking, or otherwise intensely memorable. Once the images were put in place in the imaginary setting, the practitioner simply imagined himself walking through the building again, noted each image in its place, and recalled the information it encoded.

While this procedure may seem unnecessarily complex, in practice it works extremely well, and modern practitioners have found that the traditional rules enable them to store and recall information far more quickly and efficiently than unaided memory can manage. Nonetheless, like so many of the intellectual and mental disciplines of the Renaissance, the art of memory went into western civilization's dustbin during the Industrial Revolution.

By 1700, when the golden age of secret societies in the western world was just beginning, the art of memory was already slipping into oblivion, but the methods of the art had a profound impact on secret societies nonetheless. The second Schaw Statutes, a set of rules for Scottish stonemasons issued by William Schaw in 1599, instruct lodge officers of Scottish stonemasons' lodges to test the master masons of their lodge in the art of memory and fine those who proved deficient. As these same lodges evolved into the first lodges of Freemasons, the fusion of imagery, memory, and meaning central to the art of memory found its way into early Masonic ritual, and from there to every other secret society that took Freemasonry for its model. See **Freemasonry**; **Schaw, William**.

Further reading: Stevenson 1988, Yates 1966.

Arthurian Legends

Sometime in the late fifth century CE, during the collapse of the western half of the Roman Empire, a Romano–British nobleman in the abandoned province of Britannia organized a troop of cavalry and led them in a series of successful battles against the invading Saxons. His name was probably Artorius, the name of a distinguished Roman family. At a place later chroniclers called Mount Badon, probably in southwestern Britain, his army crushed a large Saxon force and won Celtic Britain a fifty-year reprieve from invasion. His victory had a massive impact on the future of the British Isles. Neither the division of Britain into a Celtic western and an English eastern half, nor the survival of Ireland as a beacon of classical culture during the Dark Ages, might have happened if the Saxons had won the day at Badon.

Over the centuries that followed, a rich oral tradition of stories and poems gathered around Artorius and his soldiers among the descendants of the people he defended, enriched further by scraps of old pagan myth. In legend's gilded hindsight, the Romano-British nobleman and his band of horsemen turned into King Arthur, greatest of monarchs, and his Round Table of gallant knights. In this form, the stories came to the ears of French minstrels in the twelfth century CE, who recognized a gold mine when they saw it and spread the legends of King Arthur across the western world. As the Arthurian legend expanded, it drew other once-independent legends into orbit around it, so that the love affair of Tristram and Iseult and the quest for the Grail became part of the Arthurian world. See **Grail**.

While they waxed and waned in popularity, the legends of King Arthur and his knights remained part of most Europeans' mental furniture through the Middle Ages and Renaissance into the modern world. Until the birth of modern historical scholarship in the late seventeenth century, most people throughout Europe believed that Arthur was what legend said he was – a great king who had ruled Britain and several other countries during the fading years of Roman power. The dawn of the Industrial Revolution and the dominance of its mythology of progress led scholars to dismiss Arthur as empty legend, but this only encouraged those who rejected the materialist worldview of industrial society to reinterpret and reinvent the Arthurian legends for their own purposes.

Arthurian legends and symbolism played a relatively small part in the secret societies of the eighteenth century, though the Order of the Golden and Rosy Cross, an important German Rosicrucian order, boasted that they had first arrived in Britain in the days of King Arthur. Degrees in some of the irregular Masonic rites of the nineteenth century used Arthurian symbolism, and fraternal secret societies in America and elsewhere used the image of the Round Table to surround themselves with a romantic aura. The Druid movement in Britain and America in the nineteenth century also drew heavily from Arthurian sources in creating a revived Druidry, and several occult secret societies affiliated with the Druid movement claimed direct descent from the knighthood of Arthur's day. See **Druid Revival**; **high degrees**; **Order of the Golden and Rosy Cross**.

The twentieth century, for all its boasted modernity, saw more Arthurian literature produced than any other century in history, and it also witnessed an explosion in Arthurian scholarship. From the 1940s on, mainstream historians cautiously embraced the idea that the Arthur of legend was based on some kernel of solid historical fact. The two trends, literary and scholarly, fed off one another, and both helped drive an explosion of Arthurian themes among late twentieth-century secret societies. By 2000 more than a hundred newly minted secret societies, most of them linked to the late twentieth-century Pagan revival or the older occult traditions of the western world, claimed some level of connection – ranging from inspiration to direct lineal descent – from the knights, wizards, and sorceresses of Arthur's day. Most of these societies will likely prove ephemeral, but some show signs of turning into major players in the secret-society scene of the twenty-first century.

Further reading: Ashe 1972, Knight 1983.

Ascended Masters teachings

One of the few distinctively American traditions of occultism, the Ascended Masters teachings emerged out of the work of Guy Ballard (1878–1939), author (under the pen name Godfré Ray King) of numerous books on esoteric spirituality. Ballard claimed he received his teachings from the Comte de Saint-Germain and several other ascended masters after an initial meeting with the Comte on the slopes of Mount Shasta in northern California. See **Masters**; **Saint-Germain, Comte de**.

Ballard's own teaching organization, the I Am Activity, suffered from a series of internal political disputes after Ballard's death, however, and several of the groups descended from it copied its organizational structure and thus fell into the same troubles. Many students of Ballard's writings responded by pursuing their studies and practices on their own or in small study groups of like-minded people. The resulting movement drew on the voluminous writings of English–American occultist Alice Bailey (1880–1949), which Bailey claimed were dictated by the ascended master Djwal Khul, alongside those of Ballard and such Ballard-inspired writers such as Elizabeth Clare Prophet. See **Bailey, Alice**.

The resulting movement has become a large but rarely noticed undercurrent in American culture, hidden by a lack of large national organizations and a position on the cultural spectrum rarely identified with occultism. More often than not, followers of the Ascended Masters teachings tend to be socially and politically conservative, with a fervent patriotism rooted in the belief that the ascended masters themselves brought the United States into being and shaped its system of government. Most self-identify as Christians, though they revere Jesus as the highest of the Masters rather than as an incarnate deity. See **Jesus of Nazareth**.

The teachings, like most twentieth-century American occult traditions, draw heavily from Theosophy. The supreme being, I AM, exists in the higher self of every human being as the I AM Presence. Those who make contact with the I AM Presence within themselves are liberated from the wheel of reincarnation and experience ascension, leaving behind their material bodies and becoming ascended masters in their own right. The classic toolkit for achieving ascension includes decrees – spoken prayers to the I AM Presence and the masters, repeated in a meditative state – and work with the Violet Flame, which is visualized while practicing decrees to help burn away karma and encourage spiritual development. A wide range of other practices can be found among students of the Ascended Masters teachings, however, and the entire movement is in the midst of a major period of creativity and redefinition at present. See **Theosophical Society**.

Ashmole, Elias

English historian, astrologer, alchemist and Freemason. Born in Lichfield, Staffordshire, to middle-class parents, Ashmole (1617–92) studied law and worked for a short time as a solicitor, then went up to Oxford in 1644, where he became a member of Brasenose College and studied astrology and mathematics. His studies were interrupted by the final phases of the English Civil War, and he served with distinction in the Royalist cause, helping defend Oxford and Worcester against Parliamentary armies.

After the final collapse of the Royalist cause in 1646, Ashmole went to live with relatives in Cheshire. While there, on October 16, 1646, he was initiated into Freemasonry, becoming one of the first two "accepted Masons" (Masons not employed in the building trades) in England; the other, initiated on the same evening, was his brother-in-law Henry Mainwaring. He remained active in Masonry for the rest of his life and appears to have played a significant role in its spread in seventeenth-century England. See **Freemasonry**.

As the chaos of the Civil War faded, Ashmole returned to scholarship and took up the study of alchemy. He collected many of the papers of John Dee, Queen Elizabeth I's court astrologer and magus, and Dee's alchemist son Arthur. In 1651 he became the "son," or alchemical student-initiate, of the alchemist William Backhouse of Swallowfield, Berkshire. The next year he published the immense *Theatrum Chymicum Britannicum*, an invaluable anthology of English works on alchemy. In 1653, according to Ashmole's diary, Backhouse told him the secret First Matter of the philosopher's stone – though Ashmole, true to his alchemists' oaths, did not write down the name of that elusive substance. See **Alchemy**.

Ashmole's loyalty to the Royalist cause finally paid off in 1660, when Charles II returned from exile to receive the British crown. The new king, recognizing Ashmole's scholarship, gave him the position of Windsor Herald, which allowed Ashmole to carry out the research that resulted in his magisterial 1672 work *The Institution, Laws and Ceremonies of the Most Noble Order of the Garter*. Charles also gave his support to a project backed by Ashmole, among others: the foundation of "a College for the promoting of Physico-Mathematicall Experimentall Learning." As a result, 1661 saw the establishment of the Royal Society, the first institute for scientific research in the modern world, with Ashmole as one of its founding members. See **Order of the Garter**; **Royal Society**.

From 1679 to 1683 Ashmole devoted his energies to another project of great historical importance, the founding of the first public museum of the natural sciences in Britain. The Ashmolean Museum was duly established in Oxford, where it remains today, one of the world's most famous centers of scientific education. Throughout the last three decades of his life Ashmole also found time to support the rebuilding of Lichfield Cathedral, which had been wrecked by Parliamentary forces during the Civil War. He died quietly in his sleep in London in 1693.

Further reading: Churton 2004.

Assassins

Among the world's most famous secret societies, the Assassins emerged out of the Ismaili sect of Islam in the late eleventh century CE. Their founder, Hassan-i-Sabah, came from a Persian Shiite family but converted to the Ismaili sect after a long period of spiritual doubt capped by a serious illness. In 1078 he went to Cairo, then the center of Ismaili activity, and sought permission from the Caliph to spread the Ismaili faith in Persia. The Caliph agreed, but required that Hassan pledge to support the claim of the Caliph's eldest son Nizar to the Caliphate. From this pledge came the formal name of Hassan's order, the Nizaris.

In the years that followed, Hassan wandered Persia, teaching the Ismaili faith and winning converts. He seized control of the fortress at Alamut, high in the northern mountains of Iran, and made it his center of operations. As his following increased, he began to use assassination as a core strategy for dealing with opponents, and expanded his power through protection rackets backed up by the knives of his followers. In 1094, when the Caliph died and Nizar's claim to the succession failed, Hassan was strong enough to become an independent force, seizing additional mountain strongholds as far west as Syria and using these to extend his reach through the Middle East.

Hassan imposed a strict hierarchy on his followers. Members of the lowest rank of the order, who carried out assassinations, had the title of *fidai* or devotee; above these were the ranks of *lasiq* or lay brother, *rafiq* or companion, and *da'i* or teacher. A group of senior *da'i*s formed Hassan's inner circle. A rule of total obedience bound those at each level to follow orders from their superiors. According to medieval accounts, Hassan reinforced the loyalty of his followers with a clever trick. After completing a course of martial arts training, each *fidai* was given wine drugged with hashish, and taken into a hidden garden full of fruit trees, modeled on the paradise described in the Quran, where wine flowed in streams among gilded pavilions and lovely women provided every sensual delight. The *fidai* stayed there for a few days, until another dose of drugged wine returned him to his ordinary life. Convinced that Hassan had literally transported them to Paradise and back, the *fidais* readily risked their lives for him in the belief that death simply meant a one-way trip back to the garden.

Hassan died in 1124, but his first two successors pursued his policies and made the Assassins a name to be feared throughout the Muslim world. The fourth head of the order, Hassan II, pursued a different course. After becoming Sheik of the order in 1162, he proclaimed himself the Mahdi, the prophet whose arrival marked the coming of the millennium, and abandoned Islam for a religion of his own invention centered on the teaching that "nothing is true, and everything is permissible." After four years, he was murdered by his brother-in-law, and the Assassins returned to orthodox Islam, but Hassan II's troubled rule allowed the head of the Syrian branch of the Assassins, Rashid ad-Din Sinan, to break free of Alamut's control.

Syria at that time was divided between the Crusader kingdoms to the south and a Sunni Muslim kingdom centered on Aleppo in the north, and Sinan played these off against each other to maintain his own independence. When the great Arab general Saladin (Salah al-Din al-Ayyubi, 1138–93) took power in Aleppo, Sinan responded by ordering his death, but by this time Arab rulers had begun to learn Assassin ways and Sinan's agents failed twice. He was more successful against Conrad of Montferrat, King of Jerusalem, who was cut down by two Assassins in 1192. Against the Knights Templar, who owned several large castles in southern Syria and had copied many elements of Assassin discipline, Sinan was more circumspect, and at one point paid them a yearly tribute of 2000 pieces of gold to keep them at bay. See **Knights Templar**.

After Sinan's time, the Assassins moved away from their sectarian roots and became an organization of hired knives who killed for money. Like the rest of the Arab world, they were fatally unprepared for the arrival of the Mongol armies in the middle of the thirteenth century. The threat of assassination meant nothing to the Mongols, who responded to the least resistance by slaughtering entire populations. Faced with these tactics, Alamut surrendered to the Mongol warlord Hulagu Khan in 1256. The Syrian branch of the order dissolved not long afterwards, and most of its members entered the service of the Sultan of Egypt as hired killers.

Further reading: Mackenzie 1967.

ASTRONOMICAL RELIGION

One of the most important theories of comparative religion from the late eighteenth to the early twentieth century, the theory of astronomical religion argued that all religions – or rather, in most versions, all religions but Judaism and Christianity – developed out of early humanity's awe and wonder at the sun and the night-time sky. According to the theory, the gods and goddesses of pagan religions are simply poetic ways of talking about the sun, moon, planets, and seasonal phenomena on the surface of the earth. A good deal of evidence supports the idea that at least some religious thought has astronomical roots; it's not an accident, after all, that people in the western world still call the planets by the names of old gods.

The theory of astronomical religion has taken at least four standard forms, all of which have left their traces on secret societies and the secret history of the western world. One form is solar religion, the idea that ancient religion and mythology focused on the interactions between sun and earth in the cycle of the seasons. Another is planetary religion, the idea that ancient religion and mythology focused on the movement of the seven traditional planets (the sun, moon, Mercury, Venus, Mars, Jupiter, and Saturn) against the background of the stars. A third is precessional religion – the idea that ancient religion and mythology focused on the precession of the equinoxes, a vast slow wobble in the earth's movement that shifts the seasonal stations of the sun slowly backwards against the stars, and points the earth's poles toward different pole stars in a

25,920-year cycle. The fourth form is catastrophic religion, the idea that ancient religion and mythology focused on the memory of a series of vast cosmic disasters caused by comets or roving planets. All four of these offer intriguing and sometimes compelling explanations of certain myths, and none of them necessarily conflict with the others – it is entirely plausible that different myths might be talking about different heavenly events, after all.

Still, in the scholarly debates of the late nineteenth century, each version of astronomical theory – like most theories of comparative religion – was taken to extremes and turned into a supposed universal key to all mythologies. One of the most comprehensive examples was the "solar theory" of Max Müller (1823–1900), who was among the greatest philologists of the late nineteenth century and a major player in the struggles over myth's meanings during that era. Müller argued that all mythology, everywhere, retold the story of the seasonal cycle; all gods were solar and meteorological phenomena associated with the seasons, while all goddesses symbolized the earth and its changing vegetation. Müller's theory was widely accepted until it was demonstrated, a few years after his death, that by his own criteria Müller himself could be proved to be a sun god.

Long before this, however, the theory of astronomical religion found a home in the underworld of nineteenth-century secret societies. The rebirth of European paganism in the 1790s at the hands of Thomas Taylor, the great English Neoplatonist and translator of Greek texts, made pagan religious traditions increasingly attractive to nineteenth-century intellectuals, who saw them as a humane and psychologically healthy alternative to the stultifying Protestantism of the Victorian era. Druid secret societies in particular borrowed heavily from the astronomical theory and its major competitor, the theory of fertility religion, as raw material for their reconstructions of ancient Celtic spirituality. See **Druid Revival**.

This process was paralleled by a movement within Freemasonry, especially (but not only) in America, that interpreted the Masonic Craft as a descendant of the ancient pagan mysteries and drew on the astronomical theory to reinvent Freemasonry as a spirituality for thinking men. Masonic writers such as J.D. Buck and E. Valentia Straiton argued that every aspect of Masonic symbolism could be traced back to ancient mystery cults, a theme that also influenced Albert Pike, Grand Commander of the southern US jurisdiction of the Scottish Rite, in his revision of the Rite's rituals and the compilation of his sprawling Masonic sourcebook *Morals and Dogma* (1871). The spread of these ideas among a minority of Masons predictably ended up being used in the late twentieth century by Christian fundamentalists to claim that all of Freemasonry was a Satanic cult. See **Antimasonry**; **Freemasonry**; **Pike, Albert**.

The popularity of the astronomical theory of religion peaked around 1900, however, and thereafter it quickly fell from favor as psychological and social theories rose to prominence. Since then the first three versions of the theory mentioned above have had a dwindling role in the world of secret societies as well, though substantial traces can still be found in some concordant bodies of Masonry, in the older Druid orders, and in a few other occult secret societies with older roots. The one survivor is the theory of catastrophic religion, which came back into vogue in the late twentieth century and now feeds into alternative visions of approaching earth changes and ages of the world. See **ages of the world**; **earth changes**.

Further reading: Godwin 1994.

Atkinson, William Walker

American occultist, author, and secret society member. One of the leading figures in the occult scene in turn of the century America, Atkinson (1862–1932) was born to middle-class parents in Baltimore, Maryland and took up a business career, then studied law. In the late 1890s, however, his health broke down as a result of stress, and he turned to the New Thought movement in the hope of a cure. By 1900 Atkinson had completely recovered, and moved to Chicago to take up a position as an editor at *New Thought* magazine. A few years later, turning his business skills to a new purpose, he founded the Atkinson School of Mental Science and began publishing books on New Thought under his own name, books on yoga under the pen name Yogi Ramacharaka, and books on mental magnetism and occultism under the name of Theron Q. Dumont.

Atkinson soon became a leading figure in the Chicago occult community. In 1907 he was contacted by the young occultist Paul Foster Case, and the two began an extensive correspondence that lasted until the end of Atkinson's life. Sometime before 1907 Atkinson also became a member of the Chicago temple of the Alpha et Omega, the largest American branch of the Hermetic Order of the Golden Dawn, and probably also joined the Societas Rosicruciana in America (SRIA), then closely affiliated with the Alpha et Omega. Together with Case and Michael Whitty, Atkinson wrote *The Kybalion* (1912), one of the classic works of American occult philosophy. The three concealed their authorship under the anonymity of the name "Three Initiates." See **Case, Paul Foster**; **Hermetic Order of the Golden Dawn**; **Societas Rosicruciana in America (SRIA)**.

Sometime in the 1920s, Atkinson moved to California, which was rapidly becoming the center of America's occult community at that time, and remained there until his death in 1932. Many of the books he wrote as "Yogi Ramacharaka" are still in print today, though his other writings went out of print as the New Thought movement faded out in the 1940s.

Further reading: "Three Initiates" 1912.

ATLANTIS

The continent of Atlantis, according to occult lore, existed in the middle of the Atlantic Ocean until its sinking some eleven thousand years ago. A constant theme in occult secret-society teachings during the "Theosophical century" from 1875 to 1975, Atlantis remains a major presence in the current realm of rejected knowledge. Hundreds, perhaps thousands, of secret societies have claimed Atlantean origins or possession of Atlantean secrets in an effort to backdate themselves before the dawn of recorded history. Ironically, this has had the opposite effect, since Atlantis was very nearly a forgotten story until 1882, when the Irish-American politician and writer Ignatius Donnelly (1831–1901) launched it on its modern career. The presence of Atlantis as a significant theme in secret society teachings is thus good evidence that the society dates from the end of the nineteenth or the first three-quarters of the twentieth centuries. See **lost continents**; **rejected knowledge**.

Atlantis first appears in two dialogues by Plato (*c.*428–*c.*348 BCE), the *Timaeus* and the unfinished *Critias*. *Timaeus* recounts a story supposedly told by an Egyptian priest in the city of Saïs to Plato's ancestor Solon, the Athenian lawgiver. According to the story, around 9600 BCE, the city of Athens fought a war against the empire of Atlantis, a large island located in the Atlantic Ocean opposite the Strait of Gibraltar. After the defeat of the Atlantean army, earthquakes and floods destroyed Atlantis, leaving only shoals of mud in the ocean. Plato expanded on this account in the finished part of *Critias*, describing Atlantis as an island ruled by ten kings descended from the god Poseidon and a mortal woman, and explaining how it fell from virtue and wisdom into decadence.

No ancient author before Plato's time mentions anything about Atlantis, and the only classical references from after his time come from writers strongly influenced by Plato's philosophy. The philosopher Aristotle (384–322 BCE), one of Plato's students, thought that he made the whole thing up. For centuries thereafter, the Atlantis story floated in the indeterminate world of marvel tales. It gave its name to the ocean west of Europe and Africa, and nearly ended up fixed to the continent on the other side; both Richard Hakluyt, the Elizabethan explorer, and John Dee, Queen Elizabeth's court astrologer, magus, and spy, thought that the Americas should be named "Atlantis." Francis Bacon titled his scientific utopia *The New Atlantis,* and wove into the story a claim that the ancient Mexicans had been Plato's Atlantean empire. The Jesuit wizard Athanasius Kircher (1602–80) took Plato literally and put a map of Atlantis in one of his many books, and the visionary poet William Blake (1757–1827) imagined Atlantean hills beneath the waves between Britain and America, but they were exceptions. See **Bacon, Francis**.

Not until the late nineteenth century did the lost continent find its way back to the bottom of the Atlantic. Appropriately enough, pioneering science-fiction author Jules Verne (1828–1905) helped jumpstart the process in his 1869 novel *Twenty Thousand Leagues Under the Sea* by having Captain Nemo take the story's protagonist, Professor Aronnax, to the submerged ruins of Atlantis. Several other authors in the field of speculative prehistory also made use of Atlantis around this time, notably Cornelius Over den Linden and J.O. Ottema, the creators of the *Oera Linda Chronicle* (1871), which transformed the lost continent into an island in the North Sea that sank in 2193 BCE. Helena Petrovna Blavatsky (1831–91), the founder of Theosophy, put a short discussion of Atlantis into her first book, *Isis Unveiled* (1877), along with many other criticisms of conventional ideas of nature and history. The bulk of her writing on Atlantis came later, though, in response to the most influential book of alternative history ever written. See **Blavatsky, Helena Petrovna**; **Theosophical Society**.

This was the 1882 bestseller *Atlantis, The Antediluvian World* by Ignatius Donnelly. Donnelly, born to an Irish immigrant family in Philadelphia, became a lawyer and then entered politics, winning election as a US congressman from Minnesota. After retiring from politics in 1880, he vaulted into a third career as a writer. In *Atlantis,* he argued that Plato's account was based on sober fact, and that the island of Atlantis, located where the Mid-Ocean Ridge is today, was the site of the world's first civilization. He collected cultural parallels from the Old and New World and used them as evidence that an older culture, located halfway between the two, had inspired them. The book became an instant bestseller and roused interest in the lost continent around the world; British Prime Minister William Gladstone was impressed enough by Donnelly's arguments that he tried (unsuccessfully) to convince the Admiralty to send an expedition to look for the undersea ruins of Atlantean cities.

All this was grist for Blavatsky's mill, and in 1888 she raised the stakes with her sprawling two-volume *The Secret Doctrine,* a history of the universe and everything in it transmitted, as she claimed, by secluded adepts from central Asia. Atlantis, along with the lost continent of Lemuria and much else, found a place in the vast sweep of Blavatsky's vision. Her Atlantis was the homeland of the fourth of the seven root races of humanity, an island continent inhabited by an advanced civilization with pyramids, airships, and magical powers. Misuse of these last caused a series of catastrophes and the sinking of the continent. See **Lemuria**.

Blavatsky's claims provided the foundation for a vast structure of speculation about Atlantis, much of it derived by clairvoyant means and subject to the usual problems of visionary evidence. William Scott-Eliot provided much of this via his 1896 book *The Story of Atlantis*, which featured eight-foot tall red-skinned Atlanteans ruling much of the world from their capital, the City of the Golden Gates, now far undersea off the coast of Senegal. Atlantean decadence and the misuse of magic for evil ends led to a gradual submergence through repeated floods; the destruction recorded by Plato was the submergence of the very last portion of the former continent, the twin islands of Ruta and Daitya. See **Scrying**.

This was the version of Atlantis that found its way into secret societies throughout the English-speaking world and large parts of Europe from the late nineteenth century on. Few occult societies got by without some version of the Theosophical story of Atlantis. Some societies, such as Dion Fortune's Fraternity (later Society) of the Inner Light, based large elements of their ritual work and teaching on Atlantean roots, and Fortune and most of her inner circle recalled past incarnations in the Atlantean priesthood. The Austrian clairvoyant scientist Rudolf Steiner and his pupil Max Heindel (Carl Louis Grasshof), both founders of important esoteric traditions, imported Blavatsky's ideas into their own substantial writings. Even Aleister Crowley, a maverick in most other matters, found room in his voluminous writings for *Atlantis Liber LI, The Lost Continent*, a tale of Atlantean sex magic, in which the inhabitants of Atlantis spent most of their time in orgiastic rituals to create a mysterious substance, Zro, that would enable them to escape Earth and emigrate en masse to the planet Venus. See **Anthroposophical Society**; **Crowley, Aleister**; **Rosicrucian Fellowship**; **Society of the Inner Light**.

The reign of Atlantis in occult secret societies faded out, along with the rest of the legacy of Theosophy, by the last quarter of the twentieth century. Ironically, this trend paralleled the spread of these same ideas via the New Age movement into popular culture across the world. As rejected knowledge found a new mass market, first in New Age circles and then in a booming alternative-history scene, the lost continent became raw material for scores of new books, with the popular writer Charles Berlitz leading the fray with his 1969 work *The Mystery of Atlantis.* Many of these books abandoned

Plato's story altogether, drawing from Theosophical sources or popular culture. One common theme in this literature was the relocation of Atlantis to the far corners of the globe. Antarctica and Peru were among the sites proposed for ancient Atlantis, despite the fact that neither of these regions has been under water any time in the last 11,000 years. See **Antarctica**; **New Age movement**.

Other writers, notably the visionary earth-mysteries scholar John Michell, have used the term "Atlantis" as a convenient label for an ancient global civilization with no particular connection to Plato's story. In Michell's bestselling *The View Over Atlantis* (1969), the remains of the lost civilization are hidden in plain sight by their sheer size: landscape alignments and ancient monuments trace out an immense pattern across the face of the earth, the remnant of a forgotten technology of earth energies. See **leys**.

A counterpoint to the occult vision of Atlantis has been the attempt to trace the Atlantis story back to some natural event conceivable within the worldview of modern science. The most popular contender for the title is an eruption of Thera, a small volcanic island in the Mediterranean between Crete and the Greek mainland. Around 1450 BCE a cataclysmic eruption of Thera sent tidal waves crashing into Crete, sending the ancient Minoan civilization of Crete into its final decline. While the date, location, and details differ completely from Plato's story, most mainstream archeologists who deal with Atlantis at all consider the Thera eruption the origin of the legend.

An alternative vision has been offered by researchers on the fringes of conventional archeology, who have pointed out that Plato's original account makes a surprising amount of sense on its own terms: 9600 BCE is a good approximate date for the end of the last Ice Age, when temperatures spiked upward across the northern hemisphere, melting the vast continental glaciers and raising sea levels 300 feet in the course of a few centuries. Huge expanses of land, including the broad plains that once reached from southern Britain to France and the land whose mountains now break the surface as the islands of Cuba, Hispaniola, and the Antilles, sank beneath the waters of the Atlantic. Elsewhere around the globe, the same story repeated itself as tens of thousands of square miles of land were overwhelmed by rising oceans in an uncomfortably close fit to current predictions of the effects of global warming.

The other aspects of Plato's story also fit the world of 9600 BCE remarkably well. In her 1986 book *Plato Prehistorian*, Mary Settegast left Atlantis itself untouched but joined Plato's account of the ancient Mediterranean with current archeological research to demonstrate a close fit between the two. Charles Hapgood Jr.'s 1969 *Maps of the Ancient Sea Kings*, a study of early maps full of anomalous geographical knowledge, presented evidence that someone mapped large portions of the Atlantic and Mediterranean coasts, not long after the end of the last Ice Age, with a degree of accuracy not seen again until the eighteenth century. These and other lines of evidence suggest that civilization may be older than current archeological models admit, and the rising seas of 9600 BCE could well have swallowed the heartland of a relatively advanced society in the lowlands on either side of the Atlantic. Still, none of this amounts to firm proof of the reality of Atlantis, much less justification for the wilder speculations about it. See **lost civilizations**.

Further reading: de Camp 1970, Donnelly 1973, Plato 1961, Scott-Elliot 1962.

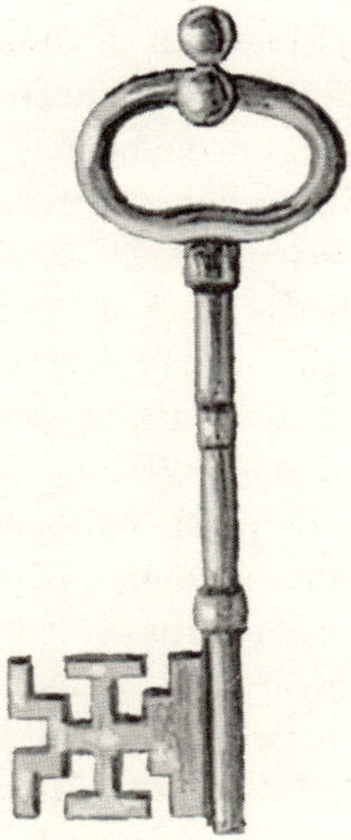

Aurum Solis

An influential occult secret society in the late twentieth-century magical community, Aurum Solis (Latin for "gold of the sun") was originally founded in 1897 by British occultists Charles Kingold and George Stanton. With interruptions during the two world wars, it remained active in a quiet way through the first two-thirds of the twentieth century. It suffered a short-lived schism in 1957, when a group of members broke away over differences in the initiation ritual; the group thus formed, the Ordo Sacri Verbi (Order of the Sacred Word), rejoined the Aurum Solis when it was reconstituted in 1971.

At the time of its reconstitution, the Aurum Solis came under the leadership of Vivian and Leon Barcynski, two London occultists who set out to break the Aurum Solis out of its rut of obscurity. Using the pen names Melita Denning and Osborne Phillips, the Barcynskis published books on the teachings of the Aurum Solis that vaulted the society into prominence throughout the English-speaking occult scene. It has had its ups and downs since that time, but remains active in Britain. The Aurum Solis symbolism and techniques covered in their books have also influenced occultists throughout the western world.

According to its internal history, the Aurum Solis is one expression of the Ogdoadic Tradition, a system of magical initiation dating back to classical Greek times. Such older organizations as the Knights Templar, the Fideli d'Amore, and Francis Bacon's Order of the Helmet are claimed as earlier expressions of the Ogdoadic Tradition. No real evidence of a distinct Ogdoadic Tradition can be found in records of occult traditions before the 1970s, however, nor do any of the Aurum Solis' distinctive symbols and practices occur in any of these older orders, so it is fair to assume that these claims are simply another example of the retrospective recruitment so common among secret societies. See **Bacon, Francis**; **Knights Templar**; **retrospective recruitment**.

The Aurum Solis works three degrees, or Halls, each with their own distinctive symbolism. The teachings of the order, however, are very closely modeled on those of the Hermetic Order of the Golden Dawn, with the same blend of Cabalistic and Enochian material and exact equivalents for every ritual practice in the Golden Dawn toolkit, a point-for-point equivalence not found in any of the other Hermetic magical orders of the time. Another source for the Aurum Solis system is the Order of Bards Ovates and Druids, to which Vivian Barcynski belonged in the late 1960s and early 1970s, and from which the Aurum Solis seems to have borrowed some of its distinctive features. These borrowings have occasionally been presented as evidence that the Aurum Solis was invented out of whole cloth in 1971, at the time of its supposed reconstitution, but this does not necessarily follow; secret societies routinely rework their teachings and training programs in the light of new information, and material from other secret societies is among the most common raw material for such projects. See **Hermetic Order of the Golden Dawn**; **Order of Bards Ovates and Druids (OBOD)**.

Further reading: Denning and Phillips 1975, Phillips 2001.

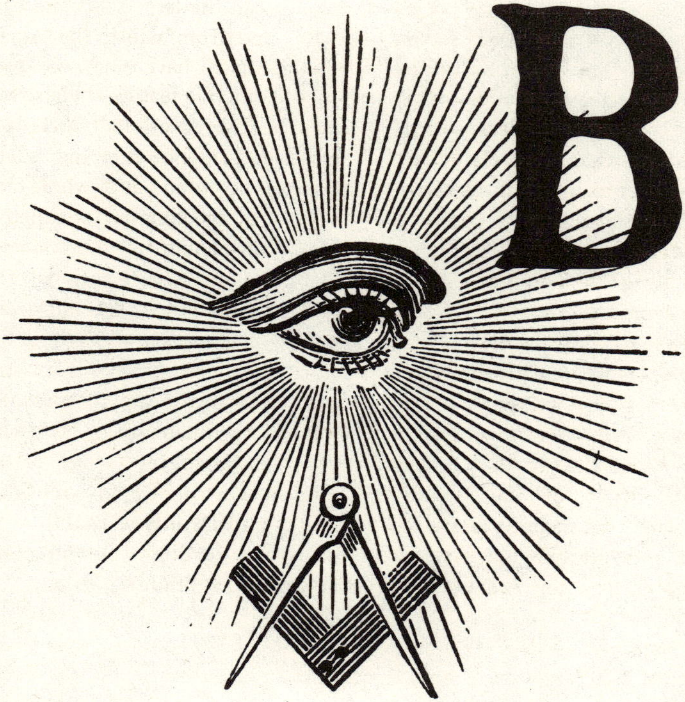

B

Babeuf, François "Gracchus"

French conspirator and secret society leader. Born into a poor family in provincial France, Babeuf (1760–97) worked as a minor functionary in the local government until the Revolution, when he went to Paris and became a journalist. During the elimination of the radical wing of the Revolution in 1795, he was thrown into prison, where he met Filippo Buonarroti, an Italian revolutionary. When they were released in October 1795, they launched the *Societé du Panthéon* (Society of the Pantheon), a semi-secret group that met to discuss egalitarian ideas and published a newspaper, the *Tribun du Peuple*. When the authorities shut down the newspaper in early 1796, Babeuf was ready to take the next step: the most committed members of the society were brought into a new secret society, the Conspiracy of Equals, and went to work under Babeuf's direction planning a *coup d'etat*. See **Conspiracy of Equals**; **French Revolution**.

A police informer within the Conspiracy alerted the authorities to the plot, and just before the planned coup, Babeuf and 200 other members were arrested. He was tried in February 1797 and executed. His friend Buonarroti landed in prison. After his release in 1806 he pursued the plans the two of them had devised together for the rest of his life, becoming the most famous figure in the political secret societies of the nineteenth century. See **Buonarroti, Filippo**.

Further reading: Roberts 1972.

Bacon, Francis

English philosopher, author, lawyer, and possible secret society member. One of the most brilliant minds of the Elizabethan age, Bacon (1561–1626) was the youngest son of Sir Nicholas Bacon, Lord Keeper of the Seal to Queen Elizabeth, and his second wife, the classical scholar Anne Cooke. Lord Burghley, Elizabeth's chief minister, was a close relative by marriage. These connections and his own precocious intellect brought him to Trinity College, Cambridge, at the age of 12. Graduating three years later, he entered Gray's Inn to study law, and was admitted to the Bar in 1582.

A brilliant and many-sided scholar, Bacon envisioned his life's work as the "Great Instauration," a complete reform of scholarship and human knowledge. His writings included *On the Advancement of Learning* (1605), which played an important role in launching the scientific revolution, and the posthumously published *The New Atlantis* (1627), a utopian novel of a society centered on a "think-tank," the House of Salomon, where all human knowledge was gathered, tested, and put to constructive use. He has also been credited with writing at least some of the works attributed to William Shakespeare. See **Shakespeare controversies**.

All this took place in the midst of a dazzling political career. In 1584 he entered the House of Commons, beginning a parliamentary career that only ended with his elevation to the peerage in 1618; 1591 saw him become a close associate of Robert Devereaux, Earl of Essex, a rising star in Elizabeth's court at that time. Only when Essex shifted from politics to rebellion did Bacon abandon him, serving as counsel for the prosecution in the trial that ended with Essex's execution in 1601. Knighted on the accession of James I, Bacon rose thereafter through the highest offices of the English civil service, becoming Lord Chancellor in 1618. In 1621 he was created Viscount St Albans, but in the same year his political enemies brought charges of bribery and corruption against him, and he was fined and imprisoned in the Tower. Pardoned by King James, he retired to his estates, where he spent the rest of his life in scientific and literary pursuits. He died in April 1626 from pneumonia contracted in an experiment to preserve a chicken by stuffing it with snow.

Bacon's level of involvement in secret societies during his lifetime remains an open question. Among the plays he wrote while at Gray's Inn includes one called *Ancient and Honourable Order of the Helmet*, and this order has accordingly been adopted into the legendary history of a number of more recent secret societies, notably the contemporary magical order Aurum Solis. In the literary and political war between the School of Night, the famous circle of freethinkers and occultists centered on Sir Walter Raleigh, and the supporters of the Earl of Essex, Bacon sided with his friend Essex, but – unless he was the author of the Shakespeare plays and poems – he does not seem to have contributed to the literary dimension of the struggle. See **Aurum Solis**; **School of Night**.

This may seem to offer only limited evidence for secret-society connections, but that has not prevented secret societies and their opponents from describing Bacon as a prominent member of esoteric secret societies, or even the leading figure in a world of secret societies underlying the Elizabethan Renaissance. Despite a complete lack of supporting evidence, he has been described as a prominent Freemason and one of the leading members of the Rosicrucian order, and some of his more enthusiastic supporters have credited him, or a secret society headed by him, with creating most of the great literature of the sixteenth and seventeenth centuries. Ironically, Bacon himself took a dim view of occult sciences, admitting at most that they ought to be searched for any scraps of real knowledge they might happen to contain. See **Freemasonry**; **Rosicrucians**.

A large part of this literature has based its claims on complex ciphers allegedly found in Bacon's own acknowledged works, as well as those attributed to Shakespeare and other writers of Bacon's period. Bacon himself was interested in ciphers, but attempts to use ciphers mentioned in his writings to decode hidden messages in Shakespeare's plays have proved equivocal at best, turning out wildly different results depending on the personal biases of the individuals employing them.

Further reading: Pott 1900.

Bailey, Alice

Anglo-American occultist and secret society founder, 1880–1949. Born in Manchester, the daughter of an engineer, Bailey was a devout Christian in her early years and went to India as a missionary. She met her first husband, the evangelist Walter Evans, in India and married him in 1907. They moved to America, where he took a position as an Episcopalian minister. The marriage proved to be unhappy, though, and ended in divorce.

Shortly after her arrival in America, Bailey encountered Theosophy for the first time and found it far more convincing than the Protestant Christianity of her youth. She came to believe that she had been receiving spiritual guidance from the Master Koot Hoomi (or Kuthumi), one of the Mahatmas of Theosophy, since the age of 15. In 1919, she experienced contact with another of the Masters, Djwal Khul, whom she called simply "the Tibetan." She spent the rest of her life writing down his teachings and communicating them to the world. See **Masters**; **Theosophical Society**.

In 1920 she married her second husband, the Freemason and fellow Theosophist Foster Bailey, and in 1923 they founded a teaching organization, the Arcane School, to pass on the Tibetan's teachings. An additional organization, the Lucis Trust, came into being later on to publish her voluminous writings. She pursued an active career in the American occult community for more than two decades thereafter until her death in 1949. See **Arcane School**.

Before the end of her life, despite a very quiet and uncontroversial career, Bailey was being named by conspiracy theorists as the leading figure in a Satanist conspiracy controlling the world. This role was the invention of Christina Stoddard, a former Golden Dawn initiate and temple chief of the Stella Matutina – the largest splinter group that emerged after the collapse of the Golden Dawn in 1900 – who later became a devout fundamentalist Christian, anticommunist, and author of classic conspiracy-theory books. Her *The Trail of the Serpent* argued that one of the major projects of the global Jewish–Satanist–Communist conspiracy was the invention of a syncretistic religion to unite the world's disparate faiths and replace conservative Protestant Christianity. At the center of this web of conspiracy, Stoddard placed Alice Bailey and her Lucis Trust. Despite a glaring lack of evidence for this claim, it has been repeated by more recent conspiracy theorists, notably the American fundamentalist writer Texe Marrs. See **fundamentalism**; **Hermetic Order of the Golden Dawn**.

Ballard, Guy

American writer and occultist. Ballard (1878–1939) was born and raised in Kansas, and worked as a mining engineer all over the western United States for nearly three decades. In the late 1920s, according to his later account, he met the Comte de Saint-Germain, one of the ascended masters, on the slopes of Mount Shasta. From the Comte and several other masters, Ballard claimed, he learned the secrets of the Violet Flame and the supreme power of the cosmos, the mighty I AM Presence. In the process he remembered his previous life as George Washington, and took part in conflicts between the servants of the ascended masters and dark forces that threatened America, which was under the Masters' special protection. See **Masters**; **Saint-Germain, Comte de**.

In 1934 he published his first book, *Unveiled Mysteries*, under the pen name Godfré Ray King, and followed it up with a series of other books. With the help of his wife Edna and son Donald, both of whom took active roles in his work, Ballard established an organization – the I Am Activity – to pass on his teachings, which included much of the Theosophical lore standard in early twentieth-century American occultism but focused specifically on the occult powers of color and light. Traveling from city to city as the sole "Accredited Representative of the Masters," Ballard pioneered the use of multimedia presentations, using colored lights and banners along with live and recorded music in his public presentations.

In the midst of this second career he died unexpectedly, an event that caused a great deal of consternation among his followers, since as a representative of the ascended masters he was expected to ascend rather than simply expire. Still, the Activity (now the Saint-Germain Foundation) survived him and remains active in a quiet way today, while Ballard's books are among the primary sources for the Ascended Masters teachings, one of the most innovative branches of American occultism today. See **Ascended Masters teachings**.

Baphomet

When King Philip IV of France rounded up the Knights Templar in his kingdom and turned them over to the Inquisition for torture, one of the offenses they were charged with was that they had worshipped an idol named Baphomet. Under torture, some of the Templars admitted to the charge, though their descriptions of Baphomet varied so wildly that it's clear they, like most victims of torture, simply said whatever would make the torturers stop. See **Knights Templar**.

During the centuries that followed, as most people forgot about the Knights Templar, references to Baphomet gathered dust in old archives. The first great transformation of the Templar myth, at the hands of Jacobite Freemasons in the middle years of the eighteenth century, left Baphomet untouched. Only when Joseph von Hammer-Purgstall, an Austrian government clerk turned historian, published his *Mysterium Baphometis Revelatum* (*The Mystery of Baphomet Revealed*, 1818) did Baphomet find its way back into the burgeoning Templar myth. Hammer-Purgstall argued that the Templars were part of an ancient Gnostic cult that practiced sexual orgies in honor of the hermaphroditic goddess Achamoth, and redefined Baphomet as the idol of Achamoth that the Templars worshipped during their obscene revels. See **Gnosticism**.

As so often happens in the history of secret societies, Hammer-Purgstall's theory was then borrowed by would-be Templars, attracted by his portrayal of Templar heresy and sexual deviance. By 1845, when Eliphas Lévi's *Dogme et Rituel de la Haute Magie* (*Doctrine and Ritual of High Magic*) took the occult scene by storm and reinvented magic for the modern world, some reference to Baphomet was all but obligatory in a French book on magic. Lévi met the demand with a description of Baphomet as a symbol of the Absolute, and an illustration: the half-human, hermaphrodite Goat of Mendes with its veiled phallus, bare breasts, and dark wings, a torch blazing between its horns and a pentagram on its brow, its hands pointing up and down in echo of the old Hermetic axiom "as above, so below." The image was a creation of Lévi's own magical imagination, inspired by Hammer-Purgstall's claims and the contemporary theory of fertility religion, but it has defined Baphomet in occult circles ever since. See **fertility religion**.

Since Lévi's time Baphomet has remained a constant presence in occult symbolism and philosophy. Predictably, given the phallic symbolism of the name, Aleister Crowley took Baphomet as his magical title as head of the Ordo Templi Orientis, the magical secret society he took over from Theodor Reuss. In some contemporary magical systems, Baphomet has become a symbol of the *spiritus mundi* or soul of the world, formed from the sum total of life energy generated by all the living things on earth. A new interpretation of the old legend surfaced in the early 1980s, when writers in the alternative-history field suggested that the idol of the Templars might have been the Shroud of Turin, a medieval forgery that claims to show the face and body of Christ miraculously imprinted on his shroud. See **Crowley, Aleister**; **Ordo Templi Orientis (OTO)**; **Reuss, Theodor**; **Shroud of Turin**.

Interpretations of the meaning of the alleged idol's name form a sideline among Baphomet researchers.

Suggestions range from German bookseller Friedrich Nicolai's claim that it derived from Greek words for "color" (and in a somewhat unlikely extension, "baptism") and "spirit," through Eliphas Lévi's proposal that it was a backwards abbreviation, TEM.O.H.P.AB, of the Latin phrase *Templum omnium hominum pacis abbas* ("abbot of the temple of peace for all men"), to Crowley's suggestion that it came from a phrase meaning "Father Mithras." It took twentieth-century scholars of medieval history to point out that "Baphomet" is the standard medieval French mispronunciation of the name of Muhammad, the Prophet of Islam, equivalent to the medieval and early modern English "Mahound." Philip IV's use of the term to blacken the Templars' reputation, in other words, was simply meant to imply that they had betrayed the Christian cause and gone over to the Muslim side.

Bavarian Illuminati

The most famous political secret society of all time, the focus of countless conspiracy theories and paranoid fantasies for more than two centuries, the Ancient Illuminated Seers of Bavaria was founded on May 1, 1776, by a professor at the University of Ingolstadt named Adam Weishaupt and four of his friends. Weishaupt was an avid student of the liberal ideas proposed by Voltaire, Diderot, and other French philosophers of the time; he hoped to foster progressive ideas in conservative, intensely Catholic Bavaria, and especially at his university, where liberal faculty members struggled against a clique of ex-Jesuits whose influence remained intact even after the Society of Jesus had been dissolved in 1773. He became a Freemason in 1774, but found the Craft's ban on political and religious discussions little to his taste. The birth of the Illuminati in 1776 was the logical result, an attempt to use the Masonic model as a tool for liberal cultural politics. See **Society of Jesus (Jesuits)**; **Weishaupt, Adam**.

From this modest start the order grew slowly. In 1779 it had 54 members, divided among five colonies (local lodges) in Bavaria. Membership growth was limited by the intensive course of study Weishaupt set out for his initiates. Weishaupt believed in the essential goodness of human nature, arguing that only the burdens of religious obscurantism and fossilized tradition stood in the way of universal human enlightenment; he originally planned to call his order the Perfectibilists, because of its focus on the possibility of human perfection, but settled on Illuminati as a reference to the enlightened attitudes he hoped to foster. Illuminati novices thus started their studies with classical moral writers such as Aristotle and Cato, and then went on to contemporary philosophers such as Holbach and Helvetius. A process of self-examination, guided by written questionnaires and the close supervision of a senior initiate, helped direct the novice toward the goal of this strenuous training program – the creation of an elite of enlightened initiates who would insinuate themselves into influential positions in Bavarian society and transform the kingdom into a Utopia.

Illuminati recruitment focused on the socially prominent, the wealthy, and the talented from the very beginning. Starting in 1779, a new and highly successful second recruitment front opened as Illuminati began to infiltrate Masonic lodges in Germany and elsewhere, recruiting Masonic leaders and taking control of lodges. Xavier Zwack, the architect of this new strategy and one of Weishaupt's senior lieutenants, started the process with the successful takeover of an important Munich lodge. By 1784 the order had spread through much of central Europe, with active colonies in Germany, Austria, Switzerland, Bohemia (now the Czech Republic), Hungary, and northern Italy, and the total number of Illuminati who had received the Illuminatus Minor degree (the basic working degree of the order) topped 650. See **Freemasonry**.

Codes, ciphers, and secret names played an important role in the Illuminati system. Each member had a code name; for example, Weishaupt was Spartacus, Zwack was Cato, and Baron von Knigge, another leader, was Philo. Places also had code names: Ingolstadt was Eleusis, Munich was Athens, and Vienna was Rome. Communications between members were always in cipher, and even the names of months were disguised.

By the period of the order's greatest growth, however, the secrecy essential to its survival had been breached. Some of its members talked too freely about the order's opposition to religious and political autocracy. In 1782, when Illuminati agents attended the great Masonic conclave at Wilhemsbad in an effort to take control of the crumbling Strict Observance, important attendees such as Jean-Baptiste Willermoz already knew enough about the order to checkmate their plans, and the Illuminati went away empty-handed. By 1784 horrifying rumors about the Illuminati were in circulation in Bavaria itself, and the Bavarian government imposed an edict banning secret organizations; 1785 saw another edict proscribing the Illuminati by name. See **Rite of Strict Observance**.

Weishaupt fled into exile, and ordered Illuminati lodges in Bavaria to go to ground, but his hopes of rebuilding the Illuminati in secret were dashed in 1786 when Bavarian police raided Xavier Zwack's house and seized copies of hundreds of the order's documents, including Weishaupt's own secret correspondence. Most of the Illuminati in Bavaria either left the kingdom or were jailed. Weishaupt himself moved to Gotha, in relatively liberal Saxony, where he settled down to a quiet career as a professor of philosophy and writer.

Most of the other Illuminati scattered in the same way, though a handful attempted to restart something close to Weishaupt's organization. Christoph Bode, an influential Illuminatus, made two visits to Paris in an attempt to interest French radicals in Weishaupt's teachings. Among his most important converts was Nicholas de Bonneville, a lawyer who went on to become one of the most influential radical journalists of the French Revolution and the founder of an important secret society, the Social Circle. Filippo Buonarroti, who would become the most influential revolutionary of the early nineteenth century, belonged to a Masonic lodge in Italy that had briefly been under Illuminati control, and he spent the rest of his long life using Illuminati methods in an attempt to foster liberal revolutions across Europe. See **Buonarroti, Filippo**; **Social Circle**; **Sublime Perfect Masters**.

The Bavarian Illuminati was one among many minor secret societies of the late eighteenth century, and might well have become nothing more than a footnote to the history of the time. Between its origins in 1776 and its suppression by the Bavarian government in 1786, it succeeded in a small way in its primary goal of spreading French Enlightenment ideas in conservative Bavaria, and won some influence over the more liberal end of German public opinion, but that was all. It is one of the great ironies of secret-society history that this modest achievement launched the most remarkable of all the myths that make up contemporary conspiracy theory, and turned Adam Weishaupt's circle of would-be reformers into the foundation of a sprawling mythology of global domination by the ultimate secret society.

The dawn of the Illuminati myth was the Bavarian government's publication of papers seized from Illuminati in 1786. The papers launched a brief furor in the conservative press of the time, but probably would have been forgotten had the French Revolution not broken out three years later. The first years of revolution saw references to the Illuminati in antimasonic publications, and now and again the suggestion that Weishaupt's society or something like it might be behind France's political troubles. The real transformation of the Illuminati from a minor episode in the history of secret societies to the centerpiece of two centuries of paranoid speculation, though, began in 1797, with the publication in London of the first two volumes of Augustin de Barruel's *Mémoires pour servir à l'histoire du Jacobinisme* (*Memoirs serving as a History of Jacobinism*).

De Barruel was an ex-Jesuit, a Catholic priest, and an author of conservative political tracts who had fled revolutionary France in 1792. He had become convinced that a widespread conspiracy was responsible for the Revolution. While he blamed Freemasons and philosophers for helping to lay the groundwork for the overthrow of the

French monarchy, he argued that an inner circle within Masonry had deliberately planned the whole affair as part of a sinister crusade against monarchy and Christianity. That hidden inner circle, he insisted, was none other than the Bavarian Illuminati. Despite the complete lack of evidence presented for the claim in de Barruel's book, his idea was taken up enthusiastically by conservatives in France and elsewhere, who found it impossible to believe that the French people might have had a reason to overthrow the most corrupt and inefficient monarchy in Europe.

In the same year that the first volumes of de Barruel's work appeared, a Scottish Freemason, John Robison, published a book of his own, with the inflammatory title *Proofs of a Conspiracy against all the Religions and Governments of Europe, carried on in the secret Meetings of Free Masons, Illuminati, and Reading Societies.* Robison's motivation was curious; he wanted to protect British Freemasonry by distancing it from the political activities of Masons in France and Italy and throwing the blame for the French Revolution on the Illuminati. Robison's book was savaged by critics for its shaky logic and lack of evidence, but was regularly reprinted and has had an immense influence on conspiracy theories in the English-speaking world ever since.

De Barruel and Robison between them caused an immediate sensation across Europe; their claims were taken up enthusiastically by conservatives as a weapon against liberal opponents. Robison's and de Barruel's ideas blended with the parallel mythology of the Knights Templar and media reports about actual nineteenth-century secret societies to make the vision of secret societies opposed to monarchy, Christianity, and property an item of faith for most European conservatives throughout the 1800s. The same beliefs found a home in a different social milieu on the far side of the Atlantic, where Robison's book sparked a brief antimasonic witch-hunt in the 1790s. The belief in sinister Illuminati plots fed into the antimasonic movement of the 1830s, became an item of faith among the Know-Nothings of the 1840s, and helped lay the foundations for the rise of fundamentalism in the early twentieth century. See **Antimasonic Party**; **fundamentalism**; **Know-Nothing Party**; **Knights Templar**.

The next stage in the development of the Illuminati mythology came in the aftermath of the First World War. *The Protocols of the Elders of Zion*, an antisemitic hoax claiming that Jews were behind an international conspiracy to enslave the world, and the success of the Bolshevik Revolution in 1917 gave a massive boost to conspiracy theories worldwide. Nesta Webster, the leading light among British conspiracy writers, responded to the Russian revolution in much the same way Robison and de Barruel had responded to the French, arguing that a vast conspiracy must have been needed to cause it. Her books argued, however, for a "One Big Conspiracy" theory in which the Bolsheviks, and the Illuminati themselves, were merely pawns in a larger game, manipulated along with countless other groups by an inner core of Jewish Satanists. These ideas found a ready audience throughout the western world, and helped feed the fascist movements of the 1920s and 1930s in Europe and America. See **Protocols of the Elders of Zion**.

The Second World War and the revelations of Nazi atrocities against the Jews made antisemitic conspiracy theories difficult to defend publicly, but did nothing to dispel the popular appeal of conspiracy theories in general. The Illuminati mythology proved more than capable of filling the void. A crucial role in the postwar expansion of Illuminati-hunting was played by Robert Welch, founder and chief ideologist of the John Birch Society. Welch started his career as an anticommunist, but became convinced that communism itself was simply a pawn in the hands of a shadowy league of wealthy "Insiders," who manipulated parties and movements across the political and social spectra. Welch drew extensively from de Barruel and Robison in his writings and explicitly identified his "Insiders" as the Illuminati. See **John Birch Society**.

Welch's claims helped make the second half of the twentieth century a golden age of speculation about the Illuminati, and did much to ensure that these speculations would proliferate free of the limits of evidence or logic. Since the original sources on Weishaupt's society had been all but forgotten, and even de Barruel and Robison were cited far more often than they were read, the shadow of the Illuminati could be stretched or cropped as needed to cover any desired collection of facts or fantasies. Thus the original Illuminati, with their dream of human moral perfection and their commitment to liberal ideals, have been completely eclipsed. Most of the conspiracy theories about the Illuminati nowadays claim that the order consists of 13 extremely wealthy families who already run the world, but who have been plotting for thousands of years to impose a Satanic dictatorship on the entire planet in the next few decades.

The result has been an extraordinary profusion of imaginative theories uniting all the world's real or imagined secret societies under the Illuminati banner. One widely quoted theory claims that the Illuminati were founded in Mesopotamia sometime around 300,000 BCE, when a group of conspirators infiltrated an existing secret society called the Brotherhood of the Snake. Since the first *Homo sapiens* apparently didn't come into being until sometime after 100,000 BCE, this theory would make the Illuminati conspiracy substantially older than our species, and indeed older than the Neanderthals. The thought of a contemporary secret society dating back to *Homo erectus* may seem dizzying at first glance, but compared to some other theories about the Illuminati – such as David Icke's claim that the world is ruled by a secret aristocracy of shape-shifting reptiles from the constellation Draco – it is relatively tame. See **Reptilians**.

The sheer diversity of Illuminati theories has driven many attempts to force some sort of order on all the confusion. Many writers simply insist that all secret societies are the Illuminati, or that the Illuminati themselves are actually another organization called Moriah Conquering Wind. Others have arranged the different groups into a neat hierarchical pyramid. The most common scheme of this sort, included in many books and websites about the Illuminati, starts at the top with the degree of the All-Seeing Eye, which is held personally by Lucifer. Next comes the Rothschild Tribunal or RT, the inner circle of Rothschild family members, whom other Illuminati allegedly regard as gods in human form. Below them is the Great Druid Council, staffed by 13 great druids who form the Rothschild family's private priesthood, although why a family of Jewish bankers would have Celtic Pagan priests is an interesting question rarely discussed. The next two levels of the pyramid are the Council of Thirty-Three, consisting of the highest Freemasons; and the Committee of 300, made up of families of satanic nobility, headed by the British Crown. Ordinary, garden-variety Illuminati fall somewhere beneath this baroque hierarchy, which brings most of the popular candidates for the post of hidden masters of the world into a single scheme. See **Committee of 300**; **Druids**; **Moriah Conquering Wind**; **Satanism**.

Predictably, all this myth-making has propelled at least two known attempts to revive the Bavarian Illuminati, at least in name. Masonic entrepreneur Theodor Reuss, better known as the originator of the Ordo Templi Orientis (OTO), was also involved in an attempt to relaunch the Illuminati. He and his associate Leopold Engel raised the Illuminati banner in 1895 in Berlin, but a split between Engel and Reuss sent the latter pursuing other projects. Engel's Illuminati continued to exist until the middle years of the twentieth century, when it merged with the Ordo Templi Orientis. See **Ordo Templi Orientis**; **Reuss, Theodor**.

Nearly half a world away, a group of Berkeley, California college students, loosely affiliated with the Discordian movement, proclaimed themselves as the Bavarian Illuminati in 1968 and sent out raucous proclamations to a bemused world for several years thereafter. See **Discordian movement**.

Further reading: Billington 1980, Roberts 1972.

Benandanti

One of the strangest cases in the files of the Italian Inquisition is the case of the *benandanti* (Italian for "good walkers"), a secret society of peasant magicians in the region of Friuli, in the far northeast of Italy. The benandanti first came to the attention of the Catholic authorities in 1575, when a member of the society was brought before the Inquisition on an unrelated charge. The inquisitors were completely baffled by what they learned, as it did not match official portrayals of Satanism or pagan religion. Investigations continued in a desultory way for the next three-quarters of a century, with over a hundred benandanti finding themselves hauled before the Inquisition and grilled about their beliefs.

According to their testimony, children born with a caul (a portion of the amniotic sac) on their head were destined to become benandanti. On the ember days – the days to either side of the solstices and equinoxes – they left their physical bodies behind and traveled in animal form to the Vale of Josaphat at the center of the world. There, using fennel stalks as their weapons, they battled the *malandanti* or "evil walkers," sorcerers armed with sorghum stalks. If the benandanti won, the harvest would be good; if the malandanti won, the crops would fail. The special powers of the benandanti gave them the ability to heal illnesses and lift curses, but their central duty was the nocturnal battle against the malandanti.

The Inquisition office in Friuli, as elsewhere in Italy, rejected the use of torture and gave accused persons certain legal rights rare north of the Alps. As a result, very few of the benandanti faced serious punishment; most were let off with penances and a stern warning to abandon their supposedly superstitious beliefs. The last trial involving benandanti was in 1644; after that time, faced with more serious threats to Catholic orthodoxy, the Friulian Inquisition abandoned the issue and no further investigations were ordered.

As historian of medieval culture Carlo Ginzburg has pointed out, the records of the benandanti are of high importance because they document one form of a tradition – found all over medieval Europe in various guises – of nocturnal journeys in animal form, often in the company of a goddess. This tradition surfaced by the ninth century, when it was condemned by the canon Episcopi, part of Catholic canon law, and can be found mentioned in Inquisition records and folklore from across Europe. See **canon Episcopi**.

Further reading: Ginzburg 1985, Ginzburg 1991.

Benevolent Protective Order of Elks [BPOE]

One of the largest and most prestigious of American fraternal orders, the Elks had their origins in a drinking club called the Jolly Corks, founded in 1867 by a group of actors and entertainers in New York City who took umbrage at the "blue laws" that forbade saloons from serving alcohol on Sundays. The group had been meeting for a few months when, just before Christmas, one of its members died, leaving his wife and children penniless. Another member of the Corks, the English-born actor Charles Vivian, was a member of a British fraternal order, and proposed to the others that they found a similar organization that would combine social drinking with a beneficial system for members. Disagreement immediately rose about the name; Vivian suggested that the new order name itself after the American buffalo, but by a vote of eight to seven the members present voted to call themselves Elks instead.

The new order was founded in February 1868 with a ritual of two degrees, and began attracting new members almost at once, first from within the theatre and entertainment industries and then from all walks of life. In these early days, Elks initiations drew heavily from the burlesque degrees of the time, as well as from Freemasonry and other fraternal orders; members even wore lambskin aprons like those used by Masons for initiation rituals. Many of these elements, however, fell out of use as the order expanded. In 1890 the second degree of initiation was eliminated; in 1895 the lambskin aprons dropped out of use; passwords stopped being used in 1899, membership badges in 1902, grips in 1904, and the use of an oath in 1911. A 1952 change eliminated the custom of blindfolding candidates. A final traditional barrier, the limitation of membership to men, went by the board in 1995. See **burlesque degrees**; **Freemasonry**.

By the last years of the nineteenth century the Elks had become one of the most prominent fraternal orders in America. Unlike most other orders of the kind, they continued to expand their membership until 1976, reaching a peak of 2200 lodges and over 1.6 million members in that year. Their success at a time when many other fraternal orders were suffering severe losses depended partly on their willingness to discard ritual practices that many twentieth-century Americans found old-fashioned, partly on the order's tradition of establishing a bar and restaurant for members in every lodge, and partly on the fact that by the early twentieth century the Elks had become the favorite social club for many members of America's political elites. US presidents Warren Harding, Franklin D. Roosevelt, Harry Truman, John F. Kennedy, and Gerald Ford were all Elks. In most US state capitals the Elks lodge can be found within a few blocks of the state government buildings, and a great deal of lobbying and informal political business was transacted there. The last quarter of the twentieth century saw some contraction in Elkdom, but the Elks remain one of the largest surviving fraternal orders at the time of writing.

The history of organizations associated with the Elks is relatively complex. Two competing ladies auxiliaries, the Emblem Club and the more exclusive Benevolent Protective Order of Does, emerged in the 1920s and still exist today. An independent Canadian Elks order was founded in 1912 and established its own ladies auxiliary, the Royal Purple, in 1914.

Another Elks order, the Improved Benevolent Protective Order of Elks of the World, was launched in 1898 in Cincinnati, Ohio by two African-American men, who were refused admission into the local Elks lodge on account of their race. The BPOE attempted to force them out of existence with a series of lawsuits but failed, and in 1918 abandoned the attempt. See **African-American secret societies**; **ladies auxiliaries**.

Bilderberg Group

One of the *bêtes noires* of contemporary conspiracy theory, the Bilderberg Group – this is not its actual name, but the title given it by its critics – is composed of the attendees of a series of informal top-level conferences among politicians, bankers, and businessmen begun in 1954 by Prince Bernhard of the Netherlands. The first meeting was held in Oosterbek, the Netherlands, in the posh Bilderberg Hotel, and subsequent annual meetings have been held in cities in Europe and the eastern seaboard of North America. The guest list for these conferences reads like a Who's Who of European and American elites, with Europeans outnumbering Americans on average by 2 to 1. The official purpose of the meetings is to foster closer ties and better understanding among political and economic leaders in the nations of the Atlantic alliance.

American conference attendees have been drawn largely from the membership of the Council on Foreign Relations (CFR) and other policy-making organizations in the upper levels of the American elite, and the entire project of having annual meetings of decision makers from many countries was probably inspired by the CFR and its European equivalents. In turn, the Bilderberg meetings probably played a role in laying foundations for the Trilateral Commission, which includes Japanese government and business leaders alongside their opposite numbers from Europe and America. See **Council on Foreign Relations (CFR)**; **Trilateral Commission**.

The role of the Bilderberg conferences in contemporary conspiracy theory began with American far-right groups, such as the John Birch Society and the Liberty Lobby, who pounced on the first conference as proof of the conspiracy of "Insiders" that John Birch Society founder Robert Welch identified as the puppet masters behind capitalism and communism alike. Since then, the "Bilderbergers" have taken a place in conspiracy literature as one among many likely candidates for the position of secret masters of the New World Order. See **John Birch Society**; **New World Order**.

BLACK BALL

In most traditional secret societies in the western world, candidates for initiation are elected to membership by a secret ballot of current members of the lodge where their application has been received. The usual method involves a wooden ballot box with a tray of white and black marbles. One at a time, members advance to the box, pick up a marble and drop it in. White marbles are favorable votes, black marbles unfavorable. In the stricter lodges, one negative vote is enough to bar a candidate from membership, while some American fraternal orders now require a majority of negative votes to exclude a potential member. See **fraternal orders**; **lodge**.

The custom of voting in members with black and white balls was widespread enough that it gave rise to the verb "to blackball," meaning to ostracize someone or block their membership in an organization.

BLACK HELICOPTERS

Central to many of the current New World Order conspiracy theories is the belief that a fleet of black military helicopters carries out secret missions in US airspace, and sometime soon will spearhead the imposition of a nationwide police state. Helicopters painted black, rather than the dark green of ordinary Army or Marine Corps craft, do exist in the US military arsenal, and have been sighted and photographed many times. The black helicopters of contemporary conspiracy theories, though, are no ordinary craft, but form the keystone of an evolving myth of immanent evil; see **New World Order**.

The first reports of black helicopters surfaced in 1971, in the early days of the cattle mutilation phenomenon. Some of the baffled farmers and ranchers whose livestock turned up dead and mutilated in otherwise unmarked pastures reported seeing mysterious black helicopters flying over their fields. The black helicopters formed only one of many purported explanations for cattle mutilations, though, and claims linking the mutilations with UFOs and Satanic cults got considerably more press. Black helicopters continued to be reported in mutilation accounts until the phenomenon faded out around 1985.

In 1993, though cattle mutilations remained a very occasional event, the black helicopters returned in force. The force behind their reappearance seems to have been the inauguration of Bill Clinton as US President after 12 years of Republican ascendancy, an event that convinced many people on the American far right that their worst fears were about to be realized. Internet chatrooms buzzed with claims that the new President, with the help of United Nations forces, was about to suspend civil rights and impose firearms laws on America comparable to those in most other developed countries. Black helicopters full of foreign troops played an important role in these fantasies. In all probability, the entire phenomenon was deliberate disinformation meant to rally the far right around the Republican Party after its stinging defeat in the 1992 national elections. See **Disinformation**.

Like many other disinformation campaigns, though, this one took on a life of its own. The image of sinister black helicopters in America's skies mirrored the fears and fantasies of too many Americans in the 1990s to fade away once it had served its political purpose. Before long talk of black helicopters spread from the far right into many other American subcultures: UFO researchers began discussing the role of black helicopters in the government's alleged UFO cover-up and dealings with alien intelligences; therapists in the Satanic ritual abuse industry began extracting stories of Satanists in black helicopters from their hypnotized clients; and radicals on the far left repeated tales that originated on the far right. By 2000 black helicopters were such a fixture in every corner of the alternative-realities scene that the phrase "the black helicopter crowd" came into widespread use as a term embracing all Americans who believed in conspiracy theories of every kind. See **Satanism**; **unidentified flying objects (UFOs)**.

Further reading: Keith 1994a.

Black Hundreds

One of the most influential conservative secret societies in prerevolutionary Russia, the Black Hundreds – more formally known as the Union of the Russian People – was founded in 1905 in St Petersburg by V. M. Purishkevich, a reactionary agitator. Russia's disastrous defeat in its 1904–05 war with Japan, along with serious economic and political troubles, forced the Tsar to grant limited political freedoms and to call the first Russian parliament, the Duma of the Empire. Purishkevich set out to discredit these changes by convincing the Russian masses that the new constitution and the Duma were part and parcel of a Jewish conspiracy against the Tsar. *The Protocols of the Elders of Zion*, a newly manufactured forgery claiming to disclose a Jewish plot for world domination, became a central element of Black Hundreds propaganda. See **Antisemitism**; **Protocols of the Elders of Zion**.

As the Union of the Russian People, the Black Hundreds ran candidates for office and held a handful of seats in the Duma. Meanwhile armed bands raised by the political wing of the organization carried out assassinations and pogroms against Jews, Freemasons, liberals, and ethnic minorities such as Armenians and Poles. The Hundreds received substantial support from Tsar Nicholas II, who wore its badge on his uniform, as well as from many influential aristocrats. It also received up to

2.5 million rubles a year from the imperial government itself.

The Black Hundreds remained a significant factor in Russian politics until the beginning of the First World War, when the government subsidies and support that kept it functioning had to be redirected to the war effort. When the Revolution broke out in 1917, most of its remaining members joined the White (anticommunist) side and were killed or exiled in the bitter civil war that followed. See **Russian revolution**.

Further reading: Cohn 1967, Laqueur 1965.

Black Lodges

In the occult scene of the late nineteenth and early twentieth centuries, a term for occult secret societies devoted to the study and practice of evil magic. Many of the occult writers of this period treat the existence and activities of the Black Lodges as a matter of common knowledge, and discuss in detail the differences between the true path of occult initiation and the corrupt and counterfeit path offered by the Black Lodges to their initiates. In practice, however, the term was used by members of rival occult orders to slander their opponents. Even Aleister Crowley, himself considered a black magician by most of his contemporaries in the occult community, used the term to describe his doctrinal opponents. See **Crowley, Aleister**; **lodge**; **Magic**.

Specific definitions of the Black Lodges varied depending on the beliefs of the lodge or occultist defining them. In the teachings of the Hermetic Brotherhood of Luxor, for example, the Black Lodges were composed of necromancers working with the energies of the mysterious Dark Satellite and its hierarch, Ob. Theosophical writings of the same period claimed that the Black Lodges glorified the separate individuality, while the Great White Lodge sought to lead all souls into the Divine Unity. See **Hermetic Brotherhood of Luxor (H.B. of L.)**; **Theosophical Society**.

In fact, to judge by all the evidence, Black Lodges of the sort described in occult literature did not actually exist in the late nineteenth and early twentieth centuries. By the last decades of the twentieth century, however, several organizations that fit the old definitions exactly had come into being and were advertising for members on the Internet. Magical orders such as the Temple of Set and the White Order of Thule, drawing on modern Satanism and the mythology of German National Socialism, duplicated the teachings and practices of the Black Lodges as described by occult writers of a century before. Fictional secret societies have inspired real ones so often that the roots of today's "black lodges" may include a good deal of inspiration from their imaginary nineteenth-century equivalents. See **Satanism**; **Temple of Set**; **White Order of Thule**.

BLACK MAGIC

In nineteenth- and twentieth-century occult parlance, a term used for systems of magic that were morally evil, as opposed to "white magic" which was, or at least claimed to be, morally good. No two definitions of black and white magic cover the same territory, but most define black magic as magical work performed with selfish intentions, while white magic has unselfish intentions and orients itself toward higher spiritual powers. In practical terms, magic that harms other people or pursues wholly selfish aims has usually been characterized as black magic. See **magic**; **white magic**.

BLACK MASS

The classic ritual of traditional Satanism, the Black Mass is a parody of the Catholic mass in which a naked woman is used as the altar, Christian symbols are defiled or inverted, and the consecrated Host (the wafer of unleavened bread that, according to Catholic theology, becomes the body of Christ) is abused in various ways. Like most transgressive forms of magic in the western world, the Black Mass seems to have started out as a fantasy of authority figures – in this case, officials of the Catholic Church – that was then adopted by opponents of authority for its shock value. See **Satanism**.

For this reason, the Black Mass has rarely been popular outside of Catholic countries. In France, where baiting the Catholic Church has been a sport for centuries, the Black Mass seems to have been practiced more often than anywhere else. In the sixteenth and seventeenth centuries, numerous French priests were burned at the stake for performing Black Masses, and though many of these cases were clearly miscarriages of justice, evidence suggests that not all of them were. At the end of the seventeenth century, the "Affair of the Poisons" turned up a flourishing trade in Black Masses reaching into the court of Louis XIV himself, and 36 people were burned alive for their roles in a plot on the king's life. The end of the nineteenth century, for its part, saw the Black Mass once again in vogue as an expression of the Decadent esthetic, and J.K. Huysmans' Satanist novel *Là-Bas* (*Down There*) drew on the author's experience of Black Masses performed in Liège.

The Black Mass had a brief vogue in England at the end of the eighteenth century, when Sir Francis Dashwood's Hell-Fire Club became notorious for its ceremonies, though these seem to have been mostly excuses for heavy drinking and sex. In the same way, Satanist-showman Anton Szandor LaVey's Church of Satan titillated audiences in the 1970s with a version of the old ritual designed to play down the religious elements and play up the display of female nudity. See **Church of Satan**; **Hell-Fire Club**.

The Black Mass has fallen almost entirely out of use among modern

Satanists, however, and traditional Satanism as a whole has been largely replaced in the last two decades by more avant-garde forms of organized wickedness, such as the Temple of Set and "dark-side" neo-Nazi lodges. The reasons behind this change are instructive. As a parody and inversion of the Catholic mass, the Black Mass depended for its effect on its contrast with the participants' memories of the grandeur of the Catholic ritual. The Second Vatican Council reforms, which banished the Latin rite, stripped away most of the mystery and power from the ceremony, and brought in such dubious entertainments as folk-music masses, left little for Satanists to parody; it's hard to imagine even the most enthusiastic Satanists getting noticeable results by singing "Kum Ba Ya" backwards. See **neo-Nazi secret societies**; **Temple of Set**.

Black Order

See **White Order of Thule (WOT)**.

Black Sun

The central symbol of contemporary neo-Nazi occultism, the Black Sun first appeared as a symbol in the writings of Erich Halik, a member of the circle that gathered around the seminal neo-Nazi thinker Wilhelm Landig in Vienna after the Second World War. Halik argued that occultists in the SS befor
ing the war had split int
tions, a Luciferian group, symbolized by the Golden Sun, who drew on the Cathar tradition and attempted to link up with secret occult centers in Tibet, and a Satanist core group, symbolized by the Black Sun, who were in contact with a mysterious Blue Island in the Arctic. He claimed that the black roundel painted just after the war on captured German aircraft had actually been the insignia of the Black Sun, proving that the Wehrmacht had reached the Blue Island before the end of the war and stationed an elite corps of SS members there to prepare a counterstroke against the victorious Allies when the time was ripe. See **Cathars**; **neo-Nazi secret societies**; **Satanism**; **SS (Schutzstaffel)**.

These ideas made their way into the broader neo-Nazi movement by way of a trilogy of novels Wilhelm Landig himself published in the last decades of the twentieth century. In *Götzen gegen Thule* (*Godlings against Thule*, 1971), *Wolfszeit um Thule* (*Wolf-time around Thule*, 1980) and *Rebellen für Thule* (*Rebels for Thule*, 1991) Landig painted a picture of secret Nazi bases in the Arctic and Antarctic, stocked with flying saucers and fighting a secret struggle against a Jewish world conspiracy. The Black Sun, which Landig explains is not black but deep purple, is the emblem of the new, magical Reich. See **Thule**.

Another neo-Nazi thriller, *Die schwarze Sonne von Tashi Lhunpo* (*The Black Sun of Tashi Lhunpo*,

1991) identified the Black Sun symbol with the sun-wheel emblem on the floor of the great tower of Wewelsburg, the SS ceremonial center in Westphalia, Germany. This version of the Black Sun, a wheel of twelve zigzag S-runes, has become a central symbol in today's neo-Nazi secret societies.

These fictional manifestations of the Black Sun launched it into the wider world of neo-Nazi occultism, where it soon became a primary symbol. In the hands of Miguel Serrano, the chief theoretician of the movement, the Black Sun represents the star around which the true home world of the Aryans circles, bathed in the "extra-galactic" light of the Green Ray. According to Serrano, when the original Aryans came to our world to battle the Demiurge and his legions of subhuman beastmen, they had superhuman powers as a result of the light of the Black Sun circulating in their veins; those powers were lost when the original Aryans mated with the beast-men to produce modern humanity. The purpose of Aryan spiritual training, according to this theory, is to open up contact with the Black Sun through the crown chakra, cleanse the self of the contamination of non-Aryan blood, and regain the lost powers of the ancient Aryans. This drastic distortion of traditional occult teaching has inspired various systems of neo-Nazi yoga and magic in recent years.

Further reading: Godwin 1993, Goodrick-Clarke 2002.

Blavatsky, Helena Petrovna

Russian author and occultist. One of the most influential figures in the history of modern occultism, Blavatsky (1831–91) – née von Hahn – was born in Yekaterinoslav in the Ukraine to a military family of German origin. Her great-grandfather, Prince Paul Dolgourouki, had been a member of the Rite of Strict Observance, the leading eighteenth-century occult Masonic order, and Blavatsky spent many hours in her youth reading occult books from his library. See **Rite of Strict Observance**.

When she was 19, her father arranged to marry her off to an elderly Russian nobleman, Nikifor Blavatsky, but she left him after a few months and traveled widely in Europe and the Near East. According to later Theosophical writings, she spent much of this time as a pupil of the Masters in Tibet, while researchers outside the Theosophical fold have argued instead that she spent these years as a circus performer, fraudulent medium, and adventuress. Her travels took her back home to the Ukraine in 1858, to the Caucasus in the 1860s, and back to Cairo, surviving shipwreck on the way, in 1871.

By the time she visited her family in 1858 she was already an accomplished spiritualist medium, and on her second trip to Cairo she established a spiritualist organization, the *Sociéte Spirite* or Spirit Society, with the help of French medium Emma

Coulombe and her husband. The Society foundered a few years later amid charges of fraud and embezzlement, and Blavatsky proceeded to Paris. In 1873 she crossed the Atlantic to New York City, where she met Col. Henry Steele Olcott, whose abilities as an organizer and publicist made Blavatsky's later career possible. Within a short time the two were living together, and had drawn up plans for an organization to teach the wisdom of the ages to the western world. Blavatsky's friend Henry Sotheran, a high-ranking Freemason and occultist, suggested the name "Theosophical Society" for the new organization, and in 1875 the movement that would dominate western occultism for a century was born at a meeting in New York. See **Theosophical Society**.

For the next two years, while the Society slowly grew around her, Blavatsky labored over the first of her two massive books, *Isis Unveiled* (1877). An all-out attack on the materialist science and orthodox religion of her time, *Isis Unveiled* presented a worldview mostly drawn from the western occultism of the time, with particularly heavily borrowings from the writings of French magus Eliphas Lévi and American Rosicrucian Paschal Beverly Randolph. An instant success, it launched the Theosophical Society on a trajectory that gave it worldwide popularity. See **Randolph, Paschal Beverly**.

In 1878 Blavatsky and Olcott went to England, and the next year arrived in India, where they established a new headquarters for the Society at Adyar, near Bombay. Blavatsky's old Cairo confidantes the Coulombes joined them there and took housekeeping positions at the headquarters building. At Adyar, Blavatsky astonished the local British community and visiting occultists by performing apparent miracles. Silverware disappeared and reappeared, and messages from mysterious Tibetan Mahatmas showed up in unlikely ways, on one occasion fluttering down from the ceiling after apparently materializing in mid air. This attracted the attention of the Society for Psychical Research (SPR) in London, and an investigator went to Adyar while Blavatsky and Olcott were conveniently away on a lecture tour. The investigation quickly turned up damning evidence of fraud, including detailed confessions from the Coulombes, who had been involved in manufacturing the "miracles."

The SPR's report, published in 1885, caused a widespread scandal, and Olcott broke with Blavatsky and forbade her to set foot in Adyar again. She returned to London and spent the next six years lecturing, writing, and organizing an inner circle of the Theosophical Society, called the Esoteric Section, to receive advanced instructions on her system of occultism. Her second major book, the massive *The Secret Doctrine* (1888), drew on material she had gathered while in India and became the essential text not only of Theosophy but also of most versions of popular occultism in the western world for the next three-quarters of a century. By the time of her death, despite the scandals, the Theosophical Society had become the largest occult organization in the world.

Further reading: Godwin 1994, Washington 1993.

BLUE LODGE

In the jargon of Freemasonry, a lodge working the three fundamental Masonic degrees of Entered Apprentice, Fellow Craft, and Master Mason. Blue is the symbolic color of these three degrees, while other degrees have their own distinctive colors; the Royal Arch and its associated degrees, for example, have red for their color. See **Freemasonry**; **Royal Arch**.

BOHEMIAN CLUB

One of dozens of private clubs in American cities that cater to the needs and interests of America's economic and political elites, the Bohemian Club in San Francisco has attracted a good deal of attention in recent years by way of the ritual performed at its annual retreat in a pristine corner of northern California. Routinely labeled occult, pagan, or Satanic worship by fundamentalists and the far right press, the Bohemian Grove ritual actually has no religious or esoteric content at all. In contemporary conspiracy theory, however, it has come to play a role far out of proportion to its actual importance. See **fundamentalism**.

The Bohemian Club was founded in San Francisco in 1872. Originally a social club catering to artists, writers, and intellectuals, it began to attract members of the city's financial elite within a few years of its founding, and by the early twentieth century was the most prestigious social club in town. Its imposing six-story building stands a few blocks from San Francisco's financial district. The Club began hosting its annual male-only retreat at the Bohemian Grove, a wooded property 65 miles north of San Francisco, in 1878, and within a few years guests from high political and economic circles began putting in appearances at the encampment. At this point the attendees at the retreat include many of the top politicians, financiers, and corporate executives in North America.

The two-week retreat, held in late June and early July, features theatrical and musical performances, informal talks by influential speakers, and many other events, but the feature that has attracted nearly all the attention lavished on the Bohemian Club focuses on the annual ritual of the Cremation of Care. In the ceremony, the body of Dull Care is brought to a funeral pyre, but comes back to life before it can be burnt and mocks the guests for thinking they can be rid of their cares during the retreat. The Bohemians beseech the Owl, the emblem of the club, for his guidance, and the Owl tells them that only the flame of the Lamp of Fellowship can incinerate Dull Care. This is duly applied, and Care gives up the ghost in a blaze of pyrotechnic glory. The ceremony is a typical piece of nineteenth-century fraternal ritual. Inevitably, though, it has been redefined by conspiracy theorists and fundamentalists as a pagan ritual of sacrifice to Satan. See **fraternal orders**; **Initiation**.

The attendee list for the Bohemian Grove retreat overlaps with the memberships of the Council on Foreign Relations, the Trilateral Commission, and the Bilderberg group, and it is often included by conspiracy theorists (together with the mythical Committee of 300) as one of the secret elite organizations intent on bringing about the New World Order. See **Bilderberg Group**; **Committee of 300**; **Council on Foreign Relations (CFR)**; **New World Order**; **Trilateral Commission**.

Further reading: Domhoff 1974, van der Zee 1974.

Book of Shadows

In modern Wicca and some related Pagan traditions, the usual name for the handwritten book of rituals and spells created by each initiate in the course of her training and copied in turn by her students. This process of transmission guarantees that Books of Shadows vary wildly, but nearly all contain ritual texts for the degrees of initiation and sabbats (seasonal celebrations) used in a given tradition, along with n[illegible] else in the way of religious, magica[illegible] and divinatory lore. Several Wiccan Books of Shadows have been published; while a few of the more strident defenders of Wiccan tradition have insisted that these have nothing to do with the "real thing," most Wiccans allow that these published versions are relatively accurate, while some Wiccan traditions now encourage students to use the published versions in place of the laborious and error-prone process of hand copying. See **Wicca**.

The term "Book of Shadows," like most of the standard terminology of Wicca, has been claimed as an inheritance from ancient European Pagans, but it appears nowhere in occult or Pagan material from before 1950, when it appears in one of Gerald Gardner's books on Wicca. He seems to have borrowed the phrase from an article in the British occult magazine *The Occult Observer* in 1949, "The Book of Shadows" by Mir Bashir, which described an alleged Hindu system of divination using the length of the querent's shadow.

Brotherhood of Luxor

According to the early writings of Helena Petrovna Blavatsky, the founder of Theosophy, a secret society active in America and elsewhere that sponsored the Theosophical Society. Some recent historians of Theosophy have suggested that the Brotherhood might have been descended from, the or Brotherhood of though, no independ- for the Brotherhood's existen... has yet surfaced, and Blavatsky changed her story completely after her first visit to India in 1879. See **Blavatsky, Helena Petrovna**; **Theosophical Society**.

Confusingly, Blavatsky's Brotherhood of Luxor appears to have had no connection to the Hermetic Brotherhood of Luxor (H.B. of L.), an occult secret society founded in Britain in the early 1880s. The Theosophical Society and the H.B. of L. ended up as bitter enemies in the late 1880s. See **Hermetic Brotherhood of Luxor (H.B. of L.)**.

Brotherhood of the Snake

According to a handful of late twentieth-century conspiracy theorists, the oldest secret society in the world, founded in prehistoric times to carry out a diabolical plot of world domination and enslavement, culminating in a New World Order scheduled to arrive sometime in the very near future. The Brotherhood of the Snake, according to several recent books, was either founded or taken over by evil forces in Mesopotamia in the year 300,000 BCE. Every secret society in history, according to these same books, is simply a branch of the Brotherhood of the Snake and cooperates with all other branches of the conspiracy, despite careful manipulation of appearances to make it look as though the different branches are distinct and even opposed to one another. See **New World Order**.

The name of this alleged society, with its reference to the serpent of the Tree of Knowledge in the biblical book of Genesis, points to the origins of the claim in fundamentalist Christian fantasies about Satanism. It may be worth adding that the writers who claim to have detected the Brotherhood of the Snake behind every secret society in history have yet to present any evidence for its existence. See **fundamentalism**; **Satanism**.

Further reading: Cooper 1991, Goodrick-Clarke 2002.

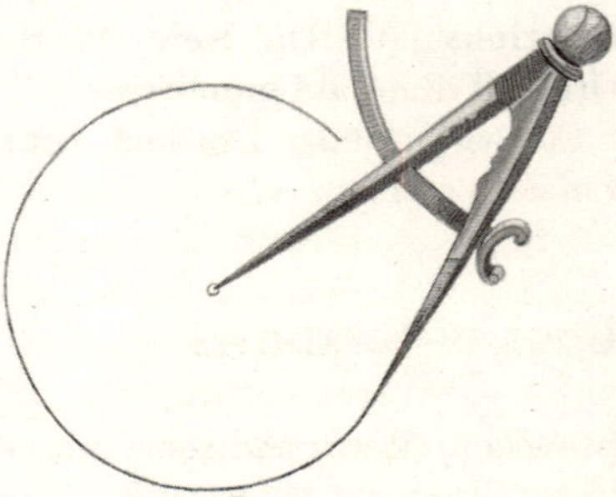

Brothering

In seventeenth- and eighteenth-century England and Scotland, ceremonies used to welcome new servants to a household or new apprentices and employees to a business were known as "brotherings." Customs varied by region and profession, but most brothering rituals began with a good deal of horseplay and pranks and finished with drinks for all paid for by the newcomer. Many Scottish brothering ceremonies included "washing the head" of the new initiate, usually by pouring a little water mixed with whiskey over him.

Most of the surviving records of brothering come from the futile efforts of Scottish civil and religious officials to suppress it. In 1639, for example, the Privy Council prohibited brothering among servants, on account of the "drinking, ryot and excesse" that took place. In 1663 the burgh council of Peebles formally denounced brothering among servants in the burgh. In 1701 the Society for the Reformation of Manners in Edinburgh petitioned the burgh council to suppress brothering in the city guard, and denounced "brothering and excessive drinking and spending thereat;" the captains of the guard promised to end the custom – a promise that may or may not have been kept – but the agitation apparently had no other effect.

Ceremonies of the brothering type can be traced back into the Middle Ages, when entry into almost every imaginable group was accompanied by some similar form of initiation, and continued in the more traditional corners of British society until the social transformations of the First World War era.

Further reading: Stevenson 1988.

Bruders Schweigen

A violent revolutionary secret society that flared and burnt out in early 1980s America, the Bruders Schweigen (German, "Silent Brotherhood") was the brainchild of Robert Mathews, a member of the racist Christian Identity movement. Mathews' conviction that racial war was brewing between "Aryan" whites and other races was inflamed by William Pierce's racist novel *The Turner Diaries* (1978), a fictional account of the overthrow of the US government by a white supremacist secret society. In 1983, Mathews decided to put the novel's scenario into practice by organizing a secret society and launching a terrorist campaign. See **Christian Identity**.

The Bruders Schweigen found recruits among members of the racist right eager to begin the long-awaited war against ZOG, the so-called "Zionist Occupation Government." To raise funds for the coming apocalypse, Mathews and his followers carried out an armored car robbery and counterfeited US money. They also assassinated Alan Berg, a Denver radio talk-show host who made a habit of baiting racists on his program. See **Zionist Occupation Government (ZOG)**.

These actions brought down a massive response from federal law-enforcement officials, who had little difficulty placing an undercover agent within the group. Mathews was cornered by federal marshals in a safe house in Washington State and gunned down, while most of the other members of the organization were arrested in 1985 and 1986 and are currently serving long prison terms. The Bruders Schweigen effectively ceased to exist with these arrests, and its complete failure to accomplish its goals did much to turn the racist right away from standard revolutionary methods and toward the occult teachings of the Black Sun and the ideology of "leaderless resistance." See **Black Sun**; **neo-Nazi secret societies**.

Further reading: Barkun 1997, Flynn and Gerhardt 1989, Goodrick-Clarke 2002.

Bruno, Giordano

Italian author, magician, and (possibly) founder of secret societies, 1548–1600. Born in the little town of Nola not far from Naples, Bruno entered the Dominican Order at the age of 15. At the time, the Dominicans made a special study of the art of memory, a method of mental training that allows the human mind to accurately store and recall large amounts of information. Bruno mastered the art so well that he was taken to Rome to display his skills to the Pope. See **art of memory**.

In 1567, however, his superiors discovered that he had taken up the study of ritual magic. Bruno abandoned his friar's habit and fled from Naples across the length of Italy, crossing the Swiss border just ahead of the Inquisition. Safe in France, where the Catholic Church had little influence at that time, he taught astronomy at the University of Toulouse for two years, then moved to Paris, where he wrote his first book on the art of memory. Thereafter he took up a wandering life, traveling through France, England, and Germany, teaching magic and the art of memory. He was suspected by the Catholic Church of founding secret groups of "Giordanisti" ("Giordanists") in Germany, though no solid evidence for these has surfaced.

In 1591 he returned to Italy, in response to an offer of money from the Venetian nobleman Zuan Mocenigo. It proved to be a fatal mistake. Mocenigo handed Bruno over to the Inquisition, and he spent eight years in church dungeons in Venice and Rome. In 1600 he was burned at the stake as a relapsed heretic at the Campo de Fiori in Rome.

Bruno's career ended in failure and a wretched death, and his circles of "Giordanisti," if they ever existed, left no traces. His impact on the later history of secret societies, though, was surprisingly large. Bruno's version of the art of memory, passed on by his disciple Alexander Dicson, was apparently prescribed for early Scottish Freemasons by William Schaw, the royal master of works who did much to foster the transition from operative to speculative Masonry at the end of the sixteenth century. In the early seventeenth century, the Irish philosopher John Toland, the founder of at least one secret society and a significant figure in the origins of modern Druidry, studied Bruno closely, translated his *Expulsion of the Triumphant Beast* into English, and reformulated Bruno's ideas into the pantheism that motivated many eighteenth-century radicals. See **Druid Revival**; **Freemasonry**; **Schaw, William**; **Toland, John**.

Further reading: Jacob 1981.

Builders of the Adytum [BOTA]

One of the major American occult societies of the twentieth century, the Builders of the Adytum started out in 1921 as the Hermetic Order of Atlantis, a small working group within the Thoth-Hermes Temple in New York City. Thoth-Hermes was a local lodge of the Alpha et Omega, one of the surviving fragments of the Hermetic Order of the Golden Dawn. The head of the working group was Paul Foster Case, who at that time was Praemonstrator (chief of instruction) of Thoth-Hermes. When Case left the Alpha et Omega in 1922, he took most of the members of the Hermetic Order of Atlantis with him, and in 1923 he renamed the group the School of Ageless Wisdom. See **Case, Paul Foster**; **Hermetic Order of the Golden Dawn**.

The School of Ageless Wisdom started out as a provider of occult correspondence courses with no group ritual or local organizations. After he was initiated into Freemasonry in 1926, however, Case revised the course, and allowed any student who had reached an advanced level of study to set up a local chapter, or Pronaos. The first Pronaoi were established in 1928. In 1938 he renamed the order the Builders of the Adytum. See **Freemasonry**.

The system of occult training and philosophy taught in BOTA started from the same intellectual foundations as the Hermetic Order of the Golden Dawn but moved in a different direction. The Tarot cards play so central a role in BOTA's training system that many people in today's occult community think of BOTA primarily as a Tarot school. Ritual magic, the core of the Golden Dawn system, has been sharply downplayed in BOTA. Case's ideas about the higher reaches of occult practice are likewise entirely his own; he claimed that intensive practice of occult meditation would cause an alchemical transformation of the practitioner's small intestine, causing him to digest food in a new and more spiritual way and thus achieve physical immortality. Unfortunately Case himself failed to achieve this, and died in the normal way in 1954.

In 1932 Case moved BOTA's headquarters to Los Angeles, the occult capital of the United States in the Depression years. Unlike many of its competitors, BOTA weathered its founder's death without noticeable disruption and has continued as one of the largest American occult orders ever since. Still based in Los

Angeles, it has Pronaoi in most large American cities and keeps most of Case's books in print.

Further reading: Case 1985b.

Buonarroti, Filippo

Italian revolutionary and secret society leader, 1761–1837. Born at Pisa to an aristocratic family, Buonarroti spent his childhood in patrician circles, serving as a page at the court of the Grand Duke of Tuscany in 1773 and becoming a cavalier in the Order of St Stephen, a military order in Tuscany, in his teen years. A headstrong and temperamental boy, he ran away to Marseilles in 1780 and spent a short time in the French army, before officials of the Grand Duke arranged to have him sent home. His rebellious streak soon landed him in radical circles; in 1786 he was initiated as a Freemason, in a lodge that had been under Illuminati control until the break-up of the order two years previously. See **Bavarian Illuminati**.

That same year the authorities raided his house and discovered seditious books. He escaped with a warning, but by 1789 Buonarroti's political activities made Tuscany too hot to hold him and he went to Corsica, where he immediately took an active role in revolutionary agitation there. In 1791 he was chased off the island by an angry Catholic mob, but returned within a month and plunged back into local politics. Visits to Paris and meetings with Robespierre brought him into the midst of the French revolutionary government, and when France invaded Italy, Buonarroti was posted to the town of Oneglia as its administrator. There he became the focus of a network of Italian exiles who wanted to copy the French revolutionary experiment in Italy. See **French Revolution**.

With the fall of Robespierre's government and the establishment of the more moderate Directory in the Thermidor *coup d'etat* of 1794, Buonarroti lost his support in Paris; in March 1795 he was recalled to the French capital and imprisoned for redistributing wealth from landowners to peasants in Oneglia. While in prison he met François "Gracchus" Babeuf, another ambitious radical. When they were released in October 1795, they plunged into politics, organizing the *Societé du Panthéon* (Society of the Pantheon) to spread egalitarian ideas and oppose the Directory's policies. When the Society was suppressed by police in February the following year, its most committed members formed a revolutionary secret society, the Conspiracy of Equals. See **Babeuf, François "Gracchus"**; **Conspiracy of Equals**.

The mass arrests that followed the failure of the Conspiracy landed Buonarroti in jail again, where he remained until 1806. While in prison he renewed contacts with his Italian associates, and managed to become a member of another secret society, the Philadelphes. On his release he moved to Geneva, where he supported himself by teaching music; he resumed his revolutionary activities, starting a Philadelphe group in the local Masonic lodge and planning a coup against Napoleon's government. He also organized another secret society, the *Sublimes Maîtres Parfaits* or Sublime Perfect Masters, which went on to become the first international political secret society of the nineteenth century. A police informant leaked news of the Philadelphe plot, but the authorities in Paris decided to bide their time, and merely ordered Buonarroti to leave Geneva. See **Philadelphes**; **Sublime Perfect Masters**.

Buonarroti spent the rest of Napoleon's reign at Grenoble, returning to Geneva at the Restoration. There, working through the Sublime Perfect Masters, he plotted a continent-wide revolution to establish republican governments and abolish private property. His efforts had some influence on the widespread risings of 1820–22. A subordinate, Alexandre Andryane, was arrested in Milan in 1822 with compromising papers, and details soon were circulated among European police officials and the general public, where they sparked a flurry of anti-secret society literature.

While Buonarroti's secret society was all but destroyed by the revelations, and Buonarroti himself was driven out of Switzerland, he gained a continent-wide reputation as the conspirator's conspirator. He went to Brussels, where he attracted a circle of young radicals who studied the art of conspiracy with him. He relaunched the Sublime Perfect Masters as *Le Monde* (The World), and published a book on the French Revolution and the conspiracies that followed it, *Conspiration pour l'Egalité* (*Conspiracy for Equality*, 1828), which became the Bible of liberal secret societies all through the nineteenth century.

In 1830, when a new revolt broke out in France, he moved to Paris, where he spent his final years pursuing his lifelong dream of revolution. In 1832 he created a new international secret society, the *Charbonnerie Réformée* or Reformed Carbonarism, and expanded it into the *Charbonnerie Démocratique Universelle* or Universal Democratic Carbonarism in 1833. He died in 1837, surrounded by friends and admirers. See **Carbonari**.

Further reading: Eisenstein 1959, Roberts 1972.

BURLESQUE DEGREES

A feature of American fraternal secret societies in the late nineteenth and early twentieth centuries, burlesque degrees were humorous ceremonies enacted for the entertainment of the members, usually at the expense of new initiates. The fashion for burlesque degrees started in the 1870s and reached a peak of popularity between 1890 and the outbreak of the First World War.

Burlesque degrees featured a combination of raucous humor and ingenious mechanical devices designed to startle a blindfolded candidate out of his wits. Examples include chairs rigged to fire a blank cartridge and collapse when someone sat on them; imitation wells containing real water, with a spark coil beneath to provide a harmless but startling shock to anyone touching the water; paddle machines designed to swat the candidate unexpectedly on the backside; and mechanical goats that candidates had to ride. See **riding the goat**.

Many burlesque degrees remained informal entertainments put on by individual lodges, but some took on a life of their own and turned into societies in their own right. Freemasonry, always quick to establish new orders, took the lead in this department with at least three major burlesque branches – the Ancient Arabic Order of Nobles of the Mystic Shrine (Shriners), the Mystic Order of Veiled Prophets of the Enchanted Realm (Grotto), and the Tall Cedars of Lebanon. A similar profusion of burlesque degrees in Odd Fellowship, including the Imperial Order of Muscovites and the Oriental Order of Humility and Perfection, underwent consolidation in 1902 into the Ancient Mystic Order of Samaritans (AMOS). The Knights of Pythias had their Dramatic Order Knights of Khorassan, and the Red Men their Order of Haymakers; even the Knights of Columbus climbed aboard the burlesque bandwagon with the International Order of Alhambra. Other organizations, such as E Clampus Vitus, were simply burlesque orders with no fraternal order behind them. See **Ancient Arabic Order of Nobles of the Mystic Shrine (AAONMS)**; **E Clampus Vitus**; **Freemasonry**; **Improved Order of Red Men**; **Knights of Columbus**; **Knights of Pythias**; **Odd Fellowship**.

During the twentieth century, changes in social habits, the rising fear of lawsuits, and a belief among fraternal secret societies that their survival depended on becoming as respectable as possible, all worked against the survival of the old burlesque degrees. Most of the burlesque orders disappeared, and many of those that survived banished the old pranks and pratfalls from their rituals and refocused their efforts on charitable causes. By the late 1960s the Shriners, who once prided themselves on throwing the wildest parties in North America, had refocused their publicity on their chain of free children's hospitals and burn treatment centers, and boasted that while alcohol could still be found in Shriner conventions, it was limited to private room parties.

Further reading: Goldsmith 2004, van Deventer 1964.

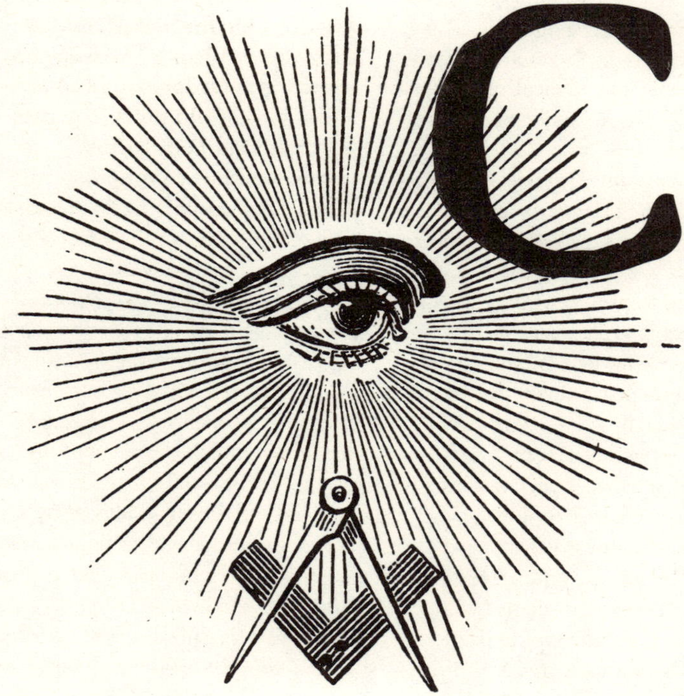
C

Cabala

One of the core elements of the western occult tradition, the Cabala emerged in Jewish mystical circles in southern France around the middle of the twelfth century CE. In English it is spelled variously Cabala, Kabbalah, and Qabala, due to the difficulty of expressing Hebrew sounds adequately in Latin letters. In recent times various branches of the tradition have adopted different spellings as a way of differentiating themselves from the competition, but the Hebrew word קבלה (QBLH) simply means "tradition," or "that which is passed down."

Like most mystical traditions, the Cabala engaged in retrospective recruitment, backdating itself centuries before its actual origin. According to some texts, the Cabala was originally revealed to Adam in the Garden of Eden by the angel Raziel. Adam's third son, Seth, when he journeyed to the gates of Paradise, then learned the Cabala from the angels who guarded the garden with a flaming sword. The patriarch Abraham is also cited as an early Cabalist, while all accounts agree that Moses received the Cabala as well as the Ten Commandments on Mount Sinai. From one or another of these beginnings, according to traditional histories, the Cabala has been passed on from master to disciple until the present. See **retrospective recruitment**.

The actual origins of the Cabala can be traced to a circle of mystics around Rabbi Isaac the Blind, a leader of the Jewish community in Narbonne, France, who died around 1235. Rabbi Isaac and his students had material from two older systems of Jewish mysticism, the *Ma'aseh Berashith* (Work of Creation), based on the Book of Genesis, and the *Ma'aseh Merkabah* (Work of the Chariot), based on the Book of Ezekiel. They also had a good working familiarity with Neoplatonism, a Greek mystical philosophy that had been borrowed and reworked extensively by Jewish, Christian, and Muslim mystics alike. An old book from the *Ma'aseh Berashith* literature, the *Sepher Yetzirah* (*Book of Formation*) and a collection of old fragments reworked by Isaac's circle into the *Sepher ha-Bahir* (*Book of Radiance*), provided essential elements for the new synthesis.

The Cabala caught on quickly in Jewish communities in Spain, where schools started by Isaac's pupils sprang up in the thirteenth century in Burgos, Gerona, and Toledo. The masterpiece of the tradition, the sprawling *Sepher ha-Zohar* (*Book of Splendor*), was written by Moses de Leon in the thirteenth century, but attributed by him to the second-century Rabbi Simeon bar Yochai. In the century or so before the expulsion of the Jews from Spain in 1492, Cabalistic ideas became all but universal in the Jewish communities of that country, and spread across the Mediterranean world.

In 1486, the Italian Hermetic philosopher and magician Giovanni

Pico Della Mirandola learned about the Cabala from a Jewish friend, and shocked intellectuals across Europe by proclaiming that, "no science can better convince us of the divinity of Jesus Christ than magic and the Cabala." By the time Pico died in 1494, the German scholar Johannes Reuchlin had published *De Verbo Mirifico* (*On the Wonder-working Word*), the first published introduction to Christian Cabala. In 1533 Henricus Cornelius Agrippa launched a Hermetic, magical Cabala with his bestselling *Three Books of Occult Philosophy*. From that point on, the Cabala was an integral part of most western occult traditions, and permeated the underworld of occult secret societies throughout the western world.

The factor that made the Cabala so pervasive is its flexibility. At its foundation is a simple act of counting. In the opening passages of the Book of Genesis, the phrase "God said" appears 10 times, while God is described as doing 22 other things in the process of creating the world. The circles of Jewish mystics around Isaac the Blind linked these divine speeches and acts to the numbers from 1 to 10 and the 22 letters of the Hebrew alphabet. Later generations of Cabalists added more layers of symbolism, resulting in an infinitely expansive symbolic matrix in which everything in the universe relates to one of the 10 *sephiroth* ("numberings" in Hebrew), and the Hebrew letters define 22 paths that connect the sephiroth together and channel energy from one to another. Together, the sephiroth and paths form a diagram called the Tree of Life.

The symbolic patterns of the Tree of Life can be used in a galaxy of different ways. Traditional Jewish Cabala applies them largely to the task of interpreting the scriptures, a task made much easier by the fact that every Hebrew letter is also a number. In Cabalistic analysis, or *gematria*, the numerical values of words, phrases, and whole sentences are added up, and their totals compared with those of others; any two words or passages that add up to exactly the same value, according to the Cabalistic tradition, have exactly the same meaning. Thus in Genesis 18:2, where God visits Abraham, the Hebrew words for the phrase "And behold, three men" adds up to the same number as the phrase "These are Michael, Raphael and Gabriel;" by this equation, Cabalists know that the "three men" were actually these three great angels. See **Gematria**.

In the Hermetic and magical branch of Cabala, by contrast, analysis of scripture plays little if any role, and the Cabala functions as the fundamental symbolic toolkit of the operative magician. A Hermetic occultist designing a ritual to bring balance into a situation, for example, starts by identifying this goal with one of the 10 sephiroth – in this case Tiphareth (Beauty), the sixth sephirah, which represents the point of balance between extremes. The occultist drapes her altar with a yellow cloth, places six candles on it, burns frankincense in the censer, and wears a crown of laurel leaves; she begins the ritual, during the day and hour assigned to the sun, by ringing a bell or chime six times, and calls on the archangel Raphael, or on solar gods such as Apollo or Ra – all these being symbols of Tiphareth. See **Magic**.

The Cabala has been one of the major sources of symbolism for secret societies of every kind. Magical secret societies such as the Hermetic Order of the Golden Dawn relied on it constantly, and most of the higher grades of Freemasonry borrowed from it extensively. It is not accidental, for example, that the Scottish Rite has 33 degrees – these represent the 10 sephiroth and 22 paths, plus one more to represent the pure potential from which the paths and sephiroth alike unfolded – or that its predecessor, the Rite of Perfection, had 22 degrees. More surprising, but equally relevant, the Independent Order of Odd Fellows – the largest fraternal order in the world a century ago – has a total of 10 degrees of initiation, and assigns 22 emblems to these degrees. In all three cases the symbolism of the degrees can be mapped onto the Cabalistic Tree of Life precisely. It is fair to say that a knowledge of the Cabala is one of the master keys to the secret society traditions of the western world. See **Ancient and Accepted Scottish Rite (AASR)**; **Hermetic Order of the Golden Dawn**; **Odd Fellowship**; **Rite of Perfection**.

Further reading: Greer 1996, Scholem 1974.

Cabiri

See **Samothracian mysteries**.

Cagliostro, Alessandro

Sicilian adventurer, 1743–95. Born Giuseppe Balsamo into a working-class family in Palermo, he spent a short time in his youth as a novice of the Brothers of Mercy, a Catholic monastic order, but was expelled after a series of scandals and launched a new career as a confidence artist and forger who claimed to have magical powers. After convincing several landowners that spirits would show him buried treasure on their property for a price, he was caught forging the title deed to an estate and fled Palermo.

He next turned up in Rome, where he met and married the beautiful blonde Lorenza Feliciani, a belt-maker's daughter in her teens with a taste for high living and no moral scruples worth mentioning. The two of them quickly found a niche preying on the highest circles of European society. Balsamo at first called himself the Marquis Pellegrini, then settled on the more dashing Count Alessandro Cagliostro, while Lorenza became the Countess Seraphina Cagliostro. He sold patent medicines and elixirs of life for inflated prices, while she marketed her charms to rich noblemen and dabbled in blackmail as well. The proceeds proved rewarding enough to ensure that Cagliostro was soon in the forefront of society, moving from city to city just often enough to keep the threat of exposure at bay.

In 1777 he was in London, and there applied for membership to a Masonic lodge affiliated with the Rite of Strict Observance, then the most popular Masonic rite in Germany. He was initiated in the first four degrees of the Rite's system, and a short time thereafter announced that he had found an old Masonic manuscript at a London bookstall, containing rituals for a system of Egyptian Masonry as old as the pyramids, full of occult and alchemical secrets. His new Egyptian Rite was launched in 1778, with Cagliostro as Grand Copht, and immediately attracted a wide following. Since the initiation fees and dues paid by members of the Rite ended up in Cagliostro's pocket, this proved much more lucrative than his previous trade in elixirs and launched the most successful phase of his career. See **Rite of Strict Observance**.

He traveled around Europe with Lorenza for most of the following decade, establishing lodges of the Egyptian Rite and spending money lavishly. In 1780 he came to Strasbourg and became an intimate of Louis, Cardinal Rohan, one of the most influential men in France. After traveling elsewhere in France, establishing the Grand Lodge of his Egyptian Rite in Lyons, Cagliostro made a triumphant entry into Paris in 1785, cutting a dashing figure in Parisian society. In August of that year, however, he was arrested along with Rohan as the "affair of the diamond necklace" came to light. This was a complicated fraud in which Rohan was duped into spending 1,600,000 livres on a diamond necklace, supposedly for the French queen Marie Antoinette, whose political and sexual favors Rohan hoped to enjoy. While Cagliostro's complicity in the hoax has never been proved, he repeatedly advised Rohan to do what the plotters wanted.

For his part in the affair, Cagliostro spent most of a year in the Bastille; in June 1786 he was released and banished from France. Through the whole affair, the French popular press mocked him unmercifully as a fraudulent alchemist and poseur. The final blow fell late in 1786, when a newspaper article by a hack journalist in London, Charles Théveneau de Morande, traced him back to his origins and revealed, behind the dashing image of Count Cagliostro, the far less impressive figure of Giuseppe Balsamo, the confidence artist from Palermo. Abandoned by his patrons, Cagliostro fled from London to Switzerland, and Lorenza, who wanted to see her family again, convinced him to go on to Rome. There, in 1789, he was arrested by the Inquisition. The Roman Catholic Church at that time considered Freemasonry to be a religious heresy; Cagliostro was condemned to death, but the pope commuted his sentence to life imprisonment. He lingered in the dungeons of the papal fortress of San Leo until 1795, when he died of a stroke.

Cagliostro's dazzling career and his dismal fate in the pope's dungeons predisposed many people in the Protestant countries of Europe to remember him as the mysterious Masonic adept he pretended to be. There are still occultists and occult traditions that insist that Cagliostro the Grand Copht and Giuseppe Balsamo the petty crook were two different people. The Fratres Lucis, a small British occult order of the late nineteenth century, claimed to have received its teachings from the spirit of Cagliostro via crystal ball.

Further reading: Butler 1948, Trowbridge 1910.

Cagoule

French for "hood." Popular name of the *Organisation Secrete de l'Action Révolutionnaire Nationale* (Secret Organization of National Revolutionary Action), a French right-wing secret society founded in 1935 to oppose the Third Republic and prepare the way for a fascist takeover. Some of its members borrowed the Ku Klux Klan's custom of wearing hoods to conceal their identity, thus their popular name, and the Klan's activities in America seem to have been a source of inspiration for the Cagoule's leaders. Much of the Cagoule's ideology, however, came from synarchy, a right-wing political ideology popular among French secret societies in the early twentieth century. See **Ku Klux Klan**; **synarchy**.

The Cagoule had a military organization and recruited heavily from other secret societies on the French right wing. Arms from Germany, Italy, and Spain provided the wherewithal for the planned seizure of power. An attempt to fake left-wing bombings of industrial employers' associations in Paris in September of 1937, though, brought the attention of the authorities down on the would-be revolutionaries. The Cagoule's leader, Eugène Deloncle, was arrested the following month, and the organization's arms dumps surfaced shortly thereafter. Stripped of their weapons and publicly humiliated, the Cagoule sank into insignificance, though many of its members collaborated with the Nazis and the Vichy regime after the French defeat in 1940.

CANON *EPISCOPI*

A text from Catholic canon law dating from ninth-century France, the canon *Episcopi* (the title comes from the Latin for the first word of the text, "Bishops") was mistakenly thought to come from the fourth-century Council of Ancyra, and found its way into several major medieval collections of canon law. In criticizing various forms of semi-pagan folk belief as superstitious and un-Christian, it provides the first solid documentation for a tradition found in many other parts of medieval and early modern Europe. The specific passage runs as follows:

> Some wicked women … profess that in the hours of the night they ride out with Diana, the goddess of the pagans and an innumerable multitude of other women, and in the silence of the dead of night they journey over vast distances of the earth, and obey her commands as their mistress, and are summoned to her service on certain nights.

This tradition of nocturnal shamanistic journeys appears in various places – a group of goddess worshippers rounded up by the Inquisition in fourteenth-century Milan, the *benandanti* ("good walkers") of northeastern Italy in the sixteenth and seventeenth centuries, the testimony of a seventeenth-century werewolf from Estonia, and many others. Exactly what was going on is difficult to tell from this distance of time, but clearly a widespread but coherent shamanistic tradition existed in organized form in medieval Europe, and survived until quite recent times in a few areas. Some scholars have argued that distorted accounts of these traditions may have helped inspire the first great wave of witchcraft persecution. See **Benandanti**; **witchcraft persecutions**.

Further reading: Ginzburg 1991.

CARBONARI

A powerful force in the European revolutionary struggles of the early nineteenth century, the Carbonari ("Charcoal Burners") traced its roots back to southeastern France around the beginning of the French Revolution, where a fraternal association called la Charbonnerie was among the most popular social groups. La Charbonnerie claimed descent from medieval charcoal burners, but probably derived from the Order of Woodcutters (*Ordre des Fendeurs*), a fraternal secret society founded by Masons and their wives in the 1740s in Paris. See **Order of Woodcutters**.

One of the initiates of la Charbonnerie, Pierre Joseph Briot, ended up in Naples after the French conquest of Italy. Briot had been a member of the House of Five Hundred, the lower house of the French revolutionary parliament under the Directory, and remained faithful to the ideals of the Revolution even after Napoleon's seizure of power. In Naples, along with other French Republicans opposed to the march toward empire, Briot blended the rituals and traditions of la Charbonnerie with elements from Masonic sources to create the Carbonari. See **Freemasonry**; **French Revolution**.

Members of the Carbonari called one another "good cousins" and pledged mutual support and protection on the blade of an ax. Their lodges were termed *venditas*, literally "shops." They worked a system of two degrees, apprentice and master; in the latter, initiates were taught the legendary origin of the Carbonari, a long tale involving St Theobald, King Francis I of France, and poor but honest Scottish charcoal burners. Members took Carbonaro names drawn from the history of the Middle Ages, and had secret signs and passwords to identify themselves to other Carbonari. All this follows patterns shared with many other secret societies of the same time. Less standard was the requirement that each Carbonaro acquire a rifle, fifty cartridges, and a dagger immediately after initiation and be prepared to use them in the struggle for liberty.

During the first four decades of the nineteenth century, the Carbonari had a remarkable degree of success in organizing political pressure and revolutionary violence across Europe. The keys to the Carbonari achievement were twofold. First was its use of popular religious symbolism instead of the symbols of esoteric spirituality; these made it more acceptable in the devoutly Catholic and Eastern Orthodox countries where it flourished. Second was its deliberate strategy of recruiting from the middle classes, who provided most government functionaries and junior army officers for the European governments of the time. The Carbonari ideal of constitutional government appealed powerfully to these classes, since it offered them a voice in government and protection against the abuses of autocracy. Carbonari venditas built on this by recruiting bureaucrats, policemen, and soldiers, with dramatic results over the following decades as the rulers of Europe's autocratic states found their own officers and civil servants on the other side of the barricades. This program of infiltration also made it easier for the Carbonari to counter the efforts made to suppress them, since the police and soldiers detailed to hunt them were as often as not members themselves.

Alongside this strategy ran an organizational flexibility that few other secret societies achieved. While a Supreme Vendita in Paris served as a central coordinating body, and High Venditas in each country had authority over venditas in their territories, the control exercised by these bodies over individual venditas was modest at best, and local venditas were, for most purposes, independent. Members of the Carbonari's second degree were also free to establish groups of their own, called *economias* ("economies"), to pursue specific goals within the broad framework of the overall Carbonari agenda. Some of the major revolutionary secret societies of the early nineteenth century started out as Carbonari *economias*, and many stayed in close contact with the Carbonari throughout their existence.

The Carbonari first flexed their muscles in 1814, during the waning days of Napoleon's power, when the order helped topple French puppet governments the length of the Italian peninsula. In 1820 and 1821, Carbonari revolts set up short-lived constitutional regimes in Spain and several Italian states, and a Greek branch of the order, the Philike Hetairia, launched a massive rising that won Greek independence after four centuries of Turkish rule. The Decembrist rising in St Petersburg and the Ukraine against Tsar Nicholas I of Russia in 1824 was largely inspired by the Carbonari example, and revolts in Paris in 1830 and central Italy in 1831 had strong backing from the Carbonari. Outside Greece, none of the Carbonari revolts succeeded in their immediate aims, as the conservative powers of Europe quickly sent troops to suppress any successful rising, but the constant threat of Carbonari risings played a large part in forcing governments across Europe to grant civil rights to their people. See **Decembrists**; **Philike Hetairia**.

Some of the most famous revolutionists of the age were members of the Carbonari at various points in their careers. The veteran conspirator Filippo Buonarroti, a tireless organizer of revolutionary secret societies, had close connections with the Carbonari during his years in Swiss exile, and made use of his Carbonaro connections in recruiting for his primary secret society, the Sublime Perfect Masters. Later in his career he reorganized the Carbonari in France in 1832 as the Reformed Carbonarism (*Charbonnerie Réformée*), renamed Universal Democratic Carbonarism (*Charbonnerie Démocratique Universelle*) the next year. Buonarroti's great opponent in the revolutionary debates of the early nineteenth century, Giuseppe Mazzini (1805–72), shared his Carbonaro background; Mazzini's main secret society, Young Italy, started out as a Carbonari *economia*. See **Buonarroti, Filippo**; **Sublime Perfect Masters**; **Young Italy**.

Further reading: Billington 1980, Hales 1956, Mackenzie 1967, Roberts 1972.

Case, Paul Foster

American musician and occultist. Born in Fairport, New York into a middle-class family, Case (1884–1956) showed remarkable talent for music in childhood and was a professional musician by his teens. After meeting the occultist Claude Bragdon in 1900, Case took up the study of occultism and yoga. In 1907 he contacted William Walker Atkinson, one of the leading figures in the occult community. The two worked together extensively; together with Michael Whitty of the Alpha et Omega – the largest Golden Dawn group in America at that time – they wrote *The Kybalion*, which was published anonymously in 1912 and went on to become one of the classics of American occult literature. See **Atkinson, William Walker**; **Hermetic Order of the Golden Dawn**.

In 1915 Case, then living in New York City, became a student of Aleister Crowley and was initiated into the Ordo Templi Orientis (OTO), rising to the third degree. He left the OTO after a few years, though, and joined the Alpha et Omega, still headed by his friend Michael Whitty. In 1918 he was initiated into New York's Thoth-Hermes Temple, taking the magical motto *Perseverantia*, and reached the grade of Adeptus Minor in 1920. When Whitty died the same year, Case was appointed Praemonstrator (chief instructional officer) in America. In 1921 he formed a study group within Thoth-Hermes Temple, calling it the Hermetic Order of Atlantis. See **Crowley, Aleister**; **Ordo Templi Orientis (OTO)**.

A series of disagreements with Moina Mathers, the Alpha et Omega's chief, came to a head in 1922, and Mathers expelled Case from the order. Unfazed, Case took most of the members of the Hermetic Order of Atlantis with him, and launched his own organization, the School of Ageless Wisdom, the next year. An occult correspondence school at first, it transformed itself into an esoteric secret society over the next decade. Case's initiation into Freemasonry in 1926 may have helped catalyze this process by convincing him that ritual work in a group setting had potentials worth exploring. In 1938 Case renamed his organization Builders of the Adytum. See **Builders of the Adytum (BOTA)**; **Freemasonry**.

The rest of Case's life was intimately tied up in the growth of BOTA into one of the premier American occult schools. In 1932 he moved the order's headquarters to Los Angeles, the most important center of American occultism during the Depression years. He continued to write and teach until shortly before his death while vacationing in Mexico in 1954.

Cathars

The last major Gnostic movement in the western world before the nineteenth century, the Cathars ("pure ones") or Albigensians ("those from Albi") emerged in northern Italy and southern France around the middle of the eleventh century. While Gnostic groups existed in those regions centuries before, the Cathar movement began with the arrival of Bogomil missionaries from the Balkans in that century. The first use of the term "Cathar" was in Monteforte, Italy, where the Gnostic community called itself by this term as early as 1030. See **Gnosticism**.

Like earlier Gnostics, the Cathars argued that the universe was created by an evil power as a prison for souls descended from a spiritual world of light. Jesus, according to their belief, descended from the world of light to show imprisoned souls the way of escape, but his teachings had been perverted by servants of the evil creator god. Cathar theologians debated whether the evil god had existed from the beginning of time, as claimed in the Cathar scripture *The Book of the Two Principles*, or whether he was a fallen servant of the true god, as claimed in another Cathar scripture, *The Gospel of the Secret Supper*. These two points of view have been called "absolute dualism" and "mitigated dualism" by modern scholars. See **dualism**.

These doctrines found such a favorable reception in southern France that in 1167 Nicetas, a leading Bogomil bishop, traveled to Toulouse. By 1200 the new Cathar Church was well on its way to becoming the majority religion in southern France and was sending out missionaries as far afield as England and western Germany. Believers fell into two classes. *Perfecti* or "perfect ones," pledged to poverty, vegetarianism, and celibacy, formed the clergy, while *credentes*, "believers" free from ascetic restrictions, formed the mass of the movement. The Gnostic belief that ignorance rather than sin barred the way to the realm of light fostered a more relaxed attitude toward sex, and helped spark a brilliant literature of love poetry.

The Cathars rejected all of the Catholic Church's sacraments and replaced them with rituals of their own. The most important of these was the Consolamentum ("consolation"), a ritual of laying on of hands by which a Cathar believer was received among the ranks of the *perfecti*. Another ritual, the Endura, consisted of deliberate suicide by starvation, and was considered a shortcut back to the world of light. Despite recent claims, the ritual of the Consolamentum has survived in several copies and contains no references to the Holy Grail, the Knights Templar, bloodlines descended from Jesus of Nazareth, or any of the other hot topics in today's alternative-history industry. See **Grail**; **Knights Templar**.

The response of the Roman Catholic Church to the rise of the Cathars was as predictable as it was brutal. In 1209, after various efforts by papal legates to bring southern France back into the Catholic fold failed dismally, Pope Innocent III pro-claimed a crusade against the Cathars. The crusaders, eventually joined by King Louis VIII of France, ravaged the south of France without mercy. By the time the last Cathar citadel at Montségur fell in 1244, the population of the region had fallen by more than half. Refugees fled into northern Italy, Catalonia, and Bosnia. In 1233, to complete the task of rooting out Catharism, Pope Gregory IX founded the Inquisition and placed it under the control of the Dominicans. The legal precedents established by the Inquisition over the next half century in the effort to exterminate the Cathar faith laid the groundwork for the witchcraft persecutions of the fifteenth, sixteenth, and seventeenth centuries. See **Roman Catholic Church**; **witchcraft persecutions**.

Like the Gnostic movement as a whole, the Cathars had a complex afterlife once Christian orthodoxy lost political power in the western world. The first revivals of Catharism appeared in southern France in the early years of the nineteenth century, and drew much of their strength from a strong current of cultural and linguistic separatism in the south of the country. The establishment of Jules Doinel's Gnostic Church in Paris in 1828 helped drive the revival of the Cathar faith by making Gnosticism a known factor in popular culture. Several independent Cathar churches now exist in France and elsewhere.

This revival also succeeded in launching the Cathars into the underworld of rejected knowledge, where the facts of the Cathar faith soon got lost beneath a torrent of fashionable beliefs and sheer invention. The Cathars featured in Madame Blavatsky's first great work, *Isis Unveiled* (1877), and found themselves adopted as ancestors by a variety of early twentieth-century occult groups via the long-established tradition of retrospective recruitment. The explosion of alternative theories of Christian origins in the late twentieth century, sparked by media treatments of Pierre Plantard's remarkable Priory of Sion hoax and the publication of the Nag Hammadi Gnostic scriptures, also enlisted the Cathars under many different (and often mutually contradictory) banners. In all this outpouring of misinformation the reality of a remarkable spiritual movement is in danger of being forgotten. See **Blavatsky, Helena Petrovna**; **Christian origins**; **Priory of Sion**; **rejected knowledge**; **retrospective recruitment**.

Further reading: Barnstone and Meyer 2003, Runciman 1995.

Catholic Order of the Rose+Cross

A minor secret society with a major impact on late nineteenth-century culture, the Catholic Order of the Rose+Cross (*Ordre Catholique de la Rose+Croix*) was founded in 1890 by Joséphin Péladan, a flamboyant French art critic, occultist and novelist who two years earlier had been one of the founders of the Kabbalistic Order of the Rose+Cross, the premier French occult secret society of its time. Péladan combined his occult beliefs with a devout if idiosyncratic Catholic faith, and had doctrinal as well as personal disagreements with Stanislaus de Guaita, the Grand Master of the Kabbalistic Order. In 1890 Péladan broke away from the latter and founded an order of his own. See **Kabbalistic Order of the Rose+Cross**.

The Catholic Order was never much more than a framework for Péladan's own artistic crusade, but Péladan was the leading defender of the Symbolist movement in art and a friend of major artists and musicians of the time. Under his order's banner, he produced six famous art exhibitions, the Salons de la Rose+Croix, which showcased Symbolist art between 1892 and 1897 and helped launch the career of eccentric French composer Erik Satie. While it never had many members, the Catholic Order, later renamed the Order of the Temple and the Grail, remained quietly active during Péladan's life.

When Péladan died in 1918, what was left of his order fragmented. His long-time personal secretary, Georges Monti, attempted to establish himself as the new Sâr or head of the order, but had little success. In Monti's last years, however, he found one student, a young man named Pierre Plantard, who later went on to model his own secret society – the undeservedly famous Priory of Sion – on the Catholic Order of the Rose+Cross. See **Priory of Sion**.

CELL SYSTEM

The basic structure of political secret societies during the nineteenth and twentieth centuries, the cell system was pioneered by Italian secret societies in the very early 1800s but spread throughout the secret society underworld within a few decades. Intended to prevent secret police from infiltrating an organization, the cell system divides up the membership of a secret society into "cells" of between 3 and 12 members. Each cell has a leader, and only the cell leader has contact with the next higher level of the organization. A group of between 3 and 12 cell leaders form a second-level cell, and only the leader of that cell has contact with the third level, which is usually the core of the organization. As new members are recruited, they become members of first-level cells, with no access to higher levels, no contact with members outside their own cells, and a very limited idea of the society's plans and objectives.

While the cell system is foolproof in theory, in practice it usually proved impossible to maintain the absolute division among cells and levels that the system required. Secret police in most countries became adept at getting agents into the upper levels of a secret society, where they could gather information on the society's membership and plans. The failure of the cell system was one of the main factors behind "leaderless resistance," a system of non-organization popular in right-wing secret societies at the end of the twentieth century.

Chevaliers of Faith

The most powerful conservative secret society in Napoleonic France, the *Chevaliers du Foi* or Chevaliers of Faith were organized in 1810 by Ferdinand de Bertier (1782–1864), whose father, the Intendant of Paris, was murdered by a mob just after the fall of the Bastille. A royalist and devout Catholic, Bertier became involved in conspiracies against Napoleon's regime in his youth. In 1809, after the pope was arrested by Napoleon's police and imprisoned in France, Bertier was thrown into prison for helping to circulate copies of the bull of excommunication against all those involved. See **French Revolution**.

After his release in 1810, Bertier joined a Masonic lodge to find out how it worked, and then launched his own secret society, the Chevaliers of Faith. Officially, the Chevaliers existed to carry out works of charity and piety, and members of the lowest level of initiation, *Associés de Charité* (Charitable Associates), learned no more than this. At the second level, *Ecuyer* (Squire), members learned that the order sought to re-establish medieval traditions of knighthood. Only at the third level, Chevalier, did initiates discover the existence of a political agenda within the order, and the nature of that agenda was revealed step-by-step in the three sub-grades of Chevalier, Hospitalier, and Chevalier of Faith; only members of this last sub-grade knew that the order aimed at Napoleon's overthrow.

By 1813 the Chevaliers of Faith had a large following in several regions of France, and they played a significant role in the collapse of Napoleon's regime the next year. Allied armies found themselves provided with detailed intelligence and guidance, and many historians hold that the Chevaliers stage-managed the Bordeaux rising in March 1814 that proclaimed Louis XVII King of France and got the Restoration under way. In the aftermath of Napoleon's final defeat, the Chevaliers seem to have faded quietly away, their work done.

Chevaliers of Jubilation

A handful of manuscript pages among the private papers of John Toland (1670–1722), the prolific Irish writer and philosopher, reveal nearly everything known about a Dutch secret society called *Les Chevaliers de la Jubilation* (the Chevaliers of Jubilation). Founded sometime before 1710 by a group of French exiles in The Hague, the Chevaliers were part dinner club, part private joke, and part serious conspiracy against French political and religious absolutism in the age of Louis XIV. See **Toland, John**.

Very little is known for certain about the Chevaliers; the surviving papers include minutes of four meetings, a short speech made by the Grand Master to the other members, and nothing else. The scanty source material includes the names of several members, the fact that the Chevaliers considered the Roman gods Mercury and Minerva to be their patrons, and the fact that they apparently drank a great deal. Toland himself was a member, and may have been the founder of the order during his stay in The Hague between 1708 and 1710.

A good deal of their reported meetings consisted of buffoonery and heavy drinking, but the Chevaliers had a serious purpose. Nearly all the members were French dissidents in exile from the autocratic government of their homeland, and several of them – Jean Rousset de Missy, Charles Levier, Michael Böhm, and possibly Toland himself – worked together to produce the most scandalous book of the eighteenth century, the *Traité des Trois Imposteurs* (*Treatise on the Three Impostors*), which argued that Moses, Jesus, and Muhammad were swindlers who manufactured bogus religions in order to manipulate people through fear and credulity, and proposed a new pantheist religion of nature.

The central target of this treatise was the intensely Catholic and conservative absolutism of Louis XIV of France. Ideas of the sort put into circulation by the Chevaliers of Jubilation, however, helped lay the foundation for radical secret societies in France and elsewhere in western Europe for more than two centuries to come.

Further reading: Jacob 1981.

Christian Identity

A radical racist movement that broke away from American Protestantism in the middle of the twentieth century, Christian Identity recast many of the dualist themes of classical Gnosticism in a violent new vein. With its call for a race war between whites and so-called "mud people," the Christian Identity movement launched a number of revolutionary secret societies in 1980s America. See **dualism**; **Gnosticism**.

The Christian Identity movement emerged out of British Israelitism, an unlikely nineteenth-century ideology that argued that the British people were actually one of the lost tribes of Israel. The British Israelite movement spread to the United States and Canada in the last decades of the nineteenth century, where it became a fringe preoccupation of a tiny faction of conservative Protestant sects. During the early twentieth century, a handful of churches in California and British Columbia combined this with the pervasive racism and antisemitism of the time, and ended up claiming they were descended from the ancient Israelites, but that modern Jews were not. See **Antisemitism**.

These views found common cause with another fringe movement in American Protestant Christianity, the "two seeds" theology of Baptist theologian Daniel Parker (1781–1844), who argued that humanity was divided into two bloodlines, an evil bloodline descending from Cain, supposedly fathered on Eve by Satan, and a good bloodline descending from Seth, whose father was Adam. This theory became popular in the South after the American Civil War and was put to use by racist ideologues at the turn of the century, who argued that the children of Seth were white while those of Cain were black.

During the 1950s and 1960s, these ideologies flowed together to form the Christian Identity movement. Wesley Swift (1913–70), the leading theoretician of the movement during its formative years, taught that the "Aryan race" (that is, light-skinned people of European ancestry) were the true Israelites and the children of God, while all other races are animals who happen to look human, and Jews are literally the biological descendants of Satan. To Wesley and his followers, a final battle between Aryans and their racial enemies was about to begin, and white people therefore needed to arm and equip themselves for a race war of extermination. This rhetoric moved from theory to practice in 1983 with the founding of the Bruders Schweigen, a racist secret society that attempted to launch a revolution against ZOG, the so-called "Zionist Occupation Government" of the United States. See **Bruders Schweigen**; **Zionist Occupation Government (ZOG)**.

The complete failure of the Bruders Schweigen project forced Christian Identity groups to reconsider their plans for racial warfare. The spread of racist paganism and neo-Nazi secret societies in the last decades of the twentieth century also drew many potential recruits away from the Christian Identity movement. It remains a significant force on the extreme right in America, however, and has substantial overlaps with contemporary neo-Nazi groups and surviving branches of the Ku Klux Klan. See **Ku Klux Klan**; **neo-Nazi secret societies**.

Further reading: Aho 1990, Barkun 1997, Gardell 1994, Goodrick-Clarke 2002.

Christian origins

As the largest religious movement in the modern world, and one of the most diverse and fractious religions in recorded history, Christianity has always had to deal with competing stories about its origins and early development. The question of Christian origins starts from the fact that for the first two centuries or so of its existence, the Christian movement was one of hundreds of tiny religious cults on the social fringes of the Roman world, and left very few traces of its existence. On the inkblot patterns of the handful of surviving sources, none of them impartial and many of them drastically edited later on, almost any set of claims can be projected.

According to the Roman Catholic and Eastern Orthodox churches, Christianity began with the career of Jesus of Nazareth, the son of the creator god of the universe, who transmitted a system of teachings, sacraments, and spiritual authority to a circle of followers before his death by crucifixion at the hands of the Roman colonial government of Judea. The books selected for inclusion in the New Testament all support this claim to one extent or another. See **Jesus of Nazareth**; **Roman Catholic Church**.

Other early Christian scriptures ex-cluded from the New Testament, many of them lost until twentieth-century archeological discoveries brought them to light again, challenge every aspect of the orthodox account but fail to establish any common ground among the alternatives. The wildly diverse Gnostic movement, which flourished from the first to the fourteenth centuries of the Common Era, presented dozens of interpretations of the nature of Jesus and the founding of Christianity. Early Jewish and Pagan sources, most of which survive only in fragments, suggest an alternative vision of Jesus of Nazareth as an itinerant wizard and folk healer on the fringes of Jewish society; while this interpretation is deeply disturbing to most Christians, it fits the evidence better than most other claims, including that of orthodoxy. See **Gnosticism**; **Magic**.

The last three centuries, however, have seen the greatest variety of alternative visions of Christian origins enter the field of debate. In the early eighteenth century, for example, French free-thinkers in a secret society titled the Chevaliers of Jubilation wrote and published one of the most scandalous books of the century, the *Traité des Trois Imposteurs* (*Treatise on the Three Impostors*), which claimed that Jesus of Nazareth was one of "three impostors" (the others being Moses and Muhammad) who manufactured fake religions and imposed them on credulous people. See **Chevaliers of Jubilation**.

It would take a volume larger than this one to describe all the accounts of Christian origins proposed during the nineteenth and twentieth centuries. Three in particular, however, require some discussion. The first of these emerged from the rebirth of Gnostic spirituality in the nineteenth century following the establishment of the *Eglise Gnostique* (Gnostic Church) by Jules Doinel in 1828. Doinel's followers resurrected the old Gnostic teaching that Jesus had actually been a Gnostic but was redefined by the orthodox churches during the suppression of Gnosticism in the third and fourth centuries CE. By the early twentieth century this idea had become widespread, and came to focus on the revision of Jesus' teaching by the apostle Paul, whose New Testament writings include most of the elements of Christian theology modern people find objectionable, and who many scholars believe played a central role in defining the version of Christian belief that ended up becoming the orthodox version of the faith.

A second theme entered the field of Christian origins via Theosophy's belief in Masters, advanced spiritual beings that watch over the course of human evolution. Many Theosophists from Christian backgrounds, searching for compromises between their new beliefs and their cultural heritage, came to see Jesus as one of the Masters, the Master of Compassion, whose teachings had been horribly distorted by the Christian churches of later times. By way of Theosophy's massive influence on the twentieth-century occult community, this set of beliefs became part of a dizzying range of alternative spiritual systems in the twentieth century. See **Masters**; **Theosophical Society**.

A final theme came into play in the late twentieth century as the underworld of rejected knowledge moved into popular culture throughout the western world. The basic claim of the rejected-knowledge scene holds that all historical and scientific theories backed by authority must be wrong, and Christian origins offered a tempting field where longstanding claims of authority could be overturned. Pierre Plantard's Priory of Sion hoax of the 1960s and 1970s, though it originally had nothing to do with Christian origins, was reworked by the trio of British authors who publicized it in the late 1970s and early 1980s into a vehicle for colorful speculations about Jesus of Nazareth, and the huge popular success of their book *The Holy Blood and the Holy Grail* (1982) established alternative theories of Christian origins as a lucrative publishing field. Since that time almost any imaginable speculation about Christian origins has found a ready market, and such speculations have become fodder for an entire genre of popular novels, including Dan Brown's bestseller *The Da Vinci Code* (2003). See **Da Vinci Code, the**; **Priory of Sion**; **rejected knowledge**.

Despite this torrent of speculation, the one thing that remains certain so far is that real evidence on the origins and development of the tiny fringe religious movement that became Christianity is very scarce. The words "We simply don't know" are among the least satisfying in the English language, but this is one situation in which they need to be used much more often than they have been to date.

Further reading: Baigent et al. 1983, Smith 1978.

Church of Light

A major player in the twentieth-century American occult scene, the Church of Light traces its ancestry back to the Hermetic Brotherhood of Luxor (H.B. of L.), one of the most influential occult secret societies of the late nineteenth century. After the H.B. of L. collapsed in a scandal in 1886, members in America reorganized as the Hermetic Brotherhood of Light in 1895. In 1900, the new organization recruited a young man named Benjamin Williams (1882–1951) who, under the name Elbert Benjamine, became a member of its governing triad in 1909 and its sole effective leader by 1914. See **Hermetic Brotherhood of Light**; **Hermetic Brotherhood of Luxor (H.B. of L.)**.

In that year he began the process of transforming the Brotherhood into a correspondence school, following the model already pioneered by the original Hermetic Brotherhood of Luxor, and 1915 saw Benjamine and the Brotherhood's headquarters move to Los Angeles, at that time a hotbed of American occultism. For the next two decades Benjamine, under the pen name C.C. Zain, wrote an immense, 210-lesson study course in astrology and occult philosophy.

In 1932, the Brotherhood of Light (as it then called itself) reorganized itself as a religious body, the Church of Light. Its members, or Stellarians, follow what Benjamine termed "the Religion of the Stars," a fusion between occult philosophy and astrological teachings. Stellarians work their way through the 21 volumes of Benjamine's study course, and receive no fewer than 50 degrees of initiation; the first 21 are earned by mastering sections of the study course, the second 21 must be earned by achieving certain psychic states, while the final 8 can be earned only by reaching advanced spiritual states. Members who receive all 50 degrees are eligible to join an inner order, the Order of the Sphinx.

Like most of the great occult correspondence schools of the period, the Church of Light passed through difficult times in the second half of the twentieth century, as membership dropped and most people interested in the occult turned away from traditional Hermetic orders toward Wicca and other more recently founded systems. In the 1990s, however, the Church's leaders came into contact with scholars researching the Hermetic Brotherhood of Luxor and its offshoots, sparking a renewed interest among Church members in their own history and roots. The relocation of the Church headquarters from a decaying Los Angeles neighborhood to a suburban location also helped buoy the organization. At present the Church of Light remains active, with a significant Internet presence, and its inner Order of the Sphinx has revived many of the old magical practices of the Hermetic Brotherhood of Luxor. See **Wicca**.

Church of Satan

Among the most colorful organizations in late twentieth-century popular occultism, the Church of Satan was founded in 1966 by San

Francisco eccentric Howard Stanton Levey (1930–77), better known by his assumed name Anton Szandor LaVey. Beginning in the late 1950s, LaVey parlayed an interest in the occult and a willingness to shock into an impressive public presence, abetted by local and national media who reported even his most outrageous claims at face value without bothering to check the facts.

As much a work of performance art as anything else, LaVey's Church of Satan became famous for public ceremonies that used all the trappings of traditional Satanism, including inverted pentagrams and female nudity. The church also taught LaVey's Satanist philosophy, a system of "rational selfishness" derived from the writings of Russian-American Objectivist philosopher Ayn Rand. Belief in the existence of Satan as an actual being was never one of the church's articles of faith; this detail completely escaped the notice of fundamentalists across the United States, who boosted LaVey's publicity campaign markedly by denouncing him at every turn. See **fundamentalism**; **Satanism**.

The late 1960s and early 1970s were the glory days of the Church of Satan, as LaVey attracted celebrities such as Jayne Mansfield and Sammy Davis Jr. to his organization, and performed Satanic weddings, baptisms, and funerals in a glare of media publicity; 1969 saw the publication of his bestselling *The Satanic Bible* and an appearance on Johnny Carson's *Tonight Show*. LaVey organized a network of local Grottoes across the United States in the following years as would-be Satanists flocked to the Church of Satan's banner. Many of these new recruits took Satanism far more seriously than LaVey did, however, and found his passion for publicity difficult to handle. In 1975 one of the Satanic priests he had ordained, Michael Aquino, broke with the Church of Satan to found a rival organization, the Temple of Set, and not long thereafter LaVey closed the Grottoes and abandoned the limelight. See **Temple of Set**.

The Church of Satan remained in existence, however, and surfaced again in the early 1990s as members of the alternative music scene adopted LaVey's kitsch Satanism as a symbol of their disaffection from society. A new book by LaVey, *The Devil's Notebook*, helped draw a new generation into the Church. The organization survived LaVey's death and remains active at the present time.

Further reading: LaVey 1969.

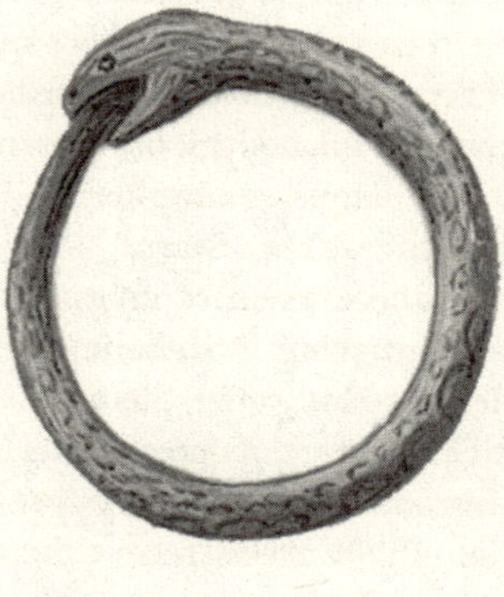

Club of Rome

One of the many organizations named in modern conspiracy literature as parts of a global plot against humanity, the Club of Rome was established in 1968 by Aurelio Peccei, former CEO of Fiat, and a select group of industrialists and social scientists to discuss responses to what Peccei termed "the problematique" – the converging crises of industrial society produced by the attempt to sustain infinite material growth on a finite planet. Shortly after its founding, the Club commissioned a group of scientists at the Massachusetts Institute of Technology to run computer simulations of future economic and demographic trends. The results were published in 1973 as the bestselling book *The Limits to Growth.* The study's results – that unrestricted economic growth leads to inevitable collapse due to resource depletion and pollution – sparked an immediate firestorm of criticism, but 30 years after the original study, its models remain among the more accurate predictions of the likely course of industrial society, with recent concerns about peaking oil production and global warming only the latest examples of "the problematique" in action.

Since the evasion of unacceptable facts is a driving force behind many modern conspiracy theories, the Club of Rome and its predictions have been grist for a good many conspiratorial mills. Several recent theories identify the Committee of 300, an alleged secret society of European industrialists, as the hidden power behind the Club of Rome. These theories claim that in order to bring about a new Dark Age and global slavery under a worldwide government, the Club publicized a fictional crisis to force the industrial countries of the world to de-industrialize and prevent Third World countries from undergoing an industrial revolution in the first place. The closure of most of America's industrial plant during the Reagan years is said to be their doing, as was the collapse of the Russian economy after the fall of Communism in 1989. See **Committee of 300**.

The Club of Rome, like most policymaking organizations and think-tanks in the industrial world today, is a secret society only in the imaginations of conspiracy theorists. Still, the widening social chasm between educated elite groups and downwardly mobile middle and working classes in the developed world has increasingly pushed class antagonisms into a conspiracy-theory mold. As resource depletion and environmental damage become even more obvious problems than they are today, claims that such problems are the result of conspiracies will doubtless become more common still.

Co-Masonry

A branch of Freemasonry that admits women as well as men to membership, Co-Masonry traces its roots to a schism in the French branch of the Ancient and Accepted Scottish Rite. One of the lodges involved in the schism, *Les Libres Penseurs* (The Free Thinkers) at Pecq in Seine-et-Oise, voted in 1881 to admit Mlle. Maria Desraimes to membership. Forbidden to do so by the Grand Loge Symbolique, their grand lodge, the lodge initiated her anyway and promptly had its charter suspended. In 1893, Mlle. Desraimes and a group of other women interested in Masonry, along with a number of male Masons who felt the exclusion of women from the Craft was unjustifiable, formed a new Grand Lodge that admitted both men and women. Over the next few years the new movement, Co-Masonry, spread rapidly; the first British lodge was founded in 1902 and the first American lodge the next year. See **Ancient and Accepted Scottish Rite (AASR)**; **Freemasonry**.

Among the members of the first lodge in London was Annie Besant, Madame Blavatsky's successor as head of the Theosophical Society. Besant quickly brought Co-Masonry in the English-speaking world into a close alliance with Theosophy and used Theosophical connections to set up Co-Masonic lodges around the world. Not all Co-Masons have found the Theosophical presence agreeable, and one of the continuing sources of strain in the movement is the relevance of Theosophy to Co-Masonry. See **Blavatsky, Helen Petrovna**; **Theosophical Society**.

Officially, all regular Masonic grand lodges condemn Co-Masonry as irregular, and regular Masons who attend Co-Masonic lodge meetings face expulsion from their lodges. How strictly this rule is enforced varies sharply from jurisdiction to jurisdiction, and there have been quiet, unofficial contacts between regular and Co-Masonic Masons for many years. Presently Co-Masonry remains active in some 50 countries around the world.

Committee of 300

One of the alleged secret societies proposed as secret masters of the world by modern conspiracy theorists, the Committee of 300 owes its existence in conspiracy literature to a passing remark in a 1909 newspaper article by Walther Rathenau, a German-Jewish industrialist and civil servant. Rathenau, in a passage criticizing industrial monopolies, commented that the European economic system was under the control of some 300 men who all knew one another. Reprinted in Rathenau's 1921 book, *Zur Kritik der Zeit* (*A Critique of the Times*), the article came to the attention of German antisemites just after the first German publication of the forged *Protocols of the Elders of Zion*. See **antisemitism**; **Protocols of the Elders of Zion**.

Erich von Ludendorff, the former general and leading right-wing politician, insisted in his 1922 book *Kriegsführung und Politik* (*Warfare *and Politics*) that the 300 men were none other than the heads of the secret Jewish world conspiracy described in the *Protocols*. Articles in German antisemitic newspapers claimed that Rathenau's knowledge of the exact number of these men proved that he himself was one of them. All this propaganda helped lay the groundwork for Rathenau's 1922 assassination by right-wing fanatics allied to the Nazi Party, then a small but rising power in German politics.

By the middle years of the twentieth century the Committee of 300 had become a fixture of European conspiracy theories, and by the end of the century it merged with other conspiracy narratives. A recent book on the Committee, John Coleman's *Conspirator's Hierarchy: The Story of the Committee of 300* (1992), describes the Committee – also known as the Olympians – as a secret society of aristocratic Satanists, and identifies them with the Bavarian Illuminati, the Bogomils, the Cathars, and the ancient Isaic and Dionysiac mysteries. The Council on Foreign Relations (CFR), a standard element of contemporary conspiracy theories, is simply a pawn in the hands of the Committee, which also sponsors the Club of Rome. See **Bavarian Illuminati**; **Cathars**; **Club of Rome**; **Council on Foreign Relations (CFR)**; **Dionysian mysteries**; **Isaic mysteries**; **Satanism**.

Despite all these impressive details, no one has actually offered any evidence that the Committee of 300 actually exists. While Rathenau's original comment was quite likely correct at the time, and is at least as likely to be true today, the loosely organized network of financiers and industrialists he meant to describe seems much more plausible than the secret Satanic conspiracy imagined by the Committee's would-be enemies.

Further reading: Cohn 1967, Coleman 1992.

Committees of Correspondence

One of the two major secret groups involved in the American Revolution, the Committees of Correspondence came into being in the 1760s among leading citizens of the American colonies who favored reforms in the colonies' relationship with Great Britain. The Committees circulated news and helped coordinate political activities across the 13 colonies. Many of their members were also involved in Freemasonry; no evidence shows a direct link between colonial Masonic lodges and the Committees, but Masonic connections likely formed a major channel by which the Committees expanded and recruited new members. See **American Revolution**; **Freemasonry**.

The Committees in New York and Boston played an important role in founding the other major secret society of the Revolution, the terrorist Sons of Liberty, and Committee members Samuel Adams and Paul Revere led the Sons of Liberty in many of their most famous actions. In 1773, as relations with Britain soured, the Committees were absorbed into colonial legislatures, and the first Continental Congress in 1776 rendered the Committees obsolete by establishing a more formal structure for cooperation between the colonies. See **Sons of Liberty**.

Communism

"A specter is haunting Europe," Karl Marx and Friedrich Engels claimed in the ringing opening lines of *The Communist Manifesto*: "the specter of Communism." The phrase proved more prophetic than they could have known. While communism existed as a philosophy and a political system, its greatest impact on the history of the nineteenth and twentieth centuries came less from these realities and more from the spectral image it cast, an image that haunted the hopes of intellectuals and the fears of ruling elites across the world.

Though it took Marx hundreds of pages of fine print to explain communism, the core concepts are simple enough. Social classes, according to Marx, are groups of people with a common relationship to the means of economic production, and the struggle between classes is the driving force of history. Industrial society is split into two classes – the bourgeoisie who own the means of production and live on their investments, and the proletariat who work the means of production and survive on wage labor. Since all economic value is the result of labor by the proletariat, the bourgeoisie are a parasitic class; the proletariat receives a fraction of the value of its labor while the bourgeoisie batten on the rest. Since competition imposes progressively lower wages and worse working conditions on the proletariat, workers will eventually rebel, overthrowing the bourgeoisie and seizing the means of production. The result, at least in Marx's theory, is communism, a society of universal justice in which economic production would serve human needs rather than bourgeois greed.

This ideology appealed powerfully to the intellectuals who made up the mainstay of the European Left through the nineteenth and twentieth centuries. Yet one of the paradoxes of communism throughout its history was that it was always at least partly a creation of its opponents. As historian James Billington pointed out, in *Fire in the Minds of Men: Origins of the Revolutionary Faith* (1980), the word "communism" appeared before there were any communists to proclaim it, and it gained most of its popularity when it was used by conservatives to attack their liberal opponents. Though the word was probably coined in French radical circles in the late 1830s, its first documented use was in a German conservative newspaper on March 11, 1840: "The Communists have in view nothing less than a levelling of society – substituting for the presently-existing order of things the absurd, immoral and impossible utopia of a community of goods" (quoted in Billington 1980, p. 246).

Since the idea of public ownership of land, housing, and factories hardly seemed absurd, immoral, or impossible to working people trapped in the fetid industrial slums of nineteenth-century Europe, attempts by conservatives to launch communism as a bogey to frighten the masses succeeded mostly in providing free publicity to the first successful radical movement to adopt the name. While a handful of political factions in France tried to lay claim to it in the early 1840s, Karl Marx made it his own later in that decade with his first significant publications on political economy. In 1847 the League of the Just – one of the major political secret societies in Europe – embraced Marxist theory and renamed itself the Communist League. Marx and his colleague Engels responded by writing *The Communist Manifesto* and permanently defined Communism in Marxist terms. See **League of the Just**.

The newborn movement grew up in a world powerfully shaped by secret societies. In the aftermath of the French Revolution, secret organizations such as the Philadelphes and the Carbonari, originally founded to oppose Napoleon's betrayal of the French Revolution, became lightning rods for nationalist aspirations and sparked more than a dozen revolutions against the conservative monarchies of the early nineteenth century. The very mixed success of these revolutions, which took power from the hands of kings and aristocracies only to hand it over to industrialists and bankers, drove a steady leftward drift in the political secret societies. Thus the Philadelphes, which started out in 1797 as a Republican secret society, by 1864 helped to create the First International. See **Carbonari**; **First International**; **Philadelphes**.

Yet communism came on the scene just as most of the radical political movements in Europe were turning away from secret societies to establish political parties, labor unions, and mass movements. The new ideology's rhetoric of mass struggle made it appealing to leftists who saw little hope in secret conspiracies. As a result, though communism borrowed some features from the older secret society tradition, it saw itself as a mass movement even when the masses wanted nothing to do with it.

This was particularly true during the long years when Marxism was only one among many movements on the Left. During the late twentieth century, propagandists for communism and capitalism alike liked to picture the history of the modern world as a contest between these two alone, but until the Second World War the options were much wider. Anarchism offered major competition to Marxist parties, and lesser-known traditions such as distributism, social credit, guild socialism, corporatism, and many others contended for influence. Many radicals criticized Marxism just as severely as capitalism. Thus Polish anarchist Waclaw Machajski, for example, argued presciently in his 1898 book *The Intellectual Worker* that a Marxist revolution would simply transfer power from business owners to government bureaucrats. See **Anarchism**.

It took a century of turmoil and two world wars to reduce the crowded playing field of political and economic ideologies to a forced choice between two contenders. The First World War and its aftermath in Russia was the major turning point in the process. The Socialist Second International had long discussed stopping a European war in its tracks by launching a general strike in the combatant nations, but in 1914 not one Socialist party or labor union followed through on these plans, and the Second International collapsed shortly after the outbreak of hostilities. See **Second International**.

In the aftermath of the Second International's failure, the Russian revolution of 1917 came like a thunderbolt. The fact that the Bolsheviks had succeeded where every other party on the Left had failed, taking absolute power in an entire nation and abolishing the capitalist system there, put them instantly at the forefront of the radical movement worldwide. Followers of most competing systems on the Left, including major leaders such as the anarchist Emma Goldman, rallied around the Bolshevik banner. The Bolsheviks made this easy by inviting anarchists, syndicalists, and non-Marxist labor unions to take part in the Third or Communist International, founded in 1919 amid widespread expectations that a proletarian revolution would follow in the rest of Europe. See **Russian revolution**; **Third International**.

Attempted communist revolutions in Hungary, Bavaria, and Yugoslavia failed, however, and as the new Russian government turned its attention to maintaining its own power, leftists who joined the Third International found themselves expected to obey orders from Moscow that focused purely on the goals of Russian foreign policy. The result was a series of schisms between pro-Russian and anti-Russian factions on the left. These splits played an important role in weakening the Left and leaving much of central Europe vulnerable to the fascist parties that seized power in the 1920s and 1930s.

The Second World War completed the transformation launched by the First. Hitler's crusade against "Jewish Bolshevism" ironically did much to save the Soviet Union from its own incompetence. German brutality bolstered Russians' wavering support of Stalin's government, while shipments of war material from the United States gave the Soviet system an economic and technological boost that helped overcome its internal problems. The establishment of the Iron Curtain after the war was made easy by the Nazi annihilation of moderate Socialist and Social Democrat parties in most eastern European countries. See **Hitler, Adolf**; **National Socialism**.

In an important sense, though, communism went out of existence in the years after the Second World War. In the bare-knuckle politics of the Cold War, "communist" came to mean nothing more than "allied with Russia." The leaders of Third World countries learned to mouth communist slogans when they wanted help disentangling themselves from the grip of American business interests, and radical parties in western Europe and elsewhere knew that using Marxist language and symbolism got them more attention than anything else, but few people anywhere went beyond slogans and symbols to study ideas that had shaken the world a century before.

By the 1990s, as the Soviet Union broke apart and China announced it was adopting a "market socialist" economy, the specter of communism haunted nothing but the history books. Its passing left a gaping void on the radical Left, which abandoned philosophy for ideology in the early twentieth century and so had few resources left for the difficult task of formulating a new critique of society, and an equally yawning gap on the radical Right, which lost most of its claim to relevance once the enemy it claimed to be fighting went out of existence. Many in both camps have tried to fill the void with resources borrowed from contemporary conspiracy theory, with the curious result that in many western countries, rhetoric about the New World Order has become the common property of both ends of the political spectrum. See **New World Order**.

Further reading: Billington 1980, Drachkovitch 1966.

Compagnonnage

An important system of secret brotherhoods in late medieval and early modern France, the institution of Compagnonnage emerged among journeymen of a variety of French trades as the medieval guild system broke down under the pressures of early capitalism and the earliest forms of industrialism. Under the original guild system, most journeymen could count on advancing to the rank of master and owning their own business, but as guild masters became owners of large business firms that hired dozens or hundreds of journeymen, access to master status and full membership in guilds was closed off. In response, journeymen in France created organizations modeled on the guilds but open to journeymen. In France, these took the name of Compagnonnage (from *compagnon*, "companion," the standard French term for a journeyman); a parallel process in Britain gave rise to Odd Fellowship, one of the major secret societies of the modern age. See **guilds, medieval**; **Odd Fellowship**.

Brotherhoods of Compagnonnage, like guilds, had their own initiation rituals, patron saints, and elected officers. Most brotherhoods belonged to one of three loose associations – the Children of Père Soubise, the Children of Maître Jacques, and the Children of Solomon – each with its own rituals and traditions. Members contributed money weekly or monthly to a common fund used to pay for sickness and funeral benefits for members and support the widows and orphans of those who died. As the institution expanded, rival brotherhoods took shape, and sometimes fought pitched battles with quarterstaffs, the traditional Compagnonnage weapon.

Compagnonnage flourished through the seventeenth and eighteenth centuries, but was largely replaced by the labor union movement in France in the nineteenth. A handful of brotherhoods survived in provincial towns, and the second half of the twentieth century has seen a modest resurgence in membership and activity. So far, Compagnonnage has had little presence in modern conspiracy theory or rejected knowledge literature, though a few books in the latter field have managed to confuse it with the builders of the Gothic cathedrals. See **rejected knowledge**.

Further reading: Truant 1994.

Concatenated Order of Hoo-Hoo

One of the oddities of American fraternalism, the Concatenated Order of Hoo-Hoo was founded in a train station in Gurdon, Arkansas in 1892, by businessmen in the wood products industry on their way home from a convention. One of the founders had been reading Lewis Carroll's nonsense-poem *The Hunting of the Snark*; this explains why the national governing body of the order, the Supreme Nine, consists of the Snark of the Universe, a Senior Hoo-Hoo, a Junior Hoo-Hoo, a Boojum, a Scrivenoter, a Jabberwock, a Custocatian, an Arcanoper, and a Gurdon. The mascot of the order is a black cat with its tail curled into the figure 9, its initiation ceremony is known as a Concatenation, and new initiates are Kittens.

According to its constitution, the objects of the order are the promotion of health, happiness, and a long life. In practice, at least in the early days of the order, these praiseworthy goals took a back seat to frivolity, and most of the wild habits of nineteenth-century burlesque orders found equivalents in Hoo-Hoo concatenations. Like many burlesque societies, however, the Hoo-Hoos gradually calmed down in the course of the twentieth century, and at this point it functions primarily as a service club in the lumber industry. Hoo-Hoo clubs exist in Canada, Australia, New Zealand, Malaysia, and South Africa as well as in the United States, and members must be employed in the wood products industry. See **burlesque degrees**.

Conspiracy of Equals

A short-lived secret society born and destroyed in the ferment of Revolutionary France, the *Conspiration des Égales* or Conspiracy of Equals was the brainchild of François "Gracchus" Babeuf and Filippo Buonarroti, two supporters of the radical Jacobin party who met in prison in 1795, after the Jacobin defeat. Babeuf had been an associate of Nicholas de Bonneville, founder of the first important secret society of the Revolution, the Social Circle. During their imprisonment, the two men discussed the Circle and its goals, and resolved to use similar methods to promote the radical agenda in France and oppose the new, more conservative government, the Directory. See **Babeuf, François "Gracchus"**; **Buonarroti, Filippo**; **French Revolution**; **Social Circle**.

On their release in October 1795, Babeuf and Buonarroti launched a political organization called the *Societé du Panthéon* (Society of the Pantheon) to promote Jacobin ideas, copying most of the details from Bonneville's organization. They also launched a radical newspaper, the *Tribun du Peuple* – a title borrowed directly from Bonneville's first paper. When the Society was suppressed by Directory authorities in February 1796, its leaders immediately organized its core members into a secret society, the Conspiracy of Equals.

Instead of trying to incite a popular rebellion, the plan Babeuf and Buonarroti devised focused on a seizure of power by a small elite of committed revolutionaries, and concentrated on recruiting government and military personnel and spreading propaganda. By May, the Conspiracy felt ready to strike, but the Directory had an informer in its inner circle and struck first, arresting 200 members. Babeuf and one other member were executed, and Buonarroti and most of the other members ended up in jail for long terms.

The Conspiracy of Equals would have been no more than a footnote to the history of the French Revolution except for the fact that Filippo Buonarroti went on to become the most famous organizer of political secret societies in the early nineteenth century. His 1828 book *Conspiration pour l'Egalité*, a history of Babeuf's conspiracy, was the Bible of liberal revolutionaries throughout Europe, and the model of revolution by elite takeover became the standard for secret societies from then on. The Bolshevik Revolution in 1917 Russia and the Nazi seizure of power in 1933 Germany are only among the most dramatic echoes of the Conspiracy's original plan. See **National Socialism**; **Russian revolution**.

Further reading: Roberts 1972.

Cosa Nostra

See **Mafia**.

Council on Foreign Relations [CFR]

Among the most prestigious of American think-tanks, and the centerpiece of most recent speculations on the New World Order, the Council on Foreign Relations was founded in New York City in 1921 by a group of leading American financiers. The seed of the CFR had been planted in Paris during the 1919 negotiations over the Versailles Treaty, when US President Woodrow Wilson's close adviser, Col. Edward M. House, assembled a group of British and American politicians at a dinner party and broached the idea of an institute to coordinate public policy in the Anglo–American alliance. The CFR came into being two years later. See **New World Order**.

The CFR's 1500 members have long included the most important movers and shakers in American politics, including four US presidents and a stellar list of ambassadors, top business executives and bureaucrats, leading academics, and cultural figures. The CFR publishes the journal *Foreign Affairs*, easily the most prestigious journal in the foreign-policy field.

Unquestionably the CFR is among the major policy-making institutions of the US upper class. Its role has been stretched out of all proportion in recent conspiracy theories, however, where it shares pride of place alongside the Trilateral Commission, the Bilderberg group, and the fictional Committee of 300 as one of the top groups behind the New World Order, supposedly a scheme to impose a global dictatorship under the control of a corporate elite. These claims, like most of contemporary conspiracy theory, fail to explain why people who allegedly run the world need to carry out a vast secret plan in order to take over the world they already run. In fact, even a cursory reading of CFR publications and the pages of *Foreign Policy* make it clear that the CFR strives – not always successfully – to find common ground among the diverse and often quarrelsome groups who form the US governing class. See **Bilderberg Group**; **Committee of 300**; **Trilateral Commission**.

Further reading: Domhoff 1974, Wilgus 1978.

Crata Repoa

According to a ritual text anonymously published at Berlin in 1770, the highest order of ancient Egyptian initiation, consisting of seven degrees. The ancient Egyptian language had not yet been deciphered in 1770, however, and the ritual of the Crata Repoa is standard eighteenth-century high degree Freemasonry with no resemblance to actual Egyptian temple ritual; the supposed Egyptian origin of the ritual is thus yet another fictitious origin story, of the sort so frequently practiced at the time. See **origin stories**.

There seems to be no evidence that the Crata Repoa existed in eighteenth-century Germany as a functioning secret society. The published ritual, however, had a surprisingly wide influence. Several groups of French occultists in the nineteenth century worked the Crata Repoa rituals, and the Ordo Templi Astarte, a currently active American magical order, uses the Crata Repoa system as the basis for its own system of initiation. See **Ordo Templi Astarte**.

Crowley, Aleister

English writer, occultist, and would-be Antichrist. One of the most colorful figures of modern occultism, Crowley (1875–1947) was born in Leamington, Warwickshire and raised in the Plymouth Brethren, a sect that invented most of modern Christian fundamentalism. Like many children from strict religious backgrounds, he rebelled against his family's beliefs in his teens. He replaced his birth names Edward Alexander with the more romantic Aleister, and convinced himself that he was the Beast 666 from the Book of Revelation. See **Antichrist**; **fundamentalism**.

In 1895 he matriculated at Trinity College, Cambridge, and briefly pursued chemistry, but left without a degree. Money inherited from his father, who died when Crowley was five, enabled him to pursue the lifestyle of a bohemian poet and self-publish two books of poetry, including a pornographic volume entitled *White Stains*. Like many young *fin-de-siècle* men of letters, he gravitated toward the occult, and in 1898 he was initiated into the Neophyte Grade of the Hermetic Order of the Golden Dawn, the premier British occult secret society of the time. See **Hermetic Order of the Golden Dawn**.

In the power struggles and schisms that beset the order just after his admission, he pledged absolute loyalty to the Order's head, Samuel Liddell Mathers, and served as Mathers' emissary to the rebellious London adepts, though his insistence on wearing full Highland dress and a black mask through the whole process cannot have helped Mathers' case. His ardor for the cause cooled, however, and in 1904 – convinced that he had been granted authority by the Secret Chiefs who ran the order – he contacted Mathers and demanded to be recognized as true head of the Golden Dawn, an act that resulted in Crowley's expulsion from Mathers' branch of the order.

The authority Crowley claimed came in a typically dramatic manner. In 1903 he married Rose Kelly, the daughter of a portrait painter, and set out with her on a world tour. Stopping in Cairo the next year, he received – by a disembodied but clearly audible voice, according to his later accounts – a communication from a spirit named Aiwass, who claimed to be the messenger of the gods who would rule the age of the world then beginning, the Aeon of Horus. Over three days, Aiwass dictated to Crowley the text of the Book of the Law, the holy scriptures of the new religion of Thelema (from the Greek word for "will"), whose central tenet was "Do what thou wilt shall be the whole of the law." See **ages of the world**.

This revelation was the turning point of Crowley's career. In the years that followed, his marriage broke apart, his literary career failed, and his occult activities took up more and more of his time, as he became convinced of his own messianic role as the prophet of the Aeon of Horus. He returned to England in 1908 and began publishing a lavish journal, *The Equinox*, to announce the good news of the arrival of Horus to the world at large. Crowley also launched his own Golden Dawn-based order, the Argenteum Astrum; however, his publication of Golden Dawn papers and rituals landed him in a court battle with Mathers. See **Argenteum Astrum**.

The journal and the court case alike brought him to the attention of Theodor Reuss and John Yarker, two major figures in irregular Masonry at the time. In 1910 Crowley was accepted into Reuss's Ordo Templi Orientis (OTO) and Yarker's Rite of Memphis and Misraim. Yarker's death in 1913 and the subsequent collapse of the Rite of Memphis and Misraim limited his activity in that field, although he did take part in the struggle to keep the order out of the hands of Annie Besant, who wanted to make it part of Co-Masonry. See **Co-Masonry**; **Ordo Templi Orientis (OTO)**; **Reuss, Theodor**; **Rite of Memphis and Misraim**; **Yarker, John**.

The Ordo Templi Orientis was another matter. In 1912, Reuss made Crowley head of the British branch of the OTO, and he proceeded to make the order a vehicle for his new religion. By 1913 he was enmeshed in bitter quarrels with Reuss and other members of the order, and in 1914 he left Britain for America, leaving a remnant of the OTO in Britain to struggle on for a few more years before collapsing after a police raid. Once in America, Crowley and his Canadian acolyte Charles Stansfield Jones attempted to spread the OTO, and once again quarreled with Reuss, who tried to recruit AMORC founder H. Spencer Lewis to spread Reuss's branch of the order instead. While in America Crowley also initiated Paul Foster Case into the OTO, though Case lost interest and became active in Mathers's branch of the Golden Dawn instead. See **Ancient Mystical Order Rosae Crucis (AMORC)**; **Case, Paul Foster**.

In 1920, after returning to Europe, Crowley gathered up a small coterie of followers and went to Cefalu in Sicily, where they established what would now be called a commune and devoted their time to sex, drugs, and magic. When one of the commune's members died of food poisoning, the media furor prompted Italian dictator Benito Mussolini to order Crowley's expulsion from Italy. After staying in Tunisia and France, becoming a heroin addict in the process, Crowley returned to England and promptly sued British sculptor Nina Hammett for referring to him in print as a "black magician," making the same mistake that ended Oscar Wilde's career. British law required Hammett to prove the accuracy of her statement in order to clear herself, and she did so to the satisfaction of the court and the public, in the process shredding what was left of Crowley's reputation and finances.

Crowley spent the remainder of his life in cheap lodgings, first in London and then at Hastings, preaching the gospel of Thelema to anyone who would listen and struggling to finance his drug habit. His small circle of friends and students at the time included Gerald Gardner, who later launched modern Wicca on its career, though there seems to be no truth to the much-quoted rumor that Gardner paid Crowley to write the original Wiccan Book of Shadows. When Crowley died in 1947, his friends performed a Thelemite funeral service for him; typically, the media reported it inaccurately as a Black Mass. See **Black Mass**; **Book of Shadows**; **Wicca**.

Further reading: Crowley 1989, King 1991.

Culdees

A Christian monastic movement in Ireland and Scotland, the Culdees (from Gaelic *celi De*, "servant of God") emerged in the seventh and eighth centuries within the Celtic Church. They adopted some elements of the Eastern Orthodox rite and lived a life of prayer and austerity in isolated hermitages. Their variations from the standard Roman Catholic practice of the time led them to be condemned as heretics once Roman authority extended to the Celtic fringe of northwest Europe, and the Culdees were gradually absorbed into more orthodox monastic traditions in the tenth and eleventh centuries. See **Roman Catholic Church**.

Very few traditions of the past have had their reputation as roughly manhandled as the Culdees. Starting in the nineteenth century, Druid Revival secret societies, which claimed connections back to the ancient Druids, redefined the Culdees as a group of Druids who nominally converted to Christianity but preserved their ancient mysteries. The neo-pagan movement of the late twentieth century borrowed this re-definition and mapped their own ideas of paganism onto it, resulting in claims that the Culdees worshipped the earth goddess and practiced free love. The reaction of the ascetic and rather puritanical Culdees themselves to this suggestion scarcely bears imagining. See **Druid Revival**.

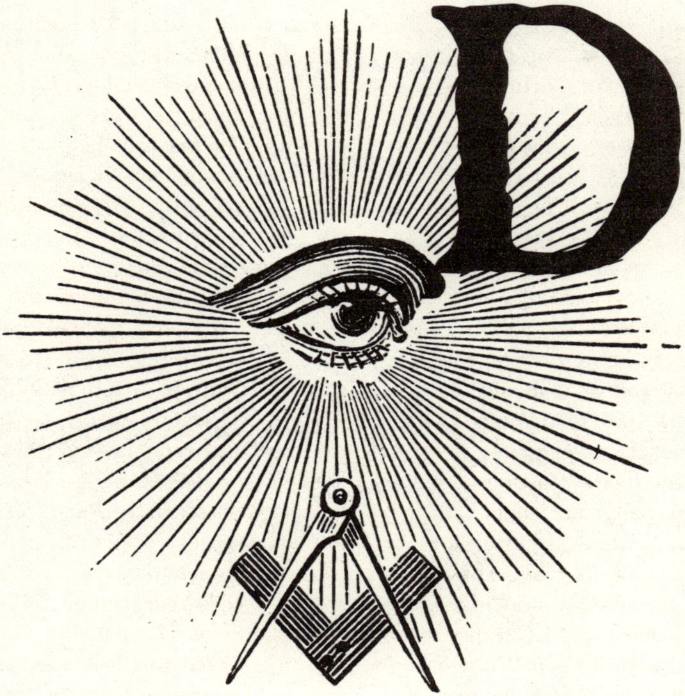
D

Damcar

See **Damear**.

Damear

A medieval city in Yemen, on the southwestern corner of the Arabian Peninsula, now called Dhamar. Damear has been an important center of Muslim theological studies since the Middle Ages. According to the original manuscript versions of the *Fama Fraternitatis* – the first Rosicrucian manifesto – Christian Rosenkreutz, the legendary founder of the Rosicrucian order, heard about the wise men of Damear while he was in Damascus, and traveled there in order to study Cabala, magic, and alchemy. See **alchemy**; **Cabala**; **Rosenkreutz, Christian**; **Rosicrucians**.

In the first printed version of the *Fama Fraternitatis*, published in 1614, the name was misspelled "Damcar," and this spelling has been repeated in nearly all Rosicrucian writings ever since.

Da Vinci Code, T

Shortly after its 2003 pu
Dan Brown's novel *The Da Vinci Code* shot to the top of the *New York Times* bestseller list and stayed there for well over half a year, and at the time of writing has sold more than 37 million copies in hardback. The *Code* is a capably written thriller, like Brown's earlier books, but the key to its phenomenal success was Brown's use of some of the most popular themes of today's alternative history industry as background for his tale. For literally millions of readers, *The Da Vinci Code* offered a first intriguing glimpse into the world of secret societies, forgotten heresies, and alternate visions of the origin of Christianity. Its success marked the coming of age of rejected knowledge in the mainstream of modern culture. See **rejected knowledge**.

The novel starts with the murder of the curator of the Louvre Museum in Paris, who is also the Grand Master of a powerful secret society, the Priory of Sion. Before he dies, he passes on a coded message to his granddaughter, Sophie Neveu, and to Harvard professor Robert Langdon, sending them on a madcap quest to discover the secret of the Holy Grail and stay ahead of the forces of orthodoxy, in the person of an albino assassin named Silas who belongs to the conservative Catholic organization Opus Dei. The secret proves to be the existence of a bloodline descended from Jesus of Nazareth and his wife Mary

Magdalene, guarded through the centuries by the Priory of Sion. The denouement takes place at Rosslyn Chapel in Scotland, where one of the two surviving heirs of the Jesus bloodline is revealed. All these themes can be found in many different combinations in the rejected-knowledge literature of the last half-century or so. See **Christian origins**; **Grail**; **Jesus of Nazareth**; **Mary Magdalene**; **Opus Dei**; **Priory of Sion**; **Roman Catholic Church**; **Rosslyn Chapel**.

The Da Vinci Code is thus at least as much a novel of ideas as it is a thriller, and its protagonist is a scholar who specializes in artistic symbolism rather than one of the hardboiled private investigators, soldiers, and spies who more often populate the pages of the thriller genre. Much of the book's appeal is in its willingness to tackle serious intellectual issues – the role of women in Christianity, the scholarly debates surrounding early Christian history, the role of secret societies in western culture, and the like – through the medium of popular fiction. This is not to say that Brown always gets his arguments straight, as many critics have been keen to point out. Central to part of the plot, for example, is Brown's claim that the letter V is always a symbol of the feminine; one wonders, just for starters, how this squares with Winston Churchill's "V for victory" sign during the Second World War. Symbolism is rarely if ever so single-voiced as Brown makes his characters suggest. See **Allegory**; **Emblems**.

Deeper issues surround the factual status of some of the historical material in the book. Brown cites several popular books from alternative-history literature in the text of his novel, but he seems to have considered them more than simply raw material for a thriller. A note on the first page describes the existence of the Priory of Sion since 1099 as a historical fact, and Brown himself has stated in public interviews that in the course of writing *The Da Vinci Code*, he went from initial skepticism to belief in the reality of the Priory of Sion, the Jesus bloodline, and the other bits of rejected knowledge that play a role in his plot. To judge by the novel's impact on popular culture, many of Brown's readers went through a similar shift in perception after encountering these ideas in his book. The irony in all this is that, in coming to this conclusion, Brown was taken in by one of the more audacious hoaxes of modern times. See **Priory of Sion**.

At the same time, however, *The Da Vinci Code* has played a significant role in bringing current scholarly debates about the origins of Christianity out of the academic community and into popular culture as a whole. Conservative Christian writers have assailed *The Da Vinci Code* for its negative portrayal of the Roman Catholic Church, leading figures in the rejected-knowledge scene have hailed it, and scholars of many different opinions have grappled thoughtfully in print with the issues raised in its pages. The resulting discussions have given Brown's work an impact on modern culture rarely achieved by a popular novel.

Further reading: Baigent et al. 1983, Bock 2004, Brown 2003, Burstein 2004.

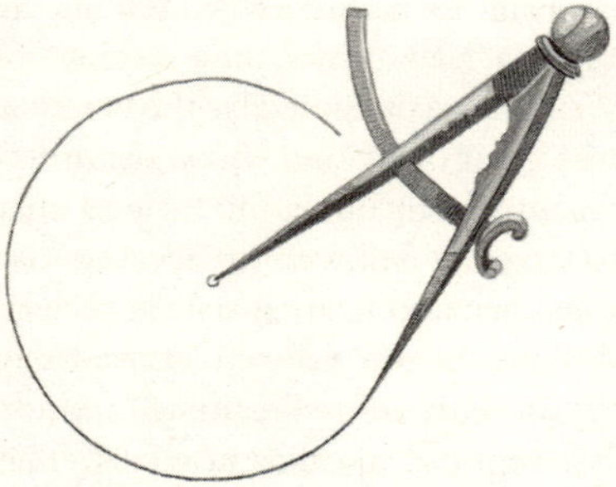

Dead Sea Scrolls

In 1947, Bedouin shepherds found a jar containing seven old scrolls in a cave in the desolate area of Qumran in Jordan, near the northwest shore of the Dead Sea. They sold the scrolls to an antiquities dealer, who sold them to an official of the Syrian Church. Eventually they came into the hands of archeologists, and the first of many excavations at the Qumran cave and the surrounding area began in 1949. These uncovered a community that, according to most scholars, belonged to the Essenes, a Jewish sect mentioned in ancient sources. See **Essenes**.

In all, the remains of around 800 manuscripts were discovered at Qumran, most in fragments. Close to half of the total consists of copies of books from the Old Testament and pseudepigrapha (alternative quasi-biblical books) known before the Qumran discoveries. The rest is made up of previously unknown pseudepigraphic books, extensive commentaries on scripture, legal documents governing the life of the Qumran community, ritual texts, a document called the War Rule, which describes an approaching 40-year war between the forces of light and darkness, and the famous Copper Scroll, which describes 64 places where immense amounts of treasure were said to be hidden.

The great majority of the Dead Sea Scrolls were published within a short time of their discovery, but the texts from Cave 4 at Qumran became the center of an international controversy. The team of scholars assigned to publish these texts released very little, and refused even to show the texts to other scholars. Biblical scholar John Allegro claimed publicly that the team, which included many Roman Catholic members, was deliberately sitting on the texts because they contained material that undermined the Christian religion. His accusations were taken up by other writers, and in 1991 unofficial versions of the unpublished scrolls saw print. This publicity finally forced the scholars to make the disputed texts available to other scholars. Despite the claims of tremendous secrets about Christian origins, the texts proved to contain nothing particularly shocking, and the refusal to release the texts proved to be based on academic politics rather than anything more sinister. See **Christian origins**; **Roman Catholic Church**.

Further reading: Shanks 1992, VanderKam 1994.

Decembrists

On December 14, 1825 a group of officers led 3000 fully armed soldiers into the Senate Square near the center of the imperial capital, St Petersburg, hoping to spark a rising in the Russian army. The attempt failed, and late that afternoon troops loyal to the Tsar opened fire on the would-be revolutionaries, killing many and scattering the rest. Another rising a few days later in the Ukraine met a similar fate. Members of both risings were called "Decembrists" after the date of their attempted revolt. When a government commission investigated, however, it discovered that the rising was the product of secret societies who had been busy for most of a decade.

The first steps toward the Decembrist rising were taken in 1816, when an organization called the Union of Salvation, or Society of True and Faithful Sons of the Fatherland, was organized in St Petersburg. Under the leadership of Pavel Pestel, a veteran of the Napoleonic Wars, the Union began drawing up plans for a constitutional monarchy and the abolition of serfdom. The Union had four degrees of initiation – Friend, Brother, Elder, and Boyar (an old Russian title of nobility), which was reserved for the original founders. Each degree had an elaborate initiation ritual. See **Initiation**.

The Union fell apart in a series of internal disputes in 1817, but in 1818 a new order, the Union of Welfare, was founded by the original core group. The new Union discarded the initiation rituals and focused on a strategy of infiltration, seeking the transformation of Russian society through liberal reforms carried out by an elite of enlightened minds assisting one another in secret. The similarities of this plan to that of the Bavarian Illuminati of the pre-Napoleonic period may not be accidental; the Illuminati had a wide influence in central Europe, and many revolutionary secret societies of the time drew ideas from Adam Weishaupt's failed conspiracy. Many members of the Union and its successor organizations were also Freemasons, at a time when Masonry was among the primary conduits for liberal ideas in Russia. The Union of Welfare also drew inspiration from the Carbonari, the most important political secret society in Europe in the post-Napoleonic period. See **Bavarian Illuminati**; **Carbonari**; **Freemasonry**.

In 1821, disagreements within the Union of Welfare split it into two groups, the Northern Society based in St Petersburg, and the Southern

Society centered in the Ukraine. The Southern Society later consolidated with another secret society with similar aims, the Society of United Slavs. Both societies drew much of their membership from the junior officer corps, men who had served in the Napoleonic Wars and absorbed liberal ideas in Paris during the occupation of France. The Southern Society was the more radical, and took an active role in distributing propaganda among ordinary soldiers; the Northern Society took a less activist approach and spent much of its time in debates about a better Russian society. Neither Society seems to have understood the challenges involved in overthrowing a government, and their plans were poorly drafted and ineffectively executed.

The Decembrist rising itself was a total failure, and the Tsar's government had little difficulty rounding up the ringleaders, executing Pestel and four others, and condemning the rest to prison or internal exile. The severity of the government response, though, had the paradoxical effect of turning the Decembrist failure into something like success. Public opinion, especially among the educated classes, strongly favored the Decembrists' aims of liberal reform, and the government's reaction convinced much of the Russian intelligentsia that revolution rather than reform would be needed to establish a progressive society on Russia's soil. The Decembrist movement thus launched Russia into the spiral of revolt and repression that culminated in the Bolshevik Revolution of 1917. See **Russian revolution**.

Further reading: Mazour 1937, Raeff 1966.

Dionysian mysteries

One of the most popular of the ancient mystery cults, the Dionysian mysteries were celebrated throughout Greece, and spread through most of the Mediterranean world after Alexander the Great's conquests imposed Greek culture on most of the Middle East. The rite was based on the Orphic myth of Dionysus, in which the god was born of Zeus and Persephone, murdered by the Titans, and resurrected in the form of humanity, which was made from the mingled ashes of the Titans and the body of Dionysus. See **Orphism**.

A few scraps of information about the Dionysian mysteries have come down via classical authors. Candidates for initiation were purified with water, dressed in the garments of the god Dionysus, and given over to a conductor, who took them on a journey through darkness. They were symbolically killed by the Titans and placed in the *pastos* or tomb, and heard lamentations for the dead god and the search for his body. Finally the candidates emerged from the *pastos* as the reborn god. All this is classic vegetation myth, with Dionysus as deity of the crops buried with the seed and reborn with the green shoot. The same pattern can be found in most of the other ancient mystery cults, as well as in the Gospel story of the life and death of Jesus of Nazareth. See **Christian origins**; **fertility religion**; **mysteries, ancient**.

In the eighteenth and nineteenth centuries, scholarly writings about the Dionysian mysteries found a ready audience in many secret societies of the time, and secret society members in search of ancient roots for their traditions routinely turned to the Dionysian mysteries, as well as other classical mystery cults. Nineteenth-century books on the origins of Freemasonry generally list the mysteries of Dionysus as one of the ancient sources of the Craft. See **Freemasonry, origins of**.

Discordian movement

One of the odder spiritual movements in America today, the Discordian movement came into being in the late 1950s when founders Gregory Hill and Kerry Thornley evolved a religion centered on Eris, the ancient Greek goddess of chaos, discord, and confusion. According to the *Principia Discordia*, the sacred scripture of the movement, the tenets of Discordianism were originally revealed to Hill and Thornley by a phantom chimpanzee late one night in a Los Angeles-area bowling alley.

Discordianism remained the private joke of a small circle of friends until the 1970s, when two publishing events launched it into the larger world. The 1970 publication of the first widely available edition of the *Principia Discordia*, by the San Francisco publishing house Rip Off Press, began this process. Then the first volume of Robert Shea and Robert Anton Wilson's *Illuminatus!* trilogy, a sprawling satire on conspiracy theories, came out in 1975 and spread Discordian ideas throughout popular culture, where they came to the attention of several avant-garde secret societies, including the Illuminates of Thanateros and Thee Temple ov Psychick Youth. See **Illuminates of Thanateros (IOT)**; **Temple ov Psychick Youth, Thee (TOPY)**.

Discordianism occupies the conceptual space between an alternative religion and an elaborate prank, and attempts to force it to make sense in conventional terms result mostly in additional amusement for Discordians. The doctrines of the faith forbid Discordians from eating hot dog buns on Thursdays, and so every Discordian is required at some point to go out on a Thursday and eat a hot dog, bun and all. Discordian organizations (which might better be termed disorganizations) such as the Paratheoanametamystik-hood of Eris Esoteric (POEE) and the Legion of Dynamic Discord add an additional layer of confusion to the mix; members join more or less by deciding to do so, and carry on whatever activities they feel like – as might be predicted for a movement worshipping a goddess of chaos.

For an extended practical joke masquerading as a religion (or a religion masquerading as an extended practical joke), Discordianism has had a surprisingly widespread impact. Several secret societies beyond the ones already mentioned, and the Chaos Magic movement, a major element of the occult community in the 1980s and 1990s, drew extensively on Discordian ideas.

Further reading: Malaclypse the Younger 1970.

Disinformation

One of the basic methods of concealment used by secret societies is disinformation, the deliberate spreading of false information. Simple concealment is rarely enough to keep a secret safe, since the absence of information rouses curiosity. By inventing a false "secret" and putting it into circulation, though, and the secret is doubly protected; those who think they know a secret rarely keep trying to find it out, and those who believe they have secret knowledge often become emotionally attached to that belief, and cling to the disinformation they have received even in the face of contrary evidence. See **Secrecy**.

A canny awareness of these factors has guided secret societies in using disinformation for centuries, and enemies of secret societies – governments, religious hierarchies, opposing secret societies, among others – have made free use of the same methods. Thus much of what passes for knowledge about secret societies nowadays in popular culture and the media consists of deliberately circulated disinformation of various kinds, some recent and some centuries old.

Secret societies have as many reasons to circulate disinformation as they have secrets to hide. Political and revolutionary secret societies conceal their plans and goals, and often their very existence; criminal secret societies conceal their illegal activities; occult secret societies conceal their teachings; even fraternal secret societies conceal the recognition signs that allow members in good standing to receive benefits from other members. Disinformation usually has a central role in concealing any or all of these.

Beyond this, secret societies have good reason to look older, larger, and more powerful than they are, since this helps attract and retain members. Disinformation plays a central role in this process. Ironically, opponents of secret societies have equally solid incentives to make secret societies look older, larger, and more powerful than they are, since this makes it easier to raise funds and attract supporters for campaigns against the supposed evil influence of secret societies! The result is that the role of secret societies in the western world over the last three centuries, important and dramatic as this has been, has been almost entirely eclipsed in the popular imagination by vast phantoms conjured into being by disinformation campaigns.

Secret society disinformation campaigns range from simple pieces of useful trickery to grand deceptions involving planted documents and years of preparation. Toward the simpler end was a project carried out by the Independent Order of Odd Fellows in the late 1850s, when that society became the target of attacks from conservative Christians after it opened its doors to men of all religions. One of the main forms taken by the attack was the publication of exposés of its signs, passwords, and rituals. The Odd Fellows responded by publishing their own exposés, with deliberate inaccuracies inserted into the signs and passwords, so that nonmembers attempting to gain admittance into Odd Fellows lodges would betray themselves. See **Odd Fellowship**.

At the other end of the spectrum is the spectacularly successful campaign carried out in the 1960s and 1970s by the *Prieuré de Sion* (Priory of Sion), a tiny French secret society. Around 1960, its Grand Master Pierre Plantard began to plant rumors and documents supporting a claim that the Priory had been active since the Middle Ages, and ultimately dated back to the Merovingian kings of sixth-century France, whose last descendant Plantard claimed to be. This disinformation campaign eventually came to the attention of three English writers, resulting in a series of popular books including the bestselling *The Holy Blood and the Holy Grail* (1982), which gave Plantard's campaign international exposure. The English researchers added material of their own to the mix, most notably a claim that Plantard himself was a lineal descendant of Jesus of Nazareth. The resulting revision of history has become a fixture in modern alternative culture and played a significant role in inspiring Dan Brown's popular novel *The Da Vinci Code* (2003). See **Christian origins**; **Knights Templar**; **Merovingians**; **Priory of Sion**.

While the worldwide publicity that came out of Plantard's disinformation campaign is unusual, it is by no means unique, and the methods he used – planting forged documents, circulating rumors, recruiting journalists and writers, and the like – have been standard practice for centuries. Successful pieces of disinformation may be reworked and recycled many times for different purposes, and competing campaigns of disinformation, positive and negative, can repeatedly redefine a single organization. Among the many ironies surrounding disinformation is that those conspiracy theorists who insist most loudly that one secret society or another has maintained total secrecy about its origins and aims are often the most likely to believe disinformation circulated by secret societies, without even taking the time to check it against basic historical facts. See **rejected knowledge**.

Dog Soldiers

A common label used among white people for Native American warrior societies of the Great Plains, the term originated among the Cheyenne tribe of the southern plains, where the Dog Soldier Society was one of the most prestigious of the tribal warrior societies in the middle years of the nineteenth century. Among the Cheyenne, the Dog Soldiers functioned as a tribal police force, enforcing traditional law codes, and also played a central role in tribal warfare.

Several other Great Plains tribes had secret societies that filled somewhat similar social functions, and inevitably the label "Dog Soldiers" was applied to these societies by whites unaware of the enormous cultural differences among native peoples. References to the Dog Soldiers as a single secret society common to all the Plains tribes can still be found in older books on secret societies. See **Native American secret societies**.

Dominionism

A radical political movement within Protestant Christianity, Dominionism (also known as "Dominion theology") emerged in the second half of the twentieth century in the writings of Armenian-American minister Rousas J. Rushdoony, whose *Institutes of Biblical Law* (1973) remains its central book. Rushdoony argued for a biblical legal system and demanded the abolition of democracy and its replacement by a Christian religious dictatorship in which slavery would be legal, women would lose civil rights, and heretics, astrologers, juvenile delinquents, and women (but not men) who had sex before marriage would suffer the death penalty.

Rushdoony's views, like Rushdoony himself, emerged from the Presbyterian branch of Protestant Christianity. Based on the writings of Swiss Protestant reformer John Calvin (1509–64), Presbyterianism has always included a strain of theocratic politics based on the doctrine of post-millennialism, which holds that the Second Coming of Christ will occur after the Millennium, the thousand years of bliss mentioned in the Book of Revelation. The opposing belief, pre-millennialism, puts the Second Coming before the Millennium. The difference may seem as relevant as the number of angels dancing on the head of a pin, but it leads to sweeping divergences in strategy. Pre-millenarians believe that Christ will cause the Millennium to happen himself, while post-millenarians believe that the task of bringing about the Millennium is up to the Christian churches. To radical post-millenarians such as Rushdoony and his followers, the process involves political action or revolutionary violence.

These views, known as Christian Reconstructionism, remained the province of a small coterie of right-wing intellectuals until the early 1990s. The failure of right-wing Christianity to gain more than token elements of their agenda from Republican administrations between 1980 and 1992, and the sweeping Democratic victory in the 1992 elections, sent many religious radicals in search of a movement less willing to compromise with the status quo. A significant minority of them found it in Rushdoony's views.

The most influential among overtly Dominionist organizations is the Coalition on Revival (COR), founded in 1984 by Rev. Jay Grimstead with the assistance of two major figures in the political wing of the Protestant churches, Rev. Tim LaHaye and Rev. Francis A. Schaeffer. Its founding document, the "Manifesto-Covenant," pledges the signers (60 members of the COR steering committee) to die, if necessary, to replace American democracy with a Christian dictatorship. Headquartered in Mountain View, California, COR trains ministers and other leadership figures in political activism, and produces and circulates propaganda supporting the abolition of the Bill of Rights and other constitutional freedoms.

The Dominionist movement nonetheless remains a relatively small faction among American Christians, and has a negligible presence outside the United States. Even within America its influence is fading, as the percentage of Americans who belong to a Protestant church has declined steadily from 72 percent in the late 1970s to 49 percent today. Like many right-wing Christian movements, it denounces secret societies such as Freemasonry but functions as a secret society itself, pursuing its subversive political agenda mostly in secret. See **Fundamentalism**.

Further reading: Barron 1992, Diamond 1995.

Druid Circle of the Universal Bond

One of the most influential Druid groups in the twentieth century, the Druid Circle of the Universal Bond claims to date from 1717, when an assembly of Druids from all over Britain met at the Apple Tree Tavern in London and established the Universal Bond. Its roots, again according to its traditional history, go back via a Mount Haemus Grove at Oxford, founded in 1245, to surviving groups of ancient Celtic Druids. Like all other stories of direct descent from the ancient Druids, this one has no evidence to support it, and may be considered another example of the common secret society habit of retrospective recruitment. No record of a Druid grove at Oxford has yet surfaced from before modern times. The 1717 meeting at the Apple Tree Tavern is plausible enough, since the Druid Revival was in its earliest stages at that time and the Apple Tree was used as a meeting place by several other secret societies active in London then, but even so, no evidence has yet surfaced to support the claim that it happened. See **Druid Revival**; **Druids**; **retrospective recruitment**.

The traceable history of the Druid Circle of the Universal Bond begins around 1904, with George Watson MacGregor-Reid, a naturopathic physician and Universalist minister in London. MacGregor-Reid's religious interests extended to Buddhism and the teachings of the ancient Druids, and sometime in the first decade of the twentieth century he began celebrating the summer solstice at Stonehenge with members of his congregation. Over the following two decades Druid activities took up a progressively larger part of MacGregor-Reid's work, until his church renamed itself the Druid Circle of the Universal Bond sometime in the 1920s. By this time, its membership included several members or former members of secret societies descended from the Hermetic Order of the Golden Dawn, and MacGregor-Reid's son Robert became an initiate of one of these societies during the 1920s. See **Hermetic Order of the Golden Dawn**.

In 1946 MacGregor-Reid died and a new minister attempted to bring his church back into conformity with the Universalist Church. In response, a number of members including Robert MacGregor-Reid quit the church and founded the Druid Circle of the Universal Bond as an independent body. For the next 20 years it was the most influential Druid group in England, with a membership that included poet and artist Ross Nichols and Gerald Gardner, the probable founder of modern Wicca. On Robert MacGregor-Reid's death in 1964 the order split, with Thomas Maughan becoming its new Chosen Chief and Ross Nichols, who had been Scribe under Robert MacGregor-Reid, breaking away to found his own Druid society, the Order of Bards Ovates and Druids. See **Order of Bards Ovates and Druids (OBOD)**; **Wicca**.

The Druid Circle of the Universal Bond remains active today, though it remains aloof from other Druid organizations and its public activities are limited.

Further reading: Nichols 1992.

Druid Revival

One of the oldest continuous traditions of pagan nature religion in the western world, the Druid Revival began in England in the early eighteenth century, and had essentially no connection to the ancient Druids whose name and image inspired it. Several Druid Revival groups have claimed direct descent from the original Celtic Druids, but all the available evidence suggests that these latter were extinct by the ninth century CE. See **Druids**.

The roots of the Druid Revival lie instead in the rediscovery by northern European nations of their own past during the sixteenth and seventeenth centuries. The ancient Druids were mentioned in classical sources such as Caesar's *Gallic Wars*, and Druids accordingly began to appear in European histories, sometimes as ignorant heathens but surprisingly often as wise custodians of a profound spiritual heritage. National pride and the lingering Renaissance faith in a primeval wisdom from the beginning of time fed into this latter image, which made attempts to lay claim to the heritage of the Druids inevitable.

The first such claim seems to have been made by the Irish philosopher John Toland (1670–1722). A radical who invented the word "pantheism" for his own beliefs, Toland founded at least one secret society, the Chevaliers of Jubilation, and the rituals in his *Pantheisticon* (1720) were at least intended to be used by another. Two modern Druid groups, the Druid Circle of the Universal Bond and the Order of Bards Ovates and Druids, claim that he also became the head of a Druid order founded in London's Apple Tree Tavern in 1717. The claim is not implausible – any number of secret societies and odd clubs came together in London and elsewhere during the first half of the eighteenth century – but no documentation has yet surfaced to support it. What is certain is that Toland was fascinated by the ancient Druids, and believed that they taught the pantheist wisdom he also traced in the pages of the *Corpus Hermeticum*. He never completed his planned history of the Druids, but his influence helped make Druids popular among British radicals. See **Chevaliers of Jubilation**; **Druid Circle of the Universal Bond**; **Hermeticism**; **Order of Bards Ovates and Druids**; **Toland, John**.

The most important figure in the eighteenth-century Druid Revival was William Stukeley (1687–1765). One of the founders of British archeology, Stukeley became convinced that the ancient Druids taught a profound and mystical religion that foreshadowed Anglican Christianity. By the 1720s he identified himself as a Druid; by the 1750s, he was the chief of the Mount Haemus Grove, a group of Druidically inclined friends who met at his home in Highgate, near London. His books on Stonehenge and Avebury, published in 1740 and

1743 respectively, put Druids on the cultural map all across Britain and made the explosion of Druid secret societies over the next century all but inevitable.

Stukeley's Mount Haemus Grove, which may or may not have been a continuation of the shadowy Druid Order headed by Toland and may or may not have continued after Stukeley's time, is the only documented Druid group from the middle of the eighteenth century. By the end of the same century, though, historians of the Revival are on firmer ground. The Ancient Order of Druids, the first solidly documented modern Druid society, was founded in 1781, probably by a London carpenter named Henry Hurle. In 1792 Edward Williams (1747–1826), a Welsh poet who adopted the Druid name Iolo Morganwg (Iolo of Glamorgan), celebrated "ancient Welsh bardic ceremonies" of his own invention on Primrose Hill in London, and over the next few decades succeeded in having them adopted by Welsh *gorseddau* (traditional bardic competitions), which still use them today. In 1833 the United Ancient Order of Druids (UAOD) broke away from the Ancient Order of Druids and began a process of growth that by the second half of the nineteenth century made them the largest Druid organization in the world. Finally, 1874 saw English Freemason and occultist Robert Wentworth Little (1840–78) found the Ancient and Archaeological Order of Druids (AAOD). Many of these groups spread outside Britain; the UAOD became a significant presence in the American, Australian, and central European secret society scene within a decade of its founding, while the AAOD chartered an American branch, the Ancient Order of Druids in America (AODA), in 1912. See **Ancient and Archaeological Order of Druids (AAOD)**; **Ancient Order of Druids**; **Ancient Order of Druids in America (AODA)**; **United Ancient Order of Druids (UAOD)**.

Toland's pantheism and Stukeley's liberal Anglican Christianity defined the spectrum of religious beliefs within which early Druid groups positioned themselves. In the course of the nineteenth century, however, theories of astronomical religion and fertility religion spread from the world of scholarship into British popular culture, and into the Druid Revival. As a result, several nineteenth-century Druid orders embraced what they thought was the pagan religion of their ancestors; most of these contained some Christian elements, but in many cases those were reshaped in ways Christian orthodoxy found difficult to tolerate. Thus the Druid Gorsedd of Pontypridd, one of many Welsh Druid groups that traced their origin to Iolo Morganwg's work, espoused a theology that fused astronomical and fertility religion and redefined Christianity in Druid terms, turning Jesus of Nazareth into a pagan symbol of the sun and the phallus. See **astronomical religion; fertility religion**.

The rise of Theosophy and other explicitly non-Christian occult traditions in the late nineteenth century had a large impact on the occult end of the Druid Revival, and so did the collapse of the Hermetic Order of the Golden Dawn in internecine struggles after 1900, a process which sent many former Golden Dawn initiates into other occult secret societies. Druidry received a sizeable fraction of these, resulting in hybrid orders such as the Ancient Order of Druid Hermetists and the Cabbalistic Order of Druids. Similarly, French Druid societies borrowed material from the lively French occult scene of the late nineteenth and early twentieth centuries, just as American Druid societies of the same period made connections with other esoteric secret societies and exchanged rituals, practices, and teachings. See **Hermetic Order of the Golden Dawn; Theosophical Society**.

The second half of the twentieth century saw the Druid Revival emerge from the underworld of secret societies and become a public presence through much of the western world. Two organizations, the Reformed Druids of North America (RDNA) and the Order of Bards Ovates and Druids (OBOD), led the way in this process. The RDNA had one of the most unlikely origins of any Druid organization, which is saying something; founded as an undergraduate prank at a small American college, it mutated into a thriving tradition of nature spirituality to which a large fraction of modern American Druid groups trace their beginnings. The OBOD, by contrast, was founded as a schism from the Druid Circle of the Universal Bond, one of the most influential Druid groups in Britain; after the death of its founder Ross Nichols, the OBOD went dormant for a period, then revived under its current chief Philip Carr-Gomm and rapidly became the most influential Druid order in the western world.

Ironically, this widespread popularity came just as the Druid Revival came under attack from within the modern Druid community. The Celtic Reconstructionist movement emerged in the 1980s among neopagans who based their systems of thought and practice on currently accepted scholarship about ancient Celtic paganism. Never more than a small faction among Druids, the Celtic Reconstructionists succeeded in polarizing the Druid community with strident attacks on Druid Revival traditions as "fake Druidry." The resulting quarrels took up a great deal of bandwidth on the Internet but did little to impact the popularity of Druid Revival groups. At the time of writing, the Druid Revival movement remains a significant presence in the occult and pagan communities throughout most of the western world.

Further reading: Green 1997, Greer 2006, Nichols 1992.

Druids

An ancient Celtic caste of loremasters and wizards, the Druids have been a favorite subject of speculation, myth-making, and retrospective recruitment since European intellectuals rediscovered them in the seventeenth century. Nearly everything that currently passes for knowledge about the Druids in popular culture came out of this fertile soil of misinformation, or out of the Druid Revival, a modern spiritual movement inspired by the ancient Druids, which took shape in Britain in the eighteenth century. See **Druid Revival**; **retrospective recruitment**.

Very little information survives about the ancient Druids, and much of what does exist is incomplete, obscure, and contradictory. Some 30 quotations in Greek and Roman authors, a somewhat larger body of Irish legend and saints' lives dating from centuries after the Druids ceased to exist, and the ambiguous evidence of archeology and comparative religion provide a very uncertain foundation of fact. According to these sources, Druids could be found in Gaul, Britain, and Ireland, but apparently not among the Celts of central Europe, the Iberian Peninsula, or Asia Minor. Some sources refer to them as philosophers, others call them wizards; modern scholars often refer to them as priests, but none of the contemporary sources describe them as such. Rather, they taught religion and philosophy, judged disputes, recited sacred verses at sacrificial rituals, and cast spells.

Would-be Druids underwent a course of study that lasted up to 20 years and required them to memorize a great deal of material in verse form, including lore about theology, astronomy, divination, and natural history. A strict taboo forbade Druids from writing down the secrets of their caste, though one Roman source comments that they used the Greek alphabet for ordinary correspondence; one unexpected confirmation of this latter claim is the fact that the name of Belenos, the Druid sun god, adds up to 365 – the number of days in a year – in Greek letters. See **Gematria**.

As the Roman Empire expanded into Gaul and Britain in the two centuries surrounding the start of the Common Era, the Druids played a significant role in rallying Celtic resistance and so were targeted for destruction after Rome's victory. Sources from the third and fourth centuries CE mention the occasional Druid or Druidess, but it is impossible to be sure whether these refer to direct descendants of the old Druids or not. In Ireland and Scotland, where Roman power never established itself, the Druids remained an active presence until the coming of Christianity. The last Druids mentioned in authentic sources lived among the Picts in present-day Scotland in the ninth century, and tried unsuccessfully to stop their people from converting to the new faith.

From then until the sixteenth century, Druids were essentially forgotten in the western world. Their rediscovery came as the Renaissance spread into northern Europe and encouraged people in Germany, France, and Britain to explore their own history. References to the Druids from classical literature, and in the pseudo-classical forgeries of Annius of Viterbo, an Italian monk who manufactured an imaginary history of northern Europe full of Druids and heroes, brought the old Celtic wizards back into prominence. By the early 1500s French, German, and Scottish historians had adopted the Druids as a colorful part of their national histories. England took a little longer to climb aboard the Druidic bandwagon, but by the later years of Elizabeth I's reign Druids had found their way into Holinshed's *Chronicles* and William Camden's *Britannia*, the two most influential British histories of their time.

Thus the Druids reached the eighteenth century, the dawn of the golden age of secret societies, as prime candidates for retrospective recruitment. First off the starting line was John Toland, who drafted them into service in the first decades of the new century as antecedents for the freethinking pantheism he helped introduce to the British cultural scene. His contemporary William Stukeley, the leading light of the eighteenth-century Druid Revival, remade them into the ancestors of his own brand of liberal Anglicanism. John Cleland – more renowned as the author of *Fanny Hill*, the most famous work of pornography in the English language – entered the lists in 1766 with a book arguing that the ancient Druids were the ancestors of the Freemasons, launching a theory of Masonic origins that still has its followers today. See **Freemasonry, origins of**; **Toland, John**.

The Druid Revival itself played a crucial role in introducing the ancient Druids to modern times. By the end of the eighteenth century Druid-inspired secret societies existed in Britain and America, and had begun the process of making the white-robed Druid with his golden sickle and mistletoe an instantly recognizable figure in popular culture. Druid gatherings at Stonehenge at the summer solstice apparently began sometime during the nineteenth century, adding another element to the popular image of the Druid.

The emergence of the neo-pagan movement in the second half of the twentieth century launched a new round of retrospective recruitment as many of the inventors of newly minted pagan faiths turned to the ancient Druids as a source of inspiration and a locus for claims of authenticity. Inevitably, the same "family tradition" origin stories circulated by Wiccans of the same period sprang up in many Druid groups, and were used to justify further redefinitions of the ancient Druids. The Druidic proto-pantheists, proto-

Anglicans and proto-Freemasons invented in the Druid Revival era made room for proto-hippies in the 1970s, proto-shamans in the 1980s, and proto-Traditionalists in the 1990s. While some of the most prominent Druid Revival groups of the present time disclaim any direct connection with the ancient Druids, ideas about Druids in popular culture throughout the western world remain remarkably confused at present. See **origin stories**; **Traditionalism**.

Further reading: Green 1997, Piggott 1975.

DUALISM

The belief that the universe is governed by competing powers of good and evil, dualism has some role in most ancient mythologies but first took center stage in the teachings of Zoroaster, the prophet of the Persian religion of Zoroastrianism. According to the Zoroastrian faith, the world is partly the creation of Ahura Mazda or Ormuzd, the god of light and goodness, and partly the creation of Angra Mainyu or Ahriman, the spirit of darkness and evil. The history of the world is the story of the struggle between these two powers, which is fated to end in Ahura Mazda's victory and Angra Mainyu's total defeat. These ideas were adopted in modified form into the Jewish faith after the Persians released the Jews from their captivity in Babylon, and became part of Christianity and Islam from the beginning.

The Gnostics of the early Common Era inherited the modified dualism of the Judeo-Christian tradition and transformed it into a teaching more radical even than Zoroaster's. To most of the Gnostics, the world and everything in it, except for a minority of human souls, had been created by the Demiurge, an evil and ignorant power who fancied himself lord of the cosmos. Certain human souls were sparks of light from another universe who had been trapped inside the Demiurge's corrupt cosmos, and the Gnostic faith claimed to offer them a way to escape from this universe and return to their true home in the World of Light. See **Gnosticism**.

These views blended with many other viewpoints in the theological free-for-all of the late classical world, and gave rise to two versions of dualism shared by later Gnostic sects such as the Manichaeans, Bogomils, and Cathars. One version, called "absolute dualism" by modern scholars, returned to the Zoroastrian vision of good and evil powers existing from the beginning of time; the other, "mitigated dualism," accepted the Judeo-Christian idea of a single good god but made the fallen archangel Satan into God's rival and the evil ruler of the material world. Until the fourteenth century, when the last Cathars were exterminated in France, these views had a sizeable following in the western world. See **Cathars**.

Thereafter the modified dualism of conventional Christianity was in the ascendant until modern times. The first modern Gnostic churches in France, which emerged in the nineteenth century, adopted various forms of dualism, some more extreme than others, while the esoteric wing of the Masonic movement during the second half of the same century borrowed ideas from Zoroastrian dualism to expand the spiritual dimensions of Freemasonry. Dualist approaches faced a serious challenge from monist beliefs of the sort promoted by the Theosophical Society and its many offshoots, but in the smorgasbord of spiritual teachings that characterized the late nineteenth and early twentieth centuries dualism was nearly always an option on the menu. See **Freemasonry**; **Theosophical Society**.

The contemporary revival of Gnosticism that began with the discovery of the Nag Hammadi Gnostic library in Egypt in 1945, ironically, has often found classic Gnostic dualism too hot to handle, and most self-proclaimed Gnostics in the contemporary spiritual scene promote a monist spirituality worlds away from the beliefs of their supposed forebears. A handful of modern Gnostic groups affirm some version of dualism at present. A far larger dualist movement, with beliefs that closely parallel those of the ancient Gnostics, is the Christian Identity movement, a racist offshoot of Christianity that defines "Aryan" peoples (that is, those descended from western Europeans) as true humans and all other peoples as soulless creations of Satan as demiurge. These views have close parallels in the neo-Nazi underground as well. See **Christian Identity**; **neo-Nazi secret societies**.

E

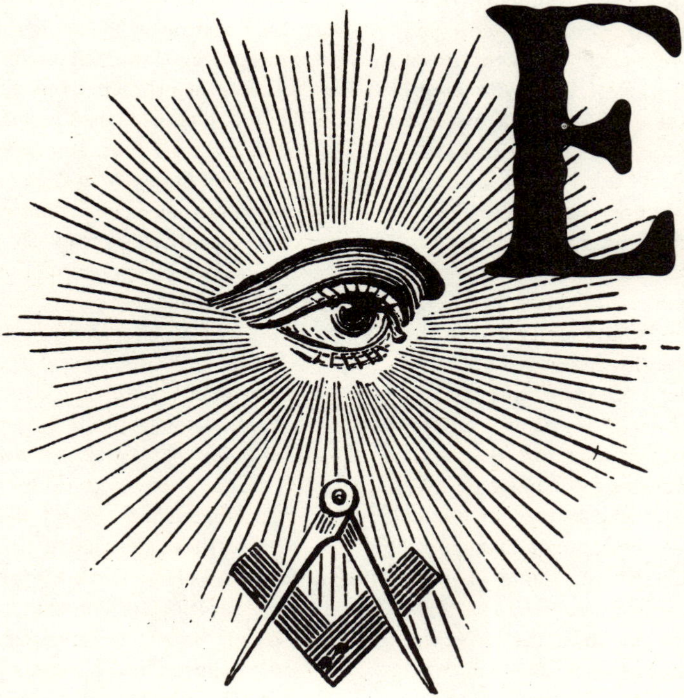

E Clampus Vitus

Among the most colorful of nineteenth-century American secret societies, E Clampus Vitus was founded by goldminers in the frontier town of Mokelumne Hill, California in 1851, in the midst of the Gold Rush. At that time most of northern California was full of little mining towns and camps whose populations shifted constantly. The Freemasons and Odd Fellows, the largest American secret societies of the time, had established lodges in many of the larger mining towns, and this inspired a group of Mokelumne Hill miners to parody these relatively formal rites with an order better suited to the rough humor and lawlessness of the frontier. E Clampus Vitus was the result. See **Freemasonry**; **Odd Fellowship**.

Meetings of E Clampus Vitus chapters – which could be held "at any time before or after a full moon" – were held in saloons, and announced by the braying of the Hewgag, a makeshift trumpet. Inside, the officers – the Noble Grand Humbug, the Royal Gyascutis, the Clamps Petrix, the Clamps Matrix, the Grand Imperturbable Hangman, and many others (as all Clampers are, by definition, officers) – presided over meetings well lubricated with beer and cheap whiskey. Initiation rituals for PBCs (Poor Blind Candidates) consisted mostly of raucous pranks. Once initiated, each candidate was given the official title of "Chairman of the Most Important Committee." Clampers also marched in parades, with a billy goat for their mascot and a banner consisting of a woman's hoop skirt and the motto, "This is the flag we fight under."

These antics coexisted with more serious activities. Life in the California mining towns was harsh and often violent, as men from every corner of the world labored and fought for their share of gold. The robust humor of the Clampers helped bring a spirit of community to the Gold Rush country. Clampers raised money to help widows and orphans, and were quick to respond when fire or flood destroyed towns and left people homeless. This combination of raucous humor and practical charity made E Clampus Vitus the largest secret society in northern California within a decade of its founding. As the gold was mined out and the mining towns dwindled, however, E Clampus Vitus faded as well, and the Hewgag announced a meeting of the original order for the last time in Quincy, California in 1916.

Pride in California's history rescued E Clampus Vitus from oblivion, however. In 1931, a new chapter of E Clampus Vitus was founded in San Francisco with the help of Adam Lee Moore, one of the few surviving members of the original order. In the years that followed the revived E Clampus Vitus spread throughout northern California and into Oregon, Nevada, and Arizona. The new order retained many of the customs and traditions of its forebear, though public drunkenness was (and is) frowned on, and interest in Gold Rush history is one of the requirements for initiation. Clampers nowadays wear red shirts, in memory of the red woolen union suits of yore, and vests bedecked with pins, patches, and medals made of tin can lids. Calling itself "a historical drinking society" (or "a drinking historical society"), it maintains a lively presence in the old mining country of northern California as of this writing.

Eagles

See **Fraternal Order of Eagles (FOE)**.

EARTH CHANGES

The idea that vast catastrophes have swept the earth in the distant past can be found in many of the ancient mythologies and philosophical traditions of the world. Plato's famous dialogue *Timaeus* speaks for traditional lore worldwide when it comments,

> There have been, and will be again, many destructions of mankind arising out of many causes; the greatest have been brought about by the agencies of fire and water, and other lesser ones by innumerable lesser causes. (Plato 1961, p. 1157)

Despite this, the theme of earth changes – past or future – played a very small role in occult traditions and secret society teachings until the last quarter of the nineteenth century. Most people in the western world before that time accepted the historical reality of the story of Noah in the Book of Genesis, and references to great floods and the changing of the earth's landscape usually referred back to that belief. The nineteenth century, however, saw nearly all geologists accept the theory of uniformitarianism, which rejected the idea of global catastrophes and argued that the earth's surface had been shaped by the same slow processes of mountain building, volcanism, erosion, and deposition that can be seen in the present-day world.

Two bestselling books by Irish-American author and politician Ignatius Donnelly (1831–1901) reintroduced the concept of catastrophic earth changes to popular culture. His *Atlantis: The Antediluvian World* (1882) argued that the lost continent of Atlantis had actually existed in the middle of the Atlantic Ocean, while his *Ragnarok: The Age of Fire and Gravel* (1883) proposed that the Ice Ages had been caused by a collision between the earth and a giant comet. His theories about Atlantis helped inspire Helena Petrovna Blavatsky (1831–91), the founder of the Theosophical Society; Blavatsky's second major book, *The Secret Doctrine* (1888), put Atlantis at center stage of a visionary prehistory of the earth. For good measure, Blavatsky added the lost continents of the Imperishable Sacred Land, Hyperborea, and Lemuria to her system; all but the first, she claimed, had been destroyed by vast cataclysms that completely changed the distribution of land and water on the earth's surface. See **Atlantis**; **Blavatsky, Helena Petrovna**; **Lemuria**; **Theosophical Society**.

The immense popularity of Theosophy during the century from 1875 to 1975 guaranteed these ideas a privileged place in the occult societies and alternative speculations of the twentieth century. Another crucial role was played by American clairvoyant Edgar Cayce (1877–1945), whose utterings in trance included a great deal of material about Atlantis. Cayce seems to have introduced the idea that another round of catastrophic earth changes was in the offing; he predicted that Atlantis would surface in 1968 or 1969, as part of a series of catastrophes that would plunge the western half of North America beneath the waves by 1998.

Long before these prophecies disproved themselves, the idea of an imminent wave of earth changes had spread throughout alternative circles, especially but not only in America. The Ascended Masters teachings, a diffuse but widespread American occult movement, proved a particularly receptive audience for earth-changes theories, and the New Age movement provided another venue for these ideas. As these currents spread, and the rejected knowledge industry became a major influence on popular culture, the idea that the world was approaching a series of vast geological catastrophes became common throughout the world. See **Ascended Masters teachings**; **New Age movement**; **rejected knowledge**.

These trends drew strength from the collapse of strict uniformitarianism in the earth sciences, beginning in the 1970s. Two major changes in scientific opinion heralded this shift. The first was the discovery of evidence suggesting that the great wave of extinctions at the end of the Cretaceous period some 70 million years ago, at the end of the age of the dinosaurs, was caused by a collision between the earth and a large asteroid. The second was the realization that much of northwest North America had been reshaped at the end of the Ice Ages by a series of immense floods of glacial meltwater let loose by the repeated breaching of ice dams in the area of modern Montana. Both showed that large-scale catastrophes had happened in the earth's past, and thus provided credibility to the idea that others might occur in the future.

The emergence of the "new catastrophism," as it has been called, resulted in a great deal of re-examination of the earth's past and a renewed willingness on the part of historians to consider the impact of climate changes, volcanic eruptions, and similar events on the human past. It also lent additional force to the warnings by environmental scientists that climate change driven by human maltreatment of the global environment might cause massive disruptions to industrial society in the relatively near future. Inevitably, though, it also provided ammunition for visionaries of various kinds who claimed advance knowledge of less credible catastrophes. The much-ballyhooed Y2K problem – the anticipated failure of computer systems worldwide to handle the transition from 1999 to 2000 – was only the largest of many false alarms to grab headlines in the western world, and divert attention from less colorful but more likely threats to the survival of industrial society.

As global temperatures rise into un-precedented territory in the early years of the twenty-first century, the possibility of widespread earth changes can hardly be dismissed. To name only one possibility, the breakup of the West Antarctic ice sheet – a process that some scientists believe has already begun – would raise sea levels 16 to 20 feet (5 to 6 meters) worldwide, drowning more than a hundred major cities. Still, such possibilities need to be assessed carefully in the light of known fact and physical possibility, and the often inaccurate claims of popular literature on such subjects may not be the best guide in these challenging times. See **Antarctica**.

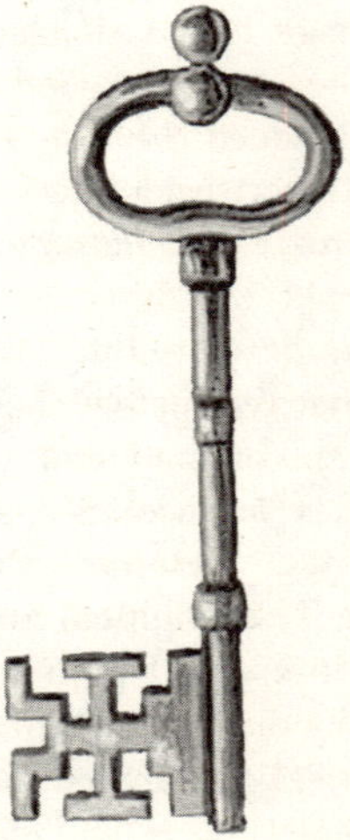

Easter Island

One of the most isolated islands in the world, this small triangular patch of land in the middle of the western Pacific is famous for the towering stone statues, or *moai*, that face inward from the island's shores. As with so many of the great works of Third World peoples, many popular writers in the industrial world refused to believe that the *moai* could have been made by the people of Easter Island, and in the twentieth century Easter Island and its statues were taken up into the canon of rejected knowledge and included in many speculations about the world's past. Along with Nan Madol, an overgrown stone city on the Micronesian archipelago most of the way across the Pacific, it has often been identified as a surviving outcropping of the lost continent of Mu. See **Mu**; **rejected knowledge**.

The islanders, who speak a dialect of the Polynesian language, say that their ancestors came by sea from a tropical island far to the west, led by a chieftain named Hotu Matu'a. After many years, another group of voyagers reached Easter Island and established itself as an aristocracy, the Hanau Eepe, a term sometimes translated as "Long Ears." Under the Hanau Eepe, the common folk of Easter Island were made to set up the great statues. Finally the commoners revolted, killed all but one of the Hanau Eepe, and destroyed many of the statues.

This account is likely based on history, but recent research has uncovered another dimension to the end of the Hanau Eepe's rule. When human beings first arrived there before 700 CE, Easter Island was covered with trees. As the native population expanded, more and more of the island was cleared of trees, and the island's people became dependent on catching fish and dolphins in deep waters that could only be reached by dugout canoes. Eventually the demand for new farmland and logs for canoes led to deforestation, severe soil erosion, and the collapse of the island's agricultural economy. With no large trees remaining, the deepwater fisheries could no longer be reached, and warfare and cannibalism broke out on the overcrowded island. The revolt against the Hanau Eepe may well have occurred in the midst of this crisis. The statues of Easter Island thus offer not a relic of alien contact or lost civilizations, but a warning to today's industrial society about the risks of ignoring ecological reality.

Further reading: Diamond 2004.

Egypt

The lost civilization *par excellence* in the imagination of western cultures, ancient Egypt has had a huge impact on secret societies and alternative history from the eighteenth century onward. Even in ancient times, Egypt had a reputation as the home of magic; a saying from the Talmud claims that all the world's magic consists of ten parts, of which nine were given to Egypt and the remaining tenth divided among all the other nations of the world. The central role of ancient Egyptian tradition in the formation of western magic, and the importance of magical practices in ancient Egyptian religion, give such claims a grounding in fact. See **lost civilizations**; **Magic**.

According to currently accepted archeological theory, ancient Egyptian civilization took shape around 4000 BCE, rising out of tribal cultures that flourished along the banks of the Nile for millennia before that time. Some alternative archeologists have argued that a handful of Egyptian relics, including the famous Sphinx of Giza, may be several thousand years older; the evidence for this is inconclusive but intriguing, and the existence of an older proto-Egyptian civilization – perhaps in the years before 6000 BCE, before the Sahara became a desert and when northern Africa was a vast grassland full of antelope, zebra, and lions – would fit easily into the prehistory of the Middle East.

Definite history begins in Egypt around 3200 BCE, when Narmer, founder of the First Dynasty, united the Nile valley from the First Cataract to the Delta into a single kingdom. Many of the central themes of ancient Egyptian civilization throughout its long lifespan, from the cult of the dead and the role of the great temple priesthoods to the regalia of the pharaohs and the pervasive presence of magic in every aspect of ancient Egyptian life, were firmly established within a few centuries of Narmer's time. Isolated from neighboring cultures by the desolate sands of the Sahara, and shaped by a traditional philosophy that looked back to *zep tepi*, the "First Time," when the gods had established the laws necessary for human life, Egypt had an immense conservatism that preserved many of its features from prehistory until the final collapse of Egyptian civilization in late Roman times.

Nearly two centuries of hard work by archeologists and linguists, beginning with the first successful translation of a hieroglyphic text by Jean François Champollion in 1822, provide a detailed picture of the history, culture, religion, magic, and daily life of the ancient Egyptians. Ironically, though, many occultists in the western world, and nearly all of the current alternative-history community, derive their ideas about Egypt from speculations from well before Champollion's time, and include misinformation discredited more than a century ago. The century or so before Champollion's work, in fact, was the great seedtime of modern inaccuracies about ancient Egypt.

The land of the Nile had been a focus of strange beliefs since the Renaissance. The *Corpus Hermeticum*, a collection of mystical documents dating from the early Common Era but backdated by its unknown authors to the time of the pharaohs, and the *Hieroglyphica of Horapollo*, a late Roman book claiming (inaccurately) to reveal the secret of Egyptian writing, had become wildly popular as early as the fifteenth century, and generated a range of misperceptions that remain active in alternative circles today. See **Emblems**; **Hermeticism**.

Much eighteenth-century speculation about Egypt, though, centered on Freemasonry, for the same period saw the manufacture of new Masonic degrees reach its all-time peak, and each freshly minted degree needed its own origin story and mythological symbolism. Ancient Egypt, as fashionable as it was mysterious, provided a tempting option. Pseudo-Egyptian rites in Masonry invented during these years included the Crata Repoa, which surfaced in 1770; Cagliostro's Egyptian Rite, founded in 1778; the Rite of Misraim, probably founded in 1805; and the Rite of Memphis, probably founded in 1814. Wolfgang Amadeus Mozart's Masonic operetta *The Magic Flute*, first performed in 1791, is a good snapshot of the age, with its mixture of Masonic and faux Egyptian symbolism, surrounding a fairy-tale plot. See **Crata Repoa**; **Freemasonry**; **high degrees**; **Rite of Memphis**; **Rite of Misraim**.

These rites pioneered the redefinition of ancient Egypt as the original homeland of early nineteenth-century occultism, and made Egypt a feature of origin stories and attempts at retrospective recruitment for two centuries thereafter. Many later secret societies borrowed just enough newly discovered material from scholarly sources to put new paint over the old misconceptions. Thus the Hermetic Order of the Golden Dawn, the premier English occult secret society in the late nineteenth century, borrowed material from the recently translated *Egyptian Book of the Dead* for its rituals, and the Ancient Mystical Order Rosae Crucis (AMORC), an American occult order founded in 1925, adopted the "heretic pharaoh" Akhenaten – then at the center of media attention due to the recent discovery of the tomb of his son Tutankhamun – as one of its forefathers. See **Akhenaten**; **Ancient Mystical Order Rosae Crucis (AMORC)**; **Hermetic Order of the Golden Dawn**; **origin stories**; **retrospective recruitment**.

The recycling of misinformation from late eighteenth- and early nineteenth-century pseudo-Egyptian rites has continued to the present. Numerous occult secret societies still teach that ancient Egyptian temples offered initiation ceremonies like those of high degree Masonry, though the *seshtau* – "that which is hidden," the secret inner rituals of ancient Egypt's temples – are known, and include nothing of the kind. Many occult orders, similarly, claim that their magical teachings were practiced in the time of the pharaohs, even though a wealth of ancient Egyptian magical lore has survived, and has almost nothing in common with the nineteenth- and twentieth-century occultism offered by today's magical secret societies. See **mysteries, ancient**.

The great irony of the contemporary flood of misinformation about ancient Egypt, as this suggests, is that authentic Egyptian traditions and spiritual teachings are readily available. The realities of ancient Egyptian magic and religion are covered in detail in hundreds of books in the scholarly literature, and the Hermetic and Gnostic traditions, both of which originated in Egypt and drew deeply from the old Egyptian lore, are also available. There is no need for those interested in classic Egyptian spirituality to settle for modern fabrications. On the other hand, neo-Egyptian systems like those of the Golden Dawn also have their value, so long as they are recognized for what they are – creations of a later age, not authentic survivals of ancient Egyptian mysteries.

Further reading: Hornung 2001.

Elect Cohens

The most influential of eighteenth-century French occult secret societies, the *Élus Coens* or Elect Cohens were the creation of Martinez de Pasqually, a Portuguese occultist of Jewish ancestry who arrived in France sometime before 1754. In that year he established his first lodge in Montpellier, calling it a lodge of Scottish Judges (*Juges Ecossais*). By 1760, when he founded a lodge in Toulouse, the term Elect Cohen first appeared. In 1766 he went to Paris to try to interest the Grand Lodge of France in his system. The attempt failed, largely because the Grand Lodge itself was wracked by disastrous political quarrels at that time. While in Paris, however, Pasqually met Jean-Baptiste Willermoz, a Mason and mystic from Lyons, who became the new system's most effective promoter, helping Pasqually establish his rite through much of France.

The Freemasonry of Knight Masons Elect Cohens of the Universe, to give the rite its full title, was in part simply another colorful system of high degree Freemasonry, like so many popular rites in late eighteenth-century France. Behind it, though, lay a complex and distinctive philosophy with roots in Gnostic traditions, and an equally distinctive system of ceremonial magic. Pasqually's one book, *Traité de la Réintégration des Etres* (*Treatise on the Reintegration of Beings*), outlines a Gnostic cosmology in which the material world was created as a prison for the fallen angels under the guardianship of Adam. In violation of the divine will, Adam desired to create beings in his own image. He and Eve, his first creation, mated without God's blessing and produced Cain; then, repenting, he sought divine blessing and fathered first Abel, who was killed by Cain, and then Seth. This third son received all the divine wisdom once possessed by Adam. Later, the descendants of Cain and Seth intermarried to produce today's humanity, but a continuous line of "Friends of Wisdom" preserved fragments of Seth's knowledge. Pasqually claimed to be the latest of the Friends of Wisdom. See **Gnosticism**; **high degrees**.

Pasqually's system of magic was evasively called *La Chose* ("The Thing"). It consisted of secret rituals performed by each high-ranking member on the days of the spring and autumn equinoxes, to conjure the intelligences of the spiritual realm into visible appearance. Success in these rites, which marked the accomplishment of reintegration, was shown by "passes" – mysterious lights and sounds experienced during the ritual. See **Magic**.

A complex and difficult man, Pasqually refused to name a successor or allow any definite organization to be established for his rite. When he left France in 1778 for Santo Domingo, in what is now the Dominican Republic, the Elect Cohens continued under the leadership of Willermoz, but Pasqually's death abroad in 1779 caused the rapid dissolution of the order. Pasqually's teachings, however, were taken up by Willermoz into the latter's rite of Beneficent Chevaliers of the Holy City, which was widely adopted in central Europe by lodges of the Rite of Strict Observance after the Congress of Wilhelmsbad in 1782, and by another of Pasqually's students, Louis-Claude de Saint-Martin, in the Rite of Martinism. In one form or another, they spread widely through the European occult community and remain a significant factor in western occultism to this day. See **Martinism**; **Rite of Strict Observance**.

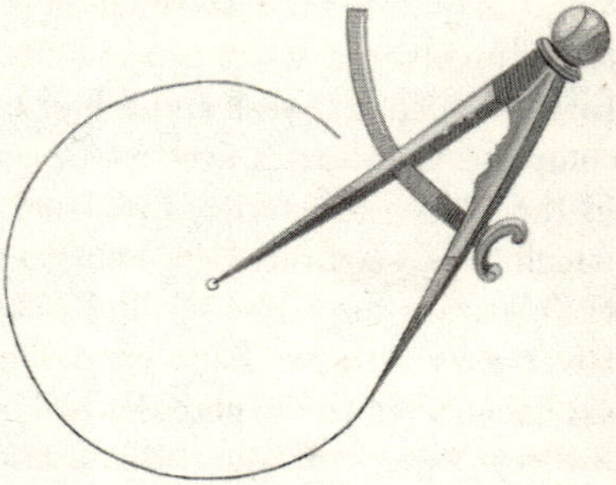

Eleusinian mysteries

Far and away the most famous of the ancient mysteries, the mystery rites of Eleusis were celebrated every September for nearly 2000 years in the small town of the same name, a few miles from Athens. Archeologists have found that by about 1500 BCE, an open space for ritual dancing had been established on the site of the later mystery temple. A century later, the first stone temple was built there, surrounded by a rough wall. Even through the Dark Age that followed the fall of Mycenae around 1250 BCE, the rites at Eleusis survived, and as Greece recovered in the eighth century BCE, the temple was rebuilt and expanded. By the beginning of the Common Era the temple had become a vast hall, the *Telesterion*, half the size of a football field. At its center was a small stone building, the *Anaktoron*, whose location remained the same through all the rebuildings of the temple.

Initiation into the Eleusinian mysteries involved a strict process that took more than a year and a half to complete. Candidates first took part in the Lesser Mysteries, the *Myesis*, which was celebrated in February each year on the banks of the Ilissos River near Athens. Each candidate sacrificed a pig to the gods, bathed in the icy waters of the Ilissos, and received instruction in the myth of Demeter, the goddess of the earth, and her daughter Persephone. The myth at the center of the mystery rite told how Persephone was carried off by Pluto, god of the underworld; how mourning Demeter deprived the earth of its fertility as she searched for her daughter; and how Zeus finally ruled that Persephone would henceforth live half the year on Mount Olympus with the gods and half in the underworld. The whole myth, like the sacred stories central to all the ancient mysteries, is an allegory of the seasons. See **fertility religion**; **mysteries, ancient**.

After the Lesser Mysteries, candidates had to wait until September of the following year before they could take part in the Greater Mysteries, called the *Teletai*. These rites formally began on the 14th of the month of Boedromion, when priestesses from Eleusis came to Athens carrying baskets. The baskets contained sacred objects that were stored in the Eleusinion, a temple in Athens; what those objects were, nobody knows. Candidates began fasting on the 10th, and on the 16th they marched in a procession down to the sea to purify themselves in its water, then went into seclusion for the next two days.

At dawn on the 19th, the candidates gathered at the Painted Porch in the central market place of Athens, donned myrtle wreaths, and formed a procession with the priestesses and their mysterious baskets. They left Athens by the Sacred Gate and proceeded along the Sacred Road toward Eleusis. At a bridge they met priests who gave each of them a carefully measured portion of a beverage called *kykeon* ("the mixture") containing water, roasted barley, and pennyroyal. At a second bridge, another detachment of priests tied a thread to the right hand and left foot of each candidate. Finally, around sunset, the procession reached Eleusis and marched by torchlight into the sacred precinct. They entered the Telesterion, where the Hierophant, the chief priest of Eleusis, sat on his throne just outside the entrance to the Anaktoron.

It is at this point that most of the surviving sources fall silent. Some ancient authors mention that a brilliant light shone out of the Telesterion, bright enough to be seen for miles. By that light, the Hierophant apparently opened the doors of the Anaktoron and showed something to the candidates. No reliable ancient source mentions what they saw. While a few people in ancient times were said to have violated the oath of secrecy demanded of initiates, and one – Diagoras of

Melos, called "the godless" – even wrote a book about what went on at Eleusis, no certain trace of their testimony remains. One late and unreliable Gnostic source claims that the secret of Eleusis was a single ear of grain, held up in silence.

According to Clement of Alexandria, a Christian writer from the fourth century, initiates of Eleusis had a special password, the *synthema*: "I have fasted, drunk the *kykeon*, taken things out of the large basket, worked with them, put them into the small basket, and then back into the large basket." Comments from many initiates indicated that whatever they saw within the Telesterion freed them from the fear of death – a point that merely deepens the mystery that surrounds Eleusis.

During the heyday of the Roman Empire, people came to Eleusis from all over the known world to seek initiation, and the prestige of the mysteries made their suppression difficult even after the Christian seizure of power. In 364 CE, when the Emperor Valentinian ordered all other nocturnal pagan ceremonies suppressed, the rites at Eleusis won a reprieve. The collapse of the Roman state in the following years proved to be less easy to survive, though. In 386 the Visigoths, who converted to Christianity earlier in the century, invaded Greece and devastated most of the surviving pagan sanctuaries in the country. The temple at Eleusis was destroyed and the mysteries lost forever.

Interest in the mysteries of Eleusis seems not to have revived until the eighteenth century, when the rapid spread of Freemasonry made the ancient world's initiation rites a subject of much speculation. Few eighteenth-century secret societies made much use of the legends of Eleusis, though Adam Weishaupt – the founder of the Bavarian Illuminati – used "Eleusis" as his code word for Ingolstadt, the site of the Illuminati headquarters. By the nineteenth century, though, attempts to reconstruct the Eleusinian mysteries had begun. One of them ended up as the seventh and highest degree of the Patrons of Husbandry, one of the most influential American secret societies of the time, and several others were in use at one time or another. See **Bavarian Illuminati**; **high degrees**; **Patrons of Husbandry (Grange)**.

Further reading: Kerenyi 1967, Mylonas 1961.

Elks

See **Benevolent Protective Order of Elks**.

Emblems

Among the most common elements of secret society symbolism and initiation ritual, emblems are visual images with specific meanings hinted at, but usually not clearly revealed, by the details of design. An example is the main emblem of the Odd Fellows, the largest fraternal secret society in late nineteenth-century America and Britain, formed by three links of a chain bearing the letters F, L, and T. Odd Fellows know that the letters stood for Friendship, Love, and Truth, and the three links for the bonds of brotherhood uniting them with other Odd Fellows; those outside Odd Fellowship generally have no notion of the emblem's meaning. The use of emblems thus ties into the complex uses of secrecy in secret societies. See **Odd Fellowship**; **Secrecy**.

The use of emblems dates from the Renaissance, when the Italian author and lawyer Andrea Alciato or Alciatus (1492–1550) launched a literary genre with his bestselling *Emblemata Liber* (1531), the first emblem book. Alciatus's book was inspired by a forgery of the fifth century CE, the *Hieroglyphica of Horapollo,* which claimed to give the secret meanings of the Egyptian hieroglyphs, but simply provided allegoric readings – a circle meant eternity, a dog fidelity, and so on. Rediscovered in 1419, the *Hieroglyphica* inspired many Renaissance intellectuals to think in imagery. While Alciatus was the first to turn this habit into a literary genre, hundreds of other authors turned out emblem books of their own during the sixteenth, seventeenth, and eighteenth centuries. These emblem books, and the social habit of using emblems to convey moral or philosophical ideas spread into Freemasonry and other secret societies toward the end of this period. After the coming of the Industrial Revolution, emblem books dropped out of popular culture, and the habit of thinking in visual symbols they once inculcated survived only in secret societies. See **Freemasonry**.

Essenes

A sect of Jewish mystics active in Palestine around the beginning of the Common Era, the Essenes were known only from scattered references in a handful of ancient books until 1947, when the Dead Sea Scrolls came to light in a cave near Qumran in Jordan. As with most of the secret traditions of the ancient world, the Essenes were woven into many theories of the history of secret societies, and turned into the ancestors of several nineteenth- and twentieth-century secret societies in the western world. Much of the misinformation still circulating about the Essenes in popular culture comes from this source. See **Dead Sea Scrolls**; **retrospective recruitment**.

Between the Dead Sea Scrolls and the references in Josephus and other ancient writers, a fairly clear history of the Essenes can be pieced together. They emerged out of the tangled religious politics of the kingdom of Judea in the second century BCE, as a group of puritanical Jews convinced that the Judaism of their time had gone astray and they themselves were the only true worshippers of the Jewish god. They left Jerusalem and, after 20 years of uncertainty, settled at Qumran under the direction of a leader called the Teacher of Righteousness. Convinced that the Messiah would soon appear, destroy their enemies, and make them rulers of the world, they remained a fringe group on the edge of the Jewish community until 68 CE, when the Qumran community was destroyed by Roman soldiers and its members killed, enslaved, or dispersed. Before the end, members of the group hid its sacred scriptures in caves near the community, where they were found nearly 2000 years later.

The possibility that the early Christian church in Jerusalem had strong parallels with the Essenes has been much discussed among scholars, and there are certainly similarities between the Essene beliefs and those of early Christianity. Still, it is a very long leap from this to the confident assertions in many recent books of alternative history that Jesus was an Essene, for example, or that the early Church and the Essene movement were the same thing. Attempts to fasten the Essenes securely into a line of initiates reaching from ancient Egypt to Freemasonry or the like are equally difficult to justify, since the "Essene" features in Freemasonry are also found in the Old Testament and the Talmud, while the distinctive elements of Essene spirituality were lost when Qumran was destroyed and cannot be found in Freemasonry or any later tradition. See **Christian origins**; **Freemasonry, origins of**; **Jesus of Nazareth**.

Further reading: Knibb 1987, VanderKam 1994.

Euhemerism

Named after the Greek philosopher Euhemerus, who introduced it in a book written around 200 BCE, euhemerism is the belief that myths and legends derive from garbled retellings of ancient historical events. Since ancient times, it has been among the most popular theories about the origins and meaning of mythology, and it has seen an enormous amount of use in today's alternative history.

Euhemerus's original idea seems to have been that the marvelous features of the Greek myths were simply poetic metaphors that ended up being taken literally. He suggested, for example, that Actaeon – who according to myth had spied on the goddess Artemis bathing, and was turned into a stag by her and torn to pieces by his own hounds – was simply a nobleman so addicted to hunting that the expense of keeping packs of hunting dogs ate up all his wealth. Most later euhemerists, though, have focused their arguments on the claim that the gods of myth are ancient kings and queens whose exploits grew in the retelling until they reached divine status. Many medieval and Renaissance retellings of Scandinavian history, for example, start with a watered-down version of Norse mythology in which Odin, the high god of the Norse, becomes a famous king of the distant past.

Most modern alternative visions of history borrow euhemerist ideas, and some rely on euhemerism nearly to the exclusion of all other methods of interpretation. The huge literature arguing that the gods and goddesses of various mythologies were actually astronauts from other planets, for example, is euhemerist through and through, insisting that the gods' miraculous powers are simply advanced alien technology as interpreted by primitive humans, and so forth. In the same way, the attempts to identify Hiram Abiff, the murdered master builder of Masonic legend, as any of several dozen different historical figures – from the Egyptian pharaoh Seqenenre II to Britain's King Charles I – are euhemerist interpretations. See **extraterrestrials**; **Hiram Abiff**.

In some circumstances, it deserves to be said, the euhemerist approach has merit. To name only two examples, the medieval legends of King Arthur probably do reflect, however dimly, the exploits of a real Romano-British cavalry commander in the sixth century CE, and many of the flood legends from around the world – including the legend of Atlantis – quite plausibly derive from dim memories of the worldwide flooding at the end of the last Ice Age in 9500 BCE. Still, it is a huge leap from this to assume that every detail of myth and legend must have some historical foundation, or even that every myth retells ancient history. Mythology is an immensely rich symbolic language, and oral cultures past and present used it for many purposes; trying to force it into the Procrustean bed of any one system of interpretation usually produces more nonsense than anything else. See **Arthurian legends**; **earth changes**.

Eulis

In the writings of American occultist Paschal Beverly Randolph (1825–75) and several secret societies that trace their descent back to him, a system of magical practice based on sex. The word "Eulis" combined a reference to Eleusis, the site of the most famous of the ancient mysteries, and the Greek word *eos*, "dawn." According to some of Randolph's writings, the teachings of Eulis were originally titled *Marek Gebel* or *Gebel el-Marek*, the Gate of Light, and were passed onto him by mystics of the Ansairehs or al-Nusairis, a Sufi order he claimed to have contacted; according to other comments in his writings, he came up with them himself. See **Randolph, Paschal Beverly**.

The basic principle of Eulis was that sexual polarity between male and female was the fundamental power of the cosmos, and could be tapped into by sexual intercourse that resulted in simultaneous mutual orgasm. Its preliminary training included "volantia," or calmly focusing the mind; "decretism," or intense focus on a single idea to the exclusion of all else; and "posism," or physical and mental receptivity. Unlike most later versions of the same theory, Randolph insisted that love between sexual partners was essential to Eulis, and placed much stress on the importance of the female orgasm.

While Randolph's career was one of almost unbroken self-induced failure, and few of the magical secret societies he founded survived more than a few months, the teachings of Eulis went on to have an extraordinary wide circulation. His ideas became the principal source for several successful magical orders, including the Hermetic Brotherhood of Luxor (H.B. of L.), the Fraternitas Rosae Crucis, and the Ordo Templi Orientis, and for much of the twentieth century most methods of sex magic practiced in the western world drew extensively on Eulis. See **Fraternitas Rosae Crucis; Hermetic Brotherhood of Luxor (H.B. of L.); Ordo Templi Orientis (OTO)**.

Further reading: Deveney 1997, Randolph 1874.

Evola, Julius

Italian philosopher, writer, occultist, and Fascist. Born Giulio Cesare Andrea Evola, into an aristocratic Sicilian family, Evola (1898–1974) rebelled against his family's strict Catholicism in his teens and became involved in avant-garde circles in Rome. After serving in the Italian army during the last year of the First World War, he began a career as a poet and painter, winning a reputation as the leading representative of the Dadaist movement in Italy. In 1922, however, he abandoned painting and plunged into an intensive study of Oriental philosophy, occultism, and magic. As a student of the famous occultist and Freemason Arturo Reghini (1878–1946), Evola became part of the UR Group, a loose association of Italian occultists, and devoted himself to alchemy and ritual magic. Reghini also introduced him to the writings of René Guénon (1886–1951), founder of the Traditionalist movement. See **Traditionalism**.

In 1925 Evola published the first of his philosophical works, *Saggi sull' Idealismo Magico* (*Essays on Magical Idealism*), and a widely praised work on Indian Tantrism, *L'Uomo comme Potenza* (translated into English as *The Yoga of Power*). These books earned him a reputation as one of the leading lights of the Italian occult scene, while his right-wing political journalism won him friends not only in Fascist Italy but throughout central Europe, where authoritarian regimes sprouted like mushrooms during the 1920s and 1930s. Later books addressed the Hermetic tradition, the Holy Grail, Pagan religion, politics, and culture, and made him the twentieth century's most influential Fascist intellectual. See **Grail**; **Hermeticism**.

Underlying all Evola's works was his conviction that the "degenerate" pacifist and egalitarian tendencies of Christianity, and the materialistic mass culture of the modern world, had to be cast aside in favor of a virile new warrior spirituality based on heroic values and hierarchy. In his most influential book, *Rivolta contra il Mondo Moderno* (*Revolt against the Modern World*, 1934), he pictured all of history as a vast war between an aristocratic, solar, and masculine Uranian Tradition, which he identified as the source of all cultural creativity, and the opposed Demetrian Tradition, earthy, egalitarian, pacifist and matriarchal, which was the source of all cultural decay and the root of Christianity, communism, and democracy. This theme, the central mythology of many of his books, shows both his knowledge of esoteric traditions and his failure to grasp their deeper dimensions; traditional occult and alchemical lore focuses on the need for a creative fusion of solar and telluric currents (and all other pairs of opposites), while Evola saw instead a power struggle that only one side could win.

His ideas predictably found a ready audience north of the Alps. Evola lectured in Germany regularly from 1934 on, but his relationship with Nazism was complex. He rejected Nazi racism as crude biological determinism, insisting that spiritual and cultural factors trumped genetic inheritance; his theory of an "Aryan-Roman race," defined by its aristocratic values and spiritual orientation rather than by blood, was actually adopted by Mussolini as the basis for Italy's race laws in 1938. He disliked other elements in Nazi theory, including its materialism and its insistence that political legitimacy comes from the *Volk*. For their part, the Nazis considered him an aristocratic reactionary, but allowed his books to be published in Germany.

Evola's differences with the Nazis did not keep him from fleeing to Vienna as the Allied armies neared Rome in 1943, or accepting a position in the SS, first as a researcher in the Ahnenerbe (the research department of the SS) and later as a liaison officer working with central European fascist leaders. In March 1945, as the Third Reich's final defenses crumpled, Evola was severely wounded in an air raid and lost the use of both legs. After the war was over, he returned to Rome, where he spent the rest of his life writing further books on politics, culture, and spirituality. His apartment on the Via Corso became a site of pilgrimage for postwar neo-fascists until his death in 1974.

By that time his writings had become required reading on the radical Right throughout continental Europe. Italian neo-fascist groups such as the *Movimento Sociale Italiano* adopted Evola as their primary theoretician in the 1950s, and the Vienna circle of neo-Nazi occultists around Wilhelm Landig adoted Evola's *Revolt against the Modern World* as their Bible during the same years. By the 1980s Evola's works were being translated into English, first in the pages of neo-Nazi magazines and then in book form, and began to attract a following in the English-speaking world as well. Most currently active neo-Nazi secret societies draw at least part of their ideological basis from Evola's works. See **neo-Nazi secret societies**.

Further reading: Evola 1995, Goodrick-Clarke 2002.

EXTRATERRESTRIALS

The twentieth century's obsession with the possibility of intelligent life on other worlds has had a massive impact on the whole range of alternative beliefs in western cultures. While evidence for the actual existence of extraterrestrial life remains equivocal and speculative at best, nearly all the traditional themes of alternative spirituality and occultism have been reworked to make room for space travelers from distant planets.

Three main themes provide core doctrines for the modern faith in extraterrestrials. The first unfolds from the belief that astronauts from other worlds came to earth at some point in the distant past and had a decisive impact on human history, which can be traced in myths as well as ancient ruins and artifacts.

The second theme derives from the belief that extraterrestrials are here on earth at the present time. Most versions of this theme draw heavily on the literature of the UFO controversy to back up the claim that visitors from other planets are present now. Some, though, argue that the aliens live on earth in underground cities, beneath the Antarctic ice cap, or walking among us in concealed form. See **Rainbow City**; **underground realms**; **unidentified flying objects**.

The third theme borrows the common apocalyptic idea that our relationship with the extraterrestrials is about to undergo a major change. From UFO enthusiasts who wait for flying saucers to land on the White House lawn, through believers in ancient astronauts who anticipate the discovery of alien artifacts, to conspiracy theorists of the David Icke school who believe the world is controlled by shape-shifting reptilians disguised as human beings, and hope to see their grip on the human race overthrown, most versions of the extraterrestrial faith include some equivalent of the messianic prophecies of more ordinary religions. See **Reptilians**.

These last similarities are not accidental, and point out the extent to which faith in extraterrestrials is ultimately a religious belief. Like the gods, angels, and spirits of older faiths, the extraterrestrials of these modern belief systems either created, engendered, or influenced humankind in the beginning; they remain present today, at least to the eyes of faith; and believers expect their reality to be revealed in an apocalyptic end of ordinary history sometime in the near future. It is indicative that many versions of the extraterrestrial faith take old religious mythologies and rewrite them with space travelers from other planets in the starring roles. To some extent this is simple euhemerism – the habit of treating myth and legend as an echo of forgotten history – but it also points to a simpler reality: aliens fill the same role in many modern minds that gods did in other times and places. The extraterrestrials, even when not omniscient and omnipotent, have advanced scientific knowledge and superior technology, and serve as a lightning rod for hopes that they will save humanity from itself. See **Euhemerism**.

F

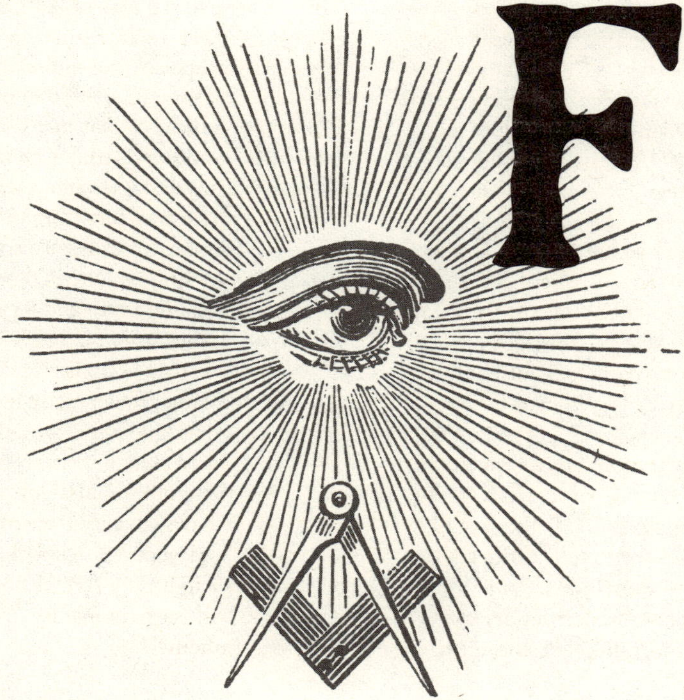

Fabian Society

An active force in British and European socialism for many years, and a significant figure in conservative conspiracy theories up to the present, the Fabian Society was founded in London in 1884 by a coterie of left-wing intellectuals who gathered around the Scottish philosopher Thomas Davidson. Author and playwright George Bernard Shaw, and Annie Besant, head of the Theosophical Society after the death of its founder Helena Petrovna Blavatsky, were among its leading early members. See **Theosophical Society**.

The Society took its name from the Roman general Fabius Maximus Cunctator, who wore down the armies of Hannibal in the second Punic War by avoiding pitched battles and using indirect tactics; the Fabians hoped to promote socialism by gradual reforms and indirect means. In the early days of the Society, its members attempted to influence the then-dominant Liberal and Conservative parties in Britain in a Socialist direction. In the first decade of the twentieth century, though, the Society helped organize the Labour Representation Committee, the seed from which the Labour Party took form in 1906. Since that time the Fabian Society has been closely associated with the Labour Party and many Labour Party leaders and members of Parliament have also belonged to the Society.

The Fabian Society's socialist platform and its use of indirect methods have given it an important role in some conservative conspiracy theories, and its activities – especially in its early years, when its efforts to diffuse socialist ideas through existing political parties made use of a certain amount of subterfuge – have provided some justification for these claims. It remains, however, simply one of many pressure groups in the complex patchwork of power in the modern world, and attempts by twentieth-century conspiracy theorists to define it as the "One Big Conspiracy" have little in common with the relatively modest reality of its influence and achievements. See **New World Order**.

Further reading: Mackenzie and Mackenzie 1977.

False Face Society

The most famous of the curing societies among the six nations of the Iroquois Confederacy, an alliance of Native American peoples living in what is now upstate New York and southern Ontario, the False Face Society is best known for its dramatic and brightly colored wooden masks, which can be found in ethnographic museums worldwide. The False Face Society performs important traditional rituals among the Iroquois tribes, including purification rites to banish disease in spring and autumn, the great midwinter ceremonial that celebrates the new year, and private feasts to commemorate a successful healing or a spiritually powerful dream. Still active today among those Iroquois who have not converted to Christianity, the False Face Society is among the Native American secret societies that have undergone a large-scale revival in recent years. See **Native American secret societies**.

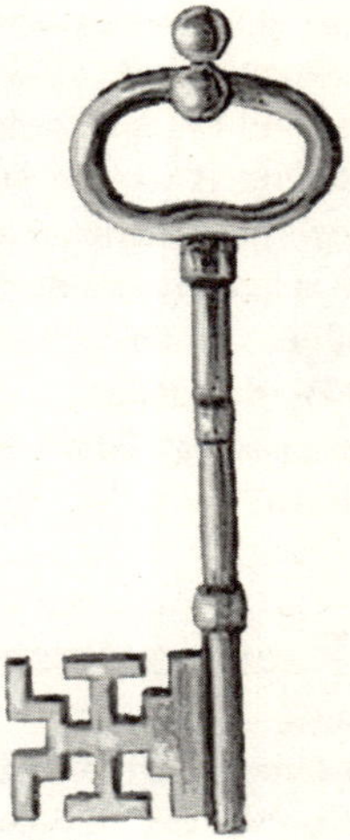

FENIAN BROTHERHOOD

The most famous of Irish revolutionary secret societies, the Fenian Brotherhood emerged after the catastrophic potato blight in Ireland in the late 1840s. The failure of British officials to provide relief for a famine that caused between one and two million deaths embittered the Irish and convinced them they had nothing to gain from continued British rule. In 1848, a planned rising was nipped in the bud by British authorities, and three of the leaders of the conspiracy – John O'Mahony, Michael Doheny, and James Stephens – fled for safety to America.

There, in 1858, they founded a secret society to pursue Irish independence, calling it the Fenian Brotherhood or Irish Republican Brotherhood. The first name came from the legendary band of warriors led by the Irish hero Fionn mac Cumhaill, while their operating structure derived from contemporary secret societies in Europe. Members swore oaths of secrecy and were grouped into cells of 10, each cell independent and unknown to all others, at least in theory. In practice, the Fenians had glaring security problems, and the British government had little problem filling its ranks with informers. The Fenians themselves did much to undermine their own security by holding large public conventions, the first in Chicago in 1863. See **cell system**.

The Fenians nonetheless posed a significant challenge to British rule over Ireland, if only because the huge Irish expatriate population in America – some 1.6 million by 1860 – provided a sizeable field for recruitment. Several attempts were made to fund a rising in Ireland, though these fell through when the British authorities used their informers to arrest leaders and seize guns and money gathered for the purpose.

The American Civil War, in which many Irish expatriates fought on the Union side, brought thousands of veterans into the Fenian ranks. This emboldened the movement and launched it on the frankly harebrained project of trying to conquer Canada as a springboard to Irish independence. In 1866, a thousand armed Fenians crossed the border and seized the town of St Armand, expecting to provoke a rising against the British government. Instead, they were quickly dispersed by Canadian troops. Two further efforts along the same lines yielded equally unimpressive results. In 1867, one final attempt at a rising in Ireland, backed by a plan to seize weapons from Chester Castle in England, fizzled quickly.

Meanwhile the Fenians faced a widening spiral of internal troubles. The organization split in half in 1866 after a series of political quarrels among its leaders, and the fragments split further in the years that followed. The consistent failure of the Fenians to accomplish any of their aims or, for that matter, even make a plausible attempt at doing so, alienated the younger generation of Irish and Irish-American activists. By the mid-1870s the Fenian Brotherhood had ceased operations in America, but Irish Fenian groups in Dublin remained active in at least a theoretical sense. The Fenian name had by this time become an embarrassment, and members typically used the name "Irish Republican Brotherhood" instead. Even under its alternative name, the Brotherhood accomplished little during the last years of the nineteenth century, and the movement was at a low ebb. Several of the most serious Irish terrorist groups of the 1880s drew their membership primarily from Irish Fenians who saw the Brotherhood as a dead end and sought to pursue the cause of Irish independence by more radical means.

By the first decades of the twentieth century British police and military intelligence had written off the Fenian movement as a negligible threat. This proved to be a disastrous mistake, as a new generation of leaders came to the fore and began preparing for an insurrection. The revitalized Brotherhood was small – it had only 2000 members in Ireland in 1914 – but it had close links to other republican organizations, including the Irish Volunteers and the Irish Citizen Army, two pro-independence militia groups. When the Brotherhood and its allies rose in revolt on the Easter weekend of 1916, they took the authorities totally by surprise. While the Easter Rising was defeated, it demonstrated the weakness of the British hold on Ireland in a way that could not be ignored, and sparked a general revolt against British rule that led to Irish independence in 1921. Thus, despite all the failures of the intervening years, the Fenian Brotherhood played a crucial role in accomplishing the goal its founders set themselves in New York back in 1858.

Further reading: Mackenzie 1967, Williams 1973.

FERTILITY RELIGION

One of the major eighteenth- and nineteenth-century theories about the origin of religion, the theory of fertility religion proposes that all religion springs from the sense of awe and delight born of humanity's experience of its own reproductive powers, and the fertility and abundance of living nature. It emerged in the second half of the eighteenth century as European scholars found themselves confronted with the contrast between the guilt and shame with which the western cultures of the time surrounded sex, and the exuberance with which ancient Greeks and Romans, modern Hindus, and people of several other non-western cultures treated sexuality as a natural part of life. English classical scholar Richard Payne Knight (1751–1824) launched the concept of fertility religion into scholarly discussion in his *A Discourse on the Worship of Priapus* (1786), and it remained a major force in comparative religion until the early twentieth century, when Sir James Frazer's massive *The Golden Bough* (1917) defended it in immense detail.

Like its rival and occasional ally, the theory of astronomical religion, the fertility religion theory started as an explanation for the origin of all religions other than Judaism and Christianity. Where the astronomical theory was often used to dismiss pagan faiths as products of human ignorance, though, a surprising number of fertility religion theorists considered the old fertility faiths better than the Judeo-Christian tradition precisely because they made room for a positive attitude toward sex. Payne Knight led the way in this, putting edgy comments about "the sour mythology of the Christians" in his book and pointing out that, whatever the supposed moral failings of the old sexual faiths, they had managed to avoid persecuting other religions. See **astronomical religion**.

Yet the quest for sexual symbolism in religion eventually opened up the possibility that Judaism and Christianity, too, might be interpreted in sexual terms. This seems to have been done first by the Welsh Druid Owen Morgan, head of a Druid order based at Pontypridd and the author of the privately printed *The Light of Britannia* (1888), a work that fused the astronomical and fertility theories of religion and interpreted Christianity in their light. To Morgan, Jesus was simply another fertility deity whose life, death, and resurrection had a primarily sexual meaning. His approach was taken up by a minority of nineteenth- and twentieth-century writers but never gained the popularity of astronomical interpretations of Christian myth. See **Christian origins**; **Druid Revival**.

The theory of fertility religion formulated by Sir James Frazer in the early twentieth century, and popularized by the many volumes of *The Golden Bough*, had a much more extensive impact by way of Margaret Murray, an Egyptologist turned medieval historian who projected Frazer's theories onto the witchcraft persecutions of the fifteenth, sixteenth, and seventeenth centuries and came to the conclusion that the witch trials were aimed at exterminating a surviving fertility cult in western Europe. Despite massive problems with issues of evidence, Murray's claim was widely accepted during the middle years of the twentieth century and gave a crucial boost to the rise of Wicca, the first widely publicized neo-pagan religion. See **Murray hypothesis**; **Wicca**.

Further reading: Godwin 1994.

First International

The *bête noire* of conservatives worldwide for more than a century after 1864, the First International and its two successors have played a huge role in the modern mythology surrounding secret societies. Though not secret societies in their own right, the Internationals drew on a long tradition of radical secret societies in western Europe, had several secret societies take an active role in their history, and gave conservatives obsessed with secret societies a visible target for their fears. Few if any of today's conspiracy theories would be the same if the First International had never existed.

The First International was founded out of the fusion of a group of French liberals, some of them in exile from Napoleon III's dictatorship, and a group of English labor unionists inspired by the possibilities of international organization. Behind the original meeting at St Martin's Hall in London on September 28, 1864 lay years of complex intrigues on the part of the Philadelphes, one of the last surviving political secret societies of the Napoleonic era. Sometime in the late 1830s the Philadelphes had taken control of the Rite of Memphis, an irregular system of Masonry with no fewer than 96 degrees of initiation. In 1850, during one of the brief periods when the Rite was able to operate legally in France, a lodge was chartered in London by a group of French emigrés with close ties to left-wing politics. After Napoleon III seized power and proclaimed the Second Empire in 1852, this lodge, and 10 other lodges connected with it, became deeply involved in intrigues against the new regime and may have taken part in some of the attempts on Napoleon III's life. See **Philadelphes**; **Rite of Memphis**.

By the early 1860s, however, the Philadelphes in England were turning toward goals more sweeping than the removal of one French tyrant. From 1855 to 1859 they operated a front organization called the International Association, which had attracted interest in America as well as Europe, and the expansion of the labor union movement in the years before 1864 opened the prospect of organizing the working classes under Philadelphe leadership. The International Workingmen's Association (IWA), as the First International was originally known, was launched under Philadelphe auspices to carry out this project.

In its first year the IWA remained essentially a Philadelphe front. Nearly a third of the members of the Association's governing board, the General Council, were members of one or another Philadelphe lodge. Yet the secret society had already brought its own nemesis aboard, in the person of a German economist named Karl Marx. Already a major figure among European radicals, Marx and his coauthor Friedrich Engels had burst on the scene in 1848 with *The Communist Manifesto*, and a growing number of radical groups across Europe were taking up Marxist ideas during the formative years of the International. Marx was indispensable, but the Philadelphes made the mistake of believing they could manipulate him to their own ends. By the end of 1865 Marx and his allies had removed the last Philadelphes from the policymaking subcommittee of the General Council and had effective control of the International.

Ironically, another secret society filled the vacuum, causing the political explosions that wrecked the First International in the 1870s. This was the International Brothers, an anarchist secret society founded and headed by the Russian radical and ex-Nihilist Mikhail Bakunin. Founded in Italy sometime around 1864, the International Brothers formed another secret society, the Secret Alliance, as a front group; they then launched a public front group for the secret one, the International Alliance of Social Democracy. In 1868 the International Alliance applied to enter the First International. The leadership of the International rejected the application, but allowed each national subdivision of the Alliance to join as a local branch of the International. See **Anarchism**; **International Brothers**; **Nihilists**.

With this as his way in, Bakunin attempted to take over the International, only to run up against the same Marxist bloc that had defeated the Philadelphes. Marx and his then-ally, French radical politician Auguste Blanqui, fought Bakunin's party for four years before finally expelling Bakunin in 1872. Though Marx ended up victorious, the struggle weakened the International fatally and drove a wedge between Marx and Blanqui. When Marx forced through new rules giving the General Council dictatorial powers over the International, the local sections rebelled. By 1873 the International was moribund, and the General Council, by then relocated to New York, formally dissolved in 1876. A new International did not begin to take shape in Europe until 1889, and when it did, it had no connection to secret societies at all.

Further reading: Billington 1980, Drachkovitch 1966.

Franklin, Benjamin

American statesman, scientist, and Freemason, 1706–90. Born in Boston to a working-class family, Franklin entered the printing trade as an apprentice to his brother, who published the *New England Courant*, a popular newspaper. In 1723, after a series of quarrels with his brother, he left Boston for Philadelphia, where he found work in a local print shop. In 1724 he went to Britain for a year and a half to improve his knowledge of the printing trade and purchase new equipment for his employer. Shortly after his return he opened his own printing business, and soon became one of the most famous printers and publishers in the American colonies, the author and publisher of the wildly successful *Poor Richard's Almanac* and a daily newspaper, *The Pennsylvania Gazette*. By 1748 his printing business had flourished to the extent that he was able to retire, leaving the business in the hands of a partner.

Masonic records from colonial Philadelphia are fragmentary enough that the exact date of Franklin's initiation into Freemasonry is still uncertain, but the most likely date was 1731. In 1734 he was elected Grand Master of the provincial Grand Lodge of Pennsylvania, and in the same year he produced an edition of Anderson's *Book of Constitutions*, a standard Masonic manual of the time, which was the first Masonic book printed in America. See **Freemasonry**.

During this time he made his mark as a leading Philadelphia citizen. He founded the city's first circulating library in 1731; a fire department in 1736; the American Philosophical Society, the colonies' first learned society, in 1743; a college, which later became the University of Pennsylvania, in 1749; and the first public hospital in Pennsylvania in 1751. From 1736 to 1751 he served as clerk of the Pennsylvania Assembly; he was elected to the Assembly in 1751, and in 1757 went to Britain as Pennsylvania's representative in London. He served in that position until 1762, then returned in 1764 and served as agent for most of the American colonies until just before the outbreak of the American Revolution. During his stay in Britain he was elected to Britain's Royal Society, frequented learned societies and clubs in London and elsewhere, and also became a member of Sir Francis Dashwood's Hell-Fire Club. See **Hell-Fire Club**; **Royal Society**.

On his return to America, Franklin was elected to the Continental Congress and helped draft the Declaration of Independence. Later in 1776, Franklin sailed for Paris and became the ambassador of the Continental Congress to the court of the French king Louis XVI. There he played a crucial role in winning French support for the American colonies. As a major cultural figure of the time, as well as a well-known Freemason, he was welcomed into lodges throughout Paris, and affiliated with the Lodge of the Nine Sisters (*Loge des Neuf Soeurs*), whose membership included many of the leading figures in French scholarship and literature. He was a member of the French commission set up to investigate the "animal magnetism" of Franz Anton Mesmer, and strongly supported its 1785 report dismissing Mesmer as a quack.

In 1778, in the aftermath of the American victory at Saratoga, Franklin negotiated an alliance with France and brought French troops and money to the support of the American army. In 1782 he began peace negotiations with Britain, and with the help of John Adams and John Jay negotiated a treaty that gave America its independence. He returned home to a hero's welcome in 1785, and despite age and ill health took part in the Constitutional Convention in Philadelphia in 1787. He died peacefully in 1790.

Further reading: Jennings 1996, van Doren 1991.

FRATERNAL BENEFIT SOCIETIES

One of the many branches of the secret society movement of the late nineteenth and early twentieth centuries, fraternal benefit societies took the benefits system of fraternal orders such as the Odd Fellows, but replaced traditional sick pay and funeral benefits with insurance policies. Joining a fraternal benefit society was equivalent to taking out an insurance policy with the society; the premiums took the form of monthly dues, and members also met regularly for business meetings, social functions, and the initiation of new candidates. See **fraternal orders**; **Odd Fellowship**.

The era of fraternal benefit societies began in 1869, when an American fraternal order, the Ancient Order of United Workmen, changed its benefit plan to a system of insurance policies for members. The economic crises of the 1870s, when more than 60 major insurance firms went bankrupt, made many Americans deeply suspicious of commercial insurance companies and encouraged them to embrace a system that seemed less vulnerable to economic vagaries. Between 1870 and 1910, accordingly, some 3500 fraternal benefit societies sprang up across America and Canada. Similar factors in the 1880s and 1890s led to a similar expansion of friendly societies, the British equivalent of North American fraternal benefit societies, in Britain itself and many parts of the British Empire. See **Ancient Order of United Workmen**.

The fraternal insurance industry became a speculative favorite in the late nineteenth century and drew a great deal of investment capital. The demand for new rituals was so great that when Lew Wallace's novel *Ben-Hur* (1880) became a nationwide bestseller in America, a group of promoters bought the fraternal-order rights from him for a substantial sum, and launched the Tribe of Ben-Hur, a fraternal benefit society with four degrees of initiation. The Tribe spread throughout the Midwest and remained in existence until 1978. Most American fraternal benefit societies, like nearly all American institutions, were segregated by race, but this simply drove the expansion of African-American fraternal benefit societies drawing on the rich heritage of secret societies in the African-American community. See **African-American secret societies**.

Most of the fraternal benefit societies, however, fell victim to their own enthusiasm and a failure to grasp the fact that insurance risk increases with age. Societies usually started with a relatively young membership and few payouts, and their bank accounts grew steadily as membership expanded. When the market for fraternal insurance was saturated, however, new memberships slowed to a trickle, payouts increased as the membership aged, and the risk of bankruptcy increased. A survey of fraternal benefit societies (cited in Palmer 1944, p. 211) found that 85 percent of the benefit societies founded between 1870 and 1910 went bankrupt, after an average lifespan of 15 years.

While most fraternal benefit societies went bankrupt, merged with others, or turned themselves into ordinary insurance firms during the twentieth century, some managed to survive and remain active today. More than a hundred fraternal benefit societies still exist today in Britain, America, Canada, and a variety of Commonwealth nations, offering insurance policies and annuities to members.

Further reading: Palmer 1944.

Fraternal Order of Eagles [FOE]

Of the fraternal secret societies of late nineteenth century, few have a more colorful origin than the Fraternal Order of Eagles. In the winter of 1898, the burlesque theatres and saloons of the Lava Beds, Seattle's notorious red light district, faced a musicians' strike. Six prominent businessmen from the Lava Beds sat down on a pile of lumber in a shipyard a few blocks from their establishments and worked out a common strategy to deal with the strike. In the course of the meeting, they decided to start meeting regularly and, half jokingly, named themselves the Independent Order of Good Things; this name shared the initials of the Independent Order of Good Templars, one of the largest temperance orders in the country. The original motto of the Seattle IOGT was "Skin 'em." See **Independent Order of Good Templars**.

In the weeks after the original meeting, other Lava Beds business owners and employees asked to join the organization, and the idea of creating a fraternal order modeled on the Elks, another order founded by people in the theatre industry, occurred to the founders. A month after the first meeting, the Independent Order of Good Things renamed itself the Fraternal Order of Eagles. The next month saw the formation of the Grand Aerie, the national grand lodge. In the next 10 years the Grand Aerie chartered 1800 aeries across the United States, Canada, and Mexico and more than 350,000 members. See **Benevolent Protective Order of Elks (BPOE)**.

Several factors contributed to this dramatic growth. At a time when most fraternal orders gave at least lip service to the temperance movement, Eagles aeries either met in saloons or, as they grew, purchased their own buildings with members-only bars. As private clubs, aeries could also evade the "blue laws" in many states that barred public saloons from selling alcohol on Sundays. The revenue from the private bars made it possible for many aeries to offer medical care, sick pay, and funeral benefits to their members. All these things made the Eagles particularly attractive to people in the theatre industry – the source of most early Eagles membership – and, as the order expanded, to many other Americans who faced the difficult economic challenges of the time, or who simply liked to drink in congenial company. See **fraternal orders**.

Unlike most fraternal orders, the Eagles continued to expand through the first half of the twentieth century. Three American presidents – Theodore Roosevelt, Franklin D.

Roosevelt, and Harry Truman – were members. The difficult years of that century's second half, which saw so many fraternal secret societies go out of existence or fade to a shadow of their former size and influence, also impacted the Eagles but left the order surprisingly strong at the century's end. The Eagles still have aeries in most American and many Canadian cities.

FRATERNAL ORDERS

A common term for those secret societies that pursue social and charitable aims, such as the Odd Fellows, Knights of Pythias, Elks, and Eagles. Freemasonry is usually included among fraternal orders in the English-speaking world, where the political dimensions of European and Latin American Masonry are usually absent. During the nineteenth and early twentieth centuries, fraternal orders had an immense influence on the western world and provided the framework on which most other secret societies modeled themselves. See **Benevolent Protective Order of Elks (BPOE)**; **Fraternal Order of Eagles (FOE)**; **Freemasonry**; **Knights of Pythias**; **Odd Fellowship**.

Freemasonry was a primary source of inspiration for the fraternal orders of the eighteenth and nineteenth centuries, though the Odd Fellows and a few others evolved from older guild structures around the same time that Masonry evolved out of the old operative stonemasons' guilds. Many other fraternal orders founded later claimed older roots, inventing origin stories with as much enthusiasm as Masons did. Still, the amount of Masonry that went into other fraternal orders varied drastically. Some were founded by Masons and borrowed symbolism and procedure from Masonic sources; others merely took a few very general ideas about lodge organization and initiation, and filled in the rest from other sources or their own inventions. See **origin stories**.

By the nineteenth century, too, other fraternal orders had risen to prominence and inspired imitators of their own. Interesting things happened when members of two or more existing orders took part in founding a new fraternal order; the founders of the Patrons of Husbandry, for example, included Odd Fellows and Freemasons, and the rituals and symbolism of the resulting order drew substantial elements from each. See **Patrons of Husbandry (Grange)**.

The expansion of fraternal orders in the nineteenth century drew much of its force from the benefits they provided to their members. In the absence of government welfare programs, fraternal lodges provided a "social safety net" for working-class and middle-class families. Most nineteenth-century fraternal orders borrowed the system of sick pay and survivor benefits developed by the Odd Fellows; in this system, each member put money into a common fund that provided sick pay for those too ill to work, funeral expenses for those who died, and support for widows and orphans. Many lodges also contracted with physicians, paying a lump sum every month in return for health care for lodge members and their families; "lodge practice" formed a significant part of many physicians' salaries until the 1940s and 1950s.

With the birth of the welfare state in most western countries during the twentieth century, though, the fraternal orders had their most important function taken away, and struggled to find new reasons for their existence. The vast majority of the smaller orders folded, and even once-giant societies such as the Independent Order of Odd Fellows – the largest secret society in the world from 1880 to 1920, surpassing even the Freemasons – saw membership rolls dwindle to a few percent of their peak numbers. Those that survive do so on a vastly reduced scale and the average age of their members is generally well above retirement age. While a trickle of new members have succeeded in keeping a few of the old fraternal orders alive, their chance of surviving long into the twenty-first century seems small as at the time of writing.

Fraternitas Rosae Crucis [FRC]

One of the major American Rosicrucian groups of the early twentieth century, the Fraternitas Rosae Crucis (Fraternity of the Rosy Cross) was the creation of R. Swinburne Clymer (1878–1966), an alternative physician and occultist with a flair for public relations, who based his work on the teachings of the charismatic American Rosicrucian Paschal Beverly Randolph (1825–75). See **Randolph, Paschal Beverly**.

According to Clymer's later writings, the FRC was founded by Randolph in 1858 and headed by Randolph's student Freeman B. Dowd (1812–1910) from 1875 to 1907, when the Grand Mastership passed to Dr. Edward H. Brown (1868–1922). On Brown's death Clymer then became the Supreme Grand Master of the Rosicrucians in the New World. Behind these claims lies a reality at least as colorful, though less marketable. Randolph's brilliance was more than matched by his erratic moods and arrogant behavior, and none of the secret societies he founded to pass on his teachings stayed together for long. Dowd, a student of Randolph in the 1860s and 1870s, was involved in several of these, and resurrected one of them – the Brotherhood of Eulis – after Randolph's suicide in 1875. Dowd's student, Edward Brown, inherited the Brotherhood in Dowd's old age; Clymer studied with Brown, and went on to contact several other initiates of Randolph's methods. On Brown's death in 1922, Clymer became head of the Brotherhood, and turned it into the basis of his own occult secret society, the Fraternitas Rosae Crucis.

Clymer's claim to be the sole head of the Rosicrucian tradition in the western hemisphere brought him into inevitable conflict with the other major contender for the title, H. Spencer Lewis, the Imperator of the Ancient Mystical Order Rosae Crucis (AMORC). Clymer struck the first blow in the quarrel, siding with several dissident ex-members of AMORC and circulating allegations about Lewis and his order. Lewis responded in kind, launching a public feud that enlivened the American occult press well into the 1930s and drew Max Heindel's Rosicrucian Fellowship into the fray. Among the many ironies in this latter-day War of the Roses was the fact that both orders were descended from Randolph and shared important elements of theory and practice derived from his teachings. See **Ancient Mystical Order Rosae Crucis (AMORC)**; **Rosicrucian Fellowship**.

The struggle faded out after Lewis's death in 1939, as Clymer had more pressing concerns by that time, notably the legal difficulties faced by alternative health care practitioners in the US at a time when the American Medical Association was forcing most natural healing systems out of existence. Despite this, Clymer maintained a successful healing practice and continued to operate the FRC until his death in 1966. His son, Emerson Clymer, succeeded to the Grand Mastership of the FRC and held it until his death in 1983, after which the position of Grand Master went to Dr. Gerald Poesnecker, a naturopathic doctor. Several high-ranking members of the FRC contested Poesnecker's election and formed a group of their own, claiming to represent the true FRC.

The FRC under Poesnecker's leadership continues to operate Beverly Hall, the 300-acre center established by R. Swinburne Clymer, as well as the Clymer Health Center in nearby Quakertown, Pennsylvania. It offers two correspondence courses to potential members – one for those interested in general occult study and one for those who seek initiation into the FRC itself. Its public material still includes criticisms of AMORC, alongside claims of an approaching time of troubles called the "Great Separation," including a series of catastrophic earth changes that will submerge much of the Old World beneath the sea. See **earth changes**.

Further reading: Deveney 1997, McIntosh 1997.

Fraternitas Rosicruciana Antiqua [FRA]

The most influential Rosicrucian order in Latin America, the Fraternitas Rosicruciana Antiqua (FRA) was founded in Mexico in 1927 by Arnoldo Krumm-Heller (1876–1949), a German expatriate businessman and occultist who had studied with the French magus Papus (Gérard

Encausse, 1865–1916), and received authority from Papus as head of the Martinist Order and Theodor Reuss, head of the Ordo Templi Orientis, to establish lodges in Latin America. See **Martinism**; **Ordo Templi Orientis (OTO)**; **Reuss, Theodor**.

Starting in 1910, Krumm-Heller began creating a network of magical lodges throughout the Latin American countries, combining the many occult traditions he had studied with the results of his own researches. In 1927, in response to the political quarrels of the European Rosicrucian scene, he founded his own organization, the FRA. He was briefly involved in the Rosicrucian wars in America, granting and then revoking a charterto H. Spencer Lewis, head of the American Rosicrucian group AMORC, and later allying with Lewis's chief rival R. Swinburne Clymer and his Fraternitas Rosae Crucis. See **Ancient Mystical Order Rosae Crucis (AMORC)**; **Fraternitas Rosae Crucis**.

After Krumm-Heller's death, the FRA fragmented, but it remains an active presence in most of the countries of Latin America. Most current FRA groups are closely associated with modern Gnostic churches. See **Gnosticism**.

Fraternitas Saturni

An influential German occult secret society, the Fraternitas Saturni was founded in 1925 by a group of German students of Aleister Crowley's magical system. It originated as a branch of another secret society, the Collegium Pansophicum, founded in the early 1920s by bookseller Heinrich Tränker. Like half the occult secret societies of the time, the Collegium claimed descent from the original Rosicrucians of seventeenth-century Germany, but its teachings and practices were fairly standard for early twentieth-century occult secret societies, with a sizeable admixture of Aleister Crowley's sexual magic. See **Crowley, Aleister**; **Rosicrucians**.

In 1925 Crowley himself went to Germany and stayed with Tränker for a time. The two occultists quarreled after a short while, and eventually Tränker went to the German authorities and had Crowley expelled from the country. Disgusted with Crowley and Tränker alike, the Berlin branch of the Collegium resigned en masse and reorganized itself as a new order, the Fraternitas Saturni (Latin for "Fraternity of Saturn"). Headed by Eugen Grosche as Grand Master, the Fraternitas became the most prominent occult order in Germany. In 1933, shortly after the Nazi seizure of power, the Fraternitas Saturni was shut down, along with all other magical lodges; Grosche revived it after the Nazi defeat in 1945 and continued to head it until his death in 1964. The Fraternitas Saturni remains active to this day.

Further reading: Godwin 1994, Howe 1997.

Freemasonry

The most famous secret society in the modern western world and the paradigm for most other secret societies over the last three centuries, Freemasonry – also known simply as Masonry or, among its members, as "the Craft" – emerged in Britain during the seventeenth century and took its modern form in the decades immediately after the founding of the first Grand Lodge of England in 1717. Its origins and history before that time have been the storm center of unending dispute for most of its history; see **Freemasonry, origins of**.

Freemasonry is a fraternal secret society limiting its membership to adult men who believe in a Supreme Being. While it absorbed a good deal of occult symbolism from its roots in Renaissance Hermeticism, and a great many male occultists have belonged to it in the last 300 years, it is not an occult order. Similarly, while it was closely associated with liberal political causes for the two centuries after 1717, and Masons such as George Washington, Simon Bolivar, and Franklin D. Roosevelt have played important roles in political affairs and world history, it is not a political organization. Non-members are often surprised to learn that its actual focus is self-improvement. Men join and practice Freemasonry to make themselves better human beings, and the rituals, symbolism, and teachings of Freemasonry focus on morality and ethics. See **Hermeticism**.

On its organizational side, Freemasonry consists of many thousands of self-governing local lodges, each of which has at least three members and may have up to several hundred. Lodges elect their officers by ballot, manage their own financial affairs, and select and initiate their members. Each lodge also sends representatives to the grand lodge with jurisdiction over the country (in America and Canada, the state or province) where it is located. The grand lodge and its officers, who are elected by the representatives, charter and supervise the local lodges. Each grand lodge is independent of all others; unlike many other fraternal secret societies, Freemasonry has no supreme grand lodge or worldwide head, and quarrels among grand lodges are not infrequent. See **grand lodge**; **lodge**.

On the ritual side, Freemasonry consists of three degrees or levels of initiation, titled Entered Apprentice, Fellow Craft, and Master Mason; the first two of these date from well before 1717, while the third was created in the early eighteenth century from material once passed on to the Worshipful Master (presiding officer) of a lodge on his installation. The first two degrees are based on the ceremonies used to initiate members of stonemasons' guilds in Scotland in the late Middle Ages, while the third enacts a medieval legend about Hiram Abiff, the murdered architect of King Solomon's Temple. Members advance from one degree to another by memorizing a catechism about the symbolism of each degree and demonstrating knowledge of the passwords, grips, and signs of recognition Masonry inherited from its medieval past. See **Hiram Abiff**; **Worshipful Master**.

Freemasonry started out as simply one of scores of clubs and societies popular in late seventeenth-century Britain, but its dramatic initiation rituals, its ethical focus, and its claim to ancient wisdom gave it a stronger appeal than most of its competitors. By the beginning of the eighteenth century it was widespread among the British middle classes and attracted a significant number of members from the aristocracy. The presence of peers in Masonic lodges gave the Craft the social cachet to spread beyond Britain's shores to Europe. The first overseas lodges were founded in France in the early 1720s, and by 1750 Masonry was active throughout Europe and the American colonies. Today it has lodges everywhere in the world except for some Muslim countries and Communist China, where it is forbidden by law. See **Initiation**.

The spread of Masonry to Europe also launched an explosion of new Masonic degrees beyond the three of the original system. These first emerged in France in the late 1730s, as Jacobites – partisans of the House of Stuart's claim on the British throne – struggled with their opponents, the Hanoverians, for control of French Masonic lodges in the years just before the Jacobite rising of 1745. These first "Scottish degrees" were originally secret but began to publicize their existence from 1750 on, and in their wake more than 2000 additional Masonic degrees came into being over the following century and a half. See **high degrees**; **Jacobites**; **Scottish degrees**.

Very few of these new degrees came under the authority of the grand lodges. The result is a bewildering tangle of independent grand bodies, which varies from country to country. In America, for example, Masonic lodges working the three degrees of Craft Masonry – "blue lodges," in Masonic parlance – answer to state grand lodges. Royal Arch chapters working one set of higher degrees answer to state grand chapters, and some of these (but not all) answer to the General Grand Chapter of the United States. Commanderies of Knights Templar working another set of higher degrees answer to state grand commanderies, which answer in turn to a national grand encampment. Local units of the Ancient and Accepted Scottish Rite, who work yet another set of higher degree, answer to one of two supreme councils, one for the northeast quarter of the United States, the other for the rest. The situation in Britain and other countries is similar. See **Ancient and Accepted Scottish Rite (AASR)**; **Royal Arch**.

What makes this even more complex than it seems is the fact that each of these grand bodies is independent of the others. The Sovereign Grand Commander of a Scottish Rite supreme council, for example, has no authority at all over the Grand Master of a state grand lodge, much less over the Grand High Priest of a state Royal Arch grand chapter, which belongs to the rival York Rite. Since quite a few American Freemasons belong to a lodge, a chapter, a commandery, and the four related bodies of the Scottish Rite at the same time, the actual authority wielded by any grand officer over a given Mason is very small. See **York Rite**.

This tangled web of organizations, jurisdictions, rituals, and degrees expanded steadily until about 1900, along with the membership of Masonry itself. In that year perhaps 8 million men belonged to Masonic lodges worldwide. Since then Masonic membership has steadily contracted, with the total number of Masons falling to a little under 2 million worldwide as of this writing. Like nearly all other modern secret societies, it flourished during an era when voluntary organizations rather than government programs took responsibility for most charitable, welfare and self-help programs, and withered as the media-driven mass society and the welfare state took over during the course of the twentieth century.

A complex role in Masonry's rise and fall has been played by organized antimasonry. Masonry's size, its social prominence, and its role as the western world's archetypal secret society has made it the target for criticism, opposition, and persecution at many times over the last three centuries. The Roman Catholic Church has been a bastion of hostility to Freemasonry since 1738, when Pope Clement XII issued the first of many bulls condemning it and excommunicating any Catholic who became a Mason, and opposition to Masonry has likewise been strong among conservative Protestant churches and some branches of Islam. The Nazi party in Germany and the Communist parties of Russia, China, and the pre-1989 Eastern Bloc all outlawed Masonry within their borders. Since the late eighteenth century, Freemasonry has also been a favorite target of conspiracy theorists in Europe and around the world. See **Antimasonry**.

Yet Masonry's steep decline in numbers and influence in the twentieth century also had much to do with changes in the Craft itself. As the most prestigious secret society in the western world in the nineteenth and early twentieth centuries, it attracted countless members whose interest in Masonry was limited to its value as a source of social connections and, especially in America, as a means of access to members only clubs and facilities. As local and grand lodges alike grew used to large budgets, maintaining and expanding membership numbers gradually took precedence over the purposes of the Craft, and led to a watering down of standards. In some jurisdictions nowadays a candidate can be entered, passed and raised (the traditional phrasing for the process of receiving the three degrees) in a single day. While these changes were put in place in an attempt to bring more men into the Craft, their effect has been to cheapen the experience of the ritual and thus remove one of the reasons men once became Masons in large numbers. At the same time, many Masonic bodies have turned away from the core Masonic purpose of self-improvement and tried to reinvent the Craft as an amateur social service agency focused on charitable projects. This has done little to slow Freemasonry's decline.

The result is a remarkable disconnection between Freemasonry's image and its reality in the opening years of the twenty-first century. People outside the Craft often see it as a polished, powerful, and monolithic institution guarding valuable secrets behind walls of wealth and privilege, while many of its members see it as a dwindling, beleaguered voluntary organization facing challenges from all sides, and struggling to define itself and its purpose in a world that increasingly treats it as an anachronistic irrelevance. Even as antimasons insist that Masonry controls the mass media, Masons complain that the mass media never portray Masonry in a positive light. While Freemasonry will probably survive its current decline, as it has weathered difficult times in the past, the clash between Masonry as it is and as it exists in the imagination of popular culture and conspiracy theory adds to the pressures against it.

Further reading: Case 1985a, MacNulty 1991, MacNulty 2002, Pike 1871, Roberts 1974, Stevenson 1988.

Freemasonry, origins of

As the most influential secret society in the modern Western world, Freemasonry has attracted a torrent of speculation from Masons and non-Masons alike, and inevitably much of that speculation has fastened on the question of Freemasonry's origins. Emerging out of obscurity in Britain in the middle of the seventeenth century, with no documented origin or founder, Freemasonry has posed a puzzle to scholarly research and provided a happy hunting ground to crackpots of all descriptions. No other social institution in the western world has been credited with so many different origins. See **Freemasonry**.

The oldest surviving Masonic documents, the Old Charges, trace the Craft back to a biblical origin. According to their account, before the Flood the sons of the patriarch Lamech invented geometry and all the other sciences. Fearing that God would punish them for their sins, they inscribed their discoveries inside two hollow pillars, a marble pillar that could endure fire and a bronze pillar that could survive flood. One of the pillars survived the Flood and was eventually found by Hermes Trismegistus, the great-grandson of Noah, who deciphered it and taught its wisdom to the Egyptians. Several generations later, King Nimrod of Babylon first set out the rules of Masonry for the builders of the Tower of Babel, and the first use of signs and gestures came after the confusion of languages during the building of the Tower, when masons unable to speak to one another learned to communicate by gesture. The regulations established by Nimrod remained in force until the time of Solomon, who reformed the Craft during the building of his temple. When the 80,000 masons employed building the temple returned to their home countries, they took Freemasonry to the four corners of the world. See **earth changes**; **Hermes Trismegistus**; **Temple of Solomon**.

This legend corresponds closely to the origin legends of many other craft guilds of the Middle Ages. By 1700, when Freemasonry began its astonishing spread through Britain and continental Europe, such legends had little credibility. While some early opponents of Masonry claimed that the Craft had been invented by the English dictator Oliver Cromwell to further his political ambitions, the vast majority of early publications related to the Craft either cited the biblical origin myths of the Old Charges or simply traced them back to craft guilds of medieval stonemasons. See **guilds, medieval**.

The link between Masonry and the old stonemasons' guilds made for good publicity in Britain, where the educated middle classes, who formed the backbone of Masonry, defined the Craft in their own image. Masonry spread to Europe, however, and became popular among French and central European aristocrats, to whom any association with manual labor seemed degrading. A new origin story was called for, and was in due time supplied by Andrew Ramsay (1686–1743), a Scottish Freemason and Jacobite in voluntary exile in France. In a famous oration written in 1736, Ramsay proposed that Masonry had actually originated with the knightly orders of the Crusades, which had somehow become mixed up with medieval stonemasons in Scotland. Ramsay specifically named the Knights Hospitaller as the order in question, but another order, far more romantic, inevitably replaced it: the Knights Templar. By the 1740s new "Scottish" degrees of Masonry explicitly named the Templars as the original source of Freemasonry. This provided Masonry with the aristocratic heritage it previously lacked, and helped the Craft expand explosively in Europe through the rest of the eighteenth century. See **Knights Templar**; **Ramsay, Andrew Michael**; **Scottish degrees**.

The prestige of the Templar story was so great that other Masonic and quasi-Masonic orders piggybacked their own origin stories onto it. This process even affected Rosicrucian orders, which had their own traditional origin story centering round the mythical fifteenth-century German sage Christian Rosenkreutz. Thus the Order of the Golden and Rosy Cross, an eighteenth-century German Rosicrucian order, claimed an origin in Egypt in 96 CE, but dated its arrival in Europe to 1188, when Knights Templar who had been initiated into the order in Palestine brought it back with them. See **Order of the Golden and Rosy Cross**; **Rosenkreutz, Christian**; **Rosicrucians**.

The Templars never managed to have Freemasonry all to themselves, however. Another influential eighteenth-century theory traced the origins of the Craft back to the ancient Druids, the priests of the Celtic peoples of Britain, Ireland, and France. That century was the seedtime of the Druid Revival – the reinvention of Druidry as a modern spiritual tradition – and it also saw Druids become a significant presence in British and French popular culture. Since scholars at the time believed the Druids built Stonehenge and other megalithic sites, their connection to a later guild of stonemasons seemed plausible, and the theory that ancient Druids had evolved into modern Masons had no shortage of enthusiastic defenders. English author John Cleland, better known as the author of *Fanny Hill*, argued for a Druid origin of Freemasonry in several books. He suggested, among other things, that the word "Mason" had originally been "May's son," referring to the Druid celebration of Beltane on May 1. American revolutionary Thomas Paine also contributed a work on the same theme. See **Druid Revival**; **Druids**.

The European rediscovery of ancient Egypt toward the end of the same century also provided Masonry with another popular source for origin stories. Alessandro Cagliostro, one of the great occult poseurs of the age, helped launch this trend in 1778 by inventing his own Egyptian Rite of Freemasonry, whose rituals he claimed he had found on a London bookstall. The Crata Repoa, a pseudo-Egyptian ritual of initiation published in Berlin in 1770, also added to the popularity of Egypt as a home of Masonry. The Rites of Memphis and Misraim, two Masonic systems of high degrees invented in the first decades of the nineteenth century, took up the banner of Egyptian Masonry and made the claim of an Egyptian origin commonplace in the occult wing of nineteenth-century Masonry. See **Cagliostro, Alessandro**; **Crata Repoa**; **Egypt**; **Rite of Memphis**; **Rite of Misraim**.

Nor were these the only theories of Masonic origins circulated and widely believed in the nineteenth century. The Dionysian artificers, a religious brotherhood of craftsmen known from a few inscriptions in the Greek city-states of Asia Minor, were given a wholly undocumented role in the building of King Solomon's Temple and thus turned into the ancestors of Masonry. The ancient Greek mysteries, much better documented but less easily linked to late medieval stonemasons, and the Essenes also ended up redefined by enthusiastic Masonic historians as ancestors of the Craft. See **Essenes**; **mysteries, ancient**.

A somewhat more plausible theory emerged from studies of ancient Roman history. From the time of the earliest Roman legal codes there existed in the city *collegia* or guilds of certain trades, and the guild of architects and builders, or *Collegium Artificum*, was established well before the beginning of the Roman Empire. In Italy, and possibly also in France and a few other places, some of the Roman guilds seem to have been the ancestors of medieval trade guilds. A seventh-century legal code of the Lombards, a German tribe that settled in northern Italy after the fall of Rome, includes two references to a guild of builders called the Comacine Masters, who took their name from the province of Como where they lived. From there, leaping the thousand-year gap between seventh-century Italy and seventeenth-century Scotland, some Masonic historians derived Freemasonry.

All these theories remained in circulation well into the twentieth century, and when they were discarded by historians they fell into the hands of the alternative-history scene, with predictable results. All the more romantic Masonic origin theories of the nineteenth century were brought back out of storage in the second half of the twentieth, so that once again Masons found themselves identified as surviving Templars, Egyptians, Essenes, and so on. Some of these efforts, such as John Robinson's restatement of the old Templar theory in his widely cited *Born In Blood* (1989), at least attempted to provide new historical evidence for the old claims. More often, though, these books argued that if a speculation couldn't be totally disproved, it must be true, or simply presented a colorful narrative and insisted that the only reason historians didn't accept it was that they were part of a conspiracy to suppress the truth. Such arguments sold books but did nothing to narrow the chasm between professional historians and authors of alternative history.

An important feature of twentieth-century conspiracy theory also had a powerful influence on theories of Masonic origins. Starting just after the First World War, when the forged *Protocols of the Elders of Zion* were circulated throughout the world, many conspiracy theorists began to insist that all secret societies, whatever their apparent motives and intentions, took orders from a single ruling circle. By the second half of the century this odd belief had become standard in the conspiracy-theory underworld and remains rarely questioned to this day. One result of this consensus is that instead of arguing over which ancient group was the ancestor of Freemasonry, many late twentieth-century writers simply insisted that they all were. See **New World Order**; **Protocols of the Elders of Zion**.

This process was catalyzed by popular works such as Christopher Knight and Robert Lomas's highly influential *The Hiram Key* (1996), which argued that the rituals of Freemasonry started as commemorations of the murder of a minor Egyptian pharaoh, which were for some reason adopted by the Hebrew tribes and passed down through the Temple of Jerusalem to the Essenes, then transmitted to the Knights Templar via documents uncovered in the foundations of the Temple following clues left by the Celtic Church of Scotland and Ireland; Templars fleeing from the destruction of their order in 1307 then brought the rituals to Scotland, where they ended up as the guild initiations of the local stonemasons. This narrative weaves together most of the popular theories about the origins of Masonry into a single tapestry, though for some reason they left out the Druids. As history, it has massive problems; knowledgeable reviewers have pointed out that its sweeping claims rest almost entirely on unsupported assumptions, speculation, and outright misinformation, but as a romantic origin story that embraces nearly every imaginable theory about Masonry's beginnings, it's hard to beat.

From the middle of the twentieth century, while speculation piled on speculation and authors in the rejected-knowledge industry had a field day with the Craft, a countertrend of sober historical scholarship has returned to the theory that Freemasonry descends from late medieval stonemasons' guilds in the British Isles. Knoop and Jones's magisterial *The Genesis of Freemasonry* (1947) made a strong case for this claim, and David Stevenson's *The Origins of Freemasonry* (1988) clinched the case by documenting many of the stages by which Scottish stonemasons' lodges began admitting people from outside the building trades, launching the transition to modern Freemasonry. None of this has even slowed down the production of new theories and the constant recycling of old ones, tracing Freemasonry to some source more romantic or sinister than the traditional ceremonies of medieval stonemasons.

Further reading: Baigent et al. 1983, Knoop and Jones 1947, Stevenson 1988.

French Revolution

The revolution of 1789–93 that toppled the Bourbon monarchy of France and set up continental Europe's first democratic government became the crucible of modern conspiracy theories and is still frequently cited by modern writers on the extreme right as the classic example of a national government subverted and destroyed by secret societies. These claims are all the more ironic in that nearly every other revolution in modern times offers more evidence of secret society activities. Where the American Revolution of 1776–83 can hardly be described without referring to the activities of the Committees of Correspondence and the Sons of Liberty and the Russian revolution of October 1917 was stage-managed by the Bolshevik Party, the role of secret societies in the French Revolution is equivocal at best. See **American Revolution; Committees of Correspondence; Russian revolution; Sons of Liberty**.

The ultimate cause of the collapse of the French monarchy in 1789 was the collision between France's ambitions as a world power and the corrupt, archaic, and inefficient system of taxation and finance that French kings relied on to fund their overseas ventures. The European wars of Louis XIV had placed the kingdom under a burden of debt that grew steadily through the reigns of his son and grandson. France's part in the American Revolution, financed almost entirely by loans, pushed the Ancien Régime to the brink; in the national budget of 1788, expenses exceeded income by 20 percent, and more than half of expenses went to service the national debt. The royal government's attempts to reorganize the tax system were systematically blocked by the aristocracy, which sought to preserve its own tax-exempt status and hoped to use the fiscal crisis to regain some of the political power it had lost during the sweeping reforms of Louis XIV.

With every other option closed to him by aristocratic intransigence, the king summoned the Estates-General, the rarely convened national parliament of France, which alone had the power to levy new taxes. Many aristocrats supported this move, as they hoped to force the king to accept a constitutional monarchy with a privileged place for the nobility. However, this plan backfired explosively on June 17, 1789 when the lowest of the three houses of the Estates-General, representing the commoners, declared itself the sole National Assembly and invited liberal members of the other two houses to join them in a new national government. While the king and conservative aristocrats bickered and temporized, the National Assembly created its own army, the National Guard. In July the Bastille in Paris, the symbol of the king's absolute rule, was seized and sacked by the Paris mob, and in October the king and his family were forced to leave Versailles for Paris as virtual prisoners of the new government.

From 1789 to 1792 the National Assembly governed France in the king's name, abolished the privileges of the aristocracy and nationalized the property of the Catholic Church in France. An attempt by the king to flee to the German border, take command of the border garrisons, and retake power was thwarted when a mob stopped him and forced him back to Paris. More serious was the outbreak of war with the Austrian Empire, which sought to return France to royal control. After the poorly equipped French army suffered a series of defeats, a group of Paris radicals seized control of the government, dissolved the National Assembly and abolished the monarchy. A new governing body, the National Convention, called up a massive new army that soon turned the tide against the invaders, driving them back beyond France's borders and launching a successful invasion of Italy.

The Convention soon broke apart in bitter internal struggles, though, and in April of 1793 Maximilien Robespierre – the head of the extremist Jacobin party – seized power and established a revolutionary dictatorship. In September of the same year the Terror began as the Jacobins started rounding up and executing their real or imagined opponents. By the time Robespierre alienated his own supporters and went to the guillotine himself, on 28 July 1794, some 40,000 people had been executed, including the king and queen. A more moderate government, the Directory, took power in 1795 and held it until 1799, when Napoleon Bonaparte, a Corsican in French service who had risen through the ranks to command the army, seized power in a coup. In 1804 he renamed himself Napoleon I, Emperor of the French. Defeated and exiled in 1814, he staged a dramatic return to power the next year, but was defeated again at the battle of Waterloo and spent the rest of his life in exile on the bleak island of St Helena in the South Atlantic.

The role of secret societies in these convulsions is complex. Freemasonry had reached France in the 1720s with Jacobite exiles; purely an aristocratic pursuit in its early years, it soon made its way down the social ladder and became popular among the educated middle classes. Many of the moderates in the revolutionary government (though relatively few of the radicals) were Freemasons. Further to the left was the Social Club, a political society headed by Louis d'Orleans, and its offspring, the Social Circle, took a position on the extreme left after its founding in 1790. Nicholas de Bonneville, the founder of the Social Circle, had connections with the Bavarian Illuminati, a liberal secret society active in Germany between 1776 and 1786. All these secret societies helped spread liberal and egalitarian social ideas before and during the Revolution. Still, evidence that any of these groups took any more active role in the Revolution is effectively absent. See **Bavarian Illuminati**; **Freemasonry**; **Social Circle**.

Ironically, the best-documented secret societies in France during the revolutionary era all opposed the governments that succeeded Louis XVI in power. The Conspiracy of Equals, a secret society headed by François "Gracchus" Babeuf and Filippo Buonarroti, attempted in 1796 to overthrow the Directorate. Later, during Napoleon's reign, the Chevaliers of Faith and the Philadelphes worked to overthrow him within France, while a dizzying array of Italian secret societies – the Raggi, the Carbonari, and others – formed to oppose French imperial pretensions in Italy. See **Carbonari**; **Chevaliers of Faith**; **Conspiracy of Equals**; **Philadelphes**; **Raggi**.

The claim that secret societies stage-managed the French Revolution – a claim that has featured in scores of conspiracy theories since that time – was a product of two conservative authors of the 1790s, the French Jesuit Augustin de Barruel and the Scottish Freemason John Robison. In sensationalistic books published within a year of one another, de Barruel and Robison both argued that the Bavarian Illuminati, acting through Freemasonry, had pursued a centuries-old vendetta, originally launched by the Knights Templar, against the French monarchy – a campaign that ultimately aimed at the violent overthrow of Christianity and all the monarchies of Europe. Both these books were wartime propaganda meant to turn public opinion against the French revolutionary government at a time when many on the left saw the spread of revolution outward from France as their own best hope of liberty. The viewpoint they presented assumed that nothing except the unseen hand of the Illuminati could explain the collapse of a corrupt, incompetent, and mismanaged French monarchy that had long since lost its legitimacy in the eyes of most of its own subjects. Despite the noticeable weaknesses in this claim, it has remained popular among reactionaries ever since. See **Knights Templar**.

Further reading: Billington 1980, Lefebvre 1947.

FRIENDLY SOCIETIES

A common term in Great Britain for fraternal benefit societies in the nineteenth and twentieth centuries. See **fraternal benefit societies**.

FUNDAMENTALISM

The word "fundamentalism" has been applied in recent years to religious extremists around the world. Properly speaking, though, it refers to an offshoot of Christianity invented in Britain in the 1820s by John Nelson Darby, the founder of a small evangelical sect called the Plymouth Brethren. Darby argued that certain Bible verses, when properly rearranged and reinterpreted, revealed a system of seven ages or "dispensations," and a detailed set of predictions about the end of the world. His influence in Britain was modest, but Darby's theories quickly gained a large following in the United States. In 1912, a 12-volume series of books titled *The Fundamentals* went into circulation in America, winning Darby's theology a sizeable audience and giving the movement its lasting name. Fundamentalist churches soon became the core of a reactionary political movement that spread through most of the English-speaking world.

Fundamentalism is not a secret society, but it has had a massive role in shaping ideas about secret societies in the western world through relentless campaigns of anti-secret society propaganda. Many fundamentalists remain convinced believers in claims of Masonic devil worship dating from the "Palladian Order" hoax of the 1880s. The New World Order mythology launched by the John Birch Society in the 1960s and claims that Freemasonry is involved in Satanic ritual abuse are also grist for fundamentalist mills. While some criticisms of Masonry and other secret societies are based on honestly held differences of opinion, others can only be described as deliberate disinformation, and seem to be motivated by the political agenda of the movement. See **disinformation**; **John Birch Society**; **New World Order**; **Palladian Order**; **Satanism**.

Ironically, the fundamentalist movement has a long history of connections with secret societies that support its agenda. In 1920s America, for example, the Ku Klux Klan and fundamentalist churches were close allies. As many as 40,000 fundamentalist ministers enrolled as Klansmen during this period. One popular Kansas City minister, Rev. E.F. Stanton, published a sermon, *Christ and Other Klansmen*, extolling the Klan as a way back to "old-fashioned" (i.e., fundamentalist) Christianity. In the early 1920s the Grand Dragons of four states and 26 of the 39 Klokards, or national lecturers, employed by the Klan were fundamentalist ministers. Other secret societies that have benefited from fundamentalist connections include the Loyal Orange Order, the Knights of Luther, and the American Protective Association. More recently, fundamentalist groups have established close ties with Dominionist organizations such as the Coalition on Revival. See **American Protective Association (APA)**; **Dominionism**; **Ku Klux Klan**; **Loyal Orange Order**.

Fundamentalism has had at least one more major impact on a secret society, this time in an unexpected direction. English magician and would-be Antichrist Aleister Crowley (1875–1947) was raised in the Plymouth Brethren, the original fundamentalist sect. His rejection of the religion of his childhood failed to erase all traces of Darby's theology from his mind, and the theology he created for his new religion of Thelema ("will") echoes Darby's ideas in many particulars, defining history as a series of dispensations ruled by different spiritual powers. This theology continues to guide the Ordo Templi Orientis, one of the largest occult secret societies in the world today. See **Crowley, Aleister**; **Ordo Templi Orientis (OTO)**.

Further reading: Boyer 1992, Marsden 1980, Stanton 1924, Wade 1987.

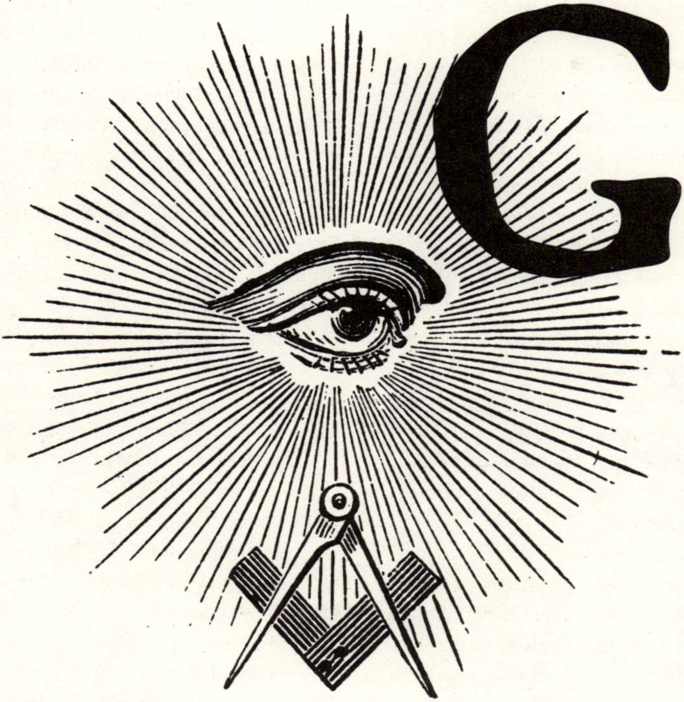
G

Gematria

A curious feature of many ancient alphabets is that each of their letters is also a number. Alphabets of this sort, called "isopsephic alphabets" by scholars, lend themselves to forms of number symbolism using the numerical value of letters, words, and sentences. In the Jewish Cabala, the mystical tradition that developed this approach most extensively, this is called gematria; the term has been adopted by most other surviving systems of number symbolism as well. See **Cabala**.

An immense amount of gematria, most of it unrecognized, occurs in the sacred writings and occult traditions of the western world. The name of the god Mithras in Greek letters, for example, adds up to 365, the number of days in a year, as do the names of the Gnostic god Abraxas and the Druid god Belenos – and it should come as no surprise that all three are solar divinities. The New Testament is especially crowded with gematria, from the name of Jesus (888 in Greek gematria) to that of the Beast of the Book of Revelation, whose number 666 has become famous in contemporary Satanism. See **Antichrist**; **Christian origins**; **Jesus of Nazareth**; **Mithraic mysteries**.

Further reading: Fideler 1993.

Germanenorden

A core element of the underground of racist secret societies that laid the foundations for the Nazi party, the Germanenorden ("Order of Germans") was founded in 1912 by Hermann Pohl, a German antisemite and right-wing political activist who belonged to the Reichshammerbund ("Reich Hammer Society"), the most influential antisemitic organization in Germany. Like most reactionaries of his time, Pohl believed devoutly in the existence of a vast Jewish conspiracy. He believed, though, that the only way to successfully counter this alleged conspiracy was to turn its own methods against it, and organize a secret society to oppose it. See **Antisemitism**.

By 1910 Pohl drafted an initiation ritual for a German antisemitic secret society. His sources include the rituals of the United Ancient Order of Druids (UAOD), a fraternal secret society that had a large presence in Germany at that time; the Ariosophical teachings of Guido von List (1848–1919), an Austrian racial mystic whose writings were a major influence all through the German far right of the time; and the musical and philosophical works of composer Richard Wagner. In 1911 Pohl and a group of fellow antisemites organized the Wotan Lodge around the new rituals. In the following year the Germanenorden drew up its bylaws and began recruiting members through the

Reichshammerbund, and by the end of the year it had six lodges and over 300 members. See **United Ancient Order of Druids (UAOD)**.

The Germanenorden quickly became a significant force on the German far right. From the beginning, though, its members disagreed on the approach the order should take. Pohl himself argued that the Germanenorden should concentrate on fostering an "Aryan-Germanic religious revival" through its ritual and occult work, but a majority of the membership wanted to concentrate on secret political action instead. These differences finally came to a head in 1916, splitting the Germanenorden in two. The more occult half, under Pohl's leadership, took the new name Germanenorden Walvater of the Holy Grail and began a systematic campaign of expansion using cover names to camouflage its existence. Walvater member Rudolf von Sebottendorf founded what would become the order's most successful local lodge in Munich, under the cover name Thule-Gesellschaft (Thule Society), which played a crucial role in bringing the Nazi party into being. See **Thule Society**.

As the Nazi party grew into the dominant party on Germany's far right, members of both branches of the Germanenorden joined it, while others helped it directly or indirectly. Adolf Hitler's inauguration as Chancellor of Germany in 1933 was thus the fulfillment of the Germanenorden's ambitions, but it also proved to be the end of the road for the order. Along with all other secret societies outside the Nazi party the Germanenorden was ordered to dissolve shortly after the Nazi takeover.

Further reading: Goodrick-Clarke 1992.

Gnosticism

A diverse and poorly understood religious movement in the ancient Mediterranean world, Gnosticism first appeared in the cultural melting pot of Hellenistic Egypt within a century of the start of the Common Era and spread throughout the Roman world over the next 200 years. Even among religious traditions, which tend to draw their inspiration from far and wide, it was remarkably eclectic in its choice of sources. Greek philosophy, pagan mystery cults, Jewish and Christian theology and myth, Egyptian magic, and (quite possibly) ideas drawn from Buddhist missionaries, who were active in the Egyptian city of Alexandria by 200 BCE, all flowed together to create a series of radical religious viewpoints that overturned the conventional ideas of every other religion of the time. See **Egypt**; **mysteries, ancient**.

Gnosticism was never a single religion, and attempts to construct a coherent doctrine out of the wild diversity of Gnostic belief fall apart in the face of the surviving evidence. A handful of core themes, though, run through nearly all Gnostic writings. The most important of these is a radical dualism that places spirit and matter in absolute opposition. The world of matter, in Gnostic thought, is a prison, and the powers who rule it are demons whose dominion over humanity is as brutal as it is unjust. The body, as a microcosm of the corrupt world of matter, is equally a prison, and the soul trapped in the body is like a living person sealed inside a tomb. The human soul has been lured into the trap of matter from another universe, a realm of light governed by timeless powers who wait for humanity to return from the material world, and these powers send messengers to call souls back to their true home. To Gnostic Christians, Jesus was such a messenger, an eternal being from the world of light who came to communicate the gift of *gnosis* ("knowledge") to those ready to receive it, because the only thing holding human souls in bondage to matter is ignorance of their true nature and the way back home. See **dualism**.

On this broad framework, a dizzying array of different theologies, teachings, and systems of practice took shape during the centuries when Gnosticism was in full flower. Some Gnostics argued that the demiurge, the evil creator of the world, was none other than the angry and jealous god of the Jews; others named the god of the Jews as the ruler of the world of light. Some Gnostic sects insisted that absolute celibacy was essential, others argued that the body was powerless to affect the spirit and indulged in total sexual freedom, while still others held that sexual rituals were the key to attaining gnosis. Since Gnostic traditions put personal spiritual experience at the center of their vision of religion, such variations were inevitable.

Some evidence suggests that the earliest Christian proto-churches were at least heavily influenced by Gnostic ideas, if not wholly Gnostic, and for the first three centuries of Christian history Gnostic interpretations of the teachings of Jesus were at least as popular as what later became the orthodox belief. Only a long struggle on the part of the emerging church hierarchy forced Gnosticism out of the Christian mainstream, and even then the result was a flurry of new heretical organizations outside of Church control. Gnosticism remained a living tradition in the western world until the fourteenth century, when the last major Gnostic movement – the Cathar church in southern France – was crushed by military force. See **Cathars**; **Christian origins**.

Gnosticism proved impossible to bury, however, and in the first decades of the nineteenth century, French occultists succeeded in reviving it. The *Église Gnostique* (Gnostic Church) of Jules Doinel, founded in Paris in 1828, launched a tradition of Gnostic churches in Europe and the Americas that remains active to this day. For more than a century, however, the Gnostic revival struggled to piece together what Theosophical writer G.R.S. Mead very appropriately termed "fragments of a faith forgotten."

All this changed in 1945, when Egyptian peasants from the village of Nag Hammadi found an ancient stone jar full of papyrus scrolls. They proved to be the library of a Gnostic monastery, hidden away at the time of the triumph of orthodox Christianity in the fifth century of the Common Era. The translation and publishing of the Nag Hammadi scrolls in the 1960s and 1970s brought Gnosticism back into the limelight and provided a wealth of material for a new generation of Gnostics. As of this writing Gnostic churches and secret societies of many kinds have proliferated throughout the world and show no sign of losing momentum any time soon.

Further reading: Barnstone and Meyer 2003, Culianu 1992, Filoramo 1990, Layton 1987.

Gormogons

See **Ancient Noble Order of Gormogons**.

Grail

The central mystery of the Arthurian legends, the Grail – also named the Grâl, Graal, or Holy Grail – was a puzzling object for which many of the Knights of the Round Table quested in the last years of Arthur's reign. Usually but not always described as a cup or goblet, it had the power to feed any number of people the food and drink they loved best. It could be found in the Castle of Carbonek, somewhere in the enchanted Waste Land, where it played the central role in a mysterious ceremony presided over by a female Grail bearer and a wounded Fisher King. In order to awaken the Grail's power, heal the wounded king, and bring fertility to the Waste Land, a wandering knight had to reach Carbonek, witness the ceremony, and ask the right question; the wording of the question varied from text to text, but the most common was "Whom does the Grail serve?" See **Arthurian legends**.

The Grail legends surfaced very suddenly around 1180, when Chrétien de Troyes – one of the first great writers of Arthurian tales – began *Perceval, ou le Conte du Graal* (*Perceval, or the Story of the Grail*), the oldest known Grail romance. It was unfinished at his death, but two other writers finished it in the following years. Wolfram von Eschenbach's German version, *Parzival*, appeared in 1207, and in the same year Walter Map's version, *Queste del Sant Graal*, reworked the Grail story to bring it closer to Christian orthodoxy, transforming it into the cup used by Jesus at the Last Supper. The production of Grail stories continued at a brisk pace until 1220, and then stopped; speculations have proliferated over the centuries, but to this day no one is sure why. See **Jesus of Nazareth**.

Scholars have argued for more than two centuries about the origin and meaning of the Grail legends. Certainly many of the core themes of the legend have roots in archaic Celtic traditions, where enchanted cauldrons that magically produce food are a common feature. Close similarities exist between the Grail procession of the legends and a ceremony known from a handful of ancient Celtic and Germanic sources, in which a woman bore a cup of mead to the king in a ceremonial proclamation of his kingship. Jessie Weston, one of the premier scholars of the Arthurian legends in the early twentieth century, argued that the rituals surrounding the Grail in the legends were echoes of an ancient mystery initiation, perhaps descended from a Gnostic sect known as the Naassenes. See **fertility religion**; **Gnosticism**; **mysteries, ancient**.

Like so much of the Arthurian legends, the Grail dropped out of popular culture at the end of the Middle Ages and received little attention until the Victorian period. Druidic secret societies in Britain and France in the late nineteenth century made room for it in their teachings, but it entered the wider realm of occult secret societies only in the twentieth century, when it was adopted as an important occult symbol by many magical traditions. Occult lodges based on the work of English magician Dion Fortune (1890–1946) use it as a central symbol, and it has also become important in some branches of Wicca and a range of secret societies inspired by the Arthurian legends. See **Druid Revival**; **Society of the Inner Light**; **Wicca**.

More recently, the Grail has been re-defined in a radically different way From the early twentieth century on, Christian occultists and mystics have made use of the pun between the medieval French *sangreal* ("holy grail") and *sang real* ("royal blood") to draw attention to the symbolic role of the Grail as the cup of the Last Supper and the symbolic or physical container for the blood of Jesus. In the last decades of the twentieth century, however, this bit of wordplay was pulled out of its context in occult teaching and turned into an element in one of the most popular branches of the contemporary rejected-knowledge scene. See **rejected knowledge**.

In their bestselling *The Holy Blood and the Holy Grail* (1982), which postulated that Jesus had a child by Mary Magdalene and founded a bloodline that survives to the present, authors Michael Baigent, Richard Leigh, and Henry Lincoln argued that the Grail was a symbol of the Jesus bloodline. This identification has been widely accepted in the rejected-knowledge community since that time, and plays a role in alternative visions of Christianity in popular fiction such as Dan Brown's bestselling novel *The Da Vinci Code* (2003). The medieval Grail romances themselves offer no noticeable support for this claim, but that has not stopped it from being stated as fact in dozens if not hundreds of books since that time. See **Da Vinci Code, the**.

Further reading: Baigent et al. 1983, Enright 1996, Matthews and Green 1986, Weston 1983.

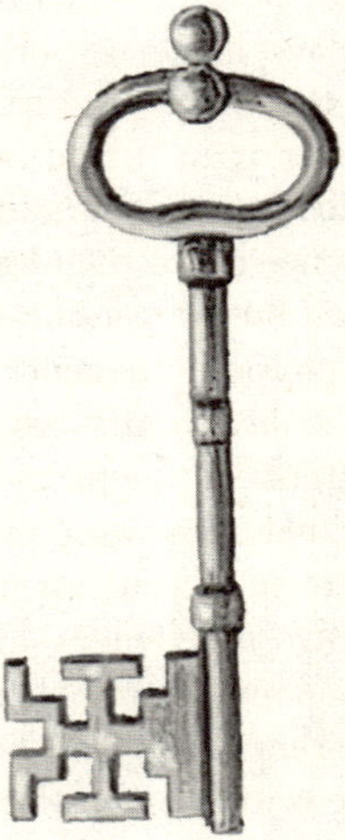

GRAND LODGE

In Freemasonry and most other fraternal secret societies, the organization that charters and supervises local lodges. The first grand lodge was created in 1717 by four Masonic lodges meeting in London, and went through a long period of political disagreements and schisms before it was accepted as the governing body of all English Masonic lodges. Other national grand lodges were founded in Scotland, Ireland, continental Europe, and elsewhere starting in the 1720s. Today every country that has Masonic lodges has at least one grand lodge; some nations have several, and the United States and Canada have a grand lodge for every state or province. See **Antient–Modern schism**; **Freemasonry**.

Freemasonry is all but unique in that each national, state, or provincial grand lodge is independent of every other. Many other fraternal orders add a third level. Thus the Independent Order of Odd Fellows, for example, has grand lodges for each American state and Canadian province, and above that a Sovereign Grand Lodge formed of delegates from each of the grand lodges. This is all the more ironic in that Freemasonry has often been accused of being a centralized conspiracy out to dominate the world, while the Odd Fellows, the Loyal Order of Moose, and other relatively centralized fraternal secret societies have escaped such accusations. See **Antimasonry**; **Loyal Order of Moose**; **Odd Fellowship**.

Like local lodges, grand lodges of different societies commonly have different names. Many Druid orders have a Grand Grove, for example; the Fraternal Order of Eagles has a Supreme Aerie, while the Shriners have an Imperial Divan. Some

Masonic jurisdictions have a Grand Orient instead of a Grand Lodge. See **Ancient Arabic Order of Nobles of the Mystic Shrine**; **Druid Revival**; **Fraternal Order of Eagles**; **Grand Orient**; **lodge**.

Grand Loge Alpina

The Swiss Grand Lodge of Freemasonry, the Grand Loge Alpina ("Alpine Grand Lodge") was founded in 1844 by the fusion of two earlier Grand Lodges in Switzerland. For more than 150 years it has exercised the usual functions of a Masonic Grand Lodge over most Swiss lodges. In the second half of the twentieth century, however, it became caught up in conspiracy theories about the Priory of Sion, a secret society allegedly dating back to the early Middle Ages but actually founded in 1956. Several of the documents forged by Priory founder Pierre Plantard and foisted off on French libraries were labeled, falsely, as Grand Loge Alpina publications. See **Priory of Sion**.

In the usual manner, once introduced into the world of conspiracy theory, the Grand Loge Alpina was promptly pulled out of its context and turned into part of the network of nefarious secret societies that allegedly control the world. The contrast between this colorful reputation and the rather dowdy reality of a very ordinary Masonic Grand Lodge is remarkable, to say the least. Like every other society, secret or otherwise, the Grand Loge Alpina has members with political interests, but investigators looking for successors to the Illuminati are likely to be disappointed. See **Bavarian Illuminati**.

Grand Orient

In Freemasonry and some secret societies descended from it, a term for a national or international grand lodge. The phrase, "Grand East" in French, was adopted for the newly founded grand lodge in France in 1773, after several decades of dispute between various claimants to the title of grand lodge of France. See **grand lodge**.

From then until 1877, through a complicated history of quarrels with grand bodies of the numerous high degrees active in France, the Grand Orient of France was a national grand lodge like any other. In the annual meeting of the Grand Orient that year, however, the delegates almost unanimously adopted a resolution removing belief in a Supreme Being from the requirements for membership. The United Grand Lodge of England and most other Masonic grand lodges immediately withdrew recognition from the Grand Orient and declared it and all its subordinate lodges irregular. Despite that ruling, which still remains in force, the Grand Orient of France remains the largest French Masonic jurisdiction today. See **Freemasonry**; **high degrees**.

Grange

See **Patrons of Husbandry (Grange)**.

Great Pyramid

The most famous monument on earth and one of the greatest works of architecture in human history, the Great Pyramid is one of three massive stone pyramids that rise from the Giza plateau, southwest of Cairo. According to traditions known to the ancient Greeks and confirmed by modern archeological research, it was built by Khufu, a pharaoh of Egypt's third dynasty, in about 2170 BCE. Its ancient name was *Akhet Khufu*, "Splendor of Khufu." See **Egypt**.

The Great Pyramid deserves its modern label. Superlative in every way, it stood 481 feet (146 meters) tall when it was complete; sheathed in smooth white limestone, it must have shone like a beacon in sunlight. Some 2.5 million limestone blocks, weighing a total near 6 million tons, were quarried from the Giza plateau to supply the bulk of the stone. The facing stone came from quarries across the Nile, while granite for the interior chambers came by raft down the Nile from Aswan 500 miles (over 800 kilometers) upstream. All those blocks of stone had to be hauled into place one at a time by human muscle. During the 20 or 30 years of its construction, a good fraction of Egypt's total labor force must have been called to Giza during the months of the Nile flood, when no work could be done in the fields. The work was not done by slaves; though equivalent records don't survive for the Great Pyramid, workers on later pyramids were paid in bread, beer, and onions, and proudly daubed the names of their work teams on the stones they quarried and hauled.

The builders of the Great Pyramid also managed an extraordinary degree of precision in their work, lining up the four sides of the pyramid to the compass points to within a tenth of a degree and making the sides equal to within 8 inches (20 centimeters). This level of accuracy does not require advanced technology; it can be achieved with simple tools and careful observation, but only when supported by a powerful motive.

The motive is one of the great mysteries of the Great Pyramid. Ancient Greek sources and modern archeological opinion agree that it was a tomb, and yet when the Arab Caliph Abdullah al-Mamun and his men forced their way past untouched granite barriers in 820 CE, they found no body in the great stone sarcophagus in the King's Chamber, and none of the treasures Egyptian kings typically brought with them into the afterlife. Unlike most Egyptian monuments, the interior of the Great Pyramid is bare of bas-reliefs and hieroglyphic inscriptions that might help explain it, and it contains three large chambers and a variety of passages and air-shafts, unlike other pyramids, which have one chamber with a single entrance. Mainstream archeologists suggest that the tomb was plundered in ancient times, but offer no evidence for the claim. Despite many arguments, no one knows for sure why *Akhet Khufu* was built or what purpose it might have served.

The sheer scale and grandeur of the Great Pyramid and the mysteries that surround it made it a magnet for strange theories. Charles Piazzi Smyth, Astronomer Royal for Scotland under Queen Victoria and a highly original religious thinker, became convinced that the ascending passage leading to the King's Chamber had been laid out in such a way that the length of its floor predicted the future history of the world and the date of the Second Coming. He also sorted through hundreds of measurements to find some that had remarkable qualities, such as a fair approximation to *pi* and the relative proportions of the earth and moon. His 1880 book, *Our Inheritance in the Great Pyramid*, launched the modern movement of pyramidology, sometimes labeled "pyramidiocy" by its critics; the term is not always deserved, but it is true that some remarkably dotty theories over the years have centered on the Great Pyramid.

One of the major themes of current pyramid speculation focuses on the age of the Great Pyramid. While it has traditionally been dated to Khufu's reign, no conclusive dating has been found within the Pyramid itself, and uncertainties surrounding the date of the nearby Sphinx – it has what might be signs of erosion by rain on its flanks, which would require it to date from before 6000 BCE – have been applied to the Great Pyramid as well. Some radical Egyptologists argue that it dates from thousands of years before the other pyramids, which were built in imitation of it. It is an interesting speculation but proof for it is still lacking.

Sheer limits of space make it impossible to list even a representative sample of the other claims that have been made about the Great Pyramid. It remains a central focus of rejected knowledge and the alternative-realities movement, and will probably continue to collect strange theories and speculative visions as long as it looms up against the desert sky of Giza. See **rejected knowledge**.

Further reading: Edwards 1985, Lehner 1997, Tompkins 1978.

Great White Lodge

In Theosophy and occult systems influenced by it, the brotherhood of advanced souls who form the hidden government of the world and direct the course of human evolution. Headed by the Lord of the World, Sanat Kumara, the Great White Lodge or Great White Brotherhood – the terms are used interchangeably – includes all the Masters. See **Masters**; **Theosophical Society**.

The concept of a vast, benevolent occult brotherhood managing the world behind the scenes developed over the course of the nineteenth century by a kind of intellectual inflation from the Unknown Superiors of eighteenth-century high degree Freemasonry. As occult secret societies competed with one another for members and prestige, claims about the importance of their respective Unknown Superiors provided a useful weapon. In such an environment, claims that one particular set of secret chiefs ran the world were an unavoidable result. Ironically, such claims played an important role in launching the distinctive conspiracy myth of the twentieth century, the theory that all the world's secret societies took orders from a single central group pursuing a malevolent plan of world domination. See **New World Order**; **Protocols of the Elders of Zion**.

Ironically, recent research by historian K. Paul Johnson has pointed out that in the writings of Madame Blavatsky, the Masters of the Great White Lodge were specifically described as ordinary, though spiritually advanced, human beings, and the Great White Lodge itself only took on its supernatural qualities in the writings of Blavatsky's successors, Annie Besant and C.W. Leadbeater. Johnson has argued that the actual "Great White Lodge" of Blavatsky's time was a network of Hindu spiritual and political leaders who worked with her during her time in India to oppose the British colonial government and the activities of Christian missionaries. These conclusions have been sharply attacked by modern Theosophists, but Johnson offers substantial evidence for his case and it cannot be dismissed out of hand. See **Blavatsky, Helena Petrovna**.

Further reading: Johnson 1994, Leadbeater 1925.

GUILDS, MEDIEVAL

Among the fundamental social institutions of European society during the Middle Ages, a guild (the word is also spelled gild) was an association of craftsmen of a particular trade in a single town. Members were divided into three classes: masters, who had expert knowledge of the craft and owned their own businesses; journeymen, fellows, or companions, who had basic skill in the craft and worked in the shops of masters for daily wages; and apprentices, who studied the craft from masters and worked for them as servants in exchange for room and board. Masters of a guild formed its voting membership and assembled at regular meetings under the leadership of an elected guild master.

Close parallels exist between the medieval guild system and the fraternal orders of the eighteenth, nineteenth and twentieth centuries in Europe and America. Like their later equivalents, guilds collected money from their members to provide funerals for members and support widows and orphans, and also did charitable work in their communities; each guild had its own symbols and origin legend, and put new apprentices, journeymen, and masters through traditional initiation rituals. Despite these parallels, the only guilds that changed directly into fraternal secret societies are a handful of stonemasons' guilds in Scotland, which began to admit members who did not belong to the building trades around 1600. These guilds became the ancestors of modern Freemasonry. See **Brothering**; **fraternal orders**; **Freemasonry, origins of**.

At least two other modern secret societies, however, have slightly less direct links to the medieval guild system. Through most of the Middle Ages, apprentices who showed reasonable skill and diligence at their craft could count on progressing to journeyman and then to master. The breakdown of the medieval social order in the fifteenth and sixteenth centuries, however, saw many guilds turn into associations of business owners who restricted access to the rank of master to themselves and their sons. In response, journeymen organized guild-like organizations of their own, with many of the same benefits as guild membership and which also assisted their efforts to gain higher wages and better working conditions. These proto-labor unions of the late Middle Ages usually had the word "journeyman," "fellow," or "companion" in their titles, and these marks remained in two traditions that descended from them – Compagnonnage and Odd Fellowship. See **Compagnonnage**; **Odd Fellowship**.

H

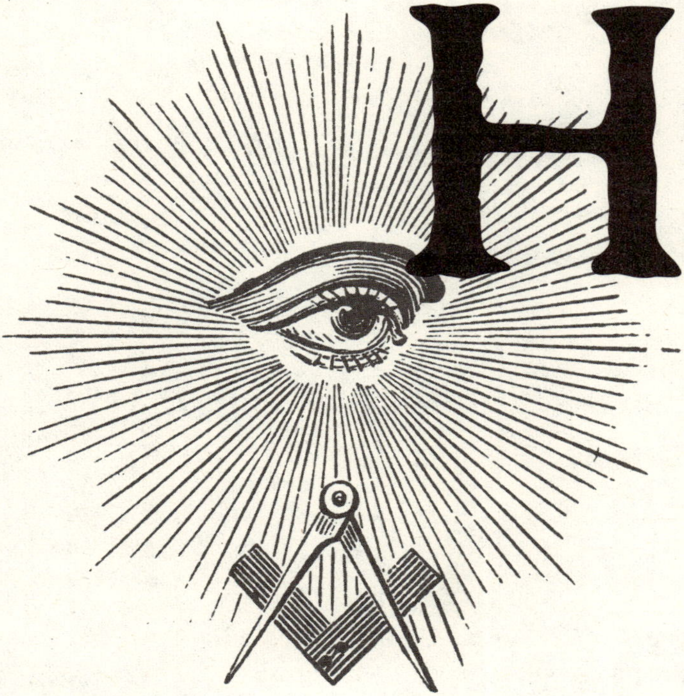

HALL, MANLY PALMER

Canadian-American occultist, 1901–90. One of the most influential figures in twentieth-century American occultism, Hall was born in Peterborough, Ontario and raised by his maternal grandmother, who took him to live in the United States in 1904. He was interested in occultism from an early age and joined the Theosophical Society in his teen years. In 1919 he left home and moved to Oceanside, California, where he spent a year as a member of Max Heindel's Rosicrucian Fellowship. See **Rosicrucian Fellowship**; **Theosophical Society**.

In 1920 he moved to New York City, where he was briefly employed on Wall Street as a stockbroker's clerk, then returned to the west coast and settled in Los Angeles, where he spent the rest of his life. In his first years there, like several other noted occultists of the time, he worked as a screenwriter in the fledgling motion picture industry, but he lectured frequently at occult organizations in the Los Angeles area as well. In 1923 he was ordained as a minister of the Church of the People, a metaphysical church in Los Angeles.

By that time he had begun work on his magnum opus, *The Secret Teachings of All Ages*, also titled *An Encyclopedic Outline of Masonic, Hermetic, Qabbalistic, and Rosicrucian Symbolical Philosophy*. Published by subscription in 1928, with gorgeous color illustrations by artist Augustus Knapp, it made Hall one of the most widely known occultists in the world. A mystery surrounds the book; in its pages, Hall speaks in glowing terms of Freemasonry and makes accurate references to its teachings and rituals, but by all accounts he was not initiated into regular Freemasonry until decades later. The most likely explanation is that he was a member of an irregular branch of the Craft, possibly a Co-Masonic lodge. Later in his life he joined a regular Masonic lodge and the Scottish Rite, rising to the rank of 33°. See **Ancient and Accepted Scottish Rite (AASR)**; **Co-Masonry**; **Freemasonry.**

The success of *The Secret Teachings* made it possible for him to pursue his lifelong dream of establishing a center for education based on ancient mystery traditions. The Philosophical Research School (PRS) was founded in 1934, and construction began on its Los Angeles headquarters the next year. For the rest of his life, Hall gave weekly lectures at the PRS, managed an extensive correspondence school, and wrote more than 200 books published by the PRS press.

The esoteric dimension of Hall's work was far less public. His contacts with Max Heindel were not the only connections Hall had with the Rosicrucian movement, and a small and very private Rosicrucian group met regularly in the PRS headquarters to practice meditations and rituals. One of the sources for his work was apparently a triangular book in cipher once in the possession of the

Comte de Saint-Germain, described as "The Holy Magic revealed to Moses discovered within an Egyptian monument and preciously preserved in Asia under the emblem of a winged dragon." The book contains a theurgic magical ritual for finding treasure and conferring health and long life; Hall owned two copies of it, and considered them among his most important possessions. See **Rosicrucians**; **Saint-Germain, Comte de**.

Hall's impact on the occult community waned after the cultural revolution of the 1960s, but he and the PRS retained a faithful audience until Hall's death in 1990. After a period of confusion and reorganization, the PRS regrouped successfully and continues to offer Hall's teachings to the world. Whether his Rosicrucian group still meets in the PRS headquarters, on the other hand, is a secret known only to its initiates.

Further reading: Hall 1988.

Hell-Fire Club

The most notorious Satanist organization in eighteenth-century Britain, the Hell-Fire Club was originally founded in London in 1719 by Philip, Duke of Wharton, a liberal politician and atheist who set out to ridicule the religious orthodoxies of his time by holding mock-Satanist ceremonies in a tavern near St James's Square, London. The Club was closed down the next year after it became a political liability to Wharton, who went on to become the Grand Master of English Freemasons in 1722, and then left Masonry the next year to organize an antimasonic order with Jacobite connections, the Gormogons. See **Ancient Noble Order of Gormogons**; **Jacobites**.

The Hell-Fire Club remained in abeyance until 1746, when Sir Francis Dashwood and a group of his friends revived it. Dashwood may have learned about the earlier club from Lady Mary Wortley Montagu, Wharton's ex-mistress, who had participated in its rites and became a friend of Dashwood's in 1739. Early meetings of the Club took place at the George and Vulture, a London pub, but operations soon moved to Medmenham Abbey, and the club continued to meet there for the remainder of its existence. The Abbey, rebuilt by Dashwood and stocked with a celebrated collection of pornography, also included a "chapter room" for private ceremonies.

According to contemporary accounts, members attended in black monastic robes and took part in burlesque pseudo-Satanic rituals along with "nuns" hired for the evening. The rites involved the consumption of impressive amounts of alcohol and ended with an orgy. Such entertainments were popular enough among the eighteenth-century English upper class to attract some of the leading figures of the time; MP John Wilkes and the Earl of Bute were members, and Benjamin Franklin took part during his second stay in England. See **Franklin, Benjamin**.

Like the great majority of Satanist organizations, the Hell-Fire Club was mostly a way for people frustrated by the moral restraints of a nominally Christian society to act out fantasies of sexual wickedness in a safe setting. In its first incarnation, though, it had echoes of a more serious purpose. Like the Chevaliers of Jubilation, a libertine secret society founded in Holland about a decade before Wharton's Hell-Fire Club, it combined ribald entertainment with calculated attacks on the dogmatic religious beliefs that underpinned political autocracy. See **Chevaliers of Jubilation**; **Satanism**.

Further reading: Towers 1986.

Hermes Trismegistus

The legendary founder of the Hermetic tradition and the inventor of astrology, alchemy, medicine, and magic, Hermes Trismegistus ("Hermes Thrice Great") was literally a figure to conjure with from the dawn of the Middle Ages until the seventeenth century. Medieval writers disagreed about his place in history; some claimed that he was the same person as Enoch, the great-grandfather of Noah, who was lifted up into heaven to become the great angel Metatron, while others held that he was the wisest of the Egyptians and lived at the time of Moses. According to the early Christian writer Eusebius, he wrote 36 books on philosophy and theology and 6 more on astronomy. See **Alchemy**; **Magic**.

The facts behind the legend are as interesting as the legend itself. After Alexander the Great conquered Egypt and installed a Greek ruling class there, Greek philosophy and Egyptian spirituality mingled freely on the banks of the Nile. In the hybrid culture that emerged, the Greek god Hermes took on many of the attributes of Thoth, the ibis-headed Egyptian god of wisdom, whose traditional titles included "Thrice Great." Just as Egyptian magical writings from the pharaonic past claimed Thoth as their author, many of the astrological, alchemical, and mystical writings produced in Hellenistic Egypt were attributed to Hermes the Thrice-Great. In the last few centuries of the Roman Empire, these writings had a wide circulation and were pressed into service by the proponents of many different traditions. Several of the early theologians of Christianity, including Augustine of Hippo, quoted the writings attributed to Hermes Trismegistus, and thus guaranteed that later generations of Christians would remember him as a wise man of the distant past. One dialogue attributed to Hermes, the *Asclepius*, survived into the Middle Ages in a Latin translation, and this and the references in old Christian sources helped build Hermes' medieval reputation.

Most of the other writings attributed to Hermes vanished forever in the chaotic years that followed the collapse of the Roman Empire. In 1453, however, a manuscript volume containing 18 short books attributed to Hermes surfaced in Greece. Translated by Marsilio Ficino, one of the greatest scholars of the age, this collection – the *Corpus Hermeticum* – launched the tradition of Renaissance Hermeticism and, directly or indirectly, became the core inspiration for most of the occult secret societies of the next 400 years. To Renaissance occultists, Hermes was an ancient Egyptian sage whose writings, older than the Bible, offered access to a purer spirituality than the Christianity of their own time. The spirited defense of magic in Hermes' writings also made it easier for Renaissance mages to justify their own practices and condemn the intolerance of their persecutors. See **Hermeticism**.

Both the medieval and the Renaissance traditions surrounding Hermes had an impact on early Freemasonry and, through it, on many other secret societies. The old medieval Masonic constitutions all refer to Hermes as one of the traditional founders of architecture and the building trades, and refer to a legend that he found and deciphered one of the two great pillars made before the Flood. These references to Hermes made it easy for the gentlemen scholars who became the first accepted Masons to read occult secrets into the medieval symbolism of Masonic initiations and reshape the old operative Masonry into modern Freemasonry. During the eighteenth and nineteenth centuries, references to Hermes in the old constitutions inspired the proliferation of high degrees containing magical, alchemical, and astrological teachings. See **accepted Mason**; **Freemasonry**; **high degrees**.

Ironically, all this came about after the historical status of Hermes himself had been convincingly debunked by British scholar Isaac Casaubon, who showed in 1612 that the *Corpus Hermeticum*, far from being more ancient than the Bible, was a product of the first few centuries of the Common Era. As a result, the occult secret societies of the next few centuries, while they drew much of their philosophy from the Hermetic writings and most of their practices from Renaissance Hermeticism, avoided references to Hermes himself. Neither the Hermetic Brotherhood of Luxor (H.B. of L.) and the Hermetic Order of the Golden Dawn, two of the most influential magical orders of the nineteenth century, made use of the legends around Hermes Trismegistus. See **Hermetic Brotherhood of Luxor (H.B. of L.)**; **Hermetic Order of the Golden Dawn**.

The emergence of Hermes as a pseudo-historical figure in the alternative-realities scene began with the founding of the Theosophical Society in 1875. Madame Blavatsky, the founder and chief theoretician of the Society, based her system of thought on the idea that everything believed by the orthodox science and religion of her time was false. Many of her followers interpreted that to mean that anything rejected by orthodox science and religion must be true. The denial of Hermes' existence by historians, by this logic, was proof that he must actually have existed. During the "Theosophical century" (1875–1975), countless writers treated Hermes as a historical person of the distant past who had written everything attributed to him. Some groups identified him with historical figures; thus the Ancient Mystical Order Rosae Crucis (AMORC), one of the premier American occult orders of the twentieth century, identified Akhenaten as "the second Hermes." See **Akhenaten**; **Ancient Mystical Order Rosae Crucis (AMORC)**; **Theosophical Society**.

The rediscovery of Renaissance Hermeticism by mainstream scholarship in the late twentieth century produced a series of excellent historical studies of the Hermetic tradition, and showed conclusively that the name "Hermes Trismegistus" was used by dozens of writers over a period of centuries. None of this mattered in the world of rejected knowledge, however, and books treating Hermes as a historical figure continue to proliferate. See **rejected knowledge**.

Further reading: Faivre 1995, Fowden 1986, Yates 1964.

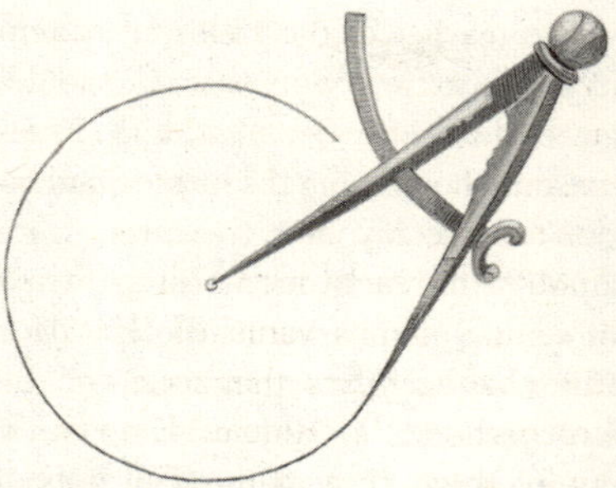

Hermetic Brotherhood of Light

The collapse of the Hermetic Brotherhood of Luxor (H.B. of L.) in 1886 left scores of initiates in Europe and America, many of them members of other occult secret societies and some of them in possession of the full teachings of the original order. Revivals were inevitable once the embarrassment of H.B. of L. secretary Thomas Burgoyne's exposure as a convicted felon had become old news. See **Hermetic Brotherhood of Luxor (H.B. of L.)**.

The most important of these revivals was the Hermetic Brotherhood of Light, founded in Boston in 1895 by a group of American H.B. of L. initiates in contact with Burgoyne, who had moved to America in 1886. Burgoyne may have played a role in launching the order, and certainly Norman Astley, a retired British

Army officer who had helped Burgoyne write a detailed resumé of H.B. of L. teachings, *The Light of Egypt* (1889), was active in the new Brotherhood. Genevieve Stebbins, an innovative teacher of the Delsarte system of exercise, and Sylvester C. Gould, an enthusiastic occultist and Freemason who became the new organization's secretary and treasurer, were among the early members. A triad of senior members ran the Exterior Circle or earthly organization of the Brotherhood; Gould was certainly one of these, though the identities of the other two remain uncertain.

Hostile publicity spread by the Theosophical Society about the original H.B. of L. and *The Light of Egypt* made the Brotherhood more than usually interested in secrecy, with the result that very little is known about the organization and its activities. It recruited candidates for membership through classified advertisements in occult periodicals and assigned each new initiate to a senior member for instruction; only after passing through a detailed course of study was the initiate allowed any contact with other members of the organization. See **Theosophical Society**.

In 1900, a young man named Benjamin Williams, later known as Elbert Benjamine, responded to one of the Brotherhood's advertisements and was accepted into its membership. He progressed rapidly through the Brotherhood's study course, and on Gould's death in 1909 he was elected to the governing triad of the order. In 1914, as effective head of the order, he began the process of transforming the Brotherhood into a correspondence school of occultism, and moved its headquarters to Los Angeles in 1915, where in 1932 it took its present name, the Church of Light. See **Church of Light**.

Further reading: Deveney 1997, Gibson 1996.

Hermetic Brotherhood of Luxor [H.B. of L.]

One of the most influential magical secret societies of the nineteenth century, the Hermetic Brotherhood of Luxor (H.B. of L.) was founded in London in 1884 by Peter Davidson and Thomas Burgoyne under the guidance of Max Theon, one of the most mysterious figures in the European occult scene of the time. Theon's original name may have been Louis Maximilian Bimstein, he was probably Jewish, and he might have been born in Poland; his death in Tlemçen, Algeria in 1927 is one of the very few firmly established facts in his biography. He apparently gave some form of occult initiation to Davidson in the early 1880s, but his precise role in launching the H.B. of L. is one of the many mysteries surrounding him.

The H.B. of L. made its first public appearance in an advertisement on the last page of a new edition of the *Corpus Hermeticum* issued in 1884 by Robert Fryar, a leading English occult publisher. The advertisement offered membership in an occult brotherhood to all "who may have been disappointed in their expectations of Sublime Wisdom being freely dispensed by HINDOO MAHATMAS". This deliberate dig at the Theosophical Society was the opening volley of a two-year struggle between the two organizations, which ended with the H.B. of L.'s collapse. Coming at a time when Theosophical pretensions had alienated many people in the occult scene, however, the H.B. of L.'s open defiance of Theosophy brought it many members and quickly made it a significant presence in Europe and America. See **Theosophical Society**.

Those who responded to the advertisement and paid the fee for membership in the H.B. of L. received a detailed postal course of instruction in practical occultism. Much of the material in the course was drawn from the work of American occultist P.B. Randolph. Another part came from the theories of Sampson Mackey, a self-taught savant of the early nineteenth century who argued for a system of world-ages based on changes in the angle of the earth's axis. Material also came from a variety of occult writers of past and present, ranging from Johannes Trithemius (1462–1516) to Eliphas Lévi (1810–75). See **ages of the world**; **earth changes**; **Eulis**; **Randolph, Paschal Beverly**.

During 1885 and 1886 the H.B. of L. reached its zenith. The order boasted a monthly periodical, *The Occult Magazine*, and attracted hundreds of members. There was, however, a skeleton in the Brotherhood's closet: its secretary Thomas Burgoyne, whose real name was Thomas Dalton, had served a jail term in 1883 for postal fraud. This came to light in 1886 and Theosophists, galled by the H.B. of L.'s ascendancy, made sure the information got into circulation throughout the occult community. The reaction was severe enough that the H.B. of L. closed its doors and both its leading members moved to America. Davidson settled in Loudsville, Georgia, and published an occult magazine for many years thereafter. Burgoyne went to Carmel, California, and became involved with the Hermetic Brotherhood of Light, the H.B. of L.'s most important successor order. See **Hermetic Brotherhood of Light**.

Despite its short life, the H.B. of L. had a major influence on the history of western occultism. Through its students and the magical secret societies they founded, Randolph's sexual teachings became the common property of dozens of occult orders, and through these connections, most contemporary sex magic in the western world derives in one way or another from the H.B. of L.

Further reading: Godwin 1994, Godwin et al. 1995.

Hermetic Order of the Golden Dawn

The most influential magical secret society of modern times, the Hermetic Order of the Golden Dawn was founded in 1887 by three English Freemasons, William Wynn Westcott, Samuel Liddell Mathers, and William Robert Woodman. According to its origin story – a variation on a very old theme – Westcott found a manuscript in cipher in a London bookstall containing rituals for a magical secret society, along with a contact address for a German adept in the society. He contacted the adept and received the charter for the Hermetic Order of the Golden Dawn. See **origin stories**; **Westcott, William Wynn**.

The actual origins of the Golden Dawn are more convoluted. The cipher manuscript actually existed, but the letters from "Fraulein Sprengel" (the alleged adept) are clumsy fakes written by someone with little knowledge of German. The most likely theory is that the cipher manuscript came from Kenneth Mackenzie, who died in 1886 and whose Masonic papers ended up in Westcott's hands. Mackenzie tried to launch an occult secret society called the Hermetic Brotherhood of Egypt, but his very dubious reputation in the British magical scene kept it from attracting members. Most likely Mackenzie's draft rituals for the Hermetic Brotherhood of Egypt provided the template for the Golden Dawn. See **Mackenzie, Kenneth**.

The new order soon became the premier occult secret society in Britain. Its success had several sources. Unlike the Masonic secret societies of the time, it admitted women as well as men; its ceremonies were splendid and dignified, and it offered a complete course of instruction in the theory and practice of occultism. Members began with the rudiments of occult symbolism and ceremonial magic and proceeded step by step from there, receiving training in every aspect of magic, divination, and alchemy. See **Alchemy**; **Magic**.

By the late 1890s the Golden Dawn had temples in Paris and several American cities. Political problems within the order, however, were building toward an explosion. Woodman died in 1891, and Westcott, the coroner for southwest London, was forced to resign in 1897 after his involvement came to the attention of his

Home Office superiors. Mathers, a brilliant but unstable magician with few organizational skills and an autocratic temper, demanded in 1899 that all members of the Second Order – the inner circle of the Golden Dawn, where the secrets of ceremonial magic were taught – sign a pledge of loyalty to him. The result was open rebellion, and Mathers was deposed.

By the time the dust settled in 1903, the Golden Dawn had broken into three orders – the Stella Matutina or Order of the Morning Star, headed by Robert W. Felkin; the Holy Order of the Golden Dawn, headed by Arthur Edward Waite; and the Alpha et Omega, a group of loyalists headed by Mathers. The first and last of these continued to teach the original Golden Dawn system, while the Holy Order replaced magic with Christian mysticism. In 1914 Waite closed the Holy Order, though he started a new organization, the Fellowship of the Rosy Cross, the next year; late in his life he also chartered an American branch of the Holy Order, which remains active today. The Alpha et Omega survived Mathers' death in 1918 but went out of existence 10 years later when Mathers' widow, Moina, died. The Stella Matutina ran into trouble after Felkin relocated to New Zealand in 1916 and the head of its London temple, Christina Stoddart, converted to fundamentalist Christianity; most of its temples went out of existence before the Second World War, though Hermes Temple in Bristol closed in 1960 and Smaragdum Thalasses in Havelock North, New Zealand, remained active until 1978.

Publication of Golden Dawn material began in 1909 when Aleister Crowley, a Golden Dawn member from 1898 to 1900 and a Mathers loyalist until 1904, printed several rituals in his magazine *The Equinox*. Most of the order's papers saw print, starting in 1937 when Israel Regardie, a member of the Stella Matutina in 1933 and 1934, published the first volume of his massive collection *The Golden Dawn*. In the 1970s, independent Golden Dawn temples sprang up in various parts of the western world, and by the end of the twentieth century more than a dozen Golden Dawn orders existed. Unfortunately many of these failed to shake off the Golden Dawn habit of bitter political quarrels, and the Golden Dawn scene today is riven by factional disputes. See **Crowley, Aleister**.

The Golden Dawn heritage found its way into the wider circle of occult secret societies as well. Several Druid orders in the early twentieth century took in members who left the Golden Dawn, and incorporated Golden Dawn practices and rituals in their own work. Crowley used large elements of Golden Dawn theory and practice in his own secret societies, the Ordo Templi Orientis and Argenteum Astrum. The American occultist Paul Foster Case, co-author of the classic occult work *The Kybalion* and founder of the Builders of the Adytum, similarly drew much from Golden Dawn sources for his own system. See **Argenteum Astrum (A∴ A∴)**; **Builders of the Adytum**; **Case, Paul Foster**; **Druid Revival**; **Ordo Templi Orientis (OTO)**.

Even more influential was English occultist Dion Fortune (Violet Firth), a member of the Alpha et Omega in its last years who later founded her own magical order, the Fraternity (later Society) of the Inner Light. Fortune combined Golden Dawn material with Theosophy to create a distinctive magical system. Several of her students, including Gareth Knight and W.E. Butler, became influential occultists in their own right, and through them Fortune's system became central to more than a dozen magical secret societies in the late twentieth century. See **Servants of the Light**; **Society of the Inner Light**.

In the occult revival of the late twentieth century the Golden Dawn system was far and away the most influential tradition of occultism in the western world. The basic philosophy and practices of Golden Dawn magic remain fundamental to more than half of all occult secret societies active today in Europe, America, and Australasia, including many who heatedly reject the notion that they owe anything at all to it.

Further reading: Howe 1972, Regardie 1971.

Hermeticism

One of the most influential spiritual movements in the western world, Hermeticism emerged in Roman Egypt in the first few centuries of the Common Era, born of the collision between traditional Egyptian spirituality and Greek philosophy in an age of radical religious change. Like Gnosticism, another movement born at the same time and in the same place, Hermeticism saw direct experience of spiritual realities as the key to inner transformation. Where Gnosticism drew massively on Judeo-Christian dualism and rejected the world of matter as a prison ruled by an evil god, however, Hermeticism celebrated the beauty of the material world as a reflection of spiritual realities. In place of the wild mythologies of Gnostic tradition, Hermetic writings present philosophy, piety, and a vision of spiritual transformation available to all those willing to turn their minds to contemplate "the things that are." Yet a deep current of magical practices and alchemy also runs through ancient as well as modern Hermeticism; the contemplation of the universe, in Hermetic thought, leads step by step to a mastery of its secret powers. See **Alchemy**; **dualism**; **Gnosticism**; **Magic**.

Three sources conveyed the Hermetic tradition to later ages. The first is the *Corpus Hermeticum*, a collection of short books attributed to the founder of the movement, the godlike sage Hermes Trismegistus; this collection survived the fall of Rome in the Byzantine Empire and reached the western world by way of a single copy bought by the Medici family, the rulers of Renaissance Florence, in 1460. The second is the *Asclepius*, a Latin translation of a lost Greek original also attributed to Hermes, which survived in medieval Europe. The third is a smattering of occult texts headed by the *Picatrix*, a collection of old Hermetic magical practices collected by an unknown Arab wizard sometime in the early Middle Ages and attributed to the great Muslim scholar al-Majriti. All of these works came to the attention of occultists and scholars in the Italian Renaissance and launched Renaissance Hermeticism. See **Hermes Trismegistus**.

Renaissance Hermeticism was the seedbed of the entire modern occult movement. In the writings of Hermetic philosophers and occultists such as Marsilio Ficino, Giovanni Pico Della Mirandola, Henricus Cornelius Agrippa, and Giordano Bruno, the teachings of the Hermetic writings became a universal philosophy in which every material object mirrors spiritual realities, and a mastery of the correspondences between stones, plants, stars, and spirits allows the Hermeticist to transform the world. These ideas flowed into nearly every corner of Renaissance culture, and formed the background of the art of memory, the notory art, and other forgotten spiritual disciplines of the age. It also underpinned the Rosicrucian movement, and became a key factor in the late medieval stonemasons' guilds that evolved into modern Freemasonry. See **art of memory**; **Bruno, Giordano**; **Freemasonry**; **Rosicrucians**.

Through these channels Hermetic ideas and teachings flowed into the secret societies of the eighteenth and nineteenth centuries. Major late nineteenth-century orders such as the Hermetic Brotherhood of Luxor and the Hermetic Order of the Golden Dawn show their roots in Hermeticism in their very names. While these orders flourished, though, the Theosophical Society had already begun the great turning toward the east that distracted most twentieth-century western mystics from their own cultural heritage and convinced four generations of seekers that wisdom was only to be found in Asia. As this conviction has faded, the secret traditions of the west have gradually found a new audience, and Hermeticism in particular has experienced a modest renaissance. How far that will extend remains one of the questions the twenty-first century will have to answer. See **Hermetic Brotherhood of Luxor (H.B. of L.)**; **Hermetic Order of the Golden Dawn**; **Theosophical Society**.

Further reading: Faivre 1995, Fowden 1986, Yates 1964.

HIGH DEGREES

In Freemasonry, all those degrees that come after the Master Mason degree, with the exception of the Royal Arch and its associated degrees, are referred to as high degrees. This usage is controversial in some circles, as Masonic tradition insists that the degree of Master Mason is the highest of all Masonic degrees. In recent years, with declining membership in all branches of Freemasonry, some Masons have insisted that the high degrees are unnecessary, and divert time and resources that should be devoted to Craft Masonry. Members of the high degrees, for their part, argue that these latter are important elements of Freemasonry and should not be discarded. See **Freemasonry**; **Royal Arch**.

The genesis of the high degrees of Masonry was a complex process, beginning in the late 1730s and continuing through the end of the nineteenth century. The catalyst for the first important series of high degrees was the famous 1736 oration of the Chevalier Ramsay, in which he argued that Masonry could trace its roots back to the knightly religious orders of the Crusades. Ramsay himself was a Jacobite – a supporter of the claims of the exiled House of Stuart to the British throne – and most of the high degrees that surfaced in Masonic circles in the two decades after his oration had close connections to the Jacobite movement. Ramsay himself is credited by some sources with the invention of the first set of high degrees, a system of three levels above Master Mason. See **Jacobites**; **Ramsay, Andrew Michael**.

In the late eighteenth and early nineteenth centuries, the manufacture of high degrees formed an important part of Masonic activity throughout Europe, and especially in France, where more than half the high degrees still worked originated. More than 2000 high degrees surfaced within Freemasonry during these years, most of them as part of degree sequences within many competing rites of Masonry. For details of the most important of these rites, see **Rite of Memphis**; **Rite of Misraim**; **Rite of Perfection**; **Rite of Strict Observance**.

Most of these rites went out of existence before 1900, or survive only as small organizations on the fringes of Freemasonry. In the English-speaking world, the two main survivors are the Ancient and Accepted Scottish Rite and the York Rite. In America, both these rites are independent of ordinary Craft Masonry; the Scottish Rite is governed by its own Supreme Councils, the York Rite by a patchwork of state and national jurisdictions bewildering to the uninitiated. In England, while the Ancient and Accepted Rite is independent, the degrees of the York Rite are under the jurisdiction of United Grand Lodge. See **Ancient and Accepted Scottish Rite**; **York Rite**.

Hiram Abiff

The central character of the legend at the core of Freemasonry, Hiram Abiff appears in the Old Testament (I Kings 7:13–40) as a master brassworker from Tyre commissioned by King Solomon to cast the brass furnishings for the Temple. In the legendary history of the medieval stoneworkers' guilds that became Freemasonry, however, Hiram turned into the master builder in charge of the Temple's construction. When the project was nearing completion, 15 of the journeymen laborers who worked on the Temple plotted to extort from him the Master's Word, which would enable them to pass as Master Masons. Twelve of them repented, but three went ahead with the plot, lying in wait for him at noon at the three entrances of the unfinished temple. When Hiram refused each of them in turn, each struck him with a tool, and the third blow killed him. The three ruffians, as they are called in Masonic writings, hid the body in a heap of rubbish until midnight, then carried it elsewhere and buried it. Hiram's death, the search for his body, and its recovery make up the core of the Master Mason degree in Masonry, while other events surrounding them appear in dozens of higher Masonic degrees, especially in the Ancient and Accepted Scottish Rite. See **Ancient and Accepted Scottish Rite (AASR)**; **Freemasonry**.

The story of Hiram Abiff can be interpreted in many ways, and most branches of Freemasonry have steadfastly refused to impose a single rigid meaning on it, preferring to allow each initiate to understand it in his own way. Books and articles over the last three centuries have suggested moral, mystical, historical, geometrical, sexual, and occult interpretations, among many others. In recent decades, though, popular books claiming to reveal the secrets of Masonry have focused almost exclusively on the historical dimension, insisting that "Hiram Abiff" is a cover name for a specific person whose life and death matched the events of the Masonic allegory.

This sort of euhemerist reading satisfies the modern craving for simplistic literal meanings, but quickly runs aground on the awkward fact that dozens of plausible candidates have been proposed for the role – ranging from Charles I of England to the minor Egyptian pharaoh Seqenenre II – and hundreds more could as readily be added. This flexibility points to the universal and archetypal dimension of the story of Hiram Abiff – a dimension too often wholly lost in interpretations fixated on the rigidities of historical fact. See **Allegory**; **Euhemerism**.

Further reading: MacNulty 2002.

Hitler, Adolf

Austrian politician and occultist, 1889–1945. Born in the small border town of Braunau-am-Inn, Hitler was a moody and difficult child with a passion for reading, philosophy, and art. He dropped out of school in 1905, and in 1907 went to Vienna in the hope of enrolling in the prestigious Vienna Academy of Art. He failed the entrance exams twice, however; unwilling to return home, he ended up on Vienna's mean streets, eking out a living as a postcard painter and male prostitute while staying in cheap rented rooms or a shelter for homeless men. A friend of his Vienna days reported that Hitler spent much of his free time reading books on occultism, astrology, hypnotism, and mysticism. He also read *Ostara*, the virulently racist Ariosophical magazine issued by the Ordo Novi Templi, one of the major occult secret societies in Austria at the time. See **Ordo Novi Templi (ONT)**.

In 1913 he emigrated to Germany and settled in Munich, finding a home in the Munich counterculture and continuing his studies. When the First World War broke out in 1914, he enlisted in the German army and served on the Western Front for the duration of the war, earning an Iron Cross for bravery under fire. He was in a military hospital, temporarily blinded by Allied poison gas, when Germany collapsed and the war ended. Thereafter he returned to Munich and earned a small salary as an informer for German army intelligence. In 1920 he attended a meeting of the German Workers' Party (*Deutsche Arbeiterpartei*, DAP), got into a heated discussion with one of its members, and was invited to join. His acceptance marked the beginning of one of the strangest political careers in modern history.

The DAP was a front group for an Ariosophical secret society, the Thule Society, which had links to right-wing occult groups across Europe. Hitler never became a member of the Thule Society, but its members and allies soon recognized his remarkable gift for oratory and brought him wealthy and influential supporters. As the DAP grew into the National Socialist German Workers' Party (*Nationalsozialistische Deutsche Arbeiterpartei*, NSDAP), Thule members Rudolf Hess and Ernst Röhm took important roles in the organization, while Thule ally Dietrich Eckart, a widely read writer and an Ariosophical occultist, became Hitler's mentor and helped him polish his manners and oratory. Eckart has often been identified as one of Hitler's occult instructors as well, and was certainly capable of filling that role, though proof one way or another is lacking. See **National Socialism**; **Thule Society**.

From the early 1920s on, Hitler's private life lay hidden behind a carefully crafted public image, and little is known for sure about his activities outside the realms of politics, diplomacy, and war. Comments preserved in his table talk, and in the memoirs of associates such as Brownshirt chief of staff Otto Wagener, show that he had not lost his interest in occultism, but most of the documented occult activities in the Third Reich's upper levels were the work of Heinrich Himmler, a passionate Ariosophist who became chief of the SS in 1929 and turned it into something even mainstream historians call "Nazi Freemasonry." See **SS (Schutzstaffel)**.

In the public sphere, Hitler and his party gained momentum slowly at first, contending with scores of other small right-wing parties in the political chaos of Weimar Germany. An early attempt at a coup in 1923 failed dismally, but Hitler's defense of his actions at his trial won the battle for popular opinion and the Nazi Party flourished thereafter. In 1933 Hitler became Chancellor, forced an Enabling Act suspending the Weimar constitution through the Reichstag, and took absolute power. For the rest of the decade he was all but invincible, transforming Germany into one of the world's great powers and bringing Austria and Czechoslovakia under German rule without a shot being fired. When Germany's invasion of Poland in 1939 began the Second World War, the British and French expected an easy victory, only to find themselves outmaneuvered at every turn by the Führer.

Yet Hitler's victories convinced him of his own infallibility and led him to make a series of disastrous mistakes, culminating in his invasion of Russia in 1941. As Germany faced a two-front war it could not win, and the Wehrmacht struggled to hold the sprawling empire it had seized, Hitler retreated more and more from the public eye. An assassination attempt in 1944 by a clique of top generals left him permanently disabled, but he held onto the reins of power in Germany until his suicide in 1945, a few days before Russian troops seized Berlin.

Hitler's occult involvements were no secret to occultists before and during the war, but in the years since his death an immense and almost totally fabricated mythology of Nazi occultism has emerged in the alternative-realities scene. Louis Pauwel and Jacques Bergier started the process with their wildly speculative *Le Matin du Magiciens* (*The Morning of the Magicians*, 1960), which linked Hitler to the Vril Society and Tibetan adepts, and Trevor Ravenscroft's 1972 book *The Spear of Destiny* built on this with a wholly fictional tale of Hitler's quest to seize and control the Spear of Longinus. From there, the new mythology of Nazism has spread to embrace every aspect of rejected knowledge, from flying saucers to the Hollow Earth. See **hollow earth**; **rejected knowledge**; **Spear of Longinus**; **unidentified flying objects (UFOs)**; **Vril Society**.

Parallel to this, and often borrowing from it, is an equally fabricated but far more noxious mythology that redefines Hitler as the messianic savior of Aryan humanity. These beliefs have become central to the growing neo-Nazi occult scene, which has largely supplanted Satanism on the dark side of contemporary occultism. See **Black Sun**; **neo-Nazi secret societies**.

Further reading: Goodrick-Clarke 1992, Hitler 1974.

Höhere Armanen-Orden [HAO]

A leading force in the proto-Nazi underworld of early twentieth-century central Europe, the Höhere Armanen-Orden (Higher Armanen Order, HAO) rose out of the Guido von List Society, an organization founded in 1908 to promote the ideas of the Austrian racial mystic Guido von List (1848–1919). List, a popular novelist famous for works that glamorized ancient German tribal customs, believed that a caste of priest-kings, the Armanen, had governed all the Germanic tribes before the coming of Christianity. Driven underground by the persecuting Catholic Church, the Armanen had disguised themselves as the Knights Templar, the Freemasons, and the Rosicrucians in order to pass their hidden knowledge down to the future. This pedigree inspired List's supporters to reconstruct the Armanen mysteries; the HAO was the result. See **Armanen**; **Freemasonry**; **Knights Templar**; **Rosicrucians**.

Very little is known about the HAO's teachings and practices, beyond the fact that it conducted pilgrimages to ancient Germanic holy places. It likely shared List's interest in runes, and seems to have been instrumental in launching and promoting Ariosophy, a racist offshoot of Theosophy that defined the Aryan peoples as the only true humans and saw the struggle between Aryan god-men and everyone else as the driving force behind human history. The membership of the HAO overlapped substantially with that of the Ordo Novi Templi (ONT), another racist secret society founded by Jörg Lanz von Liebenfels, and many ONT teachings may also have been common to the HAO. See **Ordo Novi Templi (ONT)**; **Theosophical Society**.

List himself prophesied during the First World War that a "Strong One from Above" would soon appear to liberate the Germanic peoples and lead them on a crusade against their supposed racial enemies. His prophecy came true in 1933 when Adolf Hitler, backed by many German Ariosophists, became Chancellor of Germany. Ironically, the German takeover of Austria in 1938 meant the end of the HAO and the Guido von List Society, as the Nazis enforced a strict ban on all secret societies other than their own. See **Hitler, Adolf**; **National Socialism**.

Further reading: Goodrick-Clarke 1992.

HOLLOW EARTH

The teachings of occult secret societies have included quite a few strange ideas, but among the strangest are claims that the earth we live on is hollow, and contains an unknown world inside. Hollow earth theories have deep roots in ancient traditions about the underworld, and appear in prototypical form in the writings of Renaissance savants such as Athanasius Kircher, but their modern presence on the far shores of popular culture dates from 1818.

In that year Captain John Cleves Symmes, an American veteran of the War of 1812 against Britain, announced that he had made the greatest geographical discovery of his time. The earth, he claimed, was a hollow shell containing no fewer than four undiscovered worlds inside – each one a concentric sphere, inhabitable inside and out, and accessible via openings at the poles. Symmes announced his intention to lead an expedition northwards beyond the polar ice to launch American settlement in the land inside the globe, which he modestly named "Symmzonia." In 1828, after years of lobbying by Symmes's supporters, the US Congress authorized funds for a naval expedition of three ships, but President Andrew Jackson scotched the project.

Symmes's "discovery" attracted more attention from writers and poets than from scientists, but others picked up the idea of hidden worlds within the earth and added their own stamp to the vision. At the beginning of the twentieth century, maverick geographers William Reed and Marshall Gardner argued for a single hollow globe with continents and seas inside. Their visions found their way into a seminal work of science fiction, Edgar Rice Burrough's *At the Earth's Core* (1922), before vaulting back out of fiction later in the twentieth century.

By this time, a different version of the hollow earth theory – perhaps the most striking of all – had been pioneered by the American visionary Cyrus Teed (1839–1908). Teed's "Koreshan philosophy" argued that the world was hollow, but we are already on the inside. Rejecting the idea of an infinite universe, Teed proposed in 1868 that the entire universe consisted of the hollow earth, surrounded by seven shells of different metals, with gold on the outside and literally nothing – not even empty space – beyond that. Inside, a black "counter-sun" spangled with bright points of light filled most of the intervening space, with the sun and planets whizzing through the open space between the counter-sun and the earth's inside surface. His cosmology found a receptive audience, and he established a commune in Florida that still survives and preaches Koreshanity to a mostly uninterested world.

Even in its more conventional forms, the hollow earth is a fringe concept even in the world of rejected knowledge, but the sheer power of the image has guaranteed it a place in a surprising number of alternative visions of the universe. The legendary science fiction editor Raymond Palmer, who sent sales of *Amazing Stories* to stratospheric levels in the late 1940s with pseudo-factual articles about sinister "deros" lurking in underground caverns, boosted circulation of his new periodical, *Flying Saucers*, in 1957 by revealing that UFOs actually came, not from outer space, but from within the hollow earth. Here as elsewhere, Palmer proved to be the unsung prophet of late twentieth-century popular occultism, and most of the ideas he launched in the pulp magazines he edited were recycled again and again by later and apparently more serious writers. See **Palmer, Raymond**; **unidentified flying objects (UFOs)**.

Far and away the most systematic development of his ideas, and of the hollow earth theory, has emerged from the murky underworld of neo-Nazi secret societies. The road that put Nazis inside the hollow earth was a complicated one, beginning with claims right after the Second World War that Nazi leaders, including Hitler, escaped from Germany via U-boat to Neuschwabenland, the section of the Antarctic coast claimed by Nazi Germany after a 1938 expedition. Another set of claims in the late 1940s argued that flying saucers were actually advanced Nazi aircraft flown by the "Last Battalion," a force of Luftwaffe and SS men hidden away in some distant corner of the world. Raymond Palmer's claim that flying saucers came from inside the hollow earth provided the bridge between these claims. By the 1970s pro-Nazi writers Wilhelm Landig and Ernst Zundel, among others, were arguing that Hitler, defeated on the outside of the globe, had retreated inside it to continue the war against "world Jewry" with a fleet of flying saucers that sallied forth via openings at the north and south poles. See **Antarctica**; **Hitler, Adolf**; **neo-Nazi secret societies**.

The most detailed of these neo-Nazi hollow earth theories belongs to the "esoteric Hitlerism" of the Chilean mystical fascist Miguel Serrano. In Serrano's vision, the lost polar continent of Hyperborea – the original home of the Aryans after their arrival on earth from another dimension – slid through the polar opening into the hollow earth after some of its inhabitants fell from grace by mating with non-Aryans. The descendants of the pure-blooded Hyperboreans can supposedly still be found there, in the subterranean cities of Shambhala and Agharta, and Hitler himself traveled there by U-boat after escaping from the defeated Reich, before returning via the Green Ray to the mysterious Black Sun, the extra-galactic home of the Aryans. See **Agharta**; **Black Sun**; **Shambhala**.

Despite all these speculations, by turns colorful and repellent, the fact remains that not a scrap of evidence actually supports the theory of hidden worlds within a hollow earth. Still, the vision of undiscovered realms somewhere beneath our feet remains appealing enough that new attempts to argue in favor of a hollow earth are certain to appear in the years to come.

Further reading: Godwin 1993, Goodrick-Clarke 2002, Kafton-Minkel 1989.

I

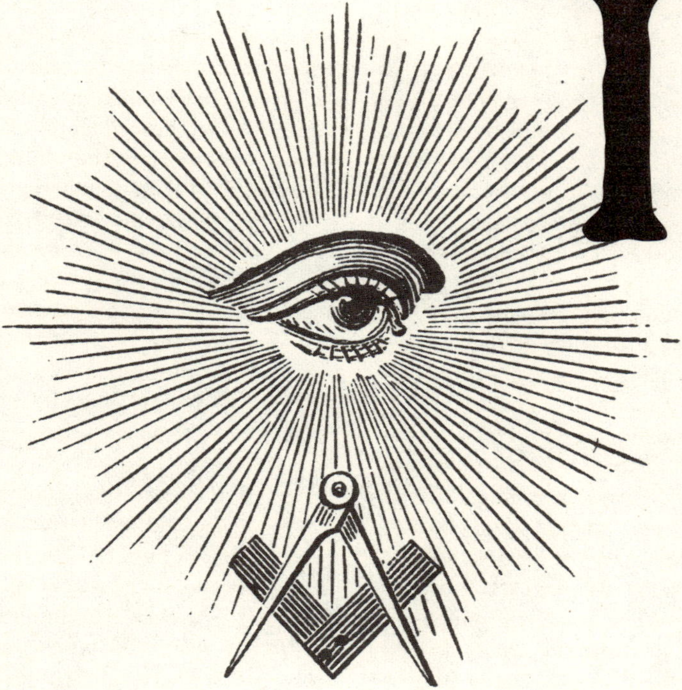

Illuminates of Thanateros [IOT]

The first magical secret society to embrace the late twentieth-century paradigm of chaos magic, the Illuminates of Thanateros was founded in Germany by two chaos magicians in 1978, drawing on materials from the Thelemic magic of Aleister Crowley's Ordo Templi Orientis and the Zos Kia Cultus of the English autoerotic mystic Austin Osman Spare. The word "Thanateros" is a fusion of the Greek words *thanatos*, "death," and *eros*, "love," and reflects the central themes of its system. See **magic**; **Ordo Templi Orientis (OTO)**; **Zos Kia Cultus**.

Chaos magic is based on the belief that the only valid parts of traditional magical teaching are its techniques for transforming consciousness and causing change, while its philosophy, cosmology, and ethical teachings should be discarded. In place of these latter, the IOT urges the rejection of all fixed patterns of belief and the use of improvised rituals centering on altered states of consciousness. The antinomian outlook of the IOT has predictably prevented it from becoming particularly large or well organized, but a recently updated Internet site lists 16 IOT temples scattered around the world.

Illuminati

See **Bavarian Illuminati**.

Improved Order of Red Men [IORM]

The first fraternal secret society original to America, the Improved Order of Red Men traces its roots back to the Sons of Liberty, a political secret society founded in Boston before the American Revolution. After the Revolution, many Sons of Liberty chapters renamed themselves the Society of St Tammany or Tamina, a name that had been taken by the Annapolis chapter as early as 1773. As the Society of St Tammany became increasingly political, members interested more in social activities than in politics founded a new organization, the Society of Red Men, which began at Fort Mifflin, Pennsylvania in 1816. Like most fraternal orders of the time, the Society met in taverns and included plenty of drinking among its activities; in 1834 members who wanted to move away from this model toward fraternal and charitable work broke away from the Society of Red Men to found their own organization, the Improved Order of Red Men. See **fraternal orders**; **Odd Fellowship**; **Society of St Tammany**; **Sons of Liberty**.

The Red Men reflected the intense ambivalence many Americans felt toward the native peoples they had displaced on the North American land. Its rituals and symbolism were based on white ideas of Native American life and spirituality, but until 1974 Native Americans themselves (along with members of all other non-white ethnic groups) were barred from membership. The order cultivated a patriotism that, as so often in nineteenth- and twentieth-century America, blended too easily with racism and xenophobia, but it also took a stand against the Ku Klux Klan in 1922, at a time when many other fraternal secret societies were covertly or openly siding with the Klan. See **Ku Klux Klan**.

The Improved Order had a slow start, and by 1850 still counted only 45 tribes (local lodges) and just over 3000 members. That same year saw a schism among the Red Men that gave rise to a competing organization, the Independent Order of Red Men, which remained in existence until the 1890s. During the second half of the nineteenth century, though, new degree rituals and the expanding popularity of fraternal orders enabled the Improved Order of Red Men to grow steadily. It established a ladies auxiliary, the Daughters of Pocahontas, in 1887, and a burlesque lodge, the National Haymakers Association, in 1878. See **burlesque degrees**; **ladies auxiliaries**.

The order reached a peak membership of more than half a million in 1920. From this high-water mark the order declined steadily, and survives today in fewer than half of the states in the US. Like most American fraternal orders, it counts several presidents among its members – Theodore Roosevelt, Warren G. Harding, Franklin D. Roosevelt, and Richard Nixon were all Red Men – but what limited political influence it once had is now long in the past.

Independent Order of Good Templars [IOGT]

Founded in 1851 in Utica, New York, the Independent Order of Good Templars was the most successful secret society in the temperance movement. Its founder, Daniel Cady, had been a member of an earlier temperance order, and felt the need for a secret society along similar lines that concentrated its efforts entirely on opposition to alcohol, instead of combining its temperance activities with fraternal benefits and other activities.

Cady's first attempt at a temperance society was the Knights of Jericho, founded in Utica in 1850. Within a year this society reorganized itself as the Order of Good Templars, drawing on the image and legends of the medieval Knights Templar as a basis for the new ritual. Members pledged never to drink alcohol, and campaigned for prohibition. A series of early political disputes saw a faction break away from the Order of Good Templars and rename itself the Independent Order of Good Templars; while the original order never got far, the IOGT expanded steadily and in 1868 established its first lodge in Great Britain at Birmingham. By 1900 it was the largest secret society in the temperance movement, with lodges in more than 30 countries.

Unlike most other secret societies of the time, the Good Templars admitted men and women on an equal basis and gave leadership positions to women. It also kept its original strict focus on temperance issues. Buoyed by these sources of strength, the IOGT became one of the major forces in the international struggle to prohibit alcohol. In 1902 it changed its name to the International Order of Good Templars.

The passage of Prohibition in the United States in 1919, however, convinced many people that the IOGT was no longer needed, now that its work was done, and the resounding failure of the new legislation in the 1920s caused it to lose credibility. The creation of Alcoholics Anonymous (AA) in 1937 posed an additional challenge, since AA quickly encroached on the IOGT's role as an organization for reformed alcoholics, and its widely copied "12 step" program proved more popular than the IOGT's moralizing approach. During the middle years of the twentieth century the IOGT abandoned the secret society traditions it had adopted from its fraternal roots, and now exists as an international federation of anti-alcohol organizations.

Independent Order of Odd Fellows [IOOF]

See **Odd Fellowship**.

Initiation

The process by which a candidate becomes a member of a secret society. Initiation is surrounded by an enormous amount of mythology, but at its core is a simple but effective process of reshaping human consciousness used by nearly all spiritual traditions worldwide, and more recently by advertisers, political movements, and many others. The core of the process is the fact that experience has a deeper impact when the subject is placed in a receptive state. Such a state can be produced in many ways; TV advertising uses immobility and the "flicker effect" of the picture tube, political rallies use the herd reactions human beings share with other social animals, and many religious traditions use the hypnotic effects of repeated prayers or mantras.

In modern secret societies in the western world, by contrast, the tool of choice is ritual, amplified by a few simple but effective psychological devices. Candidates awaiting their first initiation into a secret society are usually blindfolded, and may be bound by a cord as well. They are brought into a darkened lodge room and moved around it while voices sounding out of the darkness repeat the words of the ritual. Unable to get their bearings and moved through unfamiliar space, the candidate becomes mildly disoriented, and most secret society initiations add to this effect by startling the candidate in some way near the beginning of the ceremony. When the blindfold is finally raised, the images seen by the candidate blaze with heightened intensity, and the teachings and signs of recognition given to the candidate at that point share in that same intensity. Whenever the candidate encounters the core images of the initiation or uses the signs of recognition thereafter, what psychologists call "state-dependent memory" takes over and brings back something of the emotional tone of the moment of revelation in the initiation ritual. These effects are far from infallible – a certain percentage of candidates "fail to initiate" and usually drift out of the society in short order – but they work often enough to make the trouble of performing initiation rituals worthwhile.

As with most ritual techniques, the effects of initiation vary almost infinitely depending on the nature of the symbols and teachings presented in the initiation ceremony. Initiations into fraternal secret societies such as Odd Fellowship, for example, focus on the obligations of brotherhood and create feelings of mutual affection among members. Those of magical secret societies such as the Hermetic Order of the Golden Dawn focus on awakening the subtle powers of the self and give the initiate a foretaste of the results of magical training. Those of political secret societies encourage commitment to the society's political goals, while those of criminal secret societies foster loyalty and a sense of being unfettered by conventional rules and laws. See **fraternal orders**; **Hermetic Order of the Golden Dawn**; **Odd Fellowship**.

From 1700 to 1950, the golden age of secret societies in the western world, designers of initiation rituals experimented with many different approaches and amassed a toolkit of successful methods, which were then put to work in the rituals of the thousands of different secret societies active in those years. Some secret societies took shape around a set of successful rituals, while others, unsatisfied with their initiation ceremonies, revised or replaced them with others that seemed more likely to accomplish their goals. The rise of the Ancient and Accepted Scottish Rite from a minor Masonic body in the 1850s to the largest single rite in Masonry a century later is rightly credited to Albert Pike's brilliant revision of their rituals. See **Ancient and Accepted Scottish Rite**; **Pike, Albert**.

Nowadays, as most secret societies struggle with declining numbers and an aging membership, the quality of initiation ceremonies varies widely from order to order and indeed from local lodge to local lodge. Some lodges perform stunningly powerful rituals, while others go through the motions, awkwardly reading unfamiliar parts out of books. The common cultural assumption that ritual is by definition empty forms, and the conservative Christian assumption that any ritual but theirs must be devil worship, put additional obstacles in the way of effective initiatory work nowadays. Still, initiation is still available for those willing to seek it out, and those who have experienced its impact know that it can be a powerful tool for good.

Further reading: Greer 1998.

International Brothers

Founded by Russian ex-Nihilist Mikhail Bakunin in Italy sometime around 1864, the International Brothers were a significant presence in late nineteenth-century European politics and played an important role in the First International. The Brothers' manifesto, Bakunin's *Revolutionary Catechism* of 1866, called for capitalism's replacement by an egalitarian society in which farmers owned their own land and industry was owned and managed by workers cooperatives. In practice, however, the society was an absolute dictatorship controlled by Bakunin, and its plan of action concentrated all power in the hands of the Brothers after the revolution in an "invisible dictatorship." See **Nihilists**.

Sometime after the formation of the International Brothers, its members formed a front group, the Secret Alliance, also known as the Alliance of Social Revolutionists or the Secret Alliance of Socialist Democracy. The Secret Alliance then sponsored a public organization, the International Alliance of Socialist Democracy, which merged with the First International in 1868. Once inside the International, in time-honored fashion, they attempted to reformulate its goals and activities to fit their own vision of social revolution. See **First International**.

Bakunin's followers, however, faced opponents who had already overcome one secret society within the International. Originally sponsored in 1864 by the Philadelphes, one of the last of the old revolutionary secret societies of the Napoleonic era, the International had fallen under the control of Karl Marx and his then-ally Auguste Blanqui, another leading figure in the radical circles of the time. The co-author of the *Communist Manifesto* and the leading figure in the radical intelligentsia of his time, Marx controlled the single largest bloc of delegates on the International's General Council. See **Communism**; **Philadelphes**.

Bakunin and his followers remained in the International for four short and troubled years, but Marx and Blanqui checkmated them at every turn. Expelled in 1872 at the instigation of Marx, Bakunin tried to launch an "Anti-Authoritarian" International of his own, but this failed to attract more than a token following outside Bakunin's own organization. In 1874 Bakunin diverted the entire treasury of the Brothers to pay for improvements to his Swiss villa, causing many of the society's members to defect. Not long after he died, two years later, the International Brothers and the schismatic International they tried to control quietly went out of existence, leaving the field clear for the founding of the Second International in 1889.

Further reading: Drachkovitch 1966.

Isiac mysteries

One of the ancient mystery cults, the Isiac mysteries focused on the myth of Isis, sister and wife of the Egyptian god Osiris. They emerged in Hellenistic Egypt sometime in the second or third century BCE as Greek settlers in Egypt adopted the worship of the local goddess but reshaped her rites into forms more familiar to them. By the first century of the Common Era Iseums (temples of Isis) offering initiation into her mysteries could be found over most of the Roman Empire; even Londinium in the backwater province of Britannia boasted one. See **mysteries, ancient**.

The myth around which the Isiac mysteries built their initiations began with the death of the vegetation god Osiris at the hands of his brother Set, god of the sterile desert. Isis searched for the body of her husband and finally recovered it in the distant town of Byblos in Phoenicia. Returning with the body to the banks of the Nile, she brought Osiris back to life and coupled with him, begetting a son, Horus. Not long afterwards, Set's minions found Osiris in his hiding place and killed him a second time, hewing him to pieces and throwing them in the Nile to prevent a second resurrection. Osiris then became the god of the dead; Isis gave birth to Horus and raised him to manhood in secret, and Horus then slew Set and became the ruler of Egypt.

One of the core symbols of the Isiac mysteries was the image of Isis suckling the infant Horus. Ironically, when the Christian Church seized power in the Roman world during the fourth century CE, some statues of this sort were renamed, and became images of the Virgin Mary and the baby Jesus. Some of the famous "black Madonnas" of southern Europe, according to recent art historians, may actually be "black Isises" preserved in this way.

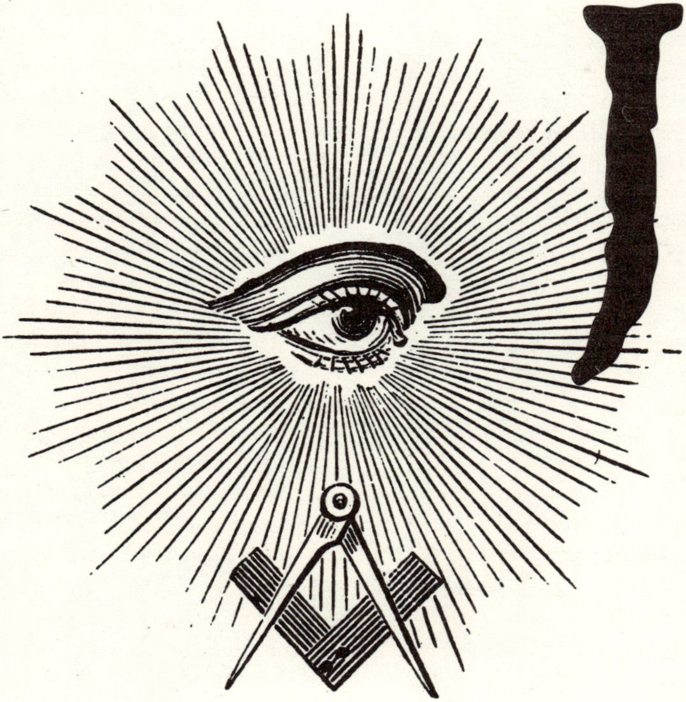

I

Jacobites

Partisans of the House of Stuart, opposed to the Hanoverian rule in Britain from 1714, the Jacobites took their title from the Latin version ("Jacobus") of the names of the exiled James II and his son, the "Old Pretender." On James's daughter Queen Anne's death in 1714, Parliament gave the throne to the minor German prince George of Hanover, a descendant of one of James I's daughters. In response, the Old Pretender landed in Scotland in 1715 and attempted to start a rebellion against the new king. The rebellion fizzled out, though, and most of James's supporters had to flee to France.

The collapse of the 1715 rising may have played a central role in one of the crucial events in Masonic history, the organization of the first Grand Lodge of England in 1717. Many of the first accepted Masons to be initiated into what were then still stonemasons' guilds, men such as Elias Ashmole and Sir Robert Moray, had been staunch supporters of the Stuarts, and a sizeable number of Jacobite exiles after the 1715 rebellion were Freemasons. The Grand Lodge, however, was firmly in the Hanoverian camp from the first, and the lodges affiliated with it followed its lead. Many Masonic historians have suggested that the Grand Lodge was at least encouraged, and may have been covertly sponsored, by supporters of the House of Hanover to deny the Jacobites a potential network for espionage and subversion. See **accepted Mason**; **Ashmole, Elias**; **grand lodge**; **Moray, Robert**.

If this was their intention, the challenge was taken up by the Jacobites. Between 1723 and 1730, Masonic lodges organized by Jacobite exiles sprang up in France. In 1732 the first French lodge chartered by the English Grand Lodge in London was founded, and from then until 1738 Jacobite and Hanoverian factions in French Masonry fought a bitter covert struggle in which the English ambassador in Paris, Lord Waldegrave, had a part. The Jacobites fared poorly in these struggles, not least because Hanoverian England had enormous prestige in eighteenth-century France.

The Jacobite loss of control over Masonry was a serious blow, but not fatal. The Jacobites responded with a double strategy that had immense consequences. First came a burst of official sanctions against French Masonic lodges. In Paris, Masonic meetings were broken up by police in 1737 and 1738, though the widespread popularity of Masonry and the high social standing of some of its members made it difficult for Cardinal Fleury, who headed the police, to go too far. More serious action came from Rome, where in 1738 Pope Clement XII issued the bull *In Eminenti*, the first Catholic condemnation of Freemasonry, which excommunicated all Masons and reserved the right to absolve them to the Pope alone. See **Antimasonry**; **Roman Catholic Church**.

The second phase of Jacobite strategy had equally sweeping results. Starting around 1740, a new form of the Craft, called "Scottish Masonry," appeared in France. Until late in the decade its presence was little more than rumor: "I am not unaware," wrote Gabriel Calabre Perau in a 1744 antimasonic book, *Les secrets de l'Ordre des Franc-Maçons dévoilés* (*The Secrets of the Order of Freemasons Unveiled*), "that a vague rumor circulates among Freemasons concerning a certain order they call Scottish, superior to ordinary Freemasonry, with its own special ceremonies and secrets" (quoted in Roberts 1972, p. 95). See **Scottish degrees**.

This "Scottish" Masonry was not Scottish at all. Scots Masonic records yield no trace of the Scottish degrees until they were imported from America in 1833. Where eighteenth-century sources talk about its origins at all, they trace it directly to the Jacobites. Providing justification for the new degrees was the famous 1737 oration of Andrew Michael Ramsay on the origins of Masonry, which for the first time traced the Craft back to the knightly orders of the Crusades; Ramsay had connections on both sides of the Stuart–Hanoverian split, but as a devout Catholic and a former tutor to the Old Pretender's two sons, his loyalties lay with the Jacobite cause. See **Ramsay, Andrew Michael**.

The Scottish degrees probably formed part of the Stuart grand strategy that led up to the 1745 rising, a strategy focused on spreading disaffection and undermining the legitimacy of the Hanoverian regime in advance of the planned revolt. Networks of Jacobite Masons in Britain and Europe played a role in these preparations. The strategy seemed to work at first; when Charles Stuart, the Young Pretender (James II's grandson), arrived in Scotland many of the Highland clans rallied to him, and his forces seized Edinburgh with little difficulty and marched south as far as Derby. But the general uprising never happened; the Jacobites never grasped the depth of popular resentment and Protestant distrust toward the Stuart line. As the British army closed in, Charles Stuart's forces retreated into Scotland and were crushed in 1746 at the battle of Culloden.

The disaster at Culloden put an end to the dream of a Stuart restoration, though it did not bring an immediate end to Jacobite activities. Masonic networks in France and Sweden that had been organized to support the rising found a new purpose helping Jacobite refugees who had fled Scotland with nothing but their lives. Yet the failure of the '45 condemned the Jacobite element in continental Masonry to death by irrelevance. In 1754 the once-secret Templar grades became public knowledge; in that year the Rite of Perfection was founded in Paris while the Rite of Strict Observance appeared in Germany. See **Rite of Perfection**; **Rite of Strict Observance**.

There the Jacobite cause rested until the Victorian period, when the Stuarts became the focus of romantic nostalgia and eccentrics could embrace the Jacobite cause with the same enthusiasm that went into schemes for universal languages and clothing reform. They had the advantage of two living claimants to the Stuart title – John Sobieski-Stuart, Count d'Albanie, and his brother Charles – who claimed to be Charles Stuart's grandsons; their actual names were John and Charles Allan and their claim has been dismissed even by modern Jacobites, but at the time they attracted much attention. A secret society titled the Order of the White Rose existed to promote the Stuart cause, and Samuel Liddell Mathers, one of the founders of the Hermetic Order of the Golden Dawn, added this to his other interests. See **Hermetic Order of the Golden Dawn**; **Order of the White Rose**.

While the claims of the House of Stuart may seem to belong on the far end of irrelevance nowadays, yet another claimant has surfaced in the rejected knowledge scene in recent years. Belgian author Michel Lafosse (1958–), who writes under the name of HRH Prince Michael of Albany, claims to be a legitimate descendant of the Young Pretender and the rightful heir to the throne of Scotland. His claims, backed by the usual lack of evidence and blatant errors of fact, have found him an enthusiastic audience in today's rejected knowledge scene. His major supporter, author Laurence Gardner, has also claimed that J.R.R. Tolkien's *Lord of the Rings* trilogy is a work of history, which may suggest something of the factual basis of "Prince Michael's" claim. See **rejected knowledge**.

Further reading: McLynn 1985, Roberts 1972.

Jesus of Nazareth

Jewish religious reformer, *c.*4 BCE–*c.*33 CE. The life of Yeshua ben Miriam, to give him his proper Hebrew name, is very poorly documented despite his role as the central figure and probable founder of Christianity, the world's largest religious movement. Little is actually known for sure about his life and teachings. The four biographies of Jesus included in the New Testament, the Gospels of Matthew, Mark, Luke, and John, were probably written between 50 and 150 years after his death, and selected out of a much larger number of gospels by church councils centuries later to form a canonical account; their value as historical sources has been hotly debated in the last two centuries. See **Christian origins**.

According to the Gospels, Jesus was the child of Mary, a young Jewish woman of the town of Nazareth in the rural northern province of Galilee, part of the Roman Empire. Mary was betrothed to Joseph, a carpenter of Nazareth, but the Gospels insist that Joseph was not Jesus' father. They state instead that Mary was made pregnant miraculously by the Holy Spirit; oddly, though, the Gospels of Matthew and Luke both trace Jesus' descent from King David through Joseph. Roman census law required Joseph and his wife to travel to the small town of Bethlehem, just south of Jerusalem, and Jesus was born there in a stable, the only lodging the couple could find.

The young Jesus grew up in Nazareth, working in Joseph's carpentry shop, and around the age of 30 went to the Jordan River to meet his older cousin, John the Baptist, an ascetic religious reformer. After being baptized by John, Jesus began preaching his own message of repentance and the imminent arrival of the kingdom of God, and soon gathered a following. The Gospel accounts credit him with a variety of miracles, including turning water into wine, feeding a large crowd of people with five loaves and two fishes, walking on water, and raising his follower Lazarus from the dead.

After some three years as an itinerant preacher, the Gospels agree, Jesus went to Jerusalem just before Passover and drew large crowds with his preaching. The Jewish religious authorities feared that he would proclaim himself the Messiah (*mashiach*, "anointed one," in Hebrew), the heir of King David, whom many Jews hoped would appear soon to restore their national independence. With the aid of Judas, a member of Jesus' inner circle who turned informer, they had Jesus seized by the temple guard. He was interrogated at a closed meeting of the Sanhedrin, the supreme Jewish religious council at the time, and then handed over to the Roman provincial government.

After a trial in the presence of Pontius Pilate, the Procurator of Judea, Jesus was executed by crucifixion, the standard Roman punishment for political crimes. He was buried in a stone tomb donated by a wealthy sympathizer. Three days later, several of his followers went to the tomb and found the entrance open and the tomb empty. Later still, according to the Gospels, members of his inner circle met the resurrected Jesus before he ascended bodily into the heavens.

In the major traditions of the Christian faith, this version of Jesus' life, death, and resurrection became the basis for a theology claiming that Jesus was the Christ (from *christos,* "anointed one," the Greek translation of *mashiach*), one of three aspects or persons of God, who incarnated as a human being and was born of the Virgin Mary in order to free those who believed in him from the original sin inherited from Adam and Eve. His crucifixion came to be seen by later Christians as a redemptive sacrifice whereby, as the Lamb of God, Jesus took on himself all the sins of the world, so that anyone who believes in his divine identity, participates in the ceremonies he instituted, and obeys the teachings of those who claim to be his successors is saved from the eternal damnation suffered by everyone else. This theology first surfaced in the writings of Saul of Tarsus (died *c.*65 CE), known to Christians as the apostle Paul, who never met Jesus in person but whose letters are the oldest documents included in the New Testament.

While this remains the most popular account of Jesus' life and death, it is far from the only one. It became standard only after centuries of dispute, and many minority views survive today. The four gospels included in today's New Testament were once part of a much larger and more varied literature of the life of Jesus, and many of the alternative gospels – the Gospel of Thomas, the Gospel of Nicodemus, the Gospel of Mary Magdalene, and more – presented radically different views of Jesus' nature, mission, and destiny. Nearly all of these were suppressed and destroyed after the Christian church seized power in the Roman world during the late fourth and early fifth centuries CE, and only the discovery of a lost Gnostic library in the twentieth century restored a handful of these alternative gospels to the light of day.

Most of the alternative gospels we know about today were the product of the orthodox church's main rival in the political struggles within the early Christian community, a diverse movement known as Gnosticism. Many of the Gnostics – the name comes from the Greek word *gnosis,* "knowledge" – taught that the material world was the creation of an ignorant and evil godling and his demonic servants, the archons, and that human souls were sparks from the true world of light who had been ensnared in the false world of matter. Jesus, according to these teachings, was one of the ruling powers of the world of light, who descended into the material world to show entrapped humanity the way to escape to their true home. See **Gnosticism**.

Another very early set of claims about Jesus came from Jewish and classical Pagan sources, and present a radically different picture. According to these sources, Jesus was a folk healer and itinerant wizard, the illegitimate son of a Jewish woman and a Roman soldier, who learned magic in Egypt after looking for work there as a young man. As historian Morton Smith showed in his groundbreaking book *Jesus the Magician* (1978), the career and recorded sayings of Jesus has many close parallels to those of other wonder-working figures of the ancient Mediterranean world, such as Apollonius of Tyana and Pythagoras, and certain elements of the Gospel accounts of Jesus find their closest parallels in Greek magical texts from Egypt dating from around the time of his life. While the idea of Jesus as a Jewish wizard makes better sense of the few solid facts about his career than most alternatives, it has understandably been ignored or denounced by nearly all sides in the debates about Christian origins. See **Egypt**; **Magic**.

The ancient Greek mysteries offer another set of intriguing parallels to early accounts of Jesus' life and death. The mysteries were pagan religious cults that focused on the life, death, and resurrection of a god or goddess. Initiates of the mysteries believed that they shared in the deity's rebirth and could count on salvation in the afterlife, in exactly the same way that Christians believe that the death and resurrection of Jesus saves them from damnation. Scholars for more than 300 years have pointed out these parallels and argued that Christianity started as nothing more than one more eastern Mediterranean mystery cult. Some of these scholars have claimed that Jesus was as mythical as Persephone or Adonis, while others have suggested that Saul of Tarsus and others overlaid the life and teachings of the real Jesus, an obscure Jewish religious reformer, with myths drawn from pagan mystery cults, in exactly the same way that an obscure Romano-British military leader in the sixth century CE was overlaid by Celtic legend to become the magnificent King Arthur of medieval romance. See **Adonis, mysteries of**; **Arthurian legends**; **Eleusinian mysteries**; **mysteries, ancient**.

Between the late fourth century CE, when the Christian church seized power and began to persecute those who disagreed with its doctrines, and the beginning of the eighteenth century, when the church's hold on society finally began to break down, very few alternative claims about Jesus appeared in the western world. The few groups rash enough to propose them, such as the medieval Gnostic movement of Catharism, faced extermination at the hands of a church far too ready to use violence against dissidents. Not until a few countries in western Europe granted religious liberty in the late seventeenth century did new interpretations begin to surface. One of the first was the work of a secret society, the Chevaliers of Jubilation, founded by the notorious freethinker and seminal Druid Revivalist John Toland sometime before 1710. Several members of the Chevaliers were responsible for the most scandalous book of the eighteenth century, the *Traité des Trois Imposteurs* (*Treatise on the Three Impostors*), which argued that Moses, Jesus, and Muhammad were fakers who invented bogus religions in order to prey on the gullible and ignorant. See **Cathars**; **Chevaliers of Jubilation**; **Toland, John**.

By the latter part of the eighteenth century these claims had been joined by a more intellectual challenge. The theory of astronomical religion, which argued that gods and goddesses were simply names for the sun, moon, planets, and other celestial bodies, included Christianity in its analysis from the beginning. Skeptical mythographers such as Charles Dupuis and William Drummond argued that Jesus was simply the sun, his twelve apostles the signs of the Zodiac, and the events of the Gospel accounts of his life mythological rewritings of the cycle of the seasons. This theory was widely accepted in the nineteenth and early twentieth centuries and still has its adherents today. See **astronomical religion**.

The chief nineteenth-century rival of astronomical religion, the theory of fertility religion, took longer to be applied to Christianity. The first writer to do so was apparently the Welsh Druid Owen Morgan, who fused the fertility and astronomical theories in his 1888 book *The Light of Britannia* to argue that Jesus was a symbol of the penis as well as the sun. Morgan's theories found few takers, though less blatantly sexual versions of fertility religion were applied to Christianity frequently in the late nineteenth and early twentieth centuries, with Jesus redefined as a vegetation god whose birth, death, burial, and resurrection symbolized the cycle of planting, growing, harvesting, and replanting grain. See **fertility religion**.

Astronomical and fertility theories of Jesus both gained a following in alternative circles, but the rise of Theosophy in the late nineteenth century introduced a much more influential theme. The Theosophical Society, the dominant force in the spiritual counterculture during those years, claimed that its teachings came from the Masters, enlightened beings who had transcended the human stage of evolution and formed the secret government of the world. Most members of the first generation of Theosophists, including the Society's founder Helena Blavatsky, rejected Christianity and everything connected with it, but by the early twentieth century the Society's new leaders, Annie Besant and Charles Leadbeater, had reinterpreted Christianity in Theosophical terms and turned Jesus into one of the Masters. This interpretation became standard through most of the occult community of the early 1900s, and spread from there into the Ascended Masters teachings and the New Age movement, two popular alternative scenes of the late twentieth and early twenty-first centuries. By way of trance mediums who claimed to be in contact with visitors from other planets, it also found its way into the UFO contactee scene, where the claim that Jesus is actually the commander of an extraterrestrial space armada is still encountered now and then. See **Ascended Masters teachings**;

Blavatsky, Helena Petrovna; **Masters**; **New Age movement**; **Theosophical Society**; **unidentified flying objects (UFOs)**.

The most popular alternative interpretation of Jesus in the late twentieth century, though, evolved by stages out of the fertility theory of religion in its latest and most scholarly form, the sacrificial king theory of Sir James Frazer. Frazer's epochal *The Golden Bough* (1917) argued that most of the world's mythology and magic related to an ancient system of fertility religion in which a sacred king, representing vegetation and the life force, was put to death to ensure the fertility of the soil and the safety of his people. Frazer said little publicly about the relevance of his theories to Christianity, but later writers such as the poet and novelist Robert Graves were less reticent. In his novel *King Jesus* (1946), Graves presented Jesus as the heir of the Jewish kingship, who married the priestess Mary Magdalene, attempted to take his ancestral throne, and was finally killed in a pagan ritual of human sacrifice. See **Mary Magdalene**.

Graves' ideas were eagerly taken up in the second half of the twentieth century and expanded in various directions by alternative thinkers. Books such as Hugh Schonfield's *The Passover Plot* (1965), which argued that Jesus and his followers staged his crucifixion and resurrection in a deliberate attempt to fulfill biblical prophecies, built a lively and lucrative market for new accounts of Christian origins, and laid the groundwork for one of the most remarkable media phenomena of modern times.

In 1969, English actor Henry Soskind (who writes under the pen name Henry Lincoln) encountered a book by Gérard de Sède, a popular French writer in the rejected-knowledge field, describing strange events that allegedly took place in the village of Rennes-le-Château around the turn of the previous century, in which a priest named Bérenger Saunière gained vast wealth after discovering a set of ancient documents hidden in the parish church. As described by de Sède, the mysterious documents had to do with the Cathars, the Knights Templar, the Merovingian kings of early medieval France, and a vast, powerful secret society called the Priory of Sion. Soskind, intrigued, began investigations of his own in the company of two other English writers, Michael Baigent and Richard Leigh. Before long they convinced themselves they had stumbled across one of the great secrets of history. See **Knights Templar**; **Merovingians**; **Priory of Sion**; **Rennes-le-Château**.

What they had actually stumbled across, however, was a trail of disinformation that had been manufactured a few years previously by Pierre Plantard, the Grand Master of the Priory of Sion. The Priory was a small and not very successful Catholic secret society created by Plantard himself in 1956. Like many secret society founders, Plantard set out to make his creation look much older and larger than it was by inventing a glamorous origin story and history for the Priory of Sion, and his methods included planting forged documents in archives and contracting with none other than Gérard de Sède to produce a book supporting the Priory's claims. See **Disinformation**; **origin stories**; **retrospective recruitment**.

Soskind and his co-authors followed the trail Plantard laid down, but then veered off in a direction of their own. Fascinated by alternative theories about Jesus, they leapt to the conclusion that the Merovingian kings were descended from a child fathered by Jesus on Mary Magdalene, that Jesus had been a claimant to the Jewish kingship, that the Knights Templar, the Cathars, and the Priory of Sion were the secret guardians of this bloodline, and that Plantard himself was the heir of King David and a lineal descendant of Jesus. These claims, which had essentially no evidence backing them and which Plantard himself rejected heatedly, became the basis for a series of wildly successful television documentaries and books, including the bestselling *The Holy Blood and the Holy Grail* (1982), and provided much of the plot and background for novelist Dan Brown's runaway bestseller *The Da Vinci Code* (2003). See **Da Vinci Code, the**.

Since the publication of *The Holy Blood and the Holy Grail*, alternative theories about Jesus have become a major growth industry. Dozens of theories now crowd the market, connecting Jesus to nearly every other popular theme in the rejected-knowledge field. One series of popular books claims that Jesus taught and practiced ancient Egyptian Freemasonry, while another argues that the Priory of Sion's role as secret guardians of the alleged Jesus bloodline actually belonged to a group of Jewish priestly families calling itself Rex Deus, which somehow became major aristocratic families in Christian medieval Europe. These and their many competitors borrow constantly from one another, treat a claim that something might possibly have happened as proof that it did, and suffer from spectacular problems of logic and evidence. None of this has prevented these books from having a remarkable influence on contemporary popular culture. See **Freemasonry**; **Rex Deus**.

The long history of arguments over who Jesus was and what he did will doubtless continue for centuries to come. The crux of the problem is that Jesus himself was a very minor figure in the context of his own time – one more local religious leader in a backwater province of the Roman Empire that was thronged with visionaries, prophets, and self-proclaimed messiahs. Nobody except for his followers apparently noticed anything special about him at the time, or for more than a century after his death, and contemporary historians outside the fledgling Christian movement saw no reason to mention him at all. Thus the facts about his life, teachings, and death may never be known for certain. This, however, has not prevented countless writers from putting forth claims about him in tones of absolute certainty.

Further reading: Baigent et al. 1983, Crossan 1991, Schonfield 2005, Smith 1978.

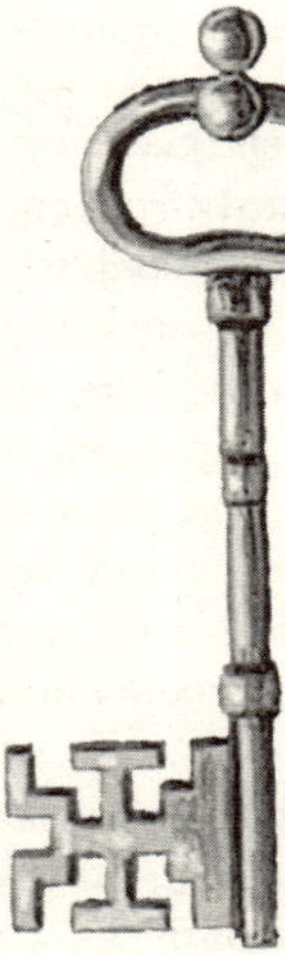

John Birch Society

The seedbed of late twentieth-century conspiracy theory in America, the John Birch Society was founded in late 1959 by Robert Welch, a successful businessman involved in right-wing politics. Like many Americans, Welch was concerned about the threat posed by communism, but he suspected that Republican as well as Democrat politicians were dupes of Moscow, and became convinced that no one in American politics was willing to do what was necessary to fight the communist threat. In 1959, he invited a group of influential conservatives to a weekend seminar in Indiana, presented his views to them, and urged the formation of a new, tightly disciplined organization to educate Americans about communism and lobby for stronger measures against it. A name for the organization came from John Birch, a Baptist missionary killed by Chinese Communists 10 days after the end of the Second World War, whom Welch considered the first casualty of the Cold War. See **Communism**.

By the end of the weekend the John Birch Society had come into being. Over the next year Welch gave 28 similar seminars in cities across the US, and the Society finished 1960 with 18,000 members. This explosive growth did not pass unnoticed, and media from the liberal and moderate sides of the political spectrum began sniping at the Society. Hostile publicity extended from the pages of *Time* and *Newsweek* to Walt Kelly's newspaper comic strip *Pogo*, which saw two of the animal residents of Okeefenokee Swamp form the Jack Acid Society and blacklist the others. Far more troubling was criticism from the right. Senator Barry Goldwater called Welch "far removed from reality and common sense," while the conservative magazine *National Review* accused Welch of "damaging the cause of anti-Communism" (cited in Goldberg 2001, p. 44).

In response to the assault, Welch and the Society moved even further to the right. The unwillingness of American conservatives to embrace the Society's viewpoint proved, at least to Welch, that the conspiracy went far beyond communism and other left-wing movements. In the early 1960s Welch encountered the writings of Augustin de Barruel and John Robison, the fathers of modern conspiracy theory, and became convinced that capitalist and communist systems alike were puppets in the hands of a sinister conspiracy of "Insiders" pursuing an agenda of world domination. These writers led him to Nesta Webster, the doyenne of early twentieth-century conspiracy theorists, who argued that a single Communist–Satanist–Jewish conspiracy headed by the Bavarian Illuminati was responsible for all the world's ills. See **Bavarian Illuminati**.

In 1964 Welch began reorienting the John Birch Society to face this larger threat. Close to a third of the membership left, but Welch was simply ahead of his time. He had embraced the distinctive theme of late twentieth-century conspiracy theory, the belief in a single global conspiracy that controls the world in secret. In 1972 he gave this theme its classic name by labeling the conspiracy's goal a "New World Order." See **New World Order**.

The 1970s saw the Society's analysis gain focus, as the Insiders were revealed as the members of the Council on Foreign Relations (CFR), a New York think-tank founded in the 1920s and supported by Rockefeller money. The CFR's international offshoot, the Trilateral Commission, soon joined it on the list of Insiders, and over the next two decades the cast expanded to include the Bilderberg Group, an annual meeting of influential politicians and businessmen in Holland; the New Age movement; and the Rockefeller, Rothschild, Baruch, Morgan, Schiff, and Warburg banking families. See **Bilderberg Group**; **Council on Foreign Relations (CFR)**; **New Age movement**; **Trilateral Commission**.

During the 1980s this vision of universal conspiracy found supporters at both ends of the political spectrum and became the most common form of conspiracy theory in America. These same years posed a serious challenge to the Society, however. Its founder suffered a crippling stroke in 1984 and died a year later, and his heir apparent, Georgia congressman Larry McDonald, was among those killed when Soviet fighters shot down a Korean airliner in October 1984. A financial crisis in 1986 nearly shut down the Society. The Reagan administration proved adept at co-opting criticism from the right, using the language of extremists while pursuing a middle-of-the-road course. The Society also came under attack from the extreme end of the Christian right because several important Society figures were Freemasons, and the Society refused to add Masonry to its enemies' list. Some modern conspiracy literature refers to the alleged inner core of Freemasons in the John Birch Society as the "Belmont Brotherhood," after the Society's headquarters in Belmont, Massachusetts. See **Antimasonry**.

The Society survived these difficulties, but has never regained its mid-1960s size and influence. It remains a small but vocal presence on the extreme right, while the ideas it launched into popular culture have become central elements of the worldviews of tens of millions of Americans.

Further reading: Goldberg 2001, Kelly 1962.

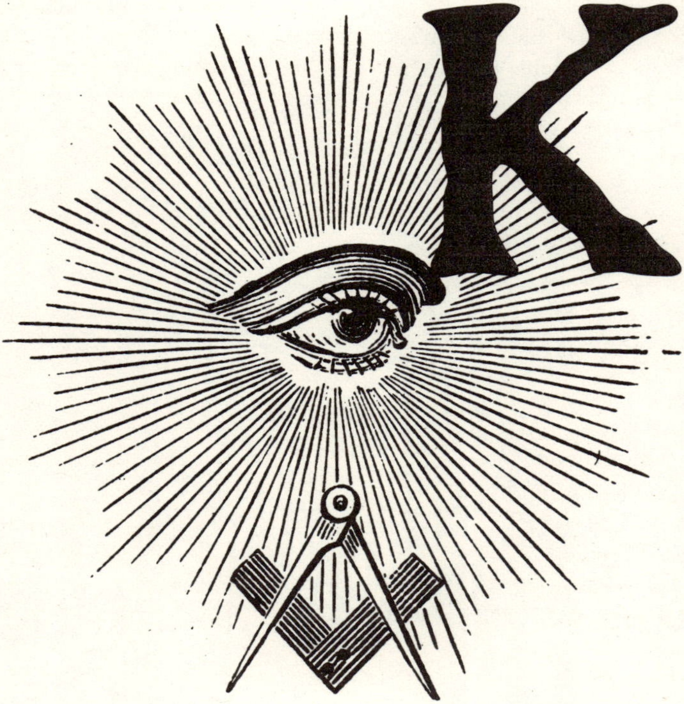
K

Kabbalistic Order of the Rose+Cross

The premier French occult secret society of the late nineteenth century, the *Ordre Kabbalistique de la Rose+Croix* (Kabbalistic Order of the Rose+Cross) was founded in 1888 by leading members of the Paris occult scene, with Stanislaus de Guaita as its first Grand Master and Joséphin Péladan, François-Charles Barlet, and Papus (Dr. Gérard Encausse) among its members. It had a governing body of 12 members, 6 of whose names were made known to members; the other 6 were concealed, according to its constitution, to enable the order to recover from any future period of decay. It claimed descent from the original Rosicrucians of medieval Germany. See **Rosicrucians**.

The order was organized as a university of magic, and the degrees offered were Bachelor, Master, and Doctor of Kabbalah, earned by attending lectures and passing examinations. This contrasts sharply with the initiatory degrees, modeled on Freemasonry, used by nearly all other magical secret societies of the time. See **Freemasonry**.

The order suffered several schisms in its history. In 1890 Péladan left to found his own Catholic Order of the Rose+Cross, which became famous for sponsoring art shows – the celebrated Salons de la Rose+Croix – but accomplished little in the occult field. Another split occurred just after the First World War, over the question of whether members of the order ought to be required to be Freemasons. Despite these controversies, the order remains active today in France and the United States. See **Catholic Order of the Rose+Cross**.

Knights of Columbus

The Knights of Columbus was the creation of Father Michael McGivney, an Irish-American Catholic priest in New Haven, Connecticut who saw the need for a men's fraternal order for Catholics. Most existing fraternal orders were formally condemned by the Vatican, which had extended its longtime rejection of Freemasonry to other secret societies during the course of the nineteenth century. The popularity of fraternal benefit societies in 1880s' America, and the very real advantages of fraternal mutual aid, made it difficult for the Catholic Church to maintain its rejection of fraternalism without providing a replacement. The Knights of Columbus was Father McGivney's solution to this problem, and with the approval of his superiors, it was founded in 1888. See **fraternal benefit societies**; **Roman Catholic Church**.

The new organization expanded quickly, and had Councils (local lodges) throughout the United States before 1900. In that year it added a new, uniformed degree, the Degree of Patriotism, to the three degrees originally created by Father McGivney and his associates, and in 1904 a burlesque degree modeled on the Shriners, the International

Order of Alhambra, was created. The Knights of Columbus currently have a presence in the US, Canada, Mexico, and the Philippines, and is in the process of establishing its first Councils in Poland as of this writing. An organization based on the Knights of Columbus, the Knights of St Columbanus, was founded in Ireland in 1915 and remains active there. See **Ancient Arabic Order of Nobles of the Mystic Shrine**; **burlesque degrees**.

The Knights of Columbus use most of the standard elements of the fraternal societies of the time, but vary them where necessary to meet the requirements of the Catholic Church's ban on secret orders. Membership in the Catholic faith is a requirement of membership, members do not take oaths, and the promise of secrecy specifically exempts the confessional. Like other fraternal benefit societies, it offers insurance policies to members; as a Catholic organization, it also raises funds for church causes and charitable works. Its founder Father McGivney has recently been proposed for sainthood, though the Vatican has not yet acted on the proposal.

Knights of Labor

The first major labor union in the United States, the Noble and Holy Order of the Knights of Labor was founded in Philadelphia in 1869 by Uriah Stephens, a tailor and labor organizer, along with eight associates. Stephens was a member of several fraternal orders of the time, including the Freemasons, the Odd Fellows, and the Knights of Pythias, and he drew much of the new order's structure and symbolism from these sources. See **Freemasonry**; **Knights of Pythias**; **Odd Fellowship**.

In its early years, the Knights were a secret society in every sense of the word, with an initiation ceremony, passwords, grips, and recognition signs. In the America of 1869, workers had few rights and most employers would fire anyone suspected of belonging to a labor union. Each Knight thus pledged, on penalty of expulsion, never to reveal the names of members to anyone outside the order. Meetings were held in secret and each Knight had to prove his identity before entering the lodge.

A second degree of initiation, the degree of the Philosopher's Stone, was created in 1878 but found few takers. By that time, however, labor violence in the Pennsylvania coal country made the use of oaths and secret meetings a political liability for labor unions, and the opposition of the Catholic Church to secret societies of every kind posed a problem at a time when many American manual laborers were immigrants from Catholic countries. In 1882 Grand Master Workman Terence Powderly abolished the rituals and made the Knights of Labor a public labor union. In the process, he opened its doors to women and African-Americans and made it, for a time, the most influential labor union in America. See **Roman Catholic Church**.

At its height in 1887, the Knights of Labor had approximately a million members, but its pursuit of a moderate line in labor disputes, and Powderly's unwillingness to support general strikes, sabotage, and violence caused it to lose ground to more radical labor organizations as the century drew to a close. The Knights also, to the embarrassment of many of their liberal supporters, took an active role in fomenting anti-Chinese sentiment, believing that Chinese immigration forced down wages. In 1917, after many years of declining membership, the Knights of Labor disbanded, and most of their members joined other labor organizations. See **labor unions**.

Further reading: Phelan 2000.

Knights of Liberty

A secret society opposed to the Ku Klux Klan, the Knights of Liberty was founded in New York in 1923 by former Klan member Andrew Padon, who had been expelled from the Invisible Empire for opposing the recruitment of undesirables in the early 1920s. Like many other anti-Klan secret societies, it flourished during the 1920s but went out of existence with the Klan's collapse at the end of the decade. See **All-American Association**; **Knights of the Flaming Circle**; **Ku Klux Klan**; **Order of Anti-Poke-Noses**.

Knights of Pythias

One of the three largest fraternal secret societies of late nineteenth- and early twentieth-century America, the Knights of Pythias were the brainchild of Justus Rathbone, a Michigan schoolteacher who came to Washington DC during the American Civil War. As early as 1858, after watching John Banim's play *Damon and Pythias* about the brotherly loyalty of two members of the Pythagorean Brotherhood in Italy in the sixth century BCE, Rathbone began drawing up plans for a fraternal order based on the legend. Rathbone was a Freemason active in the Royal Arch, and also belonged to the Improved Order of Red Men, one of the oldest purely American secret societies; he used elements of Masonic and Red Men practice in shaping his new order. See **Freemasonry**; **Improved Order of Red Men**; **Pythagorean Brotherhood**; **Royal Arch**.

Rathbone finally succeeded in organizing the first Pythian lodge, Washington #1, in 1864. The order's early years saw almost continual political struggles between Rathbone and several other founding members, and Rathbone resigned and rejoined his order several times. These quarrels failed to slow down the explosive growth of Pythian knighthood, though, and by the end of the nineteenth century the Knights of Pythias had become the third largest fraternal secret society in the United States, just behind the Freemasons and Odd Fellows. See **Odd Fellowship**.

In 1869, the Supreme Grand Lodge received a petition from a group of African-American men in Philadelphia for a lodge charter, and rejected it. Similar petitions were rejected in 1871, 1878, and 1888. This was a period when African-Americans, under the protection of post-Civil War laws, were pressing for some degree of equality, but most of the social institutions of white America closed doors in their faces. The result, as with several other fraternal orders, was the birth of a separate African-American branch of the Knights of Pythias, which remained in existence well into the twentieth century. See **African-American secret societies**.

The Knights' relationship with their own ladies auxiliary was equally complicated. Proposals for a Women's Rank were circulating in the order from 1868 onward, but the Supreme Grand Lodge refused to create one. Eventually, in 1888, an entirely independent ladies auxiliary named the Pythian Sisters was founded. Relations between the Pythian Sisters and the Knights were strained in the early years, and in 1894 the Sisters had to change their name to "Rathbone Sisters" to evade an attempt by the Knights to eliminate them; the change was not reversed until 1904. See **ladies auxiliaries**.

These confusions did not keep the Knights from trying to stay at the cutting edge of the fraternal world. The rise of fraternal benefit societies after 1868 inspired the Pythians to create a new branch, the Endowment Rank, providing fraternal insurance to Knights. Like many benefit societies, it failed to match income to expenses, and was replaced by an ordinary insurance program run by the Supreme Grand Lodge. Somewhat more successful was the Uniformed Rank, a quasi-military branch founded in 1878 to compete with the Masonic Knights Templar and other uniformed degrees. Splendid in black uniforms and white plumes, the Uniformed Rank appealed to Civil War veterans and provided color at a time when fraternal secret societies commonly marched in civic parades. Like other uniformed degrees, it faded out after the First World War and was defunct by the 1950s. See **fraternal benefit societies**.

Like most of the fraternal secret societies of nineteenth-century America, the Knights of Pythias reached their peak in the first decade of the twentieth century and declined thereafter. It still exists at the time of writing, and has lodges in approximately half the states of the US.

Knights of the Flaming Circle

Founded in 1923 in Pennsylvania, the Knights of the Flaming Circle was a secret society organized to oppose the revived Ku Klux Klan. Its members wore robes with a flaming red circle on the left breast, symbolizing truth. It welcomed Catholics, Jews, and blacks to its membership, but excluded white native-born Protestants. One of several anti-Klan secret societies founded during the 1920s, it ceased operations with the collapse of the revived Klan at the end of that decade. See **All-American Association**; **Knights of Liberty**; **Ku Klux Klan**; **Order of Anti-Poke-Noses**.

Knights of the Golden Circle

The most important pro-Southern secret society in the American Civil War, the Knights of the Golden Circle was founded in 1854 by George W.L. Bickley to support a campaign of American empire, in which US troops would conquer Mexico as a first step toward the expansion of the United States in a "Golden Circle" around the Gulf of Mexico. The Golden Circle project had a particular attraction for southerners, since the new territories were economically suited to slave plantations, and promised to make slave states a majority in the Union and thus block the influence of abolitionists in Congress. Though Bickley's project went nowhere, the order was eagerly supported by members of the Southern Rights Club, a non-secret organization founded in 1852 to oppose the Underground Railroad and Northern antislavery efforts; by 1860 the Knights functioned mostly as a secret society supporting the project of Southern independence.

In 1861, with the outbreak of hostilities between North and South, the Knights spread to the Midwestern states, where many people opposed the war. The first Castle (local lodge) north of the Mason–Dixon line was organized in Williamson County, Illinois in April 1861, and by the autumn of that year Castles existed in Ohio, Indiana, and Iowa as well as Illinois. The Knights took an active role in opposing Union enlistment and, from 1863 on, the military draft; assisting Confederate spies and escaped prisoners of war; smuggling contraband to and from the Confederate states; spreading propaganda; and organizing politically in an attempt to vote Lincoln and the Republican party out of office and force a negotiated peace. While its greatest strength was in the Midwestern states, by 1864 it had Castles (local lodges) in nearly every state of the Union, including a substantial presence in California.

The society's effective head was Clement Vallandigham, the most vocal antiwar politician in the North. After a term in the House of Representatives, Vallandigham returned to the Midwest in March 1863 and sistance to the Union. In ... s arrested by order of the ... governor of Ohio, Gen. A... Burnside, and later the same month was expelled into Confederate territory; the Confederates smuggled him through the blockade to Canada, where he resumed his leadership of the Knights. He ran for governor of Ohio on the Democratic ticket in the 1863 election, but lost. After his defeat, many members of the Knights defected to another organization, the Order of American Knights (OAK), which pursued a more direct strategy of armed revolution; Vallandigham himself accepted the office of Supreme Commander in the OAK. See **Order of American Knights**.

Like many political secret societies, the Knights found it useful to organize under many different names. Their known pseudonyms included the Mutual Protection Society, the Knights of the Mighty Host, the Circle of Honor, the Circle, and the Peace Organization. Supporters of the Union dismissed them as Copperheads (the name of a poisonous snake) or Butternuts, after the gray-brown nut that provided dye for the classic Confederate uniform.

While the Knights of the Golden Circle ceased to exist as an organized force not long after the final surrender of the Confederate armies at Appomattox in 1865, the attitudes they expressed and fostered remained active long afterwards. The same Midwestern states that formed the backbone of the Knights in the war years became the heartland of a new secret society, the revived Knights of the Ku Klux Klan, in the 1920s. See **Ku Klux Klan**.

Further reading: Benton 1972, Gray 1942.

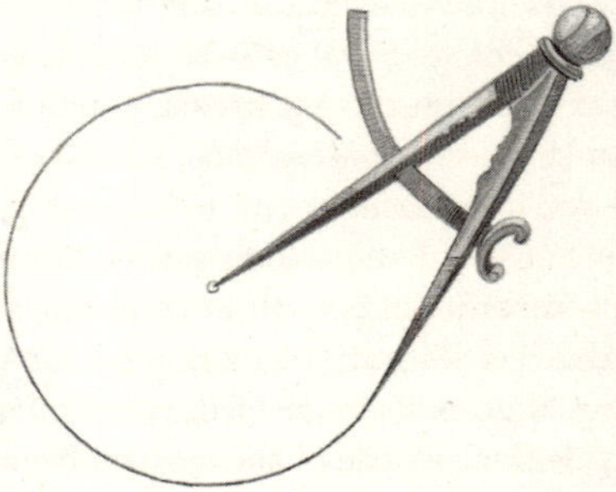

Knights Templar

In the year 1119, nine French knights living in Jerusalem formed a religious order devoted to the protection of pilgrims traveling to the Christian holy sites in that city. Together, they took monastic vows of poverty, chastity, and obedience in the presence of the patriarch of Jerusalem, and King Baldwin II gave them a place to live near the ruins of Solomon's Temple. This inspired the name of the new order, the Poor Fellow Soldiers of Christ and the Temple of Solomon, more commonly known as the Knights Templar.

Many strange claims have been floated in recent years about the founding of the order, but it made perfect sense in the context of the time. Aiding pilgrims on their way to sacred sites was a religious duty in the Middle Ages, enshrined in canon law and accepted in the popular culture of the time. The road between the port city of Joppa and Jerusalem, the principal pilgrim route, was infested by robbers and wild animals but only 40 miles (64 kilometers) long, short enough that nine competent knights devoted to the task could have a real impact on pilgrim safety.

The order remained very small for its first decade, and the title "Poor" well describes their situation; despite intermittent support from the King of Jerusalem, they had to make do on resources so limited that on occasion two brothers had to ride a single horse. A letter from the first Grand Master, Hugues de Payens, to the members in Jerusalem at the time of the Council of Troyes in 1128 makes it clear that the Poor Fellow Soldiers were struggling for survival. Fortunately for the order, help was on its way. Few people had heard of the Templars until Hugues traveled to Europe in 1128 to publicize it, but his journey brought back a torrent of donations and scores of new recruits. More valuable still, at the Council of Troyes the Catholic Church formally recognized the Templars and made their property exempt from church tithes and ordinary taxes, while the influential Bernard of Clairvaux (later canonized by the church) helped write a monastic rule for them and penned a widely circulated essay, *In Praise of the New Knighthood*, extolling the Templars and encouraging others to support them.

Within a few decades donations of land from nobles across Europe gave the Templars so much real estate that a network of local centers, called commanderies, had to be set up to manage Templar properties and send the profits to Palestine. A Templar navy had to be built to convey recruits and supplies the length of the Mediterranean, and castles rose in vulnerable points throughout the Holy Land as the Templars redirected their efforts from the protection of pilgrimage routes to the defense of the crusader kingdoms against Muslim efforts at reconquest. Even so, the Templar rule assigned ten knights to guard duty on the Joppa road as long as the crusader presence in Palestine lasted.

By 1170 the Templars had nearly a thousand brother knights in the Holy Land, divided more or less evenly between the crusader kingdoms of Jerusalem, Antioch, and Tripoli. Squires (noble recruits not yet admitted to the rank of brother knight), sergeants (cavalrymen of peasant origin), and Turcopoles (mounted archers recruited from the native Palestinian population) expanded the Templars' total fighting force to perhaps 10,000 men. Along with the two other major crusading orders of the time, the Knights Hospitallers and the Teutonic Knights, the Templars made up about half the effective fighting force of the crusader states, and their training, experience, and discipline made the military orders the iron backbone of the Crusades. The Templars' black and white banner, the Beauceant, was seen on every battlefield in the Holy Land as long as the Crusades lasted.

At the core of Templar discipline was their rule. The original or "Primitive Rule" given to the Templars at the Council of Troyes was closely modeled on the rule of the Cistercian order of monks, and had little relevance to the Templars' military life or the conditions they faced in Palestine. The rule was later expanded by *retrais* or additional sections covering the order's organization, the duties of its officers and members, and the penances imposed on those who violated its laws. The rule divided the Templars into brother knights, who were of noble birth and alone could vote in chapter meetings; chaplains, who administered the rites of the Catholic Church to the brothers; and serving brothers, a class that included squires and sergeants, as well as craftsmen such as armorers, blacksmiths, cooks, and the like, who provided all the goods and services needed to keep a medieval military force in action. A fourth class of lay affiliates consisted of men and women who pledged support to the order and received a variety of honorary membership in return.

Sensational claims about a "secret rule" were made during the trials of the Templars in the fourteenth century, and have been repeated by pro- and anti-Templar writers over the last two centuries, but the reality was more prosaic. The Templar rule has survived in numerous copies (see Upton-Ward 1992 for an English translation) and contains detailed information about Templar military tactics and procedures; for this reason one of the *retrais* requires that copies of the rule be restricted to officials of the order, so that they would not fall into enemy hands.

According to the rule, any man who applied to join the Templars had to be voted into membership by a majority of brother knights in the chapter house where the application was made. A simple initiation ritual followed, in which the new member affirmed that he was neither married or vowed to another religious order, had no debts he could not pay, had no hidden illness, had not bribed any member of the order in the hope of admission, and was not a serf. He then pledged himself to the order for the rest of his life, was received into the order, and heard a lecture on his duties and responsibilities. The ritual, which survives in numerous texts of the Templar rule, has close similarities to other medieval initiation rituals, including the reception of new members into other monastic orders and the admission of apprentices, fellow craftsmen, and masters into trade guilds. See **Brothering**; **guilds, medieval**; **Initiation**.

The Templar rule forbade any member from having any money of his own – if money was found in a brother's possessions on his death, his body was left unburied for dogs to eat – but the order itself quickly became rich. Financial systems evolved to transfer funds from Europe to the crusader kingdoms soon found other uses, and the Templars became the first international bankers in medieval Europe. From the time of King Philip Augustus of France (1165–1223) until the end of the order, the French royal house banked its treasury at the Templar center in Paris. The Grand Masters of the order served as advisers, financiers, and field marshals to crusading kings for more than a century.

The efforts of the Templars and the other military orders, however, could not save the crusader states once the Arab world united against them. Despite the Third Crusade, Jerusalem fell to the armies of Saladin (Yusuf Salah al-Din al-Ayyubi, 1138–93) in 1187, and later crusades merely slowed down the tide of Arab advances. The fall of Acre in 1291 removed the last crusader foothold in Palestine and deprived the military orders of their original reason for existence. The Knights Hospitallers moved to the Greek island of Rhodes and continued the fight from there; the Teutonic Knights returned home to Germany and launched a new holy war against the pagan Balts and Slavs of eastern Europe. The Templars alone failed to find another mission, and contented themselves with lobbying European courts for a new crusade.

This proved to be a fatal mistake. Envied for their wealth and privileges, hated for their arrogance, and blamed by many for the failure of the Crusades, the Templars offered a tempting target to any monarch bold enough to seize the opportunity. Perpetually short of money, Philip IV of France had long regarded the rich Templar properties in his country with a greedy eye. His handpicked papal candidate, Clement V, was elected Pope in 1305. All that was needed was an excuse, and rumors of Templar improprieties circulated by Esquin de Floryan, a renegade Templar from southern France, provided that.

At dawn on Friday, October 13, 1307, in an operation that would have done credit to a modern police state, royal officials carried out coordinated raids and mass arrests in every Templar chapter house in France. The charge was heresy. Two thousand Templars, of whom around a hundred were brother knights, landed in prison. Torture was used and confessions duly followed, alleging that the Templars had a secret initiation ritual requiring novices to renounce Christ, trample on a cross, and kiss their initiator on the anus, while Templar chapter meetings focused on the worship of an idol called Baphomet. This name has been subject to any number of strange interpretations over the years, but is simply the standard medieval French mispronunciation of "Muhammad," equivalent to the contemporary English "Mahound;" the implication was that the Templars, during their time in Palestine, had gone over to the enemy. See **Baphomet**.

The following year, under intense pressure from the French king, Pope

Clement decreed that Templars elsewhere in Europe be arrested and tried. Some arrests followed, but convictions were very few; in several trials, notably in Germany, the Templars were found innocent of all charges. In 1312, Clement called a general council of the Church at Vienne to condemn the Templars, but found that many of the bishops and cardinals supported the order and wanted to give them the right to formally respond to the charges against them. Clement, caught between the recalcitrant council and an enraged King Philip, summarily dissolved the Templar order on his own authority.

Outside France, the dissolution of the Templars simply involved a change of habit for its members. Most Templars found new homes in other military orders; German Templars joined the Teutonic Knights, Templars in Spain joined the Spanish military orders of Montesa and Calatrava, while the king of Portugal simply renamed the Portuguese Templars "Knights of Christ" and helped them continue as before. In England, King Edward II settled pensions on the Templars and arranged for them to transfer to monastic orders. Even in France, of the 2000 seized in the 1307 arrests, the vast majority was set free; an uncertain number died during torture, and only 60 were actually executed. One of these was the last Grand Master of the Templars, Jacques de Molay, who was burned at the stake in 1314. As he died, according to contemporary legend, he pronounced a curse against King Philip and Pope Clement. If so, the curse was a potent one, for both king and pope were dead before the year was out.

Jacques de Molay's death marked the end of the history of the Templars, but it was only the beginning of the history of the Templar myth. That myth has essentially nothing to do with the historical Knights Templar, and everything to do with the history of secret societies in the western world from the 1730s to the present.

At the time of the Templars' destruction, and for hundreds of years thereafter, almost everyone in Europe believed that Philip IV had destroyed the Templars to get at their wealth, and only a handful of propagandists for the French royal house and the official historians of the Papacy even claimed to believe the stories about heresy and the worship of Baphomet. The contemporary poet Dante Alighieri, whose great poem *The Divine Comedy* commented on most of the events of his time, referred to the Templars' fate in Canto XX of the *Purgatorio* as purely a result of Philip's greed and spite. The great Renaissance legal theorist Jean Bodin, two centuries later, cited the Templars as a classic example of a group oppressed and destroyed by an unjust monarch. Until the middle of the eighteenth century, this view and the orthodox claim that the Templars had done exactly what Philip IV said they did were the only opinions about the Templars in circulation.

Abruptly, in the late 1730s, a third set of claims began to appear, insisting that the Templars were the secret guardians of an ancient wisdom ruthlessly suppressed by the forces of orthodoxy. These first surfaced in Masonic circles in France linked to the Jacobites – supporters of the exiled House of Stuart – and drew their theme from the famous 1736 Masonic address of the Chevalier Andrew Ramsay, an influential Jacobite who argued that Freemasonry itself was descended from the knightly orders of the Crusades. See **Freemasonry**; **Jacobites**; **Ramsay, Andrew Michael**.

Within a few years of Ramsay's address, rumors circulated through the French court about a new, "Scottish" Freemasonry above the three Craft degrees of ordinary Masonry. French sources claim that the first Scottish system was launched by Ramsay himself and included the three degrees of Scottish Master, Novice, and Knight of the Temple. More degrees followed; a 1744 pamphlet from Paris claims that there were six or seven degrees above Master Mason at that time, while in 1751 most French lodges worked a system of nine degrees. See **high degrees**; **Scottish degrees**.

Central to the entire system of Scottish degrees was the claim that they descended from Templar traditions preserved in Scotland, and that the Templars themselves had been guardians of an ancient wisdom that now survived in the higher degrees of Freemasonry. Many historians of Freemasonry have argued that the entire Templar myth was created by Jacobite propagandists at this time, as part of a struggle for control of French Freemasonry between Jacobites and their opponents, and the evidence does seem to support this claim.

After the catastrophic defeat of the Jacobite rising of 1745 put an end to the hope of a Stuart restoration, several different systems of Scottish Masonry surfaced in public, among them the Royal Order of Scotland in The Hague in 1750, the Rite of Perfection (the source of today's Ancient and Accepted Scottish Rite) in Paris in 1754, and the Rite of Strict Observance in Saxony, also in 1754. All these rites had connections to the Jacobite court in exile and included, as part of their teachings, the claim that surviving Templars had carried their mysteries to Scotland in the years after 1307 and established Freemasonry there. This claim was originally a secret teaching but, like most Masonic secrets, it slipped out at an early date, and sparked a lively market for Templar degrees within Masonry. Eighteenth-century Masonry being what it was, supply soon caught up with demand, and soon more than a dozen newly minted Templar rites with no connection to the Stuart cause competed with the Scottish degrees for membership and influence. The Order of the Golden and Rosy Cross, an eighteenth-century German Rosicrucian order, also found room for the Templars in their origin story, claiming that Templars were initiated in 1188 into the Rosicrucian order, originally founded in Alexandria in 96 CE, and brought its teachings back to Europe with them. See **Ancient and Accepted Scottish Rite**; **Order of the Golden and Rosy Cross**; **Rite of Perfection**; **Rite of Strict Observance**; **Rosicrucians**; **Royal Order of Scotland**.

The next major element of the Templar myth arrived by way of the French Revolution. Many of the liberals who originally supported the National Assembly in its struggle against royal privilege in the heady days of 1789 were Freemasons. During the Revolution years, a handful of journalists turned this fact into the foundation for a claim that the Revolution itself had been hatched as a Masonic plot. One contributor to this literature was Charles-Louis Cadet de Gassicourt, a former radical whose book *Le Tombeau de Jacques Molay* (*The Tomb of Jacques Molay*, 1796) claimed that the Freemasons were exacting their vengeance against the French monarchy for the death of Jacques de Molay. Cadet de Gassicourt's book also introduced the idea that the Templars had been influenced by the Order of Assassins, and strung together more than a dozen unrelated secret societies into a supposedly continuous tradition of anarchist conspirators plotting across the centuries. See **Assassins**; **French Revolution**.

This theme was taken up readily by conservatives in the decades immediately after the Napoleonic Wars, when secret societies – many of them linked in one way or another with the Templar degrees of Freemasonry – played an important role in spreading liberal political ideas across Europe and fomenting rebellion against the attempts of autocratic regimes to stamp out the influence of the French Revolution. The two great founders of modern conspiracy theory, Augustin de Barruel and John Robison, both drew on Cadet de Gassicourt's work in claiming that Freemasonry had been infiltrated by a vast conspiracy against religions and governments. See **antimasonry**.

Far more influential than either of these authors in shaping the Templar myth, however, was the Austrian scholar Joseph von Hammer-Purgstall, whose *Mysterium Baphometis Revelatum* (*The Mystery of Baphomet Revealed*, 1818) and several later books argued that the Templars had been Gnostic heretics, practicing an orgiastic cult of the goddess Achamoth or Baphomet passed on in secret since the third century CE. Von Hammer-Purgstall was an employee of Prince Klemens von Metternich, chief minister to the Emperor of Austria and leader of the conservative reaction in post-Napoleonic Europe, and his books on the Templars were anything but disinterested scholarly research; rather, they were part of a deliberate strategy of disinformation meant to tar the revolutionary secret societies of the era with charges of sexual deviance, religious heresy, and occult practices. See **Disinformation**.

As with so much disinformation involving secret societies, however, von Hammer-Purgstall's assault on the Templars had the unintended consequence of creating new secret societies on the model of the disinformation project – in this case, making sexual deviance, religious heresy, and occult practices popular among would-be Templars. France was the scene of most of these transformations, as von Hammer-Purgstall's book arrived there in the middle of a full-blown Templar renaissance. This was launched by Bernard Fabrè-Palaprat, a Freemason who in 1804 announced that he had a charter dating back to the time of Jacques de Molay himself. According to this document, the Charter of Transmission, de Molay had passed on the Grand Mastership of the Templars to one Johannes Marcus Larmenius, who kept the order alive in secret and passed it on in his turn. The charter is an eighteenth-century forgery and Larmenius apparently never existed, but the ploy allowed Fabrè-Palaprat to launch his own Order of the Temple and attract hundreds of members.

The Templar revival quickly found common ground with the burgeoning French alternative-spirituality scene. By 1828 French Templars were claiming a direct descent from the ancient Gnostics, and Eliphas Lévi's immensely influential 1860 *Histoire de la Magie* (*History of Magic*) argued that the Templars were Gnostic sorcerers practicing the true, magical Christianity of Jesus as passed on through the "secret church" of the apostle John, and their idol Baphomet was the goat-symbol of the all-powerful Astral Light, the mysterious substance that made magic possible. See **Gnosticism**; **Magic**.

By 1903 the Aryan racial mystic Jörg Lanz von Liebenfels was laying the foundations for the Ordo Novi Templi, a racist occult order that foreshadowed Hitler's SS. In 1906 the Ordo Templi Orientis (OTO), which practiced a system of sex magic borrowed from other magical orders of its time, was established, and in 1912 Aleister Crowley, for whom sexual deviance, religious heresy, and occult practices were the breath of life, took charge of the OTO in England and America and proclaimed to his new Templars a gospel very nearly identical with von Hammer-Purgstall's fantasies. See **Crowley, Aleister**; **Ordo Novi Templi (ONT)**; **Ordo Templi Orientis (OTO)**.

Nor was this the last hurrah of the Templars. All the elements of the Templar mythology just surveyed remain live options in the alternative scene today, and many have penetrated popular culture as well. Bestselling books repeat the old claims of a Templar origin for Freemasonry and link the Templars to Gnostics, Assassins, and others. New elements have entered the myth in recent years; Pierre Plantard's extraordinary Priory of Sion hoax, and its various mutations at the hands of other authors, grafted an entirely new body of fable onto the existing mythology, centering on the Merovingian kings of Dark Age France, the alleged mysteries of Rennes-le-Château, and exotic accounts of Christian origins. These same speculative claims have also found a home in the world of popular fiction, most notably in Dan Brown's bestselling novel *The Da Vinci Code* (2003). See **Christian origins**; **Merovingians**; **Priory of Sion**; **Rennes-le-Château**.

In recent years new Templar orders of various kinds have sprouted throughout the western world, promoting almost every imaginable ideology except the orthodox Catholicism that motivated the original Templars. The reaction of the simple, devout soldier-monks of the Knights Templar to all this can scarcely be imagined.

Further reading: Barber 1978, Barber 1994, Partner 1981, Upton-Ward 1992.

Know-Nothing Party

A major force in American politics in the 1850s, the Know-Nothing Party was at one and the same time a secret society and a political party – a complicated mix, but entirely believable in nineteenth-century America, where secret societies of all kinds were in their heyday. Its formal name was the American Party; the term "Know-Nothings" came from the requirement that members answer all questions about the party and its activities with the words "I don't know."

The party's history began in 1849 when Charles B. Allen organized a secret society, the Order of the Star-Spangled Banner, in New York City. The order had two degrees of initiation and the usual lodge equipment of passwords, grips, and symbols. Its purposes, though, were strictly political; it sought to unite white Protestant Americans against the Roman Catholic Church, keep Catholics out of political office, and ban immigration from Catholic countries. The role of Catholicism in American society was a heated issue at the time, as many Americans of other religions were convinced that Catholics placed their loyalty to the Pope over their duty to their country. See **Roman Catholic Church**.

In 1852 a political party, the American Party, was founded in New York City with a platform very similar to that of the Order of the Star-Spangled Banner, and the two soon merged, absorbing several other nativist political groups in the process and drawing members and ideas from the Society of St Tammany, a descendant of the old Sons of Liberty society from the Revolutionary War era. By 1854 a new ritual of three degrees had been established, and local, district, and state Councils (local lodges) began to spring up across the United States. See **Society of St Tammany**; **Sons of Liberty**.

The Know-Nothings emerged when the Federalist (Whig) Party, until then one of the two dominant forces in American politics, was in the process of breaking apart over disputes concerning slavery. Many Whigs, especially in the southern half of the country, joined the Know-Nothing Party or supported its candidates. In 1854, the party's candidate for Governor of Maryland won election, and 1855 saw a Know-Nothing governor take office in Tennessee; there and elsewhere Know-Nothings won election to the Senate and House of Representatives, state legislatures, and a wide range of state and local offices.

In 1856 the Know-Nothing Party seemed to have a chance at the US presidency as well. Its national convention in Philadelphia that year nominated Millard Fillmore for president, and a special meeting of the National Council abolished the rituals, oaths, and other secret society aspects of the party to enable it to carry out a national political campaign. In a bitter three-way campaign against Democrat James Buchanan and John Fremont, the candidate of the recently founded Republican Party, Fillmore came in third place, with a quarter of the vote. Within a year of its defeat, the party had fallen apart as the slavery issue came to dominate the political landscape of the US and armed clashes between pro- and antislavery forces lit the fuse of the American Civil War.

Further reading: Overdyke 1950.

Ku Klux Klan

The most notorious of American secret societies, the Ku Klux Klan was founded in 1865 in Pulaski, Tennessee, by six young Confederate veterans. The name came from the Greek word *kuklos*, "circle," and the Scots word "clan," popularized in the South through the romantic novels of Sir Walter Scott. At first, the original Klansmen simply dressed as ghosts and goblins to play pranks on neighbors, but the joke turned serious – and ugly – as others joined the organization and used it to terrorize former slaves and political opponents. The original ghost costumes soon became standardized as Klansmen resurrected the old Irish custom of dressing in white for nocturnal acts of violence, a habit that dated to the eighteenth-century Whiteboys. The Klan's distinctive costume, a white robe with a tall pointed hood and cloth mask with eyeholes to cover the face, quickly became a symbol of fear across the old Confederacy. See **Whiteboys**.

By 1868 the Klan had tens of thousands of members throughout the South and had recruited Nathan Bedford Forrest, the former Confederate cavalry general, as its head. Under Forrest's leadership, the Klan evolved into an organization modeled on military lines but festooned with colorful names. The South as a whole was the Invisible Empire, headed by Forrest as Grand Wizard and his staff, the ten Genii. Each state was titled a Realm, under the authority of a Grand Dragon and eight Hydras; each congressional district was a Dominion, under a Grand Titan and six Furies; each county a Province, under a Grand Giant and four Goblins; and each town a Den, under a Grand Cyclops and two Night Hawks. How much of this organization existed in reality and how much only on paper is anyone's guess; the fact that anybody could put on a hood and pursue private vendettas under the cover of the Klan makes it impossible to tell how much of the anarchy that swept the South between 1868 and 1872 was the work of the organized Klan and how much was merely carried out in its name.

The Klan's activities brought harsh reprisals. Laws passed in 1870 and 1871 gave President Ulysses Grant the power to impose martial law and suspend habeas corpus. Federal troops moved against the Klan, and several thousand real or suspected Klansmen spent time in Federal prisons. By the late 1870s the Klan had become a memory, as Southern political and business interests made their peace with the national government and Jim Crow segregation became the law of the land south of the Mason–Dixon line.

It took one of the first successful American motion pictures, an enthusiast for secret societies, and a pair of professional promoters to bring the Klan back to life. The movie, *Birth of a Nation* (1915) by D.W. Griffith, was a masterpiece of racist propaganda that portrayed the Klan as heroic defenders of Southern womanhood against treacherous Northerners and subhuman blacks. The enthusiast, William J. Simmons, belonged to 15 fraternal orders and for a time made his living recruiting members for insurance lodges. After seeing the movie, Simmons turned his efforts to reviving the Klan as a fraternal order and wrote a new Klan ritual in which nearly every term began with the letters "kl" – the dens of the old Klan were renamed Klaverns, officers included the Klaliff, Kludd, and Kligrapp, the book of ritual was the Kloran and the songs sung during Klonvocations (Klavern meetings) were known as Klodes. Simmons proclaimed himself Imperial Wizard of the Knights of the Ku Klux Klan in 1915 and recruited a few thousand members, but the new Klan made little headway until 1920. In that year Simmons turned over public relations to Edward Young Clark and Elizabeth Tyler, who ran a firm called the Southern Publicity Association and had ample experience in fundraising and promotion.

Thereafter the Klan grew explosively, gaining 100,000 members by 1921 and more than four million nationwide by 1924. Klaverns sprouted in every American state and most Canadian provinces. Efforts to launch the Klan outside North America had little success apart from Germany, where the German Order of the Fiery Cross was founded in 1923, but the Klan's activities were a source of inspiration to the radical right throughout Europe; the Cagoule, the major French fascist secret society of the 1930s, took its name ("hood" in French) from the Klan-style headgear worn by its members. See **Cagoule**.

The key to its success was the broadening of its original white supremacist stance to include other popular American prejudices of the time. Catholics, Jews, immigrants, labor unionists, and liberals joined African-Americans on the Klan's hate list. At a time when many white Americans fretted about internal enemies undermining the American way of life, Klansmen presented themselves as defenders of "100 percent Americanism" against all comers. Publicly, Klansmen pursued their agenda through boycotts and voting drives; violence and intimidation aimed against the Klan's enemies formed the more covert dimension of Klan activity, publicly denied by the national leadership but tacitly approved by them and carried out by local Klansmen under the white Klan mask. See **Roman Catholic Church**; **Antisemitism**.

Like the Antimasonic Party and the Know-Nothings before it, the Klan drew much of its support from conservative Protestantism. The 1920s were the seedtime of the fundamentalist churches, the years when conservative Protestant denominations abandoned their commitment to social justice and turned to a rhetoric of intolerance rooted in narrow biblical literalism. Recognizing common interests, the Klan made recruitment of fundamentalist ministers a top priority. Some 40,000 fundamentalist ministers became Klansmen in the 1920s; the Grand Dragons of four states, and 26 of the 39 Klokards (national lecturers) hired by Klan headquarters, were fundamentalist ministers. This strategy paid off handsomely as Klan propaganda sounded from church pulpits and Klansmen-ministers encouraged their flocks to enter local Klaverns. See **Antimasonic Party**; **fundamentalism**; **Know-Nothing Party**.

A similar strategy aimed at influential members of other secret societies, and turned many fraternal lodges into recruiting offices for the Klan. As the most prestigious secret society in America, the Freemasons formed a major target for this project, and hostilities on the part of white Masonic lodges toward black Prince Hall Masonry rendered the Craft vulnerable to Klan rhetoric. To the lasting embarrassment of Masonry, several Masonic organizations entered into a tacit alliance with the Klan. The Southern Jurisdiction of the Ancient and Accepted Scottish Rite, with its history of hostility toward the Roman Catholic Church, was among the most heavily involved, and during the mid-1920s the head of the Scottish Rite in at least one state was also the Grand Dragon of that state's Klan. See **Ancient and Accepted**

Scottish Rite; **Freemasonry**; **Prince Hall Masonry**.

The popularity of secret societies in 1920s America made the Klan's spread spark the growth of other secret organizations, some attempting to compete with it for the same racist market and others opposing the Klan and everything it stood for. Competing orders included the American Order of Clansmen, founded in San Francisco at the same time as Simmons's Knights of the Ku Klux Klan, and the Royal Riders of the Red Robe, an order that admitted white men born outside the US (and thus excluded from Klan membership) but shared the Klan's repellent ideals. An even more colorful assortment of secret orders rose up to oppose the Klan's influence; these included the All-American Association, the Knights of Liberty, the Knights of the Flaming Circle, and the Order of Anti-Poke-Noses, an Arkansas organization founded in 1923 that opposed "any organization that attends to everyone's business but their own." See **All-American Association**; **American Order of Clansmen**; **Knights of Liberty**; **Knights of the Flaming Circle**; **Order of Anti-Poke-Noses**.

All this was prologue to the Klan's reach for political power, which occupied the national office with increasing intensity from 1923 on. The Imperial Kligrapp (national secretary) Hiram W. Evans spearheaded this project after he seized control of the Klan in a palace coup in 1922. Journalists assailed the Klan or dismissed its members as "nightie Knights," but politicians of both parties found the Klan useful. Nowhere was the Klan's political reach longer than in Indiana, where one in four white adult males was a Klan member by 1924. Indiana Grand Dragon David C. Stephenson had more control over the state government than any of its elected officials and was preparing for a Presidential campaign. In 1925, though, he abducted and raped his secretary, who took poison but lived long enough to name him and provide police with details of the crime. The media furor that followed his exposure and conviction for murder proved catastrophic for the Klan. In Indiana itself, three-fourths of the members quit in the next two years. Stephenson himself, furious at the state governor's refusal to pardon him, revealed Klan illegalities to the authorities, landing more than a dozen elected officials in jail.

Stevenson's exposure and the resulting media frenzy left the Klan in tatters. Most Klaverns outside the South went out of existence during the late 1920s as popular opinion turned against the order and politicians who had praised the Klan found that attacking it brought equal advantages. As the 1930s dawned the Klan handed an even more deadly weapon to its opponents by allying with the German-American Bund and other pro-Nazi groups in the United States. Widely suspected of disloyalty, pilloried by the media, and faced with a bill for more than half a million dollars in back taxes, the Knights of the Ku Klux Klan dissolved in 1944.

It took the civil rights struggle of the 1950s and 1960s to breathe new life into the Klan. Challenged by school desegregation and the swelling demands of black Americans for equal rights, white Southerners clinging to the Jim Crow system of racial privilege turned to the Klan in an attempt to turn back the clock. The Association of Georgia Klans (AGK) was the first Klan organization to pick up the gauntlet, launching a campaign of beatings and intimidation. In 1953 the AGK reorganized itself as the US Klans, Knights of the Ku Klux Klan, and expanded throughout the South. In 1961 the US Klans merged with another Klan group, the Alabama Knights of the Ku Klux Klan, to form the United Klans of America (UKA).

The bitter desegregation struggles of the 1960s saw the UKA take center stage as the most intransigent wing of white Southern resistance, and it grew to a total membership near 50,000. Where other racist groups launched boycotts and propaganda campaigns, members of the UKA embraced overt terrorism, firebombing black churches and murdering activists. This strategy backfired when Federal Bureau of Investigation agents infiltrated the Klan and sent dozens of its members to prison for long terms.

The Klan splintered further in the 1970s and 1980s as the South discovered it could live with desegregation, and Klan opponents discovered that civil suits could be used to bankrupt Klan groups that engaged in violent behavior. The UKA fell to this strategy when two of its officers were convicted of lynching a black teenager, and lawyers for the victim's family won a civil lawsuit that stripped the UKA of all its assets. By the late 1980s surviving Klan groups could count only a few thousand followers scattered across the United States, and their place in the racist right was rapidly being taken by neo-Nazi organizations, Christian Identity, militia groups, and racist Satanist groups such as the White Order of Thule. See **Christian Identity**; **neo-Nazi secret societies**; **New World Order**; **White Order of Thule**.

Presently the Klan is split into more than a hundred competing fragments, most of them still using revisions of Simmons's 1915 Kloran and dressing in the traditional white robe and pointed hood. Bitter internal politics and a reputation as the has-beens of the far right present a burden to further expansion that none of the current Klan leaders have been able to overcome. Still, the Klan has risen from defeat more than once in its history and the possibility of a future revival cannot be dismissed out of hand.

Further reading: Horowitz 1999, Wade 1987, Weller and Thompson 1998.

L

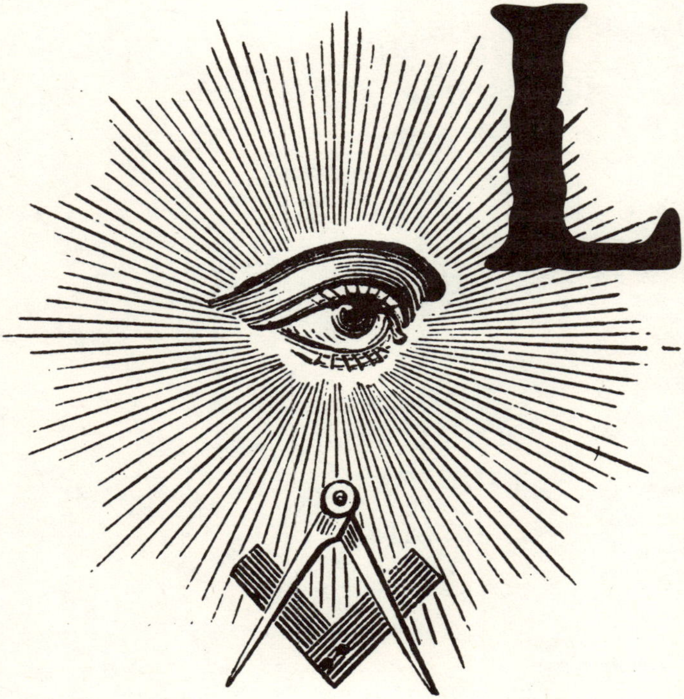

LABOR UNIONS

A major social movement throughout the western world during the nineteenth and twentieth centuries, labor unions drew on methods pioneered by the fraternal secret societies of the same period in building a movement to unite laborers for mutual aid. While attempts to organize workers to press for higher wages and improved working conditions go back to the late Middle Ages, and journeymen's associations of this sort played a role in the formation of secret societies such as Odd Fellows and Compagnonnage, the first modern labor unions emerged at the beginning of the nineteenth century. See **Compagnonnage**; **Odd Fellowship**.

In Britain and Europe, the first workers' associations drew little from the secret societies of the time, but in America, where the fraternal movement had its greatest success, many nineteenth-century unions closely resembled fraternal orders. The first American labor union to include workers of all trades, the Knights of Labor, was founded in 1869 by a labor organizer who belonged to the Freemasons, Odd Fellows, and Knights of Pythias. In its early years the Knights of Labor had an initiation ritual, passwords, secret handshakes, and all the other practices of secret societies of the time. These were dropped in 1882, and very few later labor unions made use of them, but many unions to this day follow patterns of organization modeled on secret societies. Until the last few decades, similarly, labor unions in predominantly male industries had ladies auxiliaries that were all but indistinguishable from those of fraternal orders. See **fraternal orders**; **Knights of Labor**; **Knights of Pythias**; **ladies auxiliaries**.

From the last decades of the nineteenth century on, most labor unions in Europe and America were caught up in struggles among competing leftist ideologies. Some unions, such as the Industrial Workers of the World (IWW) in America, aligned with the anarchist movement and laid plans for a nationwide general strike that would overturn the existing order; others affiliated with the Communists; still others, including the largest labor unions in Britain, aligned with the Social Democrat movement and sought to change the system gradually through peaceful political action. The first half of the twentieth century saw the gradualists win out, and labor unions became part of the system they had once set out to overturn. In the process, unions shed the last traces of their secret society ancestry – a detail that has not prevented conservative conspiracy theorists from insisting that unions are still part of a vast leftwing conspiracy. See **New World Order**.

LADIES AUXILIARIES

Most of the fraternal secret societies that flourished in Europe, America, and Australasia during the nineteenth century limited their membership to adult men. This echoed social prejudices of the time that consigned women to home and church, while defining the wider social world as a male preserve. The emergence of feminism as an active social force in the English-speaking world around the middle of the nineteenth century challenged this state of affairs and forced fraternal orders to find a place for women. A few, such as the Patrons of Husbandry, took the radical step of admitting men and women to the same lodges on an equal basis, but most compromised by creating a ladies auxiliary: a lodge for women connected to the sponsoring order by birth or marriage, with its own initiation ritual and its own passwords, signs, and grip. See **fraternal orders**; **Patrons of Husbandry (Grange)**.

Ladies auxiliaries of the nineteenth century drew some of their inspiration from the French rites of Adoptive Masonry, but America was the principal seedbed of fraternal ladies auxiliaries; the decade following the seminal 1848 conference at Seneca Falls, New York, the birthplace of American feminism, saw the first wave of auxiliaries founded. The Order of the Eastern Star, the first Masonic ladies auxiliary in America, and the Daughters of Rebekah (later simply called Rebekahs), the ladies auxiliary of the Independent Order of Odd Fellows, both appeared in 1852. By the 1880s, when dozens of new fraternal orders appeared each year, most came into existence with ladies auxiliaries already attached. See **Adoptive Masonry**; **Odd Fellowship**; **Order of the Eastern Star**.

Relations between auxiliaries and their sponsoring orders were not always cordial. The Knights of Pythias, the third largest American fraternal order, and the Pythian Sisters, their ladies auxiliary, had a stormy relationship that featured attempts by the Knights' Supreme Lodge to abolish the Sisters entirely. Two other lodges, the Modern Woodmen of America and the Woodmen of the World, found themselves out-competed by their own auxiliaries, and ended up severing the connection and sending the former auxiliaries into the world as independent fraternal benefit orders – the Degree of Honor and the Royal Neighbors of America respectively. See **fraternal benefit societies**; **Knights of Pythias**.

Even when relationships between the sponsoring order and the ladies auxiliary remained amicable, gender issues brought in complexities of their own. Brothers of the sponsoring order were also allowed to join most auxiliaries, and in the early days, ladies auxiliaries were often organized and managed by the brethren, but well before the end of the nineteenth century most ladies auxiliaries had taken control of their own affairs. In the twentieth century most auxiliaries outside Freemasonry discarded the requirement that members have some relationship to the sponsoring fraternal order; the Rebekahs led the way in this change, starting to admit women with no Odd Fellow connection in 1921.

Ladies auxiliaries remained an important part of social life in America and a few other countries well into the twentieth century, and the decline in membership that hit all fraternal orders in the last decades of the century often took longer to affect the ladies auxiliaries than the fraternal lodges that sponsored them. In many areas, lodges of the Eastern Star, the Rebekahs, the Pythian Sisters, and other auxiliaries remained large and active long after the equivalent male lodges had dwindled or disbanded. Still, the membership of most ladies auxiliaries at the century's end averaged well past retirement age, and attitudes reflected the social customs of an earlier time – two serious barriers to effective recruitment of younger women. The first years of the twenty-first century have accordingly seen most ladies auxiliaries suffer drastic losses in membership, in some cases even more dramatic than those of fraternal orders. It remains to be seen if these societies of the nineteenth century can reinvent themselves in a way that will permit them to survive into the twenty-first.

League of Outlaws

A German revolutionary secret society of the 1830s, the *Bund der Geächteten* or League of Outlaws was founded in Paris in 1834 by a group of German exiles. Its founder, Theodor Schuster, drew most of his ideas from earlier secret societies such as the Carbonari and the Philadelphes, and from the writings of Filippo Buonarroti, the most influential revolutionist of the time. The League had a hierarchical structure derived from that of Buonarroti's Universal Democratic Carbonari, with local "tents" answering to provincial "camps" that received orders from a central "focus." See **Buonarroti, Filippo**; **Carbonari**; **Philadelphes**.

While it borrowed organizational elements from these older sources, the League was among the first European revolutionary groups to push for a social revolution to abolish class barriers and eliminate exploitation of workers by capitalists. Schuster argued that the major divides in the Europe of his time were between classes, not nations, and proclaimed a future "cooperative republic" in which peasant cooperatives and government intervention would keep the influence of wealthy capitalists in check. The League thus pioneered the ideologies later claimed by Communist secret societies and regimes. See **Communism**.

At its peak, the League had perhaps 200 members, half in Paris and the rest in the westernmost states of Germany. It never achieved a coherent plan for revolution, and broke up in a series of internal disputes beginning in 1836. In early 1838, most of its remaining members left it to join a new secret society structured along the same lines, the League of the Just. See **League of the Just**.

League of the Just

In 1837, as the League of Outlaws was falling apart, several of its members in Paris drew up a new organization, the League of the Just (*Bund der Gerechten*). Like its predecessor, the League was an association of German radicals who hoped to spark revolution in the fragmented states of nineteenth-century Germany, and it drew much of its organization and strategy from the Carbonari and other early nineteenth-century political secret societies. One of the League's leading members, Johann Höckerig, was an associate of Filippo Buonarroti – the grand old man of European revolutionists at that time – in Buonarroti's last years, and echoes of Buonarroti's writings and secret societies show up all through the League's publications. See **Buonarroti, Filippo**; **Carbonari**; **League of Outlaws**.

The League broke with earlier revolutionary secret societies in combining a democratic system of internal government with the hierarchical structure common to secret societies. Each group of 10 members formed a commune, 10 communes a county, 10 counties a hall, and each of these units elected its own leaders and made many of its own decisions. This system left the League vulnerable to disagreements between its members. A schism soon developed between a moderate faction, the "carpenters," who sought political reform, and a more radical wing, the "tailors," who advocated social revolution to break the power of the rich over the working classes. "Tailor" Wilhelm Weitling, the chief theoretician of the League's early years, published a book, *Der Menschheit wie sie ist und wie sie sein sollte* (*Humanity as it Is and as it Should Be*, 1838), arguing that the artificial economy of money should be replaced by a system in which goods were priced according to the hours of labor needed to make them, and existing political systems should be abolished in favor of a "universal republic."

The League's original headquarters was in Paris, but police repression after the insurrection of 1839 forced many of the League's leaders to emigrate to Britain. There, the League found supporters in the radical wing of Chartism, a British movement for constitutional reform. An Educational Society for German Workingmen was founded in London in 1840 as a front group for the League's activities, and soon established links with revolutionary circles as far afield as Hungary, Poland, and New York. Close cooperation between the League and the Democratic Association, a radical group founded by dissident Chartists in 1837, led to an effective fusion of the two organizations during the 1840s.

Before the end of that decade the League mutated into a different, and far more famous, revolutionary organization. In 1847, impressed by the writings of a young German journalist and economic theorist then living in Brussels, the League's leadership dissolved what was left of the secret-society framework of their organization and took a new name. The journalist's name was Karl Marx, and the new name was the Communist League. Ironically, the League accomplished little before dissolving in the mid-1850s, but it popularized Marx's ideas and helped lay the groundwork for the First International. See **Communism**; **First International**.

Further reading: Billington 1980.

LEFT-HAND PATH

Hindu and Buddhist Tantric traditions are traditionally divided into two "paths" based on their attitude toward sex, alcohol, and meat. In the orthodox or "right-hand" Tantras, these are forbidden to initiates, since they cloud the awareness and distract the mind from the hard work of spiritual transformation. In the heterodox or "left-hand" Tantras, on the other hand, sex, alcohol, meat and other things forbidden to ordinary Tantric practitioners are used ritually as means to transcend the ordinary limits of the self.

These terms came west by way of the Theosophical Society, the most influential occult organization of the late nineteenth and early twentieth century, but underwent distortion in the process. In India the left-hand Tantras are considered the more risky branch of Tantrism, and practitioners sometimes have a dubious reputation, but only a minority of puritans consider them evil. In Theosophical usage, however, the term "right-hand path" became a standard term for morally pure occultism, or white magic, while "left-hand path" came to be used for evil or black magic. The overwhelming impact of Theosophy on western occultism made the left-hand path synonymous with Satanism, and this usage was soon adopted by Satanists themselves and remains in common use in those circles today. See **black magic**; **right-hand path**; **Satanism**; **Theosophical Society**; **white magic**.

LEGA NERA

The first important Italian political secret society, the Lega Nera (Italian for "Black League") took shape around 1796 in the aftermath of the French invasion of Italy. Almost nothing is known about its origins and history, except for reports in French secret police records of the time. According to these, the Lega Nera had connections to the radical

Jacobin party inside France, and planned a campaign of assassination aimed at killing French officials and military personnel. Nothing seems to have come of this plan, and by 1798 the place of the Lega Nera seems to have been taken by a more effective secret society, the Raggi. See **French Revolution**; **Raggi**.

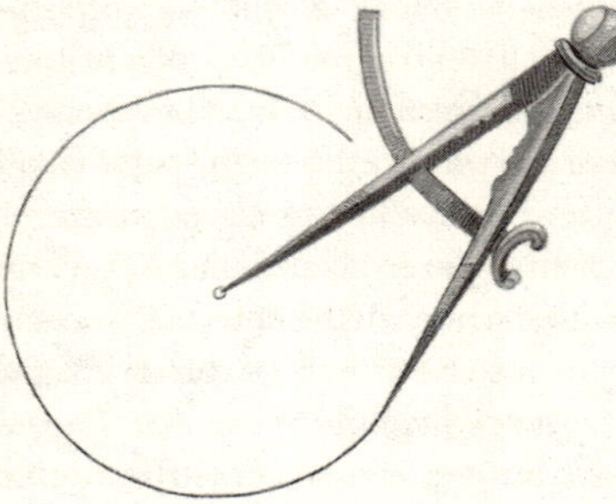

LEMURIA

The continent of Lemuria, according to modern occult traditions, existed in what is now the eastern Indian and southwestern Pacific Oceans but sank beneath the waves long before the heyday of Atlantis. The history of the concept of Lemuria offers an extraordinary glimpse into the genesis of rejected knowledge. While Lemuria is second only to Atlantis itself among the lost continents of occult lore, and has been backdated into myth and legend from around the world, the idea of a Lemurian continent dates only from the 1860s, and was first proposed not by mystics or secret society initiates but by a group of sober British geologists. See **Atlantis**; **lost continents**; **rejected knowledge**.

In the 1860s, geologists in India and South Africa noticed close similarities in rock strata and fossil animals from the two regions. Lemurs, primates now found only on Madagascar, formed the crux of the problem; lemur fossils occurred in both areas, but at that time they had been found nowhere else. The theory of continental drift had not yet been proposed, much less accepted by conventional geology, but land bridges – the most famous being the Bering Sea land bridge connecting Alaska and Siberia – were much in fashion. Thus several geologists proposed that a sunken landmass once connected southeastern Africa with the west coast of southern India. British zoologist Philip Sclater gave the concept its lasting name by suggesting that it be called "Lemuria," after the lemurs that supposedly once inhabited it.

Within a few decades, lemur fossils had been found over most of southern Asia and the Middle East, making the land bridge unnecessary, and the acceptance of continental drift in the 1970s removed the last supports for the old concept. Well before then, though, Lemuria had come to the attention of the occult philosopher Helena Petrovna Blavatsky. In her first book, *Isis Unveiled* (1877), Lemuria got a brief discussion alongside Atlantis, but the sprawling *The Secret Doctrine* (1888) placed it at center stage. To Blavatsky, Lemuria, a vast continent stretching from south and east Africa to Australia and New Zealand, was the home of the third root race of humanity, a race of hermaphroditic egg-laying apemen ancestral to the Atlantean root race and, through them, present-day humanity. See **Blavatsky, Helena Petrovna**; **Theosophical Society**.

This vision was expanded on by other Theosophical writers. The most influential of these was William Scott-Elliot, whose *The Lost Lemuria* (1904) moved the continent further out into the Pacific and pictured 12-foot-tall Lemurians leading tame plesiosaurs on leashes. According to Scott-Elliot, their modern descendants include Australian aborigines and African bushmen, and he also claimed Chinese as a language descended from ancient Lemurian. Another major source was Frederick Oliver's 1894 novel *A Dweller on Two Planets*, which he claimed to have received telepathically from a Master named Phylos the Tibetan; it included accounts of Lemurian colonies inside Mount Shasta in northern California. This launched an entire literature on underground Lemurian survivals, culminating in Richard Shaver's "Dero" tales of the 1950s.

By way of Blavatsky, Scott-Elliot, and other Theosophical writers, Lemuria quickly entered the mainstream of late nineteenth- and early twentieth-century popular culture. Among many others, American pulp fantasy writer Robert Howard wove it and most of the Theosophical worldview into the imaginary history behind his "Conan the Barbarian" stories. The rise of a rival lost continent of the Pacific, Mu, in the 1930s muddied the waters for a time but had little long-term impact, and by the 1950s many believers in lost continents simply assumed that Mu and Lemuria were actually the same continent. See **Mu**.

Buoyed by all this attention and a steady stream of publications, Lemuria became part of the stock-in-trade of occult secret societies all through the "Theosophical century" from 1875 to 1975. The revival of Rosicrucian mysticism in early twentieth-century America drew heavily on Lemurian lore, and two major American Rosicrucian societies – the Ancient Mystical Order Rosae Crucis (AMORC) and the Societas Rosicruciana in America (SRIA) – included material about Lemuria in their publications. On the other side of the Atlantic, Dion Fortune's magical secret society, the Fraternity (later Society) of the Inner Light, made room for Lemuria in its teachings, though it never had the importance there that Atlantis achieved. See **Ancient Mystical Order Rosae Crucis (AMORC)**; **Societas Rosicruciana in America (SRIA)**; **Society of the Inner Light**.

Like the rest of the Theosophical synthesis, Lemuria fell out of fashion among occult secret societies in the 1970s and remains only in a few traditional magical lodges at this point. By an irony of history, though, the same decade saw the old continent find a new home in the New Age movement. Material from early twentieth-century occultism was recycled enthusiastically in late twentieth-century New Age literature, expanded as necessary to make room for UFOs and other concerns of the post-1960s counterculture; thus, for instance, sightings of UFOs in the area of Mount Shasta were interpreted as flights to and from the Lemurian colonies inside. A parallel process saw Lemuria become popular in Japanese occult circles, where fusions of mythology from the indigenous Japanese religion of Shinto with western occult ideas led many Japanese alternative religions to claim that Japan itself was the last remnant of Lemuria above water. See **New Age movement**.

The most recent development in the history of Lemuria is in many ways the most unexpected. While the original theory behind the continent was discredited not long after Blavatsky imported it into occult lore, and the trail of Lemuria through occult secret societies and the New Age movement has been more notable for wild speculation and uncritical acceptance of visionary material than anything else, recent research has shown that there actually was a sizeable land mass, now submerged, near the middle of the area where twentieth-century Theosophists placed Lemuria. Known among today's geologists as Sundaland, this lost not-quite-continent was once a huge peninsula extending from present-day Vietnam, Cambodia, and Thailand south to Java and east beyond Borneo to the southern Philippines. At the end of the last Ice Age 11,000 years ago, when sea levels rose 300 feet in a few centuries, most of Sundaland was flooded, while its highlands remained above water as Malaysia, western Indonesia, and the Malay Peninsula. While the pet plesiosaurs Scott-Elliot described must unfortunately be relegated to the realm of occult legend, the possibility remains that the occultists who clairvoyantly saw a lost continent between the Indian and Pacific Oceans may have been onto something. See **Scrying**.

Further reading: Blavatsky 1888, Cervé 1982, de Camp 1970, Scott-Elliot 1962.

Leonardo da Vinci

Italian engineer, artist, and scientist, 1452–1519. One of the greatest geniuses of the Italian Renaissance, Leonardo da Vinci was the illegitimate son of a wealthy Florentine and his peasant mistress. At the age of 15 he was apprenticed to the famous painter Andrea del Verrocchio, and studied anatomy with Antonio Pollaiuolo. He became a member of the painters' guild in Florence in 1472, and in 1482 took a position as painter and engineer to the Duke of Milan. After the French conquest of Milan in 1499, he returned to Florence for a time, worked as a military surveyor for

Cesare Borgia, returned to Milan to work for the French viceroy there from 1506 to 1513, and in 1516 went to France at the invitation of King Francis I. He remained at Amboise, near the king's summer palace, until his death in 1519.

His life near the zenith of the Italian Renaissance brought him into contact with some of the most famous minds of the age, including the political philosopher Niccolò Macchiavelli and the master of sacred geometry Luca Pacioli. His paintings are among the most revered works of art ever made, but painting took up a relatively small part of his time, and he left most of his artistic projects unfinished. As court painter and engineer to the Duke of Milan, the French viceroy of northern Italy, and the King of France, he devoted most of his time to military and civil engineering, and to designing sets and stage machinery for the masques and entertainments fashionable in the courts of the time. His scientific and anatomical works seem to have been closest to his heart, though, and he spent most of his final years on them.

Leonardo's reputation for genius and eccentricity made him a ready target for attempts at retrospective recruitment by later secret societies. In the 1970s, Pierre Plantard's audacious Priory of Sion hoax drew Leonardo into its net along with so many others, reinventing him as one of the secret chiefs of the Priory's imaginary pre-1956 history. The Ancient Mystical Order Rosae Crucis (AMORC), whose teachings Plantard studied intensively before launching the Priory hoax, also listed Leonardo among its past chiefs. See **Ancient Mystical Order Rosae Crucis (AMORC)**; **Priory of Sion**; **retrospective recruitment**.

In the last two decades of the twentieth century, as Plantard's creation transformed itself into one of the dominant themes in rejected knowledge throughout the western world, Leonardo's supposed involvement in the Priory became a springboard from which dozens of writers launched him into countless secret intrigues and heretical traditions. Novelist Dan Brown's bestselling *The Da Vinci Code*, which used Leonardo's masterpiece *The Last Supper* as one of its main plot engines and borrowed many of Plantard's inventions, is only one of many redefinitions of Leonardo along these lines, and has predictably been taken as factual in large parts of the rejected-knowledge community. See **rejected knowledge**.

Ironically, Leonardo seems to have had less involvement in esoteric traditions, religious heresy, or secret societies than most of his contemporaries. The only initiatory organization he is known to have joined was the painters' guild in Florence, hardly a hotbed of radical ideas at the time. He had little interest in religious matters and, beyond an interest in sacred geometry partly driven by his artistic concerns and party by his friendship with Luca Pacioli, no connection with the Hermetic and Cabalistic occult traditions widespread among

Renaissance intellectuals. The doubtful gender of figures in some of his paintings, a point that has inspired wild speculations and played no small role in Brown's novel, was rooted in Leonardo's own psychology; like many of the greatest artists of his age, Leonardo was homosexual, and recent art historians have argued convincingly that his most famous painting, the *Mona Lisa*, is actually a painting of himself as a woman. See **Cabala**; **guilds, medieval**; **Hermeticism**; **sacred geometry**.

LEYS

In the summer of 1921, commercial traveler Alfred Watkins (1855–1935) was on his way through his native Herefordshire countryside when revelation struck. For years Watkins had an interest in the prehistoric monuments of Hereford. That day, as he looked across the countryside from a hilltop near Blackwardine, he saw several sites before him, and realized that they formed a straight line reaching across the landscape. A map and ruler confirmed his intuition, launching Watkins on a quest that lasted for the rest of his life and sparking a controversy that is still far from settled.

As he traced alignments on Ordnance Survey maps and followed them on foot across the British countryside, Watkins came to believe that the straight lines represented the last traces of an ancient system of trackways and navigation markers used by ancient peoples to find their way through the forests and moors of prehistoric Britain. The element "ley" appeared so often in place names along the lines that Watkins ended up calling them "leys." When he published his findings in *The Old Straight Track* (1925), orthodox archeologists dismissed them as lunacy – the magazine *Archaeology* even refused to print a paid advertisement for Watkins' book – but Watkins attracted a following. His admirers organized the Straight Track Postal Club, which linked researchers across Britain and sponsored ley walks and visits to ancient sites.

While Watkins was making and publicizing his discoveries, German researchers Josef Heinsch, Wilhelm Teudt, and Kurt Gerlach traced similar alignments in the German countryside. Heinsch discovered that the oldest Christian churches in Germany, built on the sites of old pagan temples, formed alignments at specific angles anchored by ancient holy hills and sites of sun worship. During the war years his work was extended by Kurt Gerlach, whose investigations were funded by the SS through its department of occult research, the Ahnenerbe. See **SS (Schutzstaffel)**.

The Straight Track Postal Club suspended operations at the start of the Second World War, and most of the German research was lost by the war's end. Until the 1970s the entire subject of ancient landscape alignments was nearly forgotten. The catalyst for its rediscovery was the best-selling book *The View Over Atlantis* (1969) by English occultist John Michell. An expert in sacred geometry and occult lore, Michell argued that the leys were not simply ancient trackways, but rather a network of invisible channels of subtle energy that belonged to a forgotten system of natural magic. In prehistoric times, he claimed, priest-initiates had used the ley grid to bring the sun's magical radiations together with the subtle energies of the earth and send the combined force out through the countryside to bring fertility to the soil. While his facts were not always accurate and his speculations sometimes ran wild – he argued, for example, that the huge stones of sites such as Stonehenge had literally been levitated and flown to their present positions by ancient wizards using the subtle forces of the leys – his book was one of the great works of British landscape mysticism and inspired a surge of interest in leys. See **sacred geometry**.

Two main currents of ley research rose out of the blossoming of interest in the 1970s. On the one hand, researchers such as Paul Devereaux and Nigel Pennick pursued the scientific and historical dimensions of the leys, drawing back from Michell's more extravagant ideas while still exploring the possibility that there was more to the lines than ancient tracks. Devereaux played a leading role in the Dragon Project, a research initiative that used advanced technology to study stone circles and other ancient sites. On the other hand, leys found their way into the realm of rejected knowledge, the New Age movement and other forms of popular occultism. In this setting, Michell's speculations were often rejected because they were not exotic enough, and ley research tended to focus on visionary experience, map dowsing, and sheer fantasy. Much of this material ended up being drawn into the great crop circle furor of the 1990s, and inspired many of the weirder ideas floated to explain crop circles in southern Britain and elsewhere. See **New Age movement**; **rejected knowledge**.

Both these currents of ley research remain active as of this writing. Ley researchers have amassed impressive statistical and archeological evidence that at least some leys are deliberate alignments. Similar systems of alignment elsewhere in the world offer confirmation that a ley system would have been conceivable in ancient Britain; one striking example is ancient Japan, where standing stones and burial mounds also follow straight alignments, and the traditions of the ancient Shinto religion include lore on the straight paths favored by the *kami* (Shinto gods). Even so, the one sure thing that can be said about leys is that no one today knows for certain what they are and why they were created.

Further reading: Michell 1969, Watkins 1925.

LODGE

The basic working unit of most secret societies in the western world, the lodge derives its name and many of its customs from the operative stonemasons of the Middle Ages. At each building site, the masons would construct a one-story wooden building, called a lodge, as a workplace. Meetings of stonemasons' guilds and initiations of new guild members would often be held in the lodge, with one member – the tyler, in later Masonic language – posted outside to make sure that non-members did not enter. Like most medieval guilds, stonemasons' guilds opened and closed their meetings with a brief ritual and a prayer. While the master mason in charge of the building project and his two assistants, or wardens, had absolute authority over the building site, many decisions affecting the community of working masons were made, as in other guilds, in a roughly democratic fashion, with every qualified mason having an equal vote. See **Freemasonry, origins of**.

Many of these features remained standard practice through the transition between operative stonemasons' guilds and early Freemasonry. By the eighteenth century the word "lodge" meant a local group of Freemasons under the authority of an elected Master, rather than the building (by then, usually a private room at a tavern) where they met. The simple opening and closing ritual of the operative guilds had expanded substantially, and the two degrees of initiation (Apprentice and Master) of the guilds had grown into three, with many more on the way, but lodges stillgoverned their affairs by a combination of the Master's authority and the votes of the lodge members. See **Freemasonry**.

These features were borrowed by other secret societies starting in the eighteenth century, and by the nineteenth lodges of many different secret societies shared a common language of architecture, behavior, and symbolism. Three raps with a gavel, for example, will bring the members to their feet in lodge meetings of most secret societies, and lodges of the Freemasons, Odd Fellows, and Knights of Pythias – the three largest secret societies in twentieth-century America – can all use one another's lodge rooms for meetings by shifting the positions of a few chairs. See **Knights of Pythias**; **Odd Fellowship**.

In these and nearly all other lodges, the officers sit in assigned positions around the outer edge of a rectangular lodge room, with seats for the members on the long sides of the room. The floor space is open, to allow for ritual movement; the center of the lodge may have an altar with the Bible on it, though this varies from one secret society to another – for example, Masonic and Knights of Pythias lodges have an altar in the lodge, Odd Fellows lodges do not. One lodge officer sits just inside the door to the lodge, and another is stationed outside. Members who wish to enter a lodge after it has been ritually opened must give the proper password to pass through the door, and then advance to the center of the lodge, make a secret sign of recognition, and be recognized by the presiding officer before taking a seat.

While the vast majority of traditional secret societies use standard lodge procedure, not all of them use the word "lodge" for their local groups. Even within Freemasonry, the Royal Arch has chapters rather than lodges, the Templars have commanderies or encampments (depending on jurisdiction), and the Scottish Rite has valleys in which Lodges of Perfection, Chapters of Rose-Croix, Councils of Kadosh and Consistories hold their meetings. Outside Masonry the options become much more varied. The difference in terminology, though, rarely involves a difference in practice. See **Ancient and Accepted Scottish Rite (AASR)**; **Knights Templar**; **Royal Arch**.

In recent years, however, traditional lodge practice has fallen by the wayside in some secret societies obsessed with the desire to modernize. Many more recent organizations never adopted it in the first place. While traditional secret societies remain active in most western countries, it remains to be seen whether the old lodge traditions will survive the twenty-first century.

Further reading: Greer 1998.

LOST CIVILIZATIONS

Since the coming of the Renaissance, the West has seen its vision of the past expanded many times by the discovery of lost civilizations. The Renaissance itself was launched by the recovery of Greek and Latin texts that turned the classical world of the Greek city-states and the Roman Empire from a dim memory to a massive cultural presence. The early nineteenth century saw the rediscovery of Egypt and the first translations of Egyptian hieroglyphics. By the middle of the nineteenth century Babylon and Ur had leapt off the pages of the Bible and become real cities whose clay tablet records had begun to yield their secrets to scholars, and the Mayan cities in the Yucatan jungle had been discovered. Lost civilizations became hot topics in popular culture, and inevitably found their way into occult traditions and the cultural underworld of rejected knowledge. See **Egypt**; **occultism**; **rejected knowledge**.

By the early twentieth century the existence of civilizations in the prehistoric past had become a major theme in alternative circles. Since there is no reason, after all, why people in 10,000 or 15,000 BCE couldn't have accomplished what people in 5000 BCE did, the possibility cannot be dismissed out of hand. At the same time, Egypt and Babylon got into the history books because researchers turned up plenty of hard evidence that they actually existed – tens of thousands of ruined buildings, writings, artifacts, and environmental traces of many centuries of civilization. So far, evidence on this scale for urban settlements only goes back to 9000 BCE or a little earlier, and the oldest high urban civilizations uncovered by archeologists' spades date to around 5000 BCE. The only evidence found so far for civilizations older than this consists of a handful of scattered artifacts and puzzling sites.

These can be summed up briefly. First, a handful of maps from the Middle Ages and Renaissance contain information impossible to square with the geographical knowledge of the time; examples include the Oronteus Finaeus map of 1532, the Schoner globe of 1523–4, and the Mercator map of 1538, all of which include clear and relatively accurate portrayals of Antarctica at a time when no European mariner had ever visited that continent. Second, apparent urban ruins have been found underwater, most notably in Bimini in the West Indies, at depths that were above water during the last Ice Age. Third, a few startling ancient technologies, such as the simple electric batteries found in Babylonian ruins, and legends that might refer to advanced technologies, such as the *vimanas* or flying machines that feature in ancient Indian epics, suggest the possibility of a technologically proficient civilization at some point in the distant past. Finally, certain exact details shared among ancient myths and legends of many peoples could be signs that these had diffused from a more ancient civilization in the distant past. None of this proves the existence of lost civilizations in the distant past, though taken together the points are suggestive and deserve more research than they have received.

A great deal of the debate around lost civilizations in the last century has overlapped with claims about the possible existence of Atlantis and similar lost continents. Recent geological evidence suggesting that the glaciers at the end of the last Ice Age may have melted much more quickly than previous theories had suggested, raising sea levels worldwide by some 300 feet (90 meters) in a few centuries or less, makes the Atlantis legend and its many equivalents very plausible. Again, though, none of this proves the existence of lost civilizations in the distant past. See **Atlantis**; **lost continents**.

LOST CONTINENTS

While the Atlantis legend has roots reaching back to the fourth century BCE, the belief in several lost continents in the earth's past is a much more recent phenomenon. During the century from 1875 to 1975, lost continents of varying names and locations became omnipresent in the teachings of occult secret societies of the period, and still retain a large role in today's New Age thought. This is almost wholly the result of one person, the Russian occult philosopher and founder of the Theosophical Society, Helena Petrovna Blavatsky (1831–91). See **Atlantis**; **Blavatsky, Helena Petrovna**; **Theosophical Society**.

In two massive books, *Isis Unveiled* (1877) and *The Secret Doctrine* (1888), Blavatsky launched an all-out assault on the Christian orthodoxy and scientific materialism of her time. In her first book, one of Blavatsky's basic strategies for this assault was to argue that various pieces of rejected knowledge made as much sense as the doctrines of contemporary science. By the second book, her strategy had changed to the presentation of a comprehensive vision of the origin, development, and destiny of the universe and humanity, as an alternative to Darwin's scientific mythology of progress from primeval slime to Victorian civilization. Lost continents played a large role in her vision of the past, forming the homelands of the various root races into which ancient humanity was divided. See **Occultism**; **rejected knowledge**.

The first root race of humans on earth, according to Blavatsky, dwelt on a lost continent called the Imperishable Sacred Land, located above the North Pole; etheric rather than physical, like its inhabitants, this land still exists but modern human beings are not spiritually advanced enough to perceive it. The next root race emerged in Hyperborea, located in what is now the Arctic; the third originated in Lemuria, in what is now the Indian Ocean, and the fourth in Atlantis. Except for the first, which ended with the final descent into physical matter, each root race saw its time on earth end with a vast geological catastrophe that overwhelmed its homeland, leaving a handful of scattered survivors to repopulate the world. See **Lemuria**.

The influence of the Theosophical Society and of Blavatsky's ideas was so widespread during the early twentieth century that nearly every occult secret society during that period found room for lost continents in their secret teachings. Additional lost continents such as Thule, Pan, Mu, and Isuria found their way into occult writings during those years. From the occult scene, lost continents found their way into popular culture, and in the New Age movement belief in Atlantis and Lemuria, at least, was an article of faith from the movement's earliest days. See **Mu**; **New Age movement**; **Thule**.

Ironically, at the same time that the belief in lost continents emerged as a major theme in popular culture, occult secret societies and the occult community generally lost interest in them. Partly this happened because new visions of alternative history became more popular. Many of the new feminist spiritualities of the late twentieth century adopted a belief in ancient matriarchies overwhelmed by patriarchal invaders, while the neopagan movement generally focused attention on the end of paganism and the coming of Christianity. While neither of these excluded Atlantis and other lost continents, they both filled the emotional need – the desire for a lost golden age in the past – that gave the belief in lost continents most of its power. Another important factor in the loss of interest in lost continents, though, was a growing conviction on the part of many occultists that such things actually contributed very little to the hard work of occult training and practice, which is, after all, the primary work of occultists. See **Magic**; **Matriarchy**.

The most recent chapter in the development of the lost continent theme is also the most unexpected. While all these changes were under way, a slow revolution in the geological sciences brought unexpected support to the idea that large areas once above water are now at the bottom of the sea. Research into the last Ice Age has shown that at its end, around 11,000 years ago, sea levels rose some 300 feet (90 meters), drowning hundreds of thousands of square miles of land beneath the rising waters. While the whole process took centuries, the filling and draining of vast glacial lakes in the northern hemisphere caused sea levels to rise irregularly, with some periods of rapid outflow causing sea levels to surge upwards 10 feet (3 meters) or more in as little as a few months. Behind the image of lost continents, in other words, may well lie dim memories of the catastrophic flooding of fertile lowlands as the glaciers melted and the seas rose, just a few thousand years before the birth of the first known cities. See **lost civilizations**.

Further reading: de Camp 1970.

Lost Word

According to Masonic legend, the true password of a Master Mason was lost when Hiram Abiff, the master architect of King Solomon's Temple, was murdered by three craftsmen. Since the true word was lost, King Solomon is said to have established a replacement for it, the word now used in Masonic practice as the Master's Word. See **Freemasonry**; **Hiram Abiff**.

This legend offered an obvious opportunity to the creators of higher degrees. Starting in the middle of the eighteenth century degrees were in circulation purporting to reveal the true Lost Word, and most systems of high degrees introduce at least one such word to candidates; the Scottish Rite, the most popular system of higher degrees in Masonry, presents three such words to its initiates at different points along its sequence of degrees. Many Masonic writers, however, argue that the true Lost Word is a symbol of divine truth, which can only be discovered within the self through prayer, meditation, and moral effort. See **Ancient and Accepted Scottish Rite (AASR)**; **high degrees**.

Loyal Orange Order

The most important Irish Protestant secret society, the Loyal Orange Order emerged in the bitter sectarian politics of Ireland at the end of the eighteenth century. The passage of the Catholic Relief Act of 1793 threatened the privileged place of Protestants in British-ruled Ireland, and agrarian secret societies such as the Whiteboys seemed to many Irish Protestants the forerunners of a Catholic revolution. The Peep-o'-Day Boys, a Protestant secret society of the 1780s that raided Catholic homes to search for weapons, had been met by the creation of the Defenders, a Catholic secret society that met Protestant raids with armed force. After the Battle of the Diamond, a pitched battle between Protestants and Defenders near Loughgall, Co. Armagh, on September 21, 1795, a group of radical Protestants led by James Sloan, a Loughgall innkeeper, set out to organize a secret society capable of securing the Protestant ascendancy. See **Whiteboys**.

That society, the Loyal Orange Order, took its name from William of Orange, the Dutch Protestant prince who drove the Catholic Stuart King James II off the British throne in 1688 and secured British rule over Ireland by defeating James's forces at the Battle of the Boyne in 1690. Like nearly all eighteenth-century secret societies, it borrowed most of its structure and some of its symbolism from the Freemasons, the premier secret society of the age. In the early days, members and initiation ceremonies took place behind hedges and in ruined buildings, and new initiates swore allegiance to the king of England only so long as he upheld the Protestant cause. See **Freemasonry**.

The order's leaders disavowed involvement in terror campaigns against Ulster Catholics after the Battle of the Diamond, but many members took an active role. Still, the order badly needed the support of Irish Protestant gentry and the English government, and discipline was essential for this purpose. In 1796 the order established a new degree, the Purple Degree, with an oath of initiation that forbade certain common abuses, and the 1798 rising of the United Irishmen cemented the alliance between the Orange Order and the Protestant gentry. See **Society of United Irishmen**.

Thereafter the Orange Order was a constant presence in the politics of British-ruled Ireland, essential to the British colonial government in emergencies but an embarrassment in peacetime. From 1825 to 1828, and then again from 1836 to 1846, the Orange Order was formally dissolved by order of the British government, though Orange lodges continued to meet secretly through these difficulties.

Meanwhile the order itself was expanding. The creation of the Purple degree in 1796 was only the first of a series of innovations made by local lodges and fought, with limited effect, by the Orange Grand Lodge of Ireland. By the 1840s a compromise of sorts had been reached, with ordinary Orange lodges conferring only the Orange and Purple degrees, Royal Arch Chapters conferring the Royal Purple Degree, and Black Preceptories conferring 11 more degrees, from Royal Black to Red Cross. Most of these drew heavily on Masonic high degrees. See **high degrees**; **Royal Arch**.

The Orange Order also spread outside Ireland, with lodges springing up in the English Midlands and in Scotland from the 1820s. The first overseas lodge was founded in Montreal in 1818; by the late nineteenth century, boosted by struggles between mostly Catholic Quebec and the Protestants who dominated the rest of Canada, the Orange Order ranked among the largest of Canadian secret societies. The United States had its first Orange lodge in 1820; Australia's first Orange lodge was chartered in 1845, and lodges were established in the African nations of Togo and Ghana, then British colonies, in 1917 and 1925 respectively.

Through all this, however, Ireland remained the homeland of Orangeism all through the nineteenth century, and the Orange Order took an active role in the bitter political struggles of the late nineteenth and early twentieth centuries. The 30-year battle over Irish home rule occupied much of the order's energies; eagerly pursued by Irish Catholics and many British liberals, home rule was anathema to Orangemen, who feared the power of a Catholic majority in an Irish parliament. After the partition of the country and the creation of the independent southern Irish Free State in 1921, most Orange lodges outside Northern Ireland went out of existence, while in the North the Orange Order became a major force in Protestant communities.

Today the Orange Institution, as it prefers to call itself, remains active in Northern Ireland and elsewhere in the United Kingdom, and lodges also exist in 10 American states, as well as in Canada, Australia, New Zealand, Ghana and Togo. Adherence to a Protestant Christian church remains one of the requirements for membership. Outside of Northern Ireland, the original political dimension of Orangeism has been largely replaced by charitable and fraternal activities.

Further reading: Williams 1973.

Loyal Order of Moose

One of the largest fraternal orders today, the Loyal Order of Moose was founded in Louisville, Kentucky in 1888 by Dr. John Henry Wilson and a group of friends. The founders wanted to establish a social and drinking club for working-class men to rival the Elks. The new order had a single degree of initiation to start with, and the usual panoply of robes, collars, and fezzes for the members. In the crowded fraternal world of 1880s America, however, the Moose struggled to find an audience. By 1906 Wilson himself had left the order and only two lodges, in the small Indiana towns of Crawfordsville and Frankfort, still survived. See **Benevolent Protective Order of Elks (BPOE)**; **fraternal orders**.

In that year James J. Davis joined the Crawfordsville lodge. Davis, a labor organizer and steel mill worker, became convinced that the organization could flourish if it copied other fraternal orders and offered funeral and survivor benefits. Given the title of Supreme Organizer and approval for his benefits scheme, he and a small group of organizers traveled back and forth across the United States and Canada, with dramatic results. By 1912 the Loyal Order of Moose could count more than 1000 lodges and a membership over half a million.

Three major developments occurred in 1913: the founding of a ladies auxiliary, Women of the Moose; the establishment of a second degree, the Moose Legion; and the founding of a home for orphans at Mooseheart, 38 miles (60 kilometers) west of Chicago. In 1922 the order founded a home for elderly members, Moosehaven, on the Florida coast. These steps boosted membership to new heights and made the Moose lodge a popular place to be; American presidents Theodore Roosevelt, Warren Harding, Franklin D. Roosevelt, and Harry Truman were all members of the Moose. In the aftermath of the First World War, Moose lodges began springing up in Great Britain as well, and the Grand Lodge of Great Britain, Loyal Order of Moose, was founded in 1923. See **ladies auxiliaries**.

Unlike many fraternal orders, the Moose suffered no significant loss of membership during the middle years of the twentieth century, and membership peaked at well over a million in the early 1980s. It has declined since that time, though the Loyal Order of Moose remains large and active. Most of the traditional practices of secret societies were, however, abandoned in 1992, and the order now functions as a social club with a busy charitable program.

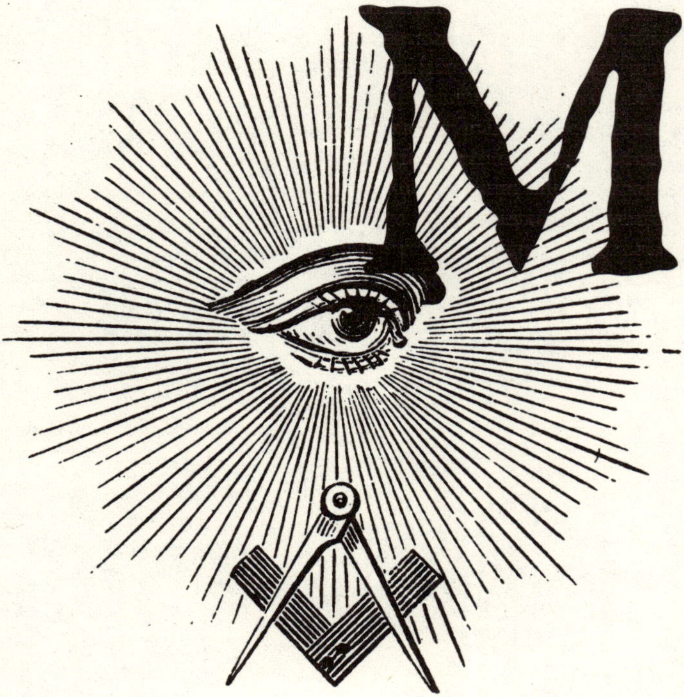
M

Mackenzie, Kenneth

English scholar, Rosicrucian, and secret society member, 1833–86. Born in London, he spent his childhood in Vienna and was educated in European schools. By the age of 18 he had returned to London and embarked on a scholarly career, producing excellent English translations of German works while contributing to *Notes and Queries* and other journals. He was elected as a Fellow of the Royal Society of Antiquaries in 1854, before his 21st birthday. These scholarly pursuits ran in parallel with an intense interest in the occult. In 1858 or 1859 he began to study magic with Frederick Hockley, an important English magician, and in 1861 he went to Paris to meet Eliphas Lévi and Allan Kardec, two leading occultists of the time.

Mackenzie never managed to live up either to his potential or his own self-image; he suffered from a serious drinking problem and a habit of blaming others for his problems. Hockley broke off his training sometime in the mid-1860s. Robert Wentworth Little sought his help in creating rituals for the Societas Rosicruciana in Anglia (SRIA), a British Rosicrucian order founded in 1866, but Mackenzie did not become a member of the SRIA until 1872 and resigned in 1875. See **Societas Rosicruciana in Anglia (SRIA)**.

His involvement in regular Freemasonry was even briefer; he was initiated in March 1870, went through the other two degrees of the Craft in April and May of the same year, and resigned in January 1871. Despite this limited background, he presented himself as an expert on Masonry in his Royal Masonic Cyclopaedia (1877). Most of Mackenzie's encyclopedia was paraphrased and condensed from standard Masonic reference works of the time, but it contains accounts of several secret societies that were Mackenzie's own inventions. See **Freemasonry**.

By the middle of the 1870s Mackenzie was hard at work trying to launch a number of occult secret societies. He attempted to interest some of the major figures in the Victorian occult scene in them, but his own reputation was bad enough and his management of the societies slapdash enough that he found few takers. Mackenzie was active in the Brotherhood of the Mystic Cross from around 1870 when it was launched by Richard Morrison, until Morrison's death in 1874 but this proved to be no more successful than Mackenzie's own ventures. From 1875 to 1878 he also took an active role in launching the Royal Oriental Order of the Sat B'hai, a quasi-Hindu secret society created by Capt. James Henry Lawrence Archer; this also failed to find a market and faded out after 1880.

Somewhat more successful was the Swedenborgian Rite of Masonry, which was imported to England from Canada in 1876; Mackenzie served as Grand Secretary for the rite in Britain until his death. In his last years Mackenzie was involved with a small working group organized for the study of alchemy, the Society of Eight. His health finally broke down as a result of his drinking, and he died on July 3, 1886, just short of his 53rd birthday. Most of his papers were bequeathed to William Wynn Westcott, who became the Swedenborgian Rite's Grand Secretary; in those papers, according to the most likely hypothesis, was the original cipher manuscript Westcott used a year later to launch the Hermetic Order of the Golden Dawn. See **Hermetic Order of the Golden Dawn; Westcott, William Wynn**.

Further reading: Godwin 1994, Howe 1997.

MADOLE, JAMES H.

American occultist and fascist, 1927–79. The forefather of American fascist occultism, James Hartung Madole was born in New York City and spent most of his life there. An avid reader of science fiction, he gravitated toward the fascist wing of the science fiction fan community in the 1940s. At the age of 18, Madole founded the Animist Party, a radical right-wing political movement drawing most of its support from among science fiction fans. When Kurt Mertig, a veteran pro-Nazi organizer, founded the National Renaissance Party (NRP) in 1949, he recruited Madole and shortly thereafter made him the NRP's leader, a position Madole held until his death 30 years later.

Madole began his career as a Nazi enthusiast, copying Hitler's hatred of communism and alliance with capitalist interests, but during the 1950s he pioneered the central theme of neo-Nazi economic theory worldwide, a "Third Way" rejecting both communism and capitalism in favor of a "corporate state" modeled on Mussolini's Italy that rejected class warfare and economic competition alike. His contributions to neo-Nazi ideology were at least as creative. Like many in his generation, he encountered the spiritual teachings of the Theosophical Society by way of popular adventure stories (such as Robert Howard's "Conan the Barbarian" series) that used Theosophy's mythic history as background. See **Theosophical Society**.

Madole borrowed much of Theosophy, combined it with Nazi antisemitism and homegrown American racism, and added dollops of science fiction and popular occult literature to create his own brand of fascist occultism. In his major treatise on the subject, *The New Atlantis: A Program for an Aryan Garden of Eden in North America*, he proposed a social order dominated by a strict caste system and racial segregation, centered on the quest to produce the God-Man, a new human species produced by "selective breeding, cosmic thinking, specialized training and Occult Initiation" (cited in Goodrick-Clarke 2002, p. 82). He despised Christianity as a Jewish invention and had close contacts with the Church of Satan and other Satanist groups. See **Church of Satan**; **Satanism**.

Despite his exotic ideology and odd appearance – when speaking in public, he always wore three-button suits with all three buttons fastened, black horn-rimmed glasses, and a white motorcycle helmet – Madole attracted a modest following. In public appearances he was always surrounded by members of the Security Echelon (SE), the NRP's storm troopers, who wore black and gray uniforms and served as security guards and brawlers in the street battles that frequently surrounded Madole's speeches. Consciously modeled after Hitler's SS, the SE combined a paramilitary ethos with occult training and the study of metaphysics. See **SS (Schutzstaffel)**.

Madole died of cancer in 1979, and his party collapsed shortly thereafter. While the NRP was never a secret society, Madole's career played a crucial role in launching fascist occultism in postwar America and spreading ideas central to the neo-Nazi secret societies of the late twentieth and early twenty-first centuries. See **neo-Nazi secret societies**.

Further reading: Goodrick-Clarke 2002.

Mafia

The world's most famous criminal secret society, the Mafia emerged in the early nineteenth century but traces its roots to bandit clans in the rugged hill country of Sicily in the Middle Ages. During much of Sicily's troubled history, foreign rulers – Arabs, Normans, Spaniards, kings of the independent kingdom of Naples, and Northern Italian elites since unification – exploited the island ruthlessly, and only the bandits of the hills offered protection against their exactions. The name Mafia probably comes from the Arabic word *mafiyya*, "place of refuge," referring to the bandit strongholds in the hills. Then as now, Mafia families were bound by a code of honor known as *omertà* that demands loyalty to the family, obedience to the family head, revenge for any harm done a family member, and refusal to cooperate with government officials or to expose family secrets.

A flexible and effective organizational system evolved with the modern Mafia and remains in place today. Mafia families united by blood or locality are headed by a capo-famiglia ("family head") elected by influential family members. Each capofamiglia has effective control of an area of Sicily, cooperates with other Mafia chieftains, and owes allegiance to the capo dei capi, the head of the Sicilian Mafia.

The Mafia took its modern form in the nineteenth century, as the old Sicilian aristocracy finally lost control over the island's wealth, and feudal estates – many of them already managed by Mafia families for absentee landlords – fell into Mafia hands. Control of the farmland, orange orchards, and sulfur mines of the island quickly amounted to control over Sicily's political and economic structure and an island-wide protection racket. When Sicily became part of the newly founded Italian state in the 1860s, the Mafia quickly learned to control local voters, and struck alliances with political parties by delivering Sicily's votes on demand. Despite occasional bursts of prosecution – the most severe of them under Mussolini's government – the tacit bargain between the Mafia and the government has remained a fixture of Italian politics since that time.

A similar bargain with more pervasive results connects the Mafia with the Roman Catholic Church. Mafia families in Sicily traditionally contribute their share of sons to the priesthood and leave Church revenues alone. Connections between the Church and the Mafia have been exposed in recent years, most notably in the links between the Mafia, the Vatican, and the renegade P2 Masonic lodge. See **P2 (Propaganda Due)**; **Roman Catholic Church**.

These compromises with power took on new forms on the far side of the Atlantic. In the late nineteenth and early twentieth centuries more than a million emigrants from Sicily arrived in America. Inevitably they brought the Mafia with them, and by the 1880s Mafia chieftains were beginning to exert authority in the port cities of America's eastern seaboard. They faced competition from the Camorra, a criminal secret society originally based in the Italian city of Naples, and from Irish and Jewish immigrant gangs as well. From the 1880s until 1929, gang warfare was a constant feature of the American underworld and few leading *mafiosi* died in their beds.

The transformation of the American Mafia from warring factions to a national crime syndicate was set in motion by Alphonse Capone. Though born in Rome, outside the network of Sicilian families who dominated the American Mafia in its early days, Capone rose through the ranks of Chicago's Italian underworld to the top of the city's Mafia hierarchy, then brokered a truce between the Mafia and the Irish, Jewish, and Polish gangs contending for shares in the lucrative bootleg liquor trade, assigning each gang a territory of its own in the city. In 1929 he organized a convention of organized crime heads in Atlantic City and applied the same logic to the United States as a whole.

Capone's truce lasted two years, until he went to prison on tax evasion charges in 1931. In his absence a bloody struggle broke out among Mafia families. In testimony to a Senate subcommittee in 1963, *mafioso* Joseph Valachi called the struggle the "Castellamarese war," after a region in Sicily where one important faction had its roots. The war ended as Charles "Lucky" Luciano, the leading figure in a younger generation of *mafiosi*, had his leading rivals gunned down and imposed a renewed truce, with himself as *capo dei capi*. Luciano and his right-hand man, Meyer Lansky, went on to become the architects of modern American organized crime.

The key to the new system pioneered by Luciano and Lansky was a refocusing of Mafia activities away from the small-time rackets of its early days into the immense profits to be gained from legitimate businesses, gambling, and the international drug trade. Lansky introduced sophisticated financial methods into Mafia operations, replacing old-fashioned money laundering techniques with a worldwide network of financial institutions.

Lansky also played a central role in the blackmail scheme that turned FBI head J. Edgar Hoover, a homosexual with a taste for cross-dressing, into an ally of organized crime. Lansky succeeded in getting compromising photos of Hoover, and used them to force the FBI chief to take the heat off organized crime. Hoover's repeated public insistence throughout the 1950s and 1960s that America had no organized crime problem, and his refusal to use FBI assets against the Mafia, was the quid pro quo that kept Lansky and his associates from releasing the photos to the press and destroying Hoover's career.

Another element in the new Mafia was a rapprochement with US intelligence services. At the beginning of the Second World War Luciano was recruited by the Office of Strategic Services (OSS), the predecessor of the Central Intelligence Agency. His first assignment was to influence New York gangsters to keep Italian-American stevedores from sabotaging Allied ships on the New York docks. When this proved successful, the OSS aimed at bigger game. In 1943, as Allied armies drove the Nazis out of North Africa and prepared for the invasion of Sicily, Luciano made contact with leading Sicilian *mafiosi* and arranged Mafia support for the invasion. The project was a spectacular success: as Allied troops landed, nearly two-thirds of the Italian troops on the island deserted, and the Mafia kidnapped the Italian commander and handed him over to American forces. These contacts between organized crime and the American intelligence services continued decades later in the 1960s, when CIA operatives employed Mafia hitmen in several attempts to assassinate Cuba's Communist leader Fidel Castro.

By the end of the twentieth century the Mafia had become part of the American scene, with a significant presence in city governments, construction firms, labor unions, and the entertainment industry, as well as in gambling and the international drug market. The protection rackets and small-time drug dealing that gave the original Mafia their start went to newly arrived immigrant gangs from Asia, eastern Europe, and elsewhere. The central insight underlying the Mafia of the late twentieth century is the recognition that organized crime is simply another facet of the American free enterprise system. As accounts of spectacular corporate fraud fill the headlines, it has become hard to distinguish a Mafia family from any other closely held family business.

Further reading: Fox 1989, Lacey 1991, Mackenzie 1967, Summers 1993.

Magic

The art and science of causing change in consciousness in accordance with will – to borrow the definition of one of its greatest twentieth-century practitioners, Dion Fortune (Violet Firth, 1890–1946). Magic is the core practice of western occultism and the main ingredient in the hidden teachings of most occult secret societies. Frequently misunderstood, dismissed as blind superstition by rationalists and condemned as devil worship by misinformed Christians, magic in reality consists of a relatively simple yet powerful set of psychophysical methods, evolved over many centuries, that allow magicians to transform their experience of the world and themselves. See **Occultism**.

In recent centuries the word "magic" has been bandied about with more enthusiasm than precision. Magic is not a religion, any more than psychotherapy or plumbing is; rather, it is a traditional set of psychophysical techniques, sharing a common history and philosophy, that can be used effectively by members of any religion, or none. Many of the great magicians of the last 1500 years have been devout Christians, and Christian magic forms a large and distinguished branch of the western occult traditions.

A more useful distinction is coded into the terms "white magic" and "black magic." The magical traditions have their ethical codes but, like psychotherapy, plumbing, or anything else, it has practitioners who consider ethics to be a waste of their time or a barrier to their desires. The fact that magic existed in a cultural underground for so many centuries has limited effective self-policing in the magical community. As a result, modern occultism includes practitioners of white magic, who maintain ethical standards and work their magic with an eye to the consequences of their actions, and practitioners of black magic, for whom magic is a tool to be used in the pursuit of their own desires. See **black magic**; **white magic**.

The very language we use to talk about magic reflects much of its history. The English word "magic" derives from *magos*, the ancient Greek word for a Persian priest and ritualist. By the fifth century BCE the term was being borrowed by Greeks, for the same reasons "swami" came into use among mystics of all varieties in twentieth-century America, and a wide range of practices – some Asian, some native Greek – were labeled *mageia*, "what *magoi* do." The equivalent terms *magus* and *magia* were borrowed into Latin a few centuries later.

By that time *magia* had almost exactly the same meaning "magic" has today. It referred to systems of ritual practice, usually performed by individuals in secret, meant to cause changes in the practitioner and the surrounding world. These systems had diverse roots, borrowing freely from ancient Egyptian, Babylonian, Jewish, and Greek traditions, and included a dizzying array of different practices. The common theme uniting them was the belief that hidden sources of power existed throughout the universe, and could be put to work by those who knew how. The magicians of Greek and Roman times, like magicians today, performed rituals to create sacred space in order to invoke spiritual forces and entities; they learned invocations that included strange divine names and words of power; they gathered herbs and roots to compound charms; they performed various kinds of divination to gauge the flow of spiritual power and the will of the gods; and they based all of these on a philosophy that envisioned the human individual as not merely a helpless plaything of fate or the gods, but as a participant in the powers of creation.

These core elements of magic have taken countless forms over the last 25 centuries, changing to fit religious and philosophical fashions. Popular Greek and Roman magic drew heavily from the mystery cults of the time, particularly the Dionysian and Orphic mysteries, while an educated tradition of magic in the same years used Greek Neoplatonic philosophy and Egyptian priestly lore as the basis for Hermetic and Gnostic magical workings. The Dark Ages, in turn, saw a remarkable flowering of Christian magic in which the names of Jesus, Mary, and the saints replaced pagan gods and spirits in ancient spells and invocations. Much of this heritage vanished forever in the holocaust of the Burning Times, but while witchcraft persecutions raged through most of Europe, Italian scholars were rediscovering the old Hermetic tradition and introducing the Cabala to non-Jewish audiences. The great magicians of the Renaissance left an extraordinary wealth of philosophy and practical methods to later students of magic and effectively defined the magical universe in which modern occultism operates. See **Cabala**; **Dionysian mysteries**; **Egypt**; **Hermeticism**; **Orphism**; **witchcraft persecutions**.

The coming of the scientific revolution forced magic underground and sparked a new epoch in the history of the tradition. Borrowing the organizational toolkit of Freemasonry, the first magical secret societies took shape in the eighteenth century and became widespread in the nineteenth. In the hothouse environment of secret lodges, the magical heritage of the Renaissance was reworked in countless ways and combined with other branches of the occult tradition, such as astrology and alchemy. Leading occult secret societies of the late nineteenth and early twentieth centuries, such as the Hermetic Order of the Golden Dawn, built on this heritage to bring the entire occult tradition of the western world into a single coherent system. It only remained for the cultural revolutions of the 1960s to launch today's occult renaissance by putting many once-secret magical traditions into circulation throughout the western world. See **Alchemy**; **Freemasonry**; **Hermetic Order of the Golden Dawn**.

For all the publicity given to occult traditions in today's world, though, the level of knowledge about magic among the general public, and even among scholars and historians, is radically lower now than it was in the Middle Ages. Poorly informed denunciations and disinformation on the part of fundamentalist Christians and scientific materialists alike have done much to muddy the waters, and far too many writers of alternative history and conspiracy theory have been content to parrot received opinion on the subject, rather than conducting their own research into authentic magical texts and practices, and finding out what magic means from the practitioner's point of view. As a result, the role of magical traditions in important historical events, such as the rise and fall of the Nazi movement in twentieth-century Germany, remains needlessly obscure. See **National Socialism**.

Further reading: Crowley 1976, Greer 1997, Greer 1998, Lévi 1972, Yates 1964.

MAGICK

An obsolete spelling of the word "magic" adopted by Aleister Crowley to distinguish his own occult teachings from those of his many rivals, magick was defined by Crowley as "the art and science of causing change in accordance with will."

Since the 1920s it has been adopted by followers of Crowley's own magical religion of Thelema, and by many others at the avant-garde end of the occult community. The adjective "magickal" and the noun "magickian" have also seen play in recent years, though neither of these were pioneered by Crowley himself. See **Crowley, Aleister**; **Magic**.

Martinism

One of the major traditions of Western esoteric spirituality, Martinism traces its roots back to Martinez de Pasqually (1727–74), whose Order of Elect Cohens (*Ordre des Élus Coens*) included several of the most influential occultists of pre-Revolutionary France. Pasqually taught a system of ceremonial magic rooted in Freemasonry, and his most famous student, French mystic and Freemason Louis-Claude de Saint-Martin (1743–1803), became expert in this system. Later in his life, though, Saint-Martin turned away from ceremonial magic and embraced the Christian mystical teachings of the German visionary Jakob Böhme. The tension between these two very different expressions of the mystic quest provides much of the strength of the later system of Martinism, but has also tended to form a fault line along which more than one Martinist organization has broken apart. See **Elect Cohens**.

While he was still committed to Pasqually's ceremonial magic, Saint-Martin founded a Masonic rite at Lyons, titled the Rectified Rite or Rite of Martinism, but this went out of existence before the French Revolution. Saint-Martin's mystical writings, however, had a powerful influence on European Freemasonry and occult traditions. The Rite of Strict Observance, the most influential Masonic order in central Europe during the third quarter of the eighteenth century, helped spread his ideas throughout educated circles in Germany and the Russian Empire, and the Asiatic Brethren, an influential occult order of the time, made his book *Des Erreurs et de la Verité* (*About Errors and the Truth*, 1775) a textbook for initiates. See **Rite of Strict Observance**.

The convulsions of the French Revolution caused most of the occult secret societies of the late eighteenth century to go out of existence. The great revival of occult studies that began with the 1845 publication of Eliphas Lévi's *Doctrine and Ritual of High Magic*, however, gradually gathered up most of the previous century's teachings in its ambit. Saint-Martin's turn came in 1884, when one of the most important members of the French occult community, Papus (Dr. Gérard Encausse, 1865–1916), launched a revived Martinist Order. The new organization had only secondhand links to Saint-Martin's original Rite of Martinism, and borrowed its degree ceremonies from other sources – Cagliostro's Egyptian Rite yielded one degree, while the

Beneficent Chevaliers of the Holy City, a degree created by Saint-Martin's fellow student Jean-Baptiste Willermoz, provided another – but it became the fount from which essentially all later Martinist orders descend.

Papus's Martinist Order fragmented after his death and spawned half a dozen competing orders, and this fragmentation has continued since that time, accompanied by the usual claims by each order that the other orders are invalid. At present more than 20 Martinist orders are active throughout the western world, offering variations on Papus's system of initiation and training. There has been surprisingly little borrowing between Martinist orders and other occult or mystical secret societies, though the American Rosicrucian order AMORC has its own Martinist organization, the Traditional Martinist Order (TMO). See **Ancient Mystical Order Rosae Crucis (AMORC)**.

Mary Magdalene

A minor figure in the New Testament but a major factor in contemporary speculations about Christian origins, Mary Magdalene – originally Miriam of Magdala – appears in the gospel accounts as a woman from Galilee who accompanied Jesus to Jerusalem, watched his crucifixion along with his mother Mary, and was the first person to see him after his resurrection. Luke adds that she was one of a group of women who provided financial support for Jesus and his inner circle of followers, and that she had had seven devils cast out of her. Medieval commentators identified her with several unnamed women in the New Testament narrative and turned her into a harlot converted to a life of sanctity by Jesus. See **Christian origins**; **Jesus of Nazareth**.

Gnostic traditions gave her a much larger role. A Gospel of Mary Magdalene was among the books suppressed by the Church councils that established the current New Testament. This and several other suppressed gospels, including the Gospel of Thomas and the Gospel of the Egyptians, describe a confrontation between the apostle Peter and Mary Magdalene in which Peter tries to discredit Mary on the grounds that she is a woman, but is rebuked by Jesus or one of the other disciples. The occurrence of this scene in several independent sources is interesting, and suggests that this passage may have been derived from a tradition current in the early Church. See **Gnosticism**.

Starting in the middle years of the twentieth century, Mary Magdalene became central to many efforts to redefine Christian origins. Speculations that she was actually the wife of Jesus appeared in English poet Robert Graves' novelistic rewriting of Christian origins, *King Jesus* (1946), and burst into popular culture with the publication of *The Holy Blood and the Holy Grail* (1982), the book that put Christian origins into the alternative-realities scene. Since then, despite the lack of definite evidence one way or another, Mary's role as the wife of Jesus has taken on nearly canonical status in alternative circles. See **Da Vinci Code, the**; **Priory of Sion**; **rejected knowledge**.

Further reading: Haskins 1987, Starbird 1993.

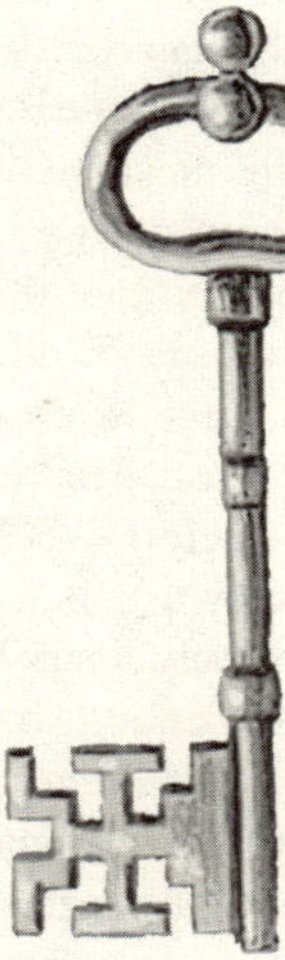

Mason Word

In the original, operative Masonry of Scottish stonemasons' lodges, a series of signs of recognition by which one Mason could identify another without any obvious communication passing between them. The first known reference to the Mason Word is in a long and amazingly bad poem, The Muses Threnodie, written by one Henry Adamson and published in 1638. The relevant lines, dealing with the rebuilding of a bridge over the River Tay, run as follows:

> For what we do presage is not in grosse,
> For we be brethren of the Rosie Crosse;
> We have the Mason Word and second sight,
> Things for to come we can foretell aright.

Other references in Scottish sources through the middle of the seventeenth century make it clear that the Mason Word was a secret passed on among Scottish stonemasons that allowed one mason to identify another at a glance. The Reverend Robert Kirk, peerless researcher of Scottish fairy lore, wrote an appendix to his 1691 book *The Secret Common-wealth of Elves, Fauns and Fairies* discussing five Scottish "Curiosities ... not much observ'd to be elsewhere," one of which was the Mason Word. Kirk wrote:

> The Mason-Word, which tho some make a Misterie of it, I will not conceal a little of what I know; it's like a Rabbinical tradition in a way of comment on Iachin and Boaz the two pillars erected in Solomon's Temple; with an addition of som secret signe delivered from hand to hand, by which they know, and become familiar one with another. (Cited in Stevenson 1988, p. 133)

See **Freemasonry**; **Temple of Solomon**.

One source, the Sloane manuscript, gives an account of the secret signs summed up by the phrase "the Mason Word." These included placing the feet or a pair of tools at right angles to one another, in the image of a square; turning the eyes toward the east and the mouth toward the west; and knocking on a door with two light knocks followed by one heavy one. A Mason visiting a building site could knock on a wall and say, "This is bose [hollow];" any Freemason present would respond by saying that it was solid.

None of these signs remained in use in Freemasonry after the early eighteenth-century reformation of the Craft, and in most Masonic works comments about "the Mason Word" refer instead to the password of the Master Mason degree. See **Freemasonry, origins of**.

Further reading: Stevenson 1988.

Masonry

See **Freemasonry**.

Masters

In Theosophy and traditions descended from it, a person who, after many cycles of reincarnation and spiritual growth, transcends the physical plane but remains active in the world as a teacher and initiator of others on the spiritual path. The Masters are also known as ascended masters or mahatmas. The concept of the Masters derives partly from Buddhist teachings about bodhisattvas, enlightened beings who refuse to enter into Nirvana until all other sentient beings are saved; partly from nineteenth-century ideas about occult initiates who secretly shape world events and pass on their teachings to a chosen few; and partly from alternative visions of Christianity that identify Jesus, not as a divine being come to earth, but as a very advanced human soul. These latter commonly treat Jesus' ascension into heaven as his most important act, showing his transcendence of human limits. The broadening of this idea to high spiritual adepts of all cultures played a crucial role in creating the concept of the Masters. See **Theosophical Society**.

Lists of known or suspected Masters vary widely. Jesus is almost always counted among them, and often ranks as the Master of Masters, while Kuthumi (Koot Hoomi) and El Morya – the spiritual masters credited by Theosophy's founder Helena Blavatsky as the source of her teachings – also rank high on the list. Djwal Khul, "the Tibetan," who inspired Alice Bailey's voluminous occult writings, also makes the short list in most accounts, and so does the Comte de Saint-Germain. Beyond this core the list broadens considerably, sometimes taking in unlikely candidates. Dion Fortune's Fraternity (later Society) of the Inner Light considered Euclid, the ancient Greek mathematician, to be one of the

Masters, while some twentieth-century American groups gave the same status to George Washington. See **Arcane School; Jesus of Nazareth; Saint-Germain, Comte de; Society of the Inner Light.**

Critics of modern occultism have had a field day with some of the more overblown descriptions of the Masters, but an experiential reality lies behind the colorful beliefs. Most practitioners of occult disciplines have had the experience of contact with disembodied entities that have distinct personalities and intellectual powers of their own – sometimes going far beyond those of the people they contact. Many of these entities claim to have been human at particular points in the past, and their speech and knowledge tends to be consistent with their claims. Thus whether the Masters exist or not, as Aleister Crowley famously said of spirits, the universe appears to behave as though they do.

At the same time, the astral cloak of the Masters has more than once served as a veil for incarnate human beings. According to K. Paul Johnson, a historian of Theosophy, Blavatsky's Masters themselves may have been Indian political and religious leaders with whom she worked in the early 1880s. Johnson has argued that the Master Koot Hoomi was actually Thakar Singh Sandhanwalia, a liberal Sikh leader of the time, while El Morya was Ranbir Singh, Maharajah of Kashmir, a Hindu who campaigned for religious tolerance; both men were closely associated with Blavatsky and helped support the Theosophical Society. Theosophists have sharply criticized Johnson's claims but his arguments have proven hard to refute. See **Blavatsky, Helena Petrovna**.

Further reading: Johnson 1994.

Matriarchy

The claim that ancient human society was governed by women rather than men has been a theme in alternative-history circles since 1861, when Swiss historian Johann Jakob Bachofen (1815–87) published his famous book *Mutterrecht* (*Mother-Right*). Like other scholars of his time, Bachofen attempted to create a universal system of human prehistory, and divided it into three periods. The first, hetairism, was a society of universal equality and sexual promiscuity, in which people worshipped the stars; the second, matriarchy, saw power held by women and the focus of worship change to the moon; in the third, patriarchy, men took control of society and the sun became the focus of religious worship. Bachofen's theory, which drew on older theories of astronomical and fertility religion, became very popular in the alternative scenes of the late nineteenth and early twentieth centuries. See **astronomical religion**; **fertility religion**.

Several other writers built on Bachofen's theories in various ways, but the modern theory of ancient matriarchies first appeared in 1903, when English classicist Jane Harrison presented it in detail in her widely read book *Themis.* According to Harrison, southeastern Europe during the Neolithic period – the last phase of the Stone Age – was a utopian society without war or crime, ruled by female elders and worshipping a mother goddess. This idyllic world was destroyed just before the beginning of recorded history by hordes of Indo-European horsemen who invaded from the east and imposed a male-dominated society. This view was widely accepted, and during the middle years of the twentieth century peaceful Neolithic matriarchies formed part of the reigning orthodoxy in archeology, especially in Britain. The belief in ancient matriarchies was so deeply rooted that sites with signs of violence were dated to the Bronze Age even when only stone tools were found there and radiocarbon dates placed them centuries too early.

Harrison and many of her followers, such as British archeologist Jacquetta Hawkes, were closely associated with conservative politics. Their ideas of matriarchy gave a privileged place to traditional female roles of nurturing and childbearing, and argued for a society in which social roles were governed by unchanging tradition; Harrison even campaigned against giving women the vote in Britain. In the 1970s, however, American feminists discovered Harrison's theories and redefined them to support a left-wing political agenda. Lithuanian-American archeologist Marija Gimbutas (1921–94) became the leading spokesperson for this view, writing a series of best-selling books that presented matriarchal "Old Europe" as a liberal feminist Utopia. These views became extremely popular throughout liberal circles in the western world, and played a major role in helping to define the Wiccan movement of the late twentieth century. See **Wicca**.

Ironically, the movement of ancient matriarchies from a conservative political theme to a liberal one happened at about the same time that archeological research finally debunked the idea that the Neolithic period had been a Utopia free of violence. Whether or not Gimbutas's "Old Europe" was ruled by women, the usual traces of warfare and social hierarchy are abundant in its archeological remains. None of this has kept the belief in a matriarchal golden age from remaining an article of faith in many alternative circles.

Further reading: Eller 2000, Gimbutas 1991.

Mau Mau

Beginning in 1948, members of the Kikuyu tribe in what was then the British colony of Kenya organized a secret society to oppose the expropriation of Kikuyu land by white farmers and drive out the colonial government. The Movement of Unity, to give it its proper name, grew out of a long history of legal Kikuyu organizations dating back to the 1920s. When legal measures and protest marches did not succeed, guerrilla war was the next logical step, and the Mau Mau movement formed in response.

The phrase "Mau Mau" evolved from the cry *Uma uma*, "Out! Out!", given to warn that police were approaching. Members took a secret oath to support the movement, in a ceremony adapted from Kikuyu tribal rituals. Committed members took another oath, the *Batuni* or platoon oath, which bound them to kill the movement's opponents on command, maintain its secrets with their lives, and protect its members.

Like most Third World insurgencies in the postwar years, the Mau Mau movement combined a sophisticated urban wing, providing support and intelligence, with guerrilla forces in isolated rural areas. The struggle that unfolded between the Mau Mau and the British government followed just as typical a pattern, with mass arrests and clumsy military actions on the part of the colonial power, matched by assassinations and atrocities on the part of the insurgents. A state of emergency was declared in 1952 and 11 infantry battalions hunted Mau Mau forces in the Aberdare range and around Mount Kenya with very mixed results.

Systematic government operations against the urban wing in Nairobi had more success, detaining some 77,000 Kikuyu on suspicion of Mau Mau involvement. Jomo Kenyatta, president of the Kenyan African Union, the political arm of the movement, was arrested in 1952 and spent nearly the entire insurgency in British colonial prisons. By 1956, harried by police and army units, Mau Mau forces in the countryside offered little further threat to the British colonial government, but by then the insurgency had achieved its goals, convincing the British government and popular opinion alike that the colonial presence in Kenya was too expensive to maintain. Kenya won its independence in 1963, with Jomo Kenyatta as its first prime minister. While a few Mau Mau bands remained in the forests after independence, claims in the British press that the Mau Mau would become a persistent problem proved inaccurate.

Mayan calendar

The calendar system of the classic Maya, the most elaborate calendar system of medieval Central America, has recently become a fixture in the New Age movement and the rejected-knowledge industry. Forgotten shortly after the conquest of Yucatan by the Spanish conquistadors, it was reconstructed in the twentieth century from scraps of information preserved in the writings of Fray Diego de Landa, a Dominican monk who accompanied the Spanish armies. See **New Age movement**; **rejected knowledge**.

Mayan timekeeping used three intersecting calendar cycles, the *haab* or civil year, the *tzolkin* or religious year, and the Long Count. The *haab* consisted of 18 months of 20 days each, plus 5 extra days, for a total of 365 days. The *tzolkin* consisted of two meshed cycles, one of 13 days and one of 20 days, for a "year" of 260 days. A Mayan date consisted of two words and two numbers; for example, 4 Ahau 8 Cumku meant the 4th day of the 13-day cycle and the day Ahau of the 20-day cycle, giving the *tzolkin* date, and the 8th day of the month Cumku, giving the *haab* date. The intersecting cycles make each date repeat every 52 years.

Alongside these, the Maya kept a sequential calendar called the Long Count, which simply gave the total number of days since a fixed point in the distant past, which works out in our calendar as August 11, 3114 BCE. The Long Count comes to an end and restarts after 13 *baktuns* of 1,872,000 days, about 5125 years. This is almost exactly one-fifth of the cycle of precession of the equinoxes, the slow wobble of earth's axis that moves the position of the sun at the solstices and equinoxes backward through the zodiac. See **astronomical religion**.

The Long Count of the Mayan calendar tracked the cycle of suns, or ages of the world; the current Fifth Sun ends on December 21, 2012. While Mayan teachings about the suns survive only in fragmentary form, other versions of the same myth are found from Peru to Oregon, and suggest that each sun ends with a catastrophe. The imminent end of the current sun has thus become a major theme in the alternative scene in recent years and feeds into speculations about approaching earth changes. See **ages of the world**; **earth changes**.

Further reading: Jenkins 1994.

Megaliths

Large stones (the meaning of the word, from Greek *megas*, "big," and *lithos*, "stone") moved and erected by human beings in the distant past, megaliths are found across much of the world. The most famous examples are in southwestern Britain and Brittany, where Stonehenge and Carnac define megaliths to the popular mind. Nearly identical megalithic structures, however, are found all across northwestern Europe, in New England and eastern Canada, in certain parts of India and Africa, and in Japan. See **Stonehenge**.

Megaliths have a terminology all their own. A menhir is a single stone set upright in the ground. A dolmen or cromlech is made of three or more stones supporting a larger capstone. A trilithon is a stone lintel atop two uprights, as at Stonehenge. A rocking stone is a single large stone balanced so delicately that it can be rocked back and forth by the pressure of a hand. A cairn is a heap of stones. Barrows are heaps of earth; a round barrow is circular in plan, while a long barrow extends along a straight line; both kinds usually have stone chambers inside them, and dolmens or cromlechs seem to be the stone chambers of old round barrows whose earth has been washed or ploughed away. A henge is a circular earthen bank with a ditch outside the bank (as at Stonehenge) or inside it (as at every other henge in the British Isles). A stone circle, finally, is exactly what it sounds like – a more or less circular pattern of big upright stones.

According to modern archeologists, the megalithic sites of northwestern Europe began to appear around 4200 BCE as long barrows rose here and there across the landscape, together with a cult of ancestor worship. Other earthworks followed, with or without stones. Around 3000 BCE long barrows dropped out of use and round barrows came in, along with dolmens and the first stone circles. Around the time Stonehenge was abandoned, megaliths stopped being raised over most of Europe, though individual menhirs were still being erected into historic times. The sequence of megalithic sites elsewhere in the world is less clear, and those in the northeast of North America have never been properly studied by archeologists at all.

The purpose behind most megalithic sites remains one of the most intractable mysteries about them. The long barrows contained the bones of many people, which were apparently used in rituals to honor the dead of a community; round barrows were burial places of the chieftains of a later people. Henges were apparently ritual sites, and at least some stone circles were probably used to track the movements of the sun and moon. Many of the sites appear to be linked together in complex sacred landscapes and alignments stretching over miles of territory, a detail that has made them of interest to ley researchers. Still, the meaning and purpose of the old megaliths remains lost in the distant past. See **leys**.

Where facts are sparse, speculation rushes in to fill the void, and nowhere more enthusiastically than with megaliths. Every popular theme in the rejected knowledge scene has been projected onto megalithic sites. The great stones have also inspired a few unique theories of their own, notably the one that they were originally stone airships levitated by earth energies and flown along ley alignments. The ancient Druids were once linked to the stones by scholars, which was at least a plausible claim in the days before radiocarbon dating. More recently, theories about ancient astronauts, lost civilizations from Atlantis onward, and earth changes past and future have all made use of megaliths in one way or another. See **Atlantis**; **Druids**; **earth changes**; **lost civilizations**; **rejected knowledge**.

Further reading: Michell 1969, Michell 1982, Souden 1997.

Merovingians

A royal house of early medieval France, the Merovingians or House of Meroveus ruled the Frankish kingdom from 476 to 751 CE. The Franks started as a tribe of German barbarians who invaded Gaul during the final collapse of the Roman Empire in the fifth century CE, and established a series of petty kingdoms in what is now north-east France. Their war leader Merowig, Meroveus in Latin, was the grandfather of Clovis I (466–511), who first consolidated the Frankish kingdoms and is considered the first Merovingian king of France. His descendants were known as the Long-Haired Kings because a traditional taboo forbade them to cut their hair. After the reign of Dagobert I (reigned 623–39), power passed to the Mayors of the Palace, a line of ambitious noblemen of the rival Carolingian family. When Charles Martel, a Mayor of the Palace, led the Frankish armies that kept the Muslims out of France at the battle of Tours in 732, a change of dynasty became inevitable. In 751 the last Merovingian king, Childeric III, was deposed and Charles's son Pepin III became King of the Franks.

The Merovingians were a footnote in the history of the Dark Ages until the 1960s, when Pierre Plantard read about them in a French magazine article and included them in the campaign of disinformation he carried out for his newly minted secret society, the Priory of Sion. The claims he circulated were picked up by a trio of British writers and used as the basis for a series of popular TV documentaries and bestselling books, including the famous *The Holy Blood and the Holy Grail* (1982). Since that time the Merovingians have become a hot property in alternative circles, by turns lauded as descendents of Jesus of Nazareth, condemned as the ancestors of today's reptilian ruling classes, and fictionalized as plot elements in popular novels such as Dan Brown's *The Da Vinci Code* (2003). See **Disinformation**; **Priory of Sion**; **Reptilians**.

Mithraic mysteries

One of the most popular mystery cults of the ancient world, the Mithraic mysteries were latecomers on the classical religious scene, emerging in what is now southeastern Turkey during the first century of the Common Era. Like the fraternal secret societies of a much later age, but unlike most of the other pagan mystery cults, they admitted only men and had several degrees of initiation. Members met once or twice a month in an underground temple, called a Mithraeum, to perform initiation rituals and share in a ceremonial meal of bread and wine. Their divine patron was Mithras, an ancient Persian deity, usually shown in Mithraic sculpture in the act of sacrificing a mighty bull, surrounded by a snake, a dog, a scorpion, a lion, and a cup. See **fraternal orders**; **mysteries, ancient**.

This image may reveal the heart of the Mithraic cult, for as historian of science David Ulansey has pointed out, it forms a star map of the constellations around Taurus. Ulansey argued that the secret of the Mithraic mysteries was the precession of the equinoxes, the slow wobble of earth's axis that shifts the sun's position at the solstices and equinoxes back through the zodiac at the rate of one degree every 72 years. In an age when the stars were gods, Mithras represented the mighty power who turned the whole structure of the heavens, and "slew" Taurus the Bull by moving it out of the sun's station at the spring equinox. See **ages of the world**; **astronomical religion**.

This theory finds an intriguing reflection in gematria, a traditional system of occult symbolism that uses the number values of alphabets such as Hebrew and Greek. In Greek letters, Mithras (ΜΕΙΘΡΑΣ) adds up to 365, the number of days in a solar year. See **Gematria**.

The Mithraic mysteries were a powerful religious force in the Roman Empire during the second and third centuries CE, but went under when the Christian Church seized political power in the Empire during the fourth century. Several nineteenth- and twentieth-century secret societies have made use of Mithraic symbolism, but so far no one seems to have attempted a full-scale revival of the mysteries of Mithras.

Further reading: Ulansey 1989.

Mopses

See **Order of Mopses**.

Moray, Robert

Scottish general, scientist, Hermeticist and Freemason, 1609–73. Moray was the son of a minor laird in Perthshire, but developed an interest in science and engineering early in life. In the 1630s he emigrated to France and, like many Scotsmen of his time, entered on a career in the French army. When the Covenanter rebellion broke out in Scotland against Charles I in 1640, however, he returned to Scotland on the orders of Cardinal Richelieu, who hoped to turn the revolt to French advantage. Moray became quartermaster general of the rebel army, and served with distinction in the Scottish invasion of the north of England in 1640–41.

In 1641 Moray was initiated as a Freemason by members of the Edinburgh lodge who were serving with the Covenanter army. He has sometimes been listed as the first Mason who was not in the building trades, but this is inaccurate; speculative Masons had been joining the Edinburgh lodge since 1634. He was also a careful student of Hermetic and Rosicrucian literature. See **Freemasonry**; **Hermeticism**; **Rosicrucians**.

With the end of hostilities between the Scottish rebels and the king, Moray returned to French service, and seems to have mended fences with Charles I, who knighted him in 1643. Later that same year, serving with the French army, he was captured by the Germans and spent two years as a prisoner in Bavaria. He was released in 1645, as the English Civil War came to an end, and divided his time thereafter between his military career with the French army and conspiracies in favor of the exiled House of Stuart. In 1651 he was in Scotland, helping Charles II in his attempt to free Scotland from Cromwell's forces, and in 1653 he played a central role in preparations for a rising against the English army of occupation in Scotland.

The failure of the rising forced Moray to flee for his life, first to the Orkneys and then to Maastricht in the Netherlands, where he waited out the short-lived English Republic. In 1660, with the restoration of Charles II to the British throne, Moray returned to London with the new monarch and spent most of the remainder of his life at court, winning a reputation as one of the few honest courtiers of Charles II. He played a central role in founding the Royal Society in 1661, and remained active in scientific pursuits until his death. See **Royal Society**.

Further reading: Stevenson 1988.

Morgan abduction

On the evening of September 12, 1826, three months before the publication of his book revealing the secrets of the first three degrees of Freemasonry, William Morgan (1774–1826?) disappeared outside the city jail in Canandaigua, New York State. Witnesses heard Morgan shout "Murder!" as he was forced into a carriage by four men. The carriage drove off into the night, and Morgan was never seen again. His disappearance launched one of the great conspiracy panics in American history.

Morgan had a checkered past and a dubious reputation. Born in Virginia, he worked as a stonemason, brewer, merchant, farmer, and clerk, and contemporary accounts describe him as a quarrelsome alcoholic, in and out of jail for unpaid debts. At some point in his life he had either become a Mason or learned enough from published exposures of Masonic ritual to pass as a Mason. No record of his initiation into the three degrees of Craft Masonry survives, though he certainly attended Masonic lodges in upstate New York in the early 1820s, and received the Royal Arch degree in 1825. See **Freemasonry**; **Royal Arch**.

He signed a petition to found a Royal Arch Chapter in Batavia, New York, but other Masons in Batavia objected to his membership and had his name removed from the petition. Morgan, infuriated, quit the Batavia lodge and decided to avenge himself on Masonry by writing a book that revealed its secrets. The hope of making money may also have played a significant part in his plans. In March 1826 he contracted with the publisher of a local newspaper and two investors to produce the book. When word got out about his plan, local Masons tried to prevent the book's publication, and Morgan and his partners received numerous threats.

On September 10, a person or persons unknown tried to burn down Miller's print shop. A day later Morgan was arrested for unpaid debts and taken to the Canandaigua jail. The next evening the Mason who had brought the charges against Morgan paid the debt and obtained Morgan's release. The jailer's wife heard a shrill whistle, went to the window, and witnessed Morgan struggling and shouting as he was forced into a carriage and taken away.

Exactly what happened to Morgan after that remains a mystery. He was apparently held prisoner for several days at the abandoned Fort Niagara, and his captors tried to convince him to accept a large cash sum, withdraw the book, and emigrate to Canada. Rumors for years thereafter claimed that he had been seen in Canada, or British Honduras, or the Turkish city of Smyrna; one account claimed that he had run away to the West and become an Indian chief, another that he had turned pirate and been hanged in Cuba. Most historians argue that the Canadian deal fell through, Morgan's captors panicked, and Morgan was tied to heavy weights and thrown into the Niagara River.

Morgan's book, *Illustrations of Masonry*, nonetheless appeared in December 1826 and was an instant bestseller. By that time the governor of New York, DeWitt Clinton, had offered rewards of $300 (a large sum by early nineteenth-century standards) for information leading to the arrest of Morgan's abductors, and a grand jury in Canandaigua had indicted four Masons for conspiracy to kidnap. Three of them pled guilty but claimed they had no idea where Morgan was. Conspiracy to kidnap was then a misdemeanor in New York, and the defendants served jail terms of between two years and three months. Three special counsels appointed by the state pursued the investigation until 1831, indicting 54 more Freemasons and convicting

10 on various charges; 13 other Masons fled the state to avoid trial.

While all this was happening, in October 1828, a badly decomposed male body was washed up on the shore of Lake Ontario. Leaders of the rapidly growing antimasonic movement insisted at once that the body was Morgan's. The original coroner's inquest noted that the corpse had a heavy beard; a second inquest, carried out at the request of the antimasons, found that the body was clean-shaven and closely resembled Morgan. Later that month, however, a Mrs. Timothy Munroe from Canada testified that her husband had disappeared and was thought to have drowned, and she was able to give an exact description of the corpse's clothing. The corpse, which had been buried at the Batavia cemetery with much antimasonic speechmaking, was then re-interred as Timothy Munroe.

The third and last special counsel, who had the remarkable name of Victory Birdseye, finished his inquiry in 1831. A few Masons involved in the abduction left deathbed confessions at various points through the nineteenth century, though none of these provided any conclusive evidence. Whatever the facts of the matter, Morgan's disappearance became the great rallying cry for the Antimasonic Party, the first significant third party in United States history, and continues to be dragged out by opponents of Masonry to this day. See **Antimasonic Party**; **Antimasonry**.

Further reading: Vaughn 1983.

Moriah Conquering Wind

According to several recent conspiracy theorists, the phrase "Moriah Conquering Wind" is the true name of the Illuminati. The origins of this odd phrase shine a revealing light into the workings of contemporary conspiracy theory. Mount Moriah, one of the hills on which the city of Jerusalem is built, was the site of the Temple of Solomon and plays an important role in biblical symbolism. The importance of the Temple of Solomon in Freemasonry ensured that Moriah became a significant word in the high degrees of the Craft, and in this way it came to the attention of conspiracy theorists convinced that high-ranking Masons actually run the world. See **Bavarian Illuminati**; **Freemasonry**; **high degrees**; **Temple of Solomon**.

The remainder of the title has a more prosaic origin. The 1960s Western musical Paint Your Wagon put the song "They Call the Wind Maria," performed by Harve Presnell, on radio stations across America. In the song "Maria" is pronounced like "Moriah," with a long "i." The first references in conspiracy literature to Moriah as the name of a wind surfaced a few years after the musical's movie version's release in 1969. By the early 1990s, conspiracy-oriented Christian fundamentalist websites were claiming that Moriah was the name of a demon representing "the destructive night wind," and from there, "Moriah Conquering Wind" required only a bit of free association. Such fusions of misunderstood secret society lore and popular media imagery are extremely common throughout today's rejected-knowledge industry. See **rejected knowledge**.

Mothers of Darkness

According to modern fundamentalist books condemning the Illuminati, the female branch of that society, headquartered at a castle in Belgium. The members wear veils and black robes lined with different colors to show their rank. Their symbolism includes the "thousand points of light," the eight-pointed star, and orchids. Barbara Bush, the wife of former US president George Bush Snr., is allegedly a member; one book shows a picture of her in a striped jacket, reading to children, and commented that she "dressed for the occasion in a hypnotic suit obviously to reinforce the Illuminati hypnotic commands given to the children surrounding her" (Springmeier 2002, p. v).

No trace of the Mothers of Darkness appears outside a handful of current anti-Illuminati tracts replete with obvious historical and factual errors. Still, it is interesting that the Illuminati, in the fashion of so many fraternal secret societies, has been credited with its own ladies auxiliary. See **Bavarian Illuminati**; **ladies auxiliaries**.

Further reading: Springmeier 2002.

Mu

One of the more recent additions to the roster of lost continents, Mu has a complex history. Its origins date back to Fray Diego de Landa, a Spanish monk of the sixteenth century who accompanied the conquistadors to Yucatan and helped to destroy most of the legacies of classical Maya culture. In the process of gathering up and destroying nearly all Mayan manuscripts, he copied down a few garbled notes on Mayan writing. He misunderstood the language completely, treating the complex hieroglyphic script as an alphabet. Until the Mayan hieroglyphs were finally deciphered in the 1980s, though, de Landa's notes were the only available information on the subject. See **lost continents**.

In 1864, the French scholar Charles-Étienne Brasseur de

Bourbourg (1814–74) obtained a copy of de Landa's notes and set out to decipher one of the four Mayan manuscripts that had survived de Landa's purge. Scholars now know that the manuscript in question is an ephemeris of the planet Venus, written and used by ancient Mayan astrologer-priests, but in Brasseur de Bourbourg's hands it seemed to present a garbled account of a volcanic catastrophe in a place called "Mu, Land of Mud." Thereafter, references to Mu cropped up in alternative writings as alleged Mayan evidence for the reality of Atlantis. See **Atlantis**.

It was in this form that American writer James Churchward came across Mu. His 1925 bestseller *The Lost Continent of Mu* claimed that Churchward had studied secret tablets in India and Central America that originated in ancient Mu. Churchward described Mu as a huge continent in the central Pacific, extending from the Marianas Islands east to Easter Island. The original home of humanity and the cradle of civilization, Mu had a population of 64 million at its height, divided into 10 tribes and ruled by a priest-king known as the Ra. Some 13,000 years ago, a series of underground gas-belts suddenly deflated, and the Land of Mud sank below the sea, leaving Easter Island, the lost city of Nan Madol, and a few other sites as echoes of its lost glory. See **Easter Island**; **Nan Madol**.

Mu was briefly in vogue among the American occult community, and several occult secret societies put material about Mu into their teachings. By the middle of the twentieth century, however, Mu became an alternate name for Lemuria, another lost continent with more cachet in occult traditions. Lemuria was originally in the western Indian Ocean, connecting India and Africa, many thousands of miles away from the supposed site of Mu. Most recent occult literature splits the difference and puts the lost continent in the area of modern Indonesia – interestingly, the area where recent archeological research suggests that many thousands of square miles of lowland were drowned by rising oceans at the end of the last Ice Age. See **Lemuria**.

Further reading: Churchward 1931, de Camp 1970.

Murray hypothesis

In a series of bestselling books, starting with *The Witch Cult in Western Europe* (1921), British Egyptologist Margaret Murray (1863–1963) popularized the theory that medieval witches were actually followers of a pagan fertility cult passed down among European peasants since pre-Christian times. During the first half of her professional career, Murray was a respected Egyptologist, a student of the renowned Sir Flinders Petrie and the author of several popular books on ancient Egyptian culture. Stranded in London by the outbreak of the First World War in 1914, she turned her attention to

British history, and was attracted by English and Scottish witchcraft. Like nearly all students of comparative religion in her time, she accepted the theories of Sir James Frazer, who had argued in his immense *The Golden Bough* (1890) that all primitive religions emerged from fertility worship. Her studies of witchcraft trials convinced her that the medieval witch cult was a Frazerian fertility religion. See **fertility religion**; **witchcraft persecutions**.

During her lifetime, that theory became widely accepted among scholars, though her later theories – which argued, among other things, that the kings of England had been deeply involved in the witch cult, and most of the assassinations in English history had been ceremonial slayings of a divine king – were quietly ignored by most historians. After her death in 1963, though, scholars re-examined the source materials Murray had used, and found massive scholarly fraud. Murray had shamelessly manipulated her data, citing passages that supported her theories while leaving out those that contradicted it, and mixed evidence from many different countries and historical periods to produce an illusion of consistency.

The debunking of the Murray hypothesis has been accepted almost universally by historians of medieval witchcraft. While the hypothesis was generally accepted, though, Murray's friend Gerald Gardner used it as the foundation for the new religion of Wicca, the first neo-pagan faith to attract a widespread following in the western world. Many people in the Wiccan and neopagan movements still treat the Murray hypothesis as an article of faith, and dismiss scholarly challenges to it as simply another round of persecution directed at their supposedly ancient faith. These same beliefs have spread outwards into a wide range of alternative spiritual contexts, where belief in medieval goddess cults suppressed by Christian brutality remains standard. See **Wicca**.

Further reading: Cohn 1975, Hutton 2000, Murray 1921, Murray 1933, Murray 1954.

MYSTERIES, ANCIENT

One of the most widespread and influential religious institutions in the ancient Greek world, the mysteries of classical times were initiatory cults in which candidates passed through rituals meant to bring them into a personal relationship with pagan divinities. Most of the mysteries centered on the mythic life, death, and rebirth of a goddess or god, and initiates participated in a re-enactment of the deity's myth. In the mysteries of Adonis, for example, candidates helped the goddess Aphrodite search for the body of Adonis, mourned him when his corpse was found, and then celebrated his resurrection. See **Adonis, mysteries of**.

Many of the most popular mysteries had close connections to the cycle of the seasons, and the god or goddess who died and rose again had close symbolic connections to grain, cut down in the harvest, buried beneath the earth at planting, and risen again in the green shoot to bring a promise of bounty to all. The mysteries of Adonis and Isis fell into this category, but the most famous of these agricultural rites was the Eleusinian mysteries, which centered on Persephone and her mother Demeter. A few mystery cults focused on different natural cycles; the Mithraic mysteries, for example, centered on the precession of the equinoxes. See **Eleusinian mysteries**; **Isiac mysteries**; **Mithraic mysteries**.

The mysteries, like nearly all other aspects of classical pagan spirituality, were suppressed after the Christian Church seized power in the Roman world during the fourth century of the Common Era. Ironically, Christianity itself probably gained a foothold in ancient times because of its close similarities to the ancient mysteries, since Christians then and now celebrate the life, death, and resurrection of Jesus of Nazareth in much the same way that initiates of the mysteries participated in the myths of their own deities. See **Christian origins**.

The mysteries were creations of ancient Greek culture, and existed only where Greek ideas and religious practices spread. The claim that ancient Egypt had mystery initiations of its own, a staple of nineteenth- and twentieth-century occultism and of today's alternative history scene, is accurate only in that Greeks brought the concept there after Egypt's conquest by Alexander the Great, and several ancient Egyptian cults, including that of Isis, were reworked into mysteries on the Greek pattern thereafter. The *seshtau* – "that which is hidden," the secret inner rituals of the Egyptian temples – were not initiations at all. See **Egypt**.

Nonetheless Egypt, and every other corner of the world, was retroactively populated with mystery cults in the eighteenth, nineteenth and twentieth centuries. As secret societies of various kinds spread to become among the most typical social institutions of the western world, the traditions of Freemasonry and several other secret orders were projected on the inkblot patterns of the past. Old books thus speak of the Gothic mysteries of northern Europe, focusing on the life and death of Baldur, son of the Norse god Odin; the Druidic mysteries, based on the adventures of Taliesin; the central American mysteries, derived from the *Popol Vuh*, a Quiché Maya sacred text; and many more. All of these were imagined as a blend of ancient Greek mystery cults and modern Masonic practice. Completely anachronistic, and unsupported by the least scrap of evidence, these "mystery cults" continue to be cited in the alternative-realities literature today. See **rejected knowledge**.

Further reading: Burkert 1985.

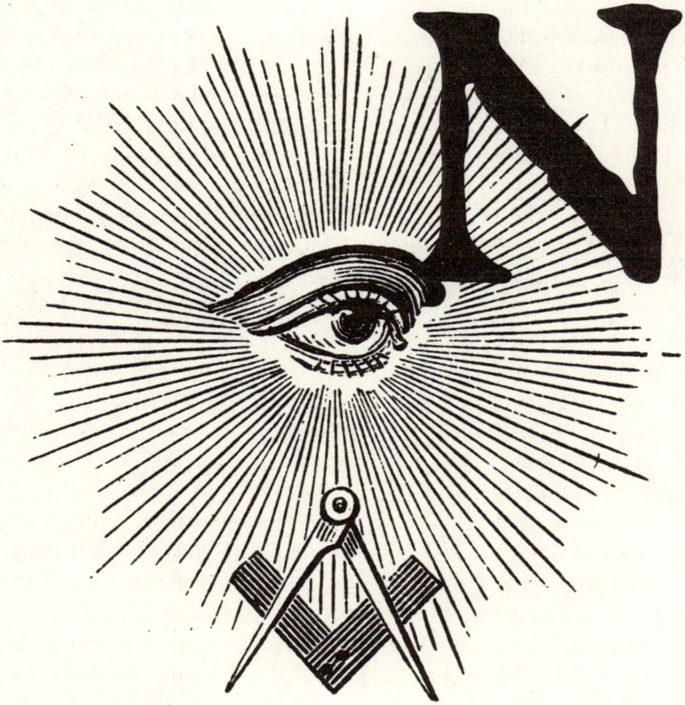
N

Nan Madol

While stories of lost cities abandoned to the jungle are common, actual examples are much less so. Nan Madol, a sprawling stone city on the island of Ponape (formerly Ascension Island) in the Caroline Islands of the western Pacific Ocean, is among the most impressive. There is nothing like it anywhere else in the South Seas. Mostly overgrown with jungle, the ruins of Nan Madol cover 175 acres (71 hectares) on an islet in Ponape's coral reef.

The city includes temples, tombs, and house platforms, separated by a maze of shallow canals and surrounded by a protective wall originally 30 feet (9 meters) tall. All the surviving structures are made of natural basalt columns stacked crib-style, like the logs in a log cabin, with chinks between "logs" filled with smaller stones, coral, and pebbles. During the years of Nan Madol's glory, archeologists agree, the stone structures served as foundations for buildings of wood and palm thatch. With no mortar, no tools capable of shaping the hard volcanic stone, and no knowledge of the arch or vault, the builders of Nan Madol nonetheless made a city splendid enough to deserve the title "the Venice of the Pacific."

According to native Ponapean legends, the city was built by two brothers, Olsihpa and Olsohpa, who came to the island from far away on a large canoe. They became the island's rulers and set out to build a stone building from which to rule. Their first three attempts were unsatisfactory, but the fourth, Nan Madol, became the island's capital. When Olsihpa died, Olsohpa became the first Saudeleur or king of Ponape. Fifteen Saudeleurs followed him, but the Ponapeans grew soft and forgot the art of war. In the reign of the sixteenth Saudeleur, the war chief Isokelekel from the island of Kusaie far to the west invaded Ponape, defeated the last Saudeleur and became king in his place. Isokelekel and his successors, the Nahnmwarkis, ruled Nan Madol for a time, but in the reign of the fifth Nahnmwarki, Luhk un Mallada, the city was finally abandoned to the jungle.

There seems no reason to doubt the Ponapean account of Nan Madol's rise and fall. Radiocarbon dates taken from remains of sacrificial turtles at one of Nan Madol's temples show that the temple was in use around 1275 CE, which fits the rough chronology established by the traditional list of reigns. The legend of the brothers Olsihpa and Olsohpa might be a folk memory of the arrival of voyagers from Indonesia or the Philippines, where buildings of stone were common long before Nan Madol was built; something as simple as a ship blown off course and wrecked on Ponape's shores might well have set the entire process in motion.

Nonetheless Nan Madol has been drafted repeatedly into the service of alternative theories of history. Claims that Nan Madol had a population of one million or more, and that it was made millions of years in the past out of 15-ton stone blocks, using engineering principles impossible for modern Ponapeans to duplicate, can be found here and there in the rejected knowledge literature, even though none of these "facts" are true. Believers in the lost continent of Mu, in particular, have redefined Nan Madol repeatedly as a lost Muvian metropolis. See **lost continents**; **Mu**; **rejected knowledge**.

Further reading: Ballinger 1978.

National Socialism

The rise and fiery end of German National Socialism between 1919 and 1945 represents one of the most puzzling phenomena of modern history, far stranger than any work of fiction. After a life on the mean streets of Vienna and Munich, an unemployed nobody named Adolf Hitler seized control of a tiny, dysfunctional party on the fringes of Munich politics, suddenly developed a talent for fiery oratory, and turned the party into one of the most terrifyingly effective political machines of modern times. Only 14 years after that party's founding, with a platform consisting mostly of medieval racist fantasies, it seized control of one of the most educated and cultured nations in the world.

In 1933, when Hitler became its Chancellor, Germany was economically, politically, and militarily prostrate, bankrupted by the Great Depression, burdened with vast reparations by the victors of the First World War, and threatened with immediate invasion if it attempted to start rebuilding its military. Seven years later German tanks and aircraft crushed the allied French and British armies, conquered France in less than two months, and came within an ace of forcing Britain out of the war. In the early part of the war Hitler and his armies forged an empire from the Atlantic to the gates of Moscow and from the Arctic Circle to the Sahara desert, and went under only after most of the world rose up in arms to crush them. As Louis Pauwels and Jacques Bergier pointed out in their seminal work on the occult dimensions of Nazism, *Le Matin du Magiciens* (*The Morning of the Magicians*, 1960), the historical arc of the Nazi movement might best be called "a few years in the absolute elsewhere."

Since 1960, a substantial literature in most western languages has pointed to occultism as a major factor in the Nazi phenomenon. Most of these works are packed with misinformation, factual inaccuracies, and blatant fabrications, and a very large number of them draw sweeping conclusions about Nazi occultism without having any clear idea of what occultism is in the first place. The irony, as a handful of pioneering historians have pointed out, is that a very solid case can be made for occultism in the National Socialist movement, but that nearly everything written about the subject has missed the actual occult dimensions of Nazism and strayed off in pursuit of fantasy and fraud instead. See **Occultism**.

The occult side of National Socialism began long before the Nazi party itself took shape, with a Germanic racist offshoot of the Theosophical movement called Ariosophy. The two chief Ariosophical theorists, Guido von List (1848–1919) and Jörg Lanz von Liebenfels (1874–1954), rejected the Theosophical faith in spiritual evolution, replacing it with a cosmology in which members of an original semi-divine Aryan race had fallen from grace and lost their superhuman powers through interbreeding with subhuman beast-men. List and Liebenfels each founded secret societies, the Höhere Armanen-Orden (Higher Armanen Order, HAO) and the Ordo Novi Templi (Order of New Templars, ONT) respectively, to promote Ariosophical teachings. The ONT published a magazine, *Ostara*, in which many of the later themes of Nazi politics and racial theory first saw print. See **Höhere Armanen-Orden**; **Ordo Novi Templi**; **Theosophical Society**.

Ariosophy found an eager audience in Germany in the years before the First World War, and in 1912 the first German Ariosophical secret society, the Germanenorden, was founded by Hermann Pohl. Originally launched as the secret wing of the largest German antisemitic organization of the time, the Hammerbund, the Germanenorden was pulled between occult and political factions and finally split in half in 1916. The Munich lodge of the Germanenorden Walvater, the magical side of the schism, operated under the cover name of the Thule-Gesellschaft (Thule Society), drawing its name from the lost continent of Thule. In 1918 members of the Thule Society organized a political party, the German Workers Party (*Deutsche Arbeiterpartei*, DAP), as a front to draw the working classes away from communism. See **Germanenorden**; **Thule**; **Thule Society**.

On the evening of September 12, 1919, an Austrian veteran named Adolf Hitler, who worked as an informer spying on Munich political parties for German Army intelligence, attended a meeting of the DAP. He joined a few days later and quickly became the party's leading figure. A longtime student of the occult and a convinced Ariosophist, Hitler soon came to the notice of important figures in the Thule Society. Thule members Rudolf Hess and Ernst Röhm became close associates of the future Führer. Another important figure was Dietrich Eckart, an Ariosophical occultist and writer associated with many Thule initiates though not actually a member himself. Eckart became Hitler's mentor; he has also been named as Hitler's occult instructor, and while no conclusive evidence supports the claim, that role was one Eckart was certainly equipped to fill. See **Hitler, Adolf**.

As the DAP transformed itself into the *Nationalsozialistische Deutsche Arbeiterpartei* (National Socialist German Workers Party, NSDAP) and became the dominant force on the German far right, many other Ariosophists and occultists flocked to it. One was Heinrich Himmler, who joined in 1919 and took over the SS (*Schutzstaffel*, Protection Force) in 1929 after a series of bitter political struggles within the party. Perhaps the most serious of Nazi occultists, Himmler believed himself to be the reincarnation of the medieval German king Heinrich I. Under his leadership the SS became an occult secret society with immense influence throughout German society, and the SS headquarters at the medieval castle of Wewelsburg became the center of the Third Reich's occult dimension as Himmler implemented many of the old ONT programs on a colossal scale. See **SS (Schutzstaffel)**.

Ironically, given the extensive occult involvements of top Nazi leaders, the history of National Socialist Germany reads like an object lesson in the dangers of negative magic. Blind to the consequences of their own actions as they lashed out at imaginary racial foes, the Nazi leadership created enemies for the regime faster than Nazi armies and concentration camps could kill them, in a spiral of violence and self-inflicted destruction that ended with Hitler's suicide, the collapse of the Nazi movement, and the total devastation of Germany itself. Any student of occult philosophy could have predicted such an outcome.

The magical dimensions of National Socialism were no secret in the occult community before or during the war. French occult periodicals discussed Hitler's occult background in the 1930s, and English magician Dion Fortune, in a series of war letters circulated among British occultists to organize anti-Nazi rituals, described the magical side of the Nazi phenomenon in plausible terms. Starting in 1960, though, this material was all but buried beneath a mountain of sensational literature that exploited rumors of Hitler's connections with the occult and the world of secret societies for all they were worth. Pauwels and Bergier's *Le Matin du Magiciens* began the trend with a colorful but inaccurate description of Hitler's occult connections. From Pauwels and Bergier come the claims that top Nazis were in contact with Tibetan masters, and that the geography professor Karl Haushofer was the secret mastermind behind Hitler's rise.

Even more influential was Trevor Ravenscroft's *The Spear of Destiny* (1972), which used ideas borrowed from Rudolf Steiner and the Austrian mystic Walter Stein to fill out a colorful story about Hitler's quest for world power through control of the Spear of Longinus, allegedly the spear that pierced the side of Jesus during his crucifixion. Ravenscroft's book has been shown to be nonsense by skeptic Ken Anderson in his book *Hitler and the Occult* (1995), but *The Spear of Destiny* remains in print and its claims have been recycled for more than three decades. See **Anthroposophical Society**; **Grail**; **Spear of Longinus**.

Another dimension of the postwar mythology of National Socialism has its roots in the rise of neo-Nazi movements and secret societies around the world. The two most important figures here are Savitri Devi (1905–82) and Miguel Serrano (1917–). Savitri Devi (born Maximiani Portas) argued that Hitler was an incarnation of the Hindu god Vishnu and the redeemer of the Aryan race in the Kali Yuga, the dark age of Hindu tradition. In her major work of Nazi theology, *The Lightning and the Sun* (1958), she argued that Hitler was a messianic figure who used the violent methods of the Kali Yuga to initiate a new Golden Age. These ideas became popular in neo-Nazi groups in the 1960s, after Devi made contact with National Socialists in Britain and America.

Chilean author and diplomat Miguel Serrano's mystical theology of Nazism, *Hitlerismo esoterico* ("esoteric Hitlerism"), reaches much more deeply into occult traditions. Trained in a Chilean magical lodge with links to right-wing French occult circles, Serrano adopted a Gnostic theology in which the distant ancestors of the Aryans, divine beings from the hidden dimension of the Green Ray descended to earth on the lost polar continent of Hyperborea to do battle with an inferior godling and the beast-men he had created. Some of the Hyperboreans interbred with the beast-men, creating today's humans, while others withdrew from the earth's surface into the hidden cities of Shambhala and Agharta inside the hollow earth. According to Serrano, Hitler was "the last avatar," a mighty being who withdrew to the hollow earth at the end of the Second World War before traveling home to the realm of the Green Ray. Despite their resemblance to third-rate science fiction, Serrano's theories have been adopted by a number of neo-Nazi secret societies. See **Black Sun**; **hollow earth**; **neo-Nazi secret societies**.

All of this postwar mythologizing, much of it carried out by people with little if any knowledge of actual occultism, has served mostly to cover the actual occult dimensions of National Socialism with many layers of nonsense. A few historians have looked into the Ariosophical background and occult activities of the National Socialist movement, but the definitive history of Nazi occultism remains to be written.

Further reading: Goodrick-Clarke 1992, Goodrick-Clarke 2002, Hakl 2000.

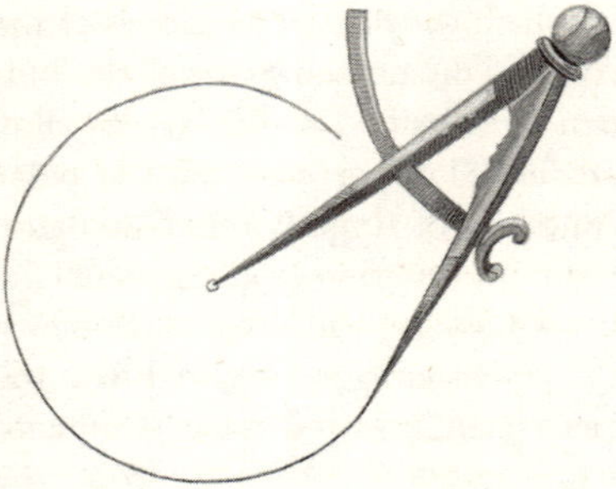

Native American secret societies

Like traditional cultures worldwide, the native peoples of North and South America have a rich and varied tradition of secret societies. A handful of Native American secret societies, including the warrior societies of the Great Plains and the shamanistic False Face Society of the Iroquois, have become fairly well known among non-native peoples in America, and commonly make brief appearances in books about secret societies around the world. Like every other aspect of Native American cultures, however, native secret societies vary dramatically from tribe to tribe, and often within individual tribes as well. Assumptions based on the traditions of one tribe rarely if ever apply to another. See **Dog Soldiers**; **False Face Society**.

One of the few generalizations that can be made about Native American secret societies is that they filled crucial functions in most native cultures, playing roles more often assigned to other forms of social organization in other cultures. Among the Lakota (Sioux) people of the northern Great Plains, for example, secret societies carried out police duties among tribespeople and enforced the traditional legal codes surrounding the buffalo hunt, while among the Hopi of the desert southwest and the Haida of the northwest coast, most traditional religious ceremonies are conducted by secret societies. Examples of other secret society functions in different tribes could be multiplied endlessly.

During the late nineteenth and early twentieth centuries, as the dominant American, Canadian, and Latin American societies tried to eliminate native cultures, most Native American secret societies faced serious restrictions and constant pressure from Christian missionaries and their converts. During the last quarter of the twentieth century, however, a widespread cultural revival among native peoples has helped revive many traditional secret societies, and ritual initiations that had not been performed for many decades are now being performed again.

Further reading: Fenton 1987, Mails 1973, Meadows 1999.

NEO-NAZI SECRET SOCIETIES

The process by which secret society fiction is recycled into secret society fact has rarely been so clearly shown as in the rise of neo-Nazi secret societies in the last decades of the twentieth century. Starting in 1960, when Louis Pauwels and Jacques Bergier published their bestselling *Le Matin du Magiciens* (*The Morning of the Magicians*), popular presses throughout the western world brought out scores of non-fiction books and hundreds of novels on Nazi occultism. A few of these drew on the actual occult connections of National Socialism, while most others invented details out of whole cloth or borrowed material from other realms of rejected knowledge, but all of them worked to create a sense in the popular imagination that the Nazi phenomenon was linked with occult mysteries and secret societies. See **National Socialism**; **rejected knowledge**.

All this was fodder for Anton Szandor LaVey (Howard Stanton Levey, 1930–97), the founder of the Church of Satan. At least as much a showman as a Satanist, LaVey produced and starred in theatrical rituals in the church's San Francisco headquarters, and the mythology of Nazi occultism inevitably found its way into his ambit. A ritual titled *Die elektrischen Vorspiele* (*The Electrical Prologue*) duly appeared, making use of the distorted perspectives of German expressionist film of the Weimar era alongside electrical equipment of the sort used in 1930s *Frankenstein* movies. Predictably, although the ritual is clearly LaVey's work, he claimed that these rituals were worked by high-ranking SS officers in Nazi Germany. See **Church of Satan**; **SS (Schutzstaffel)**.

Once launched into the Satanist community, Nazi symbolism and ritual spread quickly. By the late 1970s, Temple of Set founder Michael Aquino was working with Nazi material, a process that culminated in the foundation of the Order of the Trapezoid – a group within the Temple of Set practicing Nazi-based occult rituals – and a visit by Aquino and other Temple of Set members to the former SS ritual center at Wewelsburg, where they performed rituals to contact the forces once invoked by SS head Heinrich Himmler. The late 1970s also saw the emergence in Britain of the Order of Nine Angles, a Satanist order with close ties to the British nationalist and neo-Nazi scene. See **Order of Nine Angles**; **Temple of Set**.

The emergence of neo-Nazi occultism was also spurred by the rise and collapse of the Bruders Schweigen, a racist secret society in America that attempted to launch a guerrilla war against the US government. While its efforts ended in complete failure and the death of its founder in a hail of bullets, and most of its surviving members are still serving long prison sentences, it succeeded in bringing the existence of the Christian Identity movement, a racist offshoot of

Protestant Christianity, to the attention of the mass media. The wide publicity this gave to racist ideologies was tempered by the recognition by many racists that revolutionary violence was a risky business. This encouraged many people on the radical right to turn to occult practice as a safer way of expressing their beliefs. See **Bruders Schweigen**; **Christian Identity**.

In the last two decades of the twentieth century, well over a dozen occult secret societies using Nazi symbolism and teachings emerged. Most of these are small and localized, but close connections with the skinhead and industrial music scenes and the wider Satanist community, umbrella organizations such as the White Order of Thule, and a network of magazines, websites, and small publishing houses link them together. Despite their marginal role in contemporary culture, it might be unwise to dismiss them and their repellent creeds too lightly; the Nazi Party itself emerged out of a movement just as fragmented and marginal to its own society. See **White Order of Thule**.

Further reading: Goodrick-Clarke 2002, Gardell 1994.

New Age movement

One of the most recent branches of the alternative realities scene in the western world, the New Age movement took shape in America in the 1950s in the UFO-contactee scene, a network of people who believed they were in touch with aliens from other planets by way of trance mediums. All through the 1950s and 1960s, contactees had been bombarded with claims that an apocalypse was about to occur and usher in a new age of the world. During the 1970s, several groups in the network began to suggest that, instead of waiting for the new age to dawn, people ought to start living as though it already had. By living their lives as though the promised Utopia had arrived, they suggested, people could inspire others to do likewise and show that a living alternative to the status quo was possible. See **ages of the world**; **unidentified flying objects (UFOs)**.

These concepts caught on rapidly, and during the Seventies the movement attracted avant-garde thinkers from the scientific community. As the movement expanded, though, it became a focal point for any imaginable form of alternative thought, and the original momentum of the New Age idea faded. By the middle 1980s, nearly every form of rejected knowledge, from alternative healing and perpetual motion to conspiracy theories and the hollow earth, found a welcoming audience there A surprising amount of what makes up the New Age movement today is anything but new, and the Theosophical Society in particular contributed a huge amount to the current New Age scene. The whole New Age movement has been described as "Theosophy plus therapy," and though this is not strictly accurate, the fusion of nineteenth-century occultism with today's alternative healing methods and psychological theories does characterize a great deal of New Age thinking. See **hollow earth**; **rejected knowledge**; **Theosophical Society**.

It is hard not to sympathize with the desire to create a better world through personal example and living one's life in harmony with one's ideals, and to the extent it has fostered this project the New Age movement has contributed much to the world. In recent years, though, it has become a hunting ground for proponents of increasingly paranoid conspiracy theories, and a growing number of people who identify with the New Age have turned from radiating love to collecting guns and circulating rumors about the New World Order. While this transformation may seem surprising, much the same change occurred in the alternative spiritual scene of early twentieth-century Germany and helped lay the foundations for the Nazi movement of the 1920s and 1930s. See **Germanenorden**; **National Socialism**; **New World Order**.

New World Order

On January 16, 1991, as American aircraft bombed Baghdad in the early hours of the first Gulf War, President George H. W. Bush gave a speech proclaiming a "New World Order," in which an alliance of industrial nations would counter military aggression on the part of Third World countries worldwide. Catchy phrases of this sort have long been a staple of American political speechmaking, and Bush and his speechwriters were doubtless startled to find that within months this phrase had turned into an element in conspiracy theories around the world.

The phrase "New World Order" actually surfaced years before in the writings of John Birch Society founder Robert Welch. Once a fervent anticommunist, Welch saw conservative Republicans turn against his organization and embrace measures that, at least in his opinion, surrendered America to communist rule. His encounter with the writings of eighteenth-century Illuminati hunters Augustin de Barruel and John Robison, and their early twentieth-century followers such as Nesta Webster, explained why: conservatives no less than liberals were dupes or willing participants in an all-encompassing conspiracy. The mysterious "Insiders" who directed the plot, he believed, aimed at a global police state in which marriage, religion, private property, and individual freedom would be abolished. In 1972, he began using "New World Order" to describe the Insiders' goal. See **Bavarian Illuminati**; **John Birch Society**.

Under Welch's leadership, the John Birch Society became a major seedbed of conspiracy theory and played a central role in disseminating the distinctive secret society mythology of the late twentieth century: the belief that a single omnipotent secret society already controls the world's governments and economic systems, and is simply waiting for the right moment to cast aside the illusion of democracy and wield openly the power it currently exercises covertly. These ideas derive from the Theosophical belief in the Great White Lodge, the benevolent secret government of the planet. Antisemitic circles in late nineteenth-century Europe fused this with the conservative fear of liberal secret societies to create the myth of a single conspiracy for world domination. This provided the central theme to the *Protocols of the Elders of Zion*, the most notorious work of antisemitic literature in the twentieth century. Welch himself rejected antisemitism, but most of his claims about the Insiders simply repeat material from the *Protocols*. See **Great White Lodge**; **Protocols of the Elders of Zion**.

Writers who helped Welch put this mythology into circulation included Gary Allen, Des Griffin, and A. Ralph Epperson among others, and most got their start in the John Birch Society's magazine *American Opinion*. Gary Allen, a frequent *American Opinion* contributor, was particularly influential in the development of the New World Order idea. He argued in his *None Dare Call It Conspiracy* (1971) that the "world supra-government" behind the approaching global police state was headed by international banking families and controlled through the Council on Foreign Relations (CFR), a New York-based think-tank founded in 1923 and supported by Rockefeller money. Allen's theory was quickly adopted across the far right and became the basis of dozens of books exposing the alleged machinations of the CFR and its members. See **Council on Foreign Relations (CFR)**.

Unexpectedly, these claims also found a hearing at the other end of the political spectrum, where the collapse of the New Left in the early 1970s left many activists looking for a new ideology to replace Marxism. They found it in books such as Laurence Shoup and William Minter's *Imperial Brain Trust* (1977) and Holly Sklar's *Trilateralism* (1980), which pinpointed the CFR and its offshoot, the Trilateral Commission, as the hidden hands behind corporate imperialism in the post-Second World War world. Later works from both sides of the political spectrum drew in other familiar conspiracy theory names, such as the Committee of 300. See **Committee of 300**; **Trilateral Commission**.

Well before 1991, then, the phrase "New World Order" had become a buzzword among both left- and right-wing conspiracy theorists. Many books published in the 1980s even claimed that the phrase could be found on the back of the US dollar bill. The reverse of the Great Seal of the United States shows a pyramid topped by an eye in a triangle, and the Latin words NOVUS ORDO SECLORUM beneath; the phrase actually means "A new order for the ages" but can easily be misread "New World Order" or "New Secular Order" by those with a shaky grasp of Latin.

Thus when President Bush chose that phrase to frame his ambitions for a Pax Americana in the wake of the Soviet collapse and Iraq's defeat, the conspiracy-minded took it as confirmation of their worst fears. Bush was himself a member of the CFR and past director of the CIA. Their suspicions were heightened when Francis Fukuyama, a State Department employee with close ties to the administration, published *The End of History?*, a manifesto proclaiming the permanent ascendancy of corporate capitalism and Republican politics as the culmination of human history. To believers in conspiracy theories, Fukuyama's country club Utopia looked like a propaganda release on the part of the long-awaited global dictatorship.

Meanwhile a growing number of Christian fundamentalists were jumping on board the New World Order bandwagon. The overlap between John Birch Society political conservatives and religiously inspired social conservatives had always been large, and numerous figures on the radical fringe of the fundamentalist movement had adopted Welch's analysis in the decades before 1990. After Bush's speech, however, such talk quickly moved out of the fringes into the fundamentalist mainstream. See **fundamentalism**.

Fundamentalist minister (and presidential candidate) Pat Robertson led the way with a bestselling book, *The New World Order* (1991), that fused the John Birch Society theory of "Insiders" with Christian apocalyptic mythology. In Robertson's view, Adam Weishaupt and the Bavarian Illuminati were Satanists who initiated the Rothschild banking family into occultism and used their money to launch the French Revolution as the first move in a plot against Christianity in preparation for the coming of the Antichrist. In this way Robertson imported the entire body of twentieth-century conspiracy theory into the fundamentalist subculture. See **Antichrist**.

Even before Robertson's book made it popular, a growing number of fundamentalist writers had embraced modern conspiracy theory and adapted it to fit their religious beliefs. The huge alternative-history publishing industry, with its passion for reinterpreting Christian origins, was tailor-made for this project. Bestselling books such as *The Holy Blood and the Holy Grail* argued for the existence of a secret underworld of noble families concealing a religious tradition at odds with

Christian orthodoxy; in the hands of fundamentalist authors these became the "black nobility," an alliance of aristocrats in the service of the Antichrist.

The fundamentalist adoption of New World Order rhetoric was far from the strangest reworking of the New World Order theory. David Icke, a former BBC football commentator and Green Party candidate turned conspiracy hunter, burst onto the scene in 1995 with the first of a series of books claiming that the New World Order was under the control of alien reptiles. According to Icke, a cabal of aristocratic families, descended from lizards from another dimension, controlled the world in secret. See **Reptilians**.

As this last example suggests, the belief in an approaching New World Order has long since passed beyond the realm of history into the worlds of theology and mythic symbolism, where the mere fact that the New World Order never quite manages to arrive cannot quench the conviction of the faithful. It has also come to play an economic role as an effective marketing gimmick to boost sales of assault rifles and survival gear. These factors make it likely that the New World Order mythology will continue to unfold in the decades to come.

Further reading: Allen 1971, Fukuyama 1989, Goldberg 2001, Icke 1995, Robertson 1991, Sklar 1980.

Nihilists

A radical movement in late nineteenth-century Russia, the Nihilists emerged as the political wing of a Russian counterculture that prefigured nearly every detail of the hippie culture of the 1960s. The "New People" rebelled against the mores of Tsarist Russia with unconventional dress and manners; men grew long hair and beards, women wore their hair bobbed and refused makeup. Blue-tinted spectacles, high boots, and a passion for cigarettes formed other parts of the kit. Most were college students though few completed degrees. The New People rejected Christianity and argued for civil and sexual freedom for women, ideas that were at least as shocking in 1860s Russia as in 1960s Britain and America.

All these trends surfaced in 1855 after the death of the arch-conservative Tsar Nicholas I and the accession of his son, the more liberal Alexander II. Reforms that allowed Russian citizens to travel abroad gave many young Russians a taste of freedom and a desire for more. Many Russian students enrolled in foreign universities, especially at Heidelberg and Zurich, where they were exposed to radical ideas. In Russia, Nikolai Chernyshevsky's 1863 novel *What is to be Done?* – the story of a young woman's journey from the narrow world of middle-class St Petersburg to freedom among the New People – had the same cultural impact that Kerouac's *On the Road* had a century later among young Americans. Another novel, Ivan Turgenev's *Fathers and Sons*, attached the label of "Nihilist" to the New People, though it came to be used for the movement's political faction as the nineteenth century drew on.

This political dimension rose to prominence as Alexander II's government backed away from its more liberal reforms. Part of this withdrawal came from the Tsar's worries about the spread of radical ideas in Russia. Already in 1861 a manifesto titled *To the Younger Generation* was in circulation, calling for the Tsar to be replaced by a salaried official. Several influential writers among the New People, including Chernyshevsky himself, were imprisoned in Siberia after widely publicized trials. This served only to embitter the New People and drive more of them into revolutionary politics.

Nihilism exploded into political violence in 1866, when Dmitri Karakozov, a young student in St Petersburg, tried to assassinate the Tsar. The attempt failed, but harsh new laws passed by the Tsar's government in response launched a spiral of violence and repression that ultimately brought Russia to the threshold of the 1917 revolution. Mass arrests of suspected radicals began in 1873, but each Nihilist hanged or sent to permanent exile in Siberia was quickly replaced by others. More assassination attempts followed, some aimed at the Tsar and others targeting important government officials. A terrorist bomb thrown by Nihilists of the "People's Will" faction finally killed the Tsar on March 1, 1881.

This assassination was in many respects the last hurrah of Nihilism. By that time the New People were decidedly old news, and a younger generation of radicals was turning from the Nihilists' rejection of authority and vague belief in freedom to the new theory of social revolution proposed by a German writer named Karl Marx. See **Communism**.

Further reading: Broido 1977, Hingley 1967.

Nine Unknown Men

One of the many groups alleged to be the secret masters of the world, the Nine Unknown Men first surfaced in the writings of Louis Jacolliot (1837–90), a French colonial civil servant who wrote a number of wildly popular books on alternative history. According to Jacolliot, the order of Nine Unknown Men had been formed on the instructions of Ashoka, emperor of India in the third century BCE, as a secret government for the world. Jacolliot's claims were taken up by the mystic and writer of adventure fiction Talbot Mundy (1879–1940), who based a novel entitled *The Nine Unknowns* (1923) on the claim that the Nine remained active and influenced global politics in modern times. From there, the Nine Unknown Men found their way into modern conspiracy theory. Never as popular as the Bavarian Illuminati or the Trilateral Commission, the Nine still have their supporters among believers in one universal conspiracy that controls the world. See **Bavarian Illuminati**; **New World Order**; **Trilateral Commission**.

The Nine Unknown Men are not Jacolliot's only contribution to today's alternative-realities scene; he also invented the secret city of Agharta. See **Agharta**.

O

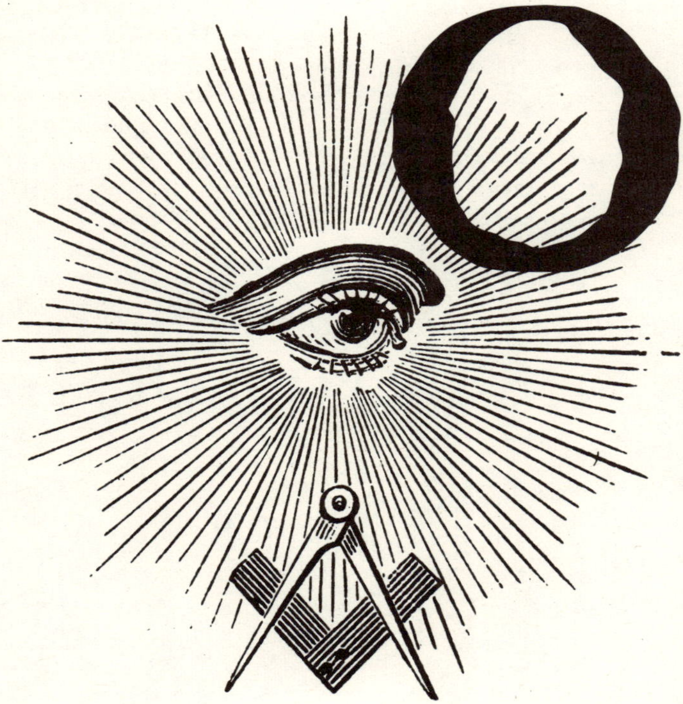

Occultism

The word "occultism" entered the English language in 1881 by way of Russian mystic Helena Petrovna Blavatsky (1831–91), founder of the Theosophical Society and one of the most influential alternative thinkers in history. The older term "occult," meaning "hidden," had been used to describe magic and related arts since the Middle Ages, but nobody before Blavatsky seems to have thought of turning the various secret traditions of magic, alchemy, astrology, and mysticism into an "ism," a system of thought and life with its own distinctive worldview. See **Blavatsky, Helena Petrovna**; **Magic**.

In the aftermath of Blavatsky's work, occultism as an organized movement and way of thought established itself throughout the world. No two occultists agree completely on what occultism is, but nearly all versions start with the idea that spiritual forces act constantly in the material world and humanity can learn to experience them directly. Disciplines such as meditation, magic, and divination are used by occultists to attune themselves to the hidden dimensions of existence, while the study of occult philosophy provides an intellectual dimension to the movement. In practice, occultism is a challenging and intensely personal path in which each individual is responsible for his or her own spiritual life.

Many current conspiracy theories insist that occultism, the New Age movement, Satanism, and rejected knowledge are the same thing, and that all secret societies are involved in the occult. This is a product of the same way of thinking that insists that all secret societies, including those that have had serious disagreements with each other for centuries, are actually one and the same. While there are points of overlap between traditional occultism, the modern New Age movement, Satanism, and the cultural underworld of rejected knowledge, the differences are much greater. See **New Age movement**; **rejected knowledge**; **Satanism**.

Secret societies, in fact, vary wildly in their attitude toward occultism. Some secret societies, such as the Hermetic Order of the Golden Dawn, exist for the purpose of teaching and practicing occultism. Others, such as Freemasonry, have had a minority of occultist members but have focused on other things. Some, such as the Knights of Pythias, have been indifferent to occultism, while others still, such as the Ku Klux Klan, have been actively hostile to it. The claim that all secret societies practice occultism is disinformation created and spread by Christian fundamentalists, who have a long history of insisting that anyone who disagrees with their worldview must secretly worship the Christian devil. See **Ancient Order of United Workmen**; **disinformation**; **Freemasonry**; **fundamentalism**; **Hermetic Order of the Golden Dawn**; **Knights of Pythias**; **Ku Klux Klan**.

Octagon Society

An American esoteric order teaching spiritual alchemy, the Octagon Society traditionally dated its founding to 1158, when members of the Knights Templar at the castle of Gisors in France devised eight spiritual laws governing the transformation of the self. The octagonal rooms within the castle's famous eight-sided tower supposedly inspired the name of the Society. In the realm of reliable history, however, the oldest surviving documents of the order date from 1958, when its Guardian, Dr. Juliet Ashley, revised the training program based on the eight laws, and those documents refer only to a 1923 text of the eight laws. This may well have been the original formulation, as the society's methods bear the stamp of early twentieth-century American esotericism and mental healing.

The spiritual alchemy taught by the society is a method of psychological healing, and the traditions of operative alchemy are used as metaphors for the transmutation of the "lead" of painful memories and psychological states into the "gold" of happiness and mental balance. The methods used have much in common with New Thought and other "mind cure" methods from the half-century before the society's apparent emergence. See **Alchemy**.

The Octagon Society has eight grades, numbered 1/8 through 8/8. Members of the 8/8 grade are eligible for advancement into two higher orders, the Temple of Solomon and the Ancient Order of Spiritual Alchemy. The Temple of Solomon claims to have been originally founded "toward the end of the first millennium, at the request of Pope John" as a military initiatory order open to single Catholic males; in its present form, it was founded in 1942 as a secret initiatory order for men and women of any religious background, and works the three degrees of Candidate, Seeker, and Student. The Ancient Order of Spiritual Alchemy was founded in 1948 by three senior members of the Octagon Society, and provides very little information about its activities to the public.

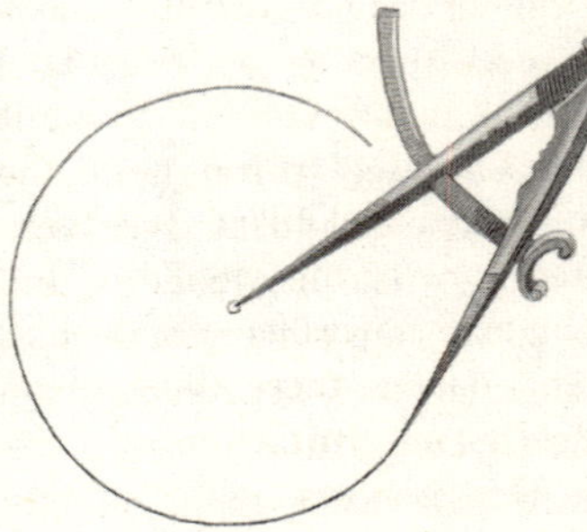

Odd Fellowship

Once the largest fraternal secret society in the world, the Odd Fellows emerged in England sometime before 1700. Documentation concerning the sources of Odd Fellowship and the origins of its quirky name did not survive the first decades of the nineteenth century, the era of the Unlawful Societies Act, but the sparse evidence suggests that the first Odd Fellows lodges evolved from craft journeymen's societies in the English Midlands and Yorkshire. The name "Odd Fellow" itself points in this direction, since "Fellow" was a standard English term for guild members of journeyman rank. See **guilds, medieval**.

Whatever its precise origin, Odd Fellowship had a significant presence in northern and central England by the early years of the eighteenth century, and some Yorkshire lodges founded before 1700 remain active today. They welcomed adult men of every profession and social standing, though the working classes always formed the majority of membership. New members were admitted by way of a single degree, called Making or Initiation, like the "brothering" rituals practiced by apprentices and servants in Scotland during these same years. See **Brothering**; **Initiation**.

The Odd Fellows quickly distinguished itself from the many other clubs and societies of the time by helping its members when they were in financial trouble. At a time when health insurance and social welfare programs were unknown, Odd Fellows lodges collected money to meet the bills of members who became ill, pay for the funerals of those who died, and support their widows and orphans. During the course of the eighteenth century this evolved into a system of regular contributions and benefits; in exchange for paying a small sum into the lodge treasury each week, members could count on fixed weekly sums for sick pay, funeral expenses, and survivor benefits. This system was widely copied by fraternal orders throughout the English-speaking world, and inspired the fraternal benefit societies of the nineteenth century. See **fraternal benefit societies**; **fraternal orders**.

With this benefit system in place, Odd Fellowship expanded steadily during the eighteenth century. Organizational stability lagged behind the growth in membership, however. In the early years of the century, each Odd Fellows lodge was effectively independent of all others. As the century went on, many lodges affiliated with one of two national organizations, the Ancient Order of Odd Fellows (which had strong Jacobite leanings) and the Patriotic Order of Odd Fellows (which was staunchly Hanoverian). See **Jacobites**.

The two orders finally united in the Grand United Order of Odd Fellows in 1802, but problems with the Grand United Order's leadership structure caused many lodges to break away from its jurisdiction within a few years. Most of those joined another Odd Fellows body, the Manchester Unity, which became the largest Odd Fellows order in Britain by 1820 and has kept that status ever since. Governed by an Annual Movable Committee, the Manchester Unity managed to negotiate the difficult years of the early nineteenth century with fair success, and expanded steadily in Britain after the ban against secret societies was removed in 1834.

As it disintegrated, the Grand United Order gained an unexpected lease of life due to American racism. In the early 1840s the Philomathean Institute, a social club for free blacks in New York City, recognized the need to provide a welfare safety net for the African-American community. Beneficial fraternal orders such as the Odd Fellows had appeared in America during the previous two decades, and the Institute applied to the Independent Order of Odd Fellows in 1843 for a charter, hoping to transform their club into an Odd Fellows lodge. Their petition was rejected out of hand by the white Odd Fellows on racial grounds. The Institute then applied to the Grand United Order of Odd Fellows in London, and promptly received a charter. When the Grand United Order finally broke apart in England a few years later, and its surviving English lodges joined the Manchester Unity, the Grand United Order's American lodges founded their own Grand Lodge and carried on. By the end of the nineteenth century the Grand United Order was one of the largest African-American fraternal orders, and also had a sizeable presence in eastern Canada and the West Indies. See **African-American secret societies**.

In the meantime, the largest and most influential of the world's Odd Fellow orders had been launched in America – the Independent Order of Odd Fellows (IOOF). In 1819, an English Odd Fellow named Thomas Wildey and four other members from England formed the first successful Odd Fellows lodge in the United States in Baltimore, Maryland. The Odd Fellows system of contributions and benefits proved popular in the new republic, and by 1830 Odd Fellows lodges existed in all the states of the Atlantic coast. In that year disputes with the Manchester Unity led the American lodges to cut their ties with Britain and found a new order, the IOOF.

The antimasonic movement in America in the 1820s and 1830s helped the new order attract members, as Odd Fellowship had not yet been tarred by the brush applied so lavishly to Freemasonry; when an attempt was made in the late 1840s to launch a similar campaign against Odd Fellowship the Independent Order weathered it easily. See **Antimasonic Party**; **Antimasonry**.

The expansion of white settlement in the West of the country brought Odd Fellowship into a period of explosive growth; as new towns sprang up across the continent Odd Fellows lodges rose with them. By 1880, soaring population growth in America and Britain, together with the founding of IOOF lodges in Australasia and Europe, the steady growth of the Grand United Order among African Americans, and the expansion of the Manchester Unity to eastern Canada, had made Odd

Fellowship the largest fraternal secret society in the world.

Paralleling this growth was an expansion of the ritual dimensions of Odd Fellowship. By the middle of the eighteenth century other degrees, many of them strongly influenced by Masonry, had been added to the single degree of the old Odd Fellows lodges. The oldest surviving ritual, dating from 1798, has Initiatory, White, Pink, and Blue Degrees, followed by the degree of the Royal Arch of Titus, modeled on the Royal Arch degree of Masonry. Organizational problems made uniformity between lodges impossible, but other Odd Fellow orders had degree sequences more or less paralleling this. See **Freemasonry**; **high degrees**; **Royal Arch**.

The most dramatic expansion of degrees took place in the Independent Order. By 1820 IOOF worked the Initiatory Degree; the White or First Degree; the Pink or Covenant Degree; the Royal Blue or Second Degree; the Green or Remembrance Degree; and the Royal Scarlet or Third Degree. In 1821 a new branch of the order appeared, the Encampment branch, modeled on the Royal Arch Chapter of Freemasonry; it had three further degrees – the Patriarchal, Golden Rule, and Royal Purple degrees – which could be received by Third Degree Odd Fellows. The birth of the first ladies auxiliary of any American fraternal order, the Daughters of Rebekah, took place in 1852, with one degree, the Rebekah Degree, and 1880 saw a major revision of the Odd Fellows Lodge rituals, which were condensed from six to four degrees. In 1885 came a uniformed branch for Odd Fellowship, the Patriarchs Militant, and a ladies auxiliary for the uniformed branch, the Ladies Auxiliary Patriarchs Militant, followed in 1903. See **ladies auxiliaries**.

The Independent Order reached its zenith around 1920, with a membership of some 9 million. The years after the First World War proved difficult for the order, however, and membership began to decline. The Great Depression was an unmitigated disaster for the order; many lodges, hoping to expand their benefit funds, invested them in the stock market of the late 1920s and lost everything in the market crash of 1929 and 1930, leaving them without assets at a time when their members needed more help than ever before. The reforms of the American New Deal in the late 1930s weakened the order further as government programs supplanted Odd Fellowship's benefit system. The 1950s saw a modest recovery, but the cultural revolution of the 1960s began a period of rapid decline as middle-aged and elderly Odd Fellows and Rebekahs, offended by the manners of the younger generation, closed the doors of their lodges against new members. The same patterns were repeated in the Manchester Unity and the Grand United Order as old customs and cultural expectations turned into barriers few potential members were willing to cross.

A new phase in Odd Fellowship's history began in 1984, when the Manchester Unity voted to admit women to regular membership in Odd Fellows lodges. After much debate, the Independent Order passed similar measures in 2000. During these same years, much-needed reforms helped encourage an influx of younger members into the Odd Fellow orders, and began to level out the steep declines in membership. At present the Independent Order remains active in the United States, Canada, and 24 other countries; the Grand United Order has lodges in the eastern half of the United States and the former British colonies in the West Indies; and the Manchester Unity has lodges throughout Britain and in eastern Canada. While the immense size and influence held by Odd Fellows a century ago is barely even remembered, all three orders seem likely to survive for the foreseeable future.

Opus Dei

The most controversial religious organization in the Roman Catholic Church today, the Prelature of the Holy Cross and Opus Dei – to give it its full name – was founded in Madrid in 1928 by a conservative Catholic priest, Josemaría Escrivá de Balaguer, as an association of Catholic laypersons. It currently has some 85,000 members in over 80 countries, primarily in Europe and the Americas. About 20 percent of those are "numeraries," single members who live in Opus Dei residential buildings and donate all their earnings to the association; the others are "supernumeraries" and "associates," who live on their own but contribute money and time to Opus Dei activities. See **Roman Catholic Church**.

Opus Dei is highly regarded by many figures in the upper reaches of the Roman Catholic hierarchy. It was granted the special status of "personal prelature" by Pope John Paul II in 1982, a status that frees its members and activities from the authority of local bishops and church officials, and its founder was elevated to sainthood in 2002. While church officials speak glowingly of Opus Dei, its many critics, including a large number of ex-members, describe it as a secret society with a right-wing political agenda, and accuse it of using unscrupulous recruitment methods.

Some of the criticisms leveled against the organization unfold from the inevitable clash between the expectations of a modern liberal society and the almost medieval form of Catholic spirituality practiced in Opus Dei, which includes various forms of physical self-torture and strict segregation of the sexes. Another factor in the controversies surrounding it is the perennial struggle between the central authority of Rome and local Catholic institutions. As a religious order free from the control of local bishops, Opus Dei has become a target for the same pressures that once focused on the Knights Templar and the Jesuits, two older orders that once possessed the same independence. On the other hand, Opus Dei's renowned secrecy and its use of cult-like recruitment techniques do provide ammunition for its detractors. See **Knights Templar**; **Society of Jesus (Jesuits)**.

Further reading: Allen 2005, Walsh 1989.

Order of American Knights [OAK]

A pro-Confederacy secret society during the American Civil War, the Order of American Knights (OAK) was founded by Phineas C. Wright in 1863 in St Louis, Missouri. Similar to the Knights of the Golden Circle but more deeply committed to a militant approach, the Order quickly spread throughout the Midwestern states, absorbing much of the membership of the Knights of the Golden Circle and spreading as far east as New York state. The leader of the Knights of the Golden Circle, Clement Vallandigham, then in exile in Canada, also accepted the post of Grand Commander of the Order of American Knights. See **Knights of the Golden Circle**.

The Order's major strength was in Ohio, Indiana, Illinois, Missouri, Kentucky, and Michigan. Its membership reached somewhere between 300,000 and 400,000 in 1864. It had a complete military organization, from the general staff of the Supreme Commander to the local township Temples, organized as companies each headed by its Captain. Despite this, the Knights never managed to oppose Federal troops effectively, and their military activities were limited to occasional guerrilla activities in Illinois and Indiana. With the backing of the Confederacy, the Order attempted to launch a revolt in the Midwest in July 1864, with the goal of breaking the entire region away from the Union, but the attempt failed dismally.

The OAK went out of existence after the defeat of the Confederacy in 1865, but its legacy can be traced in the Midwest for decades thereafter. The same states that provided the bulk of OAK membership were also, six decades later, among the most successful recruiting grounds for the revived Ku Klux Klan. See **Ku Klux Klan**.

Further reading: Gray 1942.

Order of Anti-Poke-Noses

Founded in Searcy County, Arkansas in 1923, the Order of Anti-Poke-Noses was a secret society founded to oppose the revived Ku Klux Klan. Its constitution stated that the Order was "opposed to any organization that attends to everyone's business but their own." One of several secret societies founded in the 1920s to oppose the Klan, it ceased activities around the time the revived Klan collapsed at the end of that decade. See **Knights of Liberty**; **Knights of the Flaming Circle**; **Ku Klux Klan**.

Order of Bards Ovates and Druids [OBOD]

The largest and most active Druid order in the world as of this writing, the Order of Bards Ovates and Druids (OBOD) was founded by Ross Nichols (1902–75) and a group of fellow Druids from the Druid Circle of the Universal Bond after a disputed election for the leadership of the latter group. Nichols, a poet and painter who had served as the Universal Bond's secretary for some years, focused his new order's work on the bardic arts of poetry and music, and brought in the three grades of Bard, Ovate, and Druid from Welsh traditions of Druidry. Never large, OBOD nonetheless played an important role in publicizing Druidry in Britain, but on Nichols's death in 1975 it went dormant. See **Druid Circle of the Universal Bond**; **Druid Revival**.

In 1984 one of the youngest initiates of the order in Nichols's time, Philip Carr-Gomm, was asked to take over OBOD and revive it. Carr-Gomm borrowed one of the core approaches of early twentieth-century occult groups, the postal correspondence course, and applied it to Druidry, apparently for the first time. The result was a dramatic expansion of the order. From a handful of inactive members at the time of his accession, OBOD has expanded into an international Druid order with some 60 groves and seed groups on four continents. Its members are active in tree planting and ecological causes. Carr-Gomm's books on Druidry, and his edition of Nichols's erudite work *The Book of Druidry* (1992), have been extremely influential in the modern Druid scene.

Further reading: Carr-Gomm 1993, Nichols 1992.

Order of Camels

Founded in Milwaukee, Wisconsin in 1920, the Order of Camels was a political secret society dedicated to overturning Prohibition in America. The founding members chose the camel for their emblem because it can withstand long dry periods. Members took an oath with only one clause, pledging themselves to support the legalization of alcohol. Like several other fraternal secret societies of the time, the Camels probably took part in smuggling alcohol into the United States from Canada. In 1933, with the end of Prohibition, the Order quietly went out of existence.

Order of Mopses

When Pope Clement XII formally condemned Freemasonry in 1738, many Catholic members of the Craft in Germany, France, and Austria had to renounce Masonic membership. The desire for a secret society on Masonic lines that would be acceptable to the Catholic Church inspired several Viennese ex-Masons to create a new organization, the Order of Mopses. The name of the order derived from the German word *mops*, pug dog, whose fidelity and affection were to be imitated by initiates. Members seeking admission at the door of a Mopses lodge had to bark like a pug dog. See **Antimasonry**; **Freemasonry**.

Unlike Freemasonry, the Mopses admitted women as well as men to membership, and may have played an important role in inspiring adoptive Masonry in the 1760s. The Mopses had parallel male and female officers all the way up to a Grand Master and Grand Mistress, who each had supreme authority over the order for six months out of each year. During the 1740s and 1750s, when the popularity of the Mopses was at its height, its membership included many of the most illustrious members of the German and Austrian nobility. It apparently went out of existence, however, in the early years of the French Revolution. See **Adoptive Masonry**.

Order of Nine Angles [ONA]

The most important British neo-Nazi magical order, the Order of the Nine Angles (ONA) emerged in the 1960s out of the fusion of three small British neo-pagan groups, Camlad, The Noctulians, and the Temple of the Sun. During the mid-1970s it came under the control of David Myatt (1950–), who combined a longtime interest in occultism with extensive involvement in the British skinhead and nationalist scene. Myatt had attracted headlines starting in 1974 as the head of the National Democratic Freedom Movement, a short-lived racist party with a reputation for violence, and served two prison terms for involvement in street fights. After becoming head of ONA, Myatt fused these interests and soon made the order a major presence in British Satanist circles. See **neo-Nazi secret societies**.

The ONA presents Satanism as a path of self-overcoming in a chaotic, amoral universe. The Satanist must break through his own limitations through acts generally considered illegal and evil in order to come into contact with a sinister, acausal realm of hidden magical forces. Access to those forces takes place through nine "nexions" or angles of the Tree of Wyrd, the basic symbolic diagram of the order. The nexions can only be opened by the performance of evil deeds of various kinds. Myatt's writings thus argue that human sacrifice is an important ritual practice for Satanists, and dwell at length on the proper selection of victims – primarily people reviled by society, though Christians and journalists are also suggested. These comments have landed Myatt in heated debates with Satanists such as Michael Aquino of the Temple of Set, who seek to make Satanism socially acceptable. See **Satanism**; **Temple of Set**.

Another branch of ONA teaching consists of "Aeonics," the magical study of history. Drawing on the historical writings of Oswald Spengler and Arnold Toynbee, ONA texts on Aeonics argue that the western world is imprisoned in a prolonged "time of troubles" caused by a contamination of western, Faustian ideas with an older, decadent Magian cultural pattern, which Myatt predictably identifies with the Jews. Satanic rituals help overcome the Magian contamination and hasten the arrival of Vindex, the future dictator who will establish the western world empire of the future on the heaped corpses of its opponents. See **ages of the world**.

Further reading: Goodrick-Clarke 2002, Myatt 1984.

Order of the Amaranth

One of several American orders drawing their membership from Master Masons and their female relatives, the Order of the Amaranth was originally founded in 1860 by James B. Taylor, a Freemason in New Jersey, under the name of "the Ancient Rite of Adoptive Masonry." Taylor drew his inspiration from the older French systems of adoptive Masonry, the rival Order of the Eastern Star, and a chivalric order founded by Queen Christina of Sweden in the seventeenth century. See **Adoptive Masonry**; **Freemasonry**; **Order of the Eastern Star**.

Taylor's Ancient Rite fared poorly in the scramble for popularity among fraternal orders in mid-nineteenth-century America, and by 1873 what was left of it had been taken over by Robert Macoy, one of the leading American Masonic promoters and publishers of the time. Macoy also ran the Order of the Eastern Star, and set about combining the two organizations into a single "Rite of Adoption of the World" with three degrees. The Order of the Eastern Star, in Macoy's system, became the first or Initiatory Degree; the second degree was a little-used rite named Queen of the South, while the Order of the Amaranth was the third.

The combination of the rites proved to be unworkable, however, as leading members of the Order of the Eastern Star disliked the fact that their organization was at the bottom of the degree sequence. In 1897 the Order of the Amaranth separated from the Rite of Adoption of the World and became an independent body, though its female membership remained limited to members of the Order of the Eastern Star. In 1921 this last connection was severed and the Order of the

Amaranth began admitting Master Masons and their female relatives without requiring an Eastern Star connection.

The Order of the Amaranth remains active today, although its membership has declined in recent years along with that of all Masonic concordant bodies. As a social and charitable organization, its major activities are raising money for diabetes research and assisting with other Masonic activities.

Further reading: Voorhis 1997.

Order of the Eastern Star [OES]

The largest American Masonic organization for women, the Order of the Eastern Star was the brainchild of Robert Morris, an influential American Freemason. Morris was familiar with the French system of adoptive Masonry – a rite with its own lodges and degrees for Master Masons and their female relatives – and in 1850 began to draft a ritual for an equivalent American system, using narratives from the Bible as its basis. Some evidence suggests that an earlier adoptive degree with the same name may have had a role in Morris's creation. He founded the first Constellations (as local lodges were then called) of the Eastern Star in 1852, but Morris's organizational skills proved inadequate, and his system struggled along for more than a decade with limited success. See **Adoptive Masonry**.

In 1866, before an extended trip to Palestine, Morris gave control over the Eastern Star system to Robert Macoy, one of the most enterprising Masonic promoters of the age. Macoy completely reorganized the rite, and relaunched it with much more success. In place of Constellations and Families, Macoy named local units "chapters," with state and provincial Grand Chapters and an international General Grand Chapter to govern them. In 1873, after Macoy gained control of the rival Order of the Amaranth, he joined the two degrees together with a third, the Queen of the South degree, to form the grandly titled Rite of Adoption of the World. In this rite the Order of the Eastern Star formed the first degree, the second was the Queen of the South, and the Order of the Amaranth was the third degree. See **Order of the Amaranth**.

The combined system proved unworkable, however; members of Eastern Star chapters in particular resented having their order being turned into the lowest rung of an initiatory ladder. In 1897 the Rite of Adoption broke apart and the three degrees went their separate ways. The Order of the Eastern Star proved far and away the most successful, and quickly rose to its present position as the dominant women's organization within Masonry. A social and charitable organization, its main activities today include raising money for a galaxy of charitable causes and helping to support the activities of other Masonic bodies. Like all Masonic bodies, the Order of the Eastern Star has suffered sharp declines in membership numbers in recent decades but it remains as active as any of the Craft's concordant bodies.

Morris's choice of symbolism for his newly minted order had unexpected effects in the late twentieth century, when the rise of Christian fundamentalism and conspiracy theories sparked a revival of antimasonic agitation in America and elsewhere. The emblem Morris created for his order was a five-pointed and five-colored star with one point down, bearing the initial letters of the sentence "Fairest Among Ten thousand, Altogether Lovely." This fine example of Victorian American sentimentality took on entirely different meanings a century later, when an inverted pentagram with the word FATAL in it was redefined as a Satanic symbol. The Eastern Star logo has thus appeared frequently in modern books attempting to prove that Freemasonry is a secret cult of devil worshippers. See **Antimasonry**; **Pentagram**; **Satanism**.

Order of the Garter

The premier order of chivalry in Great Britain, the Most Noble Order of the Garter is not a secret society in any sense of the word, but it has more than once been labeled a secret society by conspiracy theorists. It was originally founded by King Edward III sometime between 1344 and 1350, probably in 1348. The Order's membership was originally limited to the reigning English monarch and 25 knights. This has been expanded somewhat in recent centuries, although the extra members are not counted among the official numbers of Garter Knights. The Order's traditional patron is St George, its annual meeting is on St George's Day, and its original badge is a blue garter worn on the left leg, bearing in gold the words *Honi soit qui mal y pense*, "Shame be on him who thinks evil of it" in medieval French.

The origins of the Order and its emblem are uncertain. The traditional story has it that the king, attending a ball in Calais during his campaigns in France, happened to be nearby when a lady accidentally dropped her garter. The king picked it up, and faced down the onlookers with the words *Honi soit qui mal y pense.* He then tied the garter around his own knee and said "I will make of this, ere long, the most honourable garter that ever was worn." The story does not appear in written sources before 1550, when the notoriously inaccurate historian Polydore

Vergil mentioned it, and later historians of the Order of the Garter from Elias Ashmole on have rejected it as pure legend. See **Ashmole, Elias**.

According to the "Old Religion" hypothesis of Margaret Murray, however, this event reveals that the Order of the Garter was originally a witch coven. Murray argued that the witch persecutions of the Middle Ages were an attempt by the Catholic Church to stamp out an ancient Pagan fertility religion that worshipped a horned god of nature. The garter was allegedly one of the emblems of the Old Religion, and its sudden appearance on the floor betrayed the fact that its wearer was a high priestess of the witch cult. By picking it up Edward III indicated that the witch cult was under his personal protection, and the original Order, with its 26 members, was a double coven (2 x 13 members). The fact that its membership was entirely male, in flat contravention of normal practice in a fertility cult, does not seem to have occurred to Murray. See **Murray hypothesis**; **witchcraft persecutions**.

Further reading: de la Bere 1964.

Order of the Golden and Rosy Cross

An influential German Rosicrucian order, the Order of the Golden and Rosy Cross (*Orden des Gold- und Rosenkreutz*) was founded in the late 1750s by German Freemason and alchemist Hermann Fichtuld and a circle of fellow occultists. Like most of the occult secret societies of the time, candidates for membership had to be Master Masons in good standing. Unlike most of the Masonic rites of its time, though, the Golden and Rosy Cross was allied with the conservative movement in European politics and culture, and seems to have taken shape in opposition to the Rite of Strict Observance, a neo-Templar Masonic rite with close ties to France and links to liberal circles in Germany. See **Freemasonry**; **Rosicrucians**; **Rite of Strict Observance**.

The conservatism of the eighteenth century, unlike modern conservatism, saw nothing wrong with occult practices. The Golden and Rosy Cross was among the most active occult orders of its time, requiring students to study alchemical and mystical literature, and members of its higher degrees carried out extensive experiments in the alchemy of metals. It was among the first occult secret societies to establish a formal curriculum of study for each of its degrees. See **Alchemy**.

The origin story circulated by the order was colorful even by the standards of the time. It claimed to have been founded by Ormus, an Egyptian magician who converted to Christianity in 96 CE. He founded a secret society, the Society of Ormus, to pass on a Christianized version of ancient Egyptian wisdom, and assigned its members a red cross as their symbol. A little later, the Society of Ormus united with another secret society organized by the Essenes to form the Order of the Rose Cross. In 1188, members of the order initiated the Knights Templar in Palestine, who then traveled to Europe; three masters went to Scotland, where they founded the Order of the Masons of the East, the original version of Freemasonry. Another member, Raymond Lully (Ramon Lull), came to England and initiated Edward, Prince of Wales (later King Edward I) in 1196. The awkward facts that Edward I was not born until 1239, and that he was never Prince of Wales – he created that title for his son, the future Edward II, in 1301 – do little to lend credibility to this account. See **Essenes**; **Knights Templar**; **Ormus**.

Other claims insisted that the order had actually arrived in Britain long before the twelfth century, and was established there in the time of King Arthur; some also mentioned that each Grand Master from the beginning took the name "John" followed by a number. These claims were cited in a nineteenth-century collection of French Masonic materials, and Pierre Plantard borrowed liberally from them for his Priory of Sion hoax. See **Arthurian legends**; **Priory of Sion**.

During the late eighteenth century the Order was among the most successful secret societies of its time. Its membership included many German aristocrats, and in 1786 one of its members ascended to the throne of Prussia as King Friedrich Wilhelm II and appointed several other members to high political positions. It outlived its original rival, the Rite of Strict Observance, and carried on lively feuds with the Bavarian Illuminati and a splinter group from its own ranks, the Asiatic Brethren. After Friedrich Wilhelm's death in 1797, however, the sweeping social changes that followed the French Revolution sent the order into a steep decline, and it does not seem to have survived the Napoleonic Wars. See **Bavarian Illuminati**.

Order of the Happy

The Order of the Happy (*Ordre des Felicitaires*) was founded in 1743 in Paris. One of the first secret societies to admit women as well as men to membership, it may have been inspired by the Mopses, a Catholic secret society of the same kind founded in Vienna five years earlier. Its symbolism was entirely nautical, with candidates symbolically sailing from the Island of Felicity. The degree system included four degrees, Cabin Boy, Captain, Commodore, and Vice-Admiral, and the presiding officer of the Order's one lodge was titled the Admiral. See **Order of Mopses**.

The Order gave rise to at least one offshoot, the Knights and Ladies of the Anchor, founded in 1745. Both these organizations sank without a trace sometime in the late 1740s or early 1750s, but they helped inspire the more successful Order of Woodcutters and Adoptive Masonry later on. See **Adoptive Masonry**; **Order of Woodcutters**.

Order of the Helmet

In one of a series of plays written by Francis Bacon (1561–1626) and performed by his fellow law students at Gray's Inn before he was called to the Bar in 1582, a fictional order of chivalry called the Order of the Helmet had a role. The Order was modeled on the English chivalric orders of the Garter and the Bath, and as far as anyone has been able to tell it had no existence outside the play for which it was written. None of this has prevented secret societies from the nineteenth century onward from claiming that the Order of the Helmet was a real secret society, headed by Bacon, and placing it in their origin stories. See **Aurum Solis**; **Bacon, Francis**; **origin stories**.

Order of the Star in the East

One of several groups organized by the Theosophical Society in the early twentieth century under Annie Besant's leadership, the Order of the Star in the East was founded in 1911 at the Society's headquarters in Adyar, near Bombay. The inspiration behind it came from Charles Leadbeater, one of Besant's close allies, who became convinced that Jiddu Krishnamurti – the young son of a servant at the Adyar headquarters – was the next great World Teacher, a being on the same level of Jesus of Nazareth or the Buddha. The Order was founded to publicize these claims and prepare the world to receive Krishnamurti's teachings. See **Theosophical Society**.

The announcement of Krishnamurti's near-messianic status became an immediate bone of contention between Besant and many old-school Theosophists, and added to the stresses already caused by Besant's advocacy of Co-Masonry and the Liberal Catholic Church. The results included several major schisms within the society. The largest was the 1912 departure of Rudolf Steiner, secretary of the Society's German section, who took 90 percent of German Theosophists with him into his new Anthroposophical

Society. See **Anthroposophical Society; Co-Masonry**.

Despite these tumults, the message that a World Teacher had arrived was one that many people wanted to hear after the senseless carnage of the First World War, and through the 1920s the Order grew steadily, reaching a membership of well over 100,000 in 1929. In that year, however, it came to an abrupt end at the hands of Jiddu Krishnamurti himself. In an act of uncommon courage, addressing a mass gathering of his supporters, Krishnamurti rejected the status of World Teacher, declared that, "truth is a pathless land," and dissolved the Order. This debacle put the Theosophical Society into a decline from which it has never managed to recover. Krishnamurti went on to a long and distinguished career writing and teaching his own spiritual philosophy, but he steadfastly refused to allow any organization to be formed around him.

Order of the White Rose

One of the odder secret societies of Victorian Britain, the Order of the White Rose was founded in 1886 in London under the leadership of Bertram, Earl of Ashburnham (1840–1913) for the purpose of promoting the restoration of the House of Stuart to the British throne. The Stuart heir at that point was Princess Maria of Bavaria, a descendant of one of Charles I's daughters, while the reigning monarch, Queen Victoria, was a descendant of Charles I's sister; this may not seem like much of a distinction, but in the hothouse world of Victorian Jacobitism it served as a lightning rod for romantic fantasies and a reactionary political agenda. See **Jacobites**.

The order took its name from the white rose of York, the badge of the Stuart house during the Jacobite rebellions. Its formal purpose was to work for the restoration of the Stuart line to the British throne, to oppose all democratic tendencies, and to support the theory of the absolute power of kings by divine right. It established a newspaper, *The Royalist*, and had branches in Canada and the United States. In 1889 it arranged an exhibition on the history of the Stuarts in London, but contemporary magazine articles dismissed it as a "sleepy little society" more fond of ritual than practical action.

The Order of the White Rose had close connections to legitimist and reactionary political movements across Europe, but these international ties became its downfall. In 1914, at the outbreak of the First World War, members of the Order were appalled to hear that Prince Ruprecht of Bavaria, whom they considered Duke of Cornwall and Prince Consort to the Stuart queen Mary IV, had been appointed commander of the German forces. The Order promptly dissolved and has not been refounded since.

Order of Woodcutters

One of the first modern secret societies open to men and women alike, the Order of Woodcutters (*Ordre des Fendeurs*) was founded in Paris in 1747 by the Chevalier Beauchaine, an enthusiastic French Freemason who hoped to establish a society like his beloved Masonic lodge in which women could participate alongside men. He drew some of his inspiration from the earlier Order of the Happy, which seems to have been the first French "androgynous" lodge, but took from Masonry the idea of drawing symbolism from a working-class profession. Lodges of the Order were therefore called woodyards, symbolically surrounded by forest. The presiding officer had the title of Père-Maître (Father-Master), and members referred to one another as cousins. A single degree of initiation sufficed for the Order. See **Freemasonry**; **Order of the Happy**.

Beauchaine's Masonic connections and his skill as a ritualist guaranteed the new Order a positive reception, and it quickly became popular among the highest aristocratic circles in Paris and elsewhere in France. More than a dozen societies built on similar lines emerged in the following decade, inspired by its success. The emergence of adoptive Masonry around 1760 capped this period of expansion, and launched a movement that remains active up to the present. See **Adoptive Masonry**.

Ironically, another offshoot of the Order of Woodcutters went in a direction neither Beauchaine nor his aristocratic fellow-Masons would have approved. In the 1780s, one of the most popular societies in southeastern France called itself la Charbonnerie (the Charcoal Burners), and used a number of the Woodcutters' traditions, including the use of the term "cousin" for members. One of its initiates, Pierre Joseph Briot, drew heavily on la Charbonnerie's traditions when he launched a political secret society in Italy to oppose Napoleon Bonaparte's seizure of power there. That organization became the most widespread and feared of the radical secret societies of the early nineteenth century, the Carbonari. See **Carbonari**.

Ordo Novi Templi [ONT]

One of the most influential secret societies in the proto-Nazi underworld of early twentieth-century central Europe, the Ordo Novi Templi (Order of New Templars, ONT) was founded by Austrian occultist Jörg Lanz von Liebenfels (1874–1954) in Vienna in 1907. A defrocked Benedictine monk, Lanz (the "von Liebenfels" was an affectation) had become convinced that the mystery cults of the ancient world had all been devoted to deviant sex with subhuman dwarfs, and that the original Aryans had been godlike beings possessed of strange electrical-psychic powers, which had been lost to humanity due to inbreeding with the subhuman dwarfs. In 1905 he published his magnum opus, *Theozoologie, oder die Kunde von den Sodoms-Afflingen und dem Gotter-Elektron* (*Theozoology, or the Lore of the Sodom-Apelings and the Electron of the Gods*), which expounded this theory in vast and titillating detail.

These ideas won him a following in German and Austrian racist circles, and enabled him to launch a successful magazine, *Ostara*, which combined reactionary politics and antisemitic diatribes with long disquisitions about "theozoology" and the lost occult powers of the ancient Aryans. Lanz also became active in the Ariosophical scene, and was a founding member of the Guido von List Society, the parent body of the Höhere Armanen-Orden (Higher Armanen-Order, HAO), another Ariosophical secret society. See **Höhere Armanen-Orden (HAO)**.

In 1907 Lanz had attracted enough of a following to launch a secret society of his own. The Ordo Novi Templi was headquartered at Burg Werfenstein, a medieval castle on the Danube donated by a wealthy supporter, and combined Lanz's theories with a ritual system devoted to the new racial gnosis of "the Electron and the Holy Grail." Daily ceremonies of Matins (dawn), Prime (noon), and Compline (night) included Aryan hymns, liturgical readings, and devotional imagery modeled on Lanz's monastic background. The ONT liturgy expanded to fill seven large volumes by the time it was completed in the mid-1920s.

Advancement in the order depended largely on the candidate's percentage of Aryan blood, as determined by stringent tests devised by Lanz. Those with less than 50 percent Aryan ancestry could never advance beyond the lowest degree of Server; those with 50 percent or above could become Novices and then Masters, while a minimum of 75 percent was required to reach the degree of Canon. Masters or Canons who founded a new chapter of the order received the title of Presbyter, while Presbyters whose chapters had more than five Masters or Canons were advanced to the rank of Prior.

The racial tests and ritual life of the ONT helped inspire Heinrich Himmler's reinvention of the SS as a *Deutsche Mannerbund* ("Order of German Manhood") dedicated to racial purity and service to the Nazi cause. Despite these similarities, or just possibly because of them, the ONT was banned in Germany as soon as the Nazi government took power, and abolished in Austria after the *anschluss* of 1938. Lanz himself had the good sense to move to Switzerland in 1933, and remained there through the war years. In 1946 he returned home to Vienna, and revived the ONT. It remains active today in Austria, Germany, and several other central European countries. See **National Socialism**; **SS (Schutzstaffel)**.

Ordo Templi Astarte [OTA]

One of many occult secret societies active in America today, the Ordo Templi Astarte (Order of Templars of Astarte, OTA) was founded by American magician Carroll "Poke" Runyon in 1970. Runyon received an irregular Ordo Templi Orientis charter from Louis Culling in that year, but quickly moved away from OTO traditions to construct an eclectic magical system of his own, based on the eighteenth-century ritual system of the Crata Repoa, the teachings of the Hermetic Order of the Golden Dawn, the gods and goddesses of the ancient Phoenicians, and his own discoveries in the field of the evocation of spirits through mirror magic. See **Crata Repoa**; **Hermetic Order of the Golden Dawn**; **Ordo Templi Orientis (OTO)**; **Scrying**.

Like most of the magical orders of the late twentieth century, the Ordo Templi Astarte is relatively small, with two lodges – both in the state of California – and a membership well below 100. It has nonetheless had a significant influence on the occult scene in America and elsewhere, largely by way of Runyon's publications and the order's magazine, *The Seventh Ray*.

Ordo Templi Orientis [OTO]

One of the largest and most active occult secret societies in the world today, the Ordo Templi Orientis (Order of Oriental Templars) was created by Carl Kellner, a wealthy Austrian industrial magnate, and Theodor Reuss, a journalist and former opera singer. Both men were Freemasons interested in occultism and the more exotic Masonic degrees, and Kellner was an initiate of the Hermetic Brotherhood of Light, a secret society that taught a distinctive system of sexual magic. In 1895 the two began planning a "Masonic academy" of esoteric studies. See **Hermetic Brotherhood of Light**; **Reuss, Theodor**.

In 1902 Reuss obtained from John Yarker, the premier purveyor of fringe Masonic degrees at that time, a charter for a German grand lodge of the Ancient and Primitive Rite of Memphis and Misraim, and Reuss and Kellner put out a prospectus for their new rite the next year. A year after Kellner's death in 1905, the Ordo Templi Orientis was formally founded and began initiating members. See **Rite of Memphis and Misraim**; **Yarker, John**.

In its original form, the OTO had nine degrees drawn from the irregular Masonic systems of central Europe, with a tenth, administrative degree for the head of the order in each country. The central secret of sexual magic was reserved for the ninth degree. The order attracted many members from the European avant-garde, and an influential lodge was established in Switzerland at Zurich, near the famous Monte Veritas commune, the headquarters of the alternative scene in Europe before and during the First World War.

In 1910, hoping to expand the order further by recruiting a charismatic figure, Reuss conferred the first seven degrees of the OTO on Aleister Crowley, and in 1912 made Crowley the head of the OTO in Britain. He soon regretted the move, for Crowley reorganized the order to conform to his own eccentric beliefs, centering on his own status as prophet of the New Aeon of Horus. Crowley ordered that the *Book of the Law,* the scripture of his new religion of Thelema, be the only Volume of the Sacred Law used in OTO lodges, and by 1913 he was quarreling with most of the British members, accusing several of embezzlement and expelling others for crimes such as absenteeism and indifference. Crowley relocated to America in 1914, and the order in Britain struggled on until 1917, when British police raided the OTO's offices and seized all the order's books and property. See **Crowley, Aleister**.

The huge market for occult secret societies in the United States attracted attention from both Reuss and Crowley. In 1914 Crowley's protegé Charles Stansfield Jones established the first OTO lodge in North America, Agape Lodge in Vancouver, British Columbia. In 1915 Reuss entered into contact with H. Spencer Lewis, an American occultist who later launched the Ancient Mystical Order Rosae Crucis, and gave him a charter for an OTO lodge. In 1916 Crowley countered by making Jones head of the order in North America. The final moves in the game were made in 1921, as Reuss made Lewis a member of the European branch of the order, and raised him to the degrees of 33°, 90°, 95°, and VII° in the Scottish Rite, Rite of Memphis, Rite of Misraim, and OTO respectively. However, Lewis was already developing his own system by this time, and distanced himself from Reuss, correctly judging that there was nothing to be gained by wrestling with Crowley for the miniscule American OTO franchise. See **Ancient and Accepted Scottish Rite (AASR)**; **Ancient Mystical Order Rosae Crucis (AMORC)**.

Reuss died in 1923. On his death, Crowley proclaimed himself Outer Head of the Order, though very few of the European members of the OTO accepted his leadership. Crowley struggled for the rest of his life to establish the OTO as a Thelemic magical order, and failed completely. At the time of his death in 1947 the OTO consisted of a handful of European lodges that rejected his teachings completely, and one lodge in Pasadena, California, that went out of existence a few years later.

This situation only began to change in 1969 when Grady McMurtry (1918–85), an American student of Crowley, proclaimed that he had been given authority by Crowley to act as his Caliph or successor during a visit to Britain in 1943. All parties agreed that McMurtry did have some contact with Crowley during the Second World War and was given some sort of authority over the OTO's one American lodge, though the rest of his claims have been the subject of bitter dispute for decades. What is not disputed, though, is that McMurtry succeeded where Crowley failed, and established the OTO as the premier Thelemic organization in the world. While the OTO has been embroiled in almost constant quarrels and legal disputes over the last 30 years, and several other small bodies claim the OTO inheritance in various parts of the world, what most Thelemite occultists today call the "Caliphate OTO" has become one of the world's largest magical secret societies and has had a significant influence on the occult community worldwide.

ORIGIN STORIES

Among the standard elements of the secret society toolkit from the seventeenth century to the present are romantic origin stories that link orders and degrees back to sources in the distant past. Secret societies, like many other organizations, benefit from making themselves look larger and more important than they actually are, and claims of a glorious history are one proven way to do this. The manufacture of origin stories combines with the equally common practice of retrospective recruitment to provide secret societies with a borrowed history more glamorous than their actual origins. See **retrospective recruitment**.

Some origin stories involve direct claims that a secret society descends from some powerful organization of the past. Alessandro Cagliostro's Egyptian Rite, for example, claimed descent from rituals practiced in Egypt in the time of the pharaohs, just as each of the competing Rosicrucian societies in America in the 1920s and 1930s claimed to be the only valid offspring of the Rosicrucian order of sixteenth-century Germany. Other origin stories, however, borrow imagery or historical narratives without claiming direct descent. Many modern Druid orders, for instance, disclaim any connection to the ancient Celtic Druids but draw inspiration from them; in the same way, Masonic concordant bodies draw stories and symbols from a dizzying array of historical and legendary sources without making any claim that they derive from these sources. See **Druids**; **Rosicrucians**.

One of the less impressive habits of the current alternative-history industry is its lack of awareness that origin stories are not the same thing as historical evidence. Several of the high degrees of the Ancient and Accepted Scottish Rite of Freemasonry, for example, include origin stories that date their foundation to the Holy Land during the Crusades. A number of popular books on the origins of Freemasonry have treated these stories as valid accounts of when and where the rituals in question were invented, and assumed that they represent ancient Scottish traditions. In fact, though, the Scottish Rite's rituals were manufactured in eighteenth-century France, and the Rite did not reach Scotland at all until the 1830s, when it was imported from America. See **Ancient and Accepted Scottish Rite (AASR)**.

Ormus

According to an origin story circulated by eighteenth-century Rosicrucians, the founder of the Rosicrucian Order, an Egyptian priest and mage of Alexandria who was converted to Christianity by St Mark in the year 96 CE. He allegedly reformed Egyptian magic to fit the teachings of the Christian religion, and founded an order called the Society of Ormus to pass on his teachings. He was also known as Ormesius. See **Order of the Golden and Rosy Cross**; **origin stories**; **Rosicrucians**.

Along with many other scraps of occult lore, the name "Ormus" found its way into the disinformation campaign launched in the 1960s by Pierre Plantard for his secret society, the Priory of Sion, and it appeared in the bestselling *The Holy Blood and the Holy Grail* (1982) by Michael Baigent, Richard Leigh, and Henry Lincoln, which drew most of its material from Plantard's fabrications. Since Baigent, Leigh, and Lincoln lacked any noticeable familiarity with the occult traditions Plantard used, they offered no explanation for "Ormus" but proposed that it was probably something very important. See **Priory of Sion**.

As rejected knowledge abhors a vacuum, explanations soon surfaced. One of the more colorful describes Ormus as a mysterious substance, an alchemical form of gold that can be produced from plain water, with mysterious powers including the ability to teleport from place to place. See **Alchemy**; **rejected knowledge**.

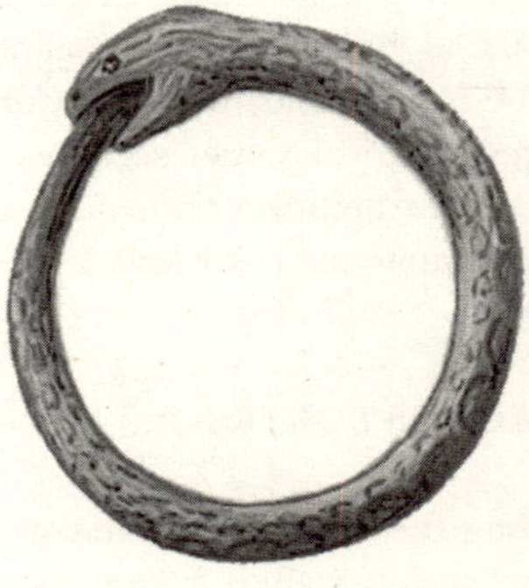

Orphic Circle

According to several accounts from the late nineteenth century, a group of occultists active in London during the 1830s and 1840s, practicing clairvoyance with crystals and magic mirrors. The sole sources of information available to date about the Circle are the anonymous *Ghost Land* (1876), a memoir allegedly by one of its members, and the autobiography of Emma Hardinge Britten, a well-known Spiritualist, who claimed to have been one of the Circle's scryers during her teen years. The Circle's members are said to have included Edward Bulwer-Lytton (1803–73), the famous author, and Richard Morrison (1795–1874), the leading figure in nineteenth-century British astrology. See **Scrying**.

The fact that Britten was also the editor (and may have been the author) of *Ghost Land* makes it difficult to use either of these sources to corroborate the other. Still, at least one major historian of nineteenth-century English occultism, Joscelyn Godwin, has shown that the accounts of occult practice in *Ghost Land* and Britten's autobiography have exact parallels with what was actually going on in Britain during the decades in question. Morrison, at least, was known to practice crystal scrying using teenage girls as scryers – he published numerous visions attained in this way in his astrological almanac – and the possibility cannot be discounted that the Orphic Circle of *Ghost Land* and Britten's memoirs is based, to a greater or lesser degree, on a real and influential organization.

Further reading: Godwin 1994.

Orphism

The system of spirituality and philosophy underlying the Dionysian mysteries, Orphism took its name from the legendary musician Orpheus, who was considered to be its founder. It was famous in ancient times for the belief that the physical body was the tomb of the spirit, expressed in a pun between the Greek words *soma* (body) and *sema* (tomb). Teachings on number symbolism and music, as well as magical practices and a detailed account of life after death were among the things passed on in books under the name of Orpheus. See **Dionysian mysteries**.

The core Orphic myth centered on the god Dionysus, said here to be the son of Zeus and Persephone, who was hidden in a cave on Crete to keep Zeus's wife Hera from learning about his existence. Hera was not fooled, though, and arranged for a band of Titans to whiten their faces with chalk, distract the infant with toys and a mirror, and then tear him to pieces and devour him. Zeus, discovering the plot too late, reduced the Titans to ashes with a thunderbolt, and from those ashes humanity was created. In Orphic writings the myth was used as an allegory of the human situation, in which the soul was the portion of Dionysus in each human being, while the body was from the Titans. See **Allegory**.

The great Greek mathematician and mystic Pythagoras derived some of his teachings from the Orphic tradition, and some ancient sources suggest that after the breakup of the Pythagorean Brotherhood the terms "Orphic" and "Pythagorean" were more or less synonymous. See **Pythagorean Brotherhood**.

Osiris, mysteries of

Unlike Isis and the Hellenistic god Serapis, the great Egyptian god Osiris, judge of the dead and lord of the underworld, did not become the center of a Greek mystery cult. This did not keep enthusiastic eighteenth- and nineteenth-century writers on mystery religions and secret societies from writing at length about the mysteries of Osiris, and inevitably high Masonic degrees and other initiatory rituals emerged during this period in which Osiris had the central role. References to mystery initiations of Osiris can still be found in books that draw too much of their material from nineteenth-century occult sources and not enough from ancient texts or modern Egyptology. See **Egypt**; **mysteries, ancient**.

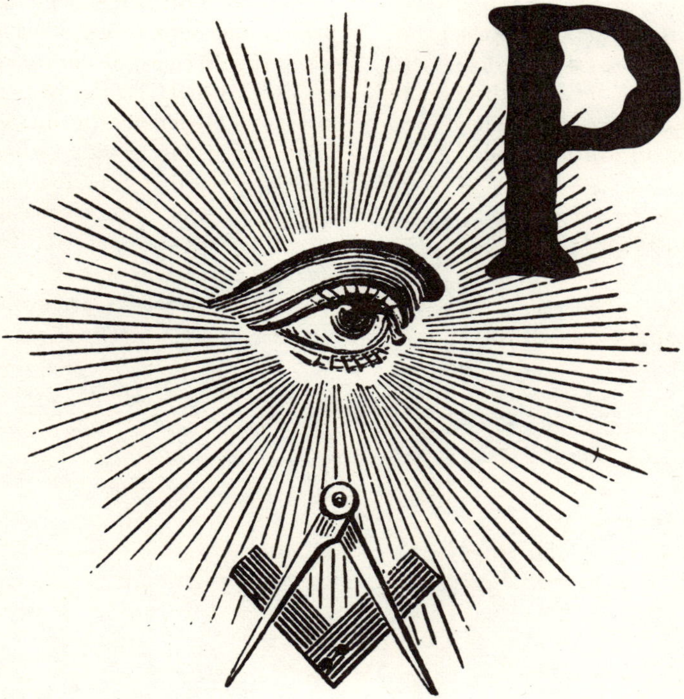
P

P2 [Propaganda Due]

Among the major political secret societies in recent European history, P2 (standing for *Propaganda Due*, "Propagation 2") was founded in Italy in 1877 as a private Masonic lodge, headed by the Grand Master of Italy, for members of the Italian parliament who wanted to become Masons but needed their membership kept secret from the Roman Catholic Church. Suppressed in 1924 by Mussolini's government, it was reactivated again in 1946. In the late 1960s, under the leadership of conservative businessman Licio Gelli, P2 reinvented itself as a political secret society. Gelli was no stranger to intrigue; he had simultaneously been a member of the Gestapo and the Italian communist underground during the Second World War. Under Gelli's leadership, P2 received CIA money as part of a project to fight communism in Italy, but the evidence suggests Gelli played the CIA and KGB off against one another and pocketed much of the proceeds. See **Freemasonry**.

P2's opposition to communism made it attractive to many people at the conservative end of the Italian political spectrum. In 1981, when its records were seized in a police raid, its membership included 3 Italian cabinet ministers, 43 members of the Italian parliament, the heads of all Italy's intelligence agencies, and many other public figures. The Mafia's traditional conservative politics made *mafiosi* another significant group within P2; members with known Mafia connections included Michele Greco, rumored to be the *capo dei capi* of Italy, and Michele Sindona, the lodge treasurer, a multimillionaire financier who managed the Mafia's profits from the transatlantic heroin trade. See **Mafia**.

The Vatican, another Italian institution with conservative leanings, also entered into a rapprochement with P2. Despite the Church's official ban on Masonic membership, Archbishop Paul Marcinkus, the head of the Vatican bank, became a member. P2 treasurer Sindona and his protégé Roberto Calvi served as key financial advisers to the Vatican. Calvi, along with Archbishop Marcinkus, created hundreds of fictitious bank accounts through which Mafia drug money was laundered. Pope Paul VI placed a large portfolio of Vatican investments under Sindona's control in 1969, an act that cost the Vatican some $240 million in losses by 1975. See **Roman Catholic Church**.

Obsessed with fighting communism on all fronts, P2's members staged at least one major terrorist attack – the bombing of the Bologna rail station in 1980 – in an attempt to discredit the Italian Communist Party and move public opinion to the right. Some investigators have argued that P2 was also behind the mysterious death of Pope John Paul I. After launching a close personal inspection of the Vatican's finances, the Pope announced on September 28, 1978, that he intended to remove

Archbishop Marcinkus and three other Sindona protégés from the Vatican bank. The next morning he was found dead; no autopsy was performed, and allegations of suppressed and destroyed evidence have dogged the Vatican ever since.

P2's plans to move Italy to the right went awry when the financial empire that supported its activities came crashing down and Italian Freemasonry turned against it. The 1974 collapse of Franklin National Bank of New York, Michele Sindona's largest American holding, set off a chain of defaults and bankruptcies that landed Sindona himself behind bars in 1980, and sparked the Italian police investigation that led to the seizure of P2's records and the public release of its membership list in 1981. At the same time, disputes between P2 and the Grand Orient of Italy – the grand lodge of Italian Freemasonry – escalated steadily; the Grand Orient formally withdrew P2's charter in 1974, and by the early 1980s one former Grand Master had been expelled from Masonry and many other Masonic officials voted out of office because of ties to P2.

In 1982, while the P2 scandal was still front-page news, Banco Ambrosiano – Italy's largest private bank, headed by Roberto Calvi – collapsed after being stripped of $1.4 billion in assets. The immediate aftermath of the collapse involved a flurry of mysterious deaths. Calvi was found hanging from Blackfriars Bridge in London. A coroner's inquest labeled the death suicide, but his widow forced the verdict to be overturned, presenting evidence that Calvi intended to name everyone involved in P2's actions, and the verdict was changed to "cause of death unknown." The same day Calvi was found hanged in London, his longtime secretary committed "suicide" by leaping from the window of her office in the Banco Ambrosiano building. Within the following year Licio Gelli vanished mysteriously from a Swiss prison cell, where he was being held for extradition, and has never been seen since, while Sindona died in a Milanese prison, claiming that he had been poisoned.

As far as anyone outside its membership knows, P2 went out of existence after it and its records became public. Still, the tradition of political secret societies runs deep in Italy and it seems likely that some of the members have reorganized under a new name.

Further reading: DiFonzo 1983, Yallop 1984.

Palladian Order

One of the most spectacular hoaxes in the history of secret societies, the Palladian Order was the brainchild of Léo Taxil (Gabriel Jorgand-Pagès), a French hack writer and Freemason who made his living writing pornography, muck-raking journalism, and anti-Catholic literature. In 1884, Pope Leo XIII issued an encyclical attacking Freemasonry, and shortly thereafter Taxil suddenly announced that he had reconciled himself to the Catholic Church. He renounced his Masonic membership, sought absolution from the local bishop, and was received back into the church after a lengthy penance. See **Roman Catholic Church**.

Within a few months of his reconciliation, Taxil began writing a series of sensational books and articles describing the Satanic inner core of Freemasonry, the Free and Regenerated Palladium or Palladian Order. Taxil's breathless prose described Palladist meetings in which the members worshipped Satan, committed horrible blasphemies and sacrileges, and practiced every sort of sexual excess with "female Masons" specially initiated for the purpose. A vast spider-web of Satanic conspiracy dedicated to undermining the Catholic Church and supporting the British Empire – the *bête noire* of conservative French opinion at the time – the order was headed by Albert Pike, "Sovereign Pontiff of Universal Freemasonry," who ruled the world in secret from his headquarters in Charleston, South Carolina. See **Pike, Albert**; **Satanism**.

All this was music to the ears of conservative French Catholics in the late nineteenth century, and Taxil's books became overnight bestsellers. French bishops and archbishops rallied to his cause, and in 1887 he received the honor of a private audience with the pope. A dozen other authors entered the lists with shocking new revelations about the Palladists. By the early 1890s a new name had appeared among the secret masters of Palladism, the Grand Priestess Diana Vaughan, whom Taxil solemnly insisted was descended from English alchemist Thomas Vaughan and a female demon. Rumors spread that Vaughan had moved operations from South Carolina to France. A new magazine appeared shortly thereafter under Diana Vaughan's name to preach the Palladist gospel to an infuriated and titillated French public; few people apparently noticed that the magazine was edited and published by Taxil himself.

By 1895 Taxil was at the storm center of a media furor, assailed by liberal writers and stoutly defended by Catholic conservatives. In that year Diana Vaughan's conversion to Catholicism made newspaper headlines over much of France. The former Grand Priestess immediately released a new magazine from Taxil's press, *Mémoires d'un ex-Palladiste* (*Memoirs of an ex-Palladist*), recounting her experiences as the head of the world's largest Satanist organization, with details of the orgiastic ceremonies over which she had presided before her conversion, and accounts of secret power struggles within the inner circle of the Palladian Order that involved some of Europe's leading political figures.

This brought matters to a head. Pressured by the media and the Catholic hierarchy to provide some evidence for his claims, Taxil announced in 1897 that Diana Vaughan had agreed to emerge from hiding for a public appearance. He rented a large hall in Paris for the event, which sold out well in advance. When the time for herappearance came, though, it was Taxil who mounted the stage. With perfect sangfroid he explained to the audience that he had made fools of them for more than a decade.

The Palladian Order and all its activities, he told them, were figments of his own imagination; Diana Vaughan was a typist who had worked for him, and who agreed to lend her name and photograph to the hoax. The other authors who had chimed in to corroborate Taxil's revelations were simply Taxil himself and one of his friends, writing under a galaxy of pen names. The entire exercise had been set in motion to show the world just how easily Catholics could be made to believe perfect nonsense. At the end of his talk, he left the stage just in time to avoid the ensuing riot. The hall had to be cleared by the gendarmes, while Taxil dined with friends at a nearby restaurant.

The consequences of Taxil's stunt were surprisingly large, and include the word "Satanist" itself, which entered the English language by way of press reports during the Palladist furor. Despite Taxil's revelation, many people have continued to believe devoutly in the existence of the Palladium and its sinister plans ever since. In the 1924 edition of *A Dictionary of Secret and Other Societies*, a standard Catholic handbook on secret societies compiled by one Arthur Preuss, the Palladium still had an entry as a real organization based in Charleston, with the comment that "this Order is not numerous and keeps its membership and proceedings so secret that little is known about them." Material from Taxil's inventions is still quoted as fact by antimasonic conspiracy theorists and fundamentalist Christians, including such public figures as American televangelist Pat Robertson. (On the other side of the balance, there were Freemasons in Italy who wanted to join the Palladian Order, who refused to believe Taxil's claim that it never existed, and who spent years trying to contact Palladian headquarters and apply for membership.) See **Antimasonry**; **fundamentalism**.

Taxil also launched a significant theological movement within Satanism itself by way of his claim that the Palladian Order was divided by a bitter theological rift between Luciferians, dualists who worshipped Lucifer as the god of light and spirit and abhorred Adonai the god of darkness and matter, and

Satanists, who simply stood Christian theology on its head and argued that the struggle between God and Satan would end with the devil's triumph. Taxil's invention has been duly repeated in hundreds of books about Satanism, and was also adopted into the mythology of Nazi occultism in the 1950s. See **Black Sun**.

Further reading: Riggs 1997, Waite 2003.

PALMER, RAYMOND

American author and magazine editor, 1910–77. One of the most influential figures in twentieth-century American alternative thought, Raymond Palmer suffered severe childhood injuries that left him partially crippled for life. Like many boys of his generation, he grew up reading science fiction, and by the late 1920s he was a significant figure in the science fiction fan community. In 1930 he published the first of many science fiction stories, and in 1933 he launched the first American prize for science fiction, the Jules Verne Prize.

In 1938 Ziff-Davis, one of the major pulp publishers of the time, hired him as managing editor for *Amazing Stories*, a failing science fiction magazine they had just purchased. Palmer's job was to save the magazine, and he accomplished this with panache. His secret was an unerring sense for the lowest common denominator of taste. Atrociously written short stories about alien monsters and buxom maidens jostled for space on *Amazing*'s pages with feature articles about the World of Tomorrow and filler pieces about a dozen different species of crackpot science. Serious science fiction readers sneered, but subscriptions soared and money poured in.

Palmer's greatest triumph began inauspiciously enough in September 1943, when Richard Shaver, a welder from Pennsylvania who claimed to hear telepathic voices while he worked, sent him a letter announcing the rediscovery of Mantong, the lost language of ancient Lemuria. Published in the December 1943 issue, the letter got a favorable response from the readership, and Palmer wrote to Shaver and asked for more. What he got was an incoherent 10,000-word letter titled "A Warning to Future Man," revealing the existence of a race of psychotic underground dwarfs called "deros" who tormented dwellers on the surface with diabolical mind-control beams. Palmer rewrote it into a 31,000-word novella titled "I Remember Lemuria!" and printed it in the March 1945 issue. The issue promptly sold out, and *Amazing*'s mailbox overflowed with 2500 letters a month asking for more information on the sinister deros. Palmer, realizing that he had stumbled upon a gold mine, spent the next three years milking the "Shaver mystery" for everything it was worth and sending *Amazing*'s sales to stratospheric levels. See **Lemuria**; **underground realms**.

Another of Palmer's oddball insights, although less profitable in the short term than Shaver's story, had more sweeping effects on modern culture. During the 1940s, looking for striking imagery for the magazine's covers, Palmer came up with the idea of a saucer-shaped airplane and had staff artists produce it. By 1947 millions of Americans had seen flying saucers on *Amazing*'s garish covers, and on June 24 of that year, pilot Kenneth Arnold reported spotting them in the sky above Mount Rainier. The modern UFO phenomenon was born. Unnervingly, many of the themes of later UFO writings appeared in fictional form in the pages of *Amazing* decades in advance; Richard Shaver's "Earth Slaves to Space" in the September 1946 issue, for example, centers on alien spaceships visiting the earth to kidnap humans for slave labor on another planet, a theme later reworked by the inventors of *Alternative 3* in the late 1970s and endlessly recycled since. See **Alternative 3**; **unidentified flying objects (UFOs)**.

By 1949, despite the sizeable profits made by Palmer's antics, the Ziff-Davis company had had enough, and told him to return *Amazing Stories* to its original science fiction focus. Palmer responded by quitting. The year before he had launched a magazine of his own, *Fate*, entirely devoted to allegedly factual accounts of strange events. When the pulp magazine industry collapsed in the fall of 1949, the victim of a stock market scheme that liquidated the last national wholesaler of pulps, *Fate* was one of the few survivors, and Palmer soon launched a second magazine, *Search*, to compete with it. A third title, *Flying Saucers From Other Worlds*, joined them in 1957, and then dropped the last three words from its title after a few months when Palmer announced that UFOs actually came from inside the hollow earth. Nearly every theme that became central to the alternative-reality scene in late twentieth-century America, from lost civilizations and the mysterious powers of crystals to alien abductions and psychic powers, found a home in the pages of these magazines long before the revival of popular occultism in the 1970s made them common currency. See **hollow earth**; **lost civilizations**.

Comfortably ensconced as the king of American lowbrow esotericism, Palmer sold *Fate* to his partners in the 1960s and concentrated on his remaining magazines, mail order sales of UFO books, and further projects with Richard Shaver until not long before his death in 1977. By that time the alternative scene had long since passed him by, but he left an indelible stamp on American popular culture.

Further reading: Keel 1989.

Patrons of Husbandry [Grange]

Among the most remarkable secret societies to emerge from the golden age of American fraternalism in the second half of the nineteenth century, the Patrons of Husbandry was launched in 1867 by Oliver H. Kelley, an employee of the federal Bureau of Agriculture, and six other men, mostly government clerks, who were concerned with the plight of small farmers after the American Civil War. Kelley was a Freemason, and the other founders were all either Masons or Odd Fellows; they felt that a fraternal secret society designed for farmers would provide them with a framework for cooperative action and mutual aid. See **Freemasonry**; **Odd Fellowship**.

The Grange, as the organization has been called from the first, copied many of the standard features of other fraternal secret societies of the time. Local lodges, called Granges, confer four degrees of initiation, based on the four seasons of the agricultural year. Three higher degrees named after Greek and Roman goddesses of agriculture and plant growth are conferred by higher levels of the organization – the Degree of Pomona by county Granges, the Degree of Flora by state Granges, and the Degree of Demeter by the National Grange. The Degree of Demeter, a reconstruction of the ancient Eleusinian mysteries, was supposedly purchased by Kelley from an Italian nobleman who claimed to have access to the original rites of Eleusis; it is sufficiently pagan that nowadays many Christian members refuse to receive it. See **Eleusinian mysteries**.

Certain features of the Grange set it apart from most other fraternal orders of its time, however. At the urging of Kelley's niece, Caroline Hall, the order admitted men and women on an equal basis, allowing women to hold every office while setting aside four positions in each local Grange that men are not allowed to hold. In addition, whereas nearly all fraternal secret societies were strictly non-political, the Grange made political activism one of its central activities, and also took on the job of organizing economic cooperatives among its members.

Recruitment was slow at first, but during the 1870s and 1880s Granges spread rapidly through America's farm belt. During these years the Patrons of Husbandry became famous for their stand against the abusive policies of

American railroads, which made it almost impossible for farmers to earn a living. Railroads were among the richest corporations in the country, with a huge degree of influence in the corrupt politics of that time, but Grange lawsuits, lobbying, and electoral organization forced through a series of laws – the "Granger Acts" – that reined in the railroad corporations and helped make possible the vast expansion of agriculture in late nineteenth- and early twentieth-century America.

Through much of the twentieth century, the local Grange hall was the center of community life in most of America's farm country, featuring a busy calendar of social events and political rallies as well as regular Grange meetings. As the percentage of farmers in the American population dwindled in the course of the century, the Grange lost ground, but it still counts some 300,000 members and 2600 local Granges, and has a significant voice in political debates over American agricultural policy.

Further reading: Howard 1992.

Pentagram

A five-pointed star formed of five equal intersecting lines, the pentagram has a complex history that has been drastically oversimplified by recent conspiracy theorists and popular occult writers. Found in most cultures worldwide, it was the ancient Babylonian symbol for "star." The Pythagorean Brotherhood is said to have used it as a secret sign of recognition. By the Middle Ages it had found a place in magic as a symbol of power, though it also appears in the English poem *Sir Gawain and the Green Knight* (*c.*1380) representing, among other things, the five wounds of Jesus and the five pure joys of the Virgin Mary. In heraldry it is known as a mullet and forms the most common star on flags and coats of arms; the stars in the American flag are pentagrams. See **Magic**; **Pythagorean Brotherhood**.

Its roles as the most important symbol of magic and the emblem of Satanism were the work of French occultist Eliphas Lévi (1810–75). Lévi essentially reinvented the western tradition of magic in a series of popular books, and much of the material he presented was of his own creation. One of these innovations was his claim that a pentagram with one point up represents good magic and God, while a pentagram with one point down represents evil magic and Satan. This interpretation was borrowed by most occultists in the late nineteenth century and has become all but universal since then. The magical religion of Wicca and twentieth-century Satanism both borrowed the pentagram from occult sources influenced by Lévi, and it was from these sources that fundamentalist Christian conspiracy hunters took it and further redefined it as the primary symbol of devil worship. See **fundamentalism**; **Satanism**; **Wicca**.

This has caused some predictable confusion in dealing with symbolism dating from before Lévi's time. The most popular ladies auxiliary in American Freemasonry, the Order of the Eastern Star, for instance, adopted a pentagram with one point down as its emblem not long after its founding in 1852. The Congressional Medal of Honor, the highest US military decoration, also features a pentagram with one point down. The Eastern Star's emblem has occasionally been cited as evidence for the alleged Satanic ideology of Freemasonry; to the present writer's knowledge no one has yet made the same claim about the Medal of Honor. See **Freemasonry**; **ladies auxiliaries**; **Order of the Eastern Star**.

PERPETUAL MOTION

A perennial interest of inventors since the Middle Ages, perpetual motion machines of various kinds have an active presence in today's alternative scene, although terms such as "zero point energy" and "over-unity devices" tend to be used for them nowadays. Some use the latest technology while others are schemes that have been tried repeatedly and unsuccessfully for centuries. All have two things in common. First, they violate the laws of thermodynamics, among the most thoroughly tested principles in modern physics, by extracting more energy out of a process than goes into it. Second, none of them work.

The oldest known perpetual motion machine is the overbalancing wheel, which first appears in a fifth-century CE astrological manuscript from India, the *Siddhanta Ciromani*. Endless variations conceal a common theme – a wheel with weights around the rim that move inward or outward as the wheel turns: inward as they rise up, and outward as they sink down. The goal is to use leverage to turn the wheel; since the same weight exerts more leverage when it's further from the hub than it does when it's nearer, the weights going down should exert more leverage than those going up, and since each weight moves in as it starts to rise and out as it starts to sink, it seems logical that the wheel should turn forever and produce useful energy in the process.

Logical or not, it doesn't work in practice. The energy gained by the out-of-balance weights is used up in moving the weights inward and outward. The best overbalancing wheels make excellent flywheels, and will run for quite a while from a single good push, but eventually the laws of thermodynamics win and they come to a halt. The same is true of perpetual motion machines that use other gravity-based methods, such as chains made of sponges designed to wring themselves out at the bottom of the loop and soak up water at the top, or self-contained hydroelectric units designed to pump water up to a tank, using energy from the same water as it pours down from the tank into a turbine or water wheel.

The repeated failures of perpetual motion schemes have not prevented thousands of inventors from trying their hand at making a working model, and devices along these same lines are still being tried today; a closed-cycle hydroelectric machine named Jeremiah 33:3 was designed and marketed by a Texas inventor in the late 1970s. Nor has there been a shortage of confidence artists whose schemes aimed at a perpetual motion of other people's money into their bank accounts. Among the greatest of these was the redoubtable John Keely (1827–98), who used concealed compressed air lines to run a "vibratory motor" that brought him millions of dollars of investment money. Even though the fraud came to light immediately after Keely's death, believers in perpetual motion continue to cite the Keely Motor as proof that free energy devices actually work.

The logic of the overbalanced wheel applied to steam turbines and internal combustion engines produce devices like the Stewart engine, a device heavily promoted in the American farm belt during the late 1970s' energy crisis. The Stewart engine supposedly extracted heat from well water and used it to run a heat engine. Hundreds of investors bought Stewart engine distributorships in 1978 and 1979, only to find the laws of thermodynamics in the way of making a profit; similar problems halted John Gamgee's zeromotor, a device along similar lines meant to run naval vessels off the heat in seawater. While liquid water (like anything else above absolute zero) contains energy in the form of heat, the energy is so diffuse that extracting the heat from it takes more energy than the extracted heat provides. Like unbalanced wheels, heat engines like the Stewart engine try to get something for nothing, and fail.

Getting something for nothing is, in fact, the keynote of all these projects, including the currently popular "zero point" technologies, whose proponents deny that their devices are perpetual motion machines and claim to extract "free energy" from quantum flux, the rotation of atomic nuclei, the universal field, or some other unquantifiable source. This thinking seems reasonable in a society that runs on the almost-free energy of petroleum and other fossil fuels, which human beings did nothing to create and are using up at a reckless pace. The possibility can't be dismissed that some ingenious inventor will come up with a way to tap some other source of energy that will allow us to continue the extravagant lifestyles currently popular in the developed world. So far, though, the utopia of infinite free energy promised by the perpetual motion industry has failed to materialize, and betting on its arrival may not be the best strategy for the future.

Further reading: Ford 1986, Ord-Hume 1980.

Philadelphes

One of the most important political secret societies of the nineteenth century, the Philadelphes began life in 1797 as a student literary club in the town of Besançon in eastern France. Like other student societies of the time, it combined rituals loosely modeled on fraternal secret society ceremonies with such innocuous activities as picnics and poetry readings. According to its chronicler, the French writer Charles Nodier, it took on a more political focus when Napoleon seized power in 1799, and gradually mutated into a widespread political conspiracy headed by Jacques-Joseph Oudet, a colonel in the French army. Organized groups of Philadelphes existed in six regiments in the army. The Philadelphes made several attempts to prepare for a rebellion against Napoleon, but none of them went far, and after Oudet was killed in action in 1809 it accomplished little more within France.

The Philadelphes reached Italy sometime after 1807, when a group of Italian exiles in Paris became members and began planning organized resistance to Napoleon. Known as Filadelfi or Adelfi in Italy, the organization played an active role in the complex politics of the early nineteenth century and, along with the Carbonari, helped coordinate preparations for the widespread revolutions of 1820 and 1821. It apparently went out of existence after that time, though many of its members were absorbed by other secret societies with similar aims. See **Carbonari**.

The accuracy of Nodier's account of the Philadelphes has been challenged by some modern scholars, but the Philadelphes certainly existed and at least attempted to play the role that Nodier painted for it. The veteran revolutionary Filippo Buonarroti became a member of the Philadelphes while in prison for his involvement in the Conspiracy of Equals, and organized a Philadelphe circle in Geneva after his release in 1806. From 1818 until at least the mid-1820s, another of Buonarroti's societies, the Sublime Perfect Masters, infiltrated the Philadelphe leadership in Italy and took control of the organization. Certainly material gathered by police spies and informers in Italy in the 1820s claimed that the Adelfi were headed by a secret directorate called the Great Firmament – the name of the governing body of the Sublime Perfect Masters. See **Buonarroti, Filippo**; **Conspiracy of Equals**; **Sublime Perfect Masters**.

The Philadelphe model of revolution by secret society dropped out of use in the 1830s, as mass movements and political parties took up the cause of political liberalization and religious freedom in Europe. A few secret groups of the old style survived in France, where they took over the Rite of Memphis, one of several irregular systems of Masonry active in Europe at the time. After the failed European revolutions of 1848 and 1849, however, many disappointed liberals returned to the secret society tradition. Exiled in London, a group of French expatriates with connections to Buonarroti's secret societies launched a new Philadelphe lodge in 1850 with a Rite of Memphis charter. When Napoleon III seized power in France in 1852 and proclaimed the Second Empire, the new lodge redefined itself as a Philadelphe Grand Lodge, formed at least 10 subordinate lodges, and launched itself into a vigorous campaign of subversion against the new French regime. See **Rite of Memphis**.

This last flourish of the old tradition had an unexpected offspring. Starting in 1855, Philadelphe initiates in England began contacting other radical groups overseas, hoping to create an international revolutionary society along the lines of Mazzini's Young Italy. The International Association lasted from 1855 to 1859 but never attracted much interest outside the French expatriate community. The growth of the labor union movement and the possibilities opened up by international organization inspired another attempt in 1864 – a front organization called the International Workingmen's Association. Later, control of the Association slipped out of Philadelphe hands into those of a German economist named Karl Marx. See **Communism**; **First International**; **Young Italy**.

Recent conspiracy theorists have almost completely neglected the Philadelphes, even when their tracks run across fields of current interest. One of the few exceptions is *The Holy Blood and the Holy Grail* (1982) by Michael Baigent, Richard Leigh, and Henry Lincoln. In the process of recycling disinformation produced by Pierre Plantard's audacious Priory of Sion hoax, Lincoln and his co-authors claim that Charles Nodier was a grand master of the Priory, and quote a line from Nodier's book on secret societies in which he mentions that behind the Philadelphes was another, more secret society, whose name he was oathbound not to reveal. The book implies that this inner circle was the Priory of Sion, but since the Priory was not founded until 1956 that possibility can be discarded. The name Nodier would not mention, rather, was that of the Sublime Perfect Masters. See **Priory of Sion**.

Further reading: Baigent et al. 1983, Billington 1980, Drachkovitch 1966, Roberts 1972.

Philike Hetairia

A Greek offshoot of the Carbonari, the Philike Hetairia ("Brotherly Association" or "Friendly Society") was founded by a group of exiled Greek patriots in Odessa, Russia, in 1814. While the exact organizational connections have proven hard to trace, it apparently rose out of Carbonari lodges (*venditas*, "shops") founded by the political agitator Rhigas Velestinlis in Vienna, Belgrade, and Bucharest shortly before his execution by the Turks in 1798. The rituals of the Hetairia show many close similarities to those of the Carbonari, and its goal of national liberation was shared by the Carbonari and its sympathizers across Europe at the time. See **Carbonari**.

The Hetairia spread quickly through the large Greek merchant communities around the Mediterranean; by 1821 lodges existed from the Russian ports on the Black Sea to Gibraltar. These maritime links allowed weapons to be smuggled into Greece in large quantities, and veterans of the Napoleonic Wars and the failed revolutions in Italy and Spain in 1820 and 1821 supported the Hetairia in large numbers. The Russian government, seeing an opportunity to weaken its longtime Turkish enemy, provided covert backing. With this help, the Hetairia launched a rising against the Turks in 1821. After a difficult five-year struggle, the rebels succeeded in freeing Greece from Turkish rule and establishing the modern Greek nation.

Pike, Albert

American soldier, author, occultist and Freemason, 1809–91. Born in Massachusetts to a working-class family, Pike showed intellectual promise from an early age and mastered Latin, Greek, and Hebrew before the age of 18. Although he was accepted at Harvard, his family was unable to afford his tuition, and so he headed west instead. Pike wound up in Fort Smith, Arkansas, where he taught for a time, edited the local newspaper, and studied law, qualifying for the Bar in 1834. In the same year he married Anne Hamilton, a wealthy local widow, and with her money went into politics in the Arkansas branch of the Know-Nothings, an anti-Catholic organization that was part secret society and part political party. Pike became the leader of the Know-Nothings in Arkansas and took an active role in the national party as well. See **Know-Nothing Party**.

Pike's military career began in 1846 during the Texan war for independence; he organized and led a regiment of volunteers against the Mexican army at the battle of Buena Vista in 1847. After the war he became involved in land disputes between settlers and local Native American peoples and took the native side in several court cases, defending the tribes against the federal government. When the American Civil War broke out in 1861, he sided with the Confederacy and was appointed commissioner of Indian affairs by Confederate president Jefferson Davis. This position placed Pike in the middle of conflicts between Indian treaty rights and the military requirements of the Confederacy, a situation that worsened when Pike was given the rank of brigadier general and put in command of Indian regiments in the western theatre of the war. In July 1862 he resigned his commission and publicly criticized the Confederate government for violating its own treaties with the Native Americans. He was thrown into jail, and then released in the autumn of 1862 as the Confederacy's western defenses collapsed. Bankrupt and with his marriage in ruins, he fled to a cabin in the Ozark hills and remained there until 1868, pursuing a project that would become his life's work.

Pike had become a Freemason during his Arkansas years, and in 1853 was initiated into the Ancient and Accepted Scottish Rite, then one of the smallest Masonic bodies in the United States, with fewer than a thousand members. Shortly after his initiation the Supreme Council appointed him to a five-man committee charged with revising the rituals. The committee never met, but Pike took on the massive task himself. In 1859, he was elected Sovereign Grand Commander of the Rite's southern jurisdiction. In his self-imposed seclusion in the Ozarks, Pike finished his revision of the rituals, including in them a wealth of material from nearly every aspect of western occult tradition. He also began the writing of his massive book *Morals and Dogma*, which was published in 1871. See **Ancient and Accepted Scottish Rite (AASR)**.

In 1868 he moved to Washington DC, where he received a congressional pardon for his wartime activities and resumed a legal career. His duties as head of the Scottish Rite took up ever more of his time as the Rite grew, however, and after a few years he abandoned his law practice and devoted the rest of his life to his Masonic involvements, which were not limited to the Scottish Rite. When the Royal Order of Scotland established a Provincial Grand Lodge for the United States in 1878, for example, Pike accepted the office of Provincial Grand Master and held it until his death. See **Royal Order of Scotland**.

In the last two decades of his life Pike was far and away the most prominent Freemason in America, and this position made him a target for conspiracy theories during and after his time. Léo Taxil's brilliant Palladian Order hoax of the late 1870s and early 1880s elevated Pike to the non-existent office of "Sovereign Pontiff of Universal Freemasonry" and head of the Palladian Order, a supposed inner circle of Satanist sex fiends inside Masonry; the title and some of the writings Taxil forged and attributed to Pike are still circulated among opponents of Freemasonry, especially fundamentalist Christians. Another inaccuracy, debunked by historians but much repeated in antimasonic circles, is the claim that Pike was a high officer in the Ku Klux Klan immediately after the Civil War. In point of fact, after his troubles with the Confederate government Pike took no further role in politics and had nothing to do with the Klan. See **Antimasonry**; **fundamentalism**; **Ku Klux Klan**; **Palladian Order**.

Further reading: Carnes 1989, Duncan 1961, Pike 1871.

Poro Society

One of the two most widespread secret societies of West Africa, the Poro Society is found all along the Upper Guinea coast from Liberia to Sierra Leone. In the past, before Christian and Muslim missionaries became influential in these areas, most boys were initiated into the Poro Society as an essential part of their transition to adulthood, while girls were initiated into the similar Sande Society. See **African secret societies**; **Sande Society**.

To be initiated into the society, candidates leave their homes and live communally for a time in the "Poro bush," a sacred grove located outside the town limits. There they are symbolically eaten by the Poro spirit, a fierce guardian entity of the forest; they spend time within the womb of the spirit's wife, and then are reborn as men with new Poro names. A council of Poro elders oversees these rites, and also traditionally manages certain community affairs and settles disputes over land or succession in aristocratic lineages. In many areas the local Poro Society wields a great deal of political and economic authority, which, however, is balanced by the influence of the women's Sande Society. In some areas, in fact, Poro and Sande elders alternate in power, with Poro elders having the final word in one year and Sande elders holding authority the next.

During the era of British rule over Sierra Leone, several colonial administrations attempted to break the economic and political authority of the Poro Society: an 1897 "Poro Ordinance" barred Poro groups from their traditional role in managing the harvest of certain trade crops, while an 1898 rising against the colonial government, the Hut Tax War, was blamed by the British on the Poro Society. Stringent repressive measures against the Society failed, however, to force it out of its traditional position, and since the collapse of colonial rule the Society has played an important part in the region. During the civil war in Sierra Leone in the 1990s, local Poro elders were even able to proclaim and enforce a "Poro curfew" forbidding night attacks in certain regions, helping local communities stay out of the crossfire between insurgents and government troops.

Further reading: Bellman 1984.

Prince Hall Masonry

Prince Hall was a black minister of West Indian origin who emigrated to Boston in 1765 and became the pastor of a Methodist church in Cambridge, Massachusetts. In 1775 he and 14 other men of African descent were entered, passed and raised by a Masonic regimental lodge in Boston. They then applied to the Grand Lodge of Massachusetts for a charter and were turned down, but an application to the Grand Lodge of England proved more successful. African Lodge #459 received a dispensation in 1784 and a charter in 1787. Seven years later it assumed the powers of a Grand Lodge and began granting charters to African-American lodges throughout the new republic. By the beginning of the Civil War "Prince Hall" lodges, as they came to be called, could be found throughout the northern states, as well as in Maryland, Virginia, and Louisiana, the states with the largest number of free African-Americans. The established (and entirely white) American Masonic lodges denounced these lodges as "clandestine," but this does not seem to have slowed the growth of black Freemasonry at all. See **Freemasonry**.

The second half of the nineteenth century saw this steady growth turn exponential as black Americans turned to fraternal orders for mutual aid and networking. Three years after the Civil War, Prince Hall lodges existed in every state of the old Confederacy. By 1900 Prince Hall Masonry was the premier African-American secret society in the United States and formed one of the core social institutions of the black middle classes. The twentieth century brought the same challenges to Prince Hall Masonry as it did to every other secret society in the western world, but it survived when many other African-American orders went under. At the time of writing, Prince Hall lodges exist in 41 US states, as well as in Canada, the Caribbean, and Liberia. See **African-American secret societies**.

In the last decades of the twentieth century, many historically white Masonic jurisdictions found themselves rethinking the old rules of racial segregation, and the issue of recognizing Prince Hall lodges formed one of the battlefields on which this was fought out. In 1989 the Grand Lodge of Connecticut formally recognized its state's Prince Hall grand lodge, a move that infuriated white Grand Masters in the deep South and saw several southern jurisdictions stop recognizing Masons from Connecticut as brothers. The movement spread, however, and at the beginning of the twenty-first century, Prince Hall Masons are recognized by 38 American grand lodges and essentially all other regular Masonic bodies around the world.

Further reading: Walkes 1979.

Priory of Sion

The most spectacular secret society hoax in recent history, the Priory of Sion (*Prieuré de Sion*) was founded in 1956 in the small town of Annemasse in southeastern France by Pierre Plantard (1920–2000), a minor figure in French right-wing occult circles. The founding papers of the organization declare that its objects were "1. The constitution of a Catholic association intended to restore antique chivalry; 2. Pursuit of the study and practice of solidarity." Its membership was limited to adult Catholics.

Behind the Priory lies two decades of failed attempts by Plantard to launch a similar organization to pursue the conservative Catholic esotericism much in vogue in early twentieth-century France. In his younger years, Plantard had been an associate of Georges Monti, the former secretary to Joséphin Péladan. Péladan had been among the most influential figures in the Paris occult scene in the 1880s and 1890s, and Monti passed onto Plantard something of Péladan's taste for aristocratic and reactionary occultism. Plantard also had a long history of involvement in reactionary political groups; before the war he was associated with members of the Cagoule, a secret society that attempted to overthrow the French government and establish a fascist state modeled on Mussolini's Italy. See **Cagoule**; **Catholic Order of the Rose+Cross**.

In 1940, not long after the German conquest of France, Plantard organized a secret society named Alpha Galates, with 12 levels of initiation culminating in the degree of Druidic Majesty, reserved for himself. Although he produced a periodical, *Vaincre* ("Conquer"), that supported the Vichy puppet government and circulated pro-Nazi propaganda, Plantard spent four months in prison when the authorities found out about it, since it had been launched without official approval. Vichy-era government documents nonetheless dismissed Plantard as a crank whose organization existed mostly in his own head. Other than his brief prison stay, he spent the war years in Paris working as a paid sexton at a Catholic church and studying lessons from the correspondence course put out by AMORC, an American Rosicrucian order based in California. See **Ancient Mystical Order Rosae Crucis (AMORC)**.

As outlined in its 1956 documents, the Priory of Sion was a new version of Alpha Galates. Even by secret society standards it was a tiny organization, and for most of its history its membership consisted mainly of Plantard himself. In its first years it either was, or masqueraded as, a committee for the right to low income housing, though these efforts were hindered by a six-month stint in prison following Plantard's conviction for fraud; he had claimed the Priory was a large organization, and sold high degrees of initiation for even higher sums of money.

Despite this setback, Plantard spent the next two decades engaged in a massive campaign of disinformation to make the Priory look larger than it was. During France's constitutional crisis of 1958, he put out publicity claiming that the Priory was behind the Committees of Public Safety that put Charles de Gaulle back in power. These efforts had little impact, but Plantard's further attempts to publicize the Priory had unexpected consequences.

Around 1960 Plantard met Noel Corbu, who opened a restaurant in the little town of Rennes-le-Château in southern France in the early 1950s, using for the purpose a stone tower built by an eccentric former parish priest named Bérenger Saunière. To publicize the restaurant, Corbu concocted a romantic tale about hidden treasure supposedly discovered by Saunière in the parish church, and turned Saunière into a man of mystery with international connections. None of Corbu's tale has the slightest basis in fact, nor can it be traced back past a 1956 magazine article for which Corbu himself was the sole source. See **Rennes-le-Château**.

Plantard took these stories, embellished them, and used them to provide a fictitious origin for the Priory of Sion, tracing it back via the Albigensian heretics and the crusading Knights Templar to the Merovingian kings of early medieval France, whose last descendant he claimed to be. In the process he borrowed liberally from the origin story of the Order of the Golden and Rosy Cross, an eighteenth-century German Rosicrucian order; he added "de St Clair" to his own name to imply a connection to the Sinclair family of Scotland, once the hereditary patrons of Scottish stonemasons' guilds, and invented a stellar list of past Nautonniers (grand masters) of the Priory, including such luminaries as Leonardo da Vinci and Isaac Newton, borrowing most of the names from lists of Rosicrucian Imperators circulated by AMORC. Along with a friend, Philippe de Chérisey, he started inserting documents backing these claims into several important French historical archives. See **Albigensians**; **Knights Templar**; **Leonardo da Vinci**; **Merovingians**; **Order of the Golden and Rosy Cross**; **origin stories**; **retrospective recruitment**; **Rosicrucians**; **Sinclair family**.

In 1964, he wrote a book detailing his claims, but was unable to find a publisher. In 1965 he arranged with Gérard de Sède, a writer of popular non-fiction, to have de Sède revise the book and publish it under his own name, with the proceeds to be split with Plantard. Plantard's friend Philippe de Chérisey was also to receive a share in return for concocting two parchments, allegedly found in a Visigothic pillar in the church at Rennes-le-Château, that contained coded messages backing up the Priory of Sion's invented Merovingian origins. The book was published, and launched the "Rennes-le-Château mystery" into French counterculture literature, but the partners fell out over the division of the royalties. In a variety of court documents and publications, Plantard and de Chérisey both admitted that the parchments had been forged, a conclusion later backed up by laboratory analysis.

None of this prevented the next stage in the unfolding of the story. In 1969, English actor Henry Soskin (who wrote under the pen name Henry Lincoln) encountered the Rennes-le-Château story by way of a second book by Gérard de Sède, and began to pursue the story, first on his own and then with the help of two other British writers, Michael Baigent and Richard Leigh. Soskin, Leigh, and Baigent soon found themselves on the receiving end of Plantard's disinformation campaign. Ironically, they realized early on that they were following a prepared trail produced by a single source (see Baigent et al. 1983, pp. 96–7), but still accepted the accuracy of the Priory's manufactured pedigree.

However, the British authors were by no means passive receptacles for all this material. They had interests of their own, focused most notably on the origins of Christianity, and managed to link Plantard's revelations into these interests, with sensational results. Their interpretation of the Priory "mystery" appeared in three TV documentaries, followed by the bestselling book *The Holy Blood and the Holy Grail* (1982), which claimed that Pierre Plantard was a descendant of Jesus of Nazareth, who had a child by Mary Magdalene – a claim Plantard himself, a devout if eccentric Catholic, rejected with some vehemence. See **Christian origins**.

In 1984, after a series of bitter quarrels with Soskin, Plantard folded up the Priory and tried to distance himself from the media circus of claims and counterclaims around the bloodline-of-Jesus theory. In 1989 he attempted to launch the Priory again, this time with a completely different set of claims about its origins, but his efforts went nowhere. An incautious claim about the Priory connections of controversial French business figure Roger-Patrice Pelat landed Plantard in court in 1993, where he admitted under oath that he had invented the Priory of Sion, its history, and its claims out of whole cloth.

From that time until his death in 2000, Plantard seems to have made no further attempts to revive the Priory. Still, his efforts succeeded in giving his small and unsuccessful group an unearned reputation as one of the most important secret societies in history, and the disinformation campaign he concocted, liberally enlarged by the imaginative contributions of more than a dozen busy writers, has redefined the history of the western world for millions of people. A bestselling novel, Dan Brown's *The Da Vinci Code* (2003), borrowed much of its theme and plot from Plantard's claims, as expanded by Soskin, Leigh, and Baigent, and at least 10 secret societies now claim either to be the authentic Priory of Sion or the current holders of its lineage. The richest irony of all is that the flurry of media attention given to the Priory of Sion has largely succeeded in distracting researchers from the activities of real secret societies in various periods of European history. See **Da Vinci Code, the**.

Further reading: Baigent et al. 1983, Richardson 1998.

Protocols of the Elders of Zion, The

The most influential book in the history of modern antisemitism and the original source for most of the key themes of contemporary conspiracy theory, *The Protocols of the Elders of Zion* first surfaced in Russia around 1895. It purports to be a plan for world conquest adopted by a secret meeting of Jewish leaders at an unspecified place and time. The 24 "protocols" or sections of the plan lay out a campaign of subversion and financial manipulation. The Elders, according to the book, already control all European political parties and economic interests, and use their control of the media to discredit authority and undermine Christianity, in order to bring the Christian kingdoms of Europe to their knees and establish a worldwide empire under a Jewish monarch. See **Antisemitism**.

In reality, *The Protocols* is a crude hoax patched together from several earlier antisemitic works. About 40 percent of the text was plagiarized from Maurice Joly's *Dialogue aux Enfers entre Montesquieu et Machiavelli* (*Dialogue in Hell between Montesquieu and Machiavelli*, 1864), a satire on the authoritarian politics of Napoleon III of France. Some of the remainder is closely modeled on a chapter from Hermann Gödsche's 1868 novel *Biarritz*, in which two characters spy on a meeting between Jewish elders and Satan in a Prague graveyard. The rest is pieced together from other antisemitic and antimasonic works popular at the time, from contemporary critiques of industrialism, and from claims about the Great White Lodge, the secret government of the world in Theosophical belief. The author, or rather compiler, of *The Protocols* was Yuliana Glinka, a Russian noblewoman living in Paris during the 1880s and 1890s, who combined an interest in Theosophy with a career as a spy for the Russian secret police. See **Great White Lodge**; **Theosophical Society**.

The Protocols was first published in an abbreviated form in a Russian newspaper in 1903, and pamphlet versions appeared in late 1905 and early 1906 from a press controlled by the Black Hundreds, the leading right-wing secret society in Russia at that time. It also appeared as an appendix to a 1905 book, *Velikoe v Malom* (*The Great in the Small*) by Sergei Nilus, a Russian Orthodox mystic whose wife was a lady-in-waiting to the Tsarina Alexandra. It quickly found a following in Russian antisemitic circles, and during the Russian revolution became standard reading material among conservative opponents of the Bolsheviks. See **Black Hundreds**; **Russian revolution**.

Refugees from the Russian civil war brought *The Protocols* with them to Germany, where it was translated at once and found an eager audience among radical right-wing parties. One minor party based in Munich adopted the Protocols with particular fervor; its leader, an Austrian veteran named Adolf Hitler, took to quoting them frequently in his speeches and writings. When Hitler took power in 1933, *The Protocols* became a standard textbook in German public schools. See **Hitler, Adolf**; **National Socialism**.

Once published in Germany, *The Protocols* quickly gained worldwide circulation, and during the 1920s copies could be found throughout Europe and the Americas. The first British and American editions appeared in 1920. The Second World War and its aftermath drove the book underground in English-speaking countries and in most of western Europe: images of Auschwitz and vivid recollections of Nazi diatribes made the fantasy of Jewish world domination too difficult to defend. However, in Latin America and the Arab world, where sympathy for the Nazis ran high during the war, *The Protocols* stayed in circulation, and editions found their way back into America and western Europe as memories of the war receded and the neo-Nazi movement took shape. See **neo-Nazi secret societies**.

Well before this happened, though, the Protocols had taken on a new life as evidence for secret masters of the world who were no longer linked to Judaism at all. This transformation began as early as 1919. In that year *The Public Ledger*, a Philadelphia newspaper, printed extracts of *The Protocols* as secret Bolshevik plans for world conquest, with all references to Jews removed. The writings of Nesta Webster and Lady Queensborough, the two most influential conspiracy theorists of 1920s Britain, adapted most of the book's ideas for the communist world conspiracy they claimed to uncover, while having little to say about the Protocols themselves. By the early 1960s, when Robert Welch's John Birch Society was redefining modern conspiracy theory, nearly all the allegations contained in *The Protocols* had been transplanted from the Jews to Welch's sinister conspiracy of Insiders and their New World Order. See **John Birch Society**; **New World Order**.

The circle completed itself in the late 1990s when copies of *The Protocols* began to appear in conspiracy theory literature, sometimes with references to Judaism deleted, sometimes not. M. William Cooper's 1991 book *Behold A Pale Horse*, required reading in conspiracy-hunting circles at the beginning of the twenty-first century, included the full text of the book, and David Icke's books, which claim that the world is actually controlled by a secret elite of shape-shifting reptiles, also quote *The Protocols* in detail. See **Reptilians**.

Further reading: Bernstein 1971, Cohn 1967, Cooper 1991.

Pythagorean Brotherhood

Among the most widely known secret societies of the classical world, the Pythagorean Brotherhood was founded by the Greek philosopher Pythagoras (*c.*570–*c.*495 BCE) in Crotona, a Greek colonial city in what is now southern Italy. Pythagoras had traveled from his native city of Samos to Egypt and Babylon to study mathematics, and then voyaged through the Greek islands to seek out mystery initiations, before settling in Crotona. His teachings, which centered on sacred geometry and numerology, combined mathematics and mysticism in a way that baffles many modern scholars but has close similarities to the practices of the old operative Masons. See **sacred geometry**.

The Pythagorean Brotherhood borrowed heavily from the ancient mystery cults but added features of its own. Candidates for membership faced a searching interview and then had to sign over all their worldly goods to the Brotherhood, to be returned if they left the society. For the first five years they had the rank of *acousmatici*, "listeners;" subject to a vow of silence, they were permitted to listen to lectures from behind a curtain but could ask no questions. After completing this probation they became *mathematici*, "mathematicians," and worked directly with Pythagoras and his inner circle of students. Members ate a vegetarian diet and lived under many taboos. Beliefs of the society also included reincarnation and a variety of moral and philosophical maxims.

The Brotherhood drew much of its membership from Crotona's upper classes and became deeply enmeshed in politics, supporting the aristocratic party in a series of social disputes that finally burst into violence. Around 500 BCE rioting broke out in Crotona and many members of the Brotherhood were killed; several ancient sources claim that most of the Brotherhood's members were trapped in their headquarters, which was burnt to the ground. Pythagoras fled to Metapontum, another city not far away, where he died a few years later. Surviving members scattered throughout the Greek world. The Brotherhood may have survived in exile for a time, but there seems to be no evidence that it existed for long thereafter – a point that has not prevented a wide range of later secret societies, including Freemasonry, from claiming Pythagorean roots. See **retrospective recruitment**.

Further reading: Burkert 1972.

R

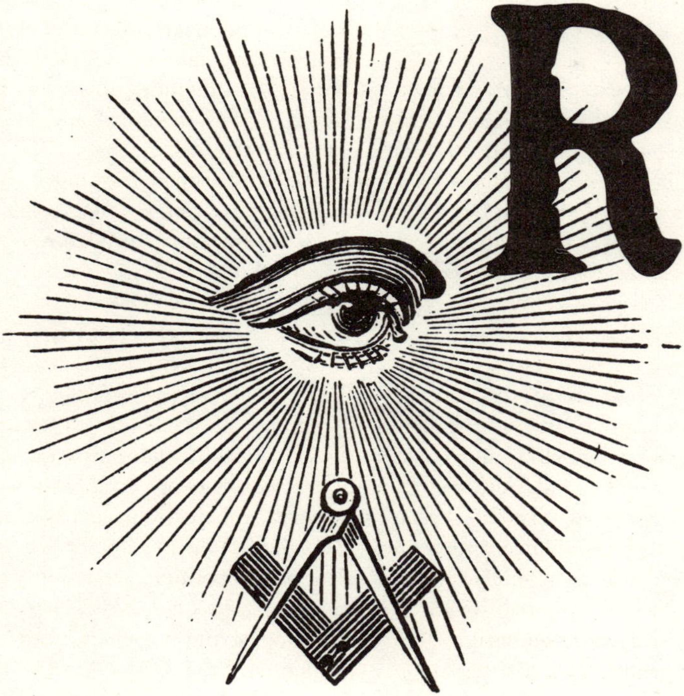

Raggi

A major secret society in early nineteenth-century Italy, the Raggi ("rays" or "radii") emerged in northern Italy sometime in 1797 in the aftermath of the French invasion. The French were originally welcomed as liberators by Italians weary of the political and religious autocracy of late eighteenth-century Italy, but soon changed their minds as the French turned the newly founded Cisalpine Republic into a puppet state subordinate to orders from Paris. Attempts to remedy the situation by legal means failed, and in response the Raggi formed and began plotting a revolt against French supremacy.

The organization, also known as the Centri ("centers") or Astronomia Platonica ("Platonic astronomy"), pioneered a system of organization that became standard throughout nineteenth-century political secret societies. Individual members, or "lines," belonged to groups of five, "rays," and members of one ray had no contact with other rays or their members; the head of each ray reported instead to one member of a "segment" or regional coordinating body. The president of each segment belonged to one of the two "hemispheres" or governing councils of the order, which were headquartered in Bologna and Milan respectively, and received instructions from the supreme directing body, the "Solar Circle." See **cell system**.

The Raggi expanded throughout Italy during the next decade; some estimates put its membership in 1804 at between 30,000 and 50,000. The Napoleonic Wars put the Raggi in a difficult situation, however, as it became increasingly clear that the alternative to French rule was a return to the old conservatism. After the fall of Napoleon, when most of the small kingdoms of Italy ended up ruled by reactionary governments backed by Austrian troops, the Raggi were apparently absorbed by the Carbonari and Philadelphes, two more militant secret societies with connections to the wider world of European revolutionary movements. See **Carbonari**; **Philadelphes**.

Rainbow City

At the extreme end of the contemporary alternative-realities spectrum is the claim that an ancient Martian city, made of multicolored plastic blocks, lies hidden somewhere beneath the icy wastes of Antarctica. Rainbow City, as this metropolis is called, is one part of a vast network of underground Martian cities established two and a half million years ago. The other cities have long since been abandoned, but Rainbow City remains inhabited by descendants of the original Martian colonists. Warm springs on all sides keep out the Antarctic cold, and ice walls 10,000 feet tall guard it from intruders – not merely humans, but also savage lizard beings from

Venus, the age-old enemies of the Martians. See **Antarctica; extraterrestrials; Reptilians; underground realms**.

These claims first surfaced in the American occult community in the 1940s in a document called the Hefferlin Manuscript, supposedly written by William and Gladys Hefferlin after their first contact with Rani Khatani, one of the "Ancient Three" who govern the Martian refuge. Rumors claim that the Hefferlins, shortly after putting their manuscript into circulation, moved to Rainbow City and are living there now, freed from old age and death by advanced Martian medical science. The tale is colorful enough that it seems almost a shame to point out that not a single scrap of evidence supports these fancies.

Further reading: Kafton-Minkel 1989.

Ramsay, Andrew Michael

Scottish Freemason and Jacobite, 1686–1743. The son of a baker in the Scottish town of Ayr, Ramsay attended Edinburgh University, then worked as a tutor for a time before relocating to London, where he encountered the writings of Archbishop François de Salignac de la Mothe-Fénelon, a noted Catholic author of the time. In 1709 he moved to the Netherlands and settled in Cambrai, where Fénelon lived. There he converted to Catholicism and became part of Fénelon's circle of friends, remaining with the archbishop until the latter's death in 1715. Shortly thereafter he was in Paris, where he associated with the Duc d'Orleans, Regent for the young King Louis XV, and became a Chevalier of the Order of St Lazare. In 1720 he published a biography of his late patron Fénelon that won him widespread acclaim.

In 1724 he went to Rome to take up a position as tutor to the two sons of the "Old Pretender" James Stuart, the exiled heir to the English throne. He held the position for some 15 months, but remained in contact with Jacobite circles in Paris and elsewhere after his return to France. Curiously, not long after his departure from Rome he was offered another position as tutor, this time to the Duke of Cumberland, second son of the Hanoverian Prince of Wales; he declined it, but returned to Britain in 1728 as a guest of the Duke of Argyll, and in 1730 – despite his religion and his Jacobite connections – was awarded a doctorate at Oxford. See **Jacobites**.

It was probably in 1728 that Ramsay was admitted to a Masonic lodge in London. On his later return to France, he became active in French Masonic circles, rising to the rank of Chancellor of the Grand Lodge of France in 1736. In that same year he wrote his most famous work, an oration on the history of Freemasonry, which traced its roots back to the Crusading knights of the Middle Ages. This was the first time that claim had been made, and it provided crucial backing for the new "Scottish" Masonry that appeared shortly thereafter in France. See **Freemasonry**; **Scottish degrees**.

Ramsay continued to write and publish until his death in 1743 at St Germain-en-Laye. His career cut across some of the most bitter political divides of the eighteenth century. He received patronage simultaneously from the Duc d'Orleans, a firm ally of the English government, and from James Stuart, who hoped to overthrow it. Mainstream historians have speculated that he might have been a double agent, working for the Jacobites and Hanoverians at the same time, while Masonic historians have suggested that he was responsible for the first Templar rite within Masonry, a rite of three degrees closely allied with the Jacobite movement. While both these claims remain unproven, his career places him near the center of some of the most complex secret intrigues of the eighteenth century, and his role in propagating the legend of a crusading origin for Freemasonry has shaped the history of secret societies ever since. See **Knights Templar**.

Further reading: Roberts 1972.

Randolph, Paschal Beverly

American occultist, spiritualist, physician, politician, author, and founder of secret societies, 1825–75. A leading figure in nineteenth-century American occultism, Randolph was the illegitimate son of Flora Clark, an African-American woman, and William Beverly Randolph, a white man, whom Randolph later claimed belonged to the wealthy Randolph family of Tidewater Virginia. Born and raised in the Five Points area, New York's most notorious slum district, Randolph lost his mother by the age of seven and had to fend for his own living thereafter. He worked as a bootblack, begged from door to door, and finally, in his teen years, found a position as a cabin boy on a merchant ship.

By 1845 he was working as a barber in upstate New York. When Spiritualism burst onto the public stage in 1848, Randolph was quickly caught up in it, first as a convert and then as one of the first African-American Spiritualist mediums. By the early 1850s he also claimed to be a "clairvoyant physician," specializing in sexual problems, and 1854 saw the publication of his first book, a novel titled *Waa-gu-Mah*. In 1855 he toured England, France, and Germany, holding Spiritualist séances and meeting with European occultists, and his reception was favorable enough that 1857 saw a second European tour.

In 1858, however, Randolph publicly renounced Spiritualism and spent the next few years on the anti-Spiritualist lecture circuit, assailing mediums as the passive victims of evil spirits. He soon quarreled with the Christian church that supported much of this activity, though, and left the country again. According to his later accounts, he spent 1861 and 1862 traveling in the Near East, making contact with the "Ansaireh" or al-Nusairi, a heretical Islamic sect in Syria, and receiving from them the principles of his later occult teachings. Whether this actually happened is anyone's guess, as Randolph's statements about his own biography changed frequently and were full of contradictions.

By the mid-1860s Randolph was back in America, helping to recruit African-American volunteers for the Union army in the Civil War, and after the war ended he made a brief and unsuccessful foray into politics. By the end of the decade he had returned to writing and occultism, and began setting forth the teachings he called Eulis or the Ansairetic Arcanum, the distinctive system of occult philosophy and sexual magic that would be his lasting legacy. Eulian magic started with the basic practices of "volantia" (calm focused concentration), "decretism" (unity of will), and "posism" (mental receptivity). These allowed the initiate to make use of the magic mirror, the primary magical instrument of Randolph's system, for clairvoyance and contact with spiritual entities, leading up through the practices of zorvoyance and aethavoyance (astral and spiritual vision) to the art of blending, Randolph's term for a conscious trance in which the initiate's consciousness fused with that of a higher spiritual being. See **Eulis**; **Scrying**.

The core teachings of Eulis, however, focused on the mysteries of sex. Randolph was far ahead of his time in his views about sex; in an era when most physicians denied the existence of the female orgasm, Randolph insisted that orgasmic release was essential to mental and physical health in women as well as men. When two lovers focused minds and wills on a common intention at the moment of mutual orgasm, Randolph believed, the result was an energy release with unlimited magical powers.

The origins of this system are a matter of much dispute. Some researchers give credence to Randolph's claims that he received them from the Rosicrucians or the al-Nusairi; others point out close similarities between Randolph's ideas and those of several important American occultists of the generation before him, notably Andrew Jackson Davis. Still others point out that Randolph himself admitted, in several places in his writings, that his teachings were entirely his own creation. It seems entirely possible that all these claims have some truth to them, and that Randolph combined scraps of older traditions with the occult teachings of his own time and his own unique insights to create his system.

Randolph's brilliance, unfortunately, coexisted with an arrogant personality that lost him friends and supporters wherever he went. He made repeated attempts to launch a magical secret society to carry on his teachings, only to quarrel with their members and dissolve them, usually within months of their founding. His personal life was no more stable, filled with broken marriages and failed businesses. In his last years his mood swings became increasingly violent, and he finally committed suicide in 1875.

The last two of his secret societies, the Brotherhood of Eulis and the Triplicate Order of Rosicrucia, Pythianae, and Eulis, both reformed after his death and played a significant role in launching other occult secret societies later on, notably R. Swinburne Clymer's Fraternitas Rosae Crucis (FRC). Moreover, two students of his work in England, Peter Davidson and Thomas Burgoyne, went on to found one of the most influential magical secret societies of the late nineteenth century, the Hermetic Brotherhood of Luxor. See **Fraternitas Rosae Crucis; Hermetic Brotherhood of Luxor (H.B. of L.).**

Further reading: Deveney 1997.

REJECTED KNOWLEDGE

The precise equivalent of religious heresy in today's secular scientific culture, the field of rejected knowledge consists of all those beliefs, ideas, and systems of thought about nature, history, and the universe that have been condemned by accepted scientific authorities. While many of the elements of today's rejected-knowledge scene date back centuries, or even millennia, a hard and fast distinction between accepted ideas and rejected ones did not begin to take shape until the second half of the nineteenth century, when scientists won the struggle with Christian religious authorities over the age of the earth and the origins of humanity.

The aftermath of the struggle saw the scientific worldview take on many of the dogmatic features of the religious worldview it had conquered. By the early twentieth century, ferocious disputes within the scientific community itself over psychic phenomena and similar subjects gave way to a consensus that ruled such fields off limits to serious research. Even inoffensive proposals such as Alfred Wegener's theory of continental drift were consigned to the dustbin by a scientific orthodoxy convinced of its own correct understanding of the world. In this climate the rise of an alternative community for rejected ideas was all but guaranteed.

The inventor of rejected knowledge as a distinct cultural phenomenon was the American politician and writer Ignatius Donnelly (1831–1901). In the later years of a long and contentious career, Donnelly wrote a series of books that launched several of the enduring themes of the rejected-knowledge scene into popular culture. His *Atlantis, The Antediluvian World* (1882) put the idea of Atlantis back on the map; his *Ragnarok, The Age of Fire and Gravel* (1883), which argued that the earth had been hit by a giant comet at the beginning of the Ice Age, reintroduced the concept of catastrophic earth changes to popular culture; and his *The Great Cryptogram* (1888) played a crucial role in bringing the Shakespeare authorship controversy to public attention. See **Atlantis**; **earth changes**; **Shakespeare controversies**.

All these themes and more were taken up by Russian mystic Helena Petrovna Blavatsky (1831–91), the founder of the Theosophical Society. Her first book, *Isis Unveiled* (1877), launched an all-out assault on the scientific and religious orthodoxies of her time in an effort to demonstrate the superiority of mystical and occult ideas. Many of the standard features of rejected knowledge in the following century, from lost continents and forgotten planetary catastrophes to suppressed technologies and the superior knowledge of ancient cultures, play central roles in *Isis Unveiled* and its sprawling sequel, *The Secret Doctrine* (1888). The enormous popular success of Theosophy ensured a wide distribution for these ideas and inspired many other intellectual dissidents to challenge the scientific mainstream with heresies of their own. See **Blavatsky, Helena Petrovna**; **Theosophical Society**.

Another central figure in the emergence of rejected knowledge was American writer and researcher Charles Hoy Fort (1874–1932). Fort made it his life's work to collect facts that refused to fit accepted scientific theories. Combing through stacks of scientific journals in the reading rooms of the New York Public Library, he compiled the raw material for his four famous books, *The Book of the Damned* (1919), *New Lands* (1923), *Lo!* (1931), and *Wild Talents* (1932). Unlike Blavatsky, who used flaws in the scientific consensus to argue for the value of her own system of mystical thought, Fort rejected all attempts at universal explanation, arguing that the universe was too bizarre for any human theory to adequately explain.

A fourth figure, American science fiction writer and editor Raymond Palmer (1910–77), fused Blavatsky's and Fort's contributions to launch rejected knowledge once and for all into popular culture. In the late 1930s, as managing editor of the science fiction magazine *Amazing Stories*, Palmer started running articles on rejected knowledge themes to fill out monthly issues when the supply of science fiction ran short. The response from the readership was so positive that more and more of the magazine came to be devoted to rejected ideas of all kinds. In 1945 he rewrote and published "I Remember Lemuria!", the first of Richard Shaver's bizarre accounts of sinister "detrimental robots" or "deros" tormenting surface dwellers with forgotten Lemurian technology from a network of abandoned tunnels far underground, and more than doubled *Amazing Stories* circulation. The UFO phenomenon that burst into popular culture two years later was more grist for Palmer's mill, and he played a crucial part in popularizing UFO lore among the general public. By 1948 Palmer was publishing and editing *Fate*, America's first monthly magazine devoted to rejected knowledge. In *Fate*'s pages, Fort's scientific skepticism and Blavatsky's mystical ideologies blended seamlessly to create the modern field of rejected knowledge. See **Lemuria**; **Palmer, Raymond**; **unidentified flying objects (UFOs)**.

The items that ended up becoming part of this field were, to some extent, a grab bag of half-forgotten traditions, anomalous experiences, and new belief systems, united mostly by the fact that scientific orthodoxy rejected them and despised their adherents. Nearly all the core elements of Blavatsky's Theosophy – lost continents, forgotten civilizations, reincarnation, disembodied masters, Asian spiritual disciplines, and unrecognized powers hidden away within the human body and mind – flowed into late twentieth-century rejected knowledge. Traditional western occultism had a much smaller role, though astrology found a place. Unexplained phenomena of every kind, from ESP and dowsing to UFOs and cattle mutilations, had a major part in defining the field.

An even larger role, though, went to alternative visions of history. Anyone who claimed to disprove the officially accepted version of history in favor of some alternative was guaranteed a hearing, and a following, among fans of rejected knowledge. From disputes about the real author of the Shakespeare poems and plays to arguments that the early history of humanity had been shaped by encounters with alien space travelers, alternative history became the backbone of the rejected-knowledge industry. Speculations about the origins of Freemasonry and Christianity became particularly popular, especially when the Priory of Sion hoax linked the two together in an appealing though completely fictional narrative. See **Christian origins**; **Freemasonry, origins of**; **Priory of Sion**.

The widespread loss of faith in the western world's institutions during and after the cultural revolutions of the late 1960s made all these ideas increasingly believable in the last quarter of the twentieth century. As evidence surfaced that government officials had lied to the public about CIA activities and that two generations of geologists had been completely wrong in dismissing continental drift, it became easy to believe that government officials were also lying about UFOs and that scientists were equally wrong in rejecting the historical reality of Atlantis. The ham-fisted efforts of self-described "skeptics" to discredit honest accounts of unexplained phenomena, and to dismiss proven but scientifically unpopular practices such as acupuncture, also helped convince millions of people that the voices of scientific authority could not be trusted. As a result, many aspects of rejected knowledge became widely accepted by the general public across most of the world, and a thriving publishing and media industry sprang up to fill the demand for new books, videos, and television programs about rejected knowledge.

The downside of this process was a complete breakdown in critical thinking on the part of many believers in rejected knowledge. Increasingly, in the last decades of the twentieth century, the only evidence that was needed to prove the reality of some piece of rejected knowledge to many people was the sheer fact that someone in science or government had dismissed it. Real anomalies and traditional systems of alternative thought and practice were shoved aside in order to make room for new and more colorful theories, many of which rested on foundations of pure fantasy and some of which had been invented from whole cloth to cash in on a lucrative market. A current of paranoia flowed into the movement as conspiracy theories gained widespread acceptance. The same period also saw alternative circles around the world embrace a "machismo of credulity," an attitude that treated a willingness to believe the most extravagant and unsupported claims as proof of one's intellectual liberation or spiritual insight.

A crucial role in this transition was played by the systematic misuse of hypnosis in several different areas of rejected knowledge. UFO researchers were first off the mark here, relying on hypnotic regression from the 1970s onward in an attempt to recover suppressed memories in people who believed that they had been abducted by aliens. Similar practices came into use after 1980 among therapists claiming to treat Satanic ritual abuse, and at about the same time hypnotherapists started recovering material from people who claimed to be unwilling experimental guinea pigs in secret government mind control projects. Despite drastic problems with therapeutic standards, objectivity, and supporting evidence, evidence from hypnosis came to be accepted without question through much of the rejected-knowledge community in the 1980s and 1990s. See **Satanism**.

By the last years of the century these trends set the stage for the emergence of theories that attempted to unite all rejected knowledge into a single coherent ideology. No two of these theories covered exactly the same ground, but the same themes did recur in them: alien astronauts who reached earth in the prehistoric past, lost civilizations and the catastrophes that overwhelmed them, sinister figures ruling the world in secret, and secret societies passing on a hidden heritage from ancient times all featured over and over again in a kaleidoscope of combinations. Some theorists, such as

English ex-football commentator and Green Party candidate David Icke, offer readers a paranoid mysticism in which all the evil in the world is caused by bloodthirsty, shape-shifting extraterrestrial reptiles who, disguised as human beings, make up the ruling class of all human societies and maintain their power through a network of diabolical secret societies practicing ritual sacrifice. Others, such as English author Graham Hancock, take the opposite viewpoint and claim that secret societies such as Freemasonry preserve valuable spiritual teachings from an ancient Martian civilization destroyed by asteroids in the distant past, and now offer timely warnings to Earth's people as they blunder toward a similar fate. These and many other writers offer powerful mythic visions of history whose emotional force too easily obscures the weaknesses in the evidence supporting them. See **lost civilizations**; **Reptilians**.

These grand narratives and unified field theories of rejected knowledge make it very difficult to sort out the wheat from the chaff, and very easy to fall into the trap of either rejecting or uncritically accepting all rejected knowledge in a lump. Just as continental drift was dismissed as a crackpot theory for most of the twentieth century, until sea floor evidence proved unequivocally that Wegener's theory was right, some elements of today's rejected knowledge have value despite the denials of contemporary authority figures: among many other points, esoteric traditions such as Hermeticism and Freemasonry offer teachings that can transform human life for the better, alternative healing methods such as acupuncture and homeopathy yield effective treatments for human illness with fewer side effects than conventional medicine, and secret societies have arguably had more impact on the history of the last four centuries or so than most mainstream historians are willing to admit. Still, none of this makes it reasonable to insist without good evidence that Queen Elizabeth II is actually a shape-shifting lizard who runs the world drug trade, or that a middle-aged American couple have attained immortality in a Martian city of giant plastic blocks near the South Pole – both claims that have been made by more than one figure in the rejected-knowledge scene in recent years.

Further reading: Blavatsky 1888, Goldberg 2001, Icke 1995, Keel 1989, Nathan and Snedecker 1995.

REMOTE VIEWING

See **Scrying**.

RENNES-LE-CHÂTEAU

A small village in the hills of southern France, located between the walled medieval city of Carcassonne to the north and the slopes of the eastern Pyrenees to the south, Rennes-le-Château was of little interest to anyone but its inhabitants until the early 1950s, when a promoter named Noel Corbu opened a restaurant in the Tour Magdala, a nineteenth-century stone building erected by a former parish priest of the village, Bérenger Saunière. Saunière earned local notoriety by his spending habits, which he financed by performing masses for money, a practice illegal under canon law that finally got him suspended by the local bishiop in 1911. Looking for publicity to attract customers to his new restaurant, Corbu heard old stories about hidden treasures from the Albigensian Crusade. He joined these tales to accounts of the free-spending Saunière to create a romantic tale about the priest's discovery of buried treasure while restoring the old parish church in the village, and talked a magazine, *La Dépêche du Midi*, into carrying an article repeating his claims in 1956. See **Cathars**.

One of the people who heard the treasure story was an acquaintance of Corbu's, Pierre Plantard, who happened to be the head of a very small secret society called the *Prieuré de Sion* or Priory of Zion. Plantard had founded the Priory himself in 1956, but like most secret societies it claimed links to the distant past, and Corbu's story apparently struck Plantard as the perfect framework for a manufactured history. Corbu's story became central to Plantard's disinformation campaign, which was taken up by a group of British writers and turned, with substantial additions, into the bestselling book *The Holy Blood and the Holy Grail* (1982). Other researchers have disputed this and argued instead that the treasure of Rennes-le-Château was the Ark of the Covenant, an extraterrestrial artifact, a coded message warning that the Earth would be struck in 2012 by a giant comet, or any of a dozen other things. The entire landscape around Rennes-le-Château has been combed for clues and turned into the background for a burgeoning subgenre in the alternative realities publishing industry. See **Ark of the Covenant**; **Christian origins**; **earth changes**; **extraterrestrials**; **Priory of Sion**.

Ironically, the entire Bérenger Saunière story had been effectively debunked by French researchers by the time *The Holy Blood and the Holy Grail* reached the bookstands. Church records and Saunière's own papers show that the vast majority of the stories circulated about Rennes-le-Château and Saunière are sheer invention, based on the modest reality of an eccentric parish priest. See **Disinformation**.

Further reading: Baigent et al. 1983, Fanthorpe 1989.

Reptilians

One of the features of the 1980s UFO scene was a series of attempts to categorize the entities reported by people who had encountered UFO occupants. These efforts foundered on the sheer variety of reported space beings, but managed to turn up a handful of common types. The so-called "grays," large-headed dwarfs with gray or brown skin, spindly limbs, and black featureless eyes were the most widely publicized variety of UFO pilot, but another variety consisted of lizard-like aliens with scaled skin and yellow eyes. These "reptilians" soon became a recognized type in UFO research circles. See **unidentified flying objects (UFOs)**.

The reptilians, like so much of the UFO phenomenon, showed remarkable parallels to the science fiction of previous decades – lizard-men from other planets were a staple of the pulp science fiction magazines – and to traditions on the fringes of the occult community. The Hefferlin manuscript, a purportedly factual document circulating in American occult circles since the 1940s, claimed that evil reptile-men from Venus invaded the earth in the distant past to do battle with benevolent humanoid Martians for control of Rainbow City, a metropolis hidden beneath the Antarctic ice cap. Despite obvious borrowings from science fiction-horror writer H.P. Lovecraft's Cthulhu mythos, the Hefferlin manuscript and an assortment of writings based on it helped popularize the idea of sinister alien reptiles and blend it with the experiences of UFO contactees. See **Rainbow City**.

A crucial role in this process of synthesis was played by an American science fiction television production (two mini-series and a short-lived weekly series) of the early 1980s. Titled *V*, these shows pitted humanity against an invasion of shape-shifting reptiles from outer space. The aliens used advanced technology and mind-control methods to manipulate humans and take over the earth's political and economic systems. Just as the cinema Satanism of the 1960s' horror movie *Rosemary's Baby* was copied in the first wave of Satanic ritual abuse claims in the late 1970s, most of *V*'s themes appeared in detail in the alien-reptile mythologies of the next decade.

By the 1990s, UFO contactees and abductees had woven the "grays," "Nordics," reptilians, and other widely reported types of UFO occupants into their narratives of alien contact. The reptilians, many contactees claimed, came from solar systems in the constellation Draco. Where the Nordics were generally portrayed in a positive light, and the grays tended to range between positive and neutral, the reptilians came in for mostly negative portrayals, playing essentially the same role they had in the *V* storyline. It was in this form that they entered the writings of David Icke, whose attempt to create a universal synthesis of all rejected knowledge gave a central role to the reptilians. See **rejected knowledge**.

Icke's reptilians are the evil aliens of the *V* series projected onto a sprawling mythology of class warfare. According to Icke, the reptilians are the secret masters of the world, a race of aliens from Draco who crossbred with human beings millennia ago to produce hybrid bloodlines that run the world on the surface, while others of pure reptile blood lurk in caverns far below. The crossbreeds, who can shape-shift from human to reptile form, include all past and present royal families of Britain, all other European royal houses, and every one of the presidents of the United States, from George Washington to George W. Bush. It is no exaggeration to say that in Icke's view every person who has ever held political, religious, or economic influence at any point in human history is a reptilian crossbreed.

While Icke insists that there are good reptilians elsewhere in the universe, he paints the ones we have here on earth in uniformly unflattering colors. As the rulers of the planet, they are personally responsible for all the evil, ignorance, and suffering on earth, manipulating humanity through a network of secret societies to cause war, poverty, and other social ills. The Knights Templar, the Illuminati, and most of the other *bêtes noires* of contemporary conspiracy theory are simply fronts for the vast reptilian conspiracy, and the establishment of the New World Order is their central goal. If this were not enough, they also passionately enjoy drinking human blood. To be fair to the reptilian crossbreeds, Icke admits that their nefarious deeds are not entirely their fault, as most of them are possessed by lizard-demons from the lower fourth dimension. See **Illuminati**; **Knights Templar**; **New World Order**.

This extraordinarily colorful mythology has found an eager audience in counterculture circles throughout the western world, and has been incorporated into the theories of several other popular conspiracy theorists. As an ideology of class conflict, which is its primary thrust, it has few equals. Not even the most extreme forms of Marxism ever accused members of the industrial world's political and economic elites of being shape-shifting extraterrestrial monsters who thirst for human blood. The evidence Icke presents is thin even by conspiracy theory standards – his claim that US president George Bush Sr. is a reptilian crossbreed, for example, depends on the testimony of one person who claimed under hypnosis to have been used as a robotic sex slave by most of the world's political leaders, and on Icke's own unsupported claim that he knows other people who saw Bush shape-shift into reptile form – but this has not prevented his books from being taken as gospel on the far ends of the political and cultural spectrum throughout Europe and America.

Further reading: Icke 1995, Icke 1999, Icke 2001.

RETROSPECTIVE RECRUITMENT

One of the primary methods used by secret societies to conceal their actual origins, retrospective recruitment was defined and satirized by a famous passage in Ambrose Bierce's *Devil's Dictionary* of 1911:

> Freemasons, n. An order with secret rites, grotesque ceremonies and fantastic costumes, which, originating in the reign of Charles II, among working artisans of London, has been joined successively by the dead of past centuries in unbroken retrogression until now it embraces all the generations of man on the hither side of Adam and is drumming up distinguished recruits among the pre-Creational inhabitants of Chaos and the Formless Void.

The basic strategy of retrospective recruitment, as this suggests, is the same as that of the person of humble origins who claims descent from some famous monarch or aristocrat. Since few people have the resources to check the claim, and fewer still are likely to devote the time and effort to the task, such claims often go unchallenged even when they are clearly bogus. Secret societies can claim prestigious forebears with even less compunction, since it is all but impossible to prove conclusively that a given public figure in the past did not belong to some secret society or another; a complete lack of evidence, after all, just shows how assiduously the person in question kept his oath of secrecy.

Such considerations have made it easy for some recently founded secret societies to claim roots reaching back hundreds or even thousands of years. One of the most widely publicized claims of this sort has been circulated by (and on behalf of) the Priory of Sion, a French secret society founded in 1956. Similar historical imagination shaped the pedigree of the Ancient Mystical Order Rosae Crucis (AMORC), an American Rosicrucian secret society founded in 1925; AMORC claimed the "heretic pharaoh" Ahkenaten, among others, in its list of forebears. See **Akhenaten**; **Ancient Mystical Order Rosae Crucis (AMORC)**; **Leonardo da Vinci**; **Priory of Sion**.

While retrospective recruitment functions mostly as an advertising gimmick nowadays, it was more important in the eighteenth and nineteenth centuries, when the Masonic custom of requiring a lodge to be chartered by a grand lodge was standard practice throughout the world of European secret societies. Innovators who devised new secret societies thus had to invent a lineage for themselves in order to gain acceptance for their creations. Romantic origin stories played a crucial role in this process, but retrospective recruitment also saw much use. See **origin stories**.

Some of the most influential secret societies in modern history equipped themselves with blatantly forged charters in order to meet this requirement. Martinez de Pasqually in 1767 founded the Elect Cohens, the fount of most contemporary French occult secret society traditions, on the basis of a charter allegedly issued by Bonnie Prince Charlie as "head of all Scottish Masonry," while the Hermetic Order of the Golden Dawn was founded by a coterie of English Masonic occultists in 1887 using an equally bogus charter supposedly issued by a German adept in Nuremberg. This same logic drove the manufacture of imaginary "family traditions" by the creators of modern Wiccan and Pagan traditions in the second half of the twentieth century. While the wholesale manufacture of roots is not as necessary now as it once was, its value as a marketing tool remains high, and retrospective recruitment will probably remain a favored tactic in secret society circles for a long time to come. See **Elect Cohens**; **Hermetic Order of the Golden Dawn**; **Wicca**.

Reuss, Theodor

German singer, journalist, Freemason and secret society founder, (1855–1923). Born in Augsburg, the son of an innkeeper, he began a musical career as a vocalist in his youth and did tolerably well, winning a part in the chorus of the first performance of Richard Wagner's opera *Parsifal* at Bayreuth. He was initiated into Freemasonry during an 1876 visit to London. In 1885 he returned to London to pursue his singing career on the English stage, and also involved himself in radical politics, becoming a member of the Socialist League; it was later alleged that he was a spy for the Prussian secret police sent to check up on links between the London socialists and anarchist circles in Germany. See **Anarchism**.

During this stay in England he also began a career as a journalist and traveled throughout Britain, Europe, and America. Until 1894 he showed no interest in occultism at all. In that year, however, he published an article on "Pranatherapy' in a German occult journal and made connections with a variety of central European occultists, above all Austrian industrialist Carl Kellner (1851–1905), an initiate of the Hermetic Brotherhood of Light. He and Kellner began to discuss the idea of a quasi-Masonic organization that would teach occultism, especially the sexual magic the Brotherhood had inherited from American occultist Paschal Beverly Randolph (1825–75).

See **Hermetic Brotherhood of Light**; **Randolph, Paschal Beverly**.

At this time, however, Reuss was active with another organization, an attempted revival of the Bavarian Illuminati, which he founded with Leopold Engel in 1895. Unlike the original Illuminati, a rationalist organization with liberal political views, Reuss's Illuminati was an occult Masonic order working five degrees – the three ordinary Craft Masonry degrees, plus the degree of St Andrew and the Rosicrucian degree. It attracted a small amount of interest, and at one point had six lodges affiliated with it. He and Engel parted company in 1902 and Reuss, leaving the Illuminati name with Engel, obtained a charter for the Rite of Memphis and Misraim from John Yarker in Britain. This proved more successful than the Illuminati, and by 1903 his order had over a hundred members; for an irregular occult Masonic order at the time, this was respectably large. See **Bavarian Illuminati**; **Rite of Memphis and Misraim**; **Rosicrucians**.

The success of the Rite of Memphis and Misraim proved fleeting, though, as the members had little patience with Reuss's demands for large sums of money. By 1906 Reuss was interested in a new project, the Ordo Templi Orientis (OTO), which would be the quasi-Masonic body he and Kellner had discussed years before. He found few takers before 1910, when he recruited Aleister Crowley. In 1912, in a move he would later richly regret, Reuss made Crowley head of the British branch of the order. Within a few years the two had fell out, and Reuss spent much of the First World War and the years immediately following it trying to undercut Crowley's position, especially in America, where he gave an OTO charter to H. Spencer Lewis, later the founder of the American Rosicrucian order AMORC. See **Ancient Mystical Order Rosae Crucis (AMORC)**; **Crowley, Aleister**; **Ordo Templi Orientis (OTO)**.

Reuss spent most of the First World War in Switzerland, and moved back to Germany in 1921. Two years later, still in the midst of quarrels with Crowley, he died in Munich.

Rex Deus

(Latin, "King God.") According to recent speculative literature, the title held by a group of European aristocratic families allegedly descended from the family lines of the 24 High Priests of the Temple of Solomon in Jerusalem, who took names from Jewish mythology corresponding to their ritual roles. In every generation, therefore, there was a Melchizedek, a Michael, a Gabriel, and so on. See **Temple of Solomon**.

The Rex Deus priesthood allegedly operated two boarding schools in the Temple complex, one for boys and one for girls, and had the privilege of ceremonially deflowering the girls when they reached childbearing age.

The girls would then be married off to husbands, who would raise the children as their own; however, the children had to be returned to the temple boarding school on their seventh birthday to receive the priesthood's training and presumably, if female, another helping of their genetic material as well. Jesus is claimed as the result of one such union, fathered by a priest with the ceremonial name of Gabriel. See **Christian origins**; **Jesus of Nazareth**.

According to the story, the Rex Deus families escaped the destruction of Jerusalem by the Romans in 68 CE and survived as an underground family tradition, surfacing in the early Middle Ages as important families of European aristocracy; how a group of Jewish families achieved this feat at a time when other Jews were confined to ghettos and subject to harsh persecution is not clear. Several founders of the Knights Templar were allegedly members of Rex Deus families, and the same families played a crucial role in the origins of the Freemasons and a variety of other currently popular historical events. The Sinclair family of Scotland is inevitably cited as one of the Rex Deus families. See **Freemasonry**; **Knights Templar**; **Sinclair family**.

The extensive surviving documentation on the ancient Jewish priesthood, ranging from the Old Testament to the writings of the Roman historian Josephus, contains no trace of the supposed Rex Deus tradition, or for that matter of 24 High Priests in the Temple, and many of the claims made for the Rex Deus priesthood include drastic violations of Jewish religious law. The evidence for the existence of the Rex Deus families, on the other hand, consists of unsupported claims made to the co-author of a book on the subject after a lecture on Rosslyn Chapel. This has not prevented the story from being repeated as fact in a number of other books on the subject of Christian origins. See **Rosslyn Chapel**.

Further reading: Hopkins et al. 2000, Knight and Lomas 1997.

Ribbonmen

The rise of the Whiteboys movement in southern Ireland in the late eighteenth century inspired Irish farmers and laborers throughout the island to consider secret societies and violence as options in the bitter economic and sectarian struggles of the time. Sometime around 1800, small groups of Ulster Catholics began organizing secret bands to attack landlords and estate managers accused of unfair practices. Members of these bands tied a colored ribbon around one arm as a uniform of sorts, a habit that soon gave them their distinctive name. See **Whiteboys**.

The Ribbonmen never had a central organization, and local Ribbon groups each took names of their own, so any attempt at a history of the Ribbon movement is fragmentary at best. Their activities rose and fell with economic cycles and harvests; when times were good and the potato harvest large, relative peace prevailed, while economic slumps and poor harvests guaranteed an upsurge in Ribbon activities. Members came predominantly from the poorest classes, who had no farms of their own and supported themselves as hired laborers. Close to the edge of survival, deprived of political rights, and more often subject to abuses and extortionate rents than others, rural laborers turned to secret organizations and nocturnal violence as their only means of any sort of redress.

The Ribbonmen flourished in the half century before the catastrophic potato blight and famine of the 1850s. As starvation and emigration reduced the Irish population to a fifth of its pre-Famine levels, the vast majority of the rural laborer class died or left the country, and the Ribbon movement dissolved.

Further reading: Williams 1973.

RIDING THE GOAT

For close to two centuries, if not longer, initiation into fraternal secret societies has been described throughout the English-speaking world as "riding the goat." The exact origins of the phrase remain obscure, but the most plausible hypothesis is that it comes from antimasonic propaganda linking Masonic initiation to the goat-headed idol Baphomet allegedly worshipped by the Knights Templar. See **Baphomet**; **Knights Templar**.

If the phrase did have its roots in antimasonry, it was quickly adopted by Masons and members of other secret societies with a vengeance, and it soon spread from secret society circles to the general public. Thus a one-act farce from 1846, *The Secrets of Odd Fellowship*, has one character bring a saddle to his initiation; if he has to ride a goat, he tells the others, he plans to do it in a dignified manner. By 1902 goat references and goat jokes were universal enough that James Pettibone of Pettibone Co., one of the premier manufacturers of secret society regalia and equipment in North America, could write and publish a book entitled *The Lodge Goat and Goat Rides: Butts and Goat Hairs, Gathered from the Lodge Rooms of every Fraternal Order*, filled with raucous stories and cartoons involving goats in lodges, complete with an introduction by "Billy the Goat."

The omnipresence of fraternal goat jokes made it inevitable that someone would attempt to stage an actual goat ride in a secret society initiation. The honor of the first such attempt belongs to the Modern Woodmen of America (MWA), a fraternal benefit society founded in the late nineteenth century. Faced with stiff competition from other benefit societies, the MWA's Head Consul, William A. Northcott, began in 1890 to add practical jokes to the MWA's initiation rituals. Mechanical goats were among the first and most popular additions to the ritual, and the company that manufactured them – DeMoulin Bros. & Co. of Greenville, Illinois, widely known as "the goat factory" – quickly became the premier supplier of "burlesque and side degree specialties" to the North American secret society market. See **burlesque degrees**; **fraternal benefit societies**.

The standard DeMoulin mechanical goat had a three-wheeled iron undercarriage, a body covered in wool, and a realistic head with curling horns. The rear axle had a zigzag in the middle connected to a push rod that moved the back end of the goat's body up and down, guaranteeing a memorable ride. As the goat business expanded, DeMoulin brought in several other designs with names such as "A Low Down Buck" and "The Rollicking Mustang Goat," rigged to deposit the rider on the lodge room floor in various ways.

Mechanical goats fell out of use in initiation rituals in the second half of the twentieth century, as customs changed and fear of lawsuits caused potentially risky elements to be eliminated by secret societies throughout the English-speaking world. The occasional DeMoulin goat, its undercarriage rusty and its woolen coat moth-eaten, turns up now and then in old lodge halls. To this day, however, candidates for initiation in American fraternal secret societies and college fraternities and sororities can expect to be teased by members about having to ride the goat. See **Initiation**.

Further reading: "A Member of the Order" 1846, Goldsmith 2004, Pettibone 1902.

RIGHT-HAND PATH

A term borrowed into western occult jargon from Indian Tantrism, this phrase originally referred to those Tantric systems that maintain the rules of behavior standard in Indian yoga traditions, including celibacy, vegetarianism, and abstention from alcohol and intoxicating drugs. The schools of the left-hand path, by contrast, permit their students to engage in sexual intercourse and in the consumption of meat, alcohol, and drugs, often using these things as tools for attaining higher awareness. See **left-hand path**.

These terms came into use in western occultism by way of the Theosophical Society but underwent a change in meaning. In late nineteenth- and early twentieth-century occultism, as a result, the phrase "right-hand path" meant roughly the same thing as "white magic" – a magical system that was, or at least claimed to be, morally good. In the same way, "left-hand path" simply became a synonym for "black" or morally evil magic. Ironically, since most western magicians then and now have sex, eat meat, and indulge in the occasional alcoholic beverage (or other intoxicant), the vast majority of self-described occultists of the right-hand path would be considered practitioners of the left-hand path in India. See **black magic; Theosophical Society; white magic.**

Rite of Memphis

One of the many systems on the fringes of regular Masonry that emerged in the nineteenth century, the Rite of Memphis was one of the most extensive, with no fewer than 95 degrees of initiation (plus an honorary 96th for its governing Grand Hierophant). According to the most widely accepted theory, it was originally founded by Samuel Honis, an expatriate Frenchman living in Egypt, in 1814. After the fall of Napoleon, Honis returned to France and brought his new rite with him, establishing one lodge, "Le Disciples de Memphis," in Montauban in 1815. It went out of existence after a year, but in the interim one Gabriel-Mathieu Marconis de Negre had received the full set of degrees.

In 1838 the Rite surfaced again in Paris with Marconis's son, Jacques-Etienne Marconis de Negre, as Grand Hierophant 96°. The younger Marconis had previously been a member of the Rite of Misraim, which boasted 90 degrees, but was expelled in 1833 and again (having joined in a different city under another name) in 1834. It has been suggested that the entire previous history of the Rite of Memphis, along with the Rite itself, was concocted by Marconis in the mid-1830s as an attempt to build a rival organization to the Rite of Misraim; conclusive evidence one way or the other is lacking, but such things happen frequently enough in the history of secret societies. See **Rite of Misraim**.

After the 1838 refounding (or founding) of the Rite, Marconis founded several lodges, but in 1841 the Rite was suppressed by the French police as a subversive secret society. To be fair, they had some justification; while Marconis seems to have been completely apolitical, the Rite of Memphis attracted attention from the radical left almost immediately it appeared, and many of its members belonged to the Philadelphes, one of the major revolutionary secret societies of the time. The suppression drove lodges underground rather than out of existence, and connections between the Rite and the Philadelphes spread during this time. See **Philadelphes**.

The revolution of 1848 brought a short-lived liberal regime into being in France, and Marconis was able to launch the Rite again under more favorable conditions. The next few years were the period of the Rite's greatest expansion, as charters for Grand Lodges went to Egypt, Romania, and the United States. French expatriates in England founded a Philadelphe lodge under the Rite's aegis in 1850. Napoleon III's seizure of power in 1852 turned this latter lodge into a major center of political opposition and conspiracy against his regime. Despite the efforts of the Grand Lodge of England to suppress the Rite of Memphis, the Philadelphe Lodge remained active at least until the end of the 1870s, and played an important role in the foundation of the First International. See **First International**.

In France, however, the Rite fell on hard times during the Second Empire; old-fashioned political secret societies such as the Philadelphes seemed out of date in an age of mass political movements. In 1862 Marconis turned what was left of the organization in France over to the Grand Orient of France, which turned its few French members into regular Freemasons and took the Memphis degrees out of circulation. Several subsequent attempts to relaunch the Rite of Memphis in Europe attracted few takers, though a handful of lodges in France, Switzerland, and Germany still work the Rite. In the United States the Rite of Memphis is in the possession of the Grand College of Rites, an organization founded for the specific purpose of taking irregular degree systems out of circulation and keeping them there. Its major descendant is the Rite of Memphis and Misraim, created by John Yarker from the remnants of Marconis's system and its most important rival. See **Rite of Memphis and Misraim**; **Yarker, John**.

Further reading: Drachkovitch 1966, Howe 1997.

Rite of Memphis and Misraim

The most extensive system of Masonic degrees ever worked, the Rite of Memphis and Misraim was the creation of John Yarker, the great promoter of fringe Masonic degrees and rites in the late nineteenth and early twentieth centuries. Yarker systematically gathered Masonic rites and high degrees from every available source, and the then-independent rites of Memphis and Misraim were among those that came into his hands. Both rites claimed ancient Egyptian origins, and both had a vast array of degrees – 90 in the Rite of Misraim, 95 in that of Memphis. Yarker hit on the scheme of combining the two, taking the best degrees from each to form the monumental 96-degree Rite of Memphis and Misraim, also called the Antient and Primitive Rite. See **high degrees**; **Rite of Memphis**; **Rite of Misraim**; **Yarker, John**.

Yarker's Sovereign Sanctuary of the Rite of Memphis and Misraim was founded at his hometown of Manchester in 1872 and immediately began conferring charters and patents (certificates of initiation) far and wide. Yarker also produced a magazine for the rite, *The Kneph*, which published occult and Masonic articles. The sheer cumbersomeness of its 96 degrees of initiation limited the appeal of the new rite, but a number of significant figures in the European occult community acquired Rite of Memphis and Misraim credentials. The most important of these was Theodor Reuss (1855–1923), who used the Rite as the basis for a quasi-Masonic magical secret society of his own, the Ordo Templi Orientis. See **Ordo Templi Orientis (OTO)**; **Reuss, Theodor**.

The Rite remained essentially Yarker's during his lifetime. Shortly after his death in 1913 his Sovereign Sanctuary became the center of a tug of war between Theosophical leaders Annie Besant and Charles Leadbeater, who wanted to annex it for Co-Masonry, and a group of Yarker loyalists backed by Aleister Crowley. The Theosophists were foiled, but the Rite passed into dormancy thereafter. It has since seen several revivals, but none of them have managed to attract more than a handful of followers. See **Co-Masonry**; **Crowley, Aleister**; **Theosophical Society**.

Rite of Misraim

Yet another of the complex systems of higher degrees born on the fringes of Freemasonry in the nineteenth century, the Rite of Misraim (also spelled Mizraim) had 90 degrees of initiation, with three additional honorary degrees for its Secret Chiefs. Its origins are obscure and have been much debated among Masonic historians; the most common theory is that it was concocted in Milan in 1805, and arrived in France in 1814 or 1815, after the fall of Napoleon, with the three Bedarride brothers. It was almost immediately attacked by the Grand Orient (Grand Lodge) of France, which declared it an irregular rite in 1816, but it proved to have more staying power than some of its rivals and has remained active in France since that time. It established a presence in England in 1870; after a few years of quarrels between its members and the Ancient and Accepted Rite, which sought to maintain its status as the only system of high degrees in Britain, it became a minor fixture in the world of British fringe Masonry. See **Ancient and Accepted Scottish Rite (AASR)**; **high degrees**.

In the 1870s, the Rite of Misraim came under the control of John Yarker, the indefatigable promoter of fringe Masonic degrees in England, and in 1878 Yarker merged it with its rival Rite of Memphis to form the Rite of Memphis and Misraim. After Yarker's death in 1913 it revived somewhat as an independent rite, mostly in France, but has attracted few followers. See **Rite of Memphis**; **Rite of Memphis and Misraim**; **Yarker, John**.

Rite of Perfection

The first known Masonic body to work the degrees that later belonged to the Scottish Rite, the Rite of Perfection was organized in Paris in 1754 by the Chevalier de Bonneville. It met in the buildings of the College of Jesuits at Clermont, thus its alternate name, the College or Rite of Clermont. Its membership included many English and Scots Jacobites in exile in France, and it seems to have played a role in reorganizing the scattered and demoralized Jacobite movement after the failure of the Stuart rising of 1745. See **Jacobites**.

The Rite of Perfection worked 22 degrees beyond the Craft Masonry degrees of Entered Apprentice, Fellow Craft, and Master Mason. Its rituals included a great deal of occult material, including alchemy, Cabala and Rosicrucian traditions, but its central teaching – certainly influenced by Andrew Ramsay's famous 1736 oration – was that Freemasonry descended from the medieval Knights Templar and that every Mason was therefore a Templar. This theory was adopted by the Rite's successor, the Council of Emperors of the East and West, which absorbed the Rite of Perfection four years after its founding. See **Freemasonry, origins of**; **Knights Templar**; **Ramsay, Andrew Michael**.

During its short lifetime, the Rite of Perfection also played a role in launching another important eighteenth-century secret society. One of its early initiates was Baron Karl Gotthelf von Hund, who went on to found the Rite of Strict Observance, one of the most important magical orders in Germany and the source of most Templar Masonry in continental Europe. See **Rite of Strict Observance**.

Rite of Strict Observance

One of the most important secret societies in Germany in the second half of the eighteenth century, the Rite of Strict Observance had its roots in the Templar Masonry invented by Jacobite exiles in France in the years just before the Stuart rebellion of 1745. Baron Karl Gotthelf von Hund, the founder and original head of the Rite, was initiated into Freemasonry in 1741 or 1742, and traveled to Paris in 1743, where he received the Templar degrees from the Earl of Kilmarnock, a Jacobite peer attached to the Stuart court in exile. See **Jacobites**; **Knights Templar**; **Scottish degrees**.

During his visit von Hund also received appointment as a Provincial Grand Master of the Templar degrees for Germany. He returned home to Saxony, and to all appearances spent the next 11 years doing nothing with the degrees and authority he had received. What exactly was going on during this period is anyone's guess, for the Templar degrees remained secret until the 1750s. Their connection to Jacobite ambitions made that secrecy something more than a ritual requirement in Germany at the time, since the House of Hanover, England's rulers since 1714 and the object of Jacobite hatreds, had close ties to many German principalities.

In 1754 von Hund went to Paris a second time. There he renewed his connections to the higher degrees by way of the Rite of Perfection, founded at the College of Clermont by the Chevalier de Bonneville that year as a public presence for the new Templar Masonry, and received new authority to promulgate the Rite in Germany. On his return to Germany, von Hund immediately launched his own organization, the Rite of Strict Observance, which took over the Templar claims of the Rite of Perfection but worked a simpler system of degrees. Masonic historians have argued that von Hund's system of 7 degrees was based on 6 degrees worked by Jacobite Masons before the creation of the 22 degrees of the Rite of Perfection. Hund himself claimed that the Rite and its secrets had been entrusted to him by a circle of Unknown Superiors, and that Charles Edward Stuart, the "Young Pretender," was its Grand Master. See **Rite of Perfection**; **Unknown Superiors**.

The Rite of Strict Observance was an immense success in Germany and other central European countries, supplanting most other Masonic systems in central Europe and expanding into Italy as well. Part of the Rite's appeal lay in the lure of new and higher degrees, and part in the Templar mythology with its attraction to German aristocrats, but von Hund also claimed to offer more tangible benefits. He claimed to have access to the secret of the philosopher's stone and the elixir of life, and many members of the Rite experimented with alchemy in the hope of preparing themselves for the final revelation that would enable them to turn lead into gold. Members of the Rite also searched for hidden Templar treasures and discussed the possibility of regaining Templar estates still held by the Knights of Malta. See **Alchemy**.

The Rite of Strict Observance faced competition from other would-be Templar Grand Masters. One of the most colorful was a man who went by the name of George Frederick Johnson, and proclaimed himself "Knight of the Great Lion of the High Order of the Lords of the Temple of Jerusalem." His real name was Leucht, and he had a shady career behind him involving other pseudonyms and claims of magical power. Johnson claimed to have received Templar degrees higher than von Hund's at a special conclave in Aberdeen, Scotland, the supposed headquarters of the Knights Templar since the fourteenth century. He surfaced in 1763 and managed to win enough of a following that von Hund at first treated him as an equal and arranged for an official meeting in 1764. When Johnson proved unable to produce any of the great secrets he claimed, von Hund denounced him as a trickster. Johnson was arrested in Magdeburg a year later for fraud, and von Hund's friends there saw to it that the "Knight of the Great Lion" languished in prison until his death in 1775.

Less easily dismissed was Johann August Starck (1741–1816), an enthusiastic Mason who went to Paris in 1766 and returned with the degrees of a new, higher Templar system, the Clerks Templar, which claimed to be an inner order of Templar clergy in possession of secrets not revealed to ordinary Templar knights. Membership in this new order was limited to Roman Catholics who had received all the degrees of the Rite of Strict Observance. In 1768 von Hund and Starck agreed to a union of the two organizations, but this never became effective and in 1775 Starck withdrew his followers from the combined rite.

By that time the Rite of Strict Observance was in steep decline. Its Achilles' heel was von Hund's claim that his Unknown Superiors were prepared to pass on important secrets. The secrets never appeared, and hard questions began to be asked about whether the Unknown Superiors existed at all. At a congress of the Rite held at Brunswick in 1775, von Hund was challenged directly on the subject, and eventually was demoted to the position of Provincial Superior, with Duke Ferdinand of Brunswick taking his place at the head of the Rite. Throughout this process, von Hund refused to reveal any information about the Rite's hidden chiefs, citing his own oath of secrecy, but his comments suggest that he was as disappointed as anyone at the failure of the Superiors to make good on their promises.

That disappointment may well not have been feigned. Contemporary writers describe von Hund as honest, enthusiastic, and credulous, and his career shows no other signs of duplicity or, for that matter, involvement in the Jacobite cause. His passion for Masonic rites seems to have landed him in the middle of intrigues whose political dimensions escaped him completely. The failure of the Jacobite cause to recover from the disaster at the battle of Culloden in 1746 explains the silence of the Unknown Superiors, since von Hund and his Rite alike had no further value to the exiled Stuart court once the hope of a restoration was past.

Hund died in 1776, still waiting for the Superiors to reveal the secrets they had promised him. The Rite continued to function for some years thereafter, though constant debates about the reality of the Unknown Superiors wracked the organization. In 1782 von Hund's successor, Duke Ferdinand, called another congress of the Rite, the Convention of Wilhelmsbad, to settle the matter once and for all. After much debate, the Convention decided that von Hund's claims of Templar connections were baseless, and replaced his higher degrees withthose of the Beneficent Chevaliers of the Holy City, a system created by the French Mason Jean-Baptiste Willermoz.

After the Convention a few initiates and lodges remained faithful to von Hund's system, and charlatans found a market for claims of access to the Unknown Superiors for years thereafter. Those members of the Rite not yet disillusioned with secret societies returned to less exotic forms of Masonry or joined the Order of the Golden and Rosy Cross, the premier German Rosicrucian order of the time, which was just then entering its period of greatest popularity. See **Order of the Golden and Rosy Cross**; **Rosicrucians**.

Further reading: Partner 1981.

Roman Catholic Church

The largest religious organization in the world today, the Roman Catholic Church claims origins dating back to Peter, one of the companions of Jesus of Nazareth. In historical terms, it emerged over several centuries in the late Roman period and early Middle Ages, as the bishops of Rome gradually expanded their power over Christian churches in Europe and claimed authority over the formerly independent bishops of other cities. Modest distinctions in theology and practice set it apart from the older Eastern Orthodox churches, from which it broke away in the eleventh century. Much greater distinctions separate it from Gnostic Christianity, which it exterminated in a series of violent actions from the fourth to the thirteenth centuries, and from the Protestant sects that broke away from it in the sixteenth century. See **Christian origins**; **Gnosticism**; **Jesus of Nazareth**.

In theory, the Roman Catholic Church is a religious monarchy in which the Pope, the bishop of Rome, is elected for a life term and has nearly unlimited power as God's representative on earth. In practice, the Pope presides over a loose federation of national churches and religious orders, each with its own traditions and prerogatives, and must depend on a sprawling medieval bureaucracy to carry out his decrees. The constant struggle to maintain the central authority of Rome in the face of powerful national and institutional constituencies makes up one of the driving forces of the Church's history.

One repeated factor in this struggle has been the emergence of new religious orders not under the control of local bishops and archbishops, and thus directly answerable to the Pope. The Benedictine Order in the seventh century, the Knights Templar in the twelfth, the Jesuits in the sixteenth, and Opus Dei in the twentieth all filled this role. All but the last eventually developed their own institutional momentum and left the Pope's direct control, each becoming another quasi-independent power bloc within the church; Opus Dei has not yet completed this process but odds are that by the twenty-second century or so it will have followed the same time-honored course. See **Knights Templar**; **Opus Dei**; **Society of Jesus (Jesuits)**.

The clash between rhetoric and reality surrounding the personal powers of the Pope has not always been grasped by people outside the Roman Catholic Church, and this has helped feed a long history of conspiracy theories surrounding it and its activities. The involvement of Catholic priests in assassination plots against England's Queen Elizabeth I and other Protestant monarchs in the sixteenth and seventeenth centuries helped give these theories credibility in their early days, and the long and inglorious history of papal involvement in European politics up until the unification of Italy in the late nineteenth century did little to dispel such ideas. Another factor was the bitter culture of hostility that developed between the Roman Catholic hierarchy and the Freemasons from the early eighteenth century onwards. The Craft's principles of religious tolerance and its long history of commitment to liberal social and political ideals, factors which gave it a profoundly positive reputation through much of the western world, were guaranteed to antagonize a church that remained wedded to a hard-line conservatism throughout the eighteenth and nineteenth centuries. See **Freemasonry**.

These and other factors sparked a conviction that the Catholic Church was, in effect, a secret society plotting world domination. This belief became extremely widespread among Protestants in the nineteenth and early twentieth centuries, and it played a large role in launching a series of anti-Catholic secret societies, including the Loyal Orange Order in Ireland and the Know-Nothings, American Protective Association, and Ku Klux Klan in the United States. See **American Protective Association**; **Know-Nothing Party**; **Ku Klux Klan**; **Loyal Orange Order**.

The explosive spread of alternative versions of Christianity and Christian origins in the second half of the twentieth century, as part of the movement of rejected knowledge from the fringes to the cultural mainstream, has added new wrinkles to this old theme. Many of the current alternative theories about Christianity's origins and history argue that the Roman Catholic Church has deliberately suppressed evidence supporting their claims. Much of this is simply an attempt to bolster a weak case with arguments that cannot be easily disproved; when specific charges have been made – for example, the claim that the Dead Sea Scrolls were being suppressed by order of the Vatican – the facts, when they came out, showed otherwise. None of this is likely to prevent conspiracy theories about the Roman Catholic Church from being recycled in the rejected-knowledge scene for many years to come. See **Dead Sea Scrolls**; **rejected knowledge**.

Rosenkreutz, Christian

Legendary German mystic and founder of the Rosicrucians, 1378–1484. According to the Fama Fraternitatis, the first of the Rosicrucian manifestoes, Rosenkreutz was born to an impoverished family of German nobility and placed in a monastery at the age of five. While still in his teens, he embarked on a pilgrimage to the Holy Land in the company of an older monk. His guide died on the island of Cyprus, but Rosenkreutz went on to Damascus, where he learned about the wise men of the city of Damear (modern Dhamar) in Yemen. He traveled there with a group of Arabs and stayed for three years, studying medicine and mathematics. He then traveled by way of Egypt to the city of Fez in Morocco, where he spent two more years studying magic and the Cabala. At the end of these journeys he returned to Europe, hoping to teach what he had learned, but European scholars dismissed his discoveries and mocked him. He returned to his old monastery in Germany and there founded the Rosicrucian society. He spent the rest of his life at the secret headquarters of the society, the College of the Holy Spirit, and was buried there in a concealed vault after his death. See Cabala; Damear; Magic; Rosicrucians.

Numerous attempts have been made over the last few centuries to claim that Rosenkreutz was a historical figure, or to identify him with various historical figures. Many occultists during the "Theosophical century" from 1875 to 1975 believed that he had been a previous incarnation of the Comte de Saint-Germain, while more recent writers have tried to identify him with the German occultist and physician Paracelsus or the Polish alchemist Michael Sendivogius. Most historians of the Rosicrucian movement, by contrast, point to the many similarities between Rosenkreutz's biography and other allegorical tales of the time, and suggest that the life of Christian Rosenkreutz ("the Christian of the Rosy Cross") is best understood as a symbolic narrative of the sort that were so abundant in alchemical and occult writings of the sixteenth and seventeenth centuries. See **Alchemy**; **Allegory**; **Saint-Germain, Comte de**.

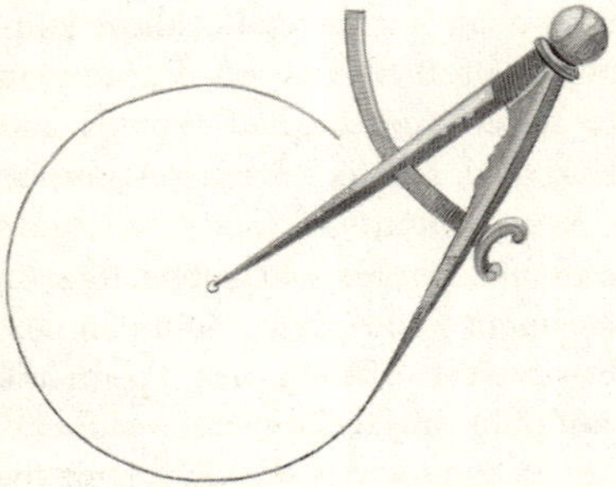

Rosicrucian Fellowship

One of the many American Rosicrucian orders of the early twentieth century, the Rosicrucian Fellowship was founded in 1907 by Max Heindel (Carl Louis Grashof), a Danish astrologer and occultist who studied with Rudolf Steiner in Germany before emigrating to America. The Fellowship was originally headquartered in Columbus, Ohio, but Heindel moved operations to Oceanside, California after a visionary experience in 1910. Like most American esoteric societies of its time, the Fellowship used the successful correspondence-course model for recruiting and training members, while reserving initiation for those who had completed the introductory training by mail. See **Anthroposophical Society**.

The Fellowship also paralleled other Rosicrucian orders of the time by claiming a link to the medieval Rosicrucians. Heindel wrote that the material in his most important book, *The Rosicrucian Cosmo-Conception*, was given to him while traveling in Europe in 1907 in a Rosicrucian temple on the border between Germany and Bohemia. The result was a long and exceptionally complex work of occult cosmology noticeably inspired by Rudolf Steiner's works and Blavatsky's *The Secret Doctrine*, though somewhat less obscure than either. These claims brought Heindel and the Fellowship in for occasional attacks in the crossfire between two other American Rosicrucian orders of the early twentieth century, H. Spencer Lewis's Ancient Mystical Order Rosae Crucis (AMORC) and R. Swinburne Clymer's Fraternitas Rosae Crucis, though Heindel behaved in a noticeably more dignified fashion than either of his assailants. See **Ancient Mystical Order Rosae Crucis (AMORC)**; **Fraternitas Rosae Crucis (FRC)**; **Theosophical Society**.

The Fellowship currently defines itself as "an international association of Christian mystics." Its correspondence school remains in operation, and it also runs a publishing house and keeps several of Heindel's books in print. Students who have been enrolled in the Fellowship for at least two years, have given up meat, tobacco, drugs, and alcohol, and are willing to renounce all other religious and occult societies except for Christian churches and fraternal lodges, are eligible to apply for the grade of Probationer and begin studies of the Fellowship's inner teachings. It remains a quiet but active presence in the American occult community at present.

Further reading: Heindel 1909.

Rosicrucian Order of the Crotona Fellowship [ROCF]

A minor occult secret society in the early twentieth-century British scene, the ROCF was the brainchild of George Alexander Sullivan, a music hall actor turned occultist. Sullivan made his first attempt to launch an occult secret society in 1911, but the Order of the Twelve, as it was called, went under early in the First World War due to travel restrictions. In 1920 he tried again, and the ROCF was the result.

Sullivan had chosen a good moment to launch a Rosicrucian order; a similar organization within the Theosophical Society, the Order of the Temple of the Rose Cross, collapsed around 1918 as Theosophical leader Annie Besant turned her attention to the Order of the Star in the East, her attempt to manufacture a messiah cult around the young Jiddu Krishnamurti. Many former members of the older order, including Besant's daughter Mabel Besant-Scott, joined Sullivan's new organization shortly after its launching, providing the funds and volunteer labor needed to make the ROCF a modest success in the occult market of the time. See **Order of the Star in the East**; **Theosophical Society**.

Those used to the colorful antics of the Theosophical leadership after Helena Blavatsky's death must have found Sullivan congenial. He took the magical name Aureolis, announced that he was none other than the immortal Comte de Saint-Germain, and proceeded to launch one of the twentieth century's more ambitious projects for an occult society, complete with its own college, the Academia Rosae Crucis, and a theatrical troupe, the Theatricum. See **Saint-Germain, Comte de**.

It must be admitted that Sullivan's reach often exceeded his grasp; he loved Latin phrases but knew little of the language, and went by the grand but ungrammatical title of Magi Supremus; he also claimed to have written all the plays attributed to Shakespeare while living in Elizabethan England under the name of Francis Bacon, and went on to write a series of new "Shakespearian" plays of uniformly dreadful quality for his theatre troupe. His claims of immortality proved to be equally overstated, as his death in 1942 proved, and the ROCF quietly disbanded not long afterward.

The ROCF had little impact on the occult community of its time, and would be utterly forgotten now except for the later career of one of its members, a wealthy retiree named Gerald Gardner, who had returned to England after spending many years in Britain's colonies in the East Indies. In the 1950s and 1960s, Gardner claimed that he had been associated with the ROCF's theatre troupe, which he called the "First Rosicrucian Theatre in England." During his time with the Theatricum, he said, he had encountered an inner circle of members who initiated him into an ancient Pagan religion that had survived in secret in the New Forest area – Wicca. See **Wicca**.

Rosicrucians

No single topic in the history of secret societies in the western world is as rich with confusion, disinformation, and wild inaccuracies as the origins and history of the Rosicrucian movement. The most common assumption about the Rosicrucians – that they are a single secret organization, active for the last 400 years if not longer – is also the most inaccurate. Since the first references to Rosicrucians appeared in print in Germany in 1614, scores of unrelated secret societies have made use of the symbol of the Rose Cross – the emblem of the movement and the source of its name, from Latin *rosa*, rose, and *crux*, cross – each claiming to be the one original Rosicrucian order, and producing disinformation to support its claims. In such a thicket of claims and counterclaims, it's necessary to step carefully. See **Disinformation**.

The established facts relating to the origin of the Rosicrucians are these. In 1614 the printer Wilhelm Wessel in Cassel, Germany, brought out a booklet with the lively title *Universal and General Reformation of the Whole Wide World; together with the* Fama Fraternitatis *of the Praiseworthy Fraternity of the Rosy Cross, written to all the Learned and Rulers of Europe; also a short reply sent by Herr Haselmayer, for which he was seized by the Jesuits and condemned to a galley; now put into print and communicated to all true hearts.* The first part of the booklet, the *Universal and General Reformation*, was a pirated German translation of one dialogue from *News from Parnassus* (1612) by the Italian author Traiano Boccalini, a raucous satire in which the god Apollo calls together a council of wise men to fix the world, listens to their preposterous proposals, and finally passes laws regulating the price of market vegetables, whereupon everyone goes home rejoicing.

The second part, the Fama Fraternitatis or "Report of the Fraternity," proclaimed the existence of a secret society, the Fraternity of the Rosy Cross. According to the Fama, this society had been founded in the fifteenth century by a Catholic monk of noble birth, whose name is given only as C.R.C. In his youth, C.R.C. traveled to the cities of Damear in Yemen and Fez in Morocco, and there was initiated into the magical secrets of nature. Returning to Europe, he found his learning rejected by most, but founded the

Fraternity of the Rosy Cross to pass on the secrets he had learned. He died in 1484, and in 1604 members of the Fraternity had rediscovered the marvelous underground vault where he had been buried, surrounded by secret books and mechanical marvels. The Fraternity therefore called on interested parties to contact them and apply for membership. The third part of the booklet, the letter from Adam Haselmayer, was just such an attempt to contact that Fraternity; its reference to the brothers of the Rose Cross as "undeceiving Jesuits" accounted for the Jesuits' annoyance with the author. See **Damear; Society of Jesus (Jesuits)**.

Within months of the booklet's publication, its account of the Fraternity of the Rose Cross had ignited a continent-wide furor. Books and pamphlets poured from European presses in a torrent; conservatives attacked the mysterious society, Hermeticists defended it, skeptics doubted its existence. In 1615, while the furor was at its height, a second booklet appeared from the same press, *A Short Consideration of the More Secret Philosophy, written by Philip à Gabella, student of Philosophy, now published for the first time together with the Confession of the R.C. Fraternity.*

The *Short Consideration* was an essay on occultism based on the *Monas Hieroglyphica*, the most baffling of the writings of the great Elizabethan wizard John Dee; the *Confession* was a second manifesto from the mysterious Fraternity, assailing the Roman Catholic Church and making veiled promises of an approaching "reformation of the whole wide world" that had religious and political dimensions. In 1616, with the furor still in full swing, a new volume, *The Chemical Wedding of Christian Rosenkreutz in the year 1549*, came from the print shop of Lazarus Zetzner in Strasbourg. Rather than a third manifesto, this was a baffling allegorical story full of alchemical symbolism. See **Alchemy**.

All three of these publications appeared anonymously. The third was apparently the first one written, and its author was Johann Valentin Andreae. He wrote it in 1605 while he was a student at Tübingen University and a member of a circle of Christian alchemists and students of occultism centered on Tobias Hess and Christoph Besold, two noted alchemists of the time. In later life a sober Lutheran pastor and theologian, Andreae did his best to distance himself from his college days, but he admitted in his autobiography that the *Chemical Wedding* was his work, though it was published against his wishes. The other two publications had more complex origins; they were written between 1606 and 1610 by one or more members of the Tübingen circle, and circulated in manuscript before their first printing. Andreae probably had a hand in them, but a comment in one of his writings lets slip the fact that Tobias Hess was also involved. They may well have been written jointly by a group of authors, a common practice at that time.

Four centuries of speculation have gone into the question of why they were written, but the *Fama*, at least, can be understood by the company it originally kept. A grand scheme of social reform, it was originally printed alongside a raucous satire on grand schemes of social reform. It's hard to avoid the implication that the *Fama* was originally an erudite joke, of the sort Renaissance scholars delighted in making. If this is true, it counts as the most influential college prank of all time.

Yet the joke turned serious as hundreds, perhaps thousands, of people across Europe tried to make contact with the mysterious Fraternity. The Adam Haselmayer whose letter and dire fate at the hands of the Jesuits made up the third section of the *Fama*'s original publication was no invention of the Tübingen circle; he was a widely respected physician, a student of the writings of the German mystic and healer Paracelsus (1493–1541), who obtained a manuscript copy of the *Fama* in 1611, published an answer to it in 1612, and served a term of five years as a galley slave because of his incautious remarks. He was not the only figure of the time to get into trouble because of the Rosicrucians; the great French philosopher René Descartes at one point in his career had to combat rumors that he was a secret Rosicrucian.

Many of those who embraced the emblem of the Rose Cross had backgrounds similar to Haselmayer's: deeply involved in alchemy, Cabala, or other branches of the occult traditions of the Renaissance. Around the manifestos emerged a lively tradition of Christian Hermeticism in which alchemy, esoteric philosophy, and Protestant mysticism blended seamlessly. Major figures in the occult scene of the time, including the German alchemist Michael Maier (1568–1622) and the English polymath Robert Fludd (1574–1637), published extensive books about the Rosicrucians. Interestingly, these two authors loudly insisted that they themselves were not Rosicrucians, but offered detailed information about the teachings and organizations of the mysterious Fraternity. Whether or not they were in on the original joke, they seem to have recognized its multiple ironies and put it to good use as a way to communicate the teachings of Renaissance occultism to a new age. See **Cabala**; **Hermeticism**.

At the same time, others made use of the same symbolism in the interests of political conspiracy. While Andreae was at Tübingen, Frederick V, Prince Palatine of the Rhine, stood at the center of a web of intrigue directed against the Catholic House of Habsburg, which then held the throne of the Holy Roman Empire. Rudolf II, king of Bohemia as well as emperor, had been forced off the throne in 1611, and his successor Matthias died eight years later. Frederick, the leading Protestant ruler in Germany, was positioning himself as the logical candidate for Bohemia's crown, a move that might have brought the Imperial crown itself within reach. Frances Yates, one of the premier historians of the Rosicrucian movement, has argued that Frederick's supporters were involved in propagating Rosicrucian documents, particularly the *Confessio*, and that the "reformation of the whole wide world" portrayed by the manifestoes was propaganda for Frederick's party.

In the end, if this was the political reality behind the Rosicrucian movement, the scheme failed disastrously. Frederick took the Bohemian throne in 1619 but was driven out by Catholic armies after the Battle of White Mountain a year later. Frederick fled to lifelong exile in Holland, and Germany plunged into the nightmare of the Thirty Years War. A handful of occult authors in Britain and a few other countries continued to produce Rosicrucian books into the middle years of the seventeenth century; Robert Fludd, Thomas Vaughan, and the master plagiarist of Jacobean British occultism John Heydon all contributed to the literature of the Rose Cross. They may have represented the last flicker of the original movement; with the coming of the scientific revolution and the hardening of attitudes against occultism, the age of the Renaissance magus had come to an end.

It took more than a century for the mythology of the Rose Cross to be pulled out of the ashes of its early seventeenth-century setting and take shape as a secret society, and this happened only because another secret society found its symbolism useful and appealing. From the beginning, the Scottish degrees of Freemasonry contained Rosicrucian elements. These degrees appeared in France in the 1740s and 1750s, and evidence suggests they were created by the Jacobites, supporters of the deposed House of Stuart, to counter the influence of mainstream British Freemasonry and further Stuart bids to regain the British throne. The Stuarts had long been involved in Renaissance traditions of courtly magic, and this may have suggested the Rosicrucian movement as a suitable subject for higher degrees. Rosicrucian degrees that entered Freemasonry by this route include the 2° of the Royal Order of Scotland, the 18° of the Ancient and Accepted Scottish Rite, and several others. See **Ancient and Accepted Scottish Rite**; **Freemasonry**; **Jacobites**; **Royal Order of Scotland**; **Scottish degrees**.

A different process launched the first solidly documented Rosicrucian order in Germany. The first Masonic lodges were established in Germany in the 1730s, and quickly became popular among Germans interested in mysteries and the occult. Since Freemasonry had little to offer aspiring occultists, the plan of establishing higher grades based on occult symbolism readily presented itself, and the symbolism of the Rose Cross offered an obvious starting point. The result was the Order of the Golden and Rosy Cross (*Orden des Gold- und Rosenkreuz*), which was founded in the 1750s by the occultist Hermann Fichtuld and spread throughout Germany and Austria in the second half of the eighteenth century, counting King Frederick William II of Prussia among its members. See **Order of the Golden and Rosy Cross**.

Despite the use of the Rosicrucian name and symbol, the legend of the *Fama* played very little role in this eighteenth-century Rosicrucianism; Christian Rosenkreutz and the mysterious vault received much less attention than claims of an Egyptian origin and attempts to graft the Rosicrucians onto the Templar myth of high-grade Freemasonry. Thus the Order of the Golden and Rosy Cross claimed that it was founded in 96 CE by Ormus, an Egyptian magus who had converted to Christianity, and reached Europe with returning Knights Templar in 1188. Membership was restricted to Master Masons. The order's training program included a great deal of material on alchemy, and members studied classic alchemical works by Basil Valentine, Arnald de Villanova, and Raymond Lully. See **Knights Templar**; **Ormus**; **Rosenkreutz, Christian**.

The Order of the Golden and Rosy Cross ceased to exist sometime after 1800, and the Rosicrucian Masonic degrees had been absorbed into the busy subculture of high-degree Masonry by the same time, but the dream of hidden philosopher-mages under the banner of the Rose Cross had enough momentum to attract new recruits in a steady stream. Rosicrucian mysteries were a constant topic of talk in nineteenth-century occult circles, and the most influential occult novel of the century, Edward Bulwer-Lytton's *Zanoni* (1842) was subtitled *A Rosicrucian Tale*; by the mid-nineteenth century it becomes meaningful to talk of a Rosicrucian movement and a specifically Rosicrucian current of occult study and practice.

Not long after 1850 the first large semi-public Rosicrucian orders began appearing in the western world. The first appears to have been the Societas Rosicruciana in Anglia (Rosicrucian Society in England), founded in 1866 by Freemason Robert Wentworth Little. Other major presences in late nineteenth-century Rosicrucianism include the Kabbalistic Order of the Rose+Cross, founded in Paris in 1888, and the Hermetic Order of the Golden Dawn, founded in London the year before. See **Hermetic Order of the Golden Dawn**; **Kabbalistic Order of the Rose+Cross**; **Societas Rosicruciana in Anglia (SRIA)**.

Yet it was in America that this later Rosicrucian movement reached its full flowering. The Rosicrucian presence in America dates back to colonial times, when German Rosicrucian sects crossed the ocean to find religious tolerance in the wilderness of Pennsylvania. The first of these, calling itself "The Woman in the Wilderness" after a passage from the Book of Revelation, arrived in 1694 and built a commune on the banks of the Wissahickon River near modern Germantown. Another, the Ephrata commune, flourished between 1735 and 1765 in Lancaster County. Both of these contributed much to American folk magic, enriching local occult lore with German sorcery, but the Rosicrucian seed they tried to plant on American soil remained dormant until nearly a century later.

The real founder of the Rosicrucian movement in America was the extraordinary Paschal Beverly Randolph (1825–75), an African-American occultist who taught a system of sexual magic and the use of magic mirrors for scrying. He claimed to be a Rosicrucian, though, as he admitted in one of his books, "Very nearly all that I have given as Rosicrucianism originated in my soul; and scarce a single thought, only suggestions, have I borrowed from those who, in ages past, have called themselves by that name" (quoted in McIntosh 1997, p. 121). Brilliant but troubled, Randolph created and then dissolved a series of Rosicrucian secret societies in America, the fragments of which were gathered up in the early twentieth century by the American Rosicrucian R. Swinburne Clymer (1878–1966) as the basis for his own Rosicrucian order, the Fraternitas Rosae Crucis. See **Fraternitas Rosae Crucis (FRC)**; **Randolph, Paschal Beverly**.

Clymer's was far from the only Rosicrucian body active in America in the first decades of the twentieth century. Its great rival, the Ancient Mystical Order Rosae Crucis (AMORC), was founded by H. Spencer Lewis (1883–1939) in 1925, though in the time-honored secret society fashion Lewis back-dated his own initiation to the end of the nineteenth century and his order to ancient Egypt. AMORC rapidly became the largest of the American Rosicrucian orders, and Clymer and Lewis spent most of the 1920s and 1930s carrying on a vitriolic public feud, with each loudly challenging the other's claims to Rosicrucian lineage and accusing the other of practicing sex magic – a charge that probably had merit in both cases, since the Rosicrucian lineages of both men derived from P.B. Randolph, Clymer's via Randolph's American students and Lewis's via the Hermetic Brotherhood of Luxor and Ordo Templi Orientis. See **Ancient Mystical Order Rosae Crucis (AMORC)**; **Hermetic Brotherhood of Luxor (H.B. of L.)**; **Ordo Templi Orientis (OTO)**.

Nor were these the only players in the crowded field of American Rosicrucian societies. Max Heindel (Carl Louis Grashof), a Danish astrologer and occultist, founded the Rosicrucian Fellowship in Columbus, Ohio in 1907, but relocated it to Oceanside, California in 1910, where it remains quietly active to this day. A split in the American branch of the SRIA in 1907 saw the founding of a rival group, the Societas Rosicruciana in America (also SRIA), which cut itself loose from its Masonic apron strings and became a major presence in American occult circles; it also remains active in a small way today. See **Rosicrucian Fellowship**; **Societas Rosicruciana in America (SRIA)**.

Another Rosicrucian order of the early twentieth century had a minor impact in its time but may have played a key role in launching one of the major religious movements of the last years of that century. In 1912 Annie Besant, then head of the Theosophical Society and an ardent Co-Mason, launched a Roscrucian organization within Theosophy, called the Order of the Temple of the Rosy Cross. Never a large organization, it folded around 1918. Many of its members in Britain joined a new society, the Rosicrucian Order of the Crotona Fellowship (ROCF), founded by British actor and occultist George Alexander Sullivan in 1920. The ROCF in turn went out of existence in the 1940s, but in the meantime it sponsored a theatrical group in the New Forest area of England. It was in this group, according to his later claims, that Gerald Gardner met the people who first initiated him into Wicca. See **Rosicrucian Order of the Crotona Fellowship (ROCF)**; **Theosophical Society**; **Wicca**.

The orders just mentioned are only a few of the Rosicrucian orders and Rosicrucian degrees within broader organizations in the western world today, and doubtless a new crop of secret societies will spring up under the Rosicrucian banner during the twenty-first century as well. Ironically, the popularity of the Rosicrucian name and its associated imagery has been gained at the cost of nearly everything distinctive about the tradition behind it. Cut loose from the Christian Hermeticism that guided the *Fama*'s authors and inspired its original audience, the movement has broadened until it is impossible to distinguish it from western occultism itself.

Further reading: Churton 2005, McIntosh 1997, Yates 1972.

Rosslyn Chapel

Located in the village of Roslin, just south of Edinburgh, Rosslyn Chapel is the sole completed portion of a large church commissioned by William Sinclair, Earl of Orkney. Construction began in 1446 and came to a halt after William's death in 1484. Only the crypt, the choir, and the eastern walls of the transepts were finished, though a baptistery was added to the west end in the nineteenth century. The finest example of late Gothic architecture in Scotland, the chapel features lavish interior carvings of the sort found in many French and English Gothic cathedrals. See **Sinclair family**.

Until the early 1980s, Rosslyn Chapel was of interest only to art historians and tourists, but the publication of *The Holy Blood and the Holy Grail* in 1982 linked it firmly in the popular imagination with the Knights Templar, the Priory of Sion, and alternative accounts of Christian origins. Since then it has featured in a torrent of books, media documentaries, and websites, and become the focus of a bumper crop of inaccuracies. Despite widely circulated claims, for example, the design of Rosslyn Chapel is no more based on the Temple of Solomon than any other Gothic church, nor is it free of Christian symbolism – a Madonna and child, crosses, and several saints may be found there. See **Christian origins**; **Freemasonry**; **Knights Templar**; **Priory of Sion**.

One possibly less specious claim about Rosslyn Chapel is the claim that its carvings show New World plants such as maize. William Sinclair was the last of three members of his family to hold the title of Earl of Orkney, and the second Sinclair earl, Henry Sinclair, may have been involved in a voyage to the New World in 1398. The earldom of Orkney had a huge stake in the north Atlantic fisheries, as well as luxury goods such as sealskins and walrus ivory; the Sinclair voyage of 1398 thus made economic sense, and the presence of depictions of maize in the chapel might have been a reflection of a successful voyage that was not followed up for more than a century. See **America, discovery of**.

Further reading: Stevenson 1988.

Royal Arch

The first of the higher degrees added to Freemasonry in the eighteenth century, the Royal Arch was probably of French origin but first surfaced in England sometime before 1744, when the first references appear to it in English Masonic writings. By that year Royal Arch lodges (not yet called chapters, as Royal Arch bodies were later termed) already existed in York and London, and possibly also in Dublin. No one has yet been able to determine who invented it. Andrew Michael Ramsay, an influential Mason in Jacobite circles in France, has been proposed as a candidate but no evidence has been found to confirm this. See **Freemasonry**; **high degrees**; **Ramsay, Andrew Michael**.

The Royal Arch in its early years was associated with the Antient side of the Antient–Modern schism that split British Masonry down the middle in the late eighteenth and early nineteenth centuries. Records of the Antient Grand Lodge in London show that the Royal Arch degree was in use among the Antients when it was still unheard of among English Moderns. In America, where the differences between the two sides were smaller, Antient and Modern grand lodges adopted the

Royal Arch with equal enthusiasm, and once the split was healed in 1813 the Royal Arch became a standard element of Masonry throughout the English-speaking world. See **Antient–Modern schism**.

For nearly a century after the degree's appearance, Masons debated where to fit it into the structure of the Craft, and different countries and Masonic rites put it in different places. In England, the Royal Arch is considered the completion of the Master Mason degree, and is under the authority of the United Grand Lodge of England. In Scotland and America, it has become the most important degree of a separate organization, the Royal Arch Chapter, which has its own national and (in North America) state and provincial grand bodies, and also confers several other degrees. In America, the Royal Arch Chapter is one of the four independent bodies that constitute the York Rite. See **York Rite**.

In France and other European countries, by contrast, it was incorporated into larger rites as one degree among many, and when these rites traveled they took their own forms of the Royal Arch with them. Thus, for example, the Royal Arch of Solomon, 13° of the Ancient and Accepted Scottish Rite, and the Grand Royal Arch, 31° of the Rite of Misraim, are essentially the same as the Holy Royal Arch worked in Chapters affiliated with the United Grand Lodge of England or the Grand Royal Arch Chapters of Scotland and the United States. Versions of the Royal Arch were also adopted into the Loyal Orange Order and several other secret societies. See **Ancient and Accepted Scottish Rite (AASR)**; **Loyal Orange Order**; **Rite of Misraim**.

Whereas the legend of the Master Mason degree deals with the loss of the Master's Word, that of the Royal Arch deals with its recovery. Three workmen, according to the legend, found an underground chamber while clearing away ruins, descended into it, and found an object marked with the true Master's Word. Curiously, different versions of the ritual put this event in different historical settings. The Scottish Rite version just mentioned, for example, places it in the time of King Solomon, not long after the death of Hiram Abiff, while the version worked in Royal Arch Chapters sets it during the rebuilding of the Temple after the Jews' Babylonian captivity. In reality, of course, the legends of this and all other Masonic degrees are symbolism, not history. See **Hiram Abiff**; **origin stories**.

The traditional color of the Royal Arch is red, contrasting with the blue of Craft Masonry (the "blue lodge"). Its emblem is the Triple Tau, a symbol formed of three capital Ts joined at the base, within a triangle.

Royal Order of Scotland

Among the oldest Masonic high degrees, the Royal Order of Scotland first surfaced in 1750, when a Provincial Grand Lodge of that order was founded at The Hague. A few years later the Provincial Grand Lodge moved to Edinburgh and became the Grand Lodge of the order, which it has remained to this day. Several eighteenth-century Masonic historians claimed that the order had previously appeared in England in 1741 or 1743, though evidence to support this claim has yet to surface. In either case, the date of its first appearance and the presence of the Knights Templar in its origin story suggest a Jacobite source. See **high degrees**; **Jacobites**.

The Order's own origin story is far more romantic. According to this account it was founded in 1314 after Robert Bruce, King of Scotland, defeated an immense English army at the battle of Bannockburn. Assisting the Scots army was a group of Knights Templar who had fled to Scotland to escape the destruction of their order by Philip IV of France. As a reward for their valor, Bruce conferred on them the title of Royal Order of Scotland. Versions of this same origin story are repeated by most of the other Masonic bodies that claim a Scottish origin. See **origin stories**; **Scottish degrees**.

It probably needs to be said that there is not a scrap of evidence supporting this story. Still, Bruce is traditionally considered to have been the first Grand Master of the order. To this day the King of Scots – since 1603, a title held by the British royal house – is considered to be the hereditary Grand Master of the order, and a vacant chair is left for him next to the presiding officer at each meeting.

The Royal Order confers two degrees, the degree of Heredom of Kilwinning and the degree of the Rosy Cross. Membership is by invitation only, and is restricted to Christian Freemasons who believe in the Trinity, have been Master Masons for at least five years, and are either 32° Scottish Rite Masons or members of the York Rite Knight Templar degrees. Originally limited to Scotland, the Royal Order established a Provincial Grand Lodge for England in London in 1872, and one for the United States in Washington, DC in 1878.

Royal Society

The world's oldest and most prestigious scientific society, the Royal Society emerged out of the underworld of English occult secret societies in the early seventeenth century. By 1645, if not earlier, small groups of English scholars, alchemists, and natural scientists had begun meeting in private homes in and near London to discuss their work. They called themselves the "Invisible College," a term made famous earlier in the same century by the Rosicrucian manifestoes. The Rosicrucian ideal of a secret brotherhood devoted to gathering and distributing knowledge, as well as Francis Bacon's projects for a renovation of natural science, played important roles in inspiring the

Invisible College and its work. See **Bacon, Francis; Rosicrucians**.

After the Restoration of 1660 put Charles II back on the British throne, the Invisible College came out of the shadows. Sir Robert Moray, a Freemason and Hermeticist who became one of the Society's founding members, played a central role in establishing it as a public body and seeking the new king's patronage for the organization. In 1662 his efforts were rewarded by a royal charter establishing the Royal Society of London for Improving Natural Knowledge. The Society has continued to meet regularly since that time, and still plays an important role in the diffusion of scientific knowledge through its publications and meetings.

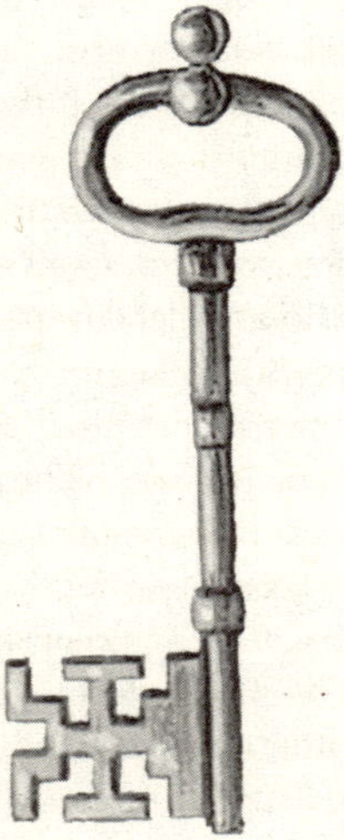

RUSSIAN REVOLUTION

The victory of the Bolshevik party in the Russian revolution of 1917 marks one of the great watersheds in the history of conspiracy theories. While the triumph of communism proved to be transitory, the 72-year lifespan of the Soviet Union played a central role in transforming modern conspiracy theory from the concern of a small fringe to a significant force in the cultural politics of the western world.

The Russian revolution, like the French Revolution before it, unfolded from the collision between the global ambitions of the country's rulers, the Tsars of the Romanov dynasty, and the corrupt and antiquated feudal system they relied on to support their regime. A previous revolution in 1905, following Russia's disastrous defeat in a war with Japan, led to the creation of an elected legislature, the Duma. After legal changes carried out by the Prime Minister, Pyotr Stolypin, in 1907, though, the Duma was almost entirely elected by the aristocracy and the Tsar's court. The extravagance of the court combined with an archaic fiscal system that exempted the aristocracy from most taxes and misguided agricultural and economic policies to hamstring the Russian economy, and in the aftermath of 1905 the peasants and urban working classes clamored for reforms that would give them economic security and a voice in government. These factors made the Tsarist regime far weaker than it appeared.

This became suddenly apparent in the autumn of 1914, when Russia declared war on Austria and Germany in the opening stages of the First World War. In September of that year, the Germans dealt the Tsarist armies the first of a series of devastating defeats, and in the spring of 1915 German and Austrian armies launched a major offensive that drove hundreds of miles into the Russian Empire. In response, Tsar Nicholas II took command of the troops in the field, leaving the government to the Tsarina Alexandra and a coterie of reactionaries whose policies worsened the crisis. By 1916 the Russian army was disintegrating, the economy had collapsed, and even the conservative parties in the Duma were calling for immediate political change.

On February 22, 1917, workers at a metalworking plant in the imperial capital of St Petersburg went on strike against the government. Over the next few days, strikes, street protests, and riots brought St Petersburg to a standstill. Army units called to quell the disturbances refused to act or joined the insurgents, and by February 28 the city was in rebel hands. As news of the rising spread, other cities rose in revolt, and mutiny spread among the armed forces. On March 2 Nicholas II abdicated and the Russian Empire came to an end.

A provisional government was formed by moderate leaders of the Duma, headed first by Georgii Lvov and later by Aleksandr Kerensky. It concentrated on restoring order and bringing the military situation under control, instead of negotiating peace and pursuing the fundamental reforms demanded by the urban working classes and peasants. A popular rising against the provisional government in July, and an attempted military coup by Gen. Lavr Kornilov in August were both barely thwarted. Meanwhile the economic situation worsened steadily and the Germans dealt the Russian army another devastating defeat. The Bolsheviks, the radical socialist party headed by Vladimir I. Lenin, seized their opportunity in late October, staging a coup against the provisional government.

The new Bolshevik regime immediately negotiated a truce with Germany and Austria. It faced civil war at home, however, as conservative forces rallied against it. From the end of 1917 to the summer of 1920, the "Red" Bolshevik government struggled for survival against a diffuse but powerful "White" opposition, supported by troops from Britain, France, the United States, and several other countries. Despite all odds, the new Soviet regime survived, and by the end of 1920 it had taken control of most of the pre-war Russian Empire.

The victory of Communist Party forces in Russia caused an immense shock to public opinion elsewhere in the world. The communist movement had been dismissed by most observers in the industrial world as a fringe group of the far left with no hope of achieving power, and very few people outside Russia before the revolution understood the catastrophic weaknesses behind the Tsarist regime's outward façade of strength. The sudden collapse of imperial Russia played a large part in fostering conspiracy theories throughout the world, particularly in Germany, Britain, and the United States, where many people on the political left openly welcomed the Russian revolution and spoke of the possibility of similar events at home. In response, government repression of left-wing political groups in many countries increased sharply, and conspiracy theories claiming that every left-of-center organization in the world was directed from Moscow became common. For the rest of the twentieth century, the Bolsheviks formed the model on which most conservatives – and from the 1970s on, many radicals and liberals – formed their own ideas of conspiracy. See **John Birch Society**; **New World Order**.

Further reading: Schapiro 1984, Wilson 1972.

S

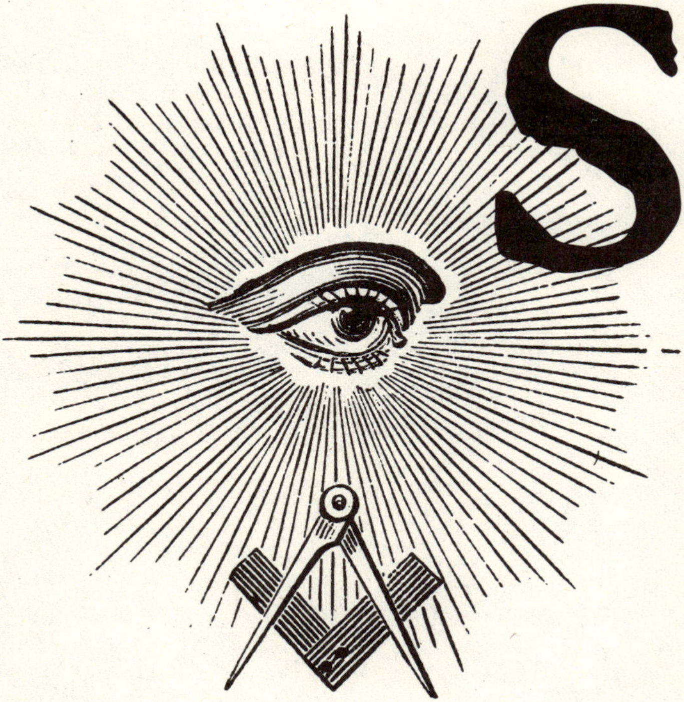

Sabbat

In European writings from the age of witchcraft persecutions, the term for a meeting of witches. The word was borrowed from the Jewish sabbath, as many medieval Christians had trouble telling the difference between members of any other religion beside their own, and antisemitism played a significant part in the creation of the medieval mythology of the witches' sabbath. See **Antisemitism**; **witchcraft persecutions**.

English Egyptologist and witchcraft theorist Margaret Murray (1863–1963) took the term from documents concerning witchcraft trials, and reshaped it to fit her theory that medieval witchcraft was actually a survival of ancient pagan religious practices. When Murray's friend Gerald Gardner (1884–1964) created modern Wicca as a supposed survival of medieval witch cults, Murray's sabbats were among his many borrowings from her writings. In the early 1950s, the term came to be associated with the eight festivals of contemporary neopaganism and is still used in that sense in pagan circles today. See **Murray hypothesis**; **Wicca**.

Modern conspiracy theories written or influenced by fundamentalist Christians have picked up the use of the term in modern pagan writings, but like their medieval equivalents have usually failed to notice the difference between Wicca and Satanism. Many of today's books of Christian conspiracy theory thus feature lurid accounts of Satanists celebrating sabbats, which is a little like claiming that Christians celebrate Yom Kippur or Americans celebrate the birthday of the Queen. See **Satanism**.

SACRED GEOMETRY

Until recently one of the most neglected branches of the western esoteric tradition, sacred geometry began to experience a renaissance in the last two decades of the twentieth century and is becoming a known factor again in the alternative scene. The links between geometry and spirituality go back to the beginnings of geometrical study in the western world, for Pythagoras, the first known teacher of geometry in the Greek world, gained his knowledge of the art in Egypt and Babylon and taught it to students as a sacred mystery surrounded by religious taboos and disciplines. See **Pythagorean Brotherhood**.

The principles behind classical sacred geometry remain essential to the tradition today. The laws governing form in geometrical constructions are understood by sacred geometers as expressions of the same timeless patterns experienced by mystics in their meditations and visions. The most significant of these laws express themselves in irrational ratios. The most widely known of these ratios is pi, π, the ratio between the diameter of a circle and its circumference. The others that have been central to sacred geometry since ancient times are $1/\sqrt{2}$, the ratio between the side of a square and its diagonal; $1/\sqrt{3}$, the ratio between the side of an equilateral triangle and twice its height; $\sqrt{5}$, the ratio between the side of a double square and its diagonal; and phi, φ, the Golden Proportion, the ratio a/b that makes a/b=b/(a+b). These ratios appear constantly in nature and art.

From its Pythagorean sources, sacred geometry became common in the ancient world and was preserved by Christian monks through the chaos that followed the collapse of the Roman Empire in the West. As the first stone cathedrals rose above European cities in the early Middle Ages, the stonemasons who put this lore into practical use became expert in the symbolic dimensions of geometry as well. While the fusion of practical and symbolic geometry went out of use in most of Europe with the rise of the universities and a growing separation between the educated and working classes, in the cultural backwater of Scotland guilds of stonemasons survived into the seventeenth century with significant elements of the old lore intact, and eventually gave rise to Freemasonry. See **Freemasonry, origins of**.

Medieval stonemasons evolved two schools of sacred geometry, based on different systems of proportion. One, the *ad quadratim* ("by the square") system, used the relationship between squares and diagonals as the basis for its designs; the other, the *ad triangulum* ("by the triangle") system, used equilateral triangles and hexagons for the same purpose. The two rival systems each had partisans, and quarrels, sometimes descending to the level of fist-fights, sometimes broke out between stonemasons of different schools working on the same building project. The Scottish stonemasons' guilds that gave rise to modern Freemasonry were partisans of the *ad quadratim* system, which is why right angles and squares play such a central part in Masonic symbolism. Continental stonemasons' guilds aligned with the *ad triangulum* approach may have had an influence on later systems of high degree Masonry, which may explain the greater importance of equilateral triangles in the higher Masonic degrees. See **high degrees**.

Long before Freemasonry emerged out of the operative stonemasons' guilds, however, sacred geometry became an integral part of the Renaissance occult tradition. Magicians of the Renaissance used geometry as one of many tools to bring themselves into harmony with the entire cosmos and call down universal powers into the human world. These methods passed at the end of the Renaissance into the underworld of occult secret societies, where they fused with Masonic lore to become essential elements of magical work. Practices based on sacred geometry remain a significant part of the teachings of many occult secret societies today; the pentagram, for example, derives its role in ritual magic from the Golden Proportion geometries that define it. By the nineteenth century, however, very few people in the occult scene understood the geometrical principles behind their rituals and practices. See **Magic**; **Pentagram**.

The revival of sacred geometry in the western world began with the work of one man, French occultist R.A. Schwaller de Lubicz (1887–1961). After decades of involvement in occult and alchemical circles in Paris and elsewhere, Schwaller went to Egypt, where he found that the geometries of ancient Egyptian art and architecture provided him with a symbolic language perfectly suited to express mystical teachings. His studies there resulted in a series of brilliant if difficult works on the subject, which introduced traditional sacred geometry to the modern occult tradition. In the 1970s, several English writers researching leys and other earth mysteries stumbled across old treatises on the subject, notably William Stirling's forgotten 1897 classic *The Canon*, and introduced the fundamentals of sacred geometry to a wider audience. Since that time, books on the subject have proliferated; some excellent work has been done, though certain authors have mixed sacred geometry with the wilder and less useful ends of the modern rejected knowledge industry, with dubious results. The field remains lively at present, and has begun to influence certain schools of architecture and design. See **Leys**; **rejected knowledge**; **Schwaller de Lubicz, René Aor**.

Further reading: Lawlor 1982, Pennick 1979, Stirling 1999.

Saint-Germain, Comte de

European adventurer, *c.*1710–1784. One of the most colorful figures of the eighteenth century, the Comte de Saint-Germain loomed large in life and even larger in the mythology that gathered around him after his death. A skilled physician, painter, chemist, musician, and composer, he was fluent in at least six languages, and by all accounts was one of the star raconteurs of an age when conversation very nearly counted as one of the fine arts. He was also vain, boastful, fond of dropping hints that he had been alive for thousands of years and had known most of the great figures of the past, and implicated in a string of very dubious financial dealings. In an age when the courts of Europe thronged with remarkable individuals who made their living by sheer personality, he was the adventurer's adventurer, admired even by those he defrauded.

He wrapped himself in a shroud of mystery so effectively that historians have yet to find any solid data about his origins and early life. Even his birth name is unknown. "Comte de Saint-Germain" was an assumed name, and he also made use of other aliases – Count Bellamare, Count Tsarogy, Count Surmont, Lord Weldon, the Marquis of Montferrat, General Soltikov, and Chevalier Schöning, among others. In his last years he claimed to be the son and heir of Francis Rákóczi, the last Prince of Transylvania, and his portraits and those of Rákóczi show what might be a family resemblance. Other claims circulated during his lifetime identified him as the son of a civil servant from Savoy named Rotondo, the son of a Jewish physician from Alsace named Wolff, the illegitimate son of a king of Portugal, and, for good measure, the son of an Arabian princess by a *jinn.*

His first documented appearance was in 1735, when he wrote a letter from Holland that is now in the British Library; 1739 saw him in Holland again, and in 1743 he arrived in London and cut a dashing figure at the court of King George II. Briefly arrested in 1745 for his supposed role in a Jacobite conspiracy, he was cleared of all charges but left the country. Between 1745 and 1757 his whereabouts are unclear, with some sources placing him in Vienna while others put him in India. From 1757 to 1760 he dazzled the French court at Versailles, but in the latter year was entrusted with a secret diplomatic mission by Louis XV and bungled it so badly that he had to flee to England to avoid a stay in the Bastille. In 1762 he was back in Holland, involved in shady financial dealings that cost a Dutch industrialist almost 100,000 gulden. From 1768 to 1774 he lived in Italy, and won an honorary commission as a Russian general for providing the Russian navy with his famous healing tea, a mild laxative made from senna pods. From 1774 on he was in Germany, living off a string of German noblemen who found his charm and conversation worth the cost of his upkeep. He died in 1784 at the home of Charles, Prince of Hesse-Cassel, the last of his patrons.

His role in the secret traditions of the time is uncertain at best. The Prince of Hesse-Cassel wrote that when the two of them discussed philosophy and religion, Saint-Germain rejected both religion and occultism and held strictly materialist views. He was initiated into Freemasonry at some point in his life, according to comments recorded by an acquaintance, but admitted that he had long since forgotten all the signs and passwords; eminent Masons and Rosicrucians who knew him were convinced that he had no real knowledge of either society, and most of the occultists of his time believed that he was a fraud. The only evidence supporting the later claim that Saint-Germain was a master occultist are two rare books that apparently came from the Comte's pen, *The Most Holy Trinosophia* ("threefold wisdom") *of the Comte de Saint-Germain* – a complex, visionary allegory of initiation – and the *Triangular Book*, a magical ritual for finding treasure and attaining long life. Conclusive evidence for or against Saint-Germain's authorship of either book has yet to surface, however.

Nonetheless the Freemasons, Theosophists, and occultists of later generations readily transformed Saint-Germain into one of the great occult masters of all time. They received a great deal of help from the eminent French forger Étienne Léon de Lamothe-Langon, who in 1836 published a set of fraudulent memoirs supposedly written by the Comtesse d'Adhemar, a lady-in-waiting to Queen Marie Antoinette on the eve of the French Revolution. The memoirs include descriptions of Saint-Germain's reappearances at Versailles years after his death, and his attempts to warn the queen about the revolution. Though the memoirs were discredited more than a century ago, Lamothe-Langon's tales continue to be cited by authors in the alternative realities field as proof that Saint-Germain did not actually die in 1784.

In the teachings of some modern occult traditions and secret societies, as well as in the New Age movement, the Comte de Saint-Germain is one of the Masters of the Great White Lodge, the benevolent secret order that supervises the evolution of humanity. Several modern occult movements, including the I Am Activity of Guy Ballard and its offspring, the Ascended Masters teachings, consider Saint-Germain to be their founder. See **Ascended Masters teachings**; **Ballard, Guy**; **Great White Lodge**; **Masters**; **New Age movement**.

Further reading: Butler 1948, Patai 1994.

Samothracian mysteries

The Samothracian mysteries, an important ancient Greek mystery cult, were celebrated on the island of Samothrace in the northwest Aegean Sea around the time of the spring equinox. Its gods were called the Cabiri; their true names were secret, but a late source gives them the names Axieros, Axiokersos, and Axiokersa, and also mentions a lesser god, Kadmillos, who was their messenger. Almost nothing is known about the ceremony of initiation except that it took place at night and included the sacrifice of a ram, the wrapping of initiates in a purple sash, and an act of confession in which each candidate was asked to name the worst deed he had ever committed. Initiates wore an iron ring after passing through the ceremony, and were believed to be immune from drowning and other dangers at sea.

Archeological evidence suggests that the mysteries of the Cabiri were celebrated on Samothrace by the seventh century BCE, and possibly earlier still. By the fifth century BCE the Samothracian mysteries were sufficiently famous to attract initiates from Athens, and they remained well known and popular around the Mediterranean, especially among sailors, until the Christian seizure of power in the fourth century CE. Like most of the ancient mysteries, the rites of Samothrace were studied intensively during the great age of secret societies in the eighteenth, nineteenth and early twentieth centuries, and references to the Cabiri appear in several nineteenth-century secret society initiation rituals. See **mysteries, ancient**.

Further reading: Burkert 1985.

Sande Society

One of the two most widespread secret societies in West Africa, the Sande Society is a women's society found along the Upper Guinea coast from Sierra Leone to Liberia. In earlier times, before Christian and Muslim missionaries gained influence in this area, most girls were initiated into the Sande Society as an essential part of their transition to womanhood, while boys became members of the similar Poro Society. See **African secret societies**; **Poro Society**.

To be initiated into the society, candidates undergo a series of ritual encounters with the Sande spirit, a female entity associated with rivers and fertility. Masked dancers wearing a distinctive wooden helmet mask represent the spirit, and pass on women's mysteries to the new initiates. A council of Sande elders oversees these rites, and also traditionally wields a great deal of political and economic authority, which, however, is balanced by the influence of the men's Poro Society. In some areas, in fact, Poro and Sande elders alternate in power, with Poro elders having the final word in one year and Sande elders holding authority the next.

Unlike the Poro Society, which faced significant legal repression during the colonial era, the Sande Society was largely neglected by colonial governments. It remains a living tradition across a sizeable area of West Africa today.

Further reading: Phillips 1995.

Satanism

The worship of Satan, the fallen archangel and spirit of evil in Christian mythology, has played a relatively minor role in secret societies in the western world, but a much larger role in the mythologies and misunderstandings that have surrounded secret societies in recent centuries. A handful of secret societies have actually embraced Satanism in one form or another, but most of the organizations accused of harboring Satanists have no actual connection to Satanism at all.

Satanism has the curious historical distinction of being almost entirely a creation of the propaganda of its enemies. The first references anywhere to the worship of Satan are in lives of Christian saints written in the late Roman period and early Middle Ages, some of which included revisionist descriptions of pagan religion as devil worship. The theme of Satanist worship had a fairly small place in Christian thought, however, until the fourteenth century.

In the aftermath of the Black Death of 1345–50, when nearly a third of the population of Europe died, rumors spread like wildfire among the survivors claiming that the plague had been caused by Jews, lepers, or Muslims, the traditional scapegoats in Christian Europe at that time. Over the next half century, these rumors mutated into a belief that a secret cult of heretics who worshipped Satan were personally responsible for much of the evil in the world. That belief launched the first great wave of witchcraft persecutions, which broke out in Switzerland and western Germany early in the following century, and remained widely accepted throughout Europe for nearly 400 years thereafter. See **witchcraft persecutions**.

The era of witchcraft persecutions also saw the first solidly attested cases of Satanist worship. The immense publicity given to the supposed Satan-worshipping witch cults during that time in effect presented Satanism as a tempting option to people dissatisfied with early modern Christianity, especially since sermons and pamphlets about witches during the age of persecutions frequently dwelt at great length on the extravagant sexual license, drunkenness, and feasting that supposedly went on at witches' sabbats, and the ability to blight their enemies' lives with magic that Satan allegedly gave to witches. Since these inevitably attracted at least as many people as they repelled, Christian propaganda directed against witchcraft ironically became publicity for Satanism. See **sabbat**.

Sorting out actual Satanists from victims of the witch-hunt hysteria can be a difficult task. In a handful of cases, though, the evidence for organized worship of the Christian devil is almost impossible to dismiss. A classic example surfaced in the "Affair of the Poisons" in late sixteenth-century France, where important figures at the court of Louis XIV, among them the king's mistress Françoise Athénaïs de Montespan, took part in black masses meant to win royal favor. The ringleader of the group was an elderly fortune-teller and abortionist who went by the name La Voisin, who also dabbled in poisons and prostitution. After members of the group made several attempts to poison the king himself, the group's existence came to light. La Voisin and 35 others were burned alive, and Madame de Montespan was forced to leave the court. See **Black Mass**.

As the witchcraft persecutions faded into memory, Satanism came to draw much of its interest from literary fashions. The craze for "Gothic" novels in eighteenth-century Britain also inspired one of the more colorful Satanist groups, the Hell-Fire Club, though this was at least as much an excuse for orgies and heavy drinking as anything. In the same way, nineteenth-century French Decadent literature inspired both the masterpiece of literary Satanism, J. K. Huysmans' harrowing *Là-Bas* (*Down There*), and a thriving subculture of Satanist groups whose rituals were as much performance art for bored gentlemen as anything else. See **Hell-Fire Club**.

Late nineteenth-century France also saw one of the defining events in the history of modern Satanism, the "Palladian Order" hoax of Léo Taxil. Taxil, a professional pornographer turned fraudulent conspiracy theorist, claimed to have uncovered a secret society of Satanist sex fiends hidden within Freemasonry, the Palladian Order, and published a torrent of books on the subject, freely inventing evidence out of whole cloth to support his claims. In the process he invented most of the rhetoric used by fundamentalist Christians and conspiracy theorists today, and in fact the word "Satanism" itself is one of Taxil's creations. See **Palladian Order**.

Satanism had little appeal, though, in the freewheeling occult scene of the late nineteenth and early twentieth centuries. Most occultists in that era were either comfortable with the relatively liberal Christianity of the time, or rejected Christian beliefs altogether to worship Pagan gods or devote themselves to Eastern systems of mysticism. Even rebel occultist and self-proclaimed Antichrist Aleister Crowley, though he dabbled in Satanism, ended up settling on a new religion of his own invention instead. At a time when almost half of all adult Americans and nearly as many Britons belonged to at least one secret society, furthermore, conservative Christian claims that secret societies all worshipped Satan behind closed doors served mostly to marginalize Christian conservatives in the eyes of the general public. In this environment neither Satanism nor accusations of Satanism flourished. See **Crowley, Aleister**.

Not until the middle years of the twentieth century did Satanism become an organized public presence in the western world, and by that time it had little to do with older ideas of devil worship. Anton Szandor LaVey (Howard Stanton Levey, 1930–97), the colorful San Francisco eccentric who founded the Church of Satan in 1966, drew his ideas from the Objectivist philosophy of Ayn Rand and used the trappings of Satanism mostly as an effective way of promoting himself. LaVey's media antics and his heavily marketed books, especially *The Satanic Bible* (1969), spawned many imitators, and a Satanist secret society with far more serious aims, the Temple of Set, broke away from LaVey's Church of Satan in 1975 and has become a significant presence in the modern occult scene. See **Church of Satan**; **Temple of Set**.

As these trends played out in the media, however, a new wave of claims about Satanism was brewing. These burst into public awareness in 1980 with the publication of *Michelle Remembers*, the book that launched the Satanic ritual abuse panic. Michelle Smith, the co-author of the book, claimed that she had been raised in a multigenerational Satanist cult in Vancouver, Canada. Her lurid narrative of torture, rape, human sacrifice, and cannibalism became a bestseller and inspired numerous imitations. By 1983 claims of Satanic ritual abuse leapt off the bookshelves and into the law courts, with the first prosecutions for Satanic ritual abuse in America.

The furor that followed these events depended on an alliance of convenience between two groups usually at opposite ends of the political spectrum. Fundamentalist Christians played a key role in launching and sustaining the panic with a torrent of books, articles, and sermons that had millions of Americans looking nervously behind every corner for signs of lurking Satanists. They also provided the vast majority of "Satanism experts," most of whom had no relevant professional training at all, but conducted seminars for law enforcement agencies and therapists across North America.

The other key group was social workers and therapists. Predisposed by their training and political views to see women and children as helpless victims of oppression needing support and advocacy, many of these turned ritual abuse cases into a personal crusade and convinced themselves that any client they encountered might be a survivor of Satanic ritual abuse. The methods they devised to help people "recover repressed memories" are textbook examples of ways to distort memory, including hypnosis, powerful drugs, suggestion, and subjection to intense emotional pressure in therapy groups to validate others' memories of abuse by coming up with mem [illegible] own. Most people subjecte [illegible] sort of "therapy" will end up be [illegible] ing whatever the therapist wants them to believe; the methods are not all that different from those used in brainwashing or the more intense forms of cult recruitment.

The furor crested and began to wane in the 1990s as law enforcement agencies found no evidence to support ritual abuse claims, investigative journalists began printing stories that uncovered awkward holes in ritual abuse stories, and the first wave of malpractice lawsuits hit therapists whose methods of extracting "recovered memories" violated accepted professional standards. By this time, however, all the noise and hype had succeeded in publicizing Satanism more effectively than anything since the great witchcraft persecutions of the fifteenth, sixteenth, and seventeenth centuries. The predictable result was a swarm of newly minted Satanist groups.

The new Satanist secret societies of the 1990s and the first years of the twenty-first century were primarily a youth phenomenon, and used the Internet as their most important forum for recruiting new members and disseminating their ideas. Fragmented and wildly diverse, these groups have almost nothing in common except total rejection of Christianity and conventional moral codes. Some aspects of the new Satanism overlap with the Ordo Templi Orientis (OTO), the ros (IOT), de magical close connec- secret societies Order of Thule. se new Satanist group ard to predict, but as long as fu mentalist churches continue to label anything they dislike as Satanic, it seems likely that Satanism will continue to thrive. See **Illuminates of Thanateros (IOT)**; **Ordo Templi Orientis (OTO)**; **White Order of Thule (WOT)**.

Further reading: Nathan and Snedecker 1995, Smith and Padzer 1980, Victor 1993.

Saunière, Bérenger

See **Priory of Sion**.

Schaw, William

Scottish builder, engineer, and Freemason, 1550–1602. The younger son of John Schaw, an influential Clackmannanshire laird, Schaw grew up close to the Scottish court. He was probably the William Schaw mentioned in court records as a page of Mary Guise, Dowager Queen of Scotland, in 1560, and received a share of his father's goods in the same year when John Schaw and four of his servants were outlawed for murdering the servant of another laird. In 1581, as one of King James VI's courtiers, he was forced to sign the Negative Confession, a denunciation of Catholicism, despite his own devout Catholic faith.

In 1583 he was appointed Master of Works by James VI, with authority over all royal building projects in Scotland. This brought him into close contact with Scottish lodges of operative masons. In 1598 he issued a set of ordinances, the first Schaw Statutes, to be observed by master stonemasons throughout Scotland. These ordinances generally follow the Old Charges, the oldest records of Masonry, but include further details of the organization and functioning of stonemasons' lodges. Apparently some lodges objected to certain elements of the first Statutes, for a revised version, the second Schaw Statutes, was enacted in 1599. These statutes are the earliest detailed records of the organization of operative masons in Scotland, and provide a crucial snapshot of the Scottish lodges early in their evolution toward Freemasonry. See **Freemasonry**.

Schaw's duties as Master of Works did not keep him from an active career as a courtier and ambassador. In 1584 he traveled to France along with Lord George Seton on a diplomatic mission, and in 1589 he accompanied James to Denmark for the king's wedding. In 1590 he became chamberlain to the queen, Anne of Denmark, and sometime after 1591 was appointed the king's master of ceremonies. On his death in 1602, Anne paid for a lavish monument in Dunfermline Abbey, where he was buried.

Further reading: Stevenson 1988.

School of Night

Among the most important occult societies in Elizabethan England, the School of Night almost certainly did not go by that name, if the group had a name at all; the phrase comes from Shakespeare, who lampooned the group in his play *Love's Labour's Lost* (*c.*1590). A circle of freethinkers, scholars, and occultists centered on the famous adventurer and courtier Sir Walter Raleigh and his magical instructor, Thomas Harriot, the School's membership included such notables as Henry, Earl of Northumberland, known as the "Wizard Earl" to his contemporaries for his involvement in alchemy and magic; Sir George Carey, later raised to the peerage as Lord Hounsdon; the playwright Christopher Marlowe; the poets George Chapman, Matthew Roydon, and William Warner; and possibly Edmund Spenser, author of *The Faerie Queene* and arguably the most important poet of the age.

Members of the School were widely thought to be atheists. A 1592 pamphlet speaks of

> Sir Walter Rawley's school of Atheisme by the way, and the Conjuror that is Master thereof, and of the diligence used to get young gentlemen of this school, wherein both Moyses and our Saviour, the olde and Newe Testamentes are jested at, and the scollers taught, among other things, to spell God backwards. (Bradbrook 1965, p. 12)

Certainly the School's members studied occult sciences – Raleigh himself was a capable alchemist – and had skeptical ideas about established religion. See **Alchemy**; **Magic**.

The School probably came into being around 1585, when Raleigh returned from his adventures in Virginia, and it died on the executioner's block with Raleigh himself in 1618. Nearly all the evidence concerning it comes from the years from 1593 to 1595. In the former year Raleigh was exiled from court and Marlowe was murdered under mysterious circumstances in Deptford, shortly after being brought before the Court of Star Chamber in London to answer charges of blasphemy and atheism. Both these events focused public attention on rumors already in circulation about Raleigh's circle, and gave Robert Devereaux, Earl of Essex – a rising star at Elizabeth's court – a chance to strike at his hated rival Raleigh.

Essex had his own playwright-poet, a man who wrote under the name of William Shakespeare (and may or may not have been the actor of that name), and Shakespeare and the School of Night sniped at one another in their writings – Shakespeare targeting Chapman's poem *The Shadow of Night* and the School generally in *Love's Labour's Lost*, Chapman retorting with a revision of *The Shadow of Night* and the later poem *Ovid's Banquet of Sense*, and other members of the School writing *Willoughbie his Avisa* as a further counterblast to *Love's Labour's Lost*. By 1596 the literary war wound up, and Essex turned his attention more and more toward the political intrigues that led to his failed *coup d'etat* and execution in 1601.

Despite the quarrel between the School of Night and the author of the Shakespeare plays and poems, several members of the School, notably Sir Walter Raleigh and Christopher Marlowe, are among the people suspected of hiding behind the mask of "William Shakespeare." See **Shakespeare controversies**.

Further reading: Bradbrook 1965, Yates 1936.

Schwaller de Lubicz, René Aor

French esoteric and secret society member, 1887–1961. One of the most influential figures in twentieth-century occultism, René Schwaller was born in Alsace and served an apprenticeship with a chemist before moving to Paris in 1905 and plunging into occult studies. A member of the Parisian branch of the Theosophical Society, he knew most of the significant figures in the French alchemical scene of the early twentieth century. An associate of the mysterious French alchemist Fulcanelli, Schwaller claimed in later life that he, not Fulcanelli, had first worked out the alchemical symbolism of French Gothic cathedrals that Fulcanelli published in his occult masterpiece *Le Mystère des Cathédrales* (*The Mystery of the Cathedrals*, 1925). See **Alchemy**; **Theosophical Society**.

In the aftermath of the First World War, like many other intellectuals of the time, Schwaller dabbled in fascist politics, organizing a group called *Les Veilleurs* (The Watchers) and publishing a journal, *L'Affranchi* (*The Liberated*). French astronomer Nicolas Camille Flammarion and Lithuanian poet O.V. de Lubicz Milosz were members, as was a young occultist from Germany who went on to become far more famous – the Nazi leader Rudolf Hess. Schwaller and Milosz became close friends, and the Lithuanian adopted Schwaller, giving him the second half of his later name and the title Chevalier de Lubicz.

Schwaller de Lubicz's political activities came to an end in 1920, when he disbanded Les Veilleurs and moved to Switzerland. Near St Moritz, he and his wife, Isha, established what would now be called a commune, Suhalia, where he and other members practiced natural healing methods and handcrafts. Suhalia broke up in 1927, and Schwaller de Lubicz moved to southern France, then to the island of Majorca, and finally, in 1938, to Egypt, where he and Isha studied the ruined temples of the Pharaohs and waited out the Second World War.

His stay in Egypt proved to be the turning point in Schwaller de Lubicz's career. Close study of Egyptian art and architecture revealed to him a complex esoteric philosophy based on sacred geometry. He and Isha returned to southern France in 1952, where he spent the rest of his life writing a series of erudite books expounding his teachings to the world. While his active involvement in secret societies seems to have ended with the disbanding of Les Veilleurs in 1920, his writings and teachings have been enormously influential in contemporary occult societies. See **sacred geometry**.

Further reading: Picknett and Prince 1999, VandenBrouck 1987.

SCOTTISH DEGREES

A series of Masonic degrees created in France in the middle of the eighteenth century. Despite the name, they have no actual connection to Scotland, and first arrived in Scotland in 1833, when the Ancient and Accepted Scottish Rite came there from America. This has not prevented incautious researchers from searching the degrees of that Rite for secrets passed down from medieval Scottish Templars. See **Ancient and Accepted Scottish Rite**; **Freemasonry**; **Knights Templar**.

The first chapters (local lodges) working Scottish degrees appeared in Paris in the late 1730s, in circles closely connected to the Jacobite exile community then planning the 1745 attempt to put Charles Edward Stuart on the British throne. The legendary origin of the degrees draws heavily on the famous Masonic oration of the Chevalier Ramsay, who first proposed that Masonry descended from the knightly orders of the medieval Crusades. Ramsay was himself a Jacobite, and it has been plausibly suggested that the oration and the new degrees were part of a single project to create a new Jacobite Masonry at a time when Jacobites were losing control of ordinary Craft lodges in France and other European countries. See **Jacobites**; **Ramsay, Andrew Michael**.

This Templar origin, according to the legend, came via Scotland. Allegedly a band of Knights Templar fled from France to escape the destruction of their order under Philip IV. They were given a safe haven in Scotland, and in gratitude fought for Robert the Bruce against the English at the battle of Bannockburn in 1314. Each of the branches of Scottish Masonry that emerged after the failure of the 1745 rebellion traced their roots back to that group of Templars; thus the Royal Order of Scotland, for instance, claims that Bruce rewarded the

Templars for their valor by instituting the Royal Order of Scotland, with the Templars as its first members and himself as the first Grand Master. See **Royal Order of Scotland**.

After the battle of Culloden put an end to Jacobite hopes in 1746, the Scottish degrees appear to have been left to their own devices, and spread through European Masonry. The Royal Order of Scotland was among the first to surface, establishing a lodge in The Hague in 1750. A much more elaborate rite of 22 degrees, the Rite of Perfection, went public in 1754 with the foundation of the Chapter of Clermont. Four years later this yielded to a new body, the Council of Emperors of the East and West, which lasted until 1781 and contended with a rival body, the Council of Emperors of the East. One or the other Council – to this day, no one is sure which – authorized a French Mason named Stephen Morin to establish the Rite of Perfection in the New World, and thus laid the foundations of the Ancient and Accepted Scottish Rite, one of the most important Masonic bodies today. See **Rite of Perfection**.

Scroll and Key Society

See **Yale secret societies**.

Scrying

One of the most common magical practices in European magic from the Middle Ages until the present, scrying is the art of seeing visions in a crystal, a magic mirror, or the scryer's own trained imagination. Since communication with the unseen is always central to occultism, scrying has often had an important role in the teachings offered by occult secret societies. It is also known as clairvoyance (from the French for "clear seeing") and, in recent New Age writings, as "remote viewing." See **New Age movement**.

The art of scrying depends on the ability to enter into a shallow trance, in which dreamlike images appear. The classic method depends on a crystal, a mirror, or some other transparent or reflective surface. Gazing into the depths of the scrying tool, the scryer can perceive cloudlike shapes and then, as the trance deepens, other images. Scrying in a crystal formed one of the key elements of English magic from the late sixteenth century until the last decades of the nineteenth. The mid-nineteenth century in particular saw it adopted by many occult secret societies, and at least one such society – the Fratres Lucis, founded by Francis Irwin in 1873 – was created using rituals and symbolism received via crystal-gazing. See **magic**.

By contrast, the great occult orders of the late nineteenth century made little use of crystal vision. The Hermetic Brotherhood of Luxor (H.B. of L.), which for a few years in the 1880s seemed likely to become the predominant magical secret society in the Western world, taught the consecration and use of magic mirrors. Although it was founded in Britain, the H.B. of L. took its scrying methods from the writings of American magus Paschal Beverly Randolph. See **Hermetic Brotherhood of Luxor (H.B. of L.)**; **Randolph, Paschal Beverly**.

The Hermetic Order of the Golden Dawn, which succeeded where the H.B. of L. had failed and redefined the entire western magical tradition for most of a century, taught its initiates to practice "scrying in the spirit vision." This method dispensed with crystals, mirrors, and scrying tools altogether; Golden Dawn exercises help spontaneous imagery rise directly into the mind's eye, turning the visual imagination into a vehicle for clairvoyant experience. See **Hermetic Order of the Golden Dawn**.

Many modern occult secret societies teach variants of the Golden Dawn methods of scrying, and a few preserve older methods of mirror and crystal scrying. The open publication of many occult techniques in recent years, though, has removed most of the veil of secrecy from these practices; it's not uncommon in modern occult lodges for students to be told to learn their scrying techniques from publicly available books on the subject.

Research on remote viewing (which is simply scrying by a different name) has shown that most people can learn to perceive images of distant places, the contents of sealed envelopes, and the like with a success rate well above chance. Not even the most gifted scryers are always accurate, however, and those who have practiced scrying know that the results can never be taken at face value without thorough checking.

This point has particular relevance to the study of hidden history, because a very large amount of the information circulated about lost continents, ancient civilizations, secret societies, and hidden traditions of the past has its origins in scrying and related techniques. In the case of Atlantis, to name only one example, the hard facts in the case consist of a few paragraphs in the writings of Plato and an assortment of equivocal details from oceanography, geology, and history; nearly everything else currently believed about the lost continent came from various kinds of scrying or the even more uncertain source of hypnotic regression, when not simply made up from whole cloth. The fact that resulting accounts of the lost continent vary drastically does not lend credence to the idea that any one of them can be taken as fact. See **Atlantis**.

The same caution should be applied to any other material from visionary sources. In today's rejected-knowledge scene, however, these concerns rarely get raised, and a huge amount of half-baked speculation and fantasy has unfortunately ended up being treated as proven fact in alternative circles. See **rejected knowledge**.

Further reading: Besterman 1965, Godwin 1994, Regardie 1971.

Second International

A major focus of conservative fears about secret societies in the late nineteenth and early twentieth centuries, the Second or Socialist International was founded in 1889 by a congress of French, English, and German Marxists and trade unionists who met in Paris to establish some common framework for working-class solidarity in the aftermath of the First International, which had imploded in a series of bitter internal quarrels in 1872. The meeting, which took place at the Salle Petrelle, had been called in a deliberate attempt to compete with another international radical congress meeting at the same time in the same city, at a hall on the Rue de Lancry; this latter meeting was dominated by anarchist groups, and the Marxists wanted an International of their own. See **Anarchism**; **Communism**; **First International**.

The congress at the Salle Petrelle laid the foundations for a new International, but it took 11 years to establish a formal organization and most power remained with the Socialist and Social Democratic parties from different countries that composed it. Annual congresses provided a venue to work out a common platform, but too often most of the International's energy went into squabbling over theoretical issues.

In the early years of the twentieth century, as the political strains that gave rise to the First World War became increasingly apparent, the Second International drew up an ambitious plan to prevent a European war by simultaneous general strikes in every country that declared war. The Stuttgart Congress of 1907 made this plan a centerpiece of Socialist policy in every major European country. When war broke out in 1914, however, every Socialist party in Europe abandoned the plan and supported its country's war effort. The mutual recriminations that followed soon tore the International apart, and a flurry of emergency congresses in 1915 failed to repair the damage. The Second International thus ended, and the Third, or Communist International, replaced it in 1919. See **Third International**.

Further reading: Drachkovitch 1966.

Secrecy

The defining characteristic of secret societies is the fact that they keep secrets. This is obvious enough. Less obvious, to those who have not participated in secret societies and paid attention to their symbolism and structure, is the deep role secrecy plays in every aspect of a secret society. The secrets of most secret societies are remarkably trivial – a few signs of recognition and the texts of initiation rituals are usually all a member promises to keep secret – and yet those secret societies that have abandoned secrecy have rarely survived for long. Secrecy, in fact, is the glue that holds secret societies together.

Yet their secrecy has played an equally central part in creating the climate of suspicion that surrounds secret societies today. M. William Cooper's 1991 conspiracy theory classic *Behold A Pale Horse* sums up the common attitude succinctly:

> You must understand that secrecy is wrong. The very fact that a meeting is secret tells me that something is going on that I would not approve. Do not ever believe that grown men meet on a regular basis just to put on fancy robes, burn candles, and glad-hand each other ... THE VERY FACT THAT SOMETHING IS SECRET MEANS THERE IS SOMETHING TO HIDE. (Cooper 1991, p. 95; emphasis in original)

Some secret societies, some of the time, have unquestionably used secrecy as a cover for reprehensible conduct. Still, it is nonsense to claim that all secrets are wrong by definition. The same people who object to the secrecy of secret societies, for example, would likely object to having the details of their finances or their sex lives printed on the front page of the daily newspaper. Equally, there are reasons for secrecy that make obvious sense even to the critics of secret societies. Political secret societies struggling to overthrow dictatorships, for example, keep their plans secret to keep the police at bay; religious secret societies condemned by intolerant religious authorities keep their meetings and beliefs secret to shield members from persecution; the fraternal secret societies common in nineteenth-century Britain and America, which provided benefits to traveling members, relied on secret signs of recognition to keep non-members from claiming benefits they had not earned.

Such concerns played a major role in creating the secret society movement of the modern western world. As secret societies spread and their members explored the psychological impact of secrecy, though, a deeper dimension came to the fore. The experience of having and keeping secrets has potent transformative effects on the self. One who has promised to keep a secret from his family and friends can no longer drift through life in the half-conscious manner usual to most of us; he must watch his words and actions, and in the process awakens to a new awareness of himself and his world. Combine this new awareness with the moral focus of traditional fraternal lodges such as Freemasonry or

Odd Fellowship, and significant moral and personal changes can result; combine it with the powerful transformative techniques of occult secret societies such as the Hermetic Order of the Golden Dawn and the initiate gains potential access to hidden worlds in the self and the universe. This is the hidden purpose of secrecy in the traditional lodge system – a secret that, like most of the inner dimensions of that system, is hidden in plain sight. See **fraternal orders**; **Freemasonry**; **Hermetic Order of the Golden Dawn**; **Odd Fellowship**.

Further reading: Greer 1998.

Servants of the Light [SOL]

One of the major occult secret societies in the western world today, the Servants of the Light began in 1965 as a correspondence course published by Helios Book Service and written by W.E. Butler and Gareth Knight, two former members of Dion Fortune's Society of the Inner Light. In 1961, the Society had abandoned much of its original magical focus for Christian mysticism, and Butler and Knight both left it around that time; the Helios Course on the Practical Qabalah, as the correspondence course was titled, was their way to disseminate Fortune's magical teachings to a new generation of occultists. See **Society of the Inner Light**.

In 1975, together with a core of students who had completed the correspondence course, Butler organized the Servants of the Light as a magical secret society, while Knight left to pursue other projects. In 1978, on Butler's death, Dolores Ashcroft-Nowicki became director of SOL and still holds that post as at the time of writing. The order still operates a correspondence course and has local lodges in Britain, North America, and Europe.

Shakespeare controversies

The identity of the writer of the plays and poems attributed to William Shakespeare (1564–1616) has been a matter of debate for nearly two centuries, and like almost everything else in the world of rejected knowledge, the controversy over Shakespeare has been drawn into the realm of secret societies. The literature on the controversy is immense and can only be outlined here; Michell 1996 offers an accessible overview of the debate. See **rejected knowledge**.

The controversy unfolds from the almost total mismatch between the historical William Shakespeare and the work attributed to him. Shakespeare came from an illiterate working-class family in the rural town of Stratford-upon-Avon. While he may have attended the local grammar school – no one is sure, as the school's records have not survived – that was the maximum extent of his education. The only surviving specimens of his handwriting are five signatures, three of them on his will, and his children were illiterate; one of them, his daughter Judith, could not even sign her own name. The same will, which specifies Shakespeare's worldly goods in detail, includes not a single book.

Shakespeare's documented life offers few clues to help resolve the matter. After a completely undistinguished childhood, he left Stratford in 1587 for a theatre career in London, leaving behind a wife eight years his senior and three young children. In an age full of diarists, satirists, and gossips, he made little impression on his contemporaries. The first reference to him in his new career is a 1592 diatribe by Robert Greene, an unsuccessful writer and dramatist, who describes him as a plagiarist who "is in his own conceit the only Shake-scene in the country." The year 1595 saw him listed as a comic actor, while court records from 1596 show him dodging taxes and give him an active role in a quarrel among Surrey gangsters, no rare thing at a time when the theatre business had close connections to organized crime.

By 1599 he had risen in the theatre world to the level of managing the Globe Theatre, and held a portion of the lease there until at least 1611. Sometime between 1604 and 1611, however, he retired to Stratford, where public records show him buying property and engaging in petty lawsuits with his neighbors for the remainder of his life. His death in 1616 was a non-event outside of Stratford; this is all the more puzzling because the deaths of other poets and playwrights of the same period were marked by outpourings of verse from their fellow writers.

Meanwhile, starting in 1598, the name William Shakespeare began appearing on the title pages of published plays. Some of them are now considered to be Shakespeare's, but others are not – *The Life of Sir John Old-Castle*, *The London Prodigall* and *A Yorkshire Tragedy* appeared in print as William Shakespeare's work, though modern experts insist he had nothing to do with them. Many of the works now attributed to Shakespeare, on the other hand, appeared anonymously or under the names of other authors years earlier, while the First Folio of 1623 included 18 plays that had never before been published and have no traceable connection to Shakespeare other than their appearance there.

The plays themselves are almost impossible to square with the life of their supposed author. They are clearly the work of an extremely well educated mind. Allusions to classical and contemporary literature, much of it unavailable in English in Shakespeare's time, appear frequently in them, as do legal turns of phrase – the author of the plays apparently had a first-rate knowledge of English law. The plays also frequently use slang unique to Cambridge University, while the Warwickshire dialect of Shakespeare's hometown is conspicuous by its absence. The plays constantly and accurately echo the habits and perspectives of Elizabethan aristocracy, from courtly manners to the complicated terminology of falconry. Whoever wrote the plays was also well-traveled by the standards of the time; plays such as *Romeo and Juliet* and *The Merchant of Venice* include detailed, accurate knowledge of north Italian geography and culture, and *Love's Labour's Lost* contains up-to-date gossip from the court of the King of Navarre. None of these things make sense if the plays were written by William Shakespeare, the glover and wool-dealer's son from Stratford-upon-Avon.

Who did write the plays then? There is no shortage of candidates. The first to be proposed was Sir Francis Bacon (1561–1626), one of the most brilliant minds of the Elizabethan age. A Cambridge man, a barrister, and a classical scholar fluent in many languages, Bacon came from a family with aristocratic connections. While studying law at Gray's Inn, he wrote plays that were performed by his fellow-students, and Bacon himself and one of his biographers, John Aubrey, call him a "concealed poet." In 1597 and 1598 two satirists, Joseph Hall and John Marston, teased Bacon (under a transparent pseudonym) for having written the poems *Venus and Adonis* and *The Rape of Lucrece*, which are usually assigned to Shakespeare.

Bacon was notorious in his lifetime as a secretive, cunning man – John Aubrey, who collected accounts from those who knew him, was told that Bacon had "the eie of a viper" – and he had an excellent motive for keeping work as a playwright secret. The public theatres of his time had roughly the same social cachet that soft-core pornography has today, and the discovery that he was responsible for the plays attributed to Shakespeare would have meant the end of his career in politics. Among secret societies, Bacon has long been a favorite candidate, and a number of important occult authors have claimed Bacon's secret authorship of the Shakespeare canon as part of a far-reaching plan to shape the collective consciousness of the Elizabethan age. See **Bacon, Francis**.

The most popular candidate nowadays is Edward de Vere, Earl of Oxford (1550–1604), another intellectual Elizabethan nobleman. Like Bacon, de Vere was educated at Cambridge and studied law, but unlike Bacon he traveled extensively in Italy and elsewhere in Europe. He had personal connections with the Elizabethan theatre – in fact, he supported a theatre company – and was widely considered the best poet among Elizabeth's courtiers; an anonymous 1589 book *The Arte of English Poesie* lists him as the foremost of the "notable gentlemen in the court that have written commendably, and suppressed it again, or else suffered it to be published without their own names to it" (quoted in Michell 1996, p. 173).

The sonnets attributed to Shakespeare offer the most support to the Oxford claim. They reflect his life and known relationships precisely, and include riddling lines in the Elizabethan style that point straight at him. A good example is Sonnet 76's line "That every word doth almost tell my name"; "every word," a near-anagram of "Edward Vere," does indeed almost tell Oxford's name. The only drawback to the Oxford claim is that he died in 1604, and plays in the Shakespeare canon kept appearing for several years afterwards, including some of the greatest; *King Lear*, *Macbeth*, and *The Tempest*, among others, had not yet been staged for the first time at Oxford's death.

Other candidates include William Stanley, Earl of Derby (1561–1642), Oxford's son-in-law, who also supported a theatre company, who was reported by a Jesuit spy of the time to be "busyed only in penning commodyes (comedies) for the common players," and who visited the court of Navarre at the right time to gather the details that appear in *Love's Labour's Lost*; Roger Manners, Earl of Rutland (1576–1612), another Cambridge man who traveled in Italy and Denmark; and Christopher Marlowe (1564–93), the first great playwright of the Elizabethan age and an agent for Queen Elizabeth's intelligence service, whose death under mysterious circumstances might possibly have been faked, leaving him alive to continue writing plays that were published under another author's name. Many theorists in recent years have argued that the plays and poems were written by two or more people working together. Each of these claims is backed by some evidence, but none can be proven conclusively.

Shakespeare's own role in all this is the least difficult of the many questions surrounding the origins of the plays and poetry bearing his name. Many entirely orthodox scholars agree that not all the plays in the Shakespeare canon are his own work; collaboration was standard practice in his time, and *Titus Andronicus* and the three parts of *Henry VI* are frequently cited as works by other playwrights lightly reworked and edited by the author of the Shakespeare plays. Robert Greene's 1592 rant about "Shake-scene," accusing Shakespeare of plagiarism, is not the only accusation. Ben Jonson, who publicly praised Shakespeare to the skies in the foreword to the 1623 First Folio, described him in a satirical epigram of 1616 as a "Poet-Ape, that would be thought our chief" who started out as a broker of plays – "At first he made low shifts, would pick and glean/Buy the reversion of old plays" (quoted in Michell 1996) – and ended up putting his own name wholesale on other people's work.

A plausible case, then, can be made that the works attributed to Shakespeare are actually the work of many different authors. This would account for the notorious variations in quality and tone among the plays, as well as the fact that the works as a whole use a vocabulary twice as large as any other writer in the English language – a likely sign that several people were involved in their creation, since every writer inevitably has a distinctive personal vocabulary. If this theory is correct, what stands behind the writings attributed to Shakespeare is not a single mind but the collected genius of an age, including the works of several noblemen who were perfectly content to have their authorship concealed behind the name of an unscrupulous play broker and actor named William Shakespeare.

Further reading: Challinor 1996, Michell 1996.

Shambhala

A hidden city in Tibetan tradition, Shambhala is said to be located somewhere north of Tibet in the desert wastelands of central Asia. Tibetan sources describe it as the original source of the Kalachakra teachings, an important branch of Tibetan Buddhist spirituality, and also claim that someday a messianic king named Rigden-Jyepo will lead his armies out from Shambhala to rid the world of evil.

References to Shambhala appear in a number of western works on Tibet from the nineteenth century, but it was Helena Petrovna Blavatsky, founder of the Theosophical Society, who put the hidden city on the western occult map. Both her major books, *Isis Unveiled* (1877) and *The Secret Doctrine* (1888), refer to the hidden city. Later Theosophical accounts describe Shambhala as a city founded by the Manu of the Fifth Root Race around 70,000 BCE on the shores of the sea that once filled the Gobi Desert. From Theosophy, Shambhala found its way into the mythic geography of the New Age movement, where it still plays a significant role. See **Blavatsky, Helena Petrovna**; **New Age movement**; **Theosophical Society**.

By the early twentieth century writers in the occult community had begun to pair Shambhala with the other hidden city of central Asia, Agharta. See **Agharta**.

Further reading: Godwin 1993.

Shickshinny Knights of Malta

One of the many secret societies who have been tabbed as the hidden puppet masters behind the New World Order, the Shickshinny Knights of Malta – also known as the American Grand Priory of the Sovereign Order of St John of Jerusalem, Knights of Malta – are headquartered in the modest town of Shickshinny, Pennsylvania, in Luzerne County, an area settled largely by German and Russian immigrants. The order, incorporated in 1956, was created in the mid-1950s by Charles Pichel and a few associates, and provided with a colorful origin story in the usual secret society manner. See **New World Order**; **origin stories**.

According to Pichel's account, the Shickshinny Knights are descended from the original Knights of Malta. When Napoleon seized the island of Malta and dispossessed the Knights of their last territorial base, a handful of knights took refuge at the court of Tsar Alexander I of Russia, where they became members of his personal honor guard but preserved a Priory of the Knights of Malta in secret. Some of their descendants emigrated from Russia to Pennsylvania and brought the knightly traditions of their forefathers with them; in 1908, the Order's Grand Priory in America was founded. By this process, the heritage of the original Knights Hospitallers made its way to Luzerne County. Not least among the ironies of the Shickshinny Knights is the close parallel between these stories and the "family tradition" origin legends of many modern Wiccan groups. See **Wicca**.

Despite their lurid reputation in certain conspiracy theories dealing with the New World Order, the Shickshinny Knights are among the smaller conservative secret societies in twenty-first-century America. Its membership has included a number of retired generals from the Second World War era, including Charles Willoughby, former chief of intelligence for General Douglas MacArthur, but very few figures with significant power or wealth. It does apparently have significant connections with other extreme right-wing groups in America and Europe – one of its members, for example, was an editor for the John Birch Society magazine *American Opinion*. See **John Birch Society**.

Shroud of Turin

A medieval relic turned modern cause célèbre, the Shroud of Turin is a 14-foot (4.2-meter) strip of linen bearing the images of the front and back of a bearded man with the marks of crucifixion. Kept at Turin Cathedral since 1578, it originally appeared in northern France around 1350. Its owner, one Geoffroy de Charny, claimed that it was the original shroud of Jesus of Nazareth, wrapped around his body after his crucifixion. See **Jesus of Nazareth**.

The local bishop investigated the matter and discovered that it was a fraud, manufactured like so many other medieval relics in order to cash in on the lucrative pilgrim trade of the time; he even managed to interview the artist who created it. The bishop's finding makes sense in the context of the time; more than 40 other "shrouds of Jesus" could be found in churches in medieval Europe in the fourteenth century, part of a cult of relics that also resulted in six different French churches claiming ownership of the one authentic relic of Jesus' circumcision. Charny hurriedly put the "holy relic" away at the time of the bishop's investigation, but brought it back out in the 1380s, prompting another investigation and a ruling from the Pope forbidding it to be called the actual shroud of Jesus.

Charny's granddaughter sold the Shroud to the Duke of Savoy in 1453, and very little was heard of it thereafter until 1969, when the Catholic Church called together a commission of experts and charged them with testing the relic's authenticity. The commission's report, published in 1976, found that pollen in the linen suggested that it might have been woven in Palestine, but that what looked like blood was actually paint. Another round of tests beginning in 1978 found that the image consisted of red ochre and vermilion, common pigments in medieval art; the "blood" was tempera paint, and radiocarbon dating of the cloth dated it to between 1260 and 1390. All these findings confirmed the original fourteenth century report.

As these results surfaced, though, the Shroud became the focus of an unusual alliance between conservative Christians, who argued that it was an authentic relic of Jesus, and proponents of rejected knowledge, who argued that it was almost anything except what the Christians said it was, but still insisted that it could not be a medieval fake. One popular theory held that it was actually the image of Jacques de Molay, the last Grand Master of the Knights Templar, imprinted on the cloth by a hypothetical chemical process after he was tortured and, according to this account, crucified by the Inquisition. The Shroud dates from the right century, and both de Molay and the figure on the shroud had beards; no other evidence supports the claim, however, and the same logic could be used to "prove" that the Shroud was in fact the burial cloth of de Molay's persecutor King Philip IV. This has not prevented this claim, and many others, from being circulated as fact in the rejected-knowledge community. See **Knights Templar**; **rejected knowledge**.

Further reading: Nickell 1987, Wilson 1979.

Sinclair family

Central to many recent theories about secret societies, the Sinclairs are a Scottish aristocratic family of

Norman extraction – their name was originally St Clair – with a historical connection to Scottish stonemasonry. In the Middle Ages, certain noble families had the right to supervise and judge disputes among members of particular professions; thus, for example, John of Gaunt, Duke of Lancaster, had supervision of all minstrels in England at the end of the fourteenth century, and the Dutton family had similar rights over all minstrels in the county of Chester in the sixteenth. The Sinclairs apparently had the same authority over stonemasons in late medieval lowland Scotland. Their position was not unique – the Coplands of Udoch had supervision over stonemasons in the shires of Aberdeen, Banff, and Kincardine, for example – but it was well enough established in tradition in the early seventeenth century that one branch of the Sinclair family was able to gain the backing of Scottish stonemasons' lodges in two attempts to re-establish their rights over the craft. The Sinclairs were also patrons of one of the masterpieces of Scottish medieval architecture, the famous Rosslyn Chapel. See **lodge**; **Rosslyn Chapel**.

During the fourteenth and fifteenth centuries the family reached its zenith, as three successive Sinclairs became Earls of Orkney and may have had connections through the north Atlantic fishing trade with early transatlantic voyages. According to a near-contemporary account the second of them, Henry Sinclair, crossed the Atlantic to what is now New England in 1398. This may explain the apparent presence of New World plants in the decorations of Rosslyn Chapel, commissioned by Henry Sinclair's son less than 50 years later. See **America, discovery of**.

The hereditary rights of the Sinclairs over Scottish masons lapsed with the transformation of Scottish stonemasons' lodges into modern Freemasonry in the seventeenth and early eighteenth centuries. In 1736, at the establishment of the Grand Lodge of Scotland, William Sinclair of Roslin formally relinquished all rights over Masonry. In return, the members of Grand Lodge made him Scotland's first elected Grand Master for a term of one year. See **Freemasonry**; **grand lodge**.

The retrospective transformation of the Sinclairs from a minor family of Scottish nobility to a focus of contemporary secret society literature began in the early 1960s, when Pierre Plantard wove their position in early Scottish Freemasonry into the tapestry of disinformation he created for his own secret society, the Priory of Sion. Plantard claimed to be descended from the Merovingian kings of early medieval France, and presented the Priory, which he had founded in 1956, as an ancient secret society that lay behind the Knights Templar and Freemasons. As part of his campaign, he added "de St Clair" to his name and claimed the Sinclairs as one branch of his imaginary Merovingian connection. Along with the rest of Plantard's inventions, this material was picked up by Henry Lincoln and his co-authors and included in their bestselling book *The Holy Blood and the Holy Grail* (1982). See **Disinformation**; **Priory of Sion**.

Once launched into the world of contemporary conspiracy literature, the Sinclairs quickly found themselves bedecked retrospectively with historically questionable honors and titles. One popular account, for example, insists that the Sinclairs had been the hereditary masters of all Scottish craft guilds, and traces their ancestry back to an imaginary group of 24 hereditary High Priests of the Temple of Jerusalem. Fundamentalist conspiracy-hunters, for their part, eagerly assigned the Sinclairs to the Satanic "black nobility" who figure prominently in current speculations about the New World Order. See **New World Order**; **Rex Deus**.

Further reading: Baigent et al. 1983, Hopkins et al. 2000, Stevenson 1988.

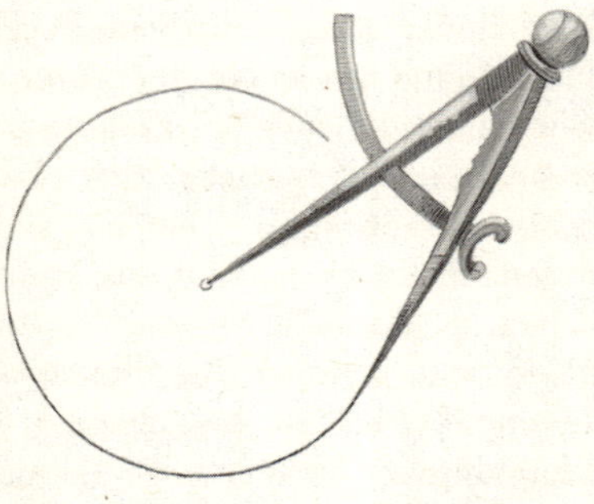

Skull and Bones Society

The most notorious college fraternity in America, the Skull and Bones Society was founded in 1832 at Yale University by valedictorian William H. Russell and 14 other undergraduates. Russell had taken time off from his Yale studies to travel in Germany, and apparently encountered a college society there that he used as a model for his new fraternity. Originally called the Eulogian Club, after its invented patron Eulogia, goddess of eloquence, the fraternity in 1833 took the pirate skull and crossbones flag as its symbol, and so became known as Skull and Bones. Like other college fraternities, it has an initiation ceremony consisting of roughly equal parts nineteenth-century melodrama and undergraduate pranks. Skull and Bones came out of a long history of similar organizations at Yale. The oldest known Yale student society, a literary society called Crotonia (after the location of Pythagoras's school in ancient Italy), was in existence before 1750. Skull and Bones, however, was the first to limit its membership. Each year, 15 members of the incoming senior class were (and are) selected for admission by vote of the existing members. Membership was restricted to male students until 1991, when the first female members were initiated. See **Yale secret societies**.

The society's headquarters, or "tomb" in Yale slang, was built in

1856 in the location it still occupies, on High Street in New Haven, Connecticut. Current members, or "knights," meet there on Thursday and Sunday nights for dinner and society activities; former members, or "patriarchs," are welcome to attend when in town, and several annual events attract large numbers back to Yale and events at the tomb. The society also owns Deer Island in the St Lawrence River, used as a vacation spot by knights, patriarchs, and their families.

As the oldest and most prestigious student society at one of America's top universities, Skull and Bones has attracted its share of members who went on to become important figures in politics and business, and three US presidents – William Howard Taft (president 1909–13), George Bush (president 1989–93), and George W. Bush (president 2000–) – were members during their time at Yale. All this is business as usual for upper-class college fraternities, and can easily be exceeded by other secret societies. The society's total of presidents measures up poorly, for example, next to the 14 presidents who have been Freemasons, or even the 5 who have been Elks. See **Benevolent Protective Order of Elks**; **Freemasonry**.

In the eyes of some recent conspiracy theorists, however, the two Bush presidencies made Skull and Bones "America's most powerful secret society." One popular book on secret societies claims that Skull and Bones forms the inner circle of the Council on Foreign Relations, an elite think-tank that is among the most popular targets for American conspiracy theorists. The Bush family connection to Skull and Bones has also brought the fraternity to center stage in many accounts of the New World Order. This sinister reputation doubtless delights the society's undergraduate members. See **Council on Foreign Relations (CFR)**; **New World Order**.

Further reading: Robbins 2002, van Helsing 1995.

SKULL AND CROSSBONES

The classic symbol of death in western culture, a skull on two crossed thighbones appears on countless tombs and other carvings from the early Middle Ages onward, and became very common after the Black Death of the mid-fourteenth century gave death imagery a prominent place in European culture. Like many elements of medieval symbolism, it survived into modern times, and was adopted by several secret societies including the Freemasons and Odd Fellows. As a symbol of death, it was also one of several flags used by pirates in the Atlantic during the sixteenth and seventeenth centuries. See **Freemasonry**; **Odd Fellowship**.

Misinterpreted as a purely Masonic symbol, the skull and crossbones has come to play a central role in recent claims that the Knights Templar discovered America. Supposedly a Templar fleet at La Rochelle in

France escaped from the roundup of French Templars in 1307 and sailed to the New World, where the descendants of its sailors became the pirates of the Caribbean. The pirates' use of the skull and crossbones, allegedly a Templar symbol also inherited by the Freemasons, is cited as proof of the claim. In fact the Templars had no fleet at La Rochelle; their fleets were in Mediterranean ports and consisted of keel-less lateenrigged craft, suitable for voyages to the Holy Land but unusable for Atlantic crossings. The Templars themselves never used the skull and crossbones as a symbol, and the alleged link between the Templars and the Freemasons was an invention of eighteenth-century Jacobite Freemasons. One could as easily argue that since Odd Fellows use the skull and crossbones, the pirates of the Caribbean were sixteenth-century Odd Fellows bolstering their widows' and orphans' funds by plundering Spanish galleons. See **America, discovery of**; **Jacobites**; **Knights Templar**; **Scottish degrees**.

Social Circle

One of the most active secret societies at the height of the French Revolution, the *Cercle Social* or Social Circle was founded by radical journalist Nicholas de Bonneville in the summer of 1790, drawing together a network of fellow radicals linked by Bonneville's journal *Le Tribun du Peuple* (*The People's Tribune*) and associated in pre-revolutionary times with the Social Club, a progressive political lobby sponsored by Philippe d'Orleans. It took up a political stance on the extreme left, insisting that the revolution had not gone far enough, and championed ideas then at the fringes of politics such as equal rights for women and a social welfare program funded by a progressive tax system.

The Circle drew much of its structure and symbolism from Freemasonry; members received the title of *francs-frères* ("free brothers") in place of *francs-maçons* (Freemasons), and a Circle publication announced that its members were "superior intelligences" who had found "a living light … in the highest spheres of Masonry" (cited in Billington 1980, p. 40). The Circle also had close links to the Bavarian Illuminati; de Bonneville was in close contact with radical circles in Germany, and was an associate of Christoph Bode, an Illuminatus who visited Paris in the summer of 1787, two years after the effective dissolution of the Bavarian organization. See **Bavarian Illuminati**; **Freemasonry**.

In many ways the Social Circle can be seen as de Bonneville's attempt to organize a secret society of his own along Illuminati lines. Like the Illuminati, the Social Circle was tightly controlled by an inner circle of members, rather than being democratically run in the Masonic style; it worked through front organizations the way the Illuminati had used Masonry and other societies; and the imagery of the light of reason illuminating the darkness of ignorance and prejudice, a staple of Illuminati propaganda, also had a central role in the Circle's imagery.

Like many political secret societies, the Circle walked a fine and wandering line between secrecy and publicity. Membersof the Circle took pseudonyms and had secret identification cards, but the Circle proclaimed its own existence loudly. Just before its formation, de Bonneville closed *Le Tribun du Peuple*, and in October 1790 he launched a new journal, *La Bouche de Fer* (*The Mouth of Iron*), as a mouthpiece for the Circle. The same month saw the appearance of a public front organization, the *Confédération Universelle des Amis de la Vérité* (Universal Confederation of the Friends of Truth), which drew 6,000 members to its opening session. While Paris remained the nerve center of the Circle, branch circles sprang up in Utrecht, Geneva, Genoa, London, and even across the Atlantic in Philadelphia.

De Bonneville himself achieved a modest political success in the course of the revolution, becoming secretary of the assembly of the Paris Commune in 1790, and his standing as the leading radical journalist of the time kept him from the guillotine during the Terror. He lobbied for left-wing causes via his own newspapers until 1800, when Napoleon closed down his journal *Le Bien-Informé* (The Well-Informed Person) after de Bonneville published an editorial comparing Napoleon to the English dictator Oliver Cromwell. The Social Circle apparently went out of existence sometime in the early 1790s, but several of its members played major roles in a later secret society, the Conspiracy of Equals. See **Conspiracy of Equals**.

Further reading: Billington 1980.

Societas Rosicruciana in America [SRIA]

The oldest of the major orders in America's twentieth-century Rosicrucian revival, the Societas Rosicruciana in America (SRIA) came into being in 1907 as the result of a schism in the Societas Rosicruciana in Civitatibus Foederatis (SRICF), the American branch of the Societas Rosicruciana in Anglia (also, confusingly, SRIA). The older, English SRIA admitted only Masons in good standing to membership. Several leading members of the SRICF's Boston College, led by Sylvester C. Gould, argued that its teachings should be available to non-Masons. After a series of disputes over this issue, the Boston College broke away from the SRICF and reorganized itself as the Societas Rosicruciana in America. Gould was its original Supreme Magus, but on his death two years later Dr. George Winslow Plummer (1876–1944) took charge of the organization. See **Rosicrucians**;

Societas Rosicruciana in Anglia (SRIA).

The English SRIA was by no means the only influence that fed into the teachings and traditions of the new order. Gould himself was an initiate of the Hermetic Brotherhood of Luxor (H.B. of L.), one of the major occult secret societies of the 1880s, and brought H.B. of L. materials into the American SRIA. Gould and his associates were also in close contact with American lodges of the Hermetic Order of the Golden Dawn. The resulting system of occult study and practice was sufficiently complex that Plummer established a correspondence course for members. In the process, he invented the standard model for occult secret societies in twentieth-century America, with a correspondence course to attract and train members, who joined or founded local lodges (in the SRIA, Colleges) once they had completed a certain level of training. The program was a resounding success and was imitated by dozens of other orders. See **Hermetic Brotherhood of Luxor (H.B. of L.)**; **Hermetic Order of the Golden Dawn**.

Like most American secret societies, the SRIA lost members and momentum in the second half of the twentieth century, but managed to survive, and in the last decade of the century it began a modest revival. It remains active as of this writing.

Further reading: Deveney 1997, Khei 1920, McIntosh 1997.

Societas Rosicruciana in Anglia [SRIA]

Among the most important esoteric Masonic orders in Britain, the Societas Rosicruciana in Anglia (SRIA) was founded by Robert Wentworth Little in 1866. Little, an employee at the United Grand Lodge of England offices in London, is said to have found a packet of old rituals there, and approached Rosicrucian scholar Kenneth Mackenzie for help deciphering them. Mackenzie is also said to have passed onto Little a Rosicrucian initiation he received in Austria from an Austrian nobleman named Count Apponyi. See **Mackenzie, Kenneth**; **Rosicrucians**.

The grades of the SRIA and some of its symbolism are based on those of the *Orden des Gold- und Rosenkreuz* (Order of the Golden and Rosy Cross), a German Rosicrucian order active in the eighteenth century, so it is at least possible that Mackenzie, who was fluent in German and had access to many rare Masonic sources via his uncle, the longtime Grand Secretary of the United Grand Lodge of England, simply borrowed freely from the older order. In 1900, when then-Supreme Magus William Wynn Westcott tried to locate any hard evidence of the society's founding, he came up empty handed. See **Order of the Golden and Rosy Cross**.

Despite the help he apparently gave Little, Mackenzie did not join the society until 1872, and even then remained a member only for a few years, resigning in 1875. Most of the major figures in the English occult scene of the time – men such as Frederick Hockley, Francis Irwin, and John Yarker – became active in the SRIA. Another member, perhaps the most important of all, was William Wynn Westcott, the London coroner and enthusiastic Mason who went on to found the Hermetic Order of the Golden Dawn, the most important magical secret society of its time. Despite the efforts he put into the Golden Dawn, the SRIA always remained Westcott's primary interest; he became its Supreme Adept in 1892 and held that position until his death in 1925. He revised the SRIA's rituals extensively, introducing a great deal of esoteric content. During his tenure additional branches were founded in other countries, notably the Societas Rosicruciana in Scotia (SRIS) in Scotland and the Societas Rosicruciana in Civitatibus Foederatis (SRICF) in the United States. See **Hermetic Order of the Golden Dawn**; **Westcott, William Wynn**.

The SRIA and its offshoots in Canada, the United States, and elsewhere are still quite active. They work a ritual of nine grades, divided into a First Order of four grades, a Second Order of three, and two honorary grades for officials. Westcott's rituals remain in use, but the esoteric dimension of the society at present is mostly limited to passages in the rituals and the activities of individual members. Membership in the society is limited to Master Masons in good standing who are recommended by a current member.

Further reading: Godwin 1994.

Society of Jesus [Jesuits]

The largest Roman Catholic religious order today, the Society of Jesus – known since the late sixteenth century as the Jesuits – was founded by Spanish priest St Ignatius Loyola (1491–1556) in 1534 as a mendicant order of priests dedicated to the propagation of Catholicism, and was formally approved by the Pope in a bull of 1540. See **Roman Catholic Church**.

Unlike older Catholic religious orders, which assign wide authority to local officials such as abbots and place important decisions in the hands of the brothers or sisters collectively, the Society of Jesus assigns absolute power to a single head, the General, who is elected for a life term by the General Congregation (a legislative assembly of provincial officials and elected delegates). The

General can do anything within the scope of the Constitutions, the written law of the Society, and can even suspend the Constitutions at will, though he cannot change them without the approval of the General Congregation. He appoints the Provincials, who govern the Society in individual countries or regions, and a variety of other officials.

Ordinary members take, alongside the usual religious vows of poverty, chastity, and obedience, a special vow of personal obedience to the Pope. In practice this requires perfect obedience to any superior in the Society. Enemies of the Jesuits have argued that this rule is used to justify Jesuit involvement in political crimes, including assassination. This has been energetically denied by the Society, but the involvement of Jesuits in attempts to assassinate England's Queen Elizabeth I and other Protestant monarchs of the sixteenth and seventeenth centuries is accepted by many historians.

The Catholic Church, while theoretically under the Pope's personal control, is in practice a diverse constellation of religious orders and regional authorities whose obedience to Rome is often a polite fiction. At the time of the Protestant Reformation, this disorganization put the survival of the Catholic Church itself at risk. The formation of an order under vows of personal obedience to the Pope was thus a godsend to Rome, and the Society received funding and encouragement from the highest levels of the Church. It repaid this by promoting Catholicism against the growth of Protestantism in France, southern Germany, and Austria, and by spearheading missionary efforts in the newly discovered lands of Asia and the Americas.

This concentration of power inevitably produced a reaction. The Jesuits aroused suspicions in France from the Wars of Religion onward, and were accused of having a role in the murder of Henri IV, who had converted from Protestantism to Catholicism before his coronation but who supported freedom of religion in France. German Protestants rightly identified the Society as the intellectual shock troops of the Catholic Counter-reformation, and attempted at several points to banish them from Germany forever. Other Catholic orders, jealous of the privileges conferred on the Society, encouraged opposition to the Jesuits even in the more staunchly Catholic countries.

The final straw, however, was economic. Jesuits used their position as missionaries in the New World to create mission plantations and mines worked by native labor, and their trade network inevitably came into conflict with the national trade policies of the colonial powers of the age. Portugal expelled its Jesuits in 1759 after a series of scandals capped by an assassination attempt on the royal chamberlain that allegedly had Jesuit backing. In France, a scandal that began with the sudden bankruptcy of the Jesuit missions on Martinique ended with the expulsion of the

Society in 1764. Spain followed suit in 1767 after the Jesuits were implicated in political activity against the government. In 1773, after many tangled negotiations, the Jesuit order was formally suppressed by Pope Clement XIV. The suppression did not take effect in Russia, however, where Catherine the Great found the Jesuits useful in her struggles with the Russian Orthodox Church, but elsewhere the Society ceased to exist.

Many Jesuits reacted to the suppression by blaming it on intrigues by the liberals of the time, many of whom were Freemasons. The rise and destruction of the Bavarian Illuminati increased hard feelings on both sides; the Illuminati crusade against former members of the Society and Catholicism in general gave ex-Jesuits reason to believe the worst about Masonry, which was seen as closely allied to Illuminism, while liberal Masons blamed ex-Jesuits for the campaign against the Illuminati by the Bavarian government. See **Bavarian Illuminati**; **Freemasonry**.

Ironically, many Masons of the time argued that some branches of Masonry had become infiltrated and controlled by the Jesuits. Johann August Starck's Order of Clerks Templar, one of the orders of high-grade Masonry active in Germany in the late eighteenth century, was one of the rites most often accused of Jesuit involvement. Writers with links to the Illuminati themselves, such as Nicholas de Bonneville, spread the charge of Jesuit infiltration more broadly, claiming that Jesuits had taken over the entire institution of Freemasonry and needed to be driven out by a secret order – presumably the Illuminati, though de Bonneville did not say so. It is worth noting in the light of all these charges that the Society is the only male Catholic religious order whose members are completely absent from lists of eighteenth- and nineteenth-century clergy in Masonry.

The sweeping European political changes that followed the French Revolution enabled a new Pope, Pius VII, to restore the Society in 1814. Penalties against the Society remained in force to varying degrees and in a variety of countries during the nineteenth century, however; as long as the Pope was a political as well as a religious figure, Jesuits were widely suspected of being his secret agents. With the absorption of the Papal States into the new nation of Italy in 1871, however, animosity against the Jesuits faded in most European countries, though many nations outside Europe have continued to treat them warily or forbid them altogether.

The Jesuits have long played a major role in conspiracy theory in Protestant countries, especially Britain, where books circulating allegations of Jesuit misdeeds have had steady sales for four centuries. Similar theories played an important part in the anti-Catholic movement in the United States, and during the first half of the twentieth century were frequently circulated in some branches of Freemasonry, particularly the Ancient and Accepted Scottish Rite (AASR). It is ironic that Freemasonry, which has so often been tarred with accusations of conspiracy, has had a major role in circulating similar allegations about another organization, but such ironies are common in the history of conspiracy theories. See **Ancient and Accepted Scottish Rite**; **Know-Nothing Party**.

Further reading: Billington 1980, Roberts 1972.

Society of St Tammany

Originally an offshoot of the radical Sons of Liberty faction in the American colonies and the early United States, the Society of St Tammany has among the most complicated and checkered careers of any American society. Its story began in Annapolis, Maryland in 1773, when the local chapter of the Sons of Liberty renamed itself the Society of St Tamina or Tammany after Tamanend, a Native American elder of the Delaware nation during the colonial period, who had earned the respect of the white immigrants as well as that of his own people. His role as patron saint of the Society was a deliberate provocation aimed at Maryland's Roman Catholic upper class, which named most of its social clubs and institutions after European Catholic saints. See **Roman Catholic Church**; **Sons of Liberty**.

In the aftermath of the American Revolution, several other Sons of Liberty chapters took the same name, including the chapter in New York City. Most members of the Sons of Liberty ended up changing their allegiance to the Society of Red Men after that organization was founded in 1816, and much of the political wing of the Society of St Tammany was drawn off into the Know-Nothing Party in the 1850s, but the New York City chapter of the older Society remained in existence. During the early decades of the nineteenth century it affiliated with the Democratic Party and became increasingly important in New York City politics. By the second half of the century Tammany Hall had become the unofficial government of the city, under the leadership of the fabulously corrupt William Marcy "Boss" Tweed (1823–78), the most notorious figure in an age of city "machine" politics. See **Improved Order of Red Men**; **Know-Nothing Party**.

The great age of political reform in the early twentieth century rooted out some of the corruption from Tammany Hall but did little to reduce its influence over city government. The social and ethnic changes that transformed most of the cities of America's east coast during the middle of the century, however, undercut the Society's power, and New York City's near-bankruptcy in the 1970s destroyed what was left. Tammany Hall still exists as a private association made up mostly of New York City's old wealth, but its days of significant influence are long past.

Society of the Inner Light

The most influential British occult secret society of the twentieth century, the Society (originally Fraternity) of the Inner Light was founded in London in 1924 by English occultist Dion Fortune (Violet Firth, 1890–1946) as a successor group to the Co-Masonic lodge founded by her occult teacher, Theodore Moriarty. Fortune had had a complicated career in the British occult community up to that point, belonging to two different Golden Dawn lodges and the Theosophical Society, and she had also participated in séances with maverick archeologist Frederick Bligh Bond, who believed he had made contact with the medieval monks of Glastonbury Abbey. All these sources flowed into Fortune's own distinctive system of magical training and initiation. See **Co-Masonry**; **Hermetic Order of the Golden Dawn**; **Theosophical Society**.

From the time of its foundation until the end of the Second World War the Fraternity was a major presence in the British occult scene. Fortune's books and magazine articles were widely read, and several of the most influential occultists of the next generation studied with her and modeled large parts of their own occult teachings on hers. When the Second World War broke out, the Fraternity took the lead in organizing a network of British occultists who set out to use magic to strengthen Britain against the German onslaught. The network remained active through the war; its importance to the war effort is by the nature of things hard to measure, but it certainly played a key role in boosting morale in the British occult community, by no means a negligible fraction of the population at that time.

Fortune died of leukemia just after the war, and her role as head of the Fraternity was taken by Arthur Chichester, who changed the organization's name to Society of the Inner Light and proceeded along the lines Fortune had established. In 1961, however, another change of leadership led to a complete reformulation of the work, in which most of the Society's occult teachings were sidelined and it focused instead on Christian mysticism. Many members left during this period, and several launched new magical secret societies of their own; the Servants of the Light, founded in 1965, is the best known of these successor orders. See **Servants of the Light**.

In 1990 the Society returned to its roots and began working with

Fortune's original set of rituals and teachings once again. Like most of today's magical secret societies, it remains relatively small, but its release of previously unpublished writings by Fortune and others has once again had a significant impact on the British occult scene.

Further reading: Fortune 1993, Knight 2000.

Society of United Irishmen

The first known Irish political secret society, the Society of United Irishmen was founded in 1791 by Theobald Wolfe Tone, a young barrister and author passionately devoted to the cause of Irish independence. Originally a public political group pressing for Catholic emancipation and a reformed Irish parliament, the Society went underground in 1793 when England declared war on Revolutionary France and several leaders of the Society were jailed as subversives.

Thereafter, it concentrated on building up a military force in the Irish countryside, with local societies answering to baronial, county, and provincial committees, and a national executive directory above all. An oath of secrecy sworn on the New Testament provided the initiation ritual, and the password was "I know U," answered by "I know N," and so on through the letters of the words "United Irishmen." Weapons were in short supply, and the Society's forces drilled with pikes while its leaders negotiated with the French to supply an army with guns and cannon. Other secret societies in Ireland at the time ranged themselves for or against the United Irishmen; the Defenders, a Catholic secret society founded to counter Protestant violence in the 1780s, allied with the United Irishmen and gave them access to extensive secret networks in south and central Ireland, while the Loyal Orange Order stood against anything that might weaken the privileged position of Protestants under British rule. See **Loyal Orange Order**.

Attempted French landings in 1796 and 1797 fizzled out, however, while a final invasion in 1798 ended in a crushing French defeat at the hands of English troops led by the viceroy Lord Cornwallis. The Irish rising in the same year failed to coordinate with the French landing, and the rebel force of 20,000 went down fighting at their camp at Vinegar Hill. Tone, captured by the English while trying to escape aboard a French ship, committed suicide.

Society of Universal Harmony

One of many esoteric secret societies in pre-Revolutionary France, the Society of Universal Harmony (*Société de l'Harmonie Universelle*) was founded in 1782 by Nicolas Bergasse and Guillaume Kornmann, two leading Parisian disciples of Franz

Anton Mesmer, the charismatic Austrian physician and inventor of Mesmerism. Bergasse and Kornmann, on behalf of the Society, paid Mesmer the substantial sum of 2400 louis d'or for all the secrets of his method. Those secrets became the teachings of the Society, given out to members in stages as they advanced through the degrees of the Society.

During its short lifetime, the Society was enormously successful, and established lodges throughout France. Its career came to an abrupt end with the coming of the Revolution, however. The tidal wave of political and social change that washed over France between 1789 and 1815 left the Society in tatters, and those of its former members who survived the Terror, the Napoleonic Wars, and the ordinary attrition of a troubled quarter-century with their interest in secret societies intact, joined new orders thereafter.

Solar Temple

The self-immolation of the Solar Temple (*Temple Solaire*), a French occult secret society of the late 1980s and early 1990s, presents one of the most troubling object lessons in the recent history of secret societies. The Solar Temple, also known as the International Chivalric Organization, Solar Tradition (*Organisation Internationale Chevaleresque Tradition Solaire*), was founded in Annemasse, Switzerland by Belgian homeopathic physician and spiritual healer Luc Jouret (1947–94), who became a successful lecturer in the New Age circuit throughout the French-speaking world and had a sizeable following in Geneva and Montreal, two cities with large occult and New Age communities in the 1980s. In 1983 he founded a group, Club Amenta, to promote his lectures, and the next year members of Club Amenta were invited to join another organization, Club Archedia, a secret society with its own initiation ceremony and teachings. See **New Age movement**.

In 1981, Jouret himself joined another secret society, the Renewed Order of the Temple, a neo-Templar secret society founded by French right-wing activist Julien Origas. He became Grand Master of the Order on Origas's death in 1983 but was forced out the next year and started his own neo-Templar order, the Solar Temple, recruiting members from Club Archedia for the new organization. The teachings of the Solar Temple came to focus on a coming apocalypse in which the earth would become uninhabitable due to pollution, and Jouret made contacts with survivalist groups in Canada and elsewhere. By 1991 these beliefs and the occult philosophy of the Solar Temple had become extreme enough that the Club Archedia dissolved in a flurry of media accusations, and the Solar Temple itself became the object of police investigations in Quebec. In 1993 Jouret pled guilty to firearms charges in a Quebec court and returned to Europe. Most of his closest followers secluded themselves in an isolated farmhouse owned by Jouret in Annemasse. They became convinced that the apocalypse had arrived and they were being called to leave their physical bodies and travel to another world orbiting around the star Sirius. On the morning of October 5, 1994, the bodies of 53 adults and children were found at the Annemasse farmhouse. Just over a year later, on November 16, 1995, 16 surviving members of the Solar Temple vanished from their homes in France; their bodies were found a few days later in an isolated forest. Three more suicides took place in the spring of 1996. The demise of the Solar Temple offers a clear example of the fatal combination of secrecy, paranoia, and apocalyptic beliefs – a mix far too common in today's alternative scene.

Further reading: Kinney 1995.

Sons of Liberty

One of two secret societies involved in the early stages of the American Revolution, the Sons of Liberty were founded in Boston and New York City in 1765 to oppose the stamp tax recently imposed on the colonies by the British Parliament. The impetus that started them seems to have come from the Committees of Correspondence, a network of leading colonial citizens formed in the early 1760s to coordinate opposition to British policies. The Sons of Liberty quickly spread to the other colonies and became a major force in the movement toward revolution. See **American Revolution**; **Committees of Correspondence**.

Where the Committees worked within the law, the Sons of Liberty engaged in terrorist activities ranging from destruction of property to mob violence against British officials and loyalists. Their most famous exploit took place in Boston in 1773, when members boarded three British ships and dumped 342 chests of tea into the harbor to protest the Tea Act. In the months before war broke out, local chapters of the Sons of Liberty formed armed bands that became the nucleus of the revolutionary army. In 1783, on the signing of the Treaty of Paris granting American independence, the Sons of Liberty dissolved.

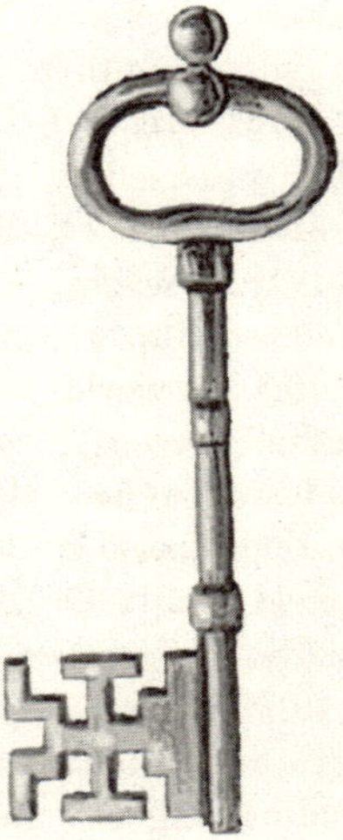

Spear of Longinus

According to a popular medieval legend, the spear that pierced the side of Jesus of Nazareth during his crucifixion, wielded by a Roman soldier named Longinus. Since Christian belief considers Jesus' blood the medium by which the sins of the world were taken away, anything that touched that blood took on special importance in medieval legend and folklore. The lively medieval industry in forged relics responded by manufacturing many allegedly authentic relics of this sort – fragments of the cross, nails used in Jesus' crucifixion, shrouds in which he was buried, and so on. A "spear of Longinus" appeared through these channels and, along with many other relics, became the property of the Emperors of Austria. See **Christian origins**; **Jesus of Nazareth**; **Shroud of Turin**.

This particular relic was of little interest to anyone until 1972, when English author Trevor Ravenscroft published his bestselling book *The Spear of Destiny*. Ravenscroft borrowed ideas from several occult traditions to back up a claim that Hitler's quest for world power had been focused on the spear of Longinus, which he had seized after the German takeover of Austria in 1938. Ravenscroft's book has since been shown to be a complete fantasy, but it is still frequently quoted by popular writers on the occult dimensions of Naziism. See **National Socialism**.

SS [Schutzstaffel]

Originally a volunteer bodyguard of Nazi thugs organized in 1925 to protect party leader Adolf Hitler on his travels around Germany, the Schutzstaffel ("Protection Force") began its rise to the summit of the Nazi system in 1929 when a series of political struggles within the party left Heinrich Himmler, a colorless young man with the manners of a college professor, in charge of the small organization. Widely dismissed within the Nazi movement as a nonentity, Himmler was a serious student of the occult and deeply committed to Ariosophy, the racist occult theory that had spawned National Socialism itself. Shortly after his promotion, he went to Hitler with a proposal to expand the SS into a volunteer elite within the Nazi movement, a *Deutsche Mannerorden* or Order of German Manhood that would ultimately reshape Germany in a Nazi mold. The Führer's approval enabled Himmler to build the organization step by step into the most powerful force in Nazi Germany. See **Hitler, Adolf**; **National Socialism**.

Himmler borrowed freely from Ariosophical sources in reinventing the SS. The SS racial purity guidelines came from the Ordo Novi Templi (ONT), an Austrian secret society with which Hitler had connections during his Vienna years, while the dagger-and-swastika emblem of the Thule Society – the organization that had originally sponsored the Nazi party – turned into the swastika armband and ceremonial dagger worn by every SS member. Ariosophical runic lore provided the new SS emblem, a double lightning-bolt S rune, which represented victory. See **Ordo Novi Templi (ONT)**; **Thule Society**.

The organization of the SS, as well as its symbolism, copied secret society methods in detail; even orthodox historians have referred to the SS as "Nazi Freemasonry." The vast majority of SS members were volunteers who worked at other jobs and attended SS meetings once or twice a week, where they took in lectures on Nazi racial and political theory and practiced military drill. Candidates for membership were vetted for character, discipline, racial purity, and political reliability; once a member, even stricter standards came into force. Members who showed promise were promoted to officer ranks. As the Nazi party became the most powerful force in German politics, the SS expanded alongside it, and Himmler's small paid staff expanded into one of the largest bureaucracies in the Nazi system.

Hitler's election as Germany's Chancellor in January 1933 and the passage of the Enabling Act giving him dictatorial powers a few months later set the stage for a massive expansion of SS power. Shortly after the passage of the Enabling Act, Hitler granted police powers to the SS, and authorized Himmler to create a new branch of his Black Order, the Waffen-SS (Armed SS), as a security and military force loyal to Hitler and the Nazi party alone. In the months that followed, the SS took a leading role in rounding up 27,000 "enemies of the state" for internment in the first concentration camps, which were guarded by special Waffen-SS units. In 1934, faced with potential revolt in the SA – the private army of "brownshirt" street thugs formed by the Nazis in their first years – Hitler turned to the SS for help, and regular SS and Waffen-SS detachments alike took part in the notorious "Night of the Long Knives" in which the SA's leaders were massacred on Hitler's orders.

By the late 1930s Himmler was the second most powerful figure in the Nazi hierarchy, and the SS was a state within a state, with immense power over every aspect of German life. The Gestapo, Nazi Germany's brutal secret police, was a branch of the SS, and the Waffen-SS formed Hitler's bodyguard, managed the new network of concentration camps, and counted Germany's best armored divisions among its membership. German intellectual and cultural life came increasingly under SS control too, as SS membership turned into a career requirement for university professors, authors, and artists, while an SS industrial empire took over a steadily growing fraction of the German economy.

Himmler's occult interests had not been forgotten in the course of SS expansion. The SS headquarters staff contained three departments dedicated to research into occult, pagan, and Ariosophical subjects. The most important of these was the *Ahnenerbe Forschungs- und Lehrgemeinschaft* (Ancestral Heritage Research and Education Society), called Ahnenerbe for short, which employed well over 100 historians and researchers, including occult luminaries such as Julius Evola. The innermost dimensions of SS occultism took place at the Wewelsburg, a medieval castle in Westphalia converted under Himmler's personal supervision into an SS ceremonial center. All records of SS Wewelsburg activities, along with the castle itself, were destroyed on Himmler's orders in the last days of the Third Reich, but it is known that he and 12 handpicked senior SS officers met there several times a year; it has been suggested plausibly that this linked into the organized magical core of the Third Reich that so many contemporary occultists sensed. See **Evola, Julius**.

After the collapse of the Nazi regime and the suicide or execution of most of the Nazi leaders, the SS went to ground. Many of its members were rounded up by the Allies, who defined the SS as a criminal organization; others fled to Spain, Latin America, or the Arab world. How much of the Black Order's traditions and inner teachings survived in exile is unknown.

Further reading: Lumsden 1997.

Stonehenge

The most famous prehistoric monument in the world, the ring of massive stones on Salisbury Plain was raised around 2400 BCE on a site that had been sacred for thousands of years before that time. As early as 8000 BCE, Mesolithic people erected massive wooden poles on the site. A circular earthen ditch and bank with two entrances and a ring of wooden posts were constructed there around 2950 BCE. More wooden posts, probably supporting buildings, went in at intervals over the next 400 years. All this was duplicated in scores of other monuments scattered over Britain. See **Megaliths**.

Then, around 2550 BCE, the first stones appeared – bluestones 6.5 to 8 feet (2 to 2.5 meters) tall, brought all the way from the Preseli Mountains in southern Wales. Within a century and a half the huge gray sarsen stones that now define the monument were hauled from the Marlborough Downs nearly 20 miles (32 kilometers) north and set up in their current positions, with a ring of uprights and lintels surrounding a horseshoe of huge trilithons open toward the midsummer sunrise. The bluestones were then arranged in a matching circle and horseshoe pattern. The final structure was probably used as a sacred calendar and observatory to track the movements of the sun and moon. Once completed, Stonehenge remained in use until 1600 BCE and then was abandoned, as the pre-Celtic civilization of ancient Britain collapsed into a dark age.

While folklore and many alternative-history theories claim that the ancient Druids used Stonehenge as a ritual site, there is very little evidence for this, though offerings were left there during the years that Britain was a Roman province. Thereafter it lay neglected for centuries, thought to be the work of giants or of the enchanter Merlin. The same rediscovery of Britain's past that sparked the Druid Revival revived interest in Stonehenge, and made it the center of a wealth of improbable theories. Almost everyone in the world except the ancient Britons was credited with building it; early archeologist and Druid William Stukeley (1687–1765) lampooned this literature with an essay crediting intelligent elephants from Africa with raising the great stones. Stukeley himself credited the Druids with building the structure and thus helped launch one of the monument's enduring legends. See **Arthurian legends**; **Druid Revival**; **Druids**.

Speculations about Stonehenge have found a home in the cultural underworld of rejected knowledge for a long time. Theories about the origins of Freemasonry that traced the Craft back to the Druids inevitably fastened on Stonehenge; the bluestones were even claimed as evidence that an ancient blue lodge had once met there! Ley hunters have also found Stonehenge as a focal point of many alignments. More recently, claims about ancient astronauts, lost civilizations, and earth changes of past and future have made much use of Stonehenge. See **earth changes**; **Leys**; **lost civilizations**; **rejected knowledge**.

Further reading: Chippindale 1994, Souden 1997.

Sublime Perfect Masters

One of the principal secret societies founded by Filippo Buonarroti, the doyen of political subversion in early nineteenth-century Europe, the *Sublimes Maîtres Parfaits* or Sublime Perfect Masters took shape in Geneva in 1809 as an inner circle of revolutionaries drawn from the Philadelphes, another secret society of the time, and from liberal Masonic circles. Unlike the Philadelphes, which focused its efforts on the destruction of Napoleon, the Sublime Perfect Masters set their sights on the rather more ambitious goal of launching revolutions throughout Europe to bring about republican governments and the abolition of private property. See **Buonarroti, Filippo**; **Philadelphes**.

The Sublime Perfect Masters followed the older, eighteenth-century pattern of political secret societies and drew heavily on Masonic symbolism and practice. Members learned very little about the society on their admission as Sublime Perfect Masters, and only those of proven loyalty were advanced through the middle degree of Sublime Elect to the Aréopagus, the guiding body of the order. Above it all was a central coordinating body, the Grand

Firmament, whose existence was kept secret from everyone outside the Aréopagus itself. This system shows close echoes to that of the Illuminati; scholars are unsure whether Buonarroti borrowed it from his early experience with an Illuminati-influenced Masonic lodge, or whether he took it from published accounts of the Illuminati, but the borrowing played a significant role in passing the eighteenth-century system of secret chiefs and progressive revelations onto nineteenth-century political secret societies. See **Illuminati**.

Under various names the Sublime Perfect Masters served primarily as a coordinating body for liberal secret societies across Europe, and at its height (around 1820) it had members in Spain, France, Belgium, Italy, Germany, Denmark, and Switzerland. Along with the Carbonari, it played a significant role in the wave of rebellions that swept Europe in 1820 and 1821, and apparently helped to coordinate risings in Italy and elsewhere. In the aftermath of these risings, informers leaked details of the order's activities to police in several countries; the results included Buonarroti's exile from Geneva and a continent-wide panic in which conservatives and police officials alike saw secret societies hiding under every bed. See **Carbonari**.

In 1828 the Sublime Perfect Masters took the new name of *Le Monde* (The World), as Buonarroti realized that the Masonic trappings of the original organization had become more of a hindrance than help. In this reorganization it added a new preliminary "grade of observation" for potential members and people in other secret societies associated with Le Monde. Under the new name, it seems to have played a role in the French and Belgian revolutions of 1830, though details are uncertain. Afterwards it appears to have been absorbed into another Buonarroti creation, the *Charbonnerie Démocratique Universelle*, a new version of the Carbonari that aimed at its founder's perennial goal of universal revolution.

Further reading: Billington 1980, Roberts 1972.

SYNARCHY

One of many political movements with secret society roots, synarchy was the creation of French occult philosopher Joseph Alexandre Saint-Yves d'Alveydre (1842–1909), perhaps the most influential figure in the French occult underground of his time. Alongside contemporaries Joséphin Péladan and Stanislaus de Guaita, Saint-Yves broke with the mostly liberal or socialist politics of earlier French occultists such as Eliphas Lévi, and launched the occult conservatism that dominated western esoteric circles until the 1960s. Synarchy was Saint-Yves' major contribution to this movement and became a major force in European politics in the twentieth century.

Drawing on the ternary logic central to nineteenth-century French occultism, synarchy sees human society as composed of the three interdependent spheres of religion, politics, and economics. In society as it existed in Saint-Yves' time (and exists today), these three spheres conflict with one another, resulting in the decline of all three, and ultimately leads to anarchy. The synarchist answer to this dilemma is the establishment of an inner circle of initiates who have positions of influence in the three spheres. This inner circle, working in secret, would coordinate the activities of the three spheres, resulting in peace. Synarchy, Saint-Yves argued, was thus the opposite of anarchy.

Like most nineteenth-century occultists, Saint-Yves also wove his theories into an alternative vision of world history. Synarchy, he believed, had been the governing system of the world under the great Universal Empire, which was founded by Rama in 6729 BCE, but had been lost when the Universal Empire fell. The great spiritual leaders of all ages – including Moses and Jesus – had attempted to re-establish it, and the Knights Templar had come close to the synarchist ideal in the Middle Ages. Saint-Yves claimed, though, that the only nation governed on synarchic principles in his own time was the underground city of Agharta, hidden deep beneath the Himalayas. Saint-Yves' book *Mission de l'Inde en Europe* (*The Mission of India in Europe*, 1910) described this hidden city in lavish detail. Its ruler was the Supreme Pontiff or Brahmatma, the head of the religious sphere, assisted by the Mahatma and Mahanga, who headed the political and economic spheres. See **Agharta**; **Knights Templar**; **underground realms**.

Despite the more colorful dimensions of Saint-Yves' theories, synarchy found a ready audience among French conservatives in the first half of the twentieth century, and its influence remains strong throughout the European far right today. The Cagoule, the most powerful of the French fascist movements before the Second World War, drew heavily on synarchy, and important policies of the Vichy regime in occupied France during the war copied synarchist ideas. Propaganda Due (P2), the rogue Masonic organization that dominated Italian politics in the 1970s, was nearly a textbook example of a synarchist organization in its attempt to bring the Italian political system, the Catholic Church, and the Mafia-controlled drug economy into an alliance that could resist Italian communists. By way of the French comparative mythologist Georges Dumézil, who projected Saint-Yves' threefold division of society back onto the ancient Indo-Europeans, synarchist ideas have found their way into a handful of modern Pagan traditions too. It remains an influential theory in many places in the world of secret societies today. See **Cagoule**; **P2 (Propaganda Due)**.

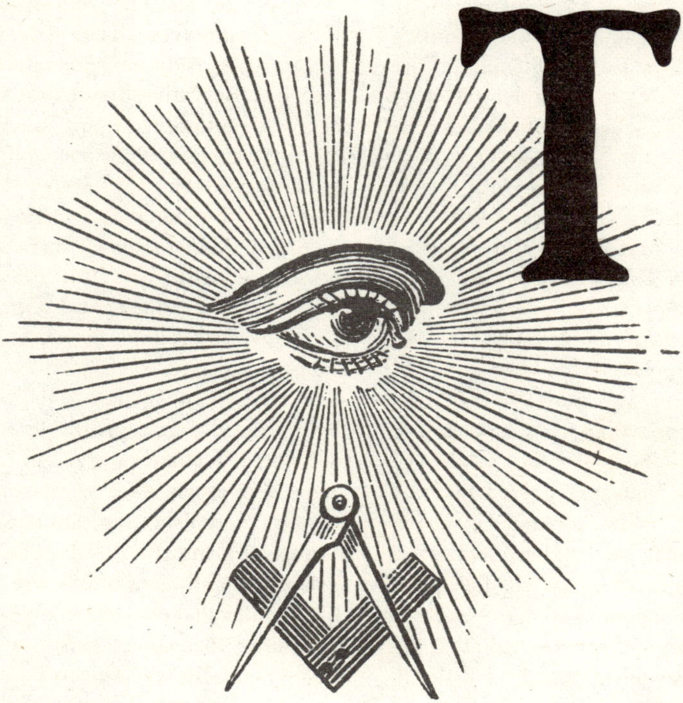
T

Temple of Set

A Satanist magical order founded by Michael Aquino in 1975, the Temple of Set began as a schism from Anton LaVey's Church of Satan, driven by disagreements between Aquino and LaVey about LaVey's penchant for putting showmanship ahead of serious Satanism. From the time of its foundation, the Temple of Set has pursued an intellectually rigorous system of Satanic spirituality and magical practice. See **Church of Satan**; **Satanism**.

The Temple's public documents distinguish between nature-worshipping religions, which include nearly all the world's religious traditions, and consciousness-worshipping religions, which consist of the Temple's own teachings and a few others. Nature-worshipping religions are dismissed as emotional crutches for those unwilling or unable to think for themselves. Intellectual clarity, self-discipline, and personal autonomy are core values of the system, and members are expected to violate conventional codes of morality to break free of the "herd mentality." The goal of Setian training is the attainment of godhood, defined as eternal, isolated self-consciousness outside of nature and the universe. The similarity of this goal to the concept of eternal damnation held by many of the world's spiritual traditions is unlikely to be accidental.

The Temple of Set is divided into Pylons, some of which are local groups while others are networks linked by the Internet, and nine Orders, special-interest groups focusing on particular magical or cultural traditions. The best known of the Orders at this point is the Order of the Trapezoid, which works with the magical currents of German National Socialism. While the Temple rejects antisemitism, and indeed counts many Jews among its membership, Aquino has claimed SS leader Heinrich Himmler as a high Satanic initiate, and has carried out intensive ritual work at the Wewelsburg, the castle formerly used by Himmler and top SS officers as a center for their own occult rituals. See **National Socialism.**

Headquartered in San Francisco, the Temple of Set is a significant force in contemporary Satanist circles. It does not release membership statistics but probably has some hundreds of members at present.

Temple of Solomon

According to Jewish legends recorded in several books of the Old Testament, a temple to the Jewish god constructed in Jerusalem in *c.*975 BCE by Solomon, king of Israel, to replace the tabernacle used to house the Ark of the Covenant since the time of Moses. According to the biblical texts the temple was a small structure, 30 feet wide and 90 feet long (9 x 27 meters), with a porch 15 feet (4.5 meters) deep in front of its doors, covered inside and out with gold leaf. The space inside was divided into a main room, the Holy Place, and an inner room, the Holy of Holies, where the Ark of the Covenant and several other sacred objects were kept. Only priests entered the Holy Place, and the high priest alone had the right once a year to enter the Holy of Holies. Outside were a series of open courts: the Court of the Priests, where sacrifices took place; the Court of the Children of Israel, where Jews gathered to worship; and the Court of the Gentiles.

According to the same sources, this First Temple was looted and destroyed during the fall of Jerusalem to the Babylonians in 586 BCE. The Second Temple was begun by Zerubbabel, a Jewish aristocrat who served the Persian empire as governor of Judah, in 535 BCE and finished in 515. The Third Temple, the most magnificent of the three, was built by Herod the Great in 18 BCE and destroyed along with the rest of Jerusalem during the Jewish revolt against Rome in 70 CE. A few traces of this final temple have been discovered by archeologists, but no definite traces of the first two have ever been found. While this seems likely enough, given the history of continued construction and reconstruction on the site, some historians have argued on this basis that the First Temple never existed outside Jewish folklore.

As the most lavishly described building project in the Bible, and a constant source of metaphors for Christian churches from the late Roman period onward, the Temple of Solomon became a central symbol in the Christian west. The Knights Templar took their name from the location of their original headquarters, near the supposed site of the Temple, and the medieval stoneworkers' guilds that eventually became Freemasonry used legends set during the Temple's construction as a basis for their rituals. See **Freemasonry**; **Hiram Abiff**; **Knights Templar**.

Temple ov Psychick Youth, Thee [TOPY]

Among the most colorful occult secret societies in the modern magical scene, Thee Temple ov Psychick Youth (TOPY) was founded in London in 1981 by Genesis P-Orridge, a popular musician in the industrial-music scene. Drawing on the Zos Kia Cultus system of English magician Austin Osman Spare, the sexual magic of Aleister Crowley's Ordo Templi Orientis, and the chaos-worshipping Discordian religion, and combining these with most of the popular trends in the 1980s and '90s counterculture, TOPY defined occultism as a means of personal liberation based on freeing the implicit powers of the human brain through sexual orgasm and the transcendence of all habitual and conventional ideas. See **Discordian movement**; **Ordo Templi Orientis (OTO)**; **Zos Kia Cultus**.

A tribal network consisting of three Stations (in Britain, Europe, and the United States) and a constantly changing assortment of local groups called Access Points, TOPY has created a non-structured structure all its own. Candidates for initiation write down a favorite sexual fantasy and, on the 23rd hour of the 23rd day of the month, anoint the paper with three different bodily fluids and hair from two parts of their body. The result is mailed to TOPY headquarters in order to build up a reservoir of magical power. When a candidate has done this 23 times, he or she becomes an initiate, and take the name "Coyote," "Kali," or "Eden" followed by a number as their magical name. As the name of the organization suggests, TOPY members and initiates are notorious in the occult community for their non-standard spellings of English. TOPY documents consistently use "coum" for "come," "ov" for "of," "thee" for "the," and "majick" for "magic." This is not simply eccentricity; it is intended, as TOPY members might express it, to majickally overcoum thee power ov habit and social convention.

For a decade after TOPY's founding in 1981, it was as much a piece of performance art as a magical (or majickal) secret society, and gained most of its members among fans of Genesis P-Orridge's musical group, Psychic TV. In 1992, after British police raided his home in the hope of finding evidence of Satanic ritual abuse, P-Orridge resigned his position as TOPY's leading member and tried to dissolve it, with no noticeable effect. TOPY remains an active presence today in the occult community, with Access Points scattered across Britain, America, and Europe, and a substantial online presence as well.

Theosophical Society

The most influential force in the great renaissance of occultism in the late nineteenth century, the Theosophical Society was founded in New York City in 1875 by the colorful Russian occultist and adventuress Helena Petrovna Blavatsky, her American promoter Col. Henry S. Olcott, and a handful of other students of the occult. According to Blavatsky, the society was sponsored and supported by the Brotherhood of Luxor, an American occult secret society. See **Blavatsky, Helena Petrovna**; **Brotherhood of Luxor**.

During its first two years the Theosophical Society was simply one more group in the crowded New York occult scene, sponsoring lectures by local authors and researchers. For a time it operated as a secret society with its own passwords and grades of initiation, though these went by the board as the fledgling Society struggled to define itself. The publication of Blavatsky's first book, *Isis Unveiled* (1877), ended this period and transformed the Society into a major player in the western world's occult scene.

Isis Unveiled was the largest and most comprehensive occult critique of religious orthodoxy and scientific materialism in its time, a sprawling two-volume work that challenged nearly all the preconceptions of its Victorian audience. Much of the material in it was drawn from the occult literature of the time, especially the writings of Eliphas Lévi and P.B. Randolph, but it presented an extraordinary and rather quirky occult philosophy all its own, different in many ways from the later system of Blavatsky's *The Secret Doctrine* (1888). See **Randolph, Paschal Beverly**.

The year after *Isis Unveiled* saw print, Blavatsky and Olcott traveled to India by way of England and established a headquarters for the Society at Adyar, near Bombay. From 1879 to 1884 Blavatsky remained at Adyar, writing articles, performing minor miracles to awe visitors, and working closely with the Arya Samaj, a movement for Indian national and religious revival, against the British colonial government. During her stay in India she stopped talking about the Brotherhood of Luxor and began claiming that her teachings came from two Tibetan Mahatmas, Koot Hoomi (Kuthumi) and El Morya. Historian K. Paul Johnson, in a controversial book on Theosophical history, has argued that these names were pseudonyms for two important Indian political and religious leaders of the time. See **Masters**.

In 1884 Blavatsky and Olcott traveled to England on a lecture tour that attracted huge crowds, and established several European sections of the Theosophical Society. During their absence from Adyar, however, an investigator from the Society for Psychical Research arrived there and learned from Blavatsky's housekeeper Emma Coulombe that the "miracles" were simple sleight-of-hand tricks. The scandal that followed earned newspaper headlines on five continents. In the aftermath of the revelations, Olcott forbade Blavatsky to stay in Adyar, and she moved to London, where she spent the rest of her life.

While at London she wrote, lectured, and debated with the Hermetic Brotherhood of Luxor, an influential magical order of the time. She also founded the Esoteric Section of the Theosophical Society, an inner circle that received instruction in practical occultism. Finally, and most significantly, she wrote a second vast book, *The Secret Doctrine*, which was published in 1888. Unlike *Isis Unveiled*, which drew most of its material from western occult sources, *The Secret Doctrine* took its inspiration from Hindu traditions and presented an immense vision of a cyclic cosmos in which souls, called monads in Theosophy, descend from cosmic unity to pass through a series of evolutionary journeys through the elemental, mineral, vegetable, animal, and human kingdoms and beyond. In order to pass through the human level, the souls of humanity must make seven "rounds" or circuits of a sequence of seven "globes" or worlds, while being reincarnated in seven different root races on each world during each sequence. Today's humanity is on the fourth globe of the fourth round; Europeans, Indians, and other Indo-Europeans are believed to belong to the fifth, or Aryan root race, while other humans belong to the fourth or Atlantean root race. See **Atlantis**; **Hermetic Brotherhood of Luxor (H.B. of L.)**.

This is only a first glimpse at a portion of the sprawling cosmos of *The Secret Doctrine*, but it may help convey the flavor of the book's dizzying complexities. After Blavatsky's death in 1891 these teachings became the Society's core doctrine, and were developed and discussed in dozens of books by later authors. The new head of the Society, Fabian socialist and liberal political activist Annie Besant, helped transform *The Secret Doctrine* into an orthodoxy, and brought the Society into alliance with Co-Masonry, an offshoot of Freemasonry that admits women as well as men to membership, and the Liberal Catholic Church, an esoteric Christian church. Schisms followed; William Quan Judge, a leading American Theosophist, broke with Besant and established a rival organization in America in 1895; widely respected occult scholar G.R.S. Mead left in 1909 to found the Quest Society, and Robert Crosbie and another dissident group founded the United Lodge of Theosophists in Los Angeles the same year. Most damaging of all was the defection of Rudolf Steiner, former secretary of the Society's German section, who left in 1912 and took 90 percent of German Theosophists with him into his newly founded Anthroposophical Society. See **Anthroposophical Society**; **Co-Masonry**; **Fabian Society**.

Steiner's split was caused by one of Besant's most serious missteps – her identification of a teenage boy named Jiddu Krishnamurti as the next World Teacher, a messianic figure who would rank with Jesus and the Buddha. In 1911 Besant and her close associate Charles Leadbeater founded the Order of the Star in the East to promote these claims. Highly successful in the years following the First World War, the Order collapsed overnight in 1929 when Krishnamurti courageously disavowed the claims made about him and disbanded it. See **Order of the Star in the East**.

The implosion of the Order of the Star in the East nearly shattered the Theosophical Society. Most Theosophical groups outside the English-speaking world quietly disbanded, while Theosophists in

Britain, America, Australasia, and India went to ground and carried on their work well out of the limelight. In the meantime, however, dozens of groups inspired by Theosophy or derived from it took over large portions of Theosophical teachings and practice. In the "Theosophical century" from 1875 to 1975, nearly every significant occult secret society in the western world drew on Theosophy as a major (though often uncredited) source. By the 1970s, as occult groups abandoned Theosophical ideas for older or newer teachings, the New Age movement stepped in and adopted Theosophy wholesale. See **New Age movement**.

Several branches of the Theosophical Society remain active today, and the last decade or so has seen a modest growth in Theosophical numbers and activity. While the Society may never again play the dominant role it once had in the occult community, it remains a living tradition with an active publishing program.

Further reading: Blavatsky 1877, Blavatsky 1888, Godwin 1994, Johnson 1994, Washington 1993.

Third International

The last of the three revolutionary Internationals, the Third International or Comintern was founded at Moscow in 1919, in the aftermath of the Bolshevik seizure of power in the Russian revolution and the civil war that followed it. As the first political party of the far left to succeed where so many others had failed, the Bolsheviks had immense prestige in radical circles, and the embarrassing failure of the Second International to follow through on its plan to prevent the First World War left the field open to a new Bolshevik international. See **Second International**.

The new International won widespread support from European leftists in the years just after its founding, but it soon became clear that to Vladimir I. Lenin, the new Russian head of state, and even more to his successor, Josef Stalin, the Third International was nothing but a tool of Russian foreign policy. Communist parties that became part of the International were expected to obey orders from Moscow without question, even when these ran counter to the stated policy of the International. The decision by Stalin to sign a non-aggression pact with Nazi Germany in 1939 was, for many people on the left, the final straw in his betrayal of Marxist ideals. With the outbreak of war later that same year the International became useless, and it was formally dissolved on Stalin's orders in 1943. See **Communism**.

Further reading: Drachkovitch 1966.

Thuggee

Among the most notorious secret societies in history, the Thugs practiced a combination of human sacrifice and highway robbery on the roads and byways of India. Bands of Thugs, 10 to 50 in number, roamed the country and lured unsuspecting travelers to journey with them. At traditional killing grounds known only to the Thugs, they turned on their hapless companions, strangled them, robbed them, and buried their mutilated bodies in concealed graves. The term "Thug" was their common name in northern India, and means "deceiver;" in southern India they were known as Phansigari, "stranglers." When Thuggee was at its height at the beginning of the nineteenth century, tens of thousands of travelers met this fate annually in every corner of the Indian subcontinent.

The origins of Thuggee are unknown. Sir William Sleeman, the British colonial official responsible for its eradication, speculated that the Thugs might have descended from members of the Sagartii, a Persian tribe described by the Greek historian Herodotus, whose members fought armed with a dagger and a leather noose. The Thugs themselves believed that they had been created by Kali, the Hindu goddess of death, during a battle against a mighty demon. When the goddess cut down the demon, more demons sprang up from its spilled blood. Kali then created the first two Thugs from the sweat on her arms, gave them strangling cloths, and sent them to kill all the demons without shedding their blood. The Thugs quickly dispatched the demons, and the goddess rewarded them by commanding them to kill and rob travelers as a sacred and profitable way of supporting themselves and their families.

Whatever their origins, the Thugs were active in India by the Middle Ages. Held at bay by the Mughal Empire at its height in the sixteenth century, they became widespread again as the Empire declined into chaos. Traditional laws ordered captured Thugs to be walled up inside pillars and left to die, or for their hands and nose to be cut off, but in many areas local rajas permitted the Thugs to operate in exchange for a share of the profits.

The Thugs themselves perfected the arts of deception in order to catch travelers off their guard. They had their own language, Ramasi, and secret gestures that allowed them to signal one another unnoticed. When not on the roads, they lived as ordinary peasants, and married only into one another's families. Strict taboos governed their killing expeditions; a sheep had to be sacrificed to Kali before the band set out, band leaders paid close attention to omens, and women and members of certain crafts and castes were not to be killed. When they struck, an absolute rule required that the only witnesses left alive be Thugs, so entire parties of travelers escaped death because one person the Thugs were forbidden to kill traveled with them.

As British rule over India spread out from coastal enclaves at the beginning of the nineteenth century, colonial administrators gradually became aware that something other than ordinary banditry was taking place on the roads. An 1816 article by Richard Sherwood, "Of the Murderers called Phansigars," helped catalyze a response. William Sleeman, then a young officer in the Bengal army, read Sherwood's paper, transferred to the civil service, and began investigating Thug activities. His discoveries pointed to the existence of a nationwide Thug organization and caused a furor in India and Britain alike. In 1830, after further investigations, he was appointed by the Governor-General to suppress Thuggee throughout central India.

Sleeman's campaign was made simpler by his ability to find informers among the Thugs, who were offered pardons in exchange for telling all they knew, and his efforts to establish schools for the children of Thugs to teach them less bloodthirsty trades. Thug families became particularly famous for carpet weaving; the magnificent carpet of the Waterloo Chamber of Windsor Palace, measuring 80 feet by 40 (24 meters by 12) and weighing two tons, was commissioned by Queen Victoria and manufactured for her by former Thugs. By 1850, pressed on all sides by British colonial authority, Thuggee was effectively extinct.

Thule

Originally *ultima Thule*, "furthest Thule" in Latin, Thule first appeared in classical Greek and Roman writings as a name for a distant island somewhere north of Britain. The Greek voyager Pytheas of Massalia claimed that he sailed there, and his description of the northern seas has enough accurate details to make the claim plausible; it is likely Pytheas sailed as far as the Orkneys, or possibly even Iceland.

In the nineteenth century the name Thule was recycled for a hypothetical lost continent somewhere in the far north. In this form it found its way into proto-Nazi occult movements in central Europe as the lost Arctic homeland of the Aryans, identical to Arktogäa and Hyperborea. See **lost continents**.

Thule Society

The National Socialist movement in early twentieth-century Germany emerged out of a complex underground of secret societies, occult traditions, and racist ideologies that historians have just begun to uncover. One crucial piece of the puzzle was an organization known as the *Thule-Gesellschaft* or Thule Society. Named after the legendary lost continent of Thule, believed by German racists of the time to be the original homeland of the Aryan peoples, the Thule Society posed as a private organization for the study of

Germanic folklore. In reality, it was the Munich lodge of an occult secret society, the Germanenorden, whose distinctive blend of racist occultism and right-wing politics defined the central commitments of the Nazi party. See **Germanenorden**.

The Thule Society was the creation of Rudolf von Sebottendorf, a German-Turkish adventurer who joined the Germanenorden in 1917 and immediately set to work organizing a Munich lodge for the order. His efforts paid off handsomely, increasing membership in Bavaria from 200 to more than 1500 by the autumn of 1918. He rented rooms for the society in the posh Hotel des Vier Jahreszeiten in Munich, and succeeded in attracting members of the Bavarian aristocracy into the organization. He also encouraged two Thule members, Karl Harrer and Anton Drexler, to organize a political circle for the Munich working class, in the hope of drawing them away from communism.

When the German imperial government collapsed in 1918, a socialist coalition seized power in Bavaria, but was then supplanted by a hardline communist faction headed by Russian exiles. Munich descended into open war, and pitched gun battles, assassinations, and summary executions by firing squad became frequent events. The Thule Society hurled itself into the struggle, networking with other conservative groups and raising a sizeable private army, the Kampfbund Thule, for the final struggle that ended the Bavarian Socialist Republic in May 1919.

By that time the political circle headed by Drexler and Harrer had already transformed itself into a political party, the *Deutsche Arbeiterpartei* (German Workers Party, DAP). Small and poorly organized, the DAP floundered for most of 1919 as most Thule members turned their attention elsewhere. In September of that year, however, the DAP gained a new recruit, an Austrian war veteran named Adolf Hitler. Not long after joining, Hitler convinced the other party members to change the organization's name to the *Nationalsozialistische Deutsche Arbeiterpartei* (National Socialist German Workers Party, NSDAP) – a name newspapers and the German public quickly shortened to "Nazi." See **Hitler, Adolf**; **National Socialism**.

As the fledgling party grew explosively, driven by Hitler's powerful oratory and impressive political skills, Thule Society members gave it vital support and direction. Thule initiate Ernst Röhm, a tough army veteran with a taste for brawling, brought many members of the Kampfbund Thule into the *Sturm-Abteilung* (Storm Troop, SA) or Brownshirts, the Nazi party's private army of street thugs. Another Thule member, Rudolf Hess, used his connections throughout the occult community in France and Germany to win support for Hitler, becoming the future Führer's right-hand man in the process. Other members introduced Hitler to wealthy conservatives in Bavaria and elsewhere in Germany, and brought him into contact with the writer and occultist Dietrich Eckart, who became Hitler's mentor.

By 1925 or a little later, the Thule Society had been completely absorbed into the growing Nazi party, and nearly all its membership, activities, and plans became part of the Nazi system. The occult aspects it had inherited from the Germanenorden ended up becoming part of the SS once Heinrich Himmler took over that organization in 1929. See **SS (Schutzstaffel)**.

Further reading: Goodrick-Clarke 1992.

"Tlön, Uqbar, Orbis Tertius"

A short story by Argentine magic realist Jorge Luis Borges, "Tlön, Uqbar, Orbis Tertius" (published in his collection *Labyrinths*, 1962) draws on the history of the Rosicrucian movement to present one of the clearest models of secret society activity in print. According to the story, sometime in the early seventeenth century, a secret society, Orbis Tertius (Third Sphere), sets out to create an imaginary country and make the world believe that it actually exists. As the project unfolds, they realize that they will have to invent an entire world to give the nation of Tlön a setting. They compile a 40-volume encyclopedia containing detailed information about every aspect of Uqbar, their invented world. With funding from an eccentric American millionaire, the encyclopedia is completed and parts of it are leaked to the outside world, and a handful of artifacts from the imaginary world begin to surface. People outside Orbis Tertius become so fascinated by Uqbar that the real world begins to imitate the imaginary one.

The historical Rosicrucian movement, intentionally or not, followed a similar trajectory from fiction to reality, as people inspired by the original Rosicrucian manifestos set out to remake themselves in the image of the adepts of the Rose Cross, launching an international movement that remains a major force in the occult community 400 years later. An even closer fit to the story can be found in the bizarre UMMO case of the 1970s, in which persons unknown faked a series of close encounters with UFOs from the planet UMMO and used the resulting publicity as a springboard to pass on hundreds of pages of Ummese philosophy, spirituality, and science to a growing community of followers. See **Rosicrucians**; **unidentified flying objects (UFOs)**.

Further reading: Borges 1970, McIntosh 1997, Vallee 1991.

Toland, John

Irish philosopher, writer, and secret society member, 1670–1722. One of the most remarkable figures of his age, John Toland was born and raised in Ardagh, on the Inishowen peninsula, and educated in Irish Catholic schools until his teen years, when he converted to the Protestant religion. In 1688 he received a scholarship to the University of Glasgow to study theology. Returning to Ireland, he published his first book, *Christianity Not Mysterious*, which dismissed the idea that any religion had sole possession of the truth and argued that anything in Christianity that offended against reason and common sense should be discarded. The book was burned by the public hangman in Dublin, and Toland had to flee to London, where he took up a career writing controversial books and pamphlets about politics and religion.

Toland invented the word "pantheism" for his own religious beliefs, and was apparently the first person ever to be called a freethinker. The sources for Toland's ideas, however, reach straight back into the radical Hermeticism of the late Renaissance. Toland was a close student of the *Corpus Hermeticum* – the writings then credited to Hermes Trismegistus, the legendary sorcerer-sage of ancient Egypt – and the works of Giordano Bruno (1548–1600), the great Renaissance magus and master of the art of memory. Toland himself prepared the first English translation of Bruno's *Expulsion of the Triumphant Beast* and had a central role in sparking a revival of interest in Bruno among English and Dutch radicals at the beginning of the eighteenth century. See **Bruno, Giordano**; **Hermeticism**.

Like many progressive intellectuals of his time, Toland was fascinated by the ancient Druids, the learned caste of the pre-Christian Celtic peoples of Britain, Ireland, and Gaul. He drew up a prospectus for a history of the Druids that was partly a vindication of his own pantheist beliefs and partly an extended satire on the Anglican Church, and tried to find a noble patron to pay for its writing and publication; not surprisingly, none appeared, and the prospectus was not published until after his death. According to several accounts Toland was involved in founding the Ancient Druid Order, the parent body of the Druid Circle of the Universal Bond, at the Apple Tree Tavern in London in 1717, though no documentation has surfaced to support this claim. See **Druid Revival**; **Druid Circle of the Universal Bond**.

Toland's involvement with two other secret societies is less speculative. During a stay in the Netherlands in 1708–10, he became a member of, and probably helped found, a secret society of freethinkers called the Chevaliers of Jubilation. Most of the Chevaliers were liberal French intellectuals in exile from the Catholic absolutism of Louis XIV, and shared Toland's disdain for dogmatic religion. Later, sometime before 1720, Toland wrote and circulated privately the *Pantheisticon*, a book of ceremonies for the meetings of a pantheist secret society; one of Toland's friends commented after Toland's death that at least one organization using the *Pantheisticon* as its ritual actually existed. See **Chevaliers of Jubilation**.

Toland's radical ideas and his abrasive personality made it difficult for him to find paying literary work as the Whig establishment in early eighteenth-century Britain grew more conservative. His health failed, and he had to sell most of his library to put food on the table in his final years. His beloved *Corpus Hermeticum* was one of the few books left to him when he died in 1722.

Further reading: Jacob 1981, Sullivan 1982.

Traditionalism

A small but vocal movement in the contemporary occult scene, Traditionalism was the creation of French philosopher and occultist René Guénon (1886–1951) and a number of followers and allies in the European esoteric scene. Originally a member of the French section of the Theosophical Society, Guénon broke with Theosophy around 1920 and denounced it categorically in his *Le Théosophisme, Histoire d'un Pseudo-religion* (*Theosophy, the History of a Pseudo-religion*, 1921). Guénon accepted the Theosophist suggestion that all religions were outer forms for a true esoteric spirituality, but dismissed the related claim that Theosophy was that esoteric core. Instead, Guénon argued, what lies behind all valid religions is a common thread of Tradition – the term is always capitalized in Traditionalist writings. See **Theosophical Society**.

Explaining Tradition is a complex matter, and few Traditionalists attempt anything like a comprehensive definition. Whatever it is, it is revealed at the beginning of each historical cycle; certain religions have it – Eastern Orthodox Christianity, Orthodox Judaism, Islam, certain Buddhist sects, conservative Hinduism and an assortment of traditions from America, Africa, and the Far East – and all others do not. Anything dating from the Middle Ages or later is, by definition, far from Tradition. Outside of Tradition, Traditionalists insist, spiritual development is impossible, and those who attempt it fall under the sway of the demonic Counter-initiation.

In practice, too often, whatever opinions a Traditionalist happens to have count as Tradition, while any dissenting opinions are tarred with the brush of Counter-initiation. Ironically, while Guénon castigates Theosophy for making a pastiche of western occultism and Hindu philosophy, his own books present exactly such a pastiche to the reader as Tradition – his *The Reign of Quantity and the Signs of the Times*, for example, fuses Hindu ideas of ages of the world with Judeo-Christian apocalyptic beliefs, complete with a cameo appearance by the Antichrist. See **ages of the world**.

One of Guénon's fellow Traditionalists, Italian philosopher and Fascist ideologue Julius Evola (1898–1974), has become far more influential than Guénon himself in the world of contemporary occult secret societies. Evola's version of Traditionalism combined Guénon's ideas with a fixation on Indo-European warrior traditions as the core example of a valid spiritual path. This combination has given him a strong appeal in neo-Nazi secret societies and to some of the more doctrinaire elements in today's neo-pagan movement. See **Evola, Julius; neo-Nazi secret societies**.

Further reading: Guénon 1953, Waterfield 1987.

Triad Society

The most powerful and widely known of Chinese secret societies, the Triad Society traces its ancestry back to five Shaolin monks who survived the destruction of their monastery in 1674 by troops of the imperial Manchu government. The five survivors, after long journeys and many struggles, banded together into a brotherhood dedicated to driving out the Manchu invaders and restoring the former native Chinese dynasty, the Ming. The slogan "Subvert the Ch'ing [Manchu], Restore the Ming" became the Triad watchword. How much of this account is true and how much legend is impossible to tell, but the first Triad organizations seem to have come into existence at some point before 1750 and an origin sometime around the traditional date is entirely possible.

The Triad system has remarkable similarities to Freemasonry and other western fraternal secret societies. New members of a Triad lodge (the Chinese word is *tang*, "hall") must be nominated by an existing member, and pass through an initiatory ceremony in which the candidate hears the story of the Triad's origins and takes an oath to obey the rules of the society, provide mutual assistance to his lodge brothers, and never betray the lodge's secrets to outsiders. Once initiated, the new members receive the secret signs of recognition that allow them to identify themselves to other Triad members. See **Freemasonry**.

The organization of Triad lodges also follows patterns akin to those of western secret societies. Officers of a Triad lodge include the Mountain Master, who presides over the lodge, and the Deputy Mountain Master, his assistant; the Incense Master and the Lead Guard, who conduct the initiation ceremony; the Red Staff, who assists the other officers; the White Fan, who serves as counselor, and the Straw Sandals, who is the messenger of the lodge. Each Triad lodge, however, is independent of all others, and the Triad system lacks a *tai tang* or Grand Lodge to judge disputes among lodges and enforce a standard code of conduct. See **grand lodge**.

Whatever their actual origins, by the beginning of the nineteenth century Triad lodges were the most popular secret society in southern China and had begun to stage risings against the Manchu government. A little later in the century, the Triads began to surface in Chinese immigrant communities overseas. Like fraternal orders in contemporary Europe and America, Triad lodges offered mutual assistance and protection to their members, while helping Chinese communities overseas cope with the prejudices and hostile treatment they often faced. Inevitably, Triad operations also spilled over into criminal activities, and by the late nineteenth century most criminal activity in the Chinese coastal ports and large Chinese communities overseas was in Triad hands. See **fraternal orders**.

The Triad lodges in China played a significant role in supporting the 1911 revolution that overthrew the Manchu and established the short-lived Chinese Republic. During the wars between the Republican government, the Japanese, and the Chinese Communist Party, different Triad lodges allied with different sides or attempted to play them against one another. The fall of the Republic in 1949 brought a campaign of violent persecution against all secret societies on the mainland as the Communist government sought to eliminate all possible rivals. In Hong Kong and throughout Chinese immigrant communities overseas, however, Triad lodges are still active, and play a significant role in organized crime activities in Asia and elsewhere.

Further reading: Chesneaux 1971.

Trilateral Commission

One of the most widely discussed (and frequently vilified) coordinating bodies among the industrial world's economic and political elites, the Trilateral Commission was founded in 1973 by American banking and petroleum magnate David Rockefeller and a consortium of politicians and businessmen from America, Europe, and Japan. The Commission drew its inspiration from Zbigniew Brzezinski's book *Between Two Ages* (1970), which argued for an alliance among the world's industrial powers as a basis for global stability. It had its period of greatest influence in the late 1970s, when Commission member Jimmy Carter was US President and Brzezinski was his national security adviser. Ronald Reagan's victory in the 1980 presidential elections, which began an era of American military and political adventurism, represented a significant defeat for the Commission's agenda, but it has continued to meet and lobby for international cooperation.

Currently the Trilateral Commission has some 350 members, drawn in approximately equal numbers from the three regions it represents. Since the Commission's founding, the Japanese sector has been expanded into an East Asian Group, and the North American Group now includes Canada and Mexico as well as the United States. Like the Council on Foreign Relations and the Bilderberg Group, its most obvious models, it holds an annual meeting in a different venue each year. Between meetings, its staff functions as a think-tank, researching issues and producing position papers on topics of interest to Commission members. See **Bilderberg Group**; **Council on Foreign Relations (CFR)**.

Within a few years of its founding, the Trilateral Commission had already been given a large role in American conspiracy theories at both ends of the political spectrum. The John Birch Society and other right-wing conspiracy watchers quickly identified it as a major player behind the attempt to abolish American independence in a global dictatorship, while their equivalents on the far left listed it as one of the major institutions behind a corporate world order aiming at the destruction of people's liberation movements worldwide and the imposition of an economic Pax Americana for the benefit of the rich. It still plays a very large role in current theories about the forthcoming New World Order. See **John Birch Society**; **New World Order**.

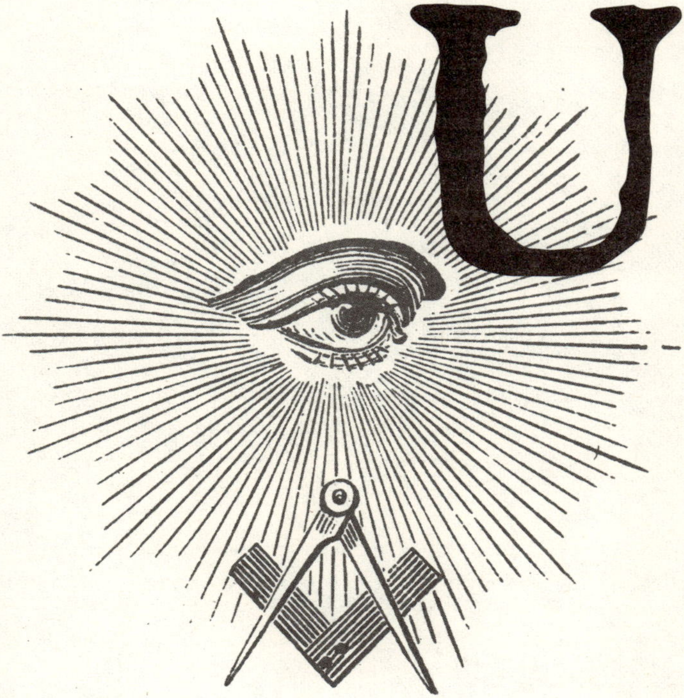
U

UFOs

See **unidentified flying objects (UFOs)**.

UNDERGROUND REALMS

Since ancient times, when myths filled the earth with underground kingdoms inhabited by monsters and goblins, the idea of hidden realms beneath the surface has captured the human imagination. As with mythology of other kinds, the truths behind the stories include spiritual and psychological symbolism, ancient astronomy and seasonal lore, visionary and shamanic experiences, and much else. Here and there, scraps of archaic history and half-forgotten memories have found their way into the mix, for – whatever else may or may not be true about the realms beneath the earth's surface – natural caves and caverns exist; so do underground structures built by human hands, and both of these have been inhabited by people, sometimes for many centuries at a time.

One example much cited by folklore scholars in the nineteenth century are the "hollow hills" of Irish legend, where the *sídhe* or fairy-folk live. Most of the fairy hills of Ireland are ancient burial mounds dating back to the Bronze Age and before, and their inhabitants are in one sense the ghosts of the people who built them, still remembered in Irish legend as the Tuatha de Danaan, the race that inhabited Ireland before the present inhabitants arrived and conquered them. Yet those same ancient people, according to archeologists, lived in earth-sheltered lodges that looked much like the tombs of their dead.

Victorian scholars of fairy lore drew on these and other parallels to suggest that survivors of the older race might have endured for centuries, hidden away in deep forests and inaccessible areas, camouflaging their traditional houses until only the keenest eye could tell them apart from natural hills. Much of the old fairy lore makes perfect sense when read as lingering memories of a Neolithic people: small, lithe, close to nature, armed with stone-tipped arrows and subtle natural poisons, by turns fighting and bargaining with their larger Iron Age neighbors. It may not be accidental, these researchers pointed out, that a common Scottish folk name for fairies is "Picts," the name of the pre-Scottish inhabitants of northern Britain, or that Hawaiian legends cheerfully admit that the *menehune*, the fairy-folk of the Hawaiian islands, are descended from ordinary humans who reached the islands from the Marquesas chain long before the ancestors of today's Hawaiians crossed the sea from Tahiti.

Yet whatever historical realities fed into legends of underground kingdoms, they became tangled up early on with material from many other sources. By the end of the Middle Ages, old Celtic and Germanic stories about "little people" living in hollow hills had been blended with Classical accounts of Hades, Christian legends of journeys to Hell, Arabic and Hindi tales that came west along the Silk Road, and much else. The result was a vision, half literary and half serious, of an earth honeycombed with countless caverns and tunnels and peopled with creatures as strange or stranger than the legendary inhabitants of fairyland.

The great Renaissance Hermeticist Athanasius Kircher (1601–80) gave a crucial boost to this process with one of his most famous and widely read books, *Mundus Subterraneus* (*The Subterranean World*, 1665). Trying to explain everything that was known of geology, including the source of volcanoes and the presence of metals in underground veins, Kircher postulated a network of underground passages through which fire, water, and air move, and a vast central passage from the north pole to the south, through which all the earth's oceans ebb and flow – an image that also provided a boost to the later idea of a hollow earth. See **hollow earth**.

Most of the writers that followed Kircher's lead, though, used fiction as their medium. Dozens of eighteenth- and nineteenth-century stories sent people from the surface into the subterranean world of caverns Kircher described. No less a figure than Giacomo Casanova the famous adventurer wrote a novel titled *Icosameron* (1788) in which his protagonists clambered down through caves in Transylvania to an underground world of "megamicros" who worshipped reptilian gods. Sir Edward Bulwer-Lytton's *The Coming Race* (1873) pictured an underground civilization wielding an omnipotent energy called *vril*. The torrent of underground adventures reached its peak in Jules Verne's classic *A Journey to the Center of the Earth* (1864), which sent a team of explorers down an extinct volcano in Iceland, only to emerge from Vesuvius in southern Italy.

The transformation of the underground realm from a setting for stories to fodder for the rejected-knowledge industry was given an immense boost by the invention of Agharta, the great underground city of the Himalayan masters. See **Agharta**.

The spread of these ideas into twentieth-century popular occultism was hastened by the career of legendary science fiction magazine editor Raymond Palmer (1910–77), who padded the pages of *Amazing Stories* in the 1940s with tales of an underground world of tunnels and artificial caverns, originally made by long-vanished Lemurians and now inhabited by deranged mutants called deros. These stories originated from Richard Shaver, a Pennsylvania welder who started hearing voices in his head while welding and ended up as one of the formative influences on today's alternative-realities scene. Shaver's stories were presented now as fiction, now as fact, and shared space in the pages of *Amazing Stories* with breathless accounts of Agharta and Shambhala, Theosophical root races, paranormal phenomena, and unexplained events. See **Palmer, Raymond**.

Real underground bases build in the Cold War provided more fodder for theories about underground realms. In the decades following the Second World War, faced with the prospect of nuclear war with the Soviet Union, the United States and many of its allies built extensive underground military complexes designed to survive direct nuclear attack. Several such bases in America, including the North American Air Defense Command (NORAD) headquarters inside Cheyenne Mountain, Wyoming, and the Strategic Air Command headquarters near Omaha, Nebraska, are a matter of public knowledge; the existence of dozens, or possibly hundreds, more is classified under national security laws. Studies carried out in the 1960s by the RAND Corporation, a military think-tank, and later released in response to Freedom of Information Act requests, suggest that plans were made for bases 5000 feet (1520 meters) or more underground and many miles in extent, serviced with their own electric railways and capable of remaining functional for years with no contact with the surface at all.

The rise of rejected knowledge from the cultural fringe to the subject of international bestsellers in the last quarter of the twentieth century set the seal on the underground realm as a standard element of alternative realities around the world. UFO literature made room for vast underground alien bases; the more outré writings on Bigfoot speculated that the giant ape might live in some hidden underground refuge and venture onto the surface for purposes of its own; conspiracy theories inflated the admittedly extensive network of underground bases built by the US government during the height of the Cold War into a vast labyrinth of subterranean cities where the black helicopters of the New World Order have their home. Some of the more exotic theories fused the underground realms with the hollow earth and filled the planet's crust with hidden passages leading from the surface to the unknown world inside. See **black helicopters**; **New World Order**; **unidentified flying objects (UFOs)**.

The earth undoubtedly remains full of mysteries. Like many other aspects of the modern rejected-knowledge industry, though, the current lore of underground realms has ignored the role of symbolism and visionary experience and imposed a rigidly literal-minded materialism on the fluid and subtle legends of hidden places within the earth. While many ancient traditions look to the earth's depths for contact with spirits and insights into reality, today's less sophisticated mystics seek tunnels full of Lemurian machinery and the hidden city of Agharta. As physical realities, at least, these are unlikely to be found beneath the earth's surface any time soon.

Further reading: Godwin 1993, Kafton-Minkel 1989, Sauder 1995.

UNIDENTIFIED FLYING OBJECTS [UFOs]

On June 24, 1947, a private pilot named Kenneth Arnold was flying past Mount Rainier in Washington State when he saw a group of "flying saucers" moving silently through the air at a tremendous speed. Arnold reported his sighting to the media shortly after landing. Hundreds of reported sightings followed in the weeks after Arnold's, ranging from obvious mistakes and blatant hoaxes to verifiable accounts of flying objects witnessed by dozens or hundreds of people and tracked on radar. The age of unidentified flying objects, or UFOs, was born.

Within a short time of Arnold's original sighting, public and scientific opinion alike had settled on two hypotheses to explain sightings of unidentified flying objects. UFO researcher Jacques Vallee has labeled these the natural phenomena hypothesis and the extraterrestrial hypothesis. According to the natural phenomena hypothesis, reports of UFOs are all the product of observational errors, recognized atmospheric phenomena, and mistaken sightings of ordinary manmade objects such as airplanes and weather balloons. According to the extraterrestrial hypothesis, reports of UFOs include sightings of spacecraft controlled by intelligent beings from another planet. Most UFO researchers, scientists, and people in general treat these two as the only possible explanations.

However, as Vallee and a handful of other researchers have pointed out in numerous books, there are many other possible explanations for the UFO phenomenon that have been almost completely neglected in the rush to judgment. Vallee himself, along with veteran UFO researcher John Keel, has argued that UFOs have close similarities to ancient traditions about elves and spirits, and might be controlled by intelligences who have been here on earth as long as humanity or longer. Another possibility rarely discussed, but at least as plausible as the more popular theories, is that the UFOs of the Cold War era may have been part of a secret military or intelligence program using wholly terrestrial technology.

Every set of imagery that carries a significant emotional charge in modern culture has been adopted and put to use by secret societies, and the UFO phenomenon is no exception. The involvement of secret societies in the UFO mystery goes back to the years immediately before Arnold's famous sightings, when members of several occult secret societies in the United States were convinced that they had received mediumistic communications from another planet. The appearance of the first flying saucers in 1947 seemed to fulfill predictions made in these channeled messages, and influential American occultists such as Dr. Meade Layne played a significant role in spreading the idea that the first wave of sightings represented the arrival of aliens from outer space. Their claims dovetailed with those of Raymond Palmer, editor of the science fiction magazine *Amazing Stories*, who had already made his magazine a haven for alternative views of reality. See **Palmer, Raymond**.

More recent secret societies have also made use of UFOs. Some occult and spiritual secret societies claim to pass on spiritual or scientific teachings received from extraterrestrial sources, while others teach explanations for UFOs that break free of the conventional wisdom; some claim, for example, that UFOs are spiritual beings such as angels or faeries rather than extraterrestrial machines, while others claim that UFOs come from secret bases on Earth or from an unknown world hidden inside the earth. All these teachings serve the usual secret society tactic of creating an alternative vision of reality for society members, and some also serve more pragmatic ends such as fundraising. See **hollow earth**; **underground realms**.

The neo-Nazi movement has proven to be a particularly fertile source of these alternate visions. By the early 1950s rumors were already being spread that UFOs were actually German secret weapons created by the Third Reich and flown by the "Last Battalion," a Nazi force based in Antarctica that was preparing a counterstrike against the victorious Allies. These claims have been recycled at intervals ever since, enhanced with ever more colorful details. One recent version claims that the Nazi flying saucers were created by the secretive Vril Society before and during the war, using technology decoded from medieval documents written by Gnostic Templars who were in contact with alien intelligences from Aldebaran. Rumors like these served to bolster the shattered morale of the defeated Nazis and help recruit members for neo-Nazi secret societies. See **Antarctica**; **neo-Nazi secret societies**; **Vril Society**.

Not all secret societies that make use of the UFO phenomenon limit themselves to interpreting existing sightings; some have gone so far as to manufacture sightings of their own. The most sophisticated attempt in this direction so far seems to be the uncanny UMMO hoax of the late 1960s and early 1970s, in which carefully faked sightings of UFOs were used to provide support for a set of documents allegedly passed on by aliens. During the late 1990s, rumors flew around the alternative-spirituality community in the United States and elsewhere that a far more dramatic attempt to fake an extraterrestrial arrival was planned for midnight on December 31, 1999, at the Great Pyramid. Nothing happened, but several groups of people and at least one secret society apparently positioned themselves to exploit the event if it happened.

At the present time it is fair to say that nobody actually knows all of the factors involved in creating and sustaining the UFO phenomenon. It has so many different ramifications, and has been adopted, adapted, manipulated, and faked by so many different groups for so many different purposes that any attempt to track the changes would be doomed to failure. Meanwhile strenuous efforts have been made to link it with other mysteries, real as well as fabricated, such as the Great Pyramid and the origins of Freemasonry. Some aspects of the UFO phenomenon remain in the hands of secret societies of various kinds, and will doubtless continue to attract secret society interest as long as the dream of visitors from another world remains a focus of human hopes and fears.

Further reading: Goodrick-Clarke 2002, Keel 1976, Keel 1989, Picknett and Prince 1999, Vallee 1991.

United Ancient Order of Druids [UAOD]

The largest and most successful Druid order of the nineteenth and early twentieth centuries, the United Ancient Order of Druids (UAOD) was founded in 1833 as a schism from the older Ancient Order of Druids (AOD). Many of the members of the Ancient Order wanted to adopt a beneficiary plan like the one introduced by the Odd Fellows, which provided sick pay and funeral benefits to members, but the AOD's Grand Grove wanted nothing to do with such a project. In the end, most of the AOD's groves (local lodges) and members broke away to form a new order, the UAOD, with a beneficiary plan. See **Ancient Order of Druids; Odd Fellowship**.

The new society spread rapidly, establishing groves in the United States from 1839 on and expanding into Europe and Australia later in the same century. The benefit system proved just as effective a draw for the Druids as it had for the Odd Fellows – the largest fraternal secret society in the world in the late nineteenth century – and the UAOD became one of the largest dozen or so secret societies in most of the countries where it had a presence at all. By popularizing the ancient Druids, it played an important role in laying the foundations for the modern Druid movement, and later orders such as the Ancient Order of Druids in America borrowed from its symbolism and rituals. See **Ancient Order of Druids in America (AODA); Druid Revival; Druids**.

Like most of the fraternal secret societies of the time, the UAOD experimented with several different degree systems, but finally settled on the three degrees of Ovate, Bard, and Druid, drawn from the Welsh branches of the Druid Revival. In America, it also created a ladies auxiliary, the Druid Circle. See **ladies auxiliaries**.

The Order's expansion in Europe, however, ended up unwittingly helping to create one of the twentieth century's great nightmares. The ancient Druids were popular in Germany in the nineteenth century, and the UAOD's expansion there attracted a minority of members from the German antisemitic far right. In 1913 some of these helped-create a new secret society, the Germanenorden, which drew heavily on UAOD ritual but pursued a racist political agenda utterly at odds with the UAOD's traditions. The Germanenorden's Bavarian branch, under the name of the Thule Society, sponsored a political front group which in 1919 became the nucleus of the Nazi Party. See **Germanenorden**; **National Socialism**; **Thule Society**.

The second half of the twentieth century was as difficult for the UAOD as for most other fraternal secret societies, and membership dropped to a small fraction of its nineteenth-century peak. It still survives in Britain, Australia, several European countries, and a handful of American states, almost completely ignored by the modern Druid movement it helped to launch.

Unknown Superiors

Many secret societies have kept the identities of their top leadership a secret, but starting in the middle years of the eighteenth century, certain secret societies made the presence of "Unknown Superiors" or "Secret Chiefs" a major element in their public relations. This habit seems to have started with the Rite of Strict Observance, a German Masonic rite publicly launched in 1754 but active for several decades before that time. Baron Karl Gotthelf von Hund, the head of the rite, insisted that he was acting on behalf of a group of unknown superiors whose names he was sworn not to reveal, but who had promised to pass on important occult secrets to the rite later on. Some evidence suggests that these original unknown superiors may have been leading figures in the Jacobite movement in exile, who hoped to use the rite for political purposes. See **Jacobites**; **Rite of Strict Observance**.

At the Convention of Wilhelmsbad in 1782, the Rite of Strict Observance rejected the belief in unknown superiors, but by that time the idea had found its way into common practice among secret societies. Much of this had political roots. The Bavarian Illuminati, which copied many of its features from Strict Observance practice, borrowed the concept of unknown superiors as well, and members of the Areopagus, the governing body of the Illuminati, were not known as such to members below the highest rank. Most of the revolutionary secret societies of the following century, such as the Sublime Perfect Masters, similarly imposed secrecy at all levels to keep secret police at bay, and a mystique of unknown superiors played an important role in this process. See **Bavarian Illuminati**; **Carbonari**; **Philadelphes**; **Sublime Perfect Masters**.

It was the occult secret societies of the nineteenth century, though, that did the most with the concept. The Hermetic Brotherhood of Luxor and the Hermetic Order of the Golden Dawn, the two most influential British magical orders of the late nineteenth century, both claimed to have been founded at the behest of unknown superiors; in the case of the Golden Dawn, the "Secret Chiefs" of the order were simply the known leadership acting under pseudonyms. The Martinist Order, an occult secret society founded in France in 1884, even had a degree of initiation titled *Superieur Inconnu* (Unknown Superior). See **Hermetic Brotherhood of Luxor (H.B. of L.)**; **Hermetic Order of the Golden Dawn**; **Martinism**.

The Theosophical Society, however, trumped all other claims of unknown superiors by insisting that it and it alone had been founded directly by members of the Great White Lodge, the mystical body of unknown superiors who formed the secret government of the world. Helena Petrovna Blavatsky (1831–91), the Russian mystic who founded the Society, originally insisted that the Masters who guided and taught her were incarnate human beings, a claim that has gained support in recent years by the work of historian K. Paul Johnson. After Blavatsky's death, however, the Mahatmas of the Great White Lodge were gradually redefined as essentially supernatural beings that had transcended ordinary human limitations many lifetimes ago. See **Blavatsky, Helena Petrovna**; **Great White Lodge**; **Masters**; **Theosophical Society**.

The redefinition of unknown superiors as superhuman beings proved highly popular and played a large role in making Theosophy the dominant influence in the occult scene during the "Theosophical century" from 1875 to 1975. Combined with the loss of trust in hierarchies common to most western societies in recent decades, though, this change has all but eliminated the old belief in unknown superiors. A handful of occult secret societies still claim to be guided by unknown superiors, but most do not, and many reject the entire concept as irrelevant.

URBAN DESIGN

In 1999, astrologer David Ovason's bestselling book *The Secret Architecture of Our Nation's Capital* proposed that a hidden pattern based on astrology and occult symbolism underlay the urban design of Washington, DC. This was not news to people inside the occult community, where the esoteric dimensions of urban design have been a subject of discussion for many years. Researchers into leys and related earth mysteries noted long ago that many towns and cities appear to be laid out according to complex patterns, some based on the positions of sun, moon, and stars, while others follow the less easily defined patterns of the ley network. As one of the major centers of ley research, Britain has been particularly well surveyed in this regard, and Alfred Watkins's classic *The Old Straight Track* (1925) includes many maps and photographs of complex urban alignments. See **leys**.

While Ovason's discoveries may not have been surprising to those familiar with the field, his work provides solid documentation of the role of esoteric symbolism in the design of a major world city. Unlike many other cities, Washington, DC did not come into being by the slow process of urban growth; it was planned and built as the capital of the new United States of America in the years immediately following the American colonies' successful revolt against Britain. The city's plan was originally laid out by Pierre Charles L'Enfant and substantially reworked by Andrew Ellicott, both of them Freemasons. They worked a rich tapestry of astrological alignments into the city plan, and this process was later echoed by other architects and builders – many of them also of the Masonic fraternity – who placed more than 30 complete zodiacs and hundreds of other astrological symbols in the architecture of the city. Much of this focuses on the constellation Virgo and on the three stars – Regulus, Arcturus, and Spica – that traditionally frame Virgo's place in the zodiac. The political importance of Virgo as a symbol of the "virgin land" of America at the time of the city's founding, no less than the constellation's deep esoteric connections to deities such as Isis and Ceres, and to the Virgin Mary in Christian myth, make this connection as obvious as it is elegant.

Few modern cities have been as comprehensively shaped by a symbolic plan as Washington, DC but most of the world's great cities (and a surprising number of the smaller cities and towns) have such geometrical and symbolic structures underlying them, as often as not half buried by a century or more of ignorant modern design and construction. Manuals of architecture and urban design, from the Roman builder Vitruvius's *Ten Books on Architecture* straight through into the early modern period, discuss the need to align streets and structures alike with winds, vistas, landforms, and heavenly bodies. These concerns blended with a vision of the world that saw the material world as a reflection of the spiritual realms to create many works of architecture that express traditional wisdom in symbolic and geometric forms. After the coming of the scientific revolution, when these approaches fell out of favor with the mainstream culture, they survived in a handful of secret societies, most specifically in Freemasonry. See **Freemasonry**.

The rediscovery of the role of Masonic symbolism in urban design has predictably sparked a great deal of discussion among antimasonic conspiracy theorists, who reworked it in search of more evidence for their belief that Freemasonry is a Satanic cult that runs the world. It has also been adopted by several authors in the fields of alternative history and rejected knowledge, who reworked it to fit their own belief that Freemasonry is a lineal descendant of the Knights Templar, the Gnostics, and other currently popular traditions of the past. Alongside Washington Rome, Paris, and an assortment of other cities have been cited as sites of Masonic geometrical design. See **Antimasonry**; **Gnosticism**; **Knights Templar**; **rejected knowledge**.

At least one other city in the world has a better claim to Masonic design than Washington, DC or any of these others, however. This is the modest American city of Sandusky, Ohio, where the street plan is laid out in the form of a Masonic square and compasses over an ordinary grid of streets. The surveyor who laid out the town, Hector Kilbourne, was also the first Master of the Masonic lodge in Sandusky – a detail that explains the source of the town plan's Masonic features. To the present writer's knowledge, however, Sandusky has yet to feature in conspiracy theory or alternate-realities literature, either as a hotbed of devil worship or as a center of the ancient mysteries.

Further reading: Kurtz 1972, Ovason 2000, Watkins 1925.

V

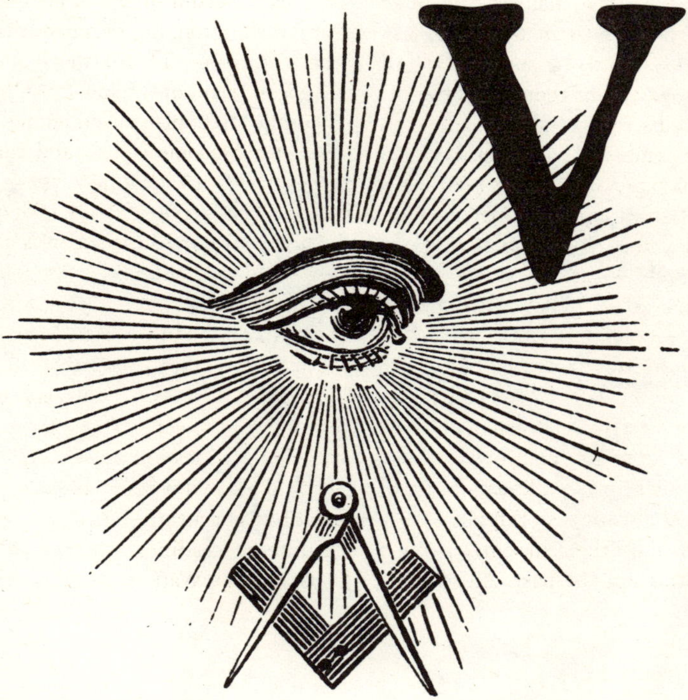

Vehm

A system of medieval courts in the old German duchy of Westphalia, east of the Rhine, the *Vehmgerichte* or "Vehm Courts" traditionally traced their origin back to Charlemagne. They first surface in written sources in the fourteenth century, when the chronicler Henry of Hervorden mentions them, and numerous sources from the fourteenth and fifteenth centuries refer to them. The Protestant Reformation seems to have crippled them, and whatever remained of them was swept away in the carnage of the Thirty Years War (1618–48).

The Vehm courts operated outside the ordinary judicial system but not outside the law. They were headed by "free judges" supported by a group of assessors. They met at dawn in the open air, and those accused of crimes under their purview were ordered to present themselves to the tribunal. If they appeared, they faced trial and would be freed if they proved their innocence, but those who failed to appear were hunted down and hanged. The Vehm had jurisdiction over religious crimes such as heresy, apostasy, perjury, and witchcraft, and serious civil crimes including rape, robbery, and murder.

The Vehm's reputation for secret justice gave them a strong appeal to the far right in the nineteenth and twentieth centuries. The National Socialist movement in Germany exploited the reputation of the Vehm in its propaganda, and more recent extremists from the Phineas Priesthood to neo-Nazi secret societies have also attempted to wrap themselves in the mantle of the Westphalian free judges. See **National Socialism**; **neo-Nazi secret societies**.

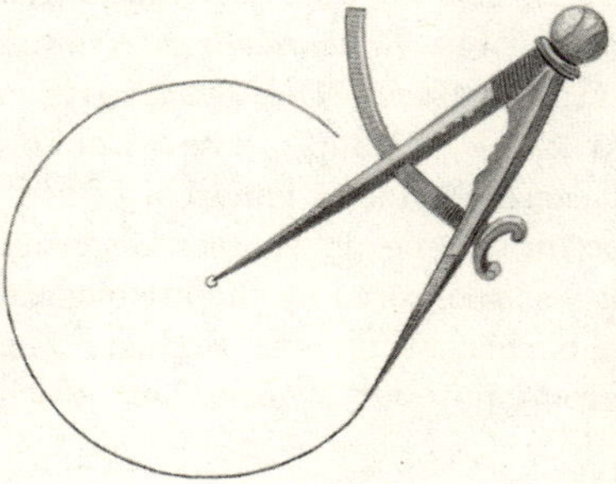

Vril Society

In a 1947 article in the American pulp magazine *Astounding Science Fiction*, rocket engineer Willy Ley mentioned a small group active in Berlin during the 1930s that he called the *Wahrheitsgesellschaft* (Truth Society). According to Ley, members meditated on a bisected apple in order to gain control of the mysterious power of "vril." Post-war books on the Nazi-occult connection built this brief reference into a claim that the organization, renamed the Vril Society, was closely affiliated with the Thule Society and the Nazi hierarchy itself and played an important role in the Third Reich's plans for world domination, putting the Nazis in contact with occult forces and reverse engineering alien technology from Aldebaran to equip the Third Reich with flying saucers. See **National Socialism**; **Thule Society**; **unidentified flying objects (UFOs)**.

The reality of the Vril Society was a good deal less impressive. Its formal name was *Reichsarbeitsgemeinschaft 'Das Kommende Deutschland'* (Reich Working Group 'The Coming Germany'); one of hundreds of little occult societies in Weimer Germany, it was sponsored by the astrological publisher Wilhelm Becker. The group put out a magazine, which apparently folded after one issue. In 1930 it also published two pamphlets, *Vril: Die kosmische Urkraft* (*Vril: The Primal Cosmic Power*) and *Weltdynamismus* (*World Dynamism*), claiming to reveal the secrets of Atlantean free energy technology. A section of the latter pamphlet shows a bisected apple as a symbol of the free energy field surrounding the earth. While this confirms Ley's account, it does nothing to back up the extravagant claims made for the Vril Society's activities and influence by later writers.

Further reading: Goodrick-Clarke 2002.

W

Weishaupt, Adam

German philosopher and founder of the Bavarian Illuminati, 1748–1811. Born in the Bavarian university town of Ingolstadt, Weishaupt came from an academic family with connections to Baron von Ickstatt, a member of the Bavarian Privy Council. Ickstatt's patronage won the young Weishaupt a scholarship at a Jesuit school. The rigidly conservative education he received there irritated Weishaupt, but the discipline and organization of the Jesuits themselves impressed him deeply. At 15 he finished his studies with the Jesuits and enrolled at the University of Ingolstadt, where he studied the writings of liberal French philosophers such as Voltaire and Diderot and quickly earned a reputation as a brilliant and independent thinker. He graduated in 1772 and immediately received a teaching position at Ingolstadt.

In the following year the Society of Jesus was dissolved by Papal edict. The conservative faction of the Ingolstadt faculty included many Jesuits, who retained their positions and opinions despite the abolition of their order, and struggles between liberal and conservative faculty broke out almost at once. Despite his youth, Weishaupt took an active part in these quarrels and was appointed to the chair of canon law at the university, which had been held by Jesuits for 90 years but became vacant in 1773. See **Society of Jesus (Jesuits)**.

The bitter struggles that followed, and the rumors that the ex-Jesuits at Ingolstadt and elsewhere had reorganized in secret, convinced Weishaupt of the need for a secret society to support progressive ideas. He considered naming it the Society of Perfectibilists, after the belief in the perfectibility of human nature he drew from the liberal French authors he loved, but finally settled on the name Ancient Illuminated Seers of Bavaria. He and four friends founded the Order of Illuminati, as it was usually called, on May 1, 1776. See **Bavarian Illuminati**.

Weishaupt spent most of the next eight years working long hours for the order, creating an extensive study program for its members, drafting rituals and symbolism, amassing a large library for the order, and corresponding constantly with its members. During the early 1780s, the glory days of the order, he and a small number of associates controlled an order with more than 650 members scattered across most of central Europe, and secretly controlled scores of Masonic lodges in Germany and elsewhere.

In 1784, when the order was exposed and the Bavarian government moved against it, Weishaupt fled the country in time to escape arrest. He found a new home at Gotha, in relatively liberal Saxony, where the reigning Duke Ernst II gave him a pension and a position as ducal counselor. Weishaupt remained there for the rest of his life. He became an important figure in the

German philosophical scene of his time, and wrote several books about the Illuminati and his experiences in Bavaria, but these received little attention amid the flood of conspiracy theories that gathered around the Illuminati in the aftermath of the French Revolution.

Further reading: Roberts 1972.

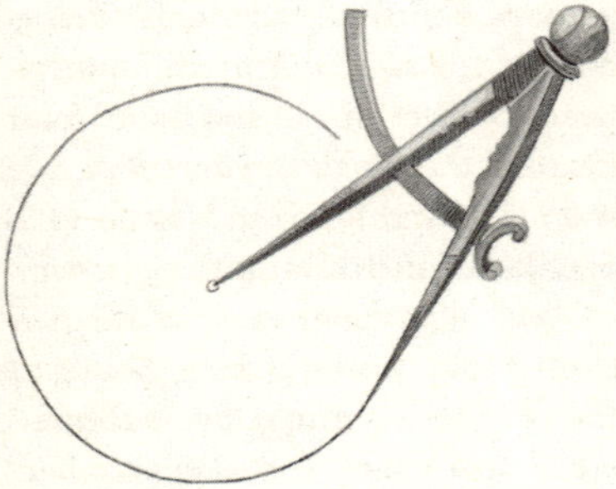

Westcott, William Wynn

English occultist and Freemason, 1848–1925. One of the most influential figures in British occultism in his time, Westcott was born at Leamington, Warwickshire, the son and nephew of physicians, and studied medicine in turn. In 1871 he joined his uncle's medical practice and began his lifelong involvement with secret societies by being initiated into the Freemasons. In 1876 he became a member of the Swedenborgian Rite, a small Masonic offshoot based on the mystical teachings of Emanuel Swedenborg. In 1879 he set aside his medical practice for two years of intensive study and practice of occultism, and in the midst of this retreat, in 1880, he joined the Societas Rosicruciana in Anglia (SRIA), the most influential Masonic esoteric order in England at the time. See **Freemasonry**; **Societas Rosicruciana in Anglia (SRIA)**.

At the end of his magical retirement in 1881, newly married and with a daughter on the way, Westcott moved to London and entered the civil service as a deputy coroner. In 1883 he was elected to the secretive Society of Eight, an order founded by the eccentric occultist Kenneth Mackenzie for the study and practice of alchemy. On Mackenzie's death in 1886 Westcott became Supreme Grand Secretary of the Swedenborgian Rite, and received all Mackenzie's Swedenborgian papers from his widow. Along with them, the evidence suggests, he received a manuscript in a simple cipher giving outlines of rituals for an occult secret society called the Hermetic Order of the Golden Dawn. See **Mackenzie, Kenneth**.

These rituals fired Westcott with the ambition to create a magical lodge of his own. With the help of fellow Freemason and occultist Samuel Liddell Mathers, who turned the ritual outlines into fully workable ceremonies, Westcott launched the Hermetic Order of the Golden Dawn in 1887 and served as one of the order's three ruling chiefs, writing many of its lectures and managing its training program. In 1897, however, Westcott was forced to resign his membership after someone informed the Home Office of his involvement in a magical society and he was told to choose between his order and his job. Westcott's resignation left Mathers in charge of the order, which led to the Golden Dawn's collapse in the early 1900s. See **Hermetic Order of the Golden Dawn**.

Westcott had remained active in the SRIA, and was elected its Supreme Magus in 1892, and was also involved in the Esoteric Section of the Theosophical Society, studying practical occultism with Helena Blavatsky until her death in 1891. The SRIA became the focus of his activities after his departure from the Golden Dawn. In 1918 he retired from the civil service and moved to Durban, South Africa, to live with his daughter and son-in-law. He died there in 1925. See **Blavatsky, Helena Petrovna**; **Theosophical Society**.

Further reading: Gilbert 1983.

White Lotus societies

One of the most influential secret movements in Chinese history, the broad spectrum of secret religious organizations commonly termed White Lotus societies can trace their ancestry back to the twelfth century CE, if not before. Their precise origin is unknown, but the movement seems to have emerged from a fusion of Taoist and Buddhist ideas in Chinese folk religion. The societies have many names – Eight Trigrams Society, Great Sword Society, and Observance Society among them; White Lotus Society was the name of one of the first such societies to become widely known, and is commonly used to refer to all of the societies of its general type.

Most White Lotus societies have a distinctive religious faith. They offer reverence to a primordial goddess of many names and titles – Wu-sheng Lao-mu (Ancient Unoriginated Mother) is among the most common – who brought the world into being and sends prophetic messengers at intervals to rescue humanity from ignorance and oppression. Most White Lotus societies believed that at some point in the near future a new messenger would appear and transform the world, restoring peace and happiness to all. In the meantime, White Lotus initiates practiced a variety of spiritual disciplines, including Taoist internal alchemy, and also commonly took up the practice of martial arts. See **Alchemy**.

In imperial China, with its traditional belief that emperors ruled by the Mandate of Heaven, the White Lotus teachings inevitably had political implications. White Lotus societies first appear in history as leading factors in the risings against the Mongols that liberated China in 1368 and put the Ming dynasty on the imperial throne. When the Ming dynasty fell to the Manchu in 1614, White Lotus groups became a significant force in the anti-Manchu underground, and staged several risings against the Manchu emperors.

Massive White Lotus-backed revolts in 1773 and 1794 were put down only after hard fighting. In response, the Eight Trigrams Society – one of the largest White Lotus organizations of its time – carried out a bold daylight attack in 1813 against the imperial palace in Beijing itself, coordinated with general uprisings in several provinces. The imperial government responded to this rising with a policy of violent persecution, but in 1861 the Black Banner Society – yet another White Lotus organization – staged another large peasant rising that lasted for two years.

White Lotus societies played only a relatively small role in the revolution that finally overthrew the Manchu dynasty in 1911 and ushered in the short-lived Chinese Republic. After the fall of the Republic in 1949, the Communist Party did its best to suppress all secret societies, and any White Lotus groups that remain on the Chinese mainland today are very well hidden. In Taiwan and many Chinese communities overseas, however, White Lotus groups remain active today, though most play down the political dimension of their teachings and focus on spiritual practices instead.

Further reading: Chesneaux 1971.

WHITE MAGIC

In nineteenth- and twentieth-century occult parlance, a term used for systems of magic that were, or at least claimed to be, morally good, as opposed to "black magic" which was morally evil. Efforts to define the boundary between the two have strayed all over the philosophical map, but most descriptions of white magic focus on the relationship between the magician and the higher spiritual powers of the universe, however these are defined. White magic, according to this definition, is magic worked with the intent of harmonizing with the purposes of higher spiritual powers, while black magic is worked with selfish intentions and with no reference to higher powers. In practical terms, most systems of white magic reject any form of magic meant to hurt or dominate another being, and look askance at magical workings carried out for purely selfish purposes. See **black magic**; **Magic**.

WHITE ORDER OF THULE [WOT]

Originally named the Black Order, this international neo-Nazi secret society was founded in January 1994 by Kerry Bolton, formerly a leader of the far-right Nationalist Workers' Party in New Zealand, who abandoned electoral politics in the late 1980s to pursue a more magical approach to fascism. In 1992 Bolton founded the Order of the Left Hand Path, renamed Ordo Sinistra Vivendi (OSV) two years later. In 1994 he and neo-Nazi Satanists in Britain, France, Germany, Italy, Sweden, Finland, Australia, New Zealand, and the United States organized the

Black Order as a network seeking to project racist and fascist ideals into popular culture in the West by way of the industrial music scene, right-wing political groups, and the Satanic end of the occult community. Functioning primarily as a support network for neo-Nazi secret societies, it keeps occult fascists worldwide updated on one another's ideas and actions through a quarterly magazine and an active book-publishing program overseen by Bolton. See **National Socialism**; **neo-Nazi secret societies**; **Satanism**.

In 1997 the absurdity of a white supremacist organization calling itself "the Black Order" finally seems to have registered, and the order changed its name to the White Order of Thule (WOT). In that same year the headquarters of the Order moved to Richmond, Virginia, as Bolton stepped down from his leadership position to concentrate on publishing projects, and in 2001 it relocated to Deer Park, Washington State, in the inland Pacific Northwest area long since staked out by American racists as the site of a future independent white nation.

Further reading: Goodrick-Clarke 2002.

Whiteboys

The first known Irish political secret society, the Whiteboys first appeared in Tipperary in the autumn of 1761. Enclosure Acts passed by the Irish Parliament permitted local landlords to seize village common pasture for their own use. In response, bands of local farmers gathered at night to destroy the ditches and fences erected by the landlords. Members of the bands took to wearing white shirts as a uniform, making recognition easy at night, and this gave them their name: Buachaillí Bána in Irish, Whiteboys in English.

As the movement spread it became a vehicle for a wider range of discontents. Almost 90 percent of the population was Catholic, but all had to pay tithes to the Protestant Church of Ireland; the right to collect tithes was commonly leased to private tithe collectors, many of whom exploited their positions shamelessly. Abusive landlords and extortionate rents for farmland provided additional motives for unrest. At a time when Irish Catholics had few legal rights, the Whiteboys offered the hope of redressing grievances. By the summer of 1762 Whiteboys could be found throughout most of the southern half of Ireland.

An initiation ritual, a simple hierarchy, and a rough code of justice formed the framework for the Whiteboys movement. The initiation was simply the taking an oath to be true and faithful to one another, to pull down any barriers raised around common land, to block attempts to repossess members' farmland, and to refuse to deal with tithe collectors. Each group of Whiteboys elected a captain and pledged to obey him. Whiteboy justice was harsh; tithe collectors who ignored Whiteboy warnings might find themselves stripped, tossed into a grave lined with brambles, and buried up to the neck, while Whiteboys who betrayed their fellows to the authorities could expect a very short lifespan thereafter.

The authorities responded to the Whiteboy activities with punitive laws and repression, and the movement went underground. The early 1770s saw a revival, as economic trouble and a series of bad harvests put pressure on Irish peasants again. In 1775 a band of Whiteboys attacked the home of a wealthy Catholic landlord, Robert Butler, the brother of the Catholic archbishop of Cashel. This brought the wrath of the Catholic hierarchy down on the head of the Whiteboys, who responded by beginning to protest against the dues and fees exacted by Catholic clergy.

A final Whiteboy outbreak in 1785 placed the question of tithes and church dues at the center of the movement. Protesting against the exactions of Protestant and Catholic churches alike, the Whiteboys, in this last major rising, won the support of large sections of the middle and upper classes, and managed to force through substantial reforms. Some historians argue that the Whiteboys' activities kept Irish landlords from engaging in the wholesale evictions that emptied huge tracts of the Scottish Highlands during the same period.

The spread of nationalist ideas from continental Europe to Ireland in the 1780s and 1790s, however, made the agrarian focus of the Whiteboys less relevant to a new generation of Irish radicals and prompted the emergence of new secret societies such as the Society of United Irishmen. The Whiteboy custom of assembling by night in white garments, however, spread to the American South by way of Irish immigrants, and was adopted after the Civil War by the Ku Klux Klan. See **Ku Klux Klan**; **Society of United Irishmen**.

Further reading: Williams 1973.

Wicca

The largest and most popular of the current neo-pagan religions, Wicca first appeared in England in the late 1940s and established a public presence immediately after the repeal of the Witchcraft Act in 1951. At that time, its principal spokesman, Gerald Gardner (1884–1964), claimed that it was descended from the witch cults of the Middle Ages and, through them, from pagan fertility cults going back to Neolithic times. His arguments for Wicca's antiquity drew on the theories of his close friend Margaret Murray (1863–1963), who popularized the idea that the witchcraft persecutions of the late Middle Ages were intended by Christian churches to stamp out a surviving pagan religion among medieval peasants. See **Murray hypothesis**; **witchcraft persecutions**.

Wicca as presented by Gardner, and practiced by the more traditionalist wing of the Wiccan community up to the present, is a nature-centered duotheistic religion; that is, its members worship two deities, a horned god of nature and an earth goddess, whose names are secrets known only to members. Membership is by initiation, after a period of probation, and there are three degrees of initiation, each with its own ceremony and traditional teachings. Each initiate must make a handwritten copy of the Book of Shadows, the sacred text of the tradition, which includes rituals, magical practices, and the rules or "Ordains" governing the tradition. Ritual nudity has an important place in the initiations, and the Great Rite of ritual intercourse between high priestess and high priest, personifying the goddess and the god, is either literally or symbolically involved in some rites. See **Book of Shadows**.

While the ancient origins of Wicca have remained an article of faith among many (though not all) Wiccans, research since Gardner's time has essentially disproved his claims. Murray's own theories were discarded during the 1970s as more careful historians showed that she had blatantly manipulated her sources to make them fit her conclusions, and half a century of hard work by folklorists in Britain and elsewhere has failed to turn up any trace of the agrarian fertility cult Murray claimed to have detected and Gardner claimed to reveal to the world. The link between modern Wicca and medieval witchcraft should be considered simply another example of the common secret society practice of retrospective recruitment, meant to give a newly launched group the patina of age by claiming antecedents far back into the past. See **retrospective recruitment**.

Yet Wicca was not simply an invention of Gardner's. In recent decades a wealth of information has surfaced about Gardner's own participation in a variety of occult secret societies where the ideas and practices of modern Wicca already existed in various combinations. Gardner's own account of his involvement with Wicca, for example, featured a theatrical performance group he called the First Rosicrucian Theatre Company in England, where, he claimed, he first met members of the witch cult. This group actually existed; it was a branch of the Rosicrucian Order of the Crotona Fellowship (ROCF), a secret society with close links to Co-Masonry, a branch of Freemasonry that admits women as well as men. Many of the elements of Wiccan initiation rituals can also be found in the ritual work practiced by Co-Masonry and the ROCF. See **Co-Masonry**; **Freemasonry**; **Rosicrucian Order of the Crotona Fellowship (ROCF)**.

Three organizations Gardner did not mention in his books on Wicca also seem to have contributed substantially to its growth. During the mid-1940s Gardner was a student of ritual magician and self-proclaimed Antichrist Aleister Crowley (1875–1947), and claimed later that he received an Ordo Templi Orientis (OTO) charter from Crowley. OTO publications from Crowley's lifetime include copious references to a system of sexual magic with close similarities to Wiccan sexual rituals. See **Crowley, Aleister**; **Ordo Templi Orientis (OTO)**.

During these same years Gardner became an associate of Ross Nichols, one of the leading figures in the Druid movement of the time, and went on to become a member of the Druid Circle of the Universal Bond. The concept of a duotheistic fertility religion worshipping one god and one goddess had been a common theme in Druid literature for most of the century before Gardner's time, and the influential Druid writer Owen Morgan had already identified duotheism, fertility religion, and ritual sexuality as the foundations of ancient British paganism in his 1887 book *The Light in Britannia*. See **Druid Circle of the Universal Bond**; **Druid Revival**; **fertility religion**.

Finally, Gardner had close connections to the English branch of Woodcraft, a youth movement founded around the beginning of the twentieth century by Canadian-American nature writer Ernest Thompson Seton (1860–1946). Starting in 1915, when Quaker groups opposed to the militarism of Lord Baden-Powell's Boy Scouts imported Woodcraft as an alternative, two Woodcraft organizations – the Order of Woodcraft Chivalry and the Kindred of the Kibbo Kift – had an active presence in the New Forest area where Gardner claimed to have worshipped with surviving witches' covens. Similarities between Wicca and English Woodcraft are particularly striking; Woodcraft ceremonies from the 1920s even include references to the earth as a goddess and to a horned god of nature, and Seton's Woodcraft included an inner, initiatory branch for adults, the Red Lodge, with three degrees of initiation. See **Woodcraft**.

All the evidence suggests that Gardner could easily have created Wicca himself out of materials ready to hand in the traditions with which he was personally acquainted. Still, the possibility exists that he was telling the truth when he claimed that he had been introduced to the system by the elderly witches who initiated him, and only expanded and developed it. All the ingredients for the creation of Wicca had been in place in the British occult community for some 30 years before Gardner's earliest publication on the subject, and it is entirely possible that someone else – perhaps members of the Rosicrucian Order of the Crotona Fellowship – first had the idea of reconstructing Murray's hypothetical witch cult using material drawn from existing occult traditions.

Whatever its actual origins, once it was launched into the public eye by a series of shrewd publicity campaigns by Gardner, Wicca attracted a growing following in Britain, Europe, America, and Australasia. Almost immediately after Gardner's first publications, though, other people began to surface, claiming that they too had been initiated into traditional witch cults; some of these were very similar to Gardner's, while others diverged from it in various ways. The second half of the twentieth century saw an extraordinary burst of religious creativity as new pagan religions modeled on Wicca sprouted throughout the western world, and older traditions such as Druidry were rediscovered and often reinvented to fit contemporary needs and concerns. This process is still underway as of this writing and bids fair to reshape the religious landscape of the twenty-first century in many western countries.

Further reading: Gardner 1954, Gardner 1959, Hutton 2000.

WITCHCRAFT PERSECUTIONS

Many human cultures have imposed legal penalties on people practicing unpopular ritual practices, and inevitably these have now and then been inflicted on innocent people. Trials for witchcraft occurred in traditional Native American and African societies, among many others, and news stories about the murder of accused witches by mobs in South Africa appear in papers even today. The immense witchcraft panics and persecutions that swept most of Europe between 1400 and 1800 unfolded from patterns common to many human societies. In their scope and brutality, though, the European witchcraft persecutions of the early modern period equal or exceed any similar example elsewhere in the world.

While organized witch-hunts in Europe did not begin until the early fifteenth century, their roots reach back centuries further into the past. The ancient Romans dreaded magic and passed laws banning most kinds of magical practice long before the Roman Empire converted to Christianity. The seizure of power by the Christian Church in the fourth century and the collapse of Roman power that followed did nothing to dispel these old fears, and Christianity added a new level of paranoia about magic. Most ancient magic either relied on invocations of the gods and spirits of the old pagan faiths, or borrowed heavily from

Gnostic sects condemned as heretical by the established Church. The medieval attitude toward magic thus blended a fear of magical attack with hostility toward religious deviance.

All through the early Middle Ages, though, this attitude was held in check by a confident belief on the part of many Christians that the power of Christ could easily resist the ineffectual workings of pagan or heretical magic. A rich heritage of Christian magical ritual evolved during this time, fusing Christian liturgies and Bible texts with old pagan ritual practices. For many centuries, so long as a ritual invoked Jesus, the Virgin, or the saints, and had a generally positive goal, official church policy held that it was prayer rather than magic, to be encouraged rather than prohibited. See **Magic**.

It took the catastrophe of the Black Death of the mid-fourteenth century, coming on the heels of half a century of crop failures and brutal warfare, to shatter this confidence and usher in an era of paranoia and mass murder. In the aftermath of the plague, which killed nearly a third of the population of Europe, rumors spread blaming various outcast groups – Jews, lepers, heretics – for causing the catastrophe. Over the next half century, the idea of a "plot against Christendom" reshaped itself into the belief that countless seemingly ordinary people were actually secret worshippers of Satan, meeting at night to sacrifice infants, violate every moral and sexual taboo, and pay homage to the powers of darkness. Convinced that the Christian world was under attack by Satan himself, civil and religious authorities alike weakened or abolished longstanding laws protecting the rights of the accused, authorized the use of torture to extract confessions from suspected witches, and thus plunged most of Europe into the 400-year ordeal that modern pagans call "the Burning Times."

The death toll from the age of witchcraft persecutions was wildly exaggerated in the early years of the modern neo-pagan revival, and the old claim of nine million deaths still surfaces in popular literature. The actual number will never be known for certain, since many records have not survived, but most scholars today place the total number of judicial murders of accused witches at around 50,000, three-fourths of them women and most of them poor. The claim that most of the accused were healers, midwives, or women in other respected traditions, which is also still repeated in popular books on the witchcraft persecutions, has no basis in fact either; surviving evidence shows clearly that the only thing that victims of the witch-hunts consistently had in common is that someone had accused them of witchcraft. Some of the victims of the persecutions no doubt practiced some form of magic or had unpopular religious beliefs, but the vast majority were ordinarily devout Christians who went to their deaths with the name of Jesus on their lips.

Pagan spiritual traditions may nonetheless have had a role in launching the first great wave of persecutions. Careful study of trial records in the last few decades has turned up traces of a set of distinctive beliefs found across much of Europe. According to these beliefs, certain chosen people, usually but not always women, left their bodies and flew through the night in the company of a goddess. Italian historian Carlo Ginzburg has suggested plausibly that these beliefs, and local cults based on them, may have provided some of the details that were woven in the aftermath of the Black Death into the legend of the witches' sabbath. These beliefs appear in the canon *Episcopi*, a text of church law dating from ninth-century France, and close equivalents can be found elsewhere in medieval records of heresy. See **Benandanti**; **canon *Episcopi***.

The system used to investigate accusations of witchcraft and try accused witches in most of Europe guaranteed the maximum possible number of innocent victims. Legal systems in most of medieval Europe before the age of witchcraft persecutions actually prohibited torture and provided the accused with some of the same legal protections now part of common law, and making a false accusation was a serious crime. In the early stages of the witchcraft panic, though, writers on witchcraft argued that these rules had to be set aside in order to combat the terrible threat posed by witches to Christian society. These same arguments had been made by lawyers for King Philip IV of France in the early fourteenth century to justify the role of torture in the destruction of the Knights Templar, and drew on older precedents for torturing heretics. See **Cathars**; **Knights Templar**.

Once the new rules were accepted, people accused of witchcraft were caught in a trap few escaped alive. Accused witches were not allowed to learn who had accused them or even what charges had been filed. In many cases they could count on being tortured until they confessed, and the torturers were encouraged to use whatever means were necessary to extract confessions. Suspects were interrogated using lists of standard questions that presupposed the inquisitors' beliefs in devil worship, and those who failed to provide the expected answers were tortured until they did. Once they had confessed, suspects were ordered to name other members of the alleged witch cult, and torture was again used to make sure that plenty of names were forthcoming. Once no more information could be extracted from them, those suspects who were not fortunate enough to die as a result of torture were handed over to the secular authorities. In most of Europe, convicted witches were burned alive, though English witches faced hanging and members of the nobility caught up in the witchcraft hysteria were usually beheaded.

The first witchcraft panics and persecutions began in Switzerland and southeastern France in the early 1400s, spread up the Rhine through western Germany, and extended east and west from there. Germany and France saw sporadic witch-hunts through the fifteenth century. From 1500 to 1550, witchcraft persecutions fell into abeyance, but broke out with renewed force after 1550 and raged through most of Europe for the next century and a half. England's last legal execution for witchcraft was in 1682, but Scotland was still executing witches as late as 1722. France's last witchcraft execution was in 1745, Germany's in 1775, and Switzerland's in 1782.

Between the end of witchcraft persecutions in Europe and the late nineteenth century, most people who discussed the witch-hunts of the past at all dismissed them as evidence of medieval superstition and barbarity. French historian of the Middle Ages Jules Michelet, however, proposed in his *Satanism and Witchcraft* (1862) that there had actually been a witch cult in the Middle Ages. His ideas were inspired and strongly influenced by the political secret societies of his own time, such as the Carbonari and the Philadelphes; Michelet's witch cult was a movement of peasants opposed to the misbehavior of the aristocracy and clergy, who turned to Satan as the image of rebellion against a social order that claimed divine sanction. Michelet's views found echoes in the writings of his contemporary, British Prime Minister Benjamin Disraeli, who thought that the secret societies of nineteenth-century Europe were descended from pagan cults of the medieval peasantry. See **Carbonari**; **Philadelphes**; **Satanism**.

American folklorist Charles Godfrey Leland built on Michelet's work in his 1899 book *Aradia, or the Gospel of the Witches.* According to Leland, while studying folklore in Italy he had contacted a surviving branch of the medieval witch cult and eventually had been entrusted with a copy of their book of secret lore, which he claimed to have translated. Like Michelet's witch cult, Leland's was a secret society of peasants who rejected Christianity as a tool of the ruling classes and embraced an alternative religion instead. Unlike Michelet's, though, Leland's witches were not Satanists, but worshippers of the goddess Diana, who believed their traditions had been revealed to them by Diana's daughter Aradia. Later research has cast substantial doubts on the authenticity of Leland's material, but at the time it found an eager audience.

The final stage in the redefinition of medieval witchcraft came in 1921, when Margaret Murray published *The Witch Cult in Western Europe*, the first of three books arguing that the witch cult had been an ancient pagan fertility religion that had been brutally suppressed by the church in the sixteenth century. See **Murray hypothesis**.

During the middle years of the twentieth century, despite severe problems with the evidence, Murray's claims were generally accepted by historians, and this provided crucial backing for the new religion of Wicca that emerged during these same years. Wicca claimed to be the witch cult described by Murray, and duplicated most of the elements of medieval witchcraft as described in her books. It also drew very heavily from Leland's *Aradia*, as well as the writings of Aleister Crowley. The fact that the first major promoter of Wicca, English author and civil servant Gerald Gardner, was a close friend of Murray's and one of her strongest supporters in the Folklore Society, as well as a student of Crowley, raised few suspicions. See **Wicca**.

In the last decades of the twentieth century, though, scholars reexamined the evidence Murray cited and found that she had shamelessly manipulated the data to support her claims. The few traces of authentic pagan practices that could be found in witch-trial records proved to have nothing in common with Murray's speculative reconstruction. Several historians also pointed out that whenever the legal system was not distorted to permit torture and anonymous accusations, witchcraft persecutions fizzled out. Even the Spanish Inquisition, which had few scruples and fewer legal limits on its activities, made a thorough investigation of the one Spanish witch panic, found no evidence of any organized witch cult, and thereafter dismissed witchcraft accusations as nonsense. Their judgment has been upheld by essentially all serious scholarship on the subject since the 1980s. Despite this, many Wiccan groups still claim to be descended from authentic medieval witch traditions. See **retrospective recruitment**.

Further reading: Cohn 1975, Ginzburg 1991, Kieckhefer 1976, Kieckhefer 1989.

Wolf's Head society

See **Yale secret societies**.

Woodcraft

A youth movement with significant pagan elements, Woodcraft was founded by Canadian-American nature writer Ernest Thompson Seton (1860–1946) in 1902, at his home in Cos Cob in suburban Connecticut. Concerned about the impact of industrialization and urban life on youth, Seton launched the movement as an attempt to bring young people into contact with nature and to teach values of self-discipline and cooperation. Seton was an early supporter of Native American rights, and drew on Native American traditions in launching his movement.

The movement started out as a single "tribe" of 42 boys in Cos Cob, but expanded dramatically over the following years, reaching a membership of 200,000 by 1910. After a brief and unsuccessful alliance with the Boy Scouts of America, Seton set up the Woodcraft League, an international organization, in 1915. Woodcraft tribes had groups for different age levels and a detailed program of activities and honors. A special inner circle for adults, the Red Lodge, had three degrees of initiation and a spiritual dimension focused on what Seton called the Red God, the spirit of wild nature and the "Buffalo Wind" that called too-civilized humanity back to its roots in living nature.

The Woodcraft League gained its first overseas members in the year of its founding, when a group of English Quakers, dissatisfied with the militaristic elements of Lord Baden-Powell's Boy Scouts, turned to Woodcraft instead and launched the Order of Woodcraft Chivalry, the first British Woodcraft group. In 1919 there was another addition to Woodcraft ranks as John Hargrave, a charismatic Scout leader, broke with the Boy Scouts and founded a Woodcraft group called the Kindred of the Kibbo Kift ("kibbo kift" being an old Kentish dialect phrase for "proof of strength"). Another Woodcraft group, the Woodcraft Folk, broke away from Hargrave's group in 1924. All three of the British Woodcraft groups set aside Seton's Native-American symbolism in favor of a mixture of Celtic and Anglo-Saxon imagery more appropriate to British youth. In the process, they helped to lay the foundations of modern Wicca. See **Wicca**.

The Woodcraft movement reached the peak of its popularity in the 1920s and 1930s, with groups active in some 20 countries around the world. The Second World War and the period of massive industrialization and Cold War militarism that followed it, however, brought a steep decline in the movement. After Seton's death in 1946 the Woodcraft League went out of existence, and the few surviving Woodcraft groups in the second half of the twentieth century continued in isolation. Woodcraft today remains an active but very small movement, with a variety of local groups linked mostly by the Internet. Whether it will survive or flicker out in the twenty-first century remains to be seen.

Further reading: Hargrave 1927, Seton 1920, Seton 1926.

Worshipful Master

The traditional title of the presiding officer of a lodge of Freemasons. The Worshipful Master of a Masonic lodge sits in a chair on the eastern end of the lodge room, presides over lodge meetings, and acts for the lodge when it is not meeting. In most jurisdictions he is elected for a one-year term. See **Freemasonry**; **lodge**.

The term "Worshipful Master" has been the subject of a great deal of speculation and innuendo in recent years. Religious opponents of Freemasonry have argued that it implies the master of the lodge is supposed to be worshipped by the other members, even though the word has this sense nowhere else in the English language. The word's original sense, preserved in Freemasonry and several other traditional uses in Britain, is "worthy" or "respected," and its modern sense, also appropriate in a Masonic context is "giving worship or reverence." Ironically, the word "reverend" – used as a title by many of Masonry's harshest critics – literally means "revered, worthy of reverence," and could be subjected to the same arguments as "Worshipful Master" with ease. See **Antimasonry**.

Y

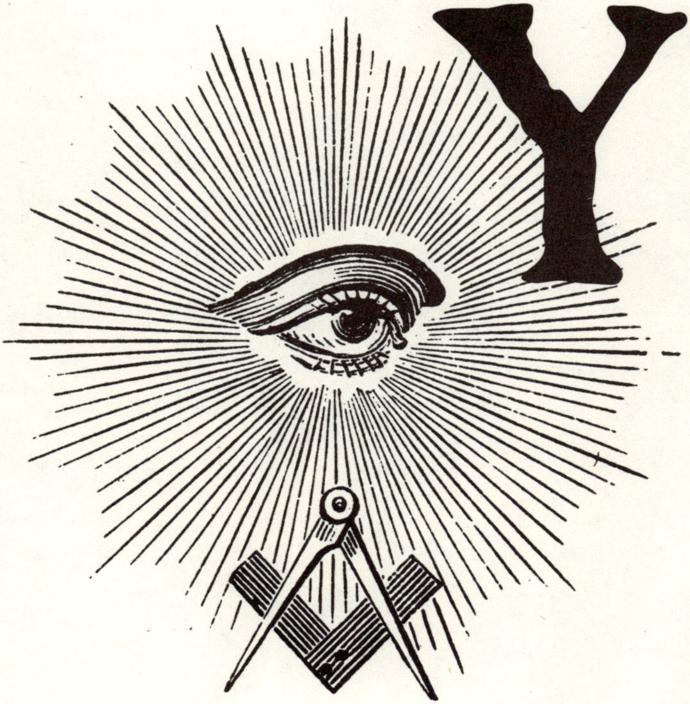

Yale secret societies

Starting in the early nineteenth century, Yale University has been home to a number of secret student societies, serving many of the same functions as student fraternities and sororities at other American universities. The oldest of these, the notorious Skull and Bones Society, was founded in 1832; its chief rival, Scroll and Key, came into being in 1842, and the third society, Wolf's Head, appeared in 1883. By the end of the twentieth century there were approximately 18 secret societies active at Yale.

While each society has its own customs and traditions, the basic pattern set by Skull and Bones in its first decades remains common to all. Each year, a society selects a fixed number of new members – usually 15 – who are initiated before the beginning of their senior year. Membership was limited to male students until the second half of the twentieth century. The society initiations, like those of college fraternities elsewhere, combine nineteenth-century ritual melodrama and undergraduate pranks. Once initiated, members take part in regular meetings twice a week. The older and wealthier societies have buildings of their own – "tombs," in Yale slang – where members dine before meetings and often spend much of their free time. After graduating, alumni are encouraged to remain involved with their society, network with other alumni, and assist them in their careers. See **Skull and Bones Society**.

The societies' secrecy, their exclusiveness, and the penchant of members for helping one another in business and politics, have long made the Yale secret societies a focus for secret society opponents and conspiracy theorists. Most of the rhetoric has been leveled at Skull and Bones, as the oldest and most prestigious of the societies, and the one with the largest number of alumni in politics. The connection between the Bush family and Skull and Bones – both George Bush Snr. (US president 1989–93) and his son, George W. Bush (US president 2000–), were Bonesmen during their time at Yale – has led some conspiracy theorists to claim that Skull and Bones is "America's most powerful secret society," a title it nonetheless shares with many other potential claimants.

Further reading: Robbins 2002.

Yarker, John

English occultist and Freemason, 1833–1913. Born in the Westmoreland village of Swindale, he moved with his parents to Lancashire in 1840 and nine years later settled in Manchester, where he would spend most of his life. At the age of 21 he became a Mason, but his interest in rare Masonic rites got him into trouble with the officials of the United Grand Lodge of England, and in 1862 he left regular Masonry behind for the less structured realms of irregular Masonic rites. He married in 1857 and led a quiet life, supporting his family as a bookseller. See **Freemasonry**; **high degrees**.

Yarker has been well described as "the universal purveyor of fringe Masonic rites" of the late nineteenth and early twentieth centuries. From his office in Manchester, charters and patents of initiation flowed out to the four quarters of the world. During and after his life he was accused of making a living by selling degrees, but even critical historians nowadays admit that his main motivation was a passion for the higher degrees of Freemasonry and a desire to see them survive. The most important of the Masonic systems he operated was the Rite of Memphis and Misraim, which he created from the older Rite of Memphis and Rite of Misraim in 1871, but he was involved in one way or another with nearly every alternative Masonic rite in Britain, and corresponded with Masonic groups overseas. See **Ordo Templi Orientis (OTO)**; **Rite of Memphis**; **Rite of Memphis and Misraim**; **Rite of Misraim**.

York Rite

One of the two major systems of Freemasonry, the York Rite derives its name and some of its rituals from the English city of York, where operative stonemasons' guilds have a very long history. Never as tightly organized as its major rival, the Scottish Rite, York Rite customs and practices vary widely from country to country. In America, where it includes nearly all ordinary Masons, it consists of four entirely independent units: the Symbolic Lodge, working the three standard degrees of Craft Masonry; the Royal Arch Chapter, working four degrees culminating in the Holy Royal Arch; the Council of Royal and Select Masters, working either two or three degrees, depending on state; and the Commandery of Knights Templar, working three degrees. In Britain, by contrast, the term "York Rite" refers only to the three fundamental degrees of Craft Masonry, the Past Master's degree, and the Holy Royal Arch. See **Ancient and Accepted Scottish Rite**; **Freemasonry**; **Knights Templar**; **Royal Arch**.

The York Rite is popular in the English-speaking countries, but has only a limited presence elsewhere in the world.

Young Italy

One of many secret societies in Italy in the tumultuous decade of the 1830s, Young Italy (*La Giovine Italia*) was founded in 1831 by Giuseppe Mazzini (1805–72) and several other Italian liberals in exile in Marseilles. Mazzini and most of his associates were members of the Carbonari, the major European revolutionary secret society of the time, and borrowed much of the new organization's structure and technique from Carbonari traditions. In place of the Carbonari emphasis on internationalism, though, Mazzini's new organization accepted only Italian members, and its goal was a nationalist revolution leading to the creation of an independent Italian republic. See **Carbonari**.

From Mazzini's headquarters in Marseilles, Young Italy established an extensive network of supporters throughout the Italian peninsula, distributed propaganda, and infiltrated the armed forces and government bureaucracies of several of the small kingdoms into which Italy was divided at the time. The most effective penetration was achieved in the Kingdom of Savoy in northwestern Italy, where large parts of the army were influenced by Young Italy propaganda. Meanwhile Mazzini, who was exiled from France in the spring of 1833, built up an army of Italian exiles in Switzerland and prepared for an invasion of Savoy to launch his planned revolt.

The Savoyard authorities discovered the plot in the summer of 1833, however; 14 members of Young Italy were executed, and many others imprisoned. This proved the beginning of the end for Young Italy. Members in other parts of Italy went to ground, fearing that they would be implicated by Savoyard members, and the planned rising in August 1833 never happened. Unfazed, Mazzini tried to launch the invasion of Savoy anyway in January of 1834, but his volunteers refused to cross the border in the absence of a revolt to support them, while members in Italy refused to revolt unless an army appeared to help them.

The complete failure of Mazzini's plan led to the rapid dissolution of Young Italy. Unwilling to admit defeat, Mazzini built ever more grandiose plans for a general European revolt until the Swiss government expelled him from the country in 1836 and he went into exile in England. His later career as a writer and Italian revolutionary proved more successful, but secret societies played essentially no part in it.

Further reading: Hales 1956.

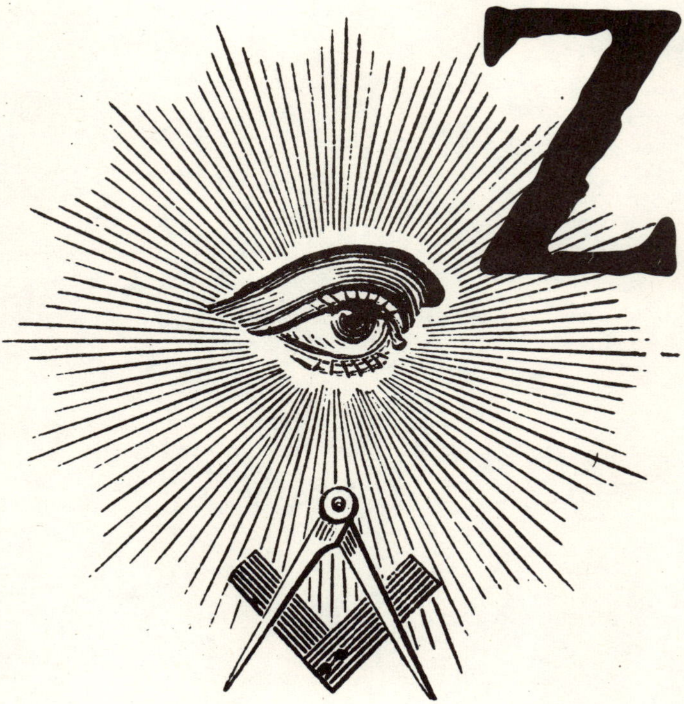
Z

ZERO POINT ENERGY

A currently popular term for machines believed to extract unlimited amounts of energy directly from the fabric of space–time, quantum flux, background radiation, or the like. Their proponents have recently attracted a large audience by claiming that the development of zero point technology offers the only effective response to fossil fuel depletion. As no working prototype of a zero point device has been produced and tested in a controlled setting, and proposed machines show close similarities to failed attempts at perpetual motion in the past, this may not be a safe bet. See **perpetual motion**.

ZIONIST OCCUPATION GOVERNMENT [ZOG]

In American neo-Nazi and radical right circles, a standard term for the US government, deriving from the theory that the Federal government is a Jewish-controlled puppet regime dedicated to the final extermination of white Americans. The term has also been adopted by British Nazis for the British government, apparently on the same basis. See **Antisemitism**; **Bruders Schweigen**; **Christian Identity**; **neo-Nazi secret societies**.

ZOS KIA CULTUS

The system of occult philosophy and practice created by English artist and magician Austin Osman Spare (1886–1956), and borrowed from his writings by chaos magicians and avant-garde occultists from the late 1970s onward. The name derives from the two primary principles of the system – Zos is the physical body in all its aspects, symbolized by the hand, while Kia is the "atmospheric I," as Spare termed the soul, and was symbolized by the phallus. The goal of the Cultus was the union of Zos and Kia; the masturbatory implications of this symbolism are intentional, as ritual masturbation was a central part of Spare's magical practice.

As a magical system, the Zos Kia Cultus was originally practiced only by Spare himself. The popularity of his writings in the last decades of the twentieth century, however, guaranteed that the Cultus would be revived in the less traditional end of the occult community. Significant elements of the Zos Kia Cultus and Spare's teachings generally have influenced such occult secret societies as the Illuminates of Thanateros (IOT) and Thee Temple ov Psychick Youth (TOPY). See **Illuminates of Thanateros (IOT)**; **Temple ov Psychick Youth, Thee (TOPY)**.

Bibliography

"A Member of the Order" (1846), *The Secrets of Odd Fellowship* (Philadelphia: Turner & Fisher)

Aho, Wayne (1990), *The Politics of Righteousness* (Seattle: University of Washington Press)

Albertus, Frater (Albert Reidel) (1960), *Alchemist's Handbook* (New York: Weiser)

Aldred, Cyril (1988), *Akhenaten, King of Egypt* (London: Thames and Hudson)

Allen, Gary (1971), *None Dare Call It Conspiracy* (Rossmoor, CA: Concord)

Allen, John L. (2005), *Opus Dei* (New York: Doubleday)

Ankerberg, John and Weldon, John (1990), *The Secret Teachings of the Masonic Lodge* (Chicago: Moody Press)

Anonymous (1994), *A Synthesis of Alchemy* (Ashland, OR: Pentarba)

Ashe, Geoffrey (1972), *Camelot and the Vision of Albion* (New York: St. Martin's Press)

Baigent, Michael, Leigh, Richard and Lincoln, Henry (1983), *Holy Blood, Holy Grail* (New York: Dell)

Baldwin, Neil (2001), *Henry Ford and the Jews: The Mass Production of Hate* (New York: Public Affairs)

Ballinger, Bill S. (1978), *Lost City of Stone: The Story of Nan Madol, the "Atlantis" of the Pacific* (New York: Simon and Schuster)

Barber, M.C. (1978), *The Trial of the Templars* (Cambridge: Cambridge University Press)

— (1994), *The New Knighthood: A History of the Knights Templars* (Cambridge: Cambridge University Press)

Barkun, Michael (1997), *Religion and the Racist Right: The Origins of the Christian Identity Movement* (Chapel Hill, NC: University of North Carolina Press)

Barnstone, Willis and Meyer, Marvin (2003), *The Gnostic Bible* (Boston: Shambhala)

Barron, Bruce (1992), *Heaven on Earth* (Grand Rapids, MI: Zondervan)

Begg, Ean (1986), *The Cult of the Black Virgin* (London: Arkana)

Bellman, Beryl (1984), *The Language of Secrecy: Symbols and*

Metaphors in Poro Ritual (New Brunswick, NJ: University of New Jersey Press)
Benham, Patrick (1993), *The Avalonians* (Glastonbury, Somerset: Gothic Image)
Benton, Elbert J. (1972), *The Movement for Peace Without a Victory During the Civil War* (New York: Da Capo Press)
Berlitz, Charles (1969), *The Mystery of Atlantis* (New York: Harper & Row)
Bernstein, Herman (1971), *The Truth About "The Protocols of Zion"* (New York: Ktav)
Besterman, Theodore (1965), *Crystal-Gazing* (New Hyde Park, NY: University Books)
Billington, James H. (1980), *Fire in the Minds of Men: Origins of the Revolutionary Faith* (New York: Basic Books)
Blavatsky, Helena Petrovna (1877), *Isis Unveiled* (New York: Theosophical Publishing House)
— (1888), *The Secret Doctrine* (Adyar: Theosophical Publishing House)
Bock, Darrell L., *Breaking the Da Vinci Code* (Nashville: Thomas Nelson, 2004)
Borges, Jorge Luis (1970), "Tlön, Uqbar, Orbis Tertius" in *Labyrinths*, trans. James E. Irby (London: Penguin)
Boyer, Paul S. (1992), *When Time Shall Be No More: Prophecy Belief in Modern American Culture* (Cambridge, MA: Belknap)
Bradbrook, M.C. (1965), *The School of Night* (New York: Russell and Russell)
Brockman, C. Lance (ed.) (1996), *Theatre of the Fraternity* (Minneapolis, MN: Frederick R. Weisman Art Museum)
Broido, Vera (1977), *Apostles into Terrorists: Women and the Revolutionary Movement in the Russia of Alexander II* (New York: Viking)
Brooke, John L. (1994), *The Refiner's Fire: The Making of Mormon Cosmology 1644–1844* (Cambridge: Cambridge University Press)
Brown, Dan, *The Da Vinci Code: A Novel* (New York: Doubleday, 2003)
Burkert, Walter (1972), *Lore and Science in Ancient Pythagoreanism* (Cambridge, MA: Harvard University Press)
— (1985), *Greek Religion* (Cambridge, MA: Harvard University Press)
— (1987), *Ancient Mystery Cults* (Cambridge, MA: Harvard University Press)
Burstein, Dan, *Secrets of the Code* (New York: CDS Books, 2004)
Butler, E.M. (1948), *The Myth of the Magus* (Cambridge: Cambridge University Press)
Butler, W.E. (1959), *The Magician: His Training and Work* (North Hollywood, CA: Wilshire)
Carnes, Mark C. (1989), *Secret Ritual and Manhood in Victorian America* (New Haven, CT: Yale University Press)
Carr-Gomm, Philip (1993), *The Druid Way* (Shaftesbury, Dorset: Element, 1993)

Case, Paul Foster (1985a), *The Masonic Letter G* (Richmond, VA: Macoy)
— (1985b), *The True and Invisible Rosicrucian Order* (York Beach, ME: Weiser)
Cervé, W.S. (H. Spencer Lewis) (1982), *Lemuria: The Lost Continent of the Pacific* (San Jose, CA: Rosicrucian Library)
Challinor, A.M. (1996), *The Alternative Shakespeare: A Modern Introduction* (Lewes, Sussex: Book Guild)
Chesneaux, Jean (1971), *Secret Societies in China*, trans. Gillian Nettle (Ann Arbor, MI: University of Michigan Press)
Childress, David Hatcher and Shaver, Richard (1999), *Lost Continents and the Hollow Earth* (Kempton, IL: Adventures Unlimited)
Chippindale, Christopher (1994), *Stonehenge Complete* (London: Thames & Hudson)
Churchward, James (1931), *The Lost Continent of Mu* (New York: Ives Washburn)
Churton, Tobias (2004), *Magus: The Invisible Life of Elias Ashmole* (Lichfield: Signal Publishing)
— (2005), *The Golden Builders: Alchemists, Rosicrucians, and the First Freemasons* (York Beach, ME: Weiser)
Cohn, Norman (1967), *Warrant for Genocide* (New York: Harper & Row)
— (1975), *Europe's Inner Demons* (New York: Basic Books)
Coleman, John (1992), *Conspirator's Hierarchy: The Story of the Committee of 300* (Carson City, NV: America West)
Cooper, M. William (1991), *Behold a Pale Horse* (Sedona, AZ: Light Technology)
Crossan, John Dominic (1991), *The Historical Jesus* (San Francisco: HarperSanFrancisco)
Crowley, Aleister (1970), *Atlantis Liber LI: The Lost Continent* (n.p., Dove Press)
— (1976), *Magick in Theory and Practice* (New York: Dover)
— (1989), *The Confessions of Aleister Crowley* (New York: Arkana)
Culianu, Ioan (1992), *The Tree of Gnosis* (San Francisco: HarperSanFrancisco)
Davidson, Gustav (1967), *A Dictionary of Angels* (New York: Macmillan)
Davis, Nancy Yaw (2000), *The Zuni Enigma* (New York: Norton)
de Camp, L. Sprague (1970), *Lost Continents* (New York: Dover)
de la Bere, Sir Ivan (1964), *The Queen's Orders of Chivalry* (London: Spring Books)
de Santillana, Giorgio and von Dechend, Hertha (1977), *Hamlet's Mill* (Boston: David R. Godine)
Denning, Melita and Phillips, Osborne (1975), *The Sword and the Serpent* (St Paul, MN: Llewellyn)
Deveney, John Patrick (1997), *Paschal Beverly Randolph* (Albany, NY: State University of New York Press)

Diamond, Jared (2004), *Collapse: How Societies Choose to Fail or Succeed* (New York: Viking)
Diamond, Sara (1995), *Roads to Dominion* (New York: Guilford)
DiFonzo, Luigi (1983), *St. Peter's Banker* (New York: Franklin Watts)
Domhoff, G. William (1974), *The Bohemian Grove and Other Retreats* (New York: Harper & Row)
Donnelly, Ignatius (1973), *Atlantis: The Antediluvian World* (Blauvelt, NY: Steinerbooks)
Drachkovitch, Milorad M. (ed.) (1966), *The Revolutionary Internationals, 1864–1943* (Stanford, CA: Stanford University Press)
Duncan, Robert L. (1961), *Reluctant General: The Life and Times of Albert Pike* (New York: Dutton)
Edwards, I.E.S. (1985), *The Pyramids of Egypt* (London: Penguin)
Eisenstein, E.L. (1959), *The First Professional Revolutionist* (Cambridge, MA: Harvard University Press)
Eller, Cynthia (2000), *The Myth of Matriarchal Prehistory* (Boston: Beacon)
Enright, Michael (1996), *Lady with a Mead Cup* (Dublin: Four Courts)
Evola, Julius (1995), *Revolt against the Modern World* (Rochester, VT: Inner Traditions)
Faivre, Antoine (1995), *The Eternal Hermes: From Greek God to Alchemical Magus* (Grand Rapids, MI: Phanes)
Fanthorpe, Lionel (1989), *The Holy Grail Revealed: The Real Secret of Rennes-le-Chateau* (San Bernardino, CA: Borgo Press)
Fenton, William N. (1987), *The False Faces of the Iroquois* (Norman, OK: University of Oklahoma Press)
Ferguson, Marilyn (1980), *The Aquarian Conspiracy* (Los Angeles: Tarcher)
Fideler, David (1993), *Jesus Christ Sun of God* (Wheaton, IL: Quest)
Filoramo, Giovanni (1990), *A History of Gnosticism* (Oxford: Blackwell)
Flynn, Kevin and Gerhardt, Gary (1989), *The Silent Brotherhood: Inside America's Racist Underground* (New York: Free Press)
Ford, R.A. (1986), *The Perpetual Motion Mystery: A Continuing Quest* (Bradley, IL: Lindsay Publications)
Fortune, Dion (1987), *Esoteric Orders and Their Work and The Training and Work of an Initiate* (Wellingborough, Northants: Aquarian)
— (1993), *The Magical Battle of Britain* (Bradford on Avon, Wilts: Golden Gates)
Fowden, Garth (1986), *The Egyptian Hermes* (Cambridge: Cambridge University Press)
Fox, Stephen (1989), *Blood and Power: Organized Crime in Twentieth-Century America* (New York: Morrow)
Frank, Emilie A. (2001), *Mt. Shasta: California's Mystic Mountain* (Hilt, CA: Photographix)

Fukuyama, Francis (1989), "The End of History?" *National Interest* (Summer), pp. 3–18
Fulcanelli (1971), *Le Mystère des Cathédrales*, trans. Mary Sworder (London: Neville Spearman)
— (1999), *The Dwellings of the Philosophers*, trans. Brigitte Donvez and Lionel Perrin (Boulder, CO: Archive)
Fuller, Robert (1995), *Naming the Antichrist* (New York: Oxford University Press)
Gardell, Matthias (1994), *Gods of the Blood: Race, Ethnicity, and the Pagan Revival* (Chapel Hill, NC: Duke University Press)
Gardner, Gerald (1954), *Witchcraft Today* (London: Rider)
— (1959), *The Meaning of Witchcraft* (London: Rider)
Gibson, Christopher (1996), "The Religion of the Stars: The Hermetic Philosophy of C.C. Zain", *Gnosis* 38 (Winter), pp. 58–63
Gilbert, R.A. (1983), *The Magical Mason* (Wellingborough, Northants: Aquarian)
— (1997), *Baphomet & Son: A Little Known Chapter in the Life of the Beast 666* (Edmonds, WA: Holmes)
Gilman, Richard (1982), *Behind World Revolution: The Strange Career of Nesta H. Webster* (Ann Arbor, MI: Insight Books)
Gimbutas, Marija (1991), *The Civilization of the Goddess* (San Francisco: HarperSanFrancisco)
Ginzburg, Carlo (1985), *The Night Battles: Witchcraft and Agrarian Cults in the Sixteenth and Seventeenth Centuries* (New York: Penguin)
— (1991), *Ecstasies: Deciphering the Witch's Sabbath* (New York: Pantheon)
Godwin, Joscelyn (1993), *Arktos: The Polar Myth in Science, Symbolism, and Nazi Survival* (Grand Rapids, MI: Phanes)
— (1994), *The Theosophical Enlightenment* (Albany, NY: State University of New York Press)
Godwin, Joscelyn, Chanel, Christian and Deveney, John P. (1995), *The Hermetic Brotherhood of Luxor* (York Beach, ME: Weiser)
Goldberg, Robert Alan (2001), *Enemies Within: The Culture of Conspiracy in Modern America* (New Haven, CT: Yale University Press)
Goldsmith, John (2004), *Three Frenchmen and a Goat: The DeMoulin Bros. Story* (Greenville, IL: Tri-State Litho)
Goodrick-Clarke, Nicholas (1992), *The Occult Roots of Nazism: Secret Aryan Cults and their Influence on Nazi Ideology* (New York: New York University Press)
— (2002), *Black Sun: Aryan Cults, Esoteric Nazism and the Politics of Identity* (New York: New York University Press)
Gray, Wood (1942), *The Hidden Civil War: The Story of the Copperheads* (New York: Viking Press)
Green, Miranda J. (1997), *The World of the Druids* (London: Thames & Hudson)

Greer, John Michael (1996), *Paths of Wisdom* (St Paul, MN: Llewellyn)
— (1997), *Circles of Power* (St Paul, MN: Llewellyn)
— (1998), *Inside A Magical Lodge* (St Paul, MN: Llewellyn)
— (2006), *The Druidry Handbook* (San Francisco: Weiser)
Greer, Mary, and Küntz, Darcy (1999), *The Chronology of the Golden Dawn* (Edmonds, WA: Holmes)
Griffin, G. Edward (1975), *The Life and Works of Robert Welch, Founder of the John Birch Society* (Thousand Oaks, CA: American Media)
Grossinger, Richard (ed.) (1983), *The Alchemical Tradition in the Late Twentieth Century* (Berkeley, CA: North Atlantic)
Guénon, René (1953), *The Reign of Quantity and the Signs of the Times* (London: Luzacs)
— (1983), *The Lord of the World* (Ellingstring: Coombe Springs)
Gustafson, Fred (1990), *The Black Madonna* (Boston: Sigo Press)
Hakl, Hans Thomas (2000), *Unknown Sources: National Socialism and the Occult* (Edmonds, WA: Holmes)
Hales, E.E.Y. (1956), *Mazzini and the Secret Societies* (New York: P.J. Kenedy)
Hall, Manly P. (ed.) (1983), *The Most Holy Trinosophia of the Comte de St.-Germain* (Los Angeles: Philosophical Research Society)
— (1988), *The Secret Teachings of All Ages* (Los Angeles: Philosophical Research Society)
Hancock, Graham (1995), *Fingerprints of the Gods* (New York: Three Rivers)
Hapgood, Charles, Jr. (1969), *Maps of the Ancient Sea Kings* (New York: Dutton)
Hargrave, John (1927), *The Confession of the Kibbo Kift* (London: Duckworth)
Harris, Robert L. (1979), "Early Black Benevolent Societies 1780–1830", *The Massachusetts Review* 20 (Autumn), pp. 603–16
Haskins, Susan (1987), *Mary Magdalene: Myth and Metaphor* (New York: Berkley)
Heindel, Max (1909), *The Rosicrucian Cosmo-Conception* (Oceanside, CA: Rosicrucian Fellowship)
Herrnleben, Johannes (2000), *Rudolf Steiner* (London: Sophia)
Hesiod (1973), "Works and Days", in *Hesiod and Theognis*, trans. Dorothea Wender (London: Penguin), pp. 59–86
Hingley, Ronald (1967), *Nihilists: Russian Radicals and Revolutionaries in the Reign of Alexander II (1855–81)* (New York: Delacorte)
Hitler, Adolf (1974), *Mein Kampf* (London: Hutchinson)
Höhne, Heinrich (1972), *The Order of the Death's Head: The Story of Hitler's SS* (London: Pan)
Hopkins, Marilyn, Simmans, Graham and Wallace-Murphy, Tim (2000), *Rex Deus* (Shaftesbury, Dorset: Element)
Hornung, Erik (2001), *The Secret Lore of Egypt* (Ithaca, NY: Cornell University Press)

Horowitz, David A. (ed.) (1999), *Inside the Klavern: the Secret History of a Ku Klux Klan of the 1920s* (Carbondale, IL: Southern Illinois University Press)
Howard, David H. (1992), *People, Pride, and Progress* (Washington, DC: The National Grange)
Howe, Ellic (1972), *The Magicians of the Golden Dawn* (London: Routledge and Kegan Paul)
— (1997), *Fringe Masonry in England 1870–1885* (Edmonds, WA: Holmes)
Hutchens, Rex R. (1995), *A Bridge to Light* (Washington, DC: Supreme Council of the Ancient and Accepted Scottish Rite, Southern Jurisdiction USA)
Hutton, Ronald (2000), *The Triumph of the Moon* (Oxford: Oxford University Press)
Icke, David (1995), *… And The Truth Shall Set You Free* (Cambridge: Bridge of Love)
— (1999), *The Biggest Secret* (Wildwood, MO: Bridge of Love, 1999)
— (2001), *Children of the Matrix* (Wildwood, MO: Bridge of Love)
Jacob, Margaret C. (1981), *The Radical Enlightenment* (London: George Allen & Unwin)
Jenkins, John Major (1994), *Tzolkin: Visionary Perspectives and Calendar Studies* (Garberville, CA: Borderlands Research Foundation)
Jennings, Francis (1996), *Benjamin Franklin, Politician* (New York: Norton)
Johnson, K. Paul (1994), *The Masters Revealed: Madame Blavatsky and the Myth of the Great White Lodge* (Albany, NY: State University of New York Press)
Johnson, Kenneth Rayner (1980), *The Fulcanelli Phenomenon* (Jersey: Neville Spearman)
Joll, James (1980), *The Anarchists* (Cambridge, MA: Harvard University Press)
Kafton-Minkel, Walter (1989), *Subterranean Worlds* (Port Townsend, WA: Loompanics)
Kauffman, Christopher J. (1982), *Faith and Fraternalism: the History of the Knights of Columbus 1882–1982* (New York: Harper & Row)
Keel, John (1976), *The Mothman Prophecies* (New York: Signet)
— (1989), "The Man who Invented Flying Saucers", in Ted Schultz (ed.), *The Fringes of Reason* (New York: Harmony Books), pp. 138–45
Keith, Jim (1994a), *Black Helicopters over America* (Lilburn, GA: IllumiNet)
— (1994b), *Casebook on Alternative 3: UFOs, Secret Societies, and World Control* (Lilburn, GA: IllumiNet)
Kelly, Walt (1962), *The Jack Acid Society Black Book* (New York: Simon and Schuster)
Kerenyi, Carl (1967), *Eleusis* (New York: Bollingen Foundation)
Khei, X° (George Winslow Plummer) (1920), *Rosicrucian Fundamentals* (New York: Flame Press)
Kieckhefer, Richard (1976), *European Witch Trials* (Berkeley,

CA: University of California Press)
— (1989), *Magic in the Middle Ages* (Cambridge: Cambridge University Press)
King, Francis (1991), *The Magical World of Aleister Crowley* (Oxford: Mandrake)
Kinney, Jay (ed.) (1995), "The Solar Temple Dossier", *Gnosis* 34 (Winter), pp. 87–96
Knibb, Michael A. (1987), *The Qumran Community* (Cambridge: Cambridge University Press)
Knight, Christopher and Lomas, Robert (1996) *The Hiram Key* (Shaftesbury, Dorset: Element)
— (1997), *The Second Messiah* (Shaftesbury, Dorset: Element)
Knight, Gareth (1983), *The Secret Tradition in Arthurian Legend* (Wellingborough, Northants: Aquarian)
— (2000), *The Story of Dion Fortune and the Inner Light* (Loughborough, Leics: Thoth)
Knoop, D. and Jones, G.P. (1947) *The Genesis of Freemasonry* (Manchester: Manchester University Press)
Kurtz, Karl W. (1972), "Laid Out in Form of Square and Compass", *California Freemason*, vol. 19 no. 3 (Summer), p. 105
Lacey, Robert (1991), *Little Man: Meyer Lansky and the Gangster Life* (Boston: Little, Brown and Co.)
Laqueur, Walter (1965), *Russia and Germany* (Boston: Little, Brown and Co.)
LaVey, Anton Szandor (1969), *The Satanic Bible* (New York: Berkley)
Lawlor, Robert (1982), *Sacred Geometry: Principles and Practice* (London: Thames & Hudson)
Layton, Bentley (1987), *The Gnostic Scriptures* (Garden City, NY: Doubleday)
Leadbeater, Charles W. (1925), *The Masters and the Path* (Adyar: Theosophical Publishing House)
Lefebvre, Georges (1947), *The Coming of the French Revolution* (Princeton, NJ: Princeton University Press)
Lehner, Mark (1997), *The Complete Pyramids* (London: Thames & Hudson)
Lévi, Eliphas (1972), *Transcendental Magic*, trans. A.E. Waite (York Beach, ME: Weiser)
Lewis, H. Spencer (1948), *Rosicrucian Manual* (San Jose, CA: AMORC)
Lumsden, Robin (1997), *Himmler's Black Order: A History of the SS, 1923–1945* (Stroud, Gloucs: Sutton)
McIntosh, Christopher (1997), *The Rosicrucians: The History, Mythology, and Rituals of an Esoteric Order* (York Beach, ME: Weiser)
McKale, Donald M. (1981), *Hitler: The Survival Myth* (New York: Stein & Day)
Mackenzie, Norman (ed.) (1967), *Secret Societies* (New York: Holt, Rinehart, and Winston)
Mackenzie, Norman and Mackenzie, Jeane (1977), *The Fabians* (New York: Simon and Schuster)
Mackey, Albert (1924), *Encyclopedia of Freemasonry*, rev. edn (Chicago: Masonic History Co.)

McLynn, Frank J. (1985), *The Jacobites* (London: Routledge & Kegan Paul)
MacNulty, W. Kirk (1991), *Freemasonry: A Journey through Ritual and Symbol* (London: Thames & Hudson)
— (2002), *The Way of the Craftsman* (Hinckley, Leics: Central Regalia)
Mails, Thomas E. (1973), *Dog Soldiers, Bear Men, and Buffalo Women: A Study of the Societies and Cults of the Plains Indians* (Englewood Cliffs, NJ: Prentice-Hall)
Malaclypse the Younger (Greg Hill) (1970), *Principia Discordia, or, How I Found Goddess And What I Did To Her When I Found Her* (San Francisco: Rip Off Press)
Marrs, Jim (2000), *Rule By Secrecy* (New York: HarperCollins)
Marrs, Texe (2000), *Circle of Intrigue* (Austin, TX: RiverCrest)
Marsden, George M. (1980), *Fundamentalism and American Culture* (New York: Oxford University Press)
Matthews, John and Green, Marian (1986), *The Grail Seeker's Companion* (Wellingborough, Northants: Aquarian)
Mazour, Anatole G. (1937), *The First Russian Revolution 1825: The Decembrist Movement* (Stanford, CA: Stanford University Press)
Meadows, William C. (1999), *Kiowa, Comanche, and Apache Military Societies* (Austin, TX: University of Texas Press)
Michell, John (1969), *The View Over Atlantis* (London: Sago Press)
— (1982), *Megalithomania* (London: Thames & Hudson)
— (1990), *New Light on the Ancient Mystery of Glastonbury* (Glastonbury, Somerset: Gothic Image Press)
— (1996), *Who Wrote Shakespeare?* (New York: Thames & Hudson)
Millegan, Kris (ed.) (2003), *Fleshing Out Skull and Bones* (Walterville, OR: Trine Day)
Murray, Margaret (1921), *The Witch Cult in Western Europe* (Oxford: Oxford University Press)
— (1933), *The God of the Witches* (Oxford: Oxford University Press)
— (1954), *The Divine King in England* (Oxford: Oxford University Press)
Myatt, David (1984), *Vindex: the Destiny of the West* (Reddy, WV: Liberty Bell Publications)
Mylonas, George E. (1961), *Eleusis and the Eleusinian Mysteries* (Princeton: Princeton University Press)
Nathan, Debbie, and Michael Snedecker (1995), *Satan's Silence: Ritual Abuse and the Making of a Modern American Witch Hunt* (New York: Basic Books)
Nichols, Ross (1992), *The Book of Druidry* (London: Thorsons)
Nickell, Joe (1987), *Verdict on the Shroud* (Buffalo, NY: Prometheus)
O'Leary, Stephen D. (1994), *Arguing the Apocalypse: A Theory of Millennial Rhetoric* (New York: Oxford University Press)
Ord-Hume, W.J.G. (1980), *Perpetual Motion: The History of an*

Obsession (New York: St Martin's Press)

Ovason, David (2000), *The Secret Architecture of Our Nation's Capital* (New York: HarperCollins)

Overdyke, W. Darrell (1950), *The Know-Nothing Party in the South* (n.p.: Louisiana State University Press)

Ownby, David (1996), *Brotherhoods and Secret Societies in Early and Mid-Qing China* (Stanford, CA: Stanford University Press)

Palmer, Edward Nelson (1944), "Negro Secret Societies", *Social Forces* 23/2 (December), pp. 207–12

Partner, Peter (1981), *The Murdered Magicians: The Knights Templar and their Myth* (Oxford: Oxford University Press)

Patai, Raphael (1994), *The Jewish Alchemists* (Princeton: Princeton University Press)

Pennick, Nigel (1979), *The Ancient Science of Geomancy* (London: Thames & Hudson)

Pettibone, James (1902), *The Lodge Goat and Goat Rides: Butts and Goat Hairs, Gathered from the Lodge Rooms of every Fraternal Order* (Cincinnati, OH: Pettibone & Co.)

Phelan, Craig (2000), *Grand Master Workman – Terence Powderly and the Knights of Labor* (Westport, CT: Greenwood)

Phillips, Osborne (2001), *Aurum Solis Initiation Ceremonies and Inner Magical Techniques* (Loughborough, Leics: Thoth)

Phillips, Ruth (1995), *Representing Woman: Sande Masquerades of the Mende of Sierra Leone* (Los Angeles: UCLA Press)

"Phylos the Tibetan" (Frederick S. Oliver) (1974), *A Dweller on Two Planets* (Blauvelt, NY: Multimedia)

Picknett, Lynn and Prince, Clive (1999), *The Stargate Conspiracy* (New York: Berkley)

Piggott, Stuart (1975), *The Druids* (London: Thames & Hudson)

Pike, Albert (1871), *Morals and Dogma of the Ancient and Accepted Scottish Rite* (Charleston, SC: Supreme Council of the Southern Jurisdiction AASR)

Plato (1961), *Collected Dialogues*, ed. Edith Hamilton and Huntington Cairns (Princeton: Princeton University Press)

Pohl, Frederick J. (1974) *Prince Henry Sinclair* (London: Davis Poynter)

Pott, Mrs. Henry (1900), *Francis Bacon and His Secret Society* (San Francisco: John Howell)

Preuss, Arthur (ed.) (1924), *A Dictionary of Secret and Other Societies* (St Louis, MO: Herder Book Co.)

Quinn, D. Michael (1987), *Early Mormonism and the Magic World View* (Salt Lake City: Signature Books)

Raeff, Marc (1966), *The Decembrist Movement* (Englewood Cliffs, NJ: Prentice-Hall)

Randolph, Paschal Beverly (1874), *Eulis!* (Toledo, OH: Randolph Publishing Co.)

Rappoport, Jon (1998), *The Secret Behind Secret Societies* (San Diego, CA: Truth Seeker)
Redford, Donald B. (1984), *Akhenaten, the Heretic King* (Princeton: Princeton University Press)
Regardie, Israel (1971), *The Golden Dawn* (St Paul, MN: Llewellyn)
Richardson, Robert (1998), *The Unknown Treasure: The Priory of Sion Fraud and the Spiritual Treasure of Rennes-le-Chateau* (Houston, TX: NorthStar)
Riggs, Brian (1997), "The Pope and the Pornographer", *Gnosis* 44 (Summer), pp. 46–50
Robbins, Alexandra (2002), *Secrets of the Tomb: Skull and Bones, the Ivy League, and the Hidden Paths of Power* (Boston: Little, Brown and Co.)
Roberts, Allen E. (1974), *The Craft and its Symbols* (Richmond, VA: Macoy)
Roberts, J.M. (1972), *The Mythology of the Secret Societies* (New York: Charles Scribner's Sons)
Robertson, Colin (2004), *The Druidic Order of the Pendragon* (Loughborough, Leics: Thoth)
Robertson, Pat (1991), *The New World Order* (Nashville, TN: Word)
Robinson, John (1989), *Born in Blood: The Lost Secrets of Freemasonry* (London: Century)
Runciman, Stephen (1995), *The Medieval Manichee* (Cambridge: Cambridge University Press)
Sauder, Richard (1995), *Underground Bases and Tunnels* (Kampton, IL: Adventures Unlimited)
Schapiro, Leonard (1984), *The Russian Revolutions of 1917* (New York: Basic Books)
Schele, Linda and Friedel, David (1990) *A Forest of Kings* (New York: William Morrow)
Scholem, Gershom (1974), *The Kabbalah* (New York: Quadrangle)
Schonfield, Hugh (2005), *The Passover Plot* (New York: The Disinformation Company)
Scott-Elliot, William (1962), *The Story of Atlantis and The Lost Lemuria* (Wheaton, IL: Theosophical Press)
Seton, Ernest Thompson (1920), *Two Little Savages* (Garden City, NY: Doubleday)
— (1926), *The Book of Woodcraft and Indian Lore* (Garden City, NY: Doubleday)
Settegast, Mary (1990), *Plato Prehistorian* (Hudson, NY: Lindisfarne)
Shanks, Hershel (ed.) (1992), *Understanding the Dead Sea Scrolls* (New York: Random House)
Sinnett, A.J. (1883), *Esoteric Buddhism* (Adyar: Theosophical Publishing House)
Sitchin, Zechariah (1976), *The 12th Planet* (Santa Fe, NM: Bear & Co.)
— (1980), *The Stairway to Heaven* (New York: St Martin's Press)
— (2002), *The Lost Book of Enki* (Rochester, VT: Bear & Co.)
Sklar, Holly (1980), *Trilateralism: The Trilateral Commission and*

Elite Planning for World Management (Boston: South End)
Smith, Michelle and Padzer, Lawrence (1980) *Michelle Remembers* (New York: Pocket Books)
Smith, Morton (1978), *Jesus the Magician* (San Francisco: Harper & Row)
Souden, David (1997), *Stonehenge Revealed* (New York: Facts on File)
Springmeier, Franz (2002), *Bloodlines of the Illuminati* (Westminster, CO: Ambassador House)
Stanton, Bill (1991), *Klanwatch: Bringing the Ku Klux Klan to Justice* (New York: Grove Weidenfeld)
Stanton, Rev. E.F. (1924), *Christ and Other Klansmen, or Lives of Love* (Kansas City: Stanton and Harper)
Starbird, Margaret (1993), *The Woman with the Alabaster Jar* (Rochester, VT: Inner Traditions)
Steiner, Rudolf (1994), *How To Know Higher Worlds* (New York: Anthroposophic Press)
Stevens, Henry (2003), *Hitler's Flying Saucers* (Kempton, IL: Adventures Unlimited)
Stevenson, David (1988), *The Origins of Freemasonry: Scotland's Century 1590–1710* (Cambridge: Cambridge University Press)
Still, William T. (1990), *New World Order: The Ancient Plan of Secret Societies* (Lafayette, LA: Huntingdon House)
Stirling, William (1999), *The Canon*, repr. (York Beach, ME: Weiser)
Sullivan, Robert E. (1982), *John Toland and the Deist Controversy* (Cambridge, MA: Harvard University Press)
Summers, Anthony (1993), *Official and Confidential: The Secret Life of J. Edgar Hoover* (New York: G.P. Putnam & Sons)
Sutton, Antony C. (1986), *America's Secret Establishment: An introduction to The Order of Skull & Bones* (Billings, MT: Liberty House)
Swedlow, Stewart A. (2002), *Blue Blood, True Blood: Conflict and Creation* (St Joseph, MI: Expansions)
Temple, Robert (1976), *The Sirius Mystery* (New York: St Martin's Press)
"Three Initiates" (1912), *The Kybalion* (Chicago: Advanced Thought)
Tompkins, Peter (1978), *Secrets of the Great Pyramid* (New York: Harper & Row)
Towers, Eric (1986), *Dashwood: The Man and the Myth* (Wellingborough, Northants: Aquarian)
Trismosin, Salomon (1991), *Splendor Solis*, trans. Joscelyn Godwin (Grand Rapids, MI: Phanes)
Trowbridge, W.R.H. (1910), *Cagliostro* (New York: Brentano's)
Truant, Cynthia Maria (1994), *The Rites of Labor: Brotherhoods of Compagnonnage in Old and New Regime France* (Ithaca, NY: Cornell University Press)

Ulansey, David (1989), *The Origin of the Mithraic Mysteries* (Oxford: Oxford University Press)
Upton-Ward, J.M., trans. (1992), *The Rule of the Templars: the French Text of the Rule of the Order of the Knights Templar* (Woodbridge, Suffolk: Boydell)
Vallee, Jacques (1979), *Messengers of Deception* (Berkeley, CA: And/Or)
— (1991), *Revelations: Alien Contact and Human Deception* (New York: Ballantine)
— (1996), *Forbidden Science* (New York: Marlowe and Co.)
VandenBrouck, André (1987), *Al-Kemi: Hermetic, Occult, Political, and Private Aspects of R.A. Schwaller de Lubicz* (Hudson, NY: Lindisfarne)
VanderKam, James C. (1994), *The Dead Sea Scrolls Today* (Grand Rapids, MI: Eerdmans)
van der Zee, John (1974), *The Greatest Men's Party on Earth: Inside the Bohemian Grove* (New York: Harcourt Brace Jovanovich)
van Deventer, Fred (1964), *Parade to Glory* (New York: Pyramid)
van Doren, Carl (1991), *Benjamin Franklin* (New York: Penguin)
van Helsing, Jan (1995), *Secret Societies and Their Power in the 20th Century* (Gran Canaria: Ewertverlag)
Vaughn, William Preston (1983), *The Antimasonic Party* (Lexington, KY: University of Kentucky Press)
Vesco, Renato and Childress, David Hatcher (1994), *Man-Made UFOs 1944–1994* (Stelle, IL: Adventures Unlimited)
Victor, Jeffrey S. (1993), *Satanic Panic* (Chicago: Open Court)
Voorhis, Harold V.B. (1997), *A Century and More of the Order of the Amaranth* (n.p.: Supreme Council of the Order of the Amaranth)
Wade, Wyn Craig (1987), *The Fiery Cross: The Ku Klux Klan in America* (New York: Simon and Schuster)
Waite, Arthur Edward (2003), *Devil Worship in France* (York Beach, ME: Weiser)
Walkes, Jr., Joseph A. (1979), *Black Square and Compass – 200 Years of Prince Hall Freemasonry* (Richmond, VA: Macoy)
Walsh, Michael (1989), *Opus Dei* (San Francisco: HarperSanFrancisco)
Washington, Peter (1993), *Madam Blavatsky's Baboon* (New York: Schocken Books)
Waterfield, Robin (1987), *René Guénon and the Future of the West* (Rochester, VT: Inner Traditions)
Watkins, Alfred (1925), *The Old Straight Track* (London: Methuen and Co.)
Watkins, Leslie, with David Ambrose and Christopher Miles (1979), *Alternative 3* (New York: Avon)
Webster, David (2002), *The Fall of the Ancient Maya* (London: Thames & Hudson)
Webster, Nesta (1949), *Spacious Days: An Autobiography* (London: Hutchinson)

— (1964), *Secret Societies and Subversive Movements* (n.p.: Christian Book Club of America)

Weller, Worth H. and Thompson, Brad (1998), *Under the Hood: Unmasking the Modern Ku Klux Klan* (North Manchester, IN: DeWitt Books)

Wells, Robert (1987), *Anarchist Handbook* (New York: Gordon Press)

Weston, Jessie (1983), *From Ritual to Romance* (Gloucester, MA: Peter Smith)

Wilgus, Neal (1978), *The Illuminoids* (Albuquerque, NM: Sun Books)

Williams, Andrew J. (1998), *Failed Imagination? New World Orders of the Twentieth Century* (Manchester: Manchester University Press)

Williams, T. Desmond (ed.) (1973), *Secret Societies in Ireland* (Dublin: Gill and Macmillan).

Wilson, Edmund (1972), *To The Finland Station* (New York: Farrar, Strauss)

Wilson, Ian (1979), *The Shroud of Turin* (Garden City, NY: Image Books)

Yallop, David (1984), *In God's Name* (New York: Bantam Books)

Yates, Frances A. (1936), *A Study of Love's Labour's Lost* (Cambridge: Cambridge University Press)

— (1964), *Giordano Bruno and the Hermetic Tradition* (Chicago: University of Chicago Press)

— (1966), *The Art of Memory* (Chicago: University of Chicago Press)

— (1972), *The Rosicrucian Enlightenment* (London: Routledge & Kegan Paul)